TESTIMONIES FOR THE CHURCH

VOLUME FIVE

TESTIMONIES

FOR

THE CHURCH

VOLUME FIVE
Comprising Testimonies Numbers 31 to 33

by
ELLEN G. WHITE

PACIFIC PRESS® PUBLISHING ASSOCIATION
Nampa, Idaho
Oshawa, Ontario, Canada

Printed in United States of America

01 02 03 04 05

CONTENTS

TESTIMONY 33 (1889)

THE TIMES OF VOLUME FIVE

A little less than a decade is spanned by *Testimonies* Nos. 31 to 33, which comprise volume 5. The first was published in 1882, but includes messages given in 1881 and onward. No. 32 was published in 1885, and No. 33 came from the press in 1889. That same year the three were united in one book—volume 5.

This was an intensely interesting period in the rapidly developing work of Seventh-day Adventists. In North America two new advanced schools were started in the year 1882, one at South Lancaster, Massachusetts, and the other at Healdsburg, California. Thus, from our denominational center at Battle Creek, the educational work was beginning to reach out toward the ends of the earth. Ten years earlier our first school had been opened at Battle Creek, and two years later its new buildings had been dedicated. During these ten years many problems incident to the pioneering of this new and important line of endeavor were met. Sometimes the issues were large, and in not a few instances special counsel was given through the spirit of prophecy to guide and guard this work. These messages dealing with problems, from discipline to curriculum, form a part of this book.

The nine-year period of this volume was also a time of extensive writing and publishing on the part of Ellen White. In 1882 arrangements were made to reprint *A Sketch of the Christian Experience and Views of Ellen G. White* and *Spiritual Gifts Volume One*. The same year these two books were united in one volume and entitled *Early Writings*. To meet the constant demand for the *Testimonies,* the first thirty numbers were reprinted in 1885 in four books—volumes 1 to 4, as they appear today. *Sketches From the Life of Paul,* the forerunner of *The Acts of the Apostles,* was published in 1883. In 1884, Mrs. White completed her work on *Spirit of Prophecy Volume Four—The Great Controversy,* and it was published immediately. It soon found its way through colporteur channels to many thousands of homes, and ten editions were rolled from the presses in three short years of time. In 1888 the enlarged *Great Controversy,* the book we know so well today, was published, taking the place of the earlier, briefer volume.

At the denominational headquarters in Battle Creek there was a steady growth. New equipment was added in the publishing house. The sanitarium and the college were greatly prospered and continued to grow. These developments brought large numbers of Seventh-day Adventists to that city. The hazards of so many Adventists gathering in one center, with the inevitable tendency to a feeling of less responsibility and toward lower standards, is pointed out in the early part of this volume. These institutional developments were also fraught with the danger that the work would become mechanical and lose its initial simplicity. Such dangers appeared especially in the publishing house. The testimonies of this volume stress economy, industry, alertness, and furnish managers and foremen with guiding instruction for their tasks.

At this same time, while problems of long-established work were being met at our headquarters, out in the Pacific Northwest new fields were being developed, and many were accepting the message. With the opening of these frontier regions, there were many new problems. Ellen White herself made two visits to the Northwest and in connection with the last trip wrote much counsel to those who were laboring there—counsel on practical subjects vital to the welfare of the work and the ministers who were working among the sturdy, independent-minded men and women who had pushed westward and established their homes in these vast, newly opened regions. These were men and women of energy, daring, rugged individuality; and many were persons of deep conviction who accepted the call of the advent message. These vigorous pioneers needed the strong, molding influence of the Spirit of God in the development of Christian character. They needed warnings against the love of money and worldly ambitions.

To the ministry were sent earnest counsels pointing out the danger that their messages might be shaped by the opinions of strong-minded church members. Counsel was given to guard against carelessness in the erection of church edifices, as seen in some instances. Warnings were also given against lightly regarding pledges of gifts to God's cause. All these and other counsels dealing with many other problems connected with the work in these new territories occupy a prominent place in this volume.

The eyes of Seventh-day Adventists were being turned more and more to the world field. For a decade we had been carrying on work in Europe. Now, in 1885, Elders S. N. Haskell and J. O. Corliss, with a company of workers, were sent to Australia to open up work in that southern continent. Africa was entered two years later by Elders D. A. Robinson and C. L. Boyd, and the message was carried to Hong Kong that same year by a layman, Brother Abraham La Rue. Then, in 1889, colporteurs commenced their work in South America. Even Mrs. White was called overseas, leaving for Europe in 1885. There she spent two and a half years traveling, counseling, speaking, and writing. In June, 1887, at Moss, Norway, she attended the first Seventh-day Adventist camp meeting held outside the United States. Her ministry overseas was much appreciated.

There was also, during the time represented by volume 5, considerable opposition on the part of a small group of disaffected souls who years earlier had left our ranks. Their attacks were leveled primarily against the agent of the prophetic gift and her writings which have strengthened and built up the church through the years. Also during the decade of this volume, one or our leading evangelists lost his way and was soon actively engaged in tearing down a work he had formerly labored to establish. Two communications written by Ellen White to restrain this man from the plunge he was about to take, are found in this book. One commences on page 571 and the other on page 621. The attempt to save him was fruitless, and he turned in bitter tirade on Mrs. White and the prophetic gift. While such attacks, of course, did not deter the work of Seventh-day Adventists, it is clear that they were recognized as distracting elements that should be counteracted.

It is not strange, then, that several vital articles touching on the prophetic gift were penned during this time. One of these forms the basis of the Introduction to *The Great Controversy,* 1888, edition. Others are found in this volume. It was at this time, too, that Mrs. White gathered from all the published *Testimonies* that which she had written on the nature and influence of the *Testimonies for the Church,* and compiled them into a thirty-eight-page article found near the close of this volume.

In the fall of 1888 an important General Conference session was held in Minneapolis, Minnesota. At this meeting there came to those assembled a broader, fuller conception of the great truths of righteousness by faith. The failure of some to open their hearts to the light which was there caused to shine so brightly spurred Mrs. White to lead out in an encouragement to diligent Bible study and to break down the barriers to advancement in the perception of truth. At the General Conference session the next year, 1889, workers and laity alike reported in their social meetings that "the past year" had "been the best of their life; the light shining forth from the word of God has been clear and distinct—justification by faith, Christ our righteousness. . . . The universal testimony from those who have spoken has been that this message of light and truth which has come to our people is just the truth for this time and wherever they go among the churches, light and relief and the blessing of God are sure to come in."—E. G. White MS. 10, 1889, quoted in *The Fruitage of Spiritual Gifts,* page 234. God's message to His people turned into a glorious victory the tide which threatened defeat.

As the writing of this volume was being brought to a close, a crisis threatened in the United States in the form of a proposed national Sunday law. In this connection there was brought before Mrs. White the views of the impending conflict and the issues which the church must meet as apostate Protestantism unites with Catholicism to enforce oppressive measures. The pathetic lethargy of those who understood the issues was clearly portrayed, and there was a call to action.

In volume 5 there is a greater diversity of subjects than in any other of the nine volumes of the *Testimonies*. This was the last of the group of *Testimony* volumes to contain "personal testimonies" addressed to various individuals. A period of eleven years was to elapse before the issuance of volume 6 of *Testimony* writings.

This volume is of great value to the church today because of the practical nature of its timely warnings and counsels. Stressed all through it are solemn statements pointing out the nearness of the end and the preparation which is needed in the light of the impending conflict. Ministers are called to deeper consecration. Executives are admonished. Physicians are counseled. Teachers are warned against adopting worldly principles and are encouraged to guide their students into soul-winning services. Colporteur evangelists are urged to higher standards of qualification. Parents are given instruction regarding home life and child training. Those with so-called new light, but with a message contrary to the fundamentals of doctrine, are reproved. The rank and file of the people are called to a revival and reformation.

The instruction and warnings of this volume exerted a steadying, sobering influence upon Seventh-day Adventists as they were launching out into greater lines of endeavor. They exert the same influence today.

THE TRUSTEES OF THE ELLEN G.
WHITE PUBLICATIONS

TESTIMONIES FOR THE CHURCH

CAMP MEETING ADDRESS

Boulder, Colorado, September 25, 1881.

Dear Brethren and Sisters Who Shall Assemble
at the Michigan Camp Meeting:*

I feel a deeper interest in this meeting than in any other that has been held this season. Michigan has not had the labor which she should have had. God has planted important institutions among you, and this brings upon you greater responsibilities than upon any other conference in the whole field. Great light has been given you, and few have responded to it, yet my heart goes out in tender solicitude for our beloved people in Michigan. The warning that the Son of man is soon to come in the clouds of heaven has become to many a familiar tale. They have left the waiting, watching position. The selfish, worldly spirit manifested in the life reveals the sentiment of the heart, "My Lord delayeth His coming." Some are enveloped in so great darkness that they openly express their unbelief, notwithstanding our Saviour's declaration that all such are unfaithful servants and their portion shall be with hypocrites and unbelievers.

Our ministers are not doing their whole duty. The attention of the people should be called to the momentous event which is so near at hand. The signs of the times should be kept fresh before their minds. The prophetic visions of Daniel and John foretell a period of moral darkness and declension; but at

---

*This appeal was written for the Michigan camp meeting, but being forgotten at that time, was read before the General Conference, December, 1881.

the time of the end, the time in which we are now living, the vision was to speak and not lie. When the signs predicted begin to come to pass, the waiting, watching ones are bidden to look up and lift up their heads and rejoice because their redemption draweth nigh.

When these things are dwelt upon as they should be, scoffers will be developed who walk after their own lusts, saying, "Where is the promise of His coming? for since the fathers fell asleep, all things continue as they were from the beginning of the creation." But "when they shall say, Peace and safety; then sudden destruction cometh upon them." "But ye, brethren, are not in darkness, that that day should overtake you as a thief." Thank God, all will not be rocked to sleep in the cradle of carnal security. There will be faithful ones who will discern the signs of the times. While a large number professing present truth will deny their faith by their works, there will be some who will endure unto the end.

The same spirit of selfishness, of conformity to the practices of the world, exists in our day as in Noah's. Many who profess to be children of God follow their worldly pursuits with an intensity that gives the lie to their profession. They will be planting and building, buying and selling, eating and drinking, marrying and giving in marriage, up to the last moment of their probation. This is the condition of a large number of our own people. Because iniquity abounds, the love of many waxes cold. To but few can it be said: "Ye are all . . . the children of the day: we are not of the night, nor of darkness."

My soul is burdened as I see the great want of spirituality among us. The fashions and customs of the world, pride, love of amusement, love of display, extravagance in dress, in houses, in lands—these are robbing the treasury of God, turning to the gratification of self the means which should be used to send forth the light of truth to the world. Selfish purposes are made the first consideration. The work of qualifying men to labor for the salvation of souls is not considered of so great consequence as worldly enterprises. Souls are perishing for want of knowledge. Those who have had the light of present truth, and yet feel no spirit of labor to warn their fellow men of the coming judgment, must give an account to God for their neglect of duty. The blood of souls will be upon their garments.

The old standard-bearers are fainting and falling. Our young men have not been educated to feel their accountability to God; little inducement is presented for them to labor in the cause, and they enter the fields that promise the largest remuneration with the least toil and responsibility. As a people we are not advancing in spirituality as we near the end. We do not realize the magnitude and importance of the work before us. Hence our plans are not becoming wider and more comprehensive. There is a sad lack of men and women prepared to carry forward the increasing work for this time.

We are not doing one-twentieth part of what God requires us to do. There has been a departure from the simplicity of the work, making it intricate, difficult to understand, and difficult to execute. The judgment and wisdom of man rather than of God has too often guided and controlled. Many feel that they have not time to watch for souls as they that must give account. And what excuse will they render for this neglect of the important work which was theirs to do?

At our college young men should be educated in as careful and thorough a manner as possible that they may be prepared to labor for God. This was the object for which the institution was brought into existence. Our brethren abroad should feel an interest not only to sustain but to guard the college, that it may not be turned away from its design and be molded after other institutions of the kind. The religious interest should be constantly guarded. Time is drawing to a close. Eternity is near. The great harvest is to be gathered. What are we doing to prepare for this work?

The leading men in our college should be men of piety and devotion. They should make the Bible the rule and guide of life, giving heed to the sure word of prophecy as to "a light that shineth in a dark place." Not one of us should dare to be off guard for a moment, for "in such an hour as ye think not the Son of man cometh." It is only those who continue faithful in well-doing that shall reap the reward. Much that has no part in Christ is allowed a place among us. Unconsecrated ministers, professors, and teachers assist Satan to plant his banner in our very strongholds.

The design of our college has been stated again and again, yet many are so blinded by the god of this world that its real object is not understood. God designed that young men should there be drawn to Him, that they should there obtain a preparation to preach the gospel of Christ, to bring out of the exhaustless treasury of God's word things both new and old for the instruction and edification of the people. Teachers and professors should have a vivid sense of the perils of this time and the work that must be accomplished to prepare a people to stand in the day of God.

Some of the teachers have been scattering from Christ instead of gathering with Him. By their own example they lead those under their charge to adopt the customs and habits of worldlings. They link the hands of the students with fashionable, amusement-loving unbelievers, and carry them an advance step toward the world and away from Christ. And they do this in the face of warnings from heaven, not only those given to the people in general, but personal appeals to themselves. The anger of the Lord is kindled for these things.

God will test the fidelity of His people. Many of the mistakes that are made by the professed servants of God are in consequence of their self-love, their desire for approval, their thirst for popularity. Blinded in this manner, they do not realize that they are elements of darkness rather than of light. "Come out from among them, and be ye separate, saith the Lord, and touch not the unclean thing; and I will receive you, and will be a Father unto you, and ye shall be My sons and daughters, saith the Lord Almighty." These are the conditions upon which we may be acknowledged as the sons of God—separation from the world, and renunciation of those things which delude, and fascinate, and ensnare.

The apostle Paul declares that it is impossible for the children of God to unite with worldlings: "Be ye not unequally yoked together with unbelievers." This does not refer to marriage alone; any intimate relation of confidence and copartnership with those who have no love for God or the truth is a snare.

The apostle continues: "For what fellowship hath righteousness with unrighteousness? and what communion hath light with darkness? and what concord hath Christ with Belial? or what part hath he that believeth with an infidel? and what agreement hath the temple of God with idols? for ye are the temple of the living God; as God hath said: I will dwell in them, and walk in them; and I will be their God, and they shall be My people." In consideration of these facts, he exclaims: "Wherefore come out from among them, and be ye separate." "Having therefore these promises, dearly beloved, let us cleanse ourselves from all filthiness of the flesh and spirit, perfecting holiness in the fear of God."

If we comply with the conditions, the Lord will fulfill to us His promises. But there is a work for us to do which we should in no wise neglect. In the strength of Jesus we can perform it aright. We may press ever onward and upward, constantly growing in grace and in a knowledge of the truth.

The children of the light and of the day are not to gather about them the shades of night and darkness which encompass the workers of iniquity. On the contrary, they are to stand faithfully at their post of duty as light bearers, gathering light from God to shed upon those in darkness. The Lord requires His people to maintain their integrity, touching not—that is, imitating not—the practices of the ungodly.

Christians will be in this world "an holy nation, a peculiar people," showing forth the praises of Him who hath called them "out of darkness into His marvelous light." This light is not to grow dim, but to shine brighter and brighter unto the perfect day. Christ's standard-bearers are never to be off duty. They have a vigilant foe who is waiting and watching to take the fort. Some of Christ's professed watchmen have invited the enemy into their stronghold, have mingled with them, and in their efforts to please have broken down the distinction between the children of God and the children of Satan.

The Lord never designed that our college should imitate other institutions of learning. The religious element should be the controlling power. If unbelievers choose this influence, it is well; if those who are in darkness choose to come to the light, it is as God would have it. But to relax our vigilance, and let the worldly element take the lead in order to secure students, is contrary to the will of God. The strength of our college is in keeping the religious element in the ascendancy. When teachers or professors shall sacrifice religious principle to please a worldly, amusement-loving class, they should be considered unfaithful to their trust and should be discharged.

The thrilling truth that has been sounding in our ears for many years, "The Lord is at hand; be ye also ready," is no less the truth today than when we first heard the message. The dearest interests of the church and people of God, and the destiny of an impenitent and ungodly world, for time and for eternity, are here involved. We are all judgment bound. "The Lord Himself shall descend from heaven with a shout, with the voice of the Archangel, and with the trump of God: and the dead in Christ shall rise first: then we which are alive and remain [unto the coming of the Lord] shall be caught up together with them in the clouds, to meet the Lord in the air: and so shall we ever be with the Lord." Christ will then be revealed from heaven, "taking vengeance on them that know not God, and that obey not the gospel."

These momentous events are nigh at hand, yet many who profess to believe the truth are asleep. They will surely be numbered with the unfaithful servant who saith in his heart, "My Lord delayeth His coming," if they remain in their present position of friendship with the world. It is only to those who are waiting in hope and faith that Christ will appear, without sin unto salvation. Many have the theory of the truth who know not the power of godliness. If the word of God dwelt in the heart, it would control the life. Faith, purity, and conformity to the will of God would testify to its sanctifying power.

RESPONSIBILITY OF MINISTERS

A solemn responsibility rests upon the watchmen. How careful should they be rightly to understand and explain the word of God. "Blessed is he that readeth, and they that hear the words of this prophecy, and keep those things which are written therein." Says the prophet Ezekiel: "The word of the Lord came unto me, saying, Son of man, speak to the children of thy people, and say unto them, When I bring the sword upon a land, if the people of the land take a man of their coasts, and set him for their watchman: if when he seeth the sword come upon the land, he blow the trumpet, and warn the people; then whosoever heareth the sound of the trumpet, and taketh not warning; if the sword come, and take him away, his blood shall be upon his own head. He heard the sound of the trumpet, and took not warning; his blood shall be upon him. But he that taketh warning shall deliver his soul. But if the watchman see the sword come, and blow not the trumpet, and the people be not warned; if the sword come, and take any person from among them, he is taken away in his iniquity; but his blood will I require at the watchman's hand. So thou, O son of man, I have set thee a watchman unto the house of Israel; therefore thou shalt hear the word at my mouth, and warn them from Me. When I say unto the wicked, O wicked man, thou shalt surely die; if thou dost not speak to warn the wicked from his way, that wicked man shall die in his iniquity; but his blood will I require at thine hand. Nevertheless, if thou warn the wicked of his way to turn from it; if he do not turn from his way, he shall die in his iniquity; but thou hast delivered thy soul."

The responsibility of the watchmen of today is as much greater than in the days of the prophet as our light is clearer and our privileges and opportunities greater than theirs. It is the minister's duty to warn every man, to teach every man, in all meekness and wisdom. He is not to conform to the practices of the world, but, as God's servant, he must contend for the faith once delivered to the saints. Satan is constantly at work to break down the strongholds which debar him from free access to souls; and, while our ministers are no more spiritually minded, while they do not connect closely with God, the enemy has great advantage, and the Lord holds the watchman accountable for his success.

I would, at this time, sound the note of warning to those who shall assemble at our camp meeting. The end of all things is at hand. My brethren, ministers and laymen, I have been shown you must work in a different manner from what you have been in the habit of working. Pride, envy, self-importance, and unsanctified independence have marred your labors. When men permit themselves to be flattered and exalted by Satan, the Lord can do little for them or through them. To what unmeasured humiliation did the Son of man descend, that He might elevate humanity! Workers for God, not the ministers only, but the people, need the meekness and lowliness of Christ if they would benefit their fellow men. As God, our Saviour humbled Himself when He took upon Him man's nature. But He went lower still. As a man, "He humbled Himself, and became obedient unto death, even the death of the cross." Would that I could find language wherewith to present these thoughts before you. Would that the veil could be rent away and you could see the cause of your spiritual weakness. Would that you could conceive of the rich supplies of grace and power awaiting your demand. Those who hunger and thirst for righteousness will be filled. We must exercise greater faith in calling upon God for all needed blessings. We must strive, agonize, to enter in at the strait gate.

Says Christ: "Come unto Me, all ye that labor and are heavy-laden, and I will give you rest. Take My yoke upon you, and learn of Me; for I am meek and lowly in heart: and ye shall find rest unto your souls." I testify to you, my dear brethren, ministers, and people, you have not yet learned this lesson. Christ endured shame and agony and death for us. "Let this mind be in you, which was also in Christ Jesus." Bear reproach and abuse without retaliation, without a spirit of revenge. Jesus died, not only to make atonement for us, but to be our pattern. Oh, wondrous condescension! matchless love! As you look upon the Prince of Life upon the cross, can you cherish selfishness? Can you indulge hatred or revenge?

Let the proud spirit bow in humiliation. Let the hard heart be broken. No longer pet and pity and exalt self. Look, oh look upon Him whom our sins have pierced. See Him descending step by step the path of humiliation to lift us up; abasing Himself till He could go no lower, and all to save us who were fallen by sin! Why will we be so indifferent, so cold, so formal, so proud, so self-sufficient?

Who of us is faithfully following the Pattern? Who of us has instituted and continued the warfare against pride of heart? Who of us has, in good earnest, brought himself to wrestle with selfishness until it should no longer dwell in the heart and be revealed in the life? Would to God the lessons given us, as we view the cross of Christ and see the signs fulfilling which bring us near to the judgment, might be so impressed upon our hearts as to render us more humble, more self-denying, more kind to one another, less self-caring, less critical, and more willing to bear one another's burdens than we are today.

I have been shown that, as a people, we are departing from the simplicity of the faith and from the purity of the gospel. Many are in great peril. Unless they change their course, they will be severed from the True Vine as useless branches. Brethren and sisters, I have been shown that we are standing upon the threshold of the eternal world. We need now to gain victories at every step. Every good deed is as a seed sown, to bear fruit unto eternal life. Every success gained places us on a higher round of the ladder of progress and gives us spiritual strength for fresh victories. Every right action prepares the way for its repetition.

Some are closing their probation; and is it well with them? have they obtained a fitness for the future life? Will not their record show wasted opportunities, neglected privileges, a life of selfishness and worldliness that has borne no fruit to the glory of God? And how much of the work which the Master has left for us to do has been left undone. All around us are souls to be warned; but how often has the time been occupied in self-serving, and the record gone up to God of souls passing to their graves unwarned and unsaved.

The Lord still has purposes of mercy toward us. There is room for repentance. We may become the beloved of God. I entreat you who have put far off the appearing of our Lord, commence now the work of redeeming the time. Study the word of God. Let all at this meeting make a covenant with God to put away light and trifling conversation and frivolous, unimportant reading, and, for the coming year, diligently and prayerfully study the Bible, that you may be able to give to every man that asketh you a reason of the hope that is within you, with meekness and fear. Will you not, without delay, humble your hearts before God and repent of your backslidings?

Let none entertain the thought that I regret or take back any plain testimony I have borne to individuals or to the people. If I have erred anywhere, it is in not rebuking sin more decidedly and firmly. Some of the brethren have taken the responsibility of criticizing my work and proposing an easier way to correct wrongs. To these persons I would say: I take God's way and not yours. What I have said or written in testimony or reproof has not been too plainly expressed.

God has given me my work, and I must meet it at the judgment. Those who have chosen their own way, who have risen up against the plain testimonies given them, and have sought to shake the faith of others in them, must settle the matter with God. I take back nothing. I soften nothing to suit their ideas or to excuse their defects of character. I have not spoken as plainly as the case required. Those who would in any way lessen the force of the sharp reproofs which God has given me to speak, must meet their work at the judgment.

Within a few weeks past, standing face to face with death, I have had a near look into eternity. If the Lord is pleased to raise me from my present state of feebleness, I hope, in the grace and strength that comes from above, to speak with fidelity the words which He gives me to speak. All through my life it has been terribly hard for me to hurt the feelings of any, or disturb their self-deception, as I deliver the testimonies given me of God. It is contrary to my nature. It costs me great pain and many sleepless nights. To those who have taken the responsibility to reprove me and, in their finite judgment, to propose a way which appears wiser to them, I repeat: I do not accept your efforts. Leave me with God, and let Him teach me. I will take the words from the Lord and speak them to the people. I do not expect that all will accept the reproof and reform their lives, but I must discharge my duty all the same. I will walk in humility before God, doing my work for time and for eternity.

God has not given my brethren the work that He has given me. It has been urged that my manner of giving reproof in public has led others to be sharp and critical and severe. If so, they must settle that matter with the Lord. If others take a responsibility which God has not laid upon them; if they disregard the instructions He has given them again and again through the humble instrument of His choice, to be kind, patient, and forbearing, they alone must answer for the results. With a sorrow-burdened heart, I have performed my unpleasant duty to my dearest friends, not daring to please myself by withholding reproof, even from my husband; and I shall not be less faithful in warning others, whether they will hear or forbear. When I am speaking to the people I say much that I have not premeditated. The Spirit of the Lord frequently comes upon me. I seem to be carried out of, and away from, myself; the life and character of different persons are clearly presented before my mind. I see their errors and dangers, and feel compelled to speak of what is thus brought before me. I dare not resist the Spirit of God.

I know that some are displeased with my testimony. It does not suit their proud, unconsecrated hearts. I feel more and more deeply the loss which our people have sustained by their failure to accept and obey the light which God has given them. My younger brethren in the ministry, I entreat you to reflect more upon your solemn responsibility. If consecrated to God, you may exert a powerful influence for good in the church and the world; but you lack heartfelt piety and devotion. God has sent you to be a light to the world by your good works as well as by your words and theories. But many of you may truly be represented by the foolish virgins, who had no oil in their lamps.

My brethren, heed the reproof and counsel of the True Witness, and God will work for you and with you. Your enemies may be strong and determined, but One mightier than they will be your helper. Let the light shine, and it will do its work. The Lord of hosts is with us; the God of Jacob is our refuge.

OUR COLLEGE*

There is danger that our college will be turned away from its original design. God's purpose has been made known, that our people should have an opportunity to study the sciences and at the same time to learn the requirements of His word. Biblical lectures should be given; the study of the Scriptures should have the first place in our system of education.

Students are sent from a great distance to attend the college at Battle Creek for the very purpose of receiving instruction from the lectures on Bible subjects. But for one or two years past there has been an effort to mold our school after other colleges. When this is done, we can give no encouragement to parents to send their children to Battle Creek College. The moral and religious influences should not be put in the background. In times past, God has worked with the efforts of the teachers, and many souls have seen the truth and embraced it,

*Read in College Hall, December, 1881, before Conference delegates and leading workers in Review and Herald office, sanitarium, and college.

and have gone to their homes to live henceforth for God, as the result of their connection with the college. As they saw that Bible study was made a part of their education, they were led to regard it as a matter of greater interest and importance.

Too little attention has been given to the education of young men for the ministry. This was the primary object to be secured in the establishment of the college. In no case should this be ignored or regarded as a matter of secondary importance. For several years, however, but few have gone forth from that institution prepared to teach the truth to others. Some who came at great expense, with the ministry in view, have been encouraged by the teachers to take a thorough course of study which would occupy a number of years, and, in order to obtain means to carry out these plans, have entered the canvassing field and given up all thought of preaching. This is entirely wrong. We have not many years to work, and teachers and principal should be imbued with the Spirit of God and work in harmony with His revealed will instead of carrying out their own plans. We are losing much every year because we do not heed what God has said upon these points.

Our college is designed of God to meet the advancing wants for this time of peril and demoralization. The study of books only cannot give students the discipline they need. A broader foundation must be laid. The college was not brought into existence to bear the stamp of any one man's mind. Teachers and principal should work together as brethren. They should consult together, and also counsel with ministers and responsible men, and, above all else, seek wisdom from above, that all their decisions in reference to the school may be such as will be approved of God.

To give students a knowledge of books merely is not the purpose of the institution. Such education can be obtained at any college in the land. I was shown that it is Satan's purpose to prevent the attainment of the very object for which the college was established. Hindered by his devices, its managers reason after the manner of the world and copy its plans and imitate its customs. But in thus doing, they will not meet the mind of the Spirit of God.

A more comprehensive education is needed, an education which will demand from teachers and principal such thought and effort as mere instruction in the sciences does not require. The character must receive proper discipline for its fullest and noblest development. The students should receive at college such training as will enable them to maintain a respectable, honest, virtuous standing in society, against the demoralizing influences which are corrupting the youth.

It would be well could there be connected with our college, land for cultivation and also workshops under the charge of men competent to instruct the students in the various departments of physical labor. Much is lost by a neglect to unite physical with mental taxation. The leisure hours of the students are often occupied with frivolous pleasures, which weaken physical, mental, and moral powers. Under the debasing power of sensual indulgence, or the untimely excitement of courtship and marriage, many students fail to reach that height of mental development which they might otherwise have attained.

The young should every day be impressed with a sense of their obligation to God. His law is continually violated, even by the children of religious parents. Some of these very youth frequent haunts of dissipation, and the powers of the mind and body suffer in consequence. This class lead others to follow their pernicious ways. Thus, while principal and teachers are giving instruction in the sciences, Satan, with hellish cunning, is exerting every energy to gain control of the minds of the pupils and lead them down to ruin.

Generally speaking, the youth have but little moral

strength. This is the result of neglected education in child-hood. A knowledge of the character of God and our obligations to Him should not be regarded as a matter of minor consequence. The religion of the Bible is the only safeguard for the young. Morality and religion should receive special attention in our educational institutions.

THE BIBLE AS A TEXTBOOK

No other study will so ennoble every thought, feeling, and aspiration as the study of the Scriptures. This Sacred Word is the will of God revealed to men. Here we may learn what God expects of the beings formed in His image. Here we learn how to improve the present life and how to secure the future life. No other book can satisfy the questionings of the mind and the craving of the heart. By obtaining a knowledge of God's word, and giving heed thereto, men may rise from the lowest depths of ignorance and degradation to become the sons of God, the associates of sinless angels.

A clear conception of what God is, and what He requires us to be, will give us humble views of self. He who studies aright the Sacred Word will learn that human intellect is not omnipotent; that, without the help which none but God can give, human strength and wisdom are but weakness and ignorance.

As an educating power the Bible is without a rival. Nothing will so impart vigor to all the faculties as requiring students to grasp the stupendous truths of revelation. The mind gradually adapts itself to the subjects upon which it is allowed to dwell. If occupied with commonplace matters only, to the exclusion of grand and lofty themes, it will become dwarfed and enfeebled. If never required to grapple with difficult problems, or put to the stretch to comprehend important truths, it will, after a time, almost lose the power of growth.

The Bible is the most comprehensive and the most instructive history which men possess. It came fresh from the fountain of eternal truth, and a divine hand has preserved its purity through all the ages. Its bright rays shine into the far distant past, where human research seeks vainly to penetrate. In God's word alone we find an authentic account of creation. Here we behold the power that laid the foundation of the earth and that stretched out the heavens. Here only can we find a history of our race, unsullied by human prejudice or human pride.

In the word of God the mind finds subject for the deepest thought, the loftiest aspiration. Here we may hold communion with patriarchs and prophets, and listen to the voice of the Eternal as He speaks with men. Here we behold the Majesty of heaven as He humbled Himself to become our substitute and surety to cope singlehanded with the powers of darkness and to gain the victory in our behalf. A reverent contemplation of such themes as these cannot fail to soften, purify, and ennoble the heart, and, at the same time, to inspire the mind with new strength and vigor.

If morality and religion are to live in a school, it must be through a knowledge of God's word. Some may urge that if religious teaching is to be made prominent our school will become unpopular; that those who are not of our faith will not patronize the college. Very well, then, let them go to other colleges, where they will find a system of education that suits their taste. Our school was established, not merely to teach the sciences, but for the purpose of giving instruction in the great principles of God's word and in the practical duties of everyday life.

This is the education so much needed at the present time. If a worldly influence is to bear sway in our school, then sell it out to worldlings and let them take the entire control; and those who have invested their means in that institution will establish another school, to be conducted, not upon the plan of popular schools, nor according to the desires of principal and teachers, but upon the plan which God has specified.

In the name of my Master I entreat all who stand in responsible positions in that school to be men of God. When the Lord requires us to be distinct and peculiar, how can we crave popularity or seek to imitate the customs and practices of the world? God has declared His purpose to have one college in the land where the Bible shall have its proper place in the education of the youth. Will we do our part to carry out that purpose?

It may seem that the teaching of God's word has but little effect on the minds and hearts of many students; but, if the teacher's work has been wrought in God, some lessons of divine truth will linger in the memory of the most careless. The Holy Spirit will water the seed sown, and often it will spring up after many days and bear fruit to the glory of God.

Satan is constantly seeking to divert the attention of the people from the Bible. The words of God to men, which should receive our first attention, are neglected for the utterances of human wisdom. How can He, who is infinite in power and wisdom, bear thus with the presumption and effrontery of men!

Through the medium of the press, knowledge of every kind is placed within the reach of all; and yet, how large a share of every community are depraved in morals and superficial in mental attainments. If the people would but become Bible readers, Bible students, we would see a different state of things.

In an age like ours, in which iniquity abounds and God's character and His law are alike regarded with contempt, special care must be taken to teach the youth to study, to reverence and obey the divine will as revealed to man. The fear of the Lord is fading from the minds of our youth because of their neglect of Bible study.

Principal and teachers should have a living connection with God, and should stand, firmly and fearlessly, as witnesses for Him. Never from cowardice or worldly policy let the word of God be placed in the background. Students will be profited. intellectually, as well as morally and spiritually, by its study.

<h2 style="text-align:center">OBJECT OF THE COLLEGE</h2>

Our college stands today in a position that God does not approve. I have been shown the dangers that threaten this important institution. If its responsible men seek to reach the world's standard, if they copy the plans and methods of other colleges, the frown of God will be upon our school.

The time has come for me to speak decidedly. The purpose of God in the establishment of our college has been plainly stated. There is an urgent demand for laborers in the gospel field. Young men who design to enter the ministry cannot spend a number of years in obtaining an education. Teachers should have been able to comprehend the situation and adapt their instruction to the wants of this class. Special advantages should have been given them for a brief yet comprehensive study of the branches most needed to fit them for their work. But I have been shown that this has not been accomplished.

Brother _____ could have done a much better work than he has done for those who were to be ministers. God is not pleased with his course in this matter. He has not adapted himself to the situation. Men who have left their fields of labor at a considerable sacrifice to learn what they could in a short time have not always received that help and encouragement which they should have had. Men who have reached mature years, even the meridian of life, and who have families of their own, have been subjected to unnecessary embarrassment. Brother _____ is himself extremely sensitive, but he does not realize that others can feel the sting of ridicule, sarcasm, or censure as keenly as he. In this he has wounded his brethren and displeased God.

TEACHERS IN THE COLLEGE

There is a work to be done for every teacher in our college. Not one is free from selfishness. If the moral and religious character of the teachers were what it should be, a better influence would be exerted upon the students. The teachers do not seek individually to perform their own work with an eye single to the glory of God. Instead of looking to Jesus, and copying His life and character, they look to self, and aim too much to meet a human standard. I wish I could impress upon every teacher a full sense of his responsibility for the influence which he exerts upon the young. Satan is untiring in his efforts to secure the service of our youth. With great care he is laying his snare for the inexperienced feet. The people of God should jealously guard against his devices.

God is the embodiment of benevolence, mercy, and love. Those who are truly connected with Him cannot be at variance with one another. His Spirit ruling in the heart will create harmony, love, and unity. The opposite of this is seen among the children of Satan. It is his work to stir up envy, strife, and jealousy. In the name of my Master I ask the professed followers of Christ: What fruit do you bear?

In the system of instruction used in the common schools the most essential part of education is neglected, namely, the religion of the Bible. Education not only affects to a great degree the life of the student in this world, but its influence extends to eternity. How important, then, that the teachers be persons capable of exerting a right influence. They should be men and women of religious experience, daily receiving divine light to impart to their pupils.

But the teacher should not be expected to do the parent's work. There has been, with many parents, a fearful neglect of duty. Like Eli, they fail to exercise proper restraint; and then they send their undisciplined children to college to receive the training which the parents should have given them at home. The teachers have a task which but few appreciate. If they succeed in reforming these wayward youth they receive but little credit. If the youth choose the society of the evil-disposed and go on from bad to worse, then the teachers are censured and the school denounced.

In many cases the censure justly belongs to the parents. They had the first and most favorable opportunity to control and train their children, when the spirit was teachable and the mind and heart easily impressed. But through the slothfulness of the parents the children are permitted to follow their own will until they become hardened in an evil course.

Let parents study less of the world and more of Christ; let them put forth less effort to imitate the customs and fashions of the world, and devote more time and effort to molding the minds and character of their children according to the divine Model. Then they could send forth their sons and daughters, fortified by pure morals and a noble purpose, to receive an education for positions of usefulness and trust. Teachers who are controlled by the love and fear of God could lead such youth still onward and upward, training them to be a blessing to the world and an honor to their Creator.

Connected with God, every instructor will exert an influence to lead his pupils to study God's word and to obey His law. He will direct their minds to the contemplation of eternal interests, opening before them vast fields for thought, grand and ennobling themes, which the most vigorous intellect may put forth all its powers to grasp and yet feel that there is an infinity beyond.

The evils of self-esteem and an unsanctified independence,

which most impair our usefulness and which will prove our ruin if not overcome, spring from selfishness. "Counsel together" is the message which has been again and again repeated to me by the angel of God. By influencing one man's judgment, Satan may endeavor to control matters to suit himself. He may succeed in misleading the minds of two persons; but, when several consult together, there is more safety. Every plan will be more closely criticized; every advance move more carefully studied. Hence there will be less danger of precipitate, ill-advised moves, which would bring confusion, perplexity, and defeat. In union there is strength. In division there is weakness and defeat.

God is leading out a people and preparing them for translation. Are we, who are acting a part in this work, standing as sentinels for God? Are we seeking to work unitedly? Are we willing to become servants of all? Are we following our great Exemplar?

Fellow laborers, we are each sowing seed in the fields of life. As is the seed, so will be the harvest. If we sow distrust, envy, jealousy, self-love, bitterness of thought and feeling, we shall reap bitterness to our own souls. If we manifest kindness, love, tender thought for the feelings of others, we shall receive the same in return.

The teacher who is severe, critical, overbearing, heedless of others' feelings, must expect the same spirit to be manifested toward himself. He who wishes to preserve his own dignity and self-respect must be careful not to wound needlessly the self-respect of others. This rule should be sacredly observed toward the dullest, the youngest, the most blundering scholars. What God intends to do with those apparently uninteresting youth you do not know. He has, in the past, accepted persons no more promising or attractive to do a great work for Him. His Spirit, moving upon the heart, has aroused every faculty to vigorous action. The Lord saw in those rough, unhewn stones, precious material that would stand the test of storm and heat and pressure. God seeth not as man sees. He judges not from appearance, but He searches the heart and judges righteously.

The teacher should ever conduct himself as a Christian gentleman. He should ever stand in the attitude of a friend and counselor to his pupils. If all our people—teachers, ministers, and lay members—would cultivate the spirit of Christian courtesy, they would far more readily find access to the hearts of the people; many more would be led to examine and receive the truth. When every teacher shall forget self and feel a deep interest in the success and prosperity of his pupils, realizing that they are God's property and that he must render an account for his influence upon their minds and character, then we shall have a school in which angels will love to linger. Jesus will look approvingly upon the work of the teachers and will send His grace into the hearts of the students.

Our college at Battle Creek is a place where the younger members of the Lord's family are to be trained according to God's plan of growth and development. They should be impressed with the idea that they are created in the image of their Maker and that Christ is the pattern which they are to follow. Our brethren permit their minds to take too narrow and too low a range. They do not keep the divine plan ever in view, but are fixing their eyes upon worldly models. Look up, where Christ sitteth at the right hand of God, and then labor that your pupils may be conformed to that perfect character.

If you lower the standard in order to secure popularity and an increase of numbers, and then make this increase a cause of rejoicing, you show great blindness. If numbers were evidence of success, Satan might claim the pre-eminence; for in this world his followers are largely in the majority. It is the degree of moral power pervading the college that is a test of its prosperity. It is the virtue, intelligence, and piety of the people composing our churches, not their numbers, that should be a source of joy and thankfulness.

Without the influence of divine grace, education will prove no real advantage; the learner becomes proud, vain, and bigoted. But that education which is received under the ennobling, refining influence of the Great Teacher will elevate man in the scale of moral value with God. It will enable him to subdue pride and passion and to walk humbly before God, as dependent upon Him for every capability, every opportunity, and every privilege.

I speak to the workers in our college: You must not only profess to be Christians, but you must exemplify the character of Christ. Let the wisdom from above pervade all your instruction. In a world of moral darkness and corruption, let it be seen that the spirit by which you are moved to action is from above, not from beneath. While you rely wholly upon your own strength and wisdom, your best efforts will accomplish little. If you are prompted by love to God, His law being your foundation, your work will be enduring. While the hay, wood, and stubble are consumed, your work will stand the test. The youth placed under your care you must meet again around the great white throne. If you permit your uncultivated manners or uncontrolled tempers to bear sway, and thus fail to influence these youth for their eternal good, you must at that day meet the grave consequences of your work. By a knowledge of the divine law, and obedience to its precepts, men may become the sons of God. By violation of that law they become servants of Satan. On the one hand they may rise to any height of moral excellence, or on the other hand they may descend to any depth of iniquity and degradation. The workers in our college should manifest a zeal and earnestness proportionate to the value of the prize at stake—the souls of their students, the approval of God, eternal life, and the joys of the redeemed.

As colaborers with Christ, with so favorable opportunities to impart the knowledge of God, our teachers should labor as if inspired from above. The hearts of the youth are not hardened, nor their ideas and opinions stereotyped, as are those of older persons. They may be won to Christ by your holy demeanor, your devotion, your Christlike walk. It would be much better to crowd them less in the study of the sciences and give them more time for religious privileges. Here a grave mistake has been made.

The object of God in bringing the college into existence has been lost sight of. Ministers of the gospel have so far shown their want of wisdom from above as to unite a worldly element with the college; they have joined with the enemies of God and the truth in providing entertainments for the students. In thus misleading the youth they have done a work for Satan. That work, with all its results, they must meet again at the bar of God. Those who pursue such a course show that they cannot be trusted. After the evil work has been done, they may confess their error; but can they as easily gather up the influence they have exerted? Will the "well done" be spoken to those who have been false to their trust? These unfaithful men have not built upon the eternal Rock. Their foundation will prove to be sliding sand. "Know ye not that the friendship of the world is enmity with God? whosoever therefore will be a friend of the world is the enemy of God."

No limit can be set to our influence. One thoughtless act may prove the ruin of many souls. The course of every worker in our college is making impressions upon the minds of the young, and these are borne away to be reproduced in others. It should be the teacher's aim to prepare every youth under his care to be a blessing to the world. This object should never be lost sight of. There are some who profess to be working for Christ, yet occasionally go over to the side of Satan and do his work. Can the Saviour pronounce these good and faithful servants? Are they as watchmen giving the trumpet a certain sound?

Every man will at the judgment receive according to the deeds done in the body, whether they be good or evil. Our Saviour bids us: "Watch ye and pray, lest ye enter into temptation." If we encounter difficulties, and in Christ's strength overcome them; if we meet enemies, and in Christ's strength put them to flight; if we accept responsibilities, and in Christ's strength discharge them faithfully, we are gaining a precious experience. We learn, as we could not otherwise have learned, that our Saviour is a present help in every time of need.

There is a great work to be done in our college, a work which demands the co-operation of every teacher; and it is displeasing to God for one to discourage another. But nearly all seem to forget that Satan is an accuser of the brethren, and they unite with the enemy in his work. While professed Christians are contending, Satan is laying his snares for the inexperienced feet of children and youth. Those who have had a religious experience should seek to shield the young from his devices. They should never forget that they themselves were once enchanted with the pleasures of sin. We need the mercy and forbearance of God every hour, and how unbecoming for us to be impatient with the errors of the inexperienced youth. So long as God bears with them, dare we, fellow sinners, cast them off?

We should ever look upon the youth as the purchase of the blood of Christ. As such they have demands upon our love, our patience, and our sympathy. If we would follow Jesus we cannot restrict our interest and affection to ourselves and our own families; we cannot give our time and attention to temporal matters and forget the eternal interests of those around us. I have been shown that it is the result of our own selfishness that there are not one hundred young men where now there is one engaged in earnest labor for the salvation of their fellow men. "Love one another, as I have loved you," is the command of Jesus. Look at His self-denial; behold the manner of love He has bestowed upon us; and then seek to imitate the Pattern.

There have been many things displeasing to God in the young men and young women who have acted as teachers at our college. You have been so absorbed in yourselves, and so devoid of spirituality, that you could not lead the youth to holiness and heaven. Many have returned to their homes more decided in their impenitence because of your lack of love for God and Christ. Walking without the spirit of Jesus, you have encouraged irreligion, lightness, and unkindness in that you have indulged these evils yourselves. The result of this course you do not realize—souls are lost that might have been saved.

Many have strong feelings against Brother _____. They accuse him of unkindness, harshness, and severity. But some of the very ones who would condemn him are no less guilty themselves. "He that is without sin among you, let him first cast a stone." Brother _____ has not always moved wisely, and he has been hard to convince where he has not taken the best course. He has not been as willing to receive counsel, and to modify his methods of instruction and his manner of dealing with his students, as he should have been. But those who would condemn him because of his defects could in their turn be justly condemned. Every man has his peculiar defects of character. One may be free from the weakness which he sees in his brother, yet he may at the same time have faults which are far more grievous in the sight of God.

This unfeeling criticism of one another is wholly satanic. I was shown Brother _____ deserves respect for the good which he has done. Let him be dealt with tenderly. He has performed the labor which three men should have shared. Let those who are so eagerly searching for his faults recount what they have done in comparison with him. He toiled when others were seeking rest and pleasure. He is worn; God would have him lay off some of these extra burdens for a while. He has so many things to divide his time and attention he can do justice to none.

Brother _____ should not permit his combative spirit to be aroused and lead him to self-justification. He has given occasion for dissatisfaction. The Lord has presented this before him in testimony.

Students should not be encouraged in their faultfinding. This complaining spirit will increase as it is encouraged, and students will feel at liberty to criticize the teachers who do not meet their liking, and a spirit of dissatisfaction and strife will rapidly increase. This must be frowned down until it shall become extinct. Shall this evil be corrected? Will teachers put away their desire for the supremacy? Will they labor in humility, in love, and harmony? Time will tell.

PARENTAL TRAINING

I have been shown that very many of the parents who profess to believe the solemn message for this time have not trained their children for God. They have not restrained themselves and have been irritated with anyone who attempted to restrain them. They have not by living faith daily bound their children upon the altar of the Lord. Many of these youth have been allowed to transgress the fourth commandment by seeking their own pleasure upon God's holy day. They have felt no compunctions of conscience in going about the streets on the Sabbath for their own amusement. Many go where they please and do what they please, and their parents are so fearful of displeasing them that, imitating the management of Eli, they lay no commands upon them.

These youth finally lose all respect for the Sabbath and have no relish for religious meetings or for sacred and eternal things. If their parents mildly remonstrate with them, they shield themselves by telling of the faults of some of the church members. In place of silencing the first approach to anything of the kind, the parents think just as their children think; if this one or that one were perfect, their children would be right. Instead of this they should teach them that the sins of others are no excuse for them. Christ is the only true pattern. The wrongs of many would not excuse one wrong in them or lessen in the least their guilt. God has given them one standard, perfect, noble, elevated. This they must meet, irrespective of the course which others may pursue. But many parents seem to lose reason and judgment in their fondness for their children, and, through these indulged, selfish, mismanaged youth, Satan in turn works effectually to ruin the parents. I was referred to the wrath of God which came upon the incredulous and disobedient of ancient Israel. Their duty to instruct their children was plainly enjoined upon them. It is just as binding upon believing parents in this generation. "Give ear, O My people, to My law: incline your ears to the words of My mouth. I will open My mouth in a parable: I will utter dark sayings of old: which we have heard and known, and our fathers have told us. We will not hide them from their children, showing to the generation to come the praises of the Lord, and His strength, and His wonderful works that He hath done."

Children are what their parents make them by their instruction, discipline, and example. Hence the overwhelming importance of parental faithfulness in training the young for the service of God. Children should early be taught the sacredness of religious obligations. This is a most important

part of their education. Our duty to God should be performed before any other. The strict observance of God's
law, from principle, should be taught and enforced. "For
He established a testimony in Jacob, and appointed a law in
Israel, which He commanded our fathers, that they should
make them known to their children: that the generation to
come might know them, even the children which should be
born; who should arise and declare them to their children:
that they might set their hope in God, and not forget the
works of God, but keep His commandments: and might not
be as their fathers, a stubborn and rebellious generation; a
generation that set not their heart aright, and whose spirit
was not steadfast with God."

Here is seen the great responsibility devolving upon parents. Children who are allowed to come up to manhood or
womanhood with the will undisciplined and the passions
uncontrolled, will generally in afterlife pursue a course which
God condemns. These are eager for frivolous enjoyments and
irreligious associates. They have been allowed to neglect religious duties and indulge the inclinations of the carnal heart,
and, as a consequence, Satan controls the mind and principles. In _____ _____ parents have given him ample room thus to
work. Most of the backsliding from God that has occurred in
that place has come in consequence of the parents' neglect to
train their children to a conscientious, religious life. The condition of these children is lamentable. They profess to be
Christians; but their parents have not taken upon themselves
the burden of teaching them how to be Christians—how to
recount the mercies of God, how to praise Him, how to exemplify in their lives the life of Christ.

When these children enter school and associate with other
students, those who have been really trying to be Christians
are ashamed to act out their faith in the presence of those who
have had so much light. They are ashamed to appear singular

and deny inclination, and so they throw away their armor at the very time when it is most needed, when the powers of darkness are working through these irreligious companions to lead them away from Christ. They enter upon a path that is full of danger without the protection and support of religious principle, because they think it will be difficult or unpleasant to carry their religion with them to the schoolroom, the playground, and into all their associations. Thus they lay bare their soul to the shafts of Satan. Where are the guardians of these youth? Who have taken a firm hold of the throne of God with one hand while with the other they encircle these youth to draw them to Christ? It is just here that these children need to know the power of religion, need to be held back with a firm hand.

Many of those who have so long rejected divine guidance and guardianship are rushing on in the path of levity and selfish pleasure, yea, more, into baser acts and defilement of the body. As a consequence their minds are polluted, and religion is distasteful to them. Some have gone so far in this downward course, and followed so earnestly in the path of the Sodomites, that they are today nigh unto cursing, and the voice of reproof and warning is lost upon them. They will never be redeemed, and the parents are guilty of their ruin. The debasing enjoyments for which they have made such an enormous sacrifice—health, peace of mind, and eternal life—are bitterness in the end.

Parents, for Christ's sake do not blunder in your most important work, that of molding the characters of your children for time and for eternity. An error on your part in neglect of faithful instruction, or in the indulgence of that unwise affection which blinds your eyes to their defects and prevents you from giving them proper restraint, will prove their ruin. Your course may give a wrong direction to all their future career. You determine for them what they will be and what they will do for Christ, for men, and for their own souls.

Deal honestly and faithfully with your children. Work bravely and patiently. Fear no crosses, spare no time or labor, burden or suffering. The future of your children will testify the character of your work. Fidelity to Christ on your part can be better expressed in the symmetrical character of your children than in any other way. They are Christ's property, bought with His own blood. If their influence is wholly on the side of Christ they are His colaborers, helping others to find the path of life. If you neglect your God-given work, your unwise course of discipline places them among the class who scatter from Christ and strengthen the kingdom of darkness.

I speak the things I know; I testify to you the things which I have seen when I say there is among our youth, among educated young men of professedly Christian parents, a grievous offense in the sight of God, which is so common that it constitutes one of the signs of the last days. It is so full of evil tendencies as to call for decided exposure and denunciation. It is the sin of regarding with levity or contempt their early vows of consecration to God. In a religious interest the Holy Spirit moved upon them to take their stand wholly under the bloodstained banner of Prince Immanuel. But the parents were so far from God themselves, so busily engaged in worldly business, or so filled with doubts and dissatisfaction in regard to their own religious experience, that they were wholly unfitted to give them instruction. These youth, in their inexperience, needed a wise, firm hand to point out the right way and to bar with counsel and restraint the wrong way.

A religious life should be shown to be in marked contrast to a life of worldliness and pleasure seeking. He who would be the disciple of Christ must take up the cross and bear it after Jesus. Our Saviour lived not to please Himself, neither must we. High spiritual attainments will require entire consecration to God. But this instruction has not been given the youth because it would contradict the life of the parents. Therefore the children have been left to gain a knowledge of the Christian life as best they could. When tempted to seek the society of worldlings and participate in worldly amusements, the fond parents, disliking to deny them any indulgence, have—if they have said or done anything in the matter—taken a position so indefinite and undecided that the children have judged for themselves that the course they desired to pursue was in keeping with the Christian life and character.

Having once started in this way, they usually continue in it until the worldly element prevails and they sneer at their former convictions. They despise the simplicity manifested when their hearts were tender, and they find excuse to elude the sacred claims of the church and of the crucified Redeemer. This class can never become what they might have been had not the convictions of conscience been stifled, the holiest, tenderest affections blunted. If in after years they become followers of Christ, they will still bear the scars which irreverence for sacred things has made upon their souls.

Parents do not see these things. They do not foresee the result of their course. They do not feel that their children need the tenderest culture, the most careful discipline in the divine life. They do not look upon them as being in a peculiar sense the property of Christ, the purchase of His blood, the trophies of His grace, and as such, skillful instruments in God's hands to be used for the upbuilding of His kingdom. Satan is ever seeking to wrest these youth from the hands of Christ, and parents do not discern that the great adversary is planting his hellish banners close by their sides. They are so blinded they think it is the banner of Christ.

By ambition or indolence, skepticism or self-indulgence, Satan allures the young from the narrow path of holiness cast up for the ransomed of the Lord to walk in. They do not generally leave this path all at once. They are won away by degrees. Having taken one wrong step, they lose the witness of the Spirit to their acceptance with God. Thus they fall into a state of discouragement and distrust. They dislike religious services because conscience condemns them. They have fallen into the snare of Satan, and there is only one way of escape. They must retrace their steps and with humility of soul confess and forsake their halfhearted course. Let them renew their first experience which they have made light of, cherish every divine aspiration, and let those holy emotions which God's Spirit only can inspire, reign in their souls. Faith in Christ's power will impart strength to sustain, and light to guide.

This practical instruction in religious experience is what Christian parents should be prepared to give their children. God requires this of you, and you neglect your duty if you fail to perform this work. Instruct your children in regard to God's chosen methods of discipline and the conditions of success in the Christian life. Teach them that they cannot serve God and have their minds absorbed in overcareful provision for this life, but do not let them cherish the thought that they have no need to toil, and may spend their leisure moments in idleness. God's word is plain on this point. Jesus, the Majesty of heaven, has left an example for the youth. He toiled in the workshop at Nazareth for His daily bread. He was subject to His parents, and sought not to control His own time or to follow His own will. By a life of easy indulgence a youth can never attain to real excellence as a man or as a Christian. God does not promise us ease, honor, or wealth in His service; but He assures us that all needed blessings will be ours, "with persecutions," and in the world to come "life everlasting." Nothing less than entire consecration to His service will Christ accept. This is the lesson which every one of us must learn.

Those who study the Bible, counsel with God, and rely upon Christ will be enabled to act wisely at all times and under all circumstances. Good principles will be illustrated in actual life. Only let the truth for this time be cordially received and become the basis of character, and it will produce steadfastness of purpose, which the allurements of pleasure, the fickleness of custom, the contempt of the world-loving, and the heart's own clamors for self-indulgence are powerless to influence. Conscience must be first enlightened, the will must be brought into subjection. The love of truth and righteousness must reign in the soul, and a character will appear which heaven can approve.

We have marked illustrations of the sustaining power of firm, religious principle. Even the fear of death could not make the fainting David drink of the water of Bethlehem, to obtain which, valiant men had risked their lives. The gaping lions' den could not keep Daniel from his daily prayers, nor could the fiery furnace induce Shadrach and his companions to fall down before the idol which Nebuchadnezzar set up. Young men who have firm principles will eschew pleasure, defy pain, and brave even the lions' den and the heated fiery furnace rather than be found untrue to God. Mark the character of Joseph. Virtue was severely tested, but its triumph was complete. At every point the noble youth endured the test. The same lofty, unbending principle appeared at every trial. The Lord was with him, and His word was law.

Such firmness and untarnished principle shines brightest in contrast with the feebleness and inefficiency of the youth of this age. With but few exceptions, they are vacillating, varying with every change of circumstance and surroundings, one thing today and another tomorrow. Let the attractions of pleasure or selfish gratification be presented, and conscience will be sacrificed to gain the coveted indulgence. Can such a person be trusted? Never! In the absence of temptation he may carry himself with such seeming propriety that your doubts and suspicions appear unjust; but let opportunity be presented, and he will betray your confidence. He is unsound at heart. Just at the time when firmness and principle are most required, you will find him giving way, and if he does not become an Arnold or a Judas, it is because he lacks a fitting opportunity.

Parents, it should be your first concern to obey the call of duty and enter, heart and soul, into the work God has given you to do. If you fail in everything else, be thorough, be efficient, here. If your children come forth from the home training pure and virtuous, if they fill the least and lowest place in God's great plan of good for the world, your life can never be called a failure and can never be reviewed with remorse.

The idea that we must submit to ways of perverse children is a mistake. Elisha, at the very commencement of his work, was mocked and derided by the youth of Bethel. He was a man of great mildness, but the Spirit of God impelled him to pronounce a curse upon those railers. They had heard of Elijah's ascension, and they made this solemn event the subject of jeers. Elisha evinced that he was not to be trifled with, by old or young, in his sacred calling. When they told him he had better go up, as Elijah had done before him, he cursed them in the name of the Lord. The awful judgment that came upon them was of God. After this, Elisha had no further trouble in his mission. For fifty years he passed in and out of the gate of Bethel, and went to and fro from city to city, passing through crowds of the worst and rudest of idle, dissolute youth, but no one ever mocked him or made light of his qualifications as the prophet of the Most High. This one instance of terrible severity in the commencement of his career was sufficient to command respect through his whole life. Had he allowed the mockery to pass unnoticed, he might have been ridiculed, reviled, and even murdered by the rabble, and his mission to instruct and save the nation in its great peril would have been defeated.

Even kindness must have its limits. Authority must be sustained by a firm severity, or it will be received by many with mockery and contempt. The so-called tenderness, the coaxing and the indulgence, used toward youth by parents and guardians is the worst evil which can come upon them. Firmness, decision, positive requirements, are essential in every family. Parents, take up your neglected responsibilities; educate your children after God's plan, showing "forth the praises of Him who hath called you out of darkness into His marvelous light."

IMPORTANT TESTIMONY

Healdsburg, California, March 28, 1882.

Dear Brother _____: Your letter was received in due time. While I was glad to hear from you, I was made sad as I read its contents. I had received similar letters from Sister _____ and from Brother _____. But I have had no communications from Brother _____ or anyone who sustains him. From your own letters I learn the course which you have pursued in the proceedings against Brother _____.

I am not surprised that such a state of things should exist in Battle Creek, but I am pained to find you, my much-esteemed brother, involved in this matter on the wrong side with those whom I know God is not leading. Some of these persons are honest, but they are deceived. They have received their impressions from another source than the Spirit of God.

I have been careful not to express my opinion to individuals concerning important matters, for unjust advantage is often taken of what I say even in the most confidential manner. Persons set themselves to work to draw out remarks from me on various points, and then they distort and misrepresent, and make my words express ideas and opinions altogether different from what I hold. But this they must meet at the bar of God.

On the occurrence of your present difficulties I determined to keep silent; I thought it might be best to let matters develop, that those who had been so ready to censure my husband might see that the spirit of murmuring existed in their own hearts and was still active, now that the man of whom they had complained was silently sleeping in the grave.

I knew that a crisis must come. God has given this people plain and pointed testimonies to prevent this state of things. Had they obeyed the voice of the Holy Spirit in warning, counsel, and entreaty they would now enjoy unity and peace. But these testimonies have not been heeded by those who professed to believe them, and as a result there has been a wide departure from God, and the withdrawal of His blessing.

To effect the salvation of men, God employs various agencies. He speaks to them by His word and by His ministers, and He sends by the Holy Spirit messages of warning, reproof, and instruction. These means are designed to enlighten the understanding of the people, to reveal to them their duty and their sins, and the blessings which they may receive, to awaken in them a sense of spiritual want, that they may go to Christ and find in Him the grace they need. But many choose to follow their own way instead of God's way. They are not reconciled to God, neither can be, until self is crucified and Christ lives in the heart by faith.

Every individual, by his own act, either puts Christ from him by refusing to cherish His spirit and follow His example, or he enters into a personal union with Christ by self-renunciation, faith, and obedience. We must, each for himself, choose Christ, because He has first chosen us. This union with Christ is to be formed by those who are naturally at enmity with Him. It is a relation of utter dependence, to be entered into by a proud heart. This is close work, and many who profess to be followers of Christ know nothing of it. They nominally accept the Saviour, but not as the sole ruler of their hearts.

Some feel their need of the atonement, and with the recognition of this need, and the desire for a change of heart, a struggle begins. To renounce their own will, perhaps their chosen objects of affection or pursuit, requires an effort, at which many hesitate and falter and turn back. Yet this battle must be fought by every heart that is truly converted. We must war against temptations without and within. We must gain the victory over self, crucify the affections and lusts; and then begins the union of the soul with Christ. As the dry and apparently lifeless branch is grafted into the living tree, so may we become living branches of the True Vine. And the fruit which was borne by Christ will be borne by all His followers. After this union is formed, it can be preserved only by continual, earnest, painstaking effort. Christ exercises His power to preserve and guard this sacred tie, and the dependent, helpless sinner must act his part with untiring energy, or Satan by his cruel, cunning power will separate him from Christ.

Every Christian must stand on guard continually, watching every avenue of the soul where Satan might find access. He must pray for divine help and at the same time resolutely resist every inclination to sin. By courage, by faith, by persevering toil, he can conquer. But let him remember that to gain the victory Christ must abide in him and he in Christ.

A union of believers with Christ will as a natural result lead to a union with one another, which bond of union is the most enduring upon earth. We are one in Christ, as Christ is one with the Father. Christians are branches, and only branches, in the living Vine. One branch is not to borrow its sustenance from another. Our life must come from the parent vine. It is only by personal union with Christ, by communion with Him daily, hourly, that we can bear the fruits of the Holy Spirit.

There has come into the church at Battle Creek a spirit that has no part in Christ. It is not a zeal for the truth, not a love for the will of God as revealed in His word. It is a self-righteous spirit. It leads you to exalt self above Jesus and to regard your own opinions and ideas as more important than union with Christ and union with one another. You are sadly lacking in brotherly love. You are a backslidden church. To know the truth, to claim union with Christ, and yet not to bring forth fruit, not to live in the exercise of constant faith—this hardens the heart in disobedience and self-confidence. Our growth in grace, our joy, our usefulness, all depend on our union with Christ and the degree of faith we exercise in Him. Here is the source of our power in the world.

Many of you are seeking honor of one another. But what is the honor or the approval of man to one who regards himself as a son of God, a joint heir with Christ? What are the pleasures of this world to him who is daily a sharer in the love of Christ which passes knowledge? What are the contempt and opposition of man to him whom God accepts through Jesus Christ? Selfishness can no more live in the heart that is exercising faith in Christ than light and darkness can exist together. Spiritual coldness, sloth, pride, and cowardice alike shrink from the presence of faith. Can those who are as closely united with Christ as the branch to the vine, talk of and to everyone but Jesus?

Are you in Christ? Not if you do not acknowledge yourselves erring, helpless, condemned sinners. Not if you are exalting and glorifying self. If there is any good in you, it is wholly attributable to the mercy of a compassionate Saviour. Your birth, your reputation, your wealth, your talents, your virtues, your piety, your philanthropy, or anything else in you or connected with you, will not form a bond of union between your soul and Christ. Your connection with the church, the manner in which your brethren regard you, will be of no avail unless you believe in Christ. It is not enough to believe *about* Him; you must believe *in* Him. You must rely wholly upon His saving grace.

Many of you at Battle Creek are living without prayer, without thoughts of Christ, and without exalting Him before those around you. You have no words to exalt Christ; you do no deeds that honor Him. Many of you are as truly strangers to Christ as though you had never heard His name. You have not the peace of Christ; for you have no true ground for peace. You have no communion with God because you are not united to Christ. Said our Saviour: "No man cometh to the Father, but by Me." You are not useful in the cause of Christ. Except ye abide in Me, says Jesus, ye can do nothing—nothing in God's sight, nothing that Christ will accept at your hands. Without Christ you can have nothing but a delusive hope, for He Himself declares: "If a man abide not in Me, he is cast forth as a branch, and is withered; and men gather them, and cast them into the fire, and they are burned."

Advancement in Christian experience is characterized by increasing humility, as the result of increasing knowledge. Everyone who is united to Christ will depart from all iniquity. I tell you, in the fear of God, I have been shown that many of you will fail of everlasting life because you are building your hopes of heaven on a false foundation. God is leaving you to yourselves, "to humble thee, and to prove thee, to know what was in thine heart." You have neglected the Scriptures. You despise and reject the testimonies because they reprove your darling sins and disturb your self-complacency. When Christ is cherished in the heart, His likeness will be revealed in the life. Humility will reign where pride was once predominant. Submission, meekness, patience, will soften down the rugged features of a naturally perverse, impetuous disposition. Love to Jesus will be manifested in love to His people. It is not fitful, not spasmodic, but calm and deep and strong. The life of the Christian will be divested of all pretense, free from all affectation, artifice, and falsehood. It is earnest, true, sublime. Christ speaks in every word. He is seen in every deed. The life is radiant with the light of an indwelling Saviour. In converse with God and in happy contemplation of heavenly things the soul is preparing for heaven and laboring to gather other souls into the fold of Christ. Our Saviour is able and willing to do for us more than we can ask or even think.

The church at Battle Creek need a self-abasing unpretending spirit. I have been shown that many are cherishing an unholy desire for the supremacy. Many love to be flattered and are jealously watching for slights or neglect. There is a hard, unforgiving spirit. There is envy, strife, emulation.

Nothing is more essential to communion with God than the most profound humility. "I dwell," says the High and Holy One, "with him also that is of a contrite and humble spirit." While you are so eagerly striving to be first, remember that you will be last in the favor of God if you fail to cherish a meek and lowly spirit. Pride of heart will cause many to fail where they might have made a success. "Before honor is humility," "and the patient in spirit is better than the proud in spirit." "When Ephraim spake trembling, he exalted himself in Israel; but when he offended in Baal, he died." "Many are called, but few are chosen." Many hear the invitation of mercy, are tested and proved; but few are sealed with the seal of the living God. Few will humble themselves as a little child, that they may enter the kingdom of heaven.

Few receive the grace of Christ with self-abasement, with a deep and permanent sense of their unworthiness. They cannot bear the manifestations of the power of God, for this would encourage in them self-esteem, pride, and envy. This is why the Lord can do so little for us now. God would have you individually seek for the perfection of love and humility in your own hearts. Bestow your chief care upon yourselves, cultivate those excellencies of character which will fit you for the society of the pure and the holy.

You all need the converting power of God. You need to seek Him for yourselves. For your soul's sake neglect this work no longer. All your trouble grows out of your separation from God. Your disunion and dissension are the fruit of an unchristian character.

I had thought to remain silent and let you go on until you should see and abhor the sinfulness of your course; but backsliding from God produces hardness of heart and blindness of mind, and there is less and less perception of the true condition, until the grace of God is finally withdrawn, as from the Jewish nation.

I wish my position to be clearly understood. I have no sympathy with the course that has been pursued toward Brother _____.The enemy has encouraged feelings of hatred in the hearts of many. The errors committed by him have been reported from one person to another, constantly growing in magnitude, as busy, gossiping tongues added fuel to the fire. Parents who have never felt the care which they should feel for the souls of their children, and who have never given them proper restraint and instruction, are the very ones who manifest the most bitter opposition when their children are restrained, reproved, or corrected at school. Some of these children are a disgrace to the church and a disgrace to the name of Adventists.

The parents despised reproof themselves, and despised the reproof given to their children, and were not careful to conceal this from them. The sin of the parents began with their mismanagement at home. The souls of some of these children will be lost because they did not receive instruction from God's word and did not become Christians at home. Instead of sympathizing with their children in a perverse course, the parents should have reproved them and sustained the faithful teacher. These parents were not united to Christ themselves, and this is the reason of their terrible neglect of duty. That which they have sown they will also reap. They are sure of a harvest.

In the school Brother _____ has not only been burdened by the wrong course of the children, but by the injudicious management of the parents, which produced and nurtured hatred of restraint. Overwork, unceasing care, with no help at home, but rather a constant irritation, have caused him at times to lose self-control and to act injudiciously. Some have taken advantage of this, and faults of minor consequence have been made to appear like grave sins.

The class of professed Sabbathkeepers who try to form a union between Christ and Belial, who take hold of the truth with one hand and of the world with the other, have surrounded their children and clouded the church with an atmosphere entirely foreign to religion and the Spirit of Christ. They dared not openly oppose the claims of truth. They dared not take a bold stand and say they did not believe the testimonies; but, while nominally believing both, they have obeyed neither. By their course of action they have denied both. They desire the Lord to fulfill to them His promises; but they refuse to comply with the conditions on which these promises are based. They will not relinquish every rival for Christ. Under the preaching of the word there is a partial suppression of worldliness, but no radical change of the affections. Worldly desires, the lust of the flesh, the lust of the eyes, and the pride of life ultimately gain the victory. This class are all professed Christians. Their names are on the church books. They live for a time a seemingly religious life and then yield their hearts, too often finally, to the predominating influence of the world.

Whatever may be Brother _____'s faults, your course is unjustifiable and unchristian. You have gone back over his history for years and have searched out everything that was unfavorable, every shadow of evil, and have made him an offender for a word. You have brought all the powers you could command to sustain yourselves in your course as accusers. Remember, God will deal in the same manner with every one of you. "With what judgment ye judge, ye shall be judged: and with what measure ye mete, it shall be measured to you again." Those who have taken part in this disgraceful proceeding will meet their work again. What influence do you think your course will have upon the students, who have ever been impatient of restraint? How will these things affect their character and their life history?

What say the testimonies concerning these things? Even one wrong trait of character, one sinful desire cherished, will eventually neutralize all the power of the gospel. The prevalence of a sinful desire shows the delusion of the soul. Every indulgence of that desire strengthens the soul's aversion to God. The pains of duty and the pleasures of sin are the cords with which Satan binds men in his snares. Those who would rather die than perform a wrong act are the only ones who will be found faithful.

A child may receive sound religious instruction; but if parents, teachers, or guardians permit his character to be biased by a wrong habit, that habit, if not overcome, will become a predominant power, and the child is lost.

The testimony borne to you by the Spirit of God is: Parley not with the enemy. Kill the thorns, or they will kill you. Break up the fallow ground of the heart. Let the work go deep and thorough. Let the plowshare of truth tear out the weeds and briers.

Said Christ to the angry, accusing Pharisees: "He that is without sin among you, let him first cast a stone." Were those

sinless who were so ready to accuse and condemn Brother
_____? Were their characters and lives to be searched as
closely and publicly as they have searched Brother _____'s,
some of them would appear far worse than they have tried to
represent him.

I dare not longer remain silent. I speak to you and to the
church at Battle Creek. You have made a great mistake.
You have treated with injustice one to whom you and your
children owe a debt of gratitude which you do not realize.
You are responsible for the influence you have exerted
upon the college. Peace has come because the students have
had their own way. In another crisis they will be as determined and persevering as they have been on this occasion;
and, if they find as able an advocate as they have found in
Brother _____, they may again accomplish their purpose.
God has been speaking to teachers and students and church
members, but you have cast His words behind you. You
have thought best to take your own course, irrespective of
consequences.

God has given us, as a people, warnings, reproofs, and
cautions, on the right hand and on the left, to lead us away
from worldly customs and worldly policy. He requires us to
be peculiar in faith and in character, to meet a standard far in
advance of worldlings. Brother _____ came among you,
unacquainted with the Lord's dealings with us. Having newly
come to the faith, he had almost everything to learn. Yet you
have unhesitatingly coincided with his judgment. You have
sanctioned in him a spirit and course of action that have
nought of Christ.

You have encouraged in the students a spirit of criticism,
which God's Spirit has sought to repress. You have led them
to betray confidence. There are not a few young persons
among us who are indebted for most valuable traits of character to the knowledge and principles received from Brother

_____. To his training many owe much of their usefulness, not only in the Sabbath school, but in various other branches of our work. Yet your influence encouraged ingratitude, and has led students to despise the things that they should cherish.

Those who have not the peculiar trials to which another is subjected may flatter themselves that they are better than he. But place them in the furnace of trial, and they might not endure it nearly as well as the one they censure and misjudge. How little we can know of the heart anguish of another. How few understand another's circumstances. Hence the difficulty of giving wise counsel. What may appear to us to be appropriate, may, in reality, be quite the reverse.

Brother _____ has been an earnest seeker after knowledge. He has sought to impress upon the students that they are responsible for their time, their talents, their opportunities. It is impossible for a man to have so much care, and carry so heavy responsibilities, without becoming hurried, weary, and nervous. Those who refuse to accept burdens which will tax their strength to the utmost know nothing of the pressure brought to bear upon those who must bear these burdens.

There are some in the college who have looked only for what has been unfortunate and disagreeable in their acquaintance with Brother _____. These persons have not that noble, Christlike spirit that thinketh no evil. They have made the most of every inconsiderate word or act, and have recalled these at a time when envy, prejudice, and jealousy were active in unchristian hearts.

A writer has said that "envy's memory is nothing but a row of hooks to hang up grudges on." There are many in the world who consider it an evidence of superiority to recount the things and persons that they "cannot bear," rather than the things and persons that they are attracted to. Not so did the great apostle. He exhorts his brethren: "Whatsoever things are honest, whatsoever things are just, whatsoever things are pure, whatsoever things are lovely, whatsoever things are of good report; if there be any virtue, and if there be any praise, think on these things."

Envy is not merely a perverseness of temper, but a distemper, which disorders all the faculties. It began with Satan. He desired to be first in heaven, and because he could not have all the power and glory he sought, he rebelled against the government of God. He envied our first parents and tempted them to sin and thus ruined them and all the human race.

The envious man shuts his eyes to the good qualities and noble deeds of others. He is always ready to disparage and misrepresent that which is excellent. Men often confess and forsake other faults, but there is little to be hoped for from the envious man. Since to envy a person is to admit that he is a superior, pride will not permit any concession. If an attempt be made to convince the envious person of his sin, he becomes even more bitter against the object of his passion, and too often he remains incurable.

The envious man diffuses poison wherever he goes, alienating friends and stirring up hatred and rebellion against God and man. He seeks to be thought best and greatest, not by putting forth heroic, self-denying efforts to reach the goal of excellence himself, but by standing where he is and diminishing the merit due to the efforts of others.

Envy has been cherished in the hearts of some in the church as well as in the college. God is displeased at your course. I entreat you, for Christ's sake, never treat another as you have treated Brother _____. A noble nature does not exult in causing others pain, or delight in discovering their deficiencies. A disciple of Christ will turn away with loathing from the feast of scandal. Some who have been active on this occasion are repeating the course pursued toward one of the Lord's servants in affliction, one who had sacrificed health and strength in their service. The Lord vindicated the cause of the oppressed and turned the light of His countenance upon His suffering servant. I then saw that God would prove these persons again, as He has now done, to reveal what was in their hearts.

When David had sinned, God granted him his choice, to receive his punishment from God or at the hand of man. The repentant king chose to fall into the hand of God. The tender mercies of the wicked are cruel. Erring, sinful man, who can himself be kept in the right path only by the power of God, is yet hardhearted, unforgiving toward his erring brother. My brethren at Battle Creek, what account will you render at the bar of God? Great light has come to you, in reproofs, warnings, and entreaties. How have you spurned its heaven-sent rays!

The tongue that delights in mischief, the babbling tongue that says, Report, and I will report it, is declared by the apostle James to be set on fire of hell. It scatters firebrands on every side. What cares the vendor of gossip that he defames the innocent? He will not stay his evil work, though he destroy hope and courage in those who are already sinking under their burdens. He cares only to indulge his scandal-loving propensity. Even professed Christians close their eyes to all that is pure, honest, noble, and lovely, and treasure up whatever is objectionable and disagreeable, and publish it to the world.

You have yourselves thrown open the doors for Satan to come in. You have given him an honored place at your investigation, or inquisition meetings. But you have shown no respect for the excellencies of a character established by years of faithfulness. Jealous, revengeful tongues have colored acts and motives to suit their own ideas. They have made black appear white, and white black. When remonstrated with for their statements, some have said: "It is true." Admitting that the fact stated is true, does that justify your course? No, no. If God should take all the accusations that might in truth be brought against you, and should braid them into a scourge to punish you, your wounds would be more and deeper than those which you have inflicted on Brother _____. Even facts may be so stated as to convey a false impression. You have no right to gather up every report against him and use them to ruin his reputation and destroy his usefulness. Should the Lord manifest toward you the same spirit which you have manifested toward your brother, you would be destroyed without mercy. Have you no compunctions of conscience? I fear not. The time has come for this satanic spell to lose its power. If Brother _____ were all that you represent him to be,—which I know he is not,—your course would still be unjustifiable.

When we listen to a reproach against our brother, we take up that reproach. To the question, "Lord, who shall abide in Thy tabernacle? who shall dwell in Thy holy hill?" the psalmist answered, "He that walketh uprightly, and worketh righteousness, and speaketh the truth in his heart. He that backbiteth not with his tongue, nor doeth evil to his neighbor, nor taketh up a reproach against his neighbor."

What a world of gossip would be prevented if every man would remember that those who tell him the faults of others will as freely publish his faults at a favorable opportunity. We should endeavor to think well of all men, especially our brethren, until compelled to think otherwise. We should not hastily credit evil reports. These are often the result of envy or misunderstanding, or they may proceed from exaggeration or a partial disclosure of facts. Jealousy and suspicion, once allowed a place, will sow themselves broadcast, like thistledown. Should a brother go astray, then is the time to show your real interest in him. Go to him kindly, pray with and for him, remembering the infinite price which Christ has paid for his redemption. In this way you may save a soul from death, and hide a multitude of sins.

A glance, a word, even an intonation of the voice, may be vital with falsehood, sinking like a barbed arrow into some heart, inflicting an incurable wound. Thus a doubt, a reproach, may be cast upon one by whom God would accomplish a good work, and his influence is blighted, his usefulness destroyed. Among some species of animals, if one of their number is wounded and falls, he is at once set upon and torn in pieces by his fellows. The same cruel spirit is indulged by men and women who bear the name of Christians. They manifest a pharisaical zeal to stone others less guilty than themselves. There are some who point to others' faults and failures to divert attention from their own, or to gain credit for great zeal for God and the church.

A few weeks since I was in a dream brought into one of your meetings for investigation. I heard the testimonies borne by students against Brother _____. Those very students had received great benefit from his thorough, faithful instruction. Once they could hardly say enough in his praise. Then it was popular to esteem him. But now the current was setting the other way. These persons have developed their true character. I saw an angel with a ponderous book open in which he wrote every testimony given. Opposite each testimony were traced the sins, defects, and errors of the one who bore it. Then there was recorded the great benefit which these individuals had received from Brother _____'s labors.

We, as a people, are reaping the fruit of Brother _____'s hard labor. There is not a man among us who has devoted more time and thought to his work than has Brother _____. He has felt that he had no one to sustain him, and has felt grateful for any encouragement.

One of the great objects to be secured in the establishment of the college was the separation of our youth from the spirit and influence of the world, from its customs, its follies, and its idolatry. The college was to build a barrier against the immorality of the present age, which makes the world as corrupt as in the days of Noah. The young are bewitched with the mania for courtship and marriage. Lovesick sentimentalism prevails. Great vigilance and tact are needed to guard the youth from these wrong influences. Many parents are blind to the tendencies of their children. Some parents have stated to me, with great satisfaction, that their sons or daughters had no desire for the attentions of the opposite sex, when in fact these children were at the same time secretly giving or receiving such attentions, and the parents were so much absorbed in worldliness and gossip that they knew nothing about the matter.

The primary object of our college was to afford young men an opportunity to study for the ministry and to prepare young persons of both sexes to become workers in the various branches of the cause. These students needed a knowledge of the common branches of education and, above all else, of the word of God. Here our school has been deficient. There has not been a man devoted to God to give himself to this branch of the work. Young men moved upon by the Spirit of God to give themselves to the ministry have come to the college for this purpose and have been disappointed. Adequate preparation for this class has not been made, and some of the teachers, knowing this, have advised the youth to take other studies and fit themselves for other pursuits. If these youth were not firm in their purpose, they were induced to give up all idea of studying for the ministry.

Such is the result of the influence exerted by unsanctified teachers, who labor merely for wages, who are not imbued with the Spirit of God and have no union with Christ. No one has been more active in this work than Brother _____. The Bible should be one of the principal subjects of study.

This book, which tells us how to spend the present life, that we may secure the future, immortal life, is of more value to students than any other. We have but a brief period in which to become acquainted with its truths. But the one who had made God's word a study, and who could more than any other teacher have helped the young to gain a knowledge of the Scriptures, has been separated from the school.

Professors and teachers have not understood the design of the college. We have put in means and thought and labor to make it what God would have it. The will and judgment of those who are almost wholly ignorant of the way in which God has led us as a people, should not have a controlling influence in that college. The Lord has repeatedly shown that we should not pattern after the popular schools. Ministers of other denominations spend years in obtaining an education. Our young men must obtain theirs in a short time. Where there is now one minister, there should be twenty whom our college had prepared with God's help to enter the gospel field.

Many of our younger ministers, and some of more mature experience, are neglecting the word of God and also despising the testimonies of His Spirit. They do not know what the testimonies contain and do not wish to know. They do not wish to discover and correct their defects of character. Many parents do not themselves seek instruction from the testimonies, and of course they cannot impart it to their children. They show their contempt for the light which God has given, by going directly contrary to His instructions. Those at the heart of the work have set the example.

You have published your contentions to the world. Do you think you stand, as a people, in a more favorable light in Battle Creek? Christ prayed that His disciples might be one, as He was one with the Father, that the world might know that God had sent Him. What testimony have you borne during the past few months? The Lord is looking into every heart. He weighs our motives. He will try every soul. Who will bear the test?

THE TESTIMONIES SLIGHTED

Healdsburg, California, June 20, 1882.

Dear Brethren and Sisters in Battle Creek: I understand that the testimony* which I sent to Brother _____, with the request that it be read to the church, was withheld from you for several weeks after it was received by him. Before sending that testimony my mind was so impressed by the Spirit of God that I had no rest day or night until I wrote to you. It was not a work that I would have chosen for myself. Before my husband's death I decided that it was not my duty to bear testimony to anyone in reproof of wrong or in vindication of right, because advantage was taken of my words to deal harshly with the erring and to unwisely exalt others whose course I had not in any degree sustained. Many explained the testimonies to suit themselves. The truth of God is not in harmony with the traditions of men, nor does it conform to their opinions. Like its divine Author, it is unchangeable, the same yesterday, today, and forever. Those who separate from God will call darkness light, and error truth. But darkness will never prove itself to be light, nor will error become truth.

The minds of many have been so darkened and confused by worldly customs, worldly practices, and worldly influences that all power to discriminate between light and darkness, truth and error, seems destroyed. I had little hope that my words would be understood; but when the Lord moved upon me so decidedly, I could not resist His Spirit. Knowing that

---

*Reference is here made to the preceding article.

you were involving yourselves in the snares of Satan, I felt that the danger was too great for me to keep silent.

For years the Lord has been presenting the situation of the church before you. Again and again reproofs and warnings have been given. October 23, 1879, the Lord gave me a most impressive testimony in regard to the church in Battle Creek. During the last months I was with you I carried a heavy burden for the church, while those who should have felt to the very depths of their souls were comparatively easy and unconcerned. I knew not what to do or what to say. I had no confidence in the course which many were pursuing, for they were doing the very things which the Lord had warned them not to do.

That God who knows their spiritual condition declares: They have cherished evil and separated from Me. They have gone astray, every one of them. Not one is guiltless. They have forsaken Me, the Fountain of living waters, and have hewed out to them broken cisterns that can hold no water. Many have corrupted their ways before Me. Envy, hatred of one another, jealousy, evil surmising, emulation, strife, bitterness, is the fruit that they bear. And they will not heed the testimony that I send them. They will not see their perverse ways and be converted, that I should heal them.

Many are looking with self-complacency upon the long years during which they have advocated the truth. They now feel that they are entitled to a reward for their past trials and obedience. But this genuine experience in the things of God in the past makes them more guilty before Him for not preserving their integrity and going forward to perfection. The faithfulness for the past year will never atone for the neglect of the present year. A man's truthfulness yesterday will not atone for his falsehood today.

Many excused their disregard of the testimonies by saying: "Sister White is influenced by her husband; the testimonies are molded by his spirit and judgment." Others were seeking to gain something from me which they could construe to justify their course or to give them influence. It was then I decided that nothing more should go from my pen until the converting power of God was seen in the church. But the Lord placed the burden upon my soul. I labored for you earnestly. How much this cost both my husband and myself, eternity will tell. Have I not a knowledge of the state of the church, when the Lord has presented their case before me again and again for years? Repeated warnings have been given, yet there has been no decided change.

I saw that the frown of God was upon His people for their assimilation to the world. I saw that the children of Brother _____ have been a snare to him. Their ideas and opinions, their feelings and statements, had an influence upon his mind and blinded his judgment. These youth are strongly inclined to infidelity. The mother's want of faith and trust in God has been given as an inheritance to her children. Her devotion to them is greater than her devotion to God. The father has neglected his duty. The result of their wrong course is revealed in their children.

As I spoke to the church I tried to impress upon parents their solemn obligation to the children, because I knew the state of these youth and what tendencies had made them what they are. But the word was not received. I know what burdens I bore in the last of my labors among you. I would never have thus tasked my strength to the utmost had I not seen your peril. I longed to arouse you to humble your hearts before God, to return to Him with penitence and faith.

Yet now when I send you a testimony of warning and reproof, many of you declare it to be merely the opinion of Sister White. You have thereby insulted the Spirit of God. You know how the Lord has manifested Himself through the spirit of prophecy. Past, present, and future have passed before me. I have been shown faces that I had never seen, and years afterward I knew them when I saw them. I have been aroused from my sleep with a vivid sense of subjects previously presented to my mind; and I have written, at midnight, letters that have gone across the continent and, arriving at a crisis, have saved great disaster to the cause of God. This has been my work for many years. A power has impelled me to reprove and rebuke wrongs that I had not thought of. Is this work of the last thirty-six years from above or from beneath?

Suppose—as some would make it appear, incorrectly however—that I was influenced to write as I did by letters received from members of the church. How was it with the apostle Paul? The news he received through the household of Chloe concerning the condition of the church at Corinth was what caused him to write his first epistle to that church. Private letters had come to him stating the facts as they existed, and in his answer he laid down general principles which if heeded would correct the existing evils. With great tenderness and wisdom he exhorts them to all speak the same things, that there be no divisions among them.

Paul was an inspired apostle, yet the Lord did not reveal to him at all times just the condition of His people. Those who were interested in the prosperity of the church, and saw evils creeping in, presented the matter before him, and from the light which he had previously received he was prepared to judge of the true character of these developments. Because the Lord had not given him a new revelation for that special time, those who were really seeking light did not cast his message aside as only a common letter. No, indeed. The Lord had shown him the difficulties and dangers which would arise in the churches, that when they should develop he might know just how to treat them.

He was set for the defense of the church. He was to watch for souls as one that must render account to God, and should he not take notice of the reports concerning their state of anarchy and division? Most assuredly; and the reproof he sent them was written just as much under the inspiration of the Spirit of God as were any of his epistles. But when these reproofs came, some would not be corrected. They took the position that God had not spoken to them through Paul, that he had merely given them his opinion as a man, and they regarded their own judgment as good as that of Paul.

So it is with many among our people who have drifted away from the old landmarks and who have followed their own understanding. What a great relief it would be to such could they quiet their conscience with the belief that my work is not of God. But your unbelief will not change the facts in the case. You are defective in character, in moral and religious experience. Close your eyes to the fact if you will, but this does not make you one particle more perfect. The only remedy is to wash in the blood of the Lamb.

If you seek to turn aside the counsel of God to suit yourselves, if you lessen the confidence of God's people in the testimonies He has sent them, you are rebelling against God as certainly as were Korah, Dathan, and Abiram. You have their history. You know how stubborn they were in their own opinions. They decided that their judgment was better than that of Moses and that Moses was doing great injury to Israel. Those who united with them were so set in their opinions that, notwithstanding the judgments of God in a marked manner destroyed the leaders and the princes, the next morning the survivors came to Moses and said: "Ye have killed the people of the Lord." We see what fearful deception will come upon the human mind. How hard it is to convince souls that have become imbued with a spirit which is not of God. As Christ's ambassador, I would say to you: Be careful what positions you take. This is God's work, and you must render to Him an account for the manner in which you treat His message.

While standing over the dying bed of my husband, I knew that had others borne their part of the burdens, he might have lived. I then pleaded, with agony of soul, that those present might no longer grieve the Spirit of God by their hardness of heart. A few days later I myself stood face to face with death. Then I had most clear revealings from God in regard to myself, and in regard to the church. In great weakness I bore to you my testimony, not knowing but it would be my last opportunity. Have you forgotten that solemn occasion? I can never forget it, for I seemed to be brought before the judgment seat of Christ. Your state of backsliding, your hardness of heart, your lack of harmony of love and spirituality, your departure from the simplicity and purity which God would have you preserve—I knew it all; I felt it all. Faultfinding, censuring, envy, strife for the highest place, were among you. I had seen it and to what it would lead. I feared that effort would cost me my life, but the interest I felt for you led me to speak. God spoke to you that day. Did it make any lasting impression?

When I went to Colorado I was so burdened for you that, in my weakness, I wrote many pages to be read at your camp meeting. Weak and trembling, I arose at three o'clock in the morning to write to you. God was speaking through clay. You might say that this communication was only a letter. Yes, it was a letter, but prompted by the Spirit of God, to bring before your minds things that had been shown me. In these letters which I write, in the testimonies I bear, I am presenting to you that which the Lord has presented to me. I do not write one article in the paper expressing merely my own ideas. They are what God has opened before me in vision—the precious rays of light shining from the throne.

After I came to Oakland I was weighted down with a sense of the condition of things at Battle Creek, and I, weak, powerless to help you. I knew that the leaven of unbelief was at work. Those who disregarded the plain injunctions of God's word were disregarding the testimonies which urged them to give heed to that word. While visiting Healdsburg last winter, I was much in prayer and burdened with anxiety and grief. But the Lord swept back the darkness at one time while I was in prayer, and a great light filled the room. An angel of God was by my side, and I seemed to be in Battle Creek. I was in your councils; I heard words uttered, I saw and heard things that, if God willed, I wish could be forever blotted from my memory. My soul was so wounded I knew not what to do or what to say. Some things I cannot mention. I was bidden to let no one know in regard to this, for much was yet to be developed.

I was told to gather up the light that had been given me and let its rays shine forth to God's people. I have been doing this in articles in the papers. I arose at three o'clock nearly every morning for months and gathered the different items written after the last two testimonies were given me in Battle Creek. I wrote out these matters and hurried them on to you; but I had neglected to take proper care of myself, and the result was that I sank under the burden; my writings were not all finished to reach you at the General Conference.

Again, while in prayer, the Lord revealed Himself. I was once more in Battle Creek. I was in many houses and heard your words around your tables. The particulars I have no liberty now to relate. I hope never to be called to mention them. I had also several most striking dreams.

What voice will you acknowledge as the voice of God? What power has the Lord in reserve to correct your errors and show you your course as it is? What power to work in the church? If you refuse to believe until every shadow of uncertainty and every possibility of doubt is removed you will never believe. The doubt that demands perfect knowledge will never yield to faith. Faith rests upon evidence, not demonstration. The Lord requires us to obey the voice of duty, when there are other voices all around us urging us to pursue an opposite course. It requires earnest attention from us to distinguish the voice which speaks from God. We must resist and conquer inclination, and obey the voice of conscience without parleying or compromise, lest its promptings cease and will and impulse control. The word of the Lord comes to us all who have not resisted His Spirit by determining not to hear and obey. This voice is heard in warnings, in counsels, in reproof. It is the Lord's message of light to His people. If we wait for louder calls or better opportunities, the light may be withdrawn, and we left in darkness.

By once neglecting to comply with the call of God's Spirit and His word, when obedience involves a cross, many have lost much—how much they will never know till the books are opened at the final day. The pleadings of the Spirit, neglected today because pleasure or inclination leads in an opposite direction, may be powerless to convince, or even impress, tomorrow. To improve the opportunities of the present, with prompt and willing hearts, is the only way to grow in grace and the knowledge of the truth. We should ever cherish a sense that, individually, we are standing before the Lord of hosts; no word, no act, no thought, even, should be indulged, to offend the eye of the Eternal One. We shall then have no fear of man or of earthly power, because a Monarch, whose empire is the universe, who holds in His hands our individual destinies for time and eternity, is taking cognizance of all our work. If we would feel that in every place we are the servants of the Most High, we would be more circumspect; our whole life would possess to us a meaning and a sacredness which earthly honors can never give.

The thoughts of the heart, the words of the lips, and every act of the life, will make our character more worthy, if the presence of God is continually felt. Let the language of the heart be: "Lo, God is here." Then the life will be pure, the character unspotted, the soul continually uplifted to the Lord. You have not pursued this course at Battle Creek. I have been shown that painful and contagious disease is upon you, which will produce spiritual death unless it is arrested.

Many are ruined by their desire for a life of ease and pleasure. Self-denial is disagreeable to them. They are constantly seeking to escape trials that are inseparable from a course of fidelity to God. They set their hearts upon having the good things of this life. This is human success, but is it not won at the expense of future, eternal interests? The great business of life is to show ourselves to be true servants of God, loving righteousness and hating iniquity. We should accept gratefully such measures of present happiness and present success as are found in the path of duty. Our greatest strength is realized when we feel and acknowledge our weakness. The greatest loss which any one of you in Battle Creek can suffer is the loss of earnestness and persevering zeal to do right, the loss of strength to resist temptation, the loss of faith in the principles of truth and duty.

Let no man flatter himself that he is a successful man unless he preserves the integrity of his conscience, giving himself wholly to the truth and to God. We should move steadily forward, never losing heart or hope in the good work, whatever trials beset our path, whatever moral darkness may encompass us. Patience, faith, and love for duty are the lessons we must learn. Subduing self and looking to Jesus is an everyday work. The Lord will never forsake the soul that trusts in Him and seeks His aid. The crown of life is placed only upon the brow of the overcomer. There is, for everyone, earnest, solemn work for God while life lasts. As Satan's power increases and his devices are multiplied, skill, aptness, and sharp generalship should be exercised by those in charge of the flock of God. Not only have we each a work to do for our own souls, but we have also a duty to arouse others to gain eternal life.

It pains me to say, my brethren, that your sinful neglect to walk in the light has enshrouded you in darkness. You may now be honest in not recognizing and obeying the light; the doubts you have entertained, your neglect to heed the requirements of God, have blinded your perceptions so that darkness is now to you light, and light is darkness. God has bidden you to go forward to perfection. Christianity is a religion of progress. Light from God is full and ample, waiting our demand upon it. Whatever blessings the Lord may give, He has an infinite supply beyond, an inexhaustible store from which we may draw. Skepticism may treat the sacred claims of the gospel with jests, scoffing, and denial. The spirit of worldliness may contaminate the many and control the few; the cause of God may hold its ground only by great exertion and continual sacrifice, yet it will triumph finally.

The word is: Go forward; discharge your individual duty, and leave all consequences in the hands of God. If we move forward where Jesus leads the way we shall see His triumph, we shall share His joy. We must share the conflicts if we wear the crown of victory. Like Jesus, we must be made perfect through suffering. Had Christ's life been one of ease, then might we safely yield to sloth. Since His life was marked with continual self-denial, suffering, and self-sacrifice, we shall make no complaint if we are partakers with Him. We can walk safely in the darkest path if we have the Light of the world for our guide.

The Lord is testing and proving you. He has counseled, admonished, and entreated. All these solemn admonitions will either make the church better or decidedly worse. The oftener the Lord speaks to correct or counsel, and you disregard His voice, the more disposed will you be to reject it again and again, till God says: "Because I have called, and ye refused; I have stretched out My hand, and no man regarded; but ye have set at nought all My counsel, and would none of My reproof: I also will laugh at your calamity; I will mock when your fear cometh; when your fear cometh as desolation, and your destruction cometh as a whirlwind; when distress and anguish cometh upon you. Then shall they call upon Me, but I will not answer; they shall seek Me early, but they shall not find me; for that they hated knowledge, and did not choose the fear of the Lord: they would none of My counsel: they despised all My reproof. Therefore shall they eat of the fruit of their own way, and be filled with their own devices."

Are you not halting between two opinions? Are you not neglecting to heed the light which God has given you? Take heed lest there be in any of you an evil heart of unbelief in departing from the living God. You know not the time of your visitation. The great sin of the Jews was that of neglecting and rejecting present opportunities. As Jesus views the state of His professed followers today, He sees base ingratitude, hollow formalism, hypocritical insincerity, pharisaical pride and apostasy.

The tears which Christ shed on the crest of Olivet were for the impenitence and ingratitude of every individual to the close of time. He sees His love despised. The soul's temple courts have been converted into places of unholy traffic. Selfishness, mammon, malice, envy, pride, passion, are all cherished in the human heart. His warnings are rejected and ridiculed, His ambassadors are treated with indifference, their words seem as idle tales. Jesus has spoken by mercies, but these mercies have been unacknowledged; He has spoken by solemn warnings, but these warnings have been rejected.

I entreat you who have long professed the faith and who still pay outward homage to Christ: Do not deceive your own souls. It is the whole heart that Jesus prizes. The loyalty of the soul is alone of value in the sight of God. "If thou hadst known, even thou, at least in this thy day, the things which belong to thy peace!" *"Thou, . . . even thou"*—Christ is at this moment addressing you personally, stooping from His throne, yearning with pitying tenderness over those who feel not their danger, who have no pity for themselves.

Many have a name to live while they have become spiritually dead. These will one day say: "Lord, Lord, have we not prophesied in Thy name? and in Thy name have cast out devils? and in Thy name done many wonderful works? And then will I profess unto them, I never knew you: depart from Me, ye that work iniquity." Woe will be pronounced against thee, if thou loiter and linger until the Sun of Righteousness shall set; the blackness of eternal night will be thy portion. Oh, that the cold, formal, worldly heart may be melted! Christ shed not only tears for us, but His own blood. Will not these manifestations of His love arouse us to deep humiliation before God? It is humility and self-abasement that we need, to be approved of God.

The man whom God is leading will be dissatisfied with himself because the light from the perfect Man shines upon him. But those who lose sight of the Pattern, and place an undue estimate upon themselves, will see faults to criticize in others; they will be sharp, suspicious, condemnatory; they will be tearing others down to build themselves up.

When the Lord last presented your case before me, and made known to me that you had not regarded the light which had been given you, I was bidden to speak to you plainly in

His name, for His anger was kindled against you. These words were spoken to me: "Your work is appointed you of God. Many will not hear you, for they refused to hear the Great Teacher; many will not be corrected, for their ways are right in their own eyes. Yet bear to them the reproofs and warnings I shall give you, whether they will hear or forbear."

I bear you the testimony of the Lord. All will hear His voice who are willing to be corrected; but those who have been deceived by the enemy are not willing now to come to the light, lest their deeds shall be reproved. Many of you cannot discern the work and presence of God. You know not that it is He. The Lord is still gracious, willing to pardon all who turn to Him with penitence and faith. Said the Lord: Many know not at what they stumble. They heed not the voice of God, but follow the sight of their own eyes and the understanding of their own hearts. Unbelief and skepticism have taken the place of faith. They have forsaken Me.

I was shown that fathers and mothers have departed from their simplicity and neglected the holy calling of the gospel. The Lord has admonished them not to corrupt themselves by adopting the customs and maxims of the world. Christ would have given them the unsearchable riches of His grace freely and abundantly, but they prove themselves unworthy.

Many are lifting up the soul unto vanity. No sooner does a person imagine that he possesses any talent which might be of use in the cause of God than he overestimates the gift and is inclined to think too highly of himself, as though he were a pillar of the church. The work which he might do with acceptance he leaves for someone else with less ability than he considers himself to possess. He thinks and talks of a higher station. He must let his light shine before men; but instead of grace, meekness, lowliness of mind, kindness, gentleness, and love shining in his life, self, important self, appears everywhere.

The spirit of Christ should so control our character and conduct that our influence may ever bless, encourage, and edify. Our thoughts, our words, our acts, should testify that we are born of God and that the peace of Christ rules in our hearts. In this way we throw around us the gracious radiance of which the Saviour speaks when He enjoins upon us to let our light shine forth to men. Thus we are leaving a bright track heavenward. In this way all who are connected with Christ may become more effectual preachers of righteousness than by the most able pulpit effort without this heavenly unction. Those light bearers shed forth the purest radiance that are the least conscious of their own brightness, as those flowers diffuse the sweetest fragrance that make the least display.

Our people are making very dangerous mistakes. We cannot praise and flatter any man without doing him a great wrong; those who do this will meet with serious disappointment. They trust too fully to finite man and not enough to God, who never errs. The eager desire to urge men into public notice is an evidence of backsliding from God and of friendship with the world. It is the spirit which characterizes the present day. It shows that men have not the mind of Jesus; spiritual blindness and poverty of soul have come upon them. Often persons of inferior minds look away from Jesus to a merely human standard, by which they are not made conscious of their own littleness, and hence have an undue estimate of their own capabilities and endowments. There is among us as a people an idolatry of human instrumentalities and mere human talent, and these even of a superficial character. We must die to self and cherish humble, childlike faith. God's people have departed from their simplicity. They have not made God their strength, and they are weak and faint, spiritually.

I have been shown that the spirit of the world is fast leavening the church. You are following the same path as did ancient Israel. There is the same falling away from your holy calling as God's peculiar people. You are having fellowship with the unfruitful works of darkness. Your concord with unbelievers has provoked the Lord's displeasure. You know not the things that belong to your peace, and they are fast being hid from your eyes. Your neglect to follow the light will place you in a more unfavorable position than the Jews upon whom Christ pronounced a woe.

I have been shown that unbelief in the testimonies has been steadily increasing as the people backslide from God. It is all through our ranks, all over the field. But few know what our churches are to experience. I saw that at present we are under divine forbearance, but no one can say how long this will continue. No one knows how great the mercy that has been exercised toward us. But few are heartily devoted to God. There are only a few who, like the stars in a tempestuous night, shine here and there among the clouds.

Many who complacently listen to the truths from God's word are dead spiritually, while they profess to live. For years they have come and gone in our congregations, but they seem only less and less sensible of the value of revealed truth. They do not hunger and thirst after righteousness. They have no relish for spiritual or divine things. They assent to the truth, but are not sanctified through it. Neither the word of God nor the testimonies of His Spirit make any lasting impression upon them. Just according to the light, the privileges, and opportunities which they have slighted will be their condemnation. Many who preach the truth to others are themselves cherishing iniquity. The entreaties of the Spirit of God, like divine melody, the promises of His word so rich and abundant, its threatenings against idolatry and disobedience —all are powerless to melt the world-hardened heart.

Many of our people are lukewarm. They occupy the position of Meroz, neither for nor against, neither cold nor hot. They hear the words of Christ, but do them not. If they remain in this state, He will reject them with abhorrence. Many of those who have had great light, great opportunities, and every spiritual advantage praise Christ and the world with the same breath. They bow themselves before God and mammon. They make merry with the children of the world, and yet claim to be blessed with the children of God. They wish to have Christ as their Saviour, but will not bear the cross and wear His yoke. May the Lord have mercy upon you; for if you go on in this way, nothing but evil can be prophesied concerning you.

The patience of God has an object, but you are defeating it. He is allowing a state of things to come that you would fain see counteracted by and by, but it will be too late. God commanded Elijah to anoint the cruel and deceitful Hazael king over Syria, that he might be a scourge to idolatrous Israel. Who knows whether God will not give you up to the deceptions you love? Who knows but that the preachers who are faithful, firm, and true may be the last who shall offer the gospel of peace to our unthankful churches? It may be that the destroyers are already training under the hand of Satan and only wait the departure of a few more standard-bearers to take their places, and with the voice of the false prophet cry, "peace, peace," when the Lord hath not spoken peace. I seldom weep, but now I find my eyes blinded with tears; they are falling upon my paper as I write. It may be that erelong all prophesyings among us will be at an end, and the voice which has stirred the people may no longer disturb their carnal slumbers.

When God shall work His strange work on the earth, when holy hands bear the ark no longer, woe will be upon the people. Oh, that thou hadst known, even thou, in this thy day, the things that belong unto thy peace! Oh, that our people may, as did Nineveh, repent with all their might and believe with all their heart, that God may turn away His fierce anger from them.

I am filled with pain and anguish as I see parents conforming to the world and allowing their children to meet the worldly standard at such a time as this. I am filled with horror as the condition of families professing present truth is opened before me. The profligacy of youth and even children is almost incredible. Parents do not know that secret vice is destroying and defacing the image of God in their children. The sins which characterized the Sodomites exist among them. The parents are responsible; for they have not educated their children to love and obey God. They have not restrained them nor diligently taught them the way of the Lord. They have allowed them to go out and to come in when they chose, and to associate with worldlings. These worldly influences which counteract parental teaching and authority are to be found largely in so-called good society. By their dress, looks, amusements, they surround themselves with an atmosphere which is opposed to Christ.

Our only safety is to stand as God's peculiar people. We must not yield one inch to the customs and fashions of this degenerate age, but stand in moral independence, making no compromise with its corrupt and idolatrous practices.

It will require courage and independence to rise above the religious standard of the Christian world. They do not follow the Saviour's example of self-denial; they make no sacrifice; they are constantly seeking to evade the cross which Christ declares to be the token of discipleship.

What can I say to arouse our people? I tell you not a few ministers who stand before the people to explain the Scriptures are defiled. Their hearts are corrupt, their hands unclean. Yet many are crying, "Peace, peace;" and the workers of iniquity are not alarmed. The Lord's hand is not shortened that He cannot save, nor His ear heavy that He cannot hear; but it is our sins that have separated us from God. The church is corrupt because of her members who defile their bodies and pollute their souls.

If all of those who come together for meetings of edification and prayer could be regarded as true worshipers, then might we hope, though much would still remain to be done for us. But it is in vain to deceive ourselves. Things are far from being what the appearance would indicate. From a distant view much may appear beautiful which, upon close examination, will be found full of deformities. The prevailing spirit of our time is that of infidelity and apostasy—a spirit of pretended illumination because of a knowledge of the truth, but in reality of the blindest presumption. There is a spirit of opposition to the plain word of God and to the testimony of His Spirit. There is a spirit of idolatrous exaltation of mere human reason above the revealed wisdom of God.

There are men among us in responsible positions who hold that the opinions of a few conceited philosophers, so called, are more to be trusted than the truth of the Bible, or the testimonies of the Holy Spirit. Such a faith as that of Paul, Peter, or John is considered old-fashioned and insufferable at the present day. It is pronounced absurd, mystical, and unworthy of an intelligent mind.

God has shown me that these men are Hazaels to prove a scourge to our people. They are wise above what is written. This unbelief of the very truths of God's word because human judgment cannot comprehend the mysteries of His work is found in every district, in all ranks of society. It is taught in most of our schools and comes into the lessons of the nurseries. Thousands who profess to be Christians give heed to lying spirits. Everywhere the spirit of darkness in the garb of religion will confront you.

If all that appears to be divine life were such in reality; if all who profess to present the truth to the world were preaching for the truth and not against it, and if they were men of God guided by His Spirit,—then might we see something cheering amid the prevailing moral darkness. But the spirit of antichrist is prevailing to such an extent as never before. Well may we exclaim: "Help, Lord; for the godly man ceaseth; for the faithful fail from among the children of men." I know that many think far too favorably of the present time. These ease-loving souls will be engulfed in the general ruin. Yet we do not despair. We have been inclined to think that where there are no faithful ministers there can be no true Christians, but this is not the case. God has promised that where the shepherds are not true He will take charge of the flock Himself. God has never made the flock wholly dependent upon human instrumentalities. But the days of purification of the church are hastening on apace. God will have a people pure and true. In the mighty sifting soon to take place we shall be better able to measure the strength of Israel. The signs reveal that the time is near when the Lord will manifest that His fan is in His hand, and He will thoroughly purge His floor.

The days are fast approaching when there will be great perplexity and confusion. Satan, clothed in angel robes, will deceive, if possible, the very elect. There will be gods many and lords many. Every wind of doctrine will be blowing. Those who have rendered supreme homage to "science falsely so called" will not be the leaders then. Those who have trusted to intellect, genius, or talent will not then stand at the head of rank and file. They did not keep pace with the light. Those who have proved themselves unfaithful will not then be entrusted with the flock. In the last solemn work few great men will be engaged. They are self-sufficient, independent of God, and He cannot use them. The Lord has faithful servants, who in the shaking, testing time will be disclosed to view. There are precious ones now hidden who have not bowed the knee to Baal. They have not had the light which has been shining in a concentrated blaze upon you. But it may be under a rough and uninviting exterior the pure brightness of a genuine Christian character will be revealed. In the daytime we look toward heaven but do not see the stars. They are there, fixed in the firmament, but the eye cannot distinguish them. In the night we behold their genuine luster.

The time is not far distant when the test will come to every soul. The mark of the beast will be urged upon us. Those who have step by step yielded to worldly demands and conformed to worldly customs will not find it a hard matter to yield to the powers that be, rather than subject themselves to derision, insult, threatened imprisonment, and death. The contest is between the commandments of God and the commandments of men. In this time the gold will be separated from the dross in the church. True godliness will be clearly distinguished from the appearance and tinsel of it. Many a star that we have admired for its brilliancy will then go out in darkness. Chaff like a cloud will be borne away on the wind, even from places where we see only floors of rich wheat. All who assume the ornaments of the sanctuary, but are not clothed with Christ's righteousness, will appear in the shame of their own nakedness.

When trees without fruit are cut down as cumberers of the ground, when multitudes of false brethren are distinguished from the true, then the hidden ones will be revealed to view, and with hosannas range under the banner of Christ. Those who have been timid and self-distrustful will declare themselves openly for Christ and His truth. The most weak and hesitating in the church will be as David—willing to do and dare. The deeper the night for God's people, the more brilliant the stars. Satan will sorely harass the faithful;

but, in the name of Jesus, they will come off more than conquerors. Then will the church of Christ appear "fair as the moon, clear as the sun, and terrible as an army with banners."

The seeds of truth that are being sown by missionary efforts will then spring up and blossom and bear fruit. Souls will receive the truth who will endure tribulation and praise God that they may suffer for Jesus. "In the world ye shall have tribulation: but be of good cheer; I have overcome the world." When the overflowing scourge shall pass through the earth, when the fan is purging Jehovah's floor, God will be the help of His people. The trophies of Satan may be exalted on high, but the faith of the pure and holy will not be daunted.

Elijah took Elisha from the plow and threw upon him his mantle of consecration. The call to this great and solemn work was presented to men of learning and position; had these been little in their own eyes and trusted fully in the Lord, He would have honored them with bearing His standard in triumph to the victory. But they separated from God, yielded to the influence of the world, and the Lord rejected them.

Many have exalted science and lost sight of the God of science. This was not the case with the church in the purest times.

God will work a work in our day that but few anticipate. He will raise up and exalt among us those who are taught rather by the unction of His Spirit than by the outward training of scientific institutions. These facilities are not to be despised or condemned; they are ordained of God, but they can furnish only the exterior qualifications. God will manifest that He is not dependent on learned, self-important mortals.

There are few really consecrated men among us, few who have fought and conquered in the battle with self. Real conversion is a decided change of feelings and motives; it is a virtual taking leave of worldly connections a hastening from their spiritual atmosphere, a withdrawing from the controlling power of their thoughts, opinions, and influences. The separation causes pain and bitterness to both parties. It is the variance which Christ declares that He came to bring. But the converted will feel a continual longing desire that their friends shall forsake all for Christ, knowing that, unless they do, there will be a final and eternal separation. The true Christian cannot, while with unbelieving friends, be light and trifling. The value of the souls for whom Christ died is too great.

He "that forsaketh not all that he hath," says Jesus, "cannot be My disciple." Whatever shall divert the affections from God must be given up. Mammon is the idol of many. Its golden chain binds them to Satan. Reputation and worldly honor are worshiped by another class. The life of selfish ease and freedom from responsibility is the idol of others. These are Satan's snares, set for unwary feet. But these slavish bands must be broken; the flesh must be crucified with the affections and lusts. We cannot be half the Lord's and half the world's. We are not God's people unless we are such entirely. Every weight, every besetting sin, must be laid aside. God's watchmen will not cry, "Peace, peace," when God has not spoken peace. The voice of the faithful watchmen will be heard: "Go ye out from thence, touch no unclean thing; go ye out of the midst of her; be ye clean that bear the vessels of the Lord."

The church cannot measure herself by the world nor by the opinion of men nor by what she once was. Her faith and her position in the world as they now are must be compared with what they would have been if her course had been continually onward and upward. The church will be weighed in the balances of the sanctuary. If her moral character and spiritual state do not correspond with the benefits and blessings God has conferred upon her, she will be found wanting.

The light has been shining clear and definite upon her pathway, and the light of 1882 calls her to an account. If her talents are unimproved, if her fruit is not perfect before God, if her light has become darkness, she is indeed found wanting. The knowledge of our state as God views it, seems to be hidden from us. We see, but perceive not; we hear, but do not understand; and we rest as unconcerned as if the pillar of cloud by day, and the pillar of fire by night, rested upon our sanctuary. We profess to know God, and to believe the truth, but in works deny Him. Our deeds are directly adverse to the principles of truth and righteousness, by which we profess to be governed.

WORKERS IN OUR COLLEGE

The very foundation of all true prosperity for our college is a close union with God on the part of teachers and students. The fear of the Lord is the beginning of wisdom. His precepts should be acknowledged as the rule of life. In the Bible the will of God is revealed to His children. Wherever it is read, in the family circle, the school, or the church, all should give quiet and devout attention as if God were really present and speaking to them.

A high religious standard has not always been maintained in our school. A majority of both teachers and students are constantly seeking to keep their religion out of sight. Especially has this been the case since worldlings have patronized the college. Christ requires from all His followers open, manly confessions of their faith. Each must take his position, and be what God designed he should be, a spectacle to the world, to angels, and to men. Every Christian is to be a light, not hid under a bushel or under a bed, but put on a candlestick, that it may give light to all that are in the house.

The teachers in our college should not conform to worldly customs or adopt worldly principles. The attributes which God prizes most are charity and purity. These attributes should be cherished by every Christian. "Everyone that loveth is born of God, and knoweth God." "If we love one another, God dwelleth in us, and His love is perfected in us." "We shall see Him as He is. And every man that hath this hope in Him purifieth himself, even as He is pure."

God has been moving upon the hearts of young men to devote themselves to the ministry. They have come to our college in the hope of finding advantages there which they could obtain nowhere else. But the solemn convictions of the Spirit of God have been lightly regarded by teachers who know but little of the worth of souls and feel but little burden for their salvation, and they have endeavored to turn the youth from the path into which God had been seeking to lead them.

The compensation of well-qualified teachers is much higher than that of our ministers, and the teacher does not labor nearly so hard or subject himself to so great inconvenience as the minister who gives himself wholly to the work. These things have been presented before the youth, and they have been encouraged to distrust God and disbelieve His promises. Many have chosen the easier course and have prepared themselves to teach the sciences or to engage in some other employment instead of preaching the truth.

Thus God's work has been hindered by unconsecrated teachers, who profess to believe the truth but who have not the love of it in their hearts. The educated young man is taught to look upon his abilities as too precious to be devoted to the service of Christ. But has God no claims upon him? Who gave the power to obtain this mental discipline and these accomplishments? Are they held on terms altogether independent of Jehovah?

Many a youth who is ignorant of the world, ignorant of his weakness, ignorant of the future, feels no need of a divine hand to point out his course. He considers himself fully competent to guide his own bark amid the breakers. Let such youth remember that, wherever they may go, they are not beyond the domain of God. They are not free to choose what they will without consulting the will of their Creator.

Talent is ever best developed and best appreciated where it is most needed. But this truth is overlooked by many eager aspirants for distinction. Though superficial in religious experience and mental attainments, their shortsighted ambition covets a higher sphere of action than that in which Providence has placed them. The Lord does not call them, as He did Joseph and Daniel, to withstand the temptations of worldly honor and high station. But they force themselves into positions of danger and desert the only post of duty for which they are fitted.

The Macedonian cry is coming to us from all directions. "Send us laborers," is the urgent appeal from East and West. All around us are fields "white already to harvest. And he that reapeth receiveth wages, and gathereth fruit unto life eternal." Is it not folly to turn from these fields to engage in a business that can yield only pecuniary gain? Christ wants no selfish workers who are seeking only for the highest wages. He calls for those who are willing to become poor for His sake, as He became poor for them. What were the inducements presented before Christ in this world? Insults, mockery, poverty, shame, rejection, betrayal, and crucifixion. Shall the undershepherds seek for an easier lot than that of their Master?

The word of God is a great simplifier of life's complicated pursuits. To every earnest seeker it imparts a divine wisdom. We should never forget that we have been redeemed by suffering. It is the precious blood of Christ that makes atonement for us. By toil and sacrifice and peril, by losses of worldly goods, and in agony of soul the gospel has been borne to the world. God calls young men in the vigor and strength of their youth to share with Him self-denial, sacrifice, and suffering. If they accept the call, He will make them His instruments to save souls for whom He died. But He would have them count the cost and enter upon their work with a full knowledge of the conditions upon which they serve a crucified Redeemer.

I can hardly express my feelings when I think how God's purpose in the establishment of our college has been disregarded. Those who have a form of godliness are denying, by their unconsecrated lives, the power of the truth to make men wise unto salvation. Look at the history of the apostles, who suffered poverty, disgrace, abuse, and even death for the truth's sake. They rejoiced that they were accounted worthy to suffer for Christ.

If great results can be attained by great efforts and great suffering, who of us that are subjects of divine grace can refuse the sacrifice? The gospel of Christ includes in its requirements every soul that has heard the message or glad tidings. What shall we render unto God for all His benefits to us? His matchless mercy can never be repaid. We can, only by willing obedience and grateful service, testify our loyalty, and crown with honor our Redeemer.

I have no higher wish than to see our youth imbued with that spirit of pure religion which will lead them to take up the cross and follow Jesus. Go forth, young disciples of Christ, controlled by principle, clad in the robes of purity and righteousness. Your Saviour will guide you into the position best suited to your talents and where you can be most useful. In the path of duty you may be sure of receiving grace sufficient for your day.

The preaching of the gospel is God's chosen agency for the salvation of souls. But our first work should be to bring our own hearts into harmony with God, and then we are prepared to labor for others. In former days there was great searching of heart among our earnest workers. They counseled together and united in humble, fervent prayer for divine guidance. There has been a decline in the true missionary spirit among ministers and teachers. Yet Christ's coming is nearer than when we believed. Every passing day leaves us one less to proclaim the message of warning to the world. Would that there were today more earnest intercession with God, greater humility, greater purity, and greater faith.

All are in constant danger. I warn the church to beware of those who preach to others the word of life but do not themselves cherish the spirit of humility and self-denial which it inculcates. Such men cannot be depended on in a crisis. They disregard the voice of God as readily as did Saul, and like him many stand ready to justify their course. When rebuked by the Lord through His prophet, Saul stoutly asserted that he had obeyed the voice of God; but the bleating sheep and lowing oxen testified that he had not. In the same manner do many today assert their loyalty to God, but their concerts and other pleasure gatherings, their worldly associations, their glorifying of self, and their eager desire for popularity all testify that they have not obeyed His voice. "As for My people, children are their oppressors, and women rule over them."

That is a high standard which the gospel sets before us. The consistent Christian is not only a new but a noble creature in Christ Jesus. He is an unfailing light to show others the way to heaven and to God. He who is drawing his life from Christ will have no desire for the frivolous, unsatisfying enjoyments of the world.

Among the youth will be found great diversity of character and education. Some have lived in an element of arbitrary restraint and harshness, which has developed in them a spirit of obstinacy and defiance. Others have been household pets, allowed by overfond parents to follow their own inclinations. Every defect has been excused, until their character is deformed. To deal successfully with these different minds the teacher needs to exercise great tact and delicacy in management, as well as firmness in government.

Dislike and even contempt for proper regulations will often be manifested. Some will exercise all their ingenuity in evading penalties, while others will display a reckless indifference to the consequences of transgression. All this will call for more patience and greater exertion on the part of those who are entrusted with their education.

One of the greatest difficulties with which teachers have had to contend is the failure on the part of parents to cooperate in administering the discipline of the college. If the parents would stand pledged to sustain the authority of the teacher, much insubordination, vice, and profligacy would be prevented. Parents should require their children to respect and obey rightful authority. They should labor with unremitting care and diligence to instruct, guide, and restrain their children until right habits are firmly established. With such training the youth would be in subjection to the institutions of society and the general restraints of moral obligation.

Both by precept and example the young should be taught simplicity of dress and manners, industry, sobriety, and economy. Many students are extravagant in expending the means furnished them by their parents. They try to show themselves superior to their associates by a lavish use of money for display and self-indulgence. In some institutions of learning this matter has been regarded of so great consequence that the dress of the student is prescribed and his use of money limited by law. But indulgent parents and indulged students will find some way to evade the law. We would resort to no such means. We ask Christian parents to take all these matters under careful, prayerful consideration, to seek counsel from the word of God, and then to endeavor to act in accordance with its teachings.

If facilities for manual labor were provided in connection with our school, and students were required to devote a portion of their time to some active employment, it would prove a safeguard against many of the evil influences that prevail in institutions of learning. Manly, useful occupations, substituted for frivolous and corrupting diversions, would give legitimate scope for the exuberance of youthful life and would promote sobriety and stability of character. All possible effort should be made to encourage a desire for moral and physical as well as mental improvement. If girls were taught how to cook, especially how to bake good bread, their education would be of far greater value. A knowledge of useful labor would prevent, to a great extent, that sickly sentimentalism which has been and is still ruining thousands. The exercise of the muscles as well as the brain will encourage taste for the homely duties of practical life.

The present age is one of show and surface work in education. Brother _____ possesses naturally a love for system and thoroughness, and these have become habit by lifelong training and discipline. He has been approved of God for this. His labors are of real worth because he will not allow students to be superficial. But in his very first efforts toward the establishment of a school he encountered many obstacles. Had he been less resolute and persevering he would have given up the struggle. Some of the parents neglected to sustain the school, and their children did not respect the teacher because he wore poor clothing. They allowed his appearance to prejudice them against him. This spirit of disrespect was rebuked of the Lord, and the teacher encouraged in his work. But the complaints and unwise reports carried home by the children strengthened the prejudice of the parents. While Brother _____ was seeking to inculcate true principles and establish right habits, overindulged children were complaining of their taxing studies. These very ones, I was shown, were suffering because the mind was not sufficiently occupied with proper subjects. Their thoughts were upon demoralizing matters, and both mind and body were enfeebled through the habit of self-abuse. It was this vile practice, not overstudy, that caused the frequent illness of these children and prevented them from making the advancement which the parents desired.

The Lord approved of the general course of Brother _____, as he was laying the foundation for the school which is now in operation. But the man has labored too hard, without a firm, blessed, strengthening home influence to lighten his burdens. Under the strain of overwork he has made some mistakes, not half so grievous, however, as those of persons who have cherished bitterness against him. In his connection with the youth he has had to meet that spirit of rebellion and defiance which the apostle declares to be one of the signs of the last days.

Some of the teachers in the college have failed to realize the responsibility of their position. They have not themselves been learners in the school of Christ, and hence they have not been prepared to instruct others.

Among the students will be found some of idle, vicious habits. These will need reproof and discipline; but if they cannot be reformed, let them not be driven further toward the pit by impatience and harshness. Teachers should ever remember that the youth under their charge are the purchase of the blood of Christ, and are younger members of the Lord's family. Christ made an infinite sacrifice to redeem them. And teachers should feel that they are to stand as missionaries, to win these students to Jesus. If they are naturally combative, let them carefully guard against the indulgence of this trait. Those who have passed the critical period of youth should never forget the temptations and trials of early life and how much they wanted sympathy, kindness, and love.

He who devotes himself to arduous public labor in the cause of humanity often finds little time to devote to his own family and, in one sense, is left almost without a family and without fireside, social influences. It has been thus with Brother _____. His mind has been constantly taxed. He had little opportunity to win the affections of his children or to give them needed restraint and guidance.

There are many in the college who need a thorough conversion. Let none seek to discern the mote that is in their brother's eye, when they have a beam in their own eye. Each should cleanse his own soul-temple from its defilement. Let envy and jealousy go with the accumulated rubbish. Exalted privileges and heavenly attainments, purchased for us at an immense cost, are freely presented for our acceptance. God holds us individually accountable for the measure of light and privileges He has given us. And if we refuse to render unto God the improvement of the talents committed to our trust we forfeit His favor.

Professor _____ would have served you well had he not been flattered by some and condemned by others. He became confused. He had traits of character that needed to be suppressed. In their enthusiasm some have given him undue confidence and praise. You have placed the man where it will be difficult for him to recover himself and find his true position. He has been sacrificed by both parties in the church, because they failed to heed the admonitions of the Spirit of God. This is injustice to him. He had newly come to the faith, and was not prepared for the developments which have been made.

How little we know of the bearing our acts will have upon the future history of ourselves and others. Many think it is of little importance what they do. It will do no harm for them to attend this concert, or unite with the world in that amusement, if they wish to do so. Thus Satan leads and controls their desires, and they do not consider that the results may be most momentous. It may be the link in the chain of events which binds a soul in the snare of Satan and determines his eternal ruin.

Every act, however small, has its place in the great drama of life. Consider that the desire for a single gratification of appetite introduced sin into our world, with its terrible consequences. Unhallowed marriages of the sons of God with the daughters of men resulted in apostasy which ended in the destruction of the world by a flood. The most trifling act of self-indulgence has resulted in great revolutions. This is the case now. There are very few who are circumspect. Like the children of Israel, they will not take heed to words of counsel, but follow their own inclination. They unite with a worldly element in attending gatherings where they will be brought into notice, and thus lead the way and others follow. What has been done once will be done again by themselves and many others. Every step these take makes a lasting impression, not only on their own consciences and habits, but upon those of others. This consideration gives awful dignity to human life.

My heart aches day after day and night after night for our churches. Many are progressing, but in the back track. "The path of the just . . . shineth more and more unto the perfect day." Their march is onward and upward. They progress from strength to strength, from grace to grace, and from glory to glory. This is the privilege of all our churches. But, oh, how different has it been with them! They need divine illumination. They must face square about. I know what I say. Unless they shall become Christians indeed, they will go from weakness to weakness, divisions will increase, and many souls will be led to perdition.

All I can say to you is: Take up the light which God has given you and follow it at any cost to yourselves. This is your only safety. You have a work to do to come into harmony, and may the Lord help you to do it even if self is crucified. Gather up the rays of light that have been slighted and rejected. Gather them up with meekness, with trembling, and with fear. The sin of ancient Israel was in disregarding the expressed will of God and following their own way according to the leadings of unsanctified hearts. Modern Israel are fast following in their footsteps, and the displeasure of the Lord is as surely resting upon them.

It is never difficult to do what we love to do, but to take a course directly against our inclinations is lifting a cross. Christ prayed that His disciples might be one as He was one with the Father. This unity is the credentials of Christ to the world that God sent Him. When self-will is renounced in reference to matters there will be a union of believers with Christ. This all should pray for and work for determinedly, thus answering as far as possible the prayer of Christ for unity in His church.

JEALOUSY AND FAULTFINDING CONDEMNED

It pains me to say that there are unruly tongues among church members. There are false tongues that feed on mischief. There are sly, whispering tongues. There is tattling, impertinent meddling, adroit quizzing. Among the lovers of gossip some are actuated by curiosity, others by jealousy, many by hatred against those through whom God has spoken to reprove them. All these discordant elements are at work. Some conceal their real sentiments, while others are eager to publish all they know, or even suspect, of evil against another.

I saw that the very spirit of perjury, that would turn truth into falsehood, good into evil, and innocence into crime, is now active. Satan exults over the condition of God's professed people. While many are neglecting their own souls, they eagerly watch for an opportunity to criticize and condemn others. All have defects of character, and it is not hard to find something that jealousy can interpret to their injury. "Now," say these self-constituted judges, "we have *facts*. We will fasten upon them an accusation from which they cannot clear themselves." They wait for a fitting opportunity and then produce their bundle of gossip and bring forth their tidbits.

In their efforts to carry a point, persons who have naturally a strong imagination are in danger of deceiving themselves and deceiving others. They gather up unguarded expressions from another, not considering that words may be uttered hastily and hence may not reflect the real sentiments of the speaker. But those unpremeditated remarks, often so trifling as to be unworthy of notice, are viewed through Satan's magnifying glass, pondered, and repeated until molehills become mountains. Separated from God, the surmisers of evil become the sport of temptation. They scarcely know the strength of their feelings or the effect of their words. While condemning the errors of others, they indulge far greater errors themselves. Consistency is a jewel.

Is there no law of kindness to be observed? Have Christians been authorized of God to criticize and condemn one another? Is it honorable, or even honest, to win from the lips of another, under the guise of friendship, secrets which have been entrusted to him, and then turn the knowledge thus gained to his injury? Is it Christian charity to gather up every floating report, to unearth everything that will cast suspicion on the character of another, and then take delight in using it to injure him? Satan exults when he can defame or wound a follower of Christ. He is "the accuser of our brethren." Shall Christians aid him in his work?

God's all-seeing eye notes the defects of all and the ruling passion of each, yet He bears with our mistakes and pities our weakness. He bids His people cherish the same spirit of tenderness and forbearance. True Christians will not exult in exposing the faults and deficiencies of others. They will turn away from vileness and deformity, to fix the mind upon that which is attractive and lovely. To the Christian every act of faultfinding, every word of censure or condemnation, is painful.

There have always been men and women who profess the truth, who have not conformed their lives to its sanctifying influence; men who are unfaithful, yet deceiving themselves and encouraging themselves in sin. Unbelief is seen in their life, their deportment, and character, and this terrible evil acts as does a canker.

Would all professed Christians use their investigative powers to see what evils needed to be corrected in themselves, instead of talking of others' wrongs, there would be a more healthy condition in the church today. Some will be honest when it costs nothing; but when policy will pay best, honesty is forgotten. Honesty and policy will not work together in the same mind. In time, either policy will be expelled, and truth and honesty reign supreme, or, if policy is cherished, honesty will be forgotten. They are never in agreement; they have nothing in common. One is the prophet of Baal, the other is the true prophet of God. When the Lord makes up His jewels, the true, the frank, the honest, will be looked upon with pleasure. Angels are employed in making crowns for such ones, and upon these star-gemmed crowns will be reflected, with splendor, the light which radiates from the throne of God.

Our ministering brethren are too often imposed upon by the relation of trials in the church, and they too frequently refer to them in their discourses. They should not encourage the members of the church to complain of one another, but should set them as spies upon their own actions. None should allow their feelings of prejudice and resentment to be aroused by the relation of the wrongs of others; all should wait patiently until they hear both sides of the question, and then believe only what stern facts compel them to believe. At all times the safe course is not to listen to an evil report until the Bible rule has been strictly carried out. This will apply to some who have worked artfully to draw out from the unsuspecting, matters which they had no business with and which would do them no good to know.

For your soul's sake, my brethren, have an eye single to the glory of God. Leave self out of your thoughts as much as possible. We are nearing the close of time. Examine your motives in the light of eternity. I know you need to be alarmed; you are departing from the old landmarks. Your science, so called, is undermining the foundation of Christian principle. I have been shown the course you would surely pursue should you disconnect from God. Do not trust to your own wisdom. I tell you, your souls are in imminent peril. For Christ's sake, search and see why you have so little love for religious exercises.

The Lord is testing and proving His people. You may be just as severe and critical with your own defective character as you please; but be kind, pitiful, and courteous toward others. Inquire every day: Am I sound to the core, or am I false-hearted? Entreat the Lord to save you from all deception on this point. Eternal interests are involved. While so many are panting after honor and greedy of gain, do you, my beloved brethren, be eagerly seeking the assurance of the love of God and crying: Who will show me how to make my calling and election sure?

Satan carefully studies the constitutional sins of men, and then he begins his work of alluring and ensnaring them. We are in the thickest of temptations, but there is victory for us if we fight manfully the battles of the Lord. All are in danger.

But if you walk humbly and prayerfully you will come forth from the proving process more precious than fine gold, even than the golden wedge of Ophir. If careless and prayerless, you will be as sounding brass and a tinkling cymbal.

Some have become almost lost in the mazes of skepticism. To such I would say: Lift your mind out of that channel. Fasten it upon God. The more closely faith and holiness bind you to the Eternal One, the clearer and brighter will the justice of His dealings appear to you. Make life, eternal life, the object of your pursuit.

I know your danger. If you lose confidence in the testimonies you will drift away from Bible truth. I have been fearful that many would take a questioning, doubting position, and in my distress for your souls I would warn you. How many will heed the warning? As you now hold the testimonies, should one be given crossing your track, correcting your errors, would you feel at perfect liberty to accept or reject any part or the whole? That which you will be least inclined to receive is the very part most needed. God and Satan never work in co-partnership. The testimonies either bear the signet of God or that of Satan. A good tree cannot bring forth corrupt fruit, neither can a corrupt tree bring forth good fruit. By their fruit ye shall know them. God has spoken. Who has trembled at His word?

THE DAY OF THE LORD AT HAND

"The great day of the Lord is near, it is near, and hasteth greatly, even the voice of the day of the Lord: the mighty man shall cry there bitterly. That day is a day of wrath, a day of trouble and distress, a day of wasteness and desolation, a day of darkness and gloominess, a day of clouds and thick darkness, a day of the trumpet and alarm against the fenced cities, and against the high towers. And I will bring distress upon men, that they shall walk like blind men, because they have sinned against the Lord."

"And it shall come to pass at that time, that I will search Jerusalem with candles, and punish the men that are settled on their lees: that say in their heart, The Lord will not do good, neither will He do evil."

"Gather yourselves together, yea, gather together, O nation not desired; before the decree bring forth, before the day pass as the chaff, before the fierce anger of the Lord come upon you, before the day of the Lord's anger come upon you. Seek ye the Lord, all ye meek of the earth, which have wrought His judgment; seek righteousness, seek meekness: it may be ye shall be hid in the day of the Lord's anger."

We are near the close of time. I have been shown that the retributive judgments of God are already in the land. The Lord has given us warning of the events about to take place. Light is shining from His word; yet darkness covers the earth, and gross darkness the people. "When they shall say, Peace and safety; then sudden destruction cometh upon them; . . . and they shall not escape."

It is our duty to inquire the cause of this terrible darkness, that we may shun the course by which men have brought upon themselves so great delusion. God has given the world an opportunity to learn and to obey His will. He has given them, in His word, the light of truth; He has sent them warning, counsel, and admonition; but few will obey His voice. Like the Jewish nation, the majority, even of professed Christians, pride themselves on their superior advantages, but make no returns to God for these great blessings. In infinite mercy a last warning message has been sent to the world, announcing that Christ is at the door and calling attention to God's broken law. But as the antediluvians rejected with scorn the warning of Noah, so will the pleasure lovers of today reject the message of God's faithful servants. The world pursues its unvarying round, absorbed as ever in its business and its pleasures, while the wrath of God is about to be visited on the transgressors of His law.

Our compassionate Redeemer, foreseeing the perils that would surround His followers at this time, has given them special warning: "Take heed to yourselves, lest at any time your hearts be overcharged with surfeiting, and drunkenness, and cares of this life, and so that day come upon you unawares. For as a snare shall it come on all them that dwell on the face of the whole earth. Watch ye therefore, and pray always, that ye may be accounted worthy to escape all these things that shall come to pass, and to stand before the Son of man." If the church pursue a course similar to that of the world, they will share the same fate. Nay, rather, as they have received greater light, their punishment will be greater than that of the impenitent.

We as a people profess to have truth in advance of every other people upon the earth. Then our life and character should be in harmony with such a faith. The day is just upon us when the righteous shall be bound like precious grain in bundles for the heavenly garner, while the wicked are, like the tares, gathered for the fires of the last great day. But the wheat and tares "grow together until the harvest." In the discharge of life's duties the righteous will to the last be brought in contact with the ungodly. The children of light are scattered among the children of darkness, that the contrast may be seen by all. Thus are the children of God to "show forth the praises of Him who hath called you out of darkness into His marvelous light." The divine love glowing in the heart, the Christlike harmony manifested in the life, will be as a glimpse of heaven granted to men of the world that they may see and appreciate its excellence.

Like will attract like. Those who are drinking from the

same fountain of blessing will draw nearer together. Truth dwelling in the hearts of believers will lead to blessed and happy assimilation. Thus will be answered the prayer of Christ that His disciples might be one even as He is one with the Father. For this oneness every truly converted heart will be striving.

With the ungodly there will be a deceptive harmony that but partially conceals a perpetual discord. In their opposition to the will and the truth of God they are united, while on every other point they are rent with hatred, emulation, jealousy, and deadly strife.

The pure and the base metal are now so mingled that only the discerning eye of the infinite God can with certainty distinguish between them. But the moral magnet of holiness and truth will attract together the pure metal, while it will repel the base and counterfeit.

"The great day of the Lord is near, it is near, and hasteth greatly;" but where do we behold the true advent spirit? Who are preparing to stand in that time of temptation which is just before us? The people to whom God has entrusted the sacred, solemn, testing truths for this time are sleeping at their post. They say by their actions: We have the truth; we are "rich, and increased with goods, and have need of nothing;" while the True Witness declares: Thou "knowest not that thou art wretched, and miserable, and poor, and blind, and naked."

With what fidelity do these words portray the present condition of the church: "*Knowest not* that thou art wretched, and miserable, and poor, and blind, and naked." Messages of warning, dictated by the Holy Spirit, are borne by the servants of God, defects of character are presented before the erring; but they say: "That does not represent my case. I do not accept the message you bring. I am doing the best I can. I believe the truth."

That evil servant who said in his heart, "My Lord delayeth

His coming," professed to be waiting for Christ. He was a "servant," outwardly devoted to the service of God while at heart he had yielded to Satan. He does not, like the scoffer, openly deny the truth, but reveals in his life the sentiment of the heart—that the Lord's coming is delayed. Presumption renders him careless of eternal interests. He accepts the world's maxims and conforms to its customs and practices. Selfishness, worldly pride, and ambitions predominate. Fearing that his brethren may stand higher than himself, he begins to disparage their efforts and impugn their motives. Thus he smites his fellow servants. As he alienates himself from the people of God he unites more and more with the ungodly. He is found eating and drinking "with the drunken"—joining with worldlings and partaking of their spirit. Thus he is lulled into a carnal security and overcome by forgetfulness, indifference, and sloth.

The very beginning of the evil was a neglect of watchfulness and secret prayer, then came a neglect of other religious duties, and thus the way was opened for all the sins that followed. Every Christian will be assailed by the allurements of the world, the clamors of the carnal nature, and the direct temptations of Satan. No one is safe. No matter what our experience has been, no matter how high our station, we need to watch and pray continually. We must be daily controlled by the Spirit of God or we are controlled by Satan.

The Saviour's instructions to His disciples were given for the benefit of His followers in every age. He had those in view who were living near the close of time, when He said: "Take heed to yourselves." It is our work, each for himself, to cherish in the heart the precious graces of the Holy Spirit.

Satan is working with unfailing perseverance and intense energy to draw into his ranks the professed followers of Christ. He is working "with all deceivableness of unrighteousness in them that perish." But Satan is not the only worker by whom the kingdom of darkness is supported. Whoever solicits to sin is a tempter. Whoever imitates the great deceiver becomes his aid. Those who give their influence to sustain an evil work are doing Satan's drudgery.

Actions reveal principles and motives. The fruit borne by many who claim to be plants in the Lord's vineyard shows them to be but thorns and briers. A whole church may sanction the wrong course of some of its members, but that sanction does not prove the wrong to be right. It cannot make grapes of thorn berries.

If some who profess to believe present truth could understand their true position, they would despair of the mercy of God. They have been exerting all their influence against the truth, against the voice of warning, against the people of God. They have been doing the work of Satan. Many have become so infatuated by his deceptions that they will never recover. Such a state of backsliding cannot exist without causing the loss of many souls.

The church has received warning after warning. The duties and dangers of God's people have been plainly revealed. But the worldly element has proved too strong for them. Customs, practices, and fashions which lead the soul away from God have been for years gaining ground in defiance of the warnings and entreaties of the Holy Spirit, until at last their ways have become right in their own eyes, and the Spirit's voice is scarcely heard. No man can tell how far he may go in sin when once he yields himself to the power of the great deceiver. Satan entered into Judas Iscariot and induced him to betray his Lord. Satan led Ananias and Sapphira to lie to the Holy Ghost. Those who are not wholly consecrated to God may be led to do the work of Satan, while yet they flatter themselves that they are in the service of Christ.

Brethren and sisters, I entreat you to "examine yourselves, whether ye be in the faith; prove your own selves." To maintain the warmth and purity of Christian love requires a constant supply of the grace of Christ. Have you employed every means that your "love may abound yet more and more," "that ye may approve things that are excellent," and be filled with the fruits of righteousness "which are by Jesus Christ, unto the glory and praise of God"?

Many who should stand firm for righteousness and truth have manifested weakness and indecision that have encouraged the assaults of Satan. Those who fail to grow in grace, not seeking to reach the highest standard in divine attainments, will be overcome.

This world is to the Christian a land of strangers and enemies. Unless he shall take for his defense the divine panoply and wield the sword of the Spirit he will become the prey of the powers of darkness. The faith of all will be tested. All will be tried as gold is tried in the fire.

The church is composed of imperfect, erring men and women, who call for the continual exercise of charity and forbearance. But there has been a long period of general lukewarmness; a worldly spirit coming into the church has been followed by alienation, faultfinding, malice, strife, and iniquity.

Should there be less sermonizing by men who are unconsecrated in heart and life, and were more time devoted to humbling the soul before God, then might we hope that the Lord would appear to your help and heal your backslidings. Much of the preaching of late begets a false security. Important interests in the cause of God cannot be wisely managed by those who have had so little real connection with God as some of our ministers have had. To entrust the work to such men is like setting children to manage great vessels at sea. Those who are destitute of heavenly wisdom, destitute of living power with God, are not competent to steer the gospel ship amid icebergs and tempests. The church is passing through severe conflicts, but in her peril many would trust her to hands that will surely wreck her. We need a pilot on board now, for we are nearing the harbor. As a people we should be the light of the world. But how many are foolish virgins, having no oil in their vessels with their lamps. May the Lord of all grace, abundant in mercy, full of forgiveness, pity and save us, that we perish not with the wicked!

In this season of conflict and trial we need all the support and consolation we can derive from righteous principles, from fixed religious convictions, from the abiding assurance of the love of Christ, and from a rich experience in divine things. We shall attain to the full stature of men and women in Christ Jesus only as the result of a steady growth in grace.

Oh, what can I say to open blind eyes, to enlighten the spiritual understanding! Sin must be crucified. A complete moral renovation must be wrought by the Holy Spirit. We must have the love of God, with living, abiding faith. This is the gold tried in the fire. We can obtain it only of Christ. Every sincere and earnest seeker will become a partaker of the divine nature. His soul will be filled with intense longing to know the fullness of that love which passes knowledge; as he advances in the divine life he will be better able to grasp the elevated, ennobling truths of the word of God, until by beholding he becomes changed and is enabled to reflect the likeness of his Redeemer.

UNWISE MARRIAGES

I have been shown that the youth of today have no true sense of their great danger. There are many of the young whom God would accept as laborers in the various branches of His work, but Satan steps in and so entangles them in his web that they become estranged from God and powerless in His work. Satan is a sharp and persevering workman. He knows just how to entrap the unwary, and it is an alarming fact that but few succeed in escaping from his wiles. They see no danger and do not guard against his devices. He prompts them to fasten their affections upon one another without seeking wisdom of God or of those whom He has sent to warn, reprove, and counsel. They feel self-sufficient and will not bear restraint.

Your own case, Brother _____, is a forcible illustration of this. You have become infatuated with the thought of marriage. As is generally the case with those who have their minds directed in this channel, the warnings of the servants of God have but little influence upon you. I have been shown how easily you are affected by surrounding influences. Should you connect with associates whose minds are cast in an inferior mold, you would become like them. Unless the love and fear of God were before you, their thoughts would be your thoughts; if they lacked reverence, you also would become irreverent, if they were frivolous and given to pleasure seeking, you would follow in the same path with a zeal and perseverance worthy of a better cause.

The young lady upon whom you have placed your affections has not depth of thought or character. Her life has been frivolous, and her mind is narrow and superficial. Yet you have steadily refused to be cautioned by your father, your loving sister, or by your friends in the church. I came to you as Christ's ambassador; but your strong feelings, your self-confidence, closed your eyes to danger and your ears to warnings. Your course has been as persistent as though no one knew quite so much as yourself or as though the salvation of your soul depended upon your following your own judgment.

Should every young man who professes the truth do as you have done, what would be the condition of families and of the church? Consider the influence of the disrespect you have shown for your parents by your self-will and self-sufficiency. You are among the class described as heady, high-minded.

This infatuation has caused you to lose your interest in religious things and to think only of yourself instead of the glory of God. No good can come of this intimacy or attachment. The blessing of God will not attend any such willful course as you are pursuing. You should not be eager to enter the marriage relation and assume the care of a family before you have thoroughly established your own character. I regard you as in great darkness but unable to realize your peril.

The truth was reforming your life and character, and you were gaining the confidence of the brethren; but Satan saw that he was losing you, and therefore he increased his efforts to entangle you in his wily snare and has succeeded wonderfully. The weakness of your nature, hitherto undiscovered, is now developed. You do not see your condition, although it is very apparent to others. Light does not come to a man who makes no effort to obtain it. When you saw that your brethren and sisters were grieved with your course, then it was time for you to stop and consider what you were doing, to pray much, and to counsel with men of experience in the church and gratefully accept their advice.

"But," say you, "should I follow the judgment of the brethren independent of my own feelings?" I answer: The church is God's delegated authority upon earth. Christ has said: "Whatsoever ye shall bind on earth shall be bound in heaven: and whatsoever ye shall loose on earth shall be loosed in heaven." There is altogether too little respect paid to the opinion of members of the same church. It is the want of deference for the opinions of the church that causes so much trouble among brethren. The eyes of the church may be able to discern in its individual members that which the erring may not see. A few persons may be as blind as the one in error, but the majority of the church is a power which should control its individual members.

The apostle Peter says: "Likewise, ye younger, submit

yourselves unto the elder. Yea, all of you be subject one to another, and be clothed with humility: for God resisteth the proud, and giveth grace to the humble." Paul exhorts: "Be kindly affectioned one to another with brotherly love; in honor preferring one another," "submitting yourselves one to another in the fear of God." "Let nothing be done through strife or vainglory; but in lowliness of mind let each esteem other better than themselves." Unless the advice and counsel of the church can be respected, it is indeed powerless. God has placed a voice in the church which must control its members.

If you are led by truth rather than error you will be willing to obey your parents and sacredly regard the voice of the church. Your prayers have been made with a determination to carry out what you regarded as right, irrespective of the wishes of your parents or of the church. All through your life you have been actuated in a large degree by selfish feelings. Ofttimes a great sacrifice of feeling has to be made in order to comply with the conditions laid down in God's word and to act from principle.

"Should parents," you ask, "select a companion without regard to the mind or feelings of son or daughter?" I put the question to you as it should be: Should a son or daughter select a companion without first consulting the parents, when such a step must materially affect the happiness of parents if they have any affection for their children? And should that child, notwithstanding the counsel and entreaties of his parents, persist in following his own course? I answer decidedly: No; not if he never marries. The fifth commandment forbids such a course. "Honor thy father and thy mother: that thy days may be long upon the land which the Lord thy God giveth thee." Here is a commandment with a promise which the Lord will surely fulfill to those who obey.

Wise parents will never select companions for their children without respect to their wishes. No one has ever proposed to do this in your case. But most of that which the youth of our day term *love* is only blind impulse, which originates with Satan to compass their destruction.

Should you, my brother, go to our college now, as you have planned, I fear for your course there. Your expressed determination to have a lady's company wherever you should go shows me that you are far from being in a position to be benefited by going to Battle Creek. The infatuation which is upon you is more satanic than divine. I do not wish to have you disappointed in regard to Battle Creek. The rules are strict there. No courting is allowed. The school would be worth nothing to students were they to become entangled in love affairs as you have been. Our college would soon be demoralized. Parents do not send their children to our college or to our offices to commence a lovesick, sentimental life, but to be educated in the sciences or to learn the printer's trade. Were the rules so lax that the youth were allowed to become bewildered and infatuated with the society of the opposite sex as you have been for some months past, the object of their going to Battle Creek would be lost. If you cannot put this entirely out of your mind and go there with the spirit of a learner and with a purpose to arouse yourself to the most earnest, humble, sincere efforts, praying that you may have a close connection with God, it would be better for you to remain at home.

Should you go you ought to be prepared to withstand temptation and to hold up the hands of professors and teachers, letting your influence be wholly on the side of discipline and order. God designs that all who work in His cause shall be subject one to another, ready to receive advice and instruction. They should train themselves by the severest mental and moral discipline, that by the assisting grace of God they may be fitted in mind and heart to train others. Fervent prayer, humility, and earnestness must be combined with God's help, for human frailties and human feelings are continually striving for the mastery. Every man must purify his soul through obedience to the truth, and with an eye single to God's glory he must abase self and exalt Jesus and His grace. By thus continually advancing toward the light he will become acquainted with God and receive His help.

Some of those who attend the college do not properly improve their time. Full of the buoyancy of youth, they spurn the restraint that is brought to bear upon them. Especially do they rebel against the rules that will not allow young gentlemen to pay their attentions to young ladies. Full well is known the evil of such a course in this degenerate age. In a college where so many youth are associated, imitating the customs of the world in this respect would turn the thoughts in a channel that would hinder them in their pursuit of knowledge and in their interest in religious things. The infatuation on the part of both young men and women in thus placing the affections upon each other during school days shows a lack of good judgment. As in your own case, blind impulse controls reason and judgment. Under this bewitching delusion the momentous responsibility felt by every sincere Christian is laid aside, spirituality dies, and the judgment and eternity lose their awful significance.

Every faculty of those who become affected by this contagious disease—blind love—is brought in subjection to it. They seem to be devoid of good sense, and their course of action is disgusting to all who behold it. My brother, you have made yourself a subject of talk and have lowered yourself in the estimation of those whose approval you should prize. With many the crisis of the disease is reached in an immature marriage, and when the novelty is past and the bewitching power of love-making is over, one or both parties awake to their true situation. They then find themselves ill-mated, but united for life. Bound to each other by the most solemn vows, they look with sinking hearts upon the miserable life they must lead. They ought then to make the best of their situation, but many will not do this. They will either prove false to their marriage vows or make the yoke which they persisted in placing upon their own necks so very galling that not a few cowardly put an end to their existence.

Associating with the vain, the superficial, and the skeptical will be productive of moral depravity and ruin. Bold, forward young gentlemen or ladies may have something pleasing in their address; they may have brilliant powers of mind and skill to make the bad appear even preferable to the good. Such persons will enchant and bewilder a certain class, and souls will be lost in consequence. The influence of every man's thoughts and actions surrounds him like an invisible atmosphere, which is unconsciously breathed in by all who come in contact with him. This atmosphere is frequently charged with poisonous influences, and when these are inhaled, moral degeneracy is the sure result.

My young brother, would that I could impress upon you your true condition. You must repent or you can never see the kingdom of heaven. Many young men and women who profess godliness do not know what it is to follow Christ. They do not imitate His example in doing good. Love and gratitude toward God are not springing up in the heart nor expressed in their words and deportment. They do not possess the spirit of self-denial, neither do they encourage each other in the way of holiness. We do not want young people to engage in the solemn work of God who profess Christ but have not the moral strength to take their position with those who are sober and watch unto prayer and who have their conversation in heaven, whence they look for the Saviour. We do not feel overanxious for youth to go to Battle Creek who profess to be Sabbath-keepers but who indicate by their choice of companions their low state of morals.

The door of our college will ever be open to those who are not professors of religion, and the youth coming to Battle Creek may have this irreligious society if it is their choice. If they have right motives in associating with these and sufficient spiritual strength to withstand their influence they may be a power for good; while they are learners they may become teachers. The true Christian does not choose the company of the unconverted for love of the atmosphere surrounding their irreligious lives or to excite admiration and secure applause, but for the purpose of communicating light and knowledge, and bringing them up to a noble, elevated standard, the broad platform of eternal truth.

One person with pure motives, intent on becoming intelligent that he may make a right use of his abilities, will be a power for good in the school. He will have a molding influence. When parents justify the complaints of their children against the authority and discipline of the school, they do not see that they are increasing the demoralizing power which now prevails to such a fearful extent. Every influence surrounding the youth needs to be on the right side, for youthful depravity is increasing.

With worldly youth, the love of society and pleasure becomes an absorbing passion. To dress, to visit, to indulge the appetite and passions, and to whirl through the round of social dissipation appears to be the great end of existence. They are unhappy if left in solitude. Their chief desire is to be admired and flattered, and to make a sensation in society; and when this desire is not gratified, life seems unendurable.

Those who will put on the whole armor of God and devote some time every day to meditation and prayer and to the study of the Scriptures will be connected with heaven and will have a saving, transforming influence upon those around them. Great thoughts, noble aspirations, clear perceptions of truth and duty to God, will be theirs. They will be yearning for purity, for light, for love, for all the graces of heavenly birth. Their earnest prayers will enter into that within the veil. This class will have a sanctified boldness to come into the presence of the Infinite One. They will feel that heaven's light and glories are for them, and they will become refined, elevated, ennobled by this intimate acquaintance with God. Such is the privilege of true Christians.

Abstract meditation is not enough; busy action is not enough; both are essential to the formation of Christian character. Strength acquired in earnest, secret prayer prepares us to withstand the allurements of society. And yet we should not exclude ourselves from the world, for our Christian experience is to be the light of the world. The society of unbelievers will do us no harm if we mingle with them for the purpose of connecting them with God and are strong enough spiritually to withstand their influence.

Christ came into the world to save it, to connect fallen man with the infinite God. Christ's followers are to be channels of light. Maintaining communion with God, they are to transmit to those in darkness and error the choice blessings which they receive of heaven. Enoch did not become polluted with the iniquities existing in his day; why need we in our day? But we may, like our Master, have compassion for suffering humanity, pity for the unfortunate, and a generous consideration for the feelings and necessities of the needy, the troubled, and the despairing.

Those who are Christians indeed will seek to do good to others and at the same time will so order their conversation and deportment as to maintain a calm, hallowed peace of mind. God's word requires that we should be like our Saviour, that we should bear His image, imitate His example, live His life. Selfishness and worldliness are not fruits of a Christian tree. No man can live for himself and yet enjoy the approbation of God.

Sept. 5, 1879.

WARNINGS AND REPROOFS

There is an element in the church at _____ that is detrimental to its spiritual interests. There is a great want of vital godliness, of experimental religion. I call no names. Let each search his own heart and understand his own imperfections. There are some who are ever leaning toward the world, ever lowering the standard of religion by their worldly conversation. They have not the love of God in their hearts. They are weak-handed when real help is needed in the church. This spiritual weakness is the result of their own unwillingness to bear burdens when and where they can help the most. When, however, there is any plan or device of their own to carry out, they are willing to assume any responsibility; to have their own way is their purpose. If that were a sanctified way, it would not be so bad; but it is not.

There is great need of zealous, disinterested workers in God's cause. One Christ-loving, devoted member will do more good in a church than one hundred half-converted, unsanctified, self-sufficient workers. It is impossible for the church to be a living, active church unless its members shall be willing to bear burdens and assume responsibilities. In church relationship are brought together different temperaments and dispositions. In the _____ church there are a few devoted, God-fearing, faithful souls who pray much, who carry the burden of the church, and whose happiness is in the prosperity of its members. Here, as elsewhere, Satan is constantly at work to drag down and demoralize. It is the business of the adversary of souls to weaken and destroy every organization which, if prospered, would glorify God.

Young men have received the truth and run well for a season, but Satan has woven his meshes about them in unwise attachments and poor marriages. This he saw would be the most successful way he could allure them from the path of holiness. For a while some of these youth bore the gospel armor with dignity and grace. Just as long as the heart and mind were in subjection to the divine will, there was prosperity; but when the eye was diverted from Jesus and attracted to unworthy objects, then it was that self asserted the sway, that carnal reason overbore wise judgment and integrity, and the Christian armor was thought too weighty to be borne by those so young in years. It would do for old, experienced soldiers of the gospel, but it was too heavy for youth. The tempter offered many suggestions calculated to cause inconstancy and vacillation in the Christian course.

The injunction of the Captain of their salvation was, "Take ye heed, watch and pray," "lest ye enter into temptation;" but it was too much trouble to faithfully guard the soul, and the deceptive power of Satan and the deceitful heart allured away from Christ. If these young men and young women had considered the words of the apostle, "Ye are not your own, for ye are bought with a price," they would not have felt at liberty to keep back from God that which He had purchased at an infinite cost.

There is not one youth in one hundred who feels his God-given responsibility. Every physical and mental capability should be carefully preserved and put to the best and highest use to advance the glory of God. Those youth who permit their powers to be perverted, thus abusing God's gifts, will be called to strict account for the good they might have done had they availed themselves of the provision made through Jesus Christ. God claims the working of every faculty.

There are youth in the _____ church who should be cultivating the grace of Christian steadfastness and growing up to be men of faith. They should become firm, unwavering, rooted and grounded in the truth. The church needs the very help which God designed they should give. Those professing His name have not consecrated their powers fully and entirely to Him, but have yielded them, in a measure, to the service of Satan. Such have been, and still are, robbing God. Like the unfaithful steward to whom were entrusted talents, they have hid the gifts of God in the world.

Another great detriment to the church at _____ has been the material which has come into it. This material needs to be melted over by the Spirit of God. The dross is seen in crude, sharp traits of character, which might have been removed had these individuals been learners of Christ. But they have not fully separated themselves from the spirit and influences of the world. They rob God by daily mingling His time, His talents, and His strength with a worldly element. These powers cannot be withheld from God without resulting in eternal ruin. You have been bought with a price, even if you perish because you will not be saved in God's appointed way.

Holy angels are watching with intense interest, to see if the individual members of the church will honor their Redeemer, to see if they will place themselves in connection with heaven and no longer defraud the Lord, whom they profess to love, honor, and serve. God calls for His own. You are His by creation, and doubly His by redemption. But when you suffer the fires of unhallowed passion to light up the eye, when you speak words that drive the holy angels from you, when you think evil of your brethren, when you profane your hands with the gains of ungodliness, you are yielding your members as instruments of unrighteousness.

Brother _____, I saw that "Wanting" was written against your name in the Ledger of Heaven—wanting in patience, in forbearance, in self-control, in lowliness and meekness. The want of these heavenly graces will surely close the gates of heaven against you. Your body, your soul, your entire being with all its capabilities, God claims as His. That hasty, uncontrolled temper must be overcome. Spiritual disease is the sure result of giving way to this fretting, complaining, murmuring spirit. And this disease of soul will be your own fault. Cease to fret, cease to be stubborn, cease to pet self, and be a noblehearted, valiant man for God. Jesus loves you. Has He not made ample provision for you, that you should have help when brought into difficult places? "What," He says, "could have been done more to My vineyard, that I have not done in it? wherefore, when I looked that it should bring forth grapes, brought it forth wild grapes?" The fruit Christ claims, after the patient care bestowed upon His church, is faith, patience, love, forbearance, heavenly-mindedness, meekness. These are clusters of fruit which mature amid storm and cloud and darkness, as well as in the sunshine.

Brother _____ is joined to the church, but not to the Lord. He has a dyspeptic religion. He is not right with God; he is filled with self. He has lost much by uniting with individuals who have not the spirit of Christ. He is lacking in almost every grace. He is useless to himself, and a great stumbling block to the church. Dear brother, Satan has controlled you to a great extent; your thoughts are unsanctified, your actions are not in accordance with the spirit of a true Christian. You have brought on your own disease; you must be your own restorer through the help of the divine Physician. Your moral powers are weak for want of nourishment. You are starving spiritually for Bible truth—the bread of life. You need to draw daily nourishment from the living Vine. The church receives no strength from you and in your present condition would be better off without you, for now, if anything arises to cross your track and you cannot control matters, you settle back with stubbornness, a dead weight on the church. You bear no burden or weight of the cause. God has borne long with you, but there is a limit to His forbearance, a line beyond which you may venture, when His Spirit will no longer strive with you, but leave you in your own perversity, defiled with selfishness, and debased with sin.

Brother _____ does not possess a right spirit. His disposition to lead hurts him, for he is not fitted for any such work. He can act a good part in the church if self is not made prominent. More meekness and lowliness will make his efforts a blessing to the church instead of a burden.

Brother and Sister _____, I saw opposite your names also, in the heavenly record, the word, "Wanting." You need to be emptied of self and the soul temple cleansed. Both of you have ability to do good, but it is unsanctified. You are greatly deficient in the simplicity of godliness. Were the church left to be molded by your standard of religion, it would be demoralized into a worldly, unconsecrated form. You might have been a great blessing to the church, but you have greatly failed. Jesus bids you come out from the spirit of the world. Sister _____, I am alarmed for you and for those who are brought in contact with your influence. You reach a low standard. "Whatsoever a man soweth, that shall he also reap." By your words and actions you are now casting the seed. You are either sowing to the flesh or to the Spirit. In the day of final reckoning everyone must take the sickle and mow down the crop his own hand has sown.

Your husband is mistaking his work. When he shall humble his heart as a little child, and when he shall feel his own importance less and his need of help from God more, then he may be where he can be used to God's glory. But, as he is, he does not realize the wants of the cause. There is so much great *I,* and so little Jesus exhibited in the life and character of many, that God will accept nothing from their hands. But few realize the solemnity of the time in which we live—the day of God's preparation. Should you both be converted and devote your ability to studying how to build up the church instead of weakening it and helping the enemy in his work of leading its members to the world you would be gaining a valuable experience every day as you pass along. Brother _____ has been a great hindrance to the church. He should not be a member of the church unless his daily life is in harmony with his profession. God does not acknowledge him as His child. He stands today under the black banner of the powers of darkness. Satan has him completely under his control.

Such strong, discouraging influences as these have been a tide almost too strong for the church to stand against. Ten members, who were walking in all humbleness of mind, would have a far greater power upon the world than has the entire church, with its present numbers and lack of unity. The more there is of the divided, inharmonious element, the less power will the church have for good in the world.

Would that I could make plain to your beclouded senses, my brethren, the great peril you are in. Every action, good or bad, prepares the way for its repetition. How was it in the case of Pharaoh? The statement in Holy Writ is that God hardened his heart, and at every repetition of light in the manifestation of God's power the statement is repeated. Every time he refused to submit to God's will his heart became harder and less impressible by the Spirit of God. He sowed the seed of obstinacy, and God left it to vegetate. He might have prevented it by a miracle, but that was not His plan. He allowed it to grow and produce a harvest of its own kind, thus, proving the truthfulness of the scripture: "Whatsoever a man soweth, that shall he also reap." When a man plants doubts, he will reap doubts. By rejecting the first light and every following ray, Pharaoh went from one degree of hardness of heart to another, until the cold, dead forms of the first-born only checked his unbelief and obstinacy for a moment. And then, determined not to yield to God's way, he continued his willful course until overwhelmed by the waters of the Red Sea.

This case is placed on record for our benefit. Just what took place in Pharaoh's heart will take place in every soul that neglects to cherish the light and walk promptly in its rays. God destroys no one. The sinner destroys himself by his own impenitence. When a person once neglects to heed the invitations, reproofs, and warnings of the Spirit of God, his conscience becomes seared, and the next time he is admonished, it will be more difficult to yield obedience than before. And thus with every repetition. Conscience is the voice of God, heard amid the conflict of human passions; when it is resisted, the Spirit of God is grieved.

We want all to understand how the soul is destroyed. It is not that God sends out a decree that man shall not be saved. He does not throw a darkness before the eyes which cannot be penetrated. But man at first resists a motion of the Spirit of God, and, having once resisted, it is less difficult to do so the second time, less the third, and far less the fourth. Then comes the harvest to be reaped from the seed of unbelief and resistance. Oh what a harvest of sinful indulgences is preparing for the sickle!

When secret prayer and reading of the Scriptures are neglected today, tomorrow they can be omitted with less remonstrance of conscience. There will be a long list of omissions, all for a single grain sown in the soil of the heart. On the other hand, every ray of light cherished will yield a harvest of light. Temptation once resisted will give power to more firmly resist the second time; every new victory gained over self will smooth the way for higher and nobler triumphs. Every victory is a seed sown to eternal life.

There is great need of zealous, faithful, self-denying workers in our churches throughout the land. No one can labor in the Sabbath school or in the temperance work without reaping a bountiful harvest, not only in the end of the world, but in the present life. In the very effort to enlighten and bless others his own views will become clearer and broader. The more we endeavor to explain the truth to others, with a love for souls, the plainer will it become to ourselves. It ever opens with new beauty and force to the understanding of the expounder.

There are some good workers in your church, and these self-denying ones will never know how much good they have accomplished by their persevering efforts in the missionary field. But the Lord has claims upon more men and women in the church than have yielded to His demands. Some of the stones composing God's holy temple reflect the light which shines upon them from Jesus Christ, while others emit no light, thus clearly revealing that they are not living stones, elect, precious. They are not devotional, but prayerless, talkative, irreligious. True Christians will copy the pattern given them by our Saviour and will be meek, lowly, forbearing, gentle, easy to be entreated, free from pomposity and stubbornness.

DANGERS OF THE YOUNG

Mr. _____ has a nature that Satan plays upon with wonderful success. This case is one that should teach the young a lesson in regard to marriage. His wife followed feeling and impulse, not reason and judgment, in selecting a companion. Was their marriage the result of true love? No, no; it was the result of impulse,—blind, unsanctified passion. Neither was at all fitted for the responsibilities of married life. When the novelty of the new order of things wore away, and each became acquainted with the other, did their love become stronger, their affection deeper, and their lives blend together in beautiful harmony? It was entirely the opposite. The worst traits of their characters began to deepen by exercise, and, instead of their married life being one of happiness, it has been one of increasing trouble, especially to the wife. God in His mercy has tested her, spared her life, and lengthened her probation in order that she might obtain a fitness for the future life.

Her husband has a very defective character. Without a thorough transformation by the grace of God he would be unfit to connect in marriage with any woman. He is so thoroughly impregnated with self, so entirely given up to habits of self-indulgence and easy indolence, that he needs to be under discipline himself, rather than have anything to do in disciplining wife or children. This man's mind has been cast in an inferior mold. He has encouraged coarseness and objectionable traits of character, until he was presented to me as having scarcely a redeeming quality in his character. There is only one hope, and that is that he will see himself, and so despise and loathe himself that he will seek a new heart, be born again, and become a new man in Christ Jesus. He should become a diligent man. Industry will be of great advantage to him. His course is offensive to God, in that he invites temptation. His rudeness, his threats, his untamable, uncourteous spirit, will make him a curse to himself and to others. His conduct toward his wife's mother has been rude and ungentlemanly. It should henceforth be the life study of both husband and wife how to avoid everything that creates contention and to keep unbroken the marriage vows.

Just such unsanctified marriages are filling up the ranks of Sabbathkeepers. God wants His children to be happy, and, if they would learn of Him, He would save them from the daily misery which comes in consequence of these unhappy unions. Many marriages can only be productive of misery; and yet the minds of the youth run in this channel because

Satan leads them there, making them believe that they must be married in order to be happy, when they have not the ability to control themselves or support a family. Those who are not willing to adapt themselves to each other's disposition, so as to avoid unpleasant differences and contentions, should not take the step. But this is one of the alluring snares of the last days, in which thousands are ruined for this life and the next. Imagination, lovesick sentimentalism, should be guarded against as would be the leprosy. Very many of the young men and women in this age of the world are lacking in virtue; therefore great caution is needed. A virtuous character is the foundation upon which to build; but if the foundation is gone, the building is worthless. Those who have preserved a virtuous character, although they may lack in other desirable qualities, may be of real moral worth.

In order for the church to prosper there must be a studious effort on the part of its members to cherish the precious plant of love. Let it have every advantage that it may flourish in the heart. Every true Christian will develop in his life the characteristics of this divine love; he will reveal a spirit of forbearance, of beneficence, and a freedom from envy and jealousy. This character developed in word and act will not repulse, and will not be unapproachable, cold, and indifferent to the interests of others. The person who cultivates the precious plant of love will be self-denying in spirit, and will not yield self-control even under provocation. He will not impute wrong motives and evil intentions to others, but will feel deeply over sin when discovered in any of the disciples of Christ.

Love vaunteth not itself. It is a humble element; it never prompts a man to boast, to exalt himself. Love for God and for our fellow men will not be revealed in acts of rashness nor lead us to be overbearing, faultfinding, or dictatorial. Love is not puffed up. The heart where love reigns will be guided to a gentle, courteous, compassionate course of conduct toward others, whether they suit our fancy or not, whether they respect us or treat us ill. Love is an active principle; it keeps the good of others continually before us, thus restraining us from inconsiderate actions lest we fail of our object in winning souls to Christ. Love seeks not its own. It will not prompt men to seek their own ease and indulgence of self. It is the respect we render to *I* that so often hinders the growth of love.

There are men of poverty and obscurity whose lives God would accept and make full of usefulness on earth and of glory in heaven, but Satan is working persistently to defeat His purposes and drag them down to perdition by marriage with those whose character is such that they throw themselves directly across the road to life. Very few come out from this entanglement triumphant. Brother _____, you are willing to experiment and try to prove that you will be an exception to the general rule. Joseph was one of the few who could withstand temptation. He showed that he had an eye single to the glory or God. He evidenced a lofty regard for God's will, alike when occupying the prisoner's cell and when standing next the throne. He carried his religion with him wherever he went and in whatever situation he was placed. True religion has an all-pervading power. It gives tone to everything man does. You need not go out of the world in order to be a Christian, but you may carry your religion, with all its sanctifying influences, into all you do and say. You may discharge well the duties belonging to the situation where God has placed you, by keeping the heart fixed upon heavenly things, and thus break the spell now upon you through unwise association. Had you followed the light you would now be able to escape the snares which those who discern not the will of God have laid to captivate your soul.

Another striking point in the character of Joseph, worthy

of imitation by all youth, is his deep filial reverence. As he meets his father with tears streaming from his eyes, he hangs upon his neck in an affectionate, loving embrace. He seems to feel that he cannot do enough for his parent's comfort and watches over his declining years with a love as tender as a mother's. No pains are spared to show his respect and love upon all occasions. Joseph is an example of what a youth should be. Love manifested for your mother would disclose a beautiful trait of character such as God would approve.

The want of respect for the counsel of a godly parent is one of the marked sins of this degenerate age. There are many lives in our land that are dark and wretched because of one step taken in the dark. By one act of disobedience many a youth has blighted his whole life and weighed down a loving mother's heart with anguish. God will not hold you guiltless if you follow in this course. By despising the counsel of a God-fearing mother, who would willingly give her life for her children, you are transgressing the fifth commandment. You know not where your steps are leading you.

I again plead a mother's claim, a mother's love. There can be no baser ingratitude than that which marks the sin of disobedience to a Christian mother. In the days of your helpless infancy she watched over you; her prayers and tears were witnessed of heaven as she affectionately cherished you. For her children she has toiled and planned, thought, prayed, and exercised self-denial. Through your whole life her true heart has been anxious and earnest for your welfare. And yet now you choose your own course; you follow your own blind, stubborn will, irrespective of the bitter harvest you will reap and the sorrow you will bring upon her.

Infirmities are gathering about your mother. She needs you; any attention you may render will be very precious to her. There are none of her other children to whom she can look. They feel under no obligation to her. But you will find the privilege which is now yours may soon be lost. Do not think, however, that should you neglect your privilege and your duty as a son, your mother would suffer. She has true friends who will feel it a privilege to do the duties from which you withdraw yourself. God loves your mother and will care for her. If her own children neglect her, He will raise up others to do the work they might have done, and receive the blessing which was offered them. It is their privilege to make her last days her best and happiest.

I tell you plainly, God is displeased with your course. There are troubles before you that you do not discern and which may be avoided if you choose to follow wise counsel. Our Saviour has made you the object of His unwearied labors and tender solicitude, that you may be wise and not ruin yourself. He yearns over you in boundless compassion and love, exclaiming: "How often would I have gathered thy children together, as a hen doth gather her brood under her wings, and ye would not!" Your foolish heart has turned from the counsel of your best friends.

Because of earnest, faithful warnings to guard you against the mistakes of a lifetime, you have imagined you were a great benefit to the church. True, you are capable, in Jesus Christ, of being useful; but, notwithstanding this, the Lord and the church can get along without you. You can join the army of Christ's followers if you will; you may share in its conflicts and triumphs. But if you choose not to do this, the self-denying army under the bloodstained banner of the cross will move on to certain victory, and leave you behind. If you choose to guide your own frail bark across life's stormy waters you must answer for the presumption and be held responsible for the result.

If you could see how you have already become weak in principle, if you could see how your honor and honesty are imperiled, you would then see that God is not with you and that you ought not to stand in the place of responsibility you now occupy; you are unworthy. My heart is sad indeed when I know what you might have been had you yielded yourself wholly to God and then see the power the enemy has had over you.

The Sabbath school work is important, and all who are interested in the truth should endeavor to make it prosperous. Brother _____ could have served well in this branch of the work had he and others in the church pursued a right course. But he has been praised and petted too much. It has nearly ruined him. The Lord can do without him, but he cannot afford to do without God. The Lord will entrust His work to men with clean hands and a pure heart; therefore it is an honor to bear responsibilities in His cause.

The temperance work is also worthy of your best endeavors. But great care should be taken to make the temperance meetings as elevated and ennobling as possible. Avoid a surface work and everything of a theatrical character. Those who realize the solemn character of this work will keep the standard high. But there is a class who have no real respect for the cause of temperance; their only concern is to show off their smartness upon the stage. The pure, the thoughtful, and those who understand the object of the work, should be encouraged to labor in these great branches of reform. They may not be intellectually great, but if pure and humble, God-fearing and true, the Lord will accept their labors.

Literary societies are quite frequently organized, but, in nine cases out of ten, they have proved a damage to souls, rather than a blessing. This is because an alliance is formed with the world or with a class whose influence and tendency is ever to lead away from the solid to the superficial, from the real to the fictitious. Literary societies would be of great advantage if controlled by a religious element; but, sooner or later, the irreligious element is almost certain to gain the ascendancy and have a controlling influence. Just so it is with our temperance societies. The solemnity of the work is all covered up with the superficial, and a continual temptation is placed before the youth whom we wish to save.

The facts are before us. The burden bearers among us are dropping off into the silent grave. The active members of the church, the true workers in all reforms, are mostly past the meridian of life, and are declining in physical and mental strength. We should anxiously contemplate who are to rise up and fill their places. To whom are to be committed the vital interests of the church? The question may be asked by us with the deepest concern, Who will bear the responsibilities of the cause of God when a few more standard-bearers fall? We can but look anxiously upon the youth of today as those who must take these burdens, and upon whom responsibilities must fall. They must take the work where others leave it; and their course will determine whether morality, religion, and vital godliness shall prevail, or whether immorality and infidelity shall corrupt and blight all that is valuable. It is the way the standard is carried now that will determine the future.

Parents, will you now show by your course of action that wholesome restraint, good order, harmony, and peace shall be the ruling principle? or, shall those whose course of life shows that they have frivolous minds and are low in the scale of moral worth have a molding, controlling influence? God calls upon His believing people to connect with Him, to purify their souls by humbly walking in the footsteps of Jesus. God calls upon you to put away pride of opinion, pride of dress, and self-exaltation, and let the good and noble faculties of the mind strengthen with use.

Will men and women professing the most solemn truths ever borne to mortals be true to principle? If they would have an influence to lead the world to serious reflection they must be; their dress and conversation must be in strict accordance with their peculiar faith. Those who are older must educate the young, by precept and example, how to discharge those claims which society and their Maker have upon them. Upon these youth must be laid grave responsibilities. The question is whether they are capable of governing themselves and standing forth in the purity of their God-given manhood, abhorring anything which savors of licentiousness and discord.

Can I say anything that will make an impression upon the young? Never before was there so much at stake; never were there such weighty results depending upon a generation as upon those now coming upon the stage of action. Not for one moment should they think that they can fill any position of trust without possessing a good character. Just as well might they expect to gather grapes of thorns or figs of thistles. A good character must be built up brick by brick, every day growing in proportion to the effort put forth. Those characteristics which they will take to heaven with them must be obtained by the diligent exercise of their own faculties, by improving every advantage Providence gives them, and by connecting with the Source of all wisdom. Aim for no low standard. Let not your minds be cast in an inferior mold. The characters of Joseph and Daniel are good models for you to follow, but Christ is the perfect pattern.

Some of the brethren and sisters in the _____ church have done a good missionary work, but their interest must not flag. A few have done more than their strength would admit, but it was their meat and drink to do it. All can act a part in this work, and none are excused. Jesus would have all who profess His name become earnest workers. It is necessary that every individual member build upon the Rock, Christ Jesus. A storm is arising that will wrench and test the spiritual foundation of every one to the utmost. Therefore avoid the sand bed; hunt for the rock. Dig deep; lay your foundation sure. Build, oh, build for eternity! Build with tears, with heartfelt prayers. Let every one of you from hence-forth make your life beautiful by good works. Calebs are the men most needed in these last days. That which will make our churches vigorous and successful in their efforts is not bustle, but quiet, humble work; not parade and bombast, but patient, prayerful, persevering effort.

"He that is not with Me," said Christ, "is against Me." It is wholehearted, thoroughly decided men and women who will stand now. Christ sifted His followers again and again, until at one time there remained only eleven and a few faithful women to lay the foundation of the Christian church. There are those who will stand back when burdens are to be borne; but when the church is all aglow, they catch the enthusiasm, sing and shout, and become rapturous; but watch them. When the fervor is gone, only a few faithful Calebs will come to the front and display unwavering principle. These are salt that retains the savor. It is when the work moves hard that the churches develop the true helpers. These will not be talking of self, vindicating self, but will lose their identity in Jesus Christ. To be great in God's kingdom is to be a little child in humility, in simplicity of faith, and in the purity of love. All pride must perish, all jealousy be overcome, all ambition for supremacy be given up, and the meekness and trust of the child be encouraged. All such will find Christ their rock of defense, their strong tower. In Him they may trust implicitly, and He will never fail them.

Oh, that all who believe present truth would be warned to seek the Lord. The thoughts of God's infinite mercy and of His matchless love should influence all to imitate His ex-ample. But this is not the case. Some of our sisters indulge too freely in a love for dress and display; they do not dress at all in harmony with our holy faith. This is true of Sister _____. The world should have a better example than this sister has given it. She should feel her God-given responsibility to cast the entire weight of her influence upon the side of Christ and seek to make those with whom she associates less worldly. She and Sister _____ would be of far greater advantage to the church if they would encourage plainness of dress in themselves and others. Those sisters who are dressmakers and who study the fashion plates frequently lead others in the church to do that which is displeasing to God by encouraging them to cut and trim their dresses in imitation of the world. The efforts of these sisters to do good would be far more acceptable to God were there seen in their lives less dressing, less cheap, worldly talking, and less visiting; less complaining and murmuring against the ministers laboring for you, and more praying and reading of the Bible.

The Lord is displeased with the course pursued by many in the church toward some of their ministering brethren. He bids you cease your cruel speeches and let words of encouragement take the place of your murmuring, your repining, your faultfinding. Christ is speaking to you in the person of His saints, and you have despised His counsel and rejected His reproof. Do this no longer. Elder _____ has a work to do, not only in the East, but in many places. God will be with him and prosper him if he hides in Jesus. He is not infallible; he may at times err in judgment. But be careful how you speak that which will make of none effect the words God bids him utter.

When he knows what the will of God is, he would not hesitate to do it should it cost him his life. While many of you plan only how you can please self and have an easy life, his whole life and interest is wrapped up in the cause of God. While studying and planning for the cause, he has sometimes exercised shrewdness and sharpness, which has led others to misjudge him. His aim was not to advantage himself, but the cause which he loved. While the Lord would have you faithfully uphold the hands of His tried servants, He would warn you against placing too great confidence in those who have newly come to the faith or with whose past life and labors you are unacquainted.

It is your privilege to be a prosperous, happy church. Let each one of you search his own heart, cleanse the defiled soul temple, and watch unto prayer. Be determined you will seek Jesus until you find Him; release not your grasp until His love dwells in your heart and you have His spirit subduing your life and fashioning your character. Then believe, and with boldness you may approach His throne, knowing that He will hear your prayers.

LABORERS FOR GOD

Fellow laborers in the great harvest field, we have but little time left in which to labor. Now is the most favorable opportunity we shall ever have, and how carefully ought every moment to be employed. So devoted was our Redeemer to the work of saving souls that He even longed for His baptism of blood. The apostles caught the zeal of their Master and firmly, steadily, zealously went forward to the accomplishment of their great work, fighting against principalities and powers, and spiritual wickedness in high places.

We are living in a time when even greater earnestness is needed than in the apostles' day. But among many of the ministers of Christ there is a feeling of unrest, a desire to imitate the romantic style of modern revivalists, a desire to do something great, to create a sensation, to be accounted able speakers, and to gain for themselves honor and distinction. If such could encounter perils and receive the honor given to heroes, they would engage in the work with unflagging energy. But to live and labor almost unknown, to toil and sacrifice for Jesus in obscurity, receiving no special praise from men—this requires a soundness of principle and a steadfastness of purpose that but few possess. Were there a greater effort to walk humbly with God, looking away from men and laboring only for Christ's sake, far more would be accomplished.

My ministering brethren, seek Jesus with all lowliness and meekness. Do not try to draw the attention of the people to yourselves. Let them lose sight of the instrument, while you exalt Jesus. Talk of Jesus; lose self in Jesus. There is too much bustle and stir about our religion, while Calvary and the cross are forgotten.

We are in the greatest peril when we receive praise of one another, when we enter into a confederacy to exalt one another. The great burden of the Pharisees was to secure the praise of men; and Christ told them that that was all the reward they would ever receive. Let us take up our appointed work and do it for Christ; if we suffer privation, let it be for His sake. Our divine Lord was made perfect through suffering. Oh, when shall we see men laboring as He labored!

The word of God is our standard. Every act of love, every word of kindness, every prayer in behalf of the suffering and oppressed, is reported before the eternal throne and placed on heaven's imperishable record. The divine word pours light into the most darkened understanding, and that light makes the most cultivated feel their inefficiency and sinfulness.

The enemy is buying souls today very cheap. "Ye have sold yourselves for nought," is the language of Scripture. One is selling his soul for the world's applause, another for money; one to gratify base passions, another for worldly amusement. Such bargains are made daily. Satan is bidding for the purchase of Christ's blood and buying them cheap, notwithstanding the infinite price which has been paid to ransom them.

Great blessings and privileges are ours. We may secure the most valuable heavenly treasures. Let ministers and people remember that gospel truth ruins if it does not save. The soul that refuses to listen to the invitations of mercy from day to day can soon listen to the most urgent appeals without an emotion stirring his soul.

As laborers with God we need more fervent piety and less self-exaltation. The more self is exalted, the more will faith in the testimonies of the Spirit of God be lessened. Those who are the most closely connected with God are the ones who know His voice when He speaks to them. Those who are spiritual discern spiritual things. Such will feel grateful that the Lord has pointed out their errors, while those who trust wholly in themselves will see less and less of God in the testimonies of His Spirit.

Our work must be accompanied with deep humiliation, fasting, and prayer. We must not expect all peace and joy. There will be sadness; but if we sow in tears we shall reap in joy. Darkness and despondency may at times enter the heart of the self-sacrificing ones; but this is not against them. It may be God's design to cause them to seek Him more earnestly.

What we need now is Calebs, men who are faithful and true. Indolence marks the lives of too many at the present day. They turn their shoulders from the wheel just when they should persevere and bring all their powers into active exercise. Ministers of Christ, "awake thou that sleepest, and arise from the dead, and Christ shall give thee light." Your labors taste so strongly of self that Christ is forgotten. Some of you are pampered and flattered too much. As in the days of Noah, there is too much eating and drinking, planting and building. The world has stolen the energies of the servants of Christ. Brethren, if you would have your religion honored by unbelievers, honor it yourselves by corresponding works. By a close connection with God and a strict adherence to Bible truth in the face of difficulty and worldly pressure, you may infuse the spirit of the truth into the hearts of your children so that they will work effectually with you as instruments in God's hands for good.

Many are incapacitated for labor both mentally and physically by overeating and the gratification of the lustful passions. The animal propensities are strengthened, while the moral and spiritual nature is enfeebled. When we shall stand around the great white throne, what a record will the lives of many then present. Then will they see what they might have done had they not debased their God-given powers. Then will they realize what height of intellectual greatness they might have attained had they given to God all the physical and mental strength He had entrusted to them. In their agony of remorse they will long to have their lives to live over again.

I call upon those who profess to be light bearers—ensamples to the flock—to depart from all iniquity. Use well the little remnant of time now left you. Have you that strong hold of God, that consecration to His service, that your religion will not fail you in the face of direst persecution? The deep love of God alone will sustain the soul amid the trials which are just upon us.

Self-denial and the cross are our portion. Will we accept it? None of us need expect that when the last great trials come upon us a self-sacrificing, patriotic spirit will be developed in a moment because needed. No, indeed, this spirit must be blended with our daily experience, and infused into the minds and hearts of our children, both by precept and example. Mothers in Israel may not be warriors themselves, but they may raise up warriors who shall gird on the whole armor and fight manfully the battles of the Lord.

Ministers and people need the converting power of grace before they will be able to stand in the day of the Lord. The world is fast approaching that point in iniquity and human depravity when God's interference will become necessary. And at that time His professed followers should be more marked for their fidelity to His holy law. Their prayer will be as that of David: "It is time for Thee, Lord, to work: for they have made void Thy law." And by their conduct they will say: "Therefore I love Thy commandments above gold; yea, above fine gold." The very contempt that is shown to the law of God is sufficient reason why His commandment-keeping people should come to the front and show their esteem and reverence for His downtrodden law.

"And because iniquity shall abound, the love of many shall wax cold." The very atmosphere is polluted with sin. Soon God's people will be tested by fiery trials, and the great proportion of those who now appear to be genuine and true will prove to be base metal. Instead of being strengthened and confirmed by opposition, threats, and abuse, they will cowardly take the side of the opposers. The promise is: "Them that honor Me I will honor." Shall we be less firmly attached to God's law because the world at large have attempted to make it void?

Already the judgments of God are abroad in the land, as seen in storms, in floods, in tempests, in earthquakes, in peril by land and by sea. The great I AM is speaking to those who make void His law. When God's wrath is poured out upon the earth, who will then be able to stand? Now is the time for God's people to show themselves true to principle. When the religion of Christ is most held in contempt, when His law is most despised, then should our zeal be the warmest, and our courage and firmness the most unflinching. To stand in defense of truth and righteousness when the majority forsake us, to fight the battles of the Lord when champions are few—this will be our test. At this time we must gather warmth from the coldness of others, courage from their cowardice, and loyalty from their treason. The nation will be on the side of the great rebel leader.

The test will surely come. Thirty-six years ago I was shown that what is now transpiring would take place, that the observance of an institution of the papacy would be enforced upon the people by a Sunday law, while the sanctified rest day of Jehovah would be trampled underfoot.

The Captain of our salvation will strengthen His people for the conflict in which they must engage. How often when Satan has brought all his forces to bear against the followers of Christ, and death stares them in the face, have earnest prayers put up in faith brought the Captain of the Lord's host upon the field of action and turned the tide of battle and delivered the oppressed.

Now is the time when we should closely connect with God, that we may be hid when the fierceness of His wrath is poured upon the sons of men. We have wandered away from the old landmarks. Let us return. If the Lord be God, serve Him; if Baal, serve him. Which side will you be on?

AGENTS OF SATAN

Satan uses men and women as agents to solicit to sin and make it attractive. These agents he faithfully educates to so disguise sin that he can more successfully destroy souls and rob Christ of His glory. Satan is the great enemy of God and man. He transforms himself through his agents into angels of light. In the Scriptures he is called a destroyer, an accuser of the brethren, a deceiver, a liar, a tormentor, and a murderer. Satan has many in his employ, but is most successful when he can use professed Christians for his satanic work. And the greater their influence, the more elevated their position, the more knowledge they profess of God and His service, the more successfully can he use them. Whoever entices to sin is his agent.

While attending one of the Eastern camp meetings I was introduced one Friday to a man who occupied a tent with several women and children. That night I was unable to sleep; my soul was deeply burdened. While pleading with God in the night season a vision given years ago at the time when the course of Nathan Fuller was reproved was distinctly revived in my mind. At that time I was shown three men whom I should meet who would be pursuing the same course of iniquity under the profession of godliness. This man was one of the three. As I bore my testimony in the morning meeting, the power and Spirit of God rested upon me; but I did not mention individual cases. Later in the day I felt clear in reference to my duty and bore my testimony, referring to his case as most marked. By this course of action this man was going exactly contrary to the direction of the apostle to "abstain from all appearance of evil." He was breaking the seventh commandment, while professedly keeping the fourth. By his deception he was gathering around him a company of women who followed him from place to place, as a faithful wife would accompany her husband.

As a people, we are looked upon as peculiar. Our position and faith distinguish us from every other denomination. If we are in life and character no better than worldlings, they will point the finger of scorn at us and say: "These are Seventh-day Adventists." "We have here a sample of the people who keep the seventh day for Sunday." The stigma which should be rightfully attached to such a class is thus placed upon all who are conscientiously keeping the seventh day. Oh, how much better it would be if such a class would not make any pretension to obey the truth!

I felt led out to rebuke this man in the name of the Lord and to call upon the women who were with him to separate from him and withdraw their misplaced confidence, for unhappiness and ruin were in the path they had entered upon.

The Ledger of Heaven testifies of this man thus: "A deceiver, an adulterer, creeping into houses and leading captive silly women." How many souls he will destroy with his satanic sophistry the judgment alone will reveal. Such men ought to be rebuked and discountenanced at once, that they may not bring a continual reproach upon the cause.

As we near the close of earth's history, perils and dangers thicken around us. A mere profession of godliness will not avail. There must be a living connection with God, that we may have spiritual eyesight to discern the wickedness which is in a most artful and secret manner creeping into our midst through those who make a profession of our faith. The greatest sins are brought in through those who profess to be sanctified and claim that they cannot sin. Yet many of this class are sinning daily and are corrupt in heart and life. Such are self-sufficient and self-righteous, making their own standard of righteousness and utterly failing to meet the Bible standard. Notwithstanding their high claims, they are strangers to the covenant of promise. It is in great mercy that God bears with their perversity and that they are not cut down as cumberers of the ground, but still remain within the possibilities of forgiveness. The forbearance of God is continually presumed upon and His mercy abused. David in his day thought that men had exceeded the boundaries of the long-suffering of God, and that He must interfere to vindicate His honor and restrain unrighteousness.

Mr. _____ is a teacher of doctrines that defile the temple of God. There is scarcely a ray of hope for him; he has deceived himself and deluded others so long that Satan has almost entire control of his mind and body. If his professed robe of righteousness can be torn from him and his vile purposes and thoughts be exposed, so that he will not continue to lead others in the paths of hell, it will be all we may expect.

The warnings of God he first hated and then resisted because they brought his own wicked course to be seen in the light of God's law. It is one of the saddest evidences of the blinding influence of sin that months and years roll on and there is no awaking to repentance. With a firm persistence he has pursued his downward course. He has no bitter feelings of remorse, no dread of heaven's vengeance. If by lies and deception he can cover his sins from observation he is content. All sense of right and wrong is dead within him. A harvest is before him that he will be horrified to reap.

The worst feature in this case is that all his satanic work is done under pretense of being a representative of Jesus Christ. One sinner dressed up as an angel of light can do incalculable harm. Dark and fearful plans are deliberately made to separate man and wife. Said the apostle: "Of this sort are they which creep into houses, and lead captive silly women laden with sins, led away with divers lusts." These licentious characters even creep into respectable families and by their deceptive wiles and intrigues lead astray the conscientious. Damnable heresies are received as truth, and the most revolting sins committed as acts of righteousness, for conscience becomes confused and stupefied.

This man embraced the unpopular doctrine that the seventh day is the Sabbath of the Lord, in order to give to his religious experience a semblance of honesty. Our views have been clearly defined in our publications, but, concealing this fact, he mixed with truth his own defiling heresies and tried to make others believe that God had given him new light upon the Bible. By thus professing to have great light for the people on the Sabbath of the fourth commandment and kindred truth he had to the unsuspecting an appearance of really being led of God. But when once the confidence is gained, he commences his satanic work of wresting the Scriptures from their true meaning by seeking to show that adultery condemned in the law of God does not mean what it is generally understood to mean. He really tries to make sensible women believe it not offensive to God for wives to be untrue to their marriage vows. He will not even admit that this would be breaking the seventh commandment. Satan rejoices to have sinners enter the church as professed Sabbathkeepers while they allow him to control their minds and affections, using them to deceive and corrupt others.

In this degenerate age many will be found who are so blinded to the sinfulness of sin that they choose a licentious life because it suits the natural and perverse inclination of the heart. Instead of facing the mirror, the law of God, and bringing their hearts and characters up to God's standard, they allow Satan's agents to erect his standard in their hearts. Corrupt men think it easier to misinterpret the Scriptures to sustain them in their iniquity than to yield up their corruption and sin and be pure in heart and life.

There are more men of this stamp than many have imagined, and they will multiply as we draw near the end of time. Unless they are rooted and grounded in the truth of the Bible, and have a living connection with God, many will be infatuated and deceived. Dangers unseen beset our path. Our only safety is in constant watchfulness and prayer. The nearer we live to Jesus, the more will we partake of His pure and holy character; and the more offensive sin appears to us, the more exalted and desirable will appear the purity and brightness of Christ.

In order to cover his corrupt life and make his sins appear harmless, this man will bring up instances recorded in the Bible where good men have fallen under temptation. Paul met with just such men in his day, and the church has been cursed with them in all ages. At Miletus Paul called the elders of the church together and warned them in regard to what they would meet: "Take heed therefore unto yourselves, and to all the flock, over the which the Holy Ghost hath made you overseers, to feed the church of God, which He hath purchased with His own blood. For I know this, that after my departing shall grievous wolves enter in among you, not sparing the flock. Also of your own selves shall men arise, speaking perverse things, to draw away disciples after them. Therefore watch, and remember, that by the space of three years I ceased not to warn everyone night and day with tears."

He who holds the truth in unrighteousness, who declares his belief in it, and yet wounds it every day by his inconsistent life, is surrendering himself to the service of Satan and leading souls to ruin. This class hold intercourse with fallen angels and are aided by them in gaining the control of minds. When Satan's bewitching power controls a person, God is forgotten, and man who is filled with corrupt purposes is extolled. Secret licentiousness is practiced by these deceived souls as a virtue. This is a species of witchcraft. The question of the apostle to the Galatians may well be asked: "Who hath bewitched you, that ye should not obey the truth, before whose eyes Jesus Christ hath been evidently set forth, crucified among you?" There is always a bewitching power in heresies and in licentiousness. The mind is so deluded that it cannot reason intelligently, and an illusion is continually leading it from purity. The spiritual eyesight becomes blurred, and persons of hitherto untainted morals become confused under the delusive sophistry of those agents of Satan who profess to be messengers of light. It is this delusion which gives these agents power. Should they come out boldly and make their advances openly they would be repulsed without a moment's hesitation; but they work first to gain sympathy and secure confidence in themselves as holy, self-sacrificing men of God. As His special messengers they then begin their artful work of drawing away souls from the path of rectitude by attempting to make void the law of God.

When ministers thus take advantage of the confidence the people place in them and lead souls to ruin, they make themselves as much more guilty than the common sinner as their profession is higher. In the day of God, when the great Ledger of Heaven is opened, it will be found to contain the names of many ministers who have made pretensions to purity of heart and life and professed to be entrusted with the gospel of Christ, but who have taken advantage of their position to allure souls to transgress the law of God.

When men and women fall under the corrupting power of Satan, it is almost impossible to recover them out of the horrible snare so that they will ever again have pure thoughts and clear conceptions of God's requirements. Sin, to their deluded minds, has been sanctified by the minister, and it is never again regarded in the loathsome light that God looks upon it. After the moral standard has been lowered in the minds of men, their judgment becomes perverted, and they look upon sin as righteousness, and righteousness as sin. By associating with these, whose inclinations and habits are not elevated and pure, others become like them. Their tastes and principles are almost unconsciously adopted.

If the society of a man of impure mind and licentious habits is chosen in preference to that of the virtuous and pure, it is a sure indication that the tastes and inclinations harmonize, that a low level of morals is reached. This level is called by these deceived, infatuated souls, a high and holy affinity of spirit—a spiritual harmony. But the apostle terms it "spiritual wickedness in high places," against which we are to institute a vigorous warfare.

When the deceiver commences his work of deception, he frequently finds dissimilarity of tastes and habits; but by great pretensions to godliness he gains the confidence, and when this is done, his wily, deceptive power is exercised in his own way to carry out his devices. By associating with this dangerous element, women become accustomed to breathe the atmosphere of impurity and almost insensibly become permeated with the same spirit. Their identity is lost; they become the shadow of their seducer.

Men professing to have new light, claiming to be reformers, will have great influence over a certain class who are convinced of the heresies that exist in the present age and who are not satisfied with the spiritual condition of the churches. With true, honest hearts, these desire to see a change for the better, a coming up to a higher standard. If the faithful servants of Christ would present the truth, pure and unadulterated, to this class, they would accept it, and purify themselves by obeying it. But Satan, ever vigilant, sets upon the track of these inquiring souls. Someone making high profession as a reformer comes to them, as Satan came to Christ disguised as an angel of light, and draws them still further from the path of right.

The unhappiness and degradation that follow in the train of licentiousness cannot be estimated. The world is defiled under its inhabitants. They have nearly filled up the measure of their iniquity; but that which will bring the heaviest retribution is the practice of iniquity under the cloak of godliness. The Redeemer of the world never spurned true repentance, however great the guilt; but He hurls burning denunciations against Pharisees and hypocrites. There is more hope for the open sinner than for this class.

"And for this cause [not receiving the love of the truth] God shall send them strong delusion, that they should believe a lie: that they all might be damned who believed not the truth, but had pleasure in unrighteousness." This man and those deceived by him love not the truth but have pleasure in unrighteousness. And what stronger delusion could come upon them than that there is nothing displeasing to God in licentiousness and adultery? The Bible contains many warnings against these sins. Paul writes to Titus of those who "profess that they know God; but in works they deny Him, being abominable, and disobedient, and unto every good work reprobate." "But there were false prophets also among the people, even as there shall be false teachers among you, who privily [not openly] shall bring in damnable heresies, even denying the Lord that bought them, and bring upon themselves swift destruction. And many shall follow their pernicious ways; by reason of whom the way of truth shall be evil spoken of." The ones here referred to are not those who openly claim to have no faith in Christ, but those who profess to *believe* the truth and by their vileness of character bring a reproach upon it, causing it to be evil spoken of.

"And through covetousness shall they with feigned words make merchandise of you: whose judgment now of a long time lingereth not, and their damnation slumbereth not." "But these, as natural brute beasts, made to be taken and destroyed, speak evil of the things that they understand not; and shall utterly perish in their own corruption; and shall receive the reward of unrighteousness, as they that count it pleasure to riot in the daytime. Spots they are and blemishes, sporting themselves with their own deceivings while they feast with you; having eyes full of adultery, and that cannot cease from sin; beguiling unstable souls: an heart they have exercised with covetous practices; cursed children: which have forsaken the right way, and are gone astray, following the way of Balaam the son of Bosor, who loved the wages of unrighteousness."

"These are wells without water, clouds that are carried with a tempest; to whom the mist of darkness is reserved forever. For when they speak great swelling words of vanity," boasting of their light, their knowledge and their love of the truth, "they allure through the lusts of the flesh, through much wantonness, those that were clean escaped from them who live in error."

In this age of corruption when our adversary the devil, as a roaring lion, walketh about seeking whom he may devour, I see the necessity of lifting my voice in warning. "Watch ye and pray, lest ye enter into temptation." There are many who possess brilliant talents who wickedly devote them to the service of Satan. What warning can I give to a people who profess to have come out from the world and to have left its works of darkness? to a people whom God has made the repositories of His law, but who, like the pretentious fig tree, flaunt their apparently flourishing branches in the very face of the Almighty, yet bear no fruit to the glory of God? Many of them cherish impure thoughts, unholy imaginations, unsanctified desires, and base passions. God hates the fruit borne upon such a tree. Angels, pure and holy, look upon the course of such with abhorrence, while Satan exults. Oh, that men and women would consider what is to be gained by transgressing God's law! Under any and every circumstance, transgression is a dishonor to God and a curse to man. We must regard it thus, however fair its guise, and by whomsoever committed.

As Christ's ambassador, I entreat you who profess present truth to promptly resent any approach to impurity and forsake the society of those who breathe an impure suggestion. Loathe these defiling sins with the most intense hatred. Flee from those who would, even in conversation, let the mind run in such a channel; "for out of the abundance of the heart the mouth speaketh."

As those who practice these defiling sins are steadily increasing in the world and would intrude themselves into our churches, I warn you to give no place to them. Turn from the seducer. Though a professed follower of Christ, he is Satan in the form of man; he has borrowed the livery of heaven that he may the better serve his master. You should not for one moment give place to an impure, covert suggestion; for even this will stain the soul, as impure water defiles the channel through which it passes.

Choose poverty, reproach, separation from friends, or any suffering rather than to defile the soul with sin. Death before dishonor or the transgression of God's law should be the motto of every Christian. As a people professing to be reformers, treasuring the most solemn, purifying truths of God's word, we must elevate the standard far higher than it is at the present time. Sin and sinners in the church must be promptly dealt with, that others may not be contaminated. Truth and purity require that we make more thorough work to cleanse the camp from Achans. Let those in responsible positions not suffer sin in a brother. Show him that he must either put away his sins or be separated from the church.

When the individual members of the church shall act as true followers of the meek and lowly Saviour, there will be less covering up and excusing of sin. All will strive to act as if in God's presence. They will realize that His all-seeing eye is ever upon them and that the most secret thought is known to Him. The character, the motives, the desires and purposes, are as clear as the light of the sun to the eye of the Omnipotent. But few bear this in mind. The larger class by far do not realize what a fearful account must be rendered at the bar of God by all the transgressors of His law.

Can you who have professed to receive such great light be content with a low level? Oh, how earnestly and constantly should we seek for the divine presence and a realization of the solemn truths that the end of all things is at hand and that the Judge of all the earth stands at the door! How can you disregard His just and holy requirements? How can you transgress in the very face of Jehovah? How can you cherish unholy thoughts and base passions in full view of the pure angels and of the Redeemer, who gave Himself for you that He might redeem you from all iniquity and purify unto Himself a peculiar people, zealous of good works? As you contemplate the matter in the light which shines from the cross of Christ, will not sin appear too mean, too perilous, to be indulged when standing upon the very borders of the eternal world?

I speak to our people. If you draw close to Jesus and seek to adorn your profession by a well-ordered life and godly conversation, your feet will be kept from straying into forbidden paths. If you will only watch, continually watch unto prayer, if you will do everything as if you were in the immediate presence of God, you will be saved from yielding to temptation, and may hope to be kept pure, spotless, and undefiled till the last. If you hold the beginning of your confidence firm unto the end, your ways will be established in God; and what grace has begun, glory will crown in the kingdom of our God. The fruits of the Spirit are "love, joy, peace, long-suffering, gentleness, goodness, faith, meekness, temperance: against such there is no law." If Christ be within us, we shall crucify the flesh with the affections and lusts.

WILL A MAN ROB GOD?

The Lord has made the diffusion of light and truth in the earth dependent on the voluntary efforts and offerings of those who have been partakers of the heavenly gifts. Comparatively few are called to travel as ministers or missionaries, but multitudes are to co-operate in spreading the truth with their means.

The history of Ananias and Sapphira is given us that we may understand the sin of deception in regard to our gifts and offerings. They had voluntarily promised to give a portion of their property for the promotion of the cause of Christ; but when the means was in their hands they declined to fulfill that obligation, at the same time wishing it to appear to others that they had given all. Their punishment was marked in order that it might serve as a perpetual warning to Christians of all ages. The same sin is fearfully prevalent at the present time, yet we hear of no such signal punishment. The Lord shows men once with what abhorrence He regards such an offense against His sacred claims and dignity, and then they are left to follow the general principles of the divine administration.

Voluntary offerings and the tithe constitute the revenue of the gospel. Of the means which is entrusted to man, God claims a certain portion—a tithe; but He leaves all free to say how much the tithe is, and whether or not they will give more than this. They are to give as they purpose in their hearts. But when the heart is stirred by the influence of the Spirit of God, and a vow is made to give a certain amount, the one who vowed has no longer any right to the consecrated portion. He has given his pledge before men, and they are called to witness to the transaction. At the same time he has incurred an obligation of the most sacred character to co-operate with the Lord in building up His kingdom on earth. Promises of this kind made to men would be considered binding. Are they not more sacred and binding when made to God? Are promises tried in the court of conscience less binding than written agreements with men?

When the divine light is shining into the heart with unusual clearness and power, habitual selfishness relaxes its grasp, and there is a disposition to give to the cause of God. None need expect that they will be allowed to fulfill the promises then made without a protest on the part of Satan. He is not pleased to see the Redeemer's kingdom on earth built up. He suggests that the pledge made was too much, that it may cripple them in their efforts to acquire property or gratify the desires of their families. The power Satan has over the human mind is wonderful. He labors most earnestly to keep the heart bound up in self.

The only means which God has ordained to advance His cause is to bless men with property. He gives them the sunshine and the rain; He causes vegetation to flourish; He gives health and ability to acquire means. All our blessings come from His bountiful hand. In turn He would have men and women show their gratitude by returning Him a portion in tithes and offerings—in thank offerings, in freewill offerings, in trespass offerings.

The hearts of men become hardened through selfishness, and, like Ananias and Sapphira, they are tempted to withhold part of the price while pretending to come up to the rules of tithing. Will a man rob God? Should means flow into the treasury exactly according to God's plan,—a tenth of all the increase,—there would be abundance to carry forward His work.

Well, says one, the calls keep coming to give to the cause; I am weary of giving. Are you? Then let me ask: Are you weary of receiving from God's beneficent hand? Not until He ceases to bless you will you cease to be under bonds to return to Him the portion He claims. He blesses you that it may be in your power to bless others. When you are weary of receiving, then you may say: I am weary of so many calls to give. God reserves to Himself a portion of all that we receive. When this is returned to Him, the remaining portion is blessed, but when it is withheld, the whole is sooner or later cursed. God's claim is first; every other is secondary.

In every church there should be established a treasury for the poor. Then let each member present a thank offering to God once a week or once a month, as is most convenient. This offering will express our gratitude for the gifts of health, of food, and of comfortable clothing. And according as God has blessed us with these comforts will we lay by for the poor, the suffering, and the distressed. I would call the attention of our brethren especially to this point. Remember the poor. Forego some of your luxuries, yea, even comforts, and help those who can obtain only the most meager food and clothing. In doing for them you are doing for Jesus in the person of His saints. He identifies Himself with suffering humanity. Do not wait until your imaginary wants are all satisfied. Do not trust to your feelings and give when you feel like it and withhold when you do not feel like it. Give regularly, either ten, twenty, or fifty cents a week, as you would like to see upon the heavenly record in the day of God.

Your good wishes we will thank you for, but the poor cannot keep comfortable on good wishes alone. They must have tangible proofs of your kindness in food and clothing. God does not mean that any of His followers should beg for bread. He has given you an abundance that you may supply those of their necessities which by industry and economy they are not able to supply. Do not wait for them to call your attention to their needs. Act as did Job. The thing that he knew not he searched out. Go on an inspecting tour and learn what is needed and how it can be best supplied.

I have been shown that many of our people are robbing the Lord in tithes and in offerings, and as the result His work is greatly hindered. The curse of God will rest upon those who are living upon God's bounties and yet close their hearts and do nothing or next to nothing to advance His cause. Brethren and sisters, how can the beneficent Father continue to make you His stewards, furnishing you with means to use for Him, when you grasp it all, selfishly claiming that it is yours!

Instead of rendering to God the means He has placed in their hands, many invest it in more land. This evil is growing with our brethren. They had before all they could well care for, but the love of money or a desire to be counted as well off as their neighbors leads them to bury their means in the world and withhold from God His just dues. Can we be surprised if they are not prospered? if God does not bless their crops and they are disappointed? Could our brethren remember that God can bless twenty acres of land and make them as productive as one hundred, they would not continue to bury themselves in lands, but would let their means flow into God's treasury. "Take heed," said Christ, "lest at any time your hearts be overcharged with surfeiting, and drunkenness, and cares of this life." Satan is pleased to have you increase your farms and invest your means in worldly enterprises, for by so doing you not only hinder the cause from advancing, but by anxiety and overwork lessen your prospect for eternal life.

We ought now to be heeding the injunction of our Saviour: "Sell that ye have, and give alms; provide yourselves bags which wax not old, a treasure in the heavens that faileth not." It is now that our brethren should be cutting down their possessions instead of increasing them. We are about to move to a better country, even a heavenly. Then let us not be dwellers upon the earth, but be getting things into as compact a compass as possible.

The time is coming when we cannot sell at any price. The decree will soon go forth prohibiting men to buy or sell of any man save him that hath the mark of the beast. We came near having this realized in California a short time since; but this was only the threatening of the blowing of the four winds. As yet they are held by the four angels. We are not just ready. There is a work yet to be done, and then the angels will be bidden to let go, that the four winds may blow upon the earth. That will be a decisive time for God's children, a time of trouble such as never was since there was a nation. Now is our opportunity to work.

There is among many professing the truth a spirit of unrest. Some want to go to another county or state, buy large lands, and carry on an extensive business; others want to go into the city. Thus little churches are left in weakness and discouragement to die, when, had the ones who left them been content to work on a smaller scale, doing their little with fidelity, they might have made their families comfortable and been free to keep their own souls in the love of God. Many who move are disappointed. They lose what little property they had, lose health, and finally give up the truth.

The Lord is coming. Let everyone show his faith by his works. Faith in Christ's near advent is dying out of the churches, and selfishness is causing them to rob God to serve their own personal interests. When Christ is abiding in us, we shall be self-denying like Him.

In times past there has been great liberality on the part of our people. They have not been backward to respond to calls for help in the various branches of the work. But of late a change has come. There has been, especially with our Eastern brethren, a withholding of means, while worldliness and love of possessions have been increasing. There is a growing disregard of promises made to help our various institutions and enterprises. Subscriptions to build a church, to endow a college, or to assist in the missionary work are looked upon as promises which persons are under no obligation to fulfill if it is not convenient. These promises were made under the holy impressions of the Spirit of God. Then do not rob Him by withholding what rightfully belongs to Him. Brethren and sisters, look over your past life and see if you have dealt faithfully with God. Have you any unredeemed pledges? If so, resolve that you will pay them if it is within your power.

Listen to the counsel of the Lord: "Bring ye all the tithes into the storehouse, that there may be meat in Mine house, and prove Me now herewith, . . . if I will not open you the windows of heaven, and pour you out a blessing, that there shall not be room enough to receive it. And I will rebuke the devourer for your sakes, and he shall not destroy the fruits of your ground; neither shall your vine cast her fruit before the time in the field." "And all nations shall call you blessed: for ye shall be a delightsome land."

Are you not willing to accept the promises which the Lord here makes and to put selfishness from you and begin to work earnestly to advance His cause? Do not strengthen your hold on this world by taking advantage of your poorer neighbor, for God's eye is upon you; He reads every motive and weighs you in the balances of the sanctuary.

I saw that many withhold from the cause while they live, quieting their consciences that they will be charitable at death; they hardly dare exercise faith and trust in God to give anything while living. But this deathbed charity is not what Christ requires of His followers; it cannot excuse the selfishness of the living. Those who hold fast their property till the last moment, surrender it to death rather than to the cause. Losses are occurring continually. Banks fail, and property is consumed in very many ways. Many purpose to do something, but they delay the matter, and Satan works to prevent the means from coming into the treasury at all. It is lost before it is returned to God, and Satan exults that it is so.

If you would do good with your means, do it at once lest Satan get it in his hands and thus hinder the work of God. Many times, when the Lord has opened the way for brethren to handle their means to advance His cause, the agents of Satan have presented some enterprise by which they were positive the brethren could double their means. They take the bait; their money is invested, and the cause, and frequently themselves, never receive a dollar.

Brethren, remember the cause, and when you have means at your command lay up for yourselves a good foundation against the time to come, that you may lay hold on eternal life. Jesus for your sakes became poor, that you through His poverty might be made rich in heavenly treasure. What will you give for Jesus, who has given all for you?

It will not do for you to depend on making your charity gifts in testamentary bequests at death. You cannot calculate with the least degree of surety that the cause will ever be benefited by them. Satan works with acute skill to stir up the relatives, and every false position is taken to gain to the world that which was solemnly dedicated to the cause of God. Much less than the sum willed is always received. Satan even puts it into the hearts of men and women to protest against their relatives' doing what they wish in the bestowment of their property. They seem to regard everything given to the Lord as robbing the relatives of the deceased. If you want your means to go to the cause, appropriate it, or all that you do not really need for a support, while you live. A few of the brethren are doing this and enjoying the pleasure of being their own executors. Will the covetousness of men make it necessary that they shall be deprived of life in order that the property which God has lent them shall not be useless forever? Let none of you draw upon yourselves the doom of the unprofitable servant who hid his Lord's money in the earth.

Dying charity is a poor substitute for living benevolence. Many will to their friends and relatives all except a very small pittance of their property. This they leave for their supreme Friend, who became poor for their sakes, who suffered insult, mockery, and death, that they might become sons and daughters of God. And yet they expect when the righteous dead shall come forth to immortal life that this Friend will take them into His everlasting habitations.

The cause of Christ is robbed, not by a mere passing thought, not by an unpremeditated act. No. By your own deliberate act you made your will, placing your property at the disposal of unbelievers. After having robbed God during your lifetime, you continue to rob Him after your death, and you do this with the full consent of all your powers of mind, in a document called your will. What do you think will be your Master's will toward you for thus appropriating His goods? What will you say when an account is demanded of your stewardship?

Brethren, awake from your life of selfishness, and act like consistent Christians. The Lord requires you to economize your means and let every dollar not needed for your comfort flow into the treasury. Sisters, take that ten cents, that twenty cents, that dollar which you were about to spend for candies, for ruffles, or for ribbons, and donate it to God's cause. Many of our sisters earn good wages, but it is nearly all spent in gratifying their pride of dress.

The wants of the cause will continually increase as we near the close of time. Means is needed to give young men a short course of study in our schools, to prepare them for efficient work in the ministry and in different branches of the cause. We are not coming up to our privilege in this matter. All schools among us will soon be closed up. How much more might have been done had men obeyed the requirements of Christ in Christian beneficence! What an influence would this readiness to give all for Christ have had upon the world! It would have been one of the most convincing arguments in favor of the truth we profess to believe—an argument which the world could not misunderstand nor gainsay. The Lord would have distinguished us with His blessing even before the eyes of the world.

The first Christian church had not the privileges and opportunities we have. They were a poor people, but they felt the power of the truth. The object before them was sufficient to lead them to invest all. They felt that the salvation or the loss of a world depended upon their instrumentality. They cast in their all and held themselves in readiness to go or come at the Lord's bidding.

We profess to be governed by the same principles, to be influenced by the same spirit. But instead of giving all for Christ many have taken the golden wedge and a goodly Babylonish garment and hid them in the camp. If the presence of one Achan was sufficient to weaken the whole camp of Israel, can we be surprised at the little success which attends our efforts when every church and almost every family has its Achan? Let us individually go to work to stimulate others by our example of disinterested benevolence. The work might have gone forward with far greater power had all done what they could to supply the treasury with means.

POWER OF THE TRUTH

The word of God was preached by His ministers in early days "in demonstration of the Spirit and of power." The hearts of men were stirred by the proclamation of the gospel. Why is it that the preaching of the truth has now so little power to move the people? Is God less willing to bestow His blessing upon the laborers in His cause in this age than in the apostles' day?

The warning which we bear to the world must prove to them a savor of life unto life or of death unto death. And will the Lord send forth His servants to proclaim this fearfully solemn message and withhold from them His Holy Spirit? Shall frail, erring men, without special grace and power from God, dare to stand between the living and the dead to speak the words of everlasting life? Our Lord is rich in grace, mighty in power; He will abundantly bestow these gifts upon all who come to Him in faith. He is more willing to give the Holy Spirit to them that ask Him than are parents to give good gifts to their children. The reason why the precious, important truth for this time is not powerful to save is that we do not work in faith.

We should pray as earnestly for the descent of the Holy Spirit as the disciples prayed on the day of Pentecost. If they needed it at that time, we need it more today. Moral darkness, like a funeral pall, covers the earth. All manner of false doctrines, heresies, and satanic deceptions are misleading the minds of men. Without the Spirit and power of God it will be in vain that we labor to present the truth.

It is by contemplating Christ, by exercising faith in Him, by experiencing for ourselves His saving grace, that we are qualified to present Him to the world. If we have learned of Him, Jesus will be our theme; His love, burning upon the altar of our hearts, will reach the hearts of the people. The truth will be presented, not as a cold, lifeless theory, but in the demonstration of the Spirit.

Many of our ministers in their discourses dwell too largely upon theory and not enough on practical godliness. They have an intellectual knowledge of the truth, but their hearts are untouched with the genuine fervor of the love of Christ. Many have gained by the study of our publications a knowledge of the arguments that sustain the truth, but they have not become Bible students for themselves. They are not constantly seeking for a deeper and more thorough knowledge of the plan of salvation as revealed in the Scriptures. While preaching to others, they are becoming dwarfs in religious growth. They do not often go before God to plead for His Spirit and grace that they may rightly present Christ to the world.

Human strength is weakness, human wisdom is folly. Our success does not depend on our talents or learning, but on our living connection with God. The truth is shorn of its power when preached by men who are seeking to display their own learning and ability. Such men display also that they know very little of experimental religion, that they are unsanctified in heart and life and are filled with vain conceit. They do not learn of Jesus. They cannot present to others a Saviour with whom they themselves are not acquainted. Their own hearts are not softened and subdued by a vivid sense of the great sacrifice which Christ has made to save perishing man. They do not feel that it is a privilege to deny self and to suffer for His dear sake. Some exalt self, and talk of self; they prepare sermons and write articles to call the attention of the people to the minister, fearing that he will not receive due honor. Had there been more lifting up of Jesus and less extolling the minister, more praise rendered to the Author of truth and less to its messengers, we would occupy a more favorable position before God than we do today.

The plan of salvation is not presented in its simplicity for the reason that few ministers know what simple faith is. An intellectual knowledge of the truth is not enough; we must know its power upon our own hearts and lives. Ministers need to come to Christ as little children. Seek Jesus, brethren, confess your sins, plead with God day and night, until you know that for Christ's sake you are pardoned and accepted. Then will you love much because you have been forgiven much. Then you can point others to Christ as a sin-pardoning Redeemer. Then you can present the truth from the fullness of a heart that feels its sanctifying power. I fear for you, my brethren. I counsel you to tarry at Jerusalem, as did the early disciples, until, like them, you receive the baptism of the Holy Spirit. Never feel at liberty to go into the desk until you have by faith grasped the arm of your strength.

If we have the spirit of Christ we shall work as He worked; we shall catch the very ideas of the Man of Nazareth and present them to the people. If, in the place of formal professors and unconverted ministers, we were indeed followers of Christ, we would present the truth with such meekness and fervor, and would so exemplify it in our lives, that the world would not be continually questioning whether we believe what we profess. The message borne in the love of Christ, with the worth of souls constantly before us, would win even from worldlings the decision: "They are like Jesus."

If we desire to reform others we must ourselves practice the principles which we would enforce upon them. Words, however good, will be powerless if contradicted by the daily life. Ministers of Christ, I admonish you: "Take heed unto thyself, and unto the doctrine." Do not excuse sins in yourselves which you reprove in others. If you preach on meekness and love, let these graces be exemplified in your own life. If you urge others to be kind, courteous, and attentive at home, let your own example give force to your admonitions. As you have received greater light than others, so is your responsibility increased. You will be beaten with many stripes if you neglect to do your Master's will.

Satan's snares are laid for us as verily as they were laid for the children of Israel just prior to their entrance into the land of Canaan. We are repeating the history of that people. Lightness, vanity, love of ease and pleasure, selfishness, and impurity are increasing among us. There is need now of men who are firm and fearless in declaring the whole counsel of God; men who will not sleep as do others, but watch and be sober. Knowing as I do the great lack of holiness and power with our ministers, I am deeply pained to see the efforts for self-exaltation. If they could but see Jesus as He is, and themselves as they are, so weak, so inefficient, so unlike their Master, they would say: If my name may be written in the obscurest part of the book of life, it is enough for me, so unworthy am I of His notice.

It is your work to study and to imitate the Pattern. Was

Christ self-denying? so must you be. Was He meek and lowly? so must you be. Was He zealous in the work of saving souls? so must you be. Did He labor to promote the glory of His Father? so must you. Did He often seek help from God? so must you. Was Christ patient? so will you be patient. As Christ forgave His enemies, so will you forgive.

It is not so much the religion of the pulpit as the religion of the family that reveals our real character. The minister's wife, his children, and those who are employed as helpers in his family are best qualified to judge of his piety. A good man will be a blessing to his household. Wife, children, and helpers will all be the better for his religion.

Brethren, carry Christ into the family, carry Him into the pulpit, carry Him with you wherever you go. Then you need not urge upon others the necessity of appreciating the ministry, for you will bear the heavenly credentials which will prove to all that you are servants of Christ. Carry Jesus with you in your hours of solitude. Remember that He was often in prayer, and His life was constantly sustained by fresh inspirations of the Holy Spirit. Let your thoughts, your inner life, be such that you will not be ashamed to meet its record in the day of God.

Heaven is not closed against the fervent prayers of the righteous. Elijah was a man subject to like passions as we are, yet the Lord heard and in a most striking manner answered his petitions. The only reason for our lack of power with God is to be found in ourselves. If the inner life of many who profess the truth were presented before them, they would not claim to be Christians. They are not growing in grace. A hurried prayer is offered now and then, but there is no real communion with God.

We must be much in prayer if we would make progress in the divine life. When the message of truth was first proclaimed, how much we prayed. How often was the voice of intercession heard in the chamber, in the barn, in the orchard, or the grove. Frequently we spent hours in earnest prayer, two or three together claiming the promise; often the sound of weeping was heard and then the voice of thanksgiving and the song of praise. Now the day of God is nearer than when we first believed, and we should be more earnest, more zealous, and fervent than in those early days. Our perils are greater now than then. Souls are more hardened. We need now to be imbued with the spirit of Christ, and we should not rest until we receive it.

Brethren and sisters, have you forgotten that your prayers should go out, like sharp sickles, with the laborers in the great harvest field? As young men go forth to preach the truth, you should have seasons of prayer for them. Pray that God will connect them with Himself and give them wisdom, grace, and knowledge. Pray that they may be guarded from the snares of Satan and kept pure in thought and holy in heart. I entreat you who fear the Lord to waste no time in unprofitable talk or in needless labor to gratify pride or to indulge the appetite. Let the time thus gained be spent in wrestling with God for your ministers. Hold up their hands as did Aaron and Hur the hands of Moses.

OUR CAMP MEETINGS

I have been shown that some of our camp meetings are far from being what the Lord designed they should be. The people come unprepared for the visitation of God's Holy Spirit. Generally the sisters devote considerable time before the meeting to the preparation of garments for the outward adorning, while they entirely forget the inward adorning, which is in the sight of God of great price. There is also much time spent in needless cooking, in the preparation of rich pies and cakes and other articles of food that do positive injury to those who partake of them. Should our sisters provide good bread and some other healthful kinds of food, both they and their families would be better prepared to appreciate the words of life and far more susceptible to the influence of the Holy Spirit.

Often the stomach is overburdened with food which is seldom as plain and simple as that eaten at home, where the amount of exercise taken is double or treble. This causes the mind to be in such a lethargy that it is difficult to appreciate eternal things; and the meeting closes, and they are disappointed in not having enjoyed more of the Spirit of God.

While preparing for the meeting each individual should closely and critically examine his own heart before God. If there have been unpleasant feelings, discord, or strife in families, it should be one of the first acts of preparation to confess these faults one to another and pray with and for one another. Humble yourselves before God, and make an earnest effort to empty the soul temple of all rubbish—all envyings, all jealousies all suspicions, all faultfindings. "Cleanse your hands, ye sinners; and purify your hearts, ye double-minded. Be afflicted, and mourn, and weep: let your laughter be turned to mourning, and your joy to heaviness. Humble yourselves in the sight of the Lord, and He shall lift you up."

The Lord speaks; enter into your closet, and in silence commune with your own heart; listen to the voice of truth and conscience. Nothing will give such clear views of self as secret prayer. He who seeth in secret and knoweth all things will enlighten your understanding and answer your petitions. Plain, simple duties that must not be neglected will open before you. Make a covenant with God to yield yourselves and all your powers to His service. Do not carry this undone work to the camp meeting. If it is not done at home, your own soul will suffer, and others will be greatly injured by your coldness, your stupor, your spiritual lethargy.

I have seen the condition of the people professing the truth. The words of the prophet Ezekiel are applicable to them at this time: "Son of man, these men have set up their idols in their heart, and put the stumbling block of their iniquity before their face: should I be inquired of at all by them? Therefore speak unto them, and say unto them, Thus saith the Lord God; Every man of the house of Israel that setteth up his idols in his heart, and putteth the stumbling block of his iniquity before his face, and cometh to the prophet; I the Lord will answer him that cometh according to the multitude of his idols."

If we love the things of the world and have pleasure in unrighteousness or fellowship with the unfruitful works of darkness, we have put the stumbling block of our iniquity before our face and have set up idols in our heart. And unless by determined effort we put them away we shall never be acknowledged as the sons and daughters of God.

Here is a work for families to engage in before coming up to our holy convocations. Let the preparation for eating and dressing be a secondary matter, but let deep heart searching commence at home. Pray three times a day, and, like Jacob, be importunate. At home is the place to find Jesus; then take Him with you to the meeting, and how precious will be the hours you spend there. But how can you expect to feel the presence of the Lord and see His power displayed when the individual work of preparation for that time is neglected?

For your soul's sake, for Christ's sake, and for the sake of others, work at home. Pray as you are not accustomed to pray. Let the heart break before God. Set your house in order. Prepare your children for the occasion. Teach them that it is not of so much consequence that they appear with fine clothes as that they appear before God with clean hands and pure hearts. Remove every obstacle that may have been in their way,—all differences that may have existed among themselves or between you and them. By so doing you will invite the Lord's presence into your homes, and holy angels will attend you as you go up to the meeting, and their light and presence will press back the darkness of evil angels. Even unbelievers will feel the holy atmosphere as they enter the encampment. Oh, how much is lost by neglecting this important work! You may be pleased with the preaching, you may become animated and revived, but the converting, reforming power of God will not be felt in the heart, and the work will not be so deep, thorough, and lasting as it should be. Let pride be crucified and the soul be clad with the priceless robe of Christ's righteousness, and what a meeting will you enjoy. It will be to your soul even as the gate of heaven.

The same work of humiliation and heart-searching should also go on in the church, so that all differences and alienations among brethren may be laid aside before appearing before the Lord at these annual gatherings. Set about this work in earnest, and rest not until it is accomplished; for if you come up to the meeting with your doubts, your murmurings, your disputings, you bring evil angels into the camp and carry darkness wherever you go.

I have been shown that for want of this preparation these yearly meetings have accomplished but little. The ministers are seldom prepared to labor for God. There are many speakers,—those who can say sharp, crank things, going out of the way to whip other churches and ridicule their faith,—but there are but few earnest laborers for God. These sharp, self-important speakers profess to have truth in advance of every other people, but their manner of labor and their religious zeal in no way correspond with their profession of faith.

I looked to see the humility of soul that should ever sit as a fitting garment upon our ministers, but it was not upon them. I looked for the deep love for souls that the Master said they should possess, but they had it not. I listened for the earnest prayers offered with tears and anguish of soul because of the impenitent and unbelieving in their own homes and in the church, but heard them not. I listened for the appeals made in the demonstration of the Spirit, but these were missing. I looked for the burden bearers, who in such a time as this should be weeping between the porch and the altar, crying, Spare Thy people, Lord, and give not Thine heritage to reproach; but I heard no such supplications. A few earnest, humble ones were seeking the Lord. At some of these meetings one or two ministers felt the burden and were weighed down as a cart beneath sheaves. But a large majority of the ministers had no more sense of the sacredness of their work than children.

I saw what these yearly gatherings might be, and what they should be—meetings of earnest labor. Ministers should seek a heart preparation before entering upon the work of helping others, for the people are far in advance of many of the ministers. They should untiringly wrestle in prayer until the Lord blesses them. When the love of God is burning on the altar of their hearts, they will not preach to exhibit their own smartness, but to present Christ who taketh away the sins of the world.

In the early church Christianity was taught in its purity; its precepts were given by the voice of inspiration; its ordinances were uncorrupted by the device of men. The church revealed the spirit of Christ and appeared beautiful in its simplicity. Its adorning was the holy principles and exemplary lives of its members. Multitudes were won to Christ, not by display or learning, but by the power of God which attended the plain preaching of His word. But the church has become corrupt. And now there is greater necessity than ever that ministers should be channels of light.

There are many flippant talkers of Bible truth, whose souls are as barren of the Spirit of God as were the hills of Gilboa of dew and rain. But what we need is men who are thoroughly converted themselves and can teach others how to give their hearts to God. The power of godliness has almost ceased to be in our churches. And why is this? The Lord is still waiting to be gracious; He has not closed the windows of heaven. We have separated ourselves from Him. We need to fix the eye of faith upon the cross and believe that Jesus is our strength, our salvation.

As we see so little burden of the work resting upon ministers and people, we inquire: When the Lord comes, shall He find faith on the earth? It is faith that is lacking. God has an abundance of grace and power awaiting our demand. But the reason we do not feel our great need of it is because we look to ourselves and not to Jesus. We do not exalt Jesus and rely wholly upon His merits.

Would that I could impress upon ministers and people the necessity of a deeper work of grace in the heart and more thorough preparation to enter into the spirit and labor of our camp meetings, that they may receive the greatest possible benefit from these meetings. These yearly gatherings may be seasons of special blessing or they may be a great injury to spirituality. Which shall they be to you, dear reader? It remains for each to decide for himself.

BROTHERLY LOVE

"By this shall all men know that ye are My disciples, if ye have love one to another." The more closely we resemble our Saviour in character, the greater will be our love toward those for whom He died. Christians who manifest a spirit of unselfish love for one another are bearing a testimony for Christ which unbelievers can neither gainsay nor resist. It is impossible to estimate the power of such an example. Nothing will so successfully defeat the devices of Satan and his emissaries, nothing will so build up the Redeemer's kingdom, as will the love of Christ manifested by the members of the church. Peace and prosperity can be enjoyed only as meekness and love are in active exercise.

In his First Epistle to the Corinthians the apostle Paul sets forth the importance of that love which should be cherished by the followers of Christ: "Though I speak with the tongues of men and of angels, and have not charity, I am become as sounding brass, or a tinkling cymbal. And though I have the gift of prophecy, and understand all mysteries, and all knowledge; and though I have all faith, so that I could remove mountains, and have not charity, I am nothing. And though I bestow all my goods to feed the poor, and though I give my body to be burned, and have not charity, it profiteth me nothing."

No matter how high his profession, he whose heart is not imbued with love for God and for his fellow men is not a disciple of Christ. Though he should possess great faith, and even have power to work miracles, yet without love his faith would be worthless. He might display great liberality, but should he from some other motive than genuine love bestow all his goods to feed the poor, the act would not commend him to the favor of God. In his zeal he might even meet a martyr's death, yet if destitute of the gold of love he would be regarded by God as a deluded enthusiast or an ambitious hypocrite.

The apostle proceeds to specify the fruits of love: "Charity suffereth long, and is kind; charity envieth not." The divine love ruling in the heart exterminates pride and selfishness. "Charity vaunteth not itself, is not puffed up." The purest joy springs from the deepest humiliation. The strongest and noblest characters rest upon the foundation of patience and love, and trusting submission to the will of God.

Charity "doth not behave itself unseemly, seeketh not her own, is not easily provoked, thinketh no evil." The heart in which love rules will not be filled with passion or revenge, by injuries which pride and self-love would deem unbearable. Love is unsuspecting, ever placing the most favorable construction upon the motives and acts of others. Love will never needlessly expose the faults of others. It does not listen eagerly to unfavorable reports, but rather seeks to bring to mind some good qualities of the one defamed.

Love "rejoiceth not in iniquity, but rejoiceth in the truth." He whose heart is imbued with love is filled with sorrow at the errors and weaknesses of others; but when truth triumphs, when the cloud that darkened the fair fame of another is removed, or when sins are confessed and wrongs corrected, he rejoices.

"Beareth all things, believeth all things, hopeth all things, endureth all things." Love not only bears with others' faults, but cheerfully submits to whatever suffering or inconvenience such forbearance makes necessary. This love "never faileth." It can never lose its value; it is the attribute of heaven. As a precious treasure it will be carried by its possessor through the portals of the city of God.

The fruit of the Spirit is love, joy, and peace. Discord and strife are the work of Satan and the fruit of sin. If we would as a people enjoy peace and love, we must put away our sins; we must come into harmony with God, and we shall be in harmony with one another. Let each ask himself: Do I possess the grace of love? Have I learned to suffer long and to be kind? Talents, learning, and eloquence, without this heavenly attribute, will be as meaningless as sounding brass or a tinkling cymbal. Alas that this precious treasure is so lightly valued and so little sought by many who profess the faith!

Paul writes to the Colossians: "Put on therefore, as the elect of God, holy and beloved, bowels of mercies, kindness, humbleness of mind, meekness, long-suffering; forbearing one another, and forgiving one another, if any man have a quarrel against any: even as Christ forgave you, so also do ye. And above all these things put on charity, which is the bond of perfectness. And let the peace of God rule in your hearts, to the which also ye are called in one body; and be ye thankful." "And whatsoever ye do in word or deed, do all in the name of the Lord Jesus, giving thanks to God and the Father by Him."

The fact that we are under so great obligation to Christ places us under the most sacred obligation to those whom He died to redeem. We are to manifest toward them the same sympathy, the same tender compassion and unselfish love, which Christ has manifested toward us. Selfish ambition, desire for supremacy, will die when Christ takes possession of the affections.

Our Saviour taught His disciples to pray: "Forgive us our debts, as we forgive our debtors." A great blessing is here asked upon conditions. We ourselves state these conditions. We ask that the mercy of God toward us may be measured by the mercy which we extend to others. Christ declares that this is the rule by which the Lord will deal with us. "If ye forgive men their trespasses, your heavenly Father will also forgive you: but if ye forgive not men their trespasses, neither will your Father forgive your trespasses." Wonderful terms! but how little are they understood or heeded. One of the most common sins, and one that is attended with most pernicious results, is the indulgence of an unforgiving spirit. How many will cherish animosity or revenge and then bow before God and ask to be forgiven as they forgive. Surely they can have no true sense of the import of this prayer or they would not dare to take it upon their lips. We are dependent upon the pardoning mercy of God every day and every hour; how then can we cherish bitterness and malice toward our fellow sinners! If, in all their daily intercourse, Christians would carry out the principles of this prayer, what a blessed change would be wrought in the church and in the world! This would be the most convincing testimony that could be given to the reality of Bible religion.

God requires more of His followers than many realize. If we would not build our hopes of heaven upon a false foundation we must accept the Bible as it reads and believe that the Lord means what He says. He requires nothing of us that He will not give us grace to perform. We shall have no excuse to offer in the day of God if we fail to reach the standard set before us in His word.

We are admonished by the apostle: "Let love be without dissimulation. Abhor that which is evil, cleave to that which is good. Be kindly affectioned one to another with brotherly love; in honor preferring one another." Paul would have us distinguish between the pure, unselfish love which is prompted by the spirit of Christ, and the unmeaning, deceitful pretense with which the world abounds. This base counterfeit has misled many souls. It would blot out the distinction between right and wrong, by agreeing with the transgressor instead of faithfully showing him his errors. Such a course never springs from real friendship. The spirit by which it is prompted dwells only in the carnal heart. While the Christian will be ever kind, compassionate, and forgiving, he can feel no harmony with sin. He will abhor evil and cling to that which is good, at the sacrifice of association or friendship with the ungodly. The spirit of Christ will lead us to hate sin, while we are willing to make any sacrifice to save the sinner.

"This I say therefore, and testify in the Lord, that ye henceforth walk not as other Gentiles walk, in the vanity of their mind, having the understanding darkened, being alienated from the life of God through the ignorance that is in them, because of the blindness of their heart: who being past feeling have given themselves over unto lasciviousness, to work all uncleanness with greediness." The apostle admonishes his brethren, in the name and by the authority of the Lord Jesus, that after having professed the gospel they should not conduct themselves as did the Gentiles, but should show by their daily deportment that they had been truly converted.

"Put off concerning the former conversation the old man, which is corrupt according to the deceitful lusts; and be renewed in the spirit of your mind; and that ye put on the new man, which after God is created in righteousness and true holiness." Once they were corrupt, degraded, enslaved by lustful passions; they were drugged by worldly opiates, blinded, bewildered, and betrayed by Satan's devices. Now that they had been taught the truth as it is in Jesus, there must be a decided change in their life and character.

The accession of members who have not been renewed in heart and reformed in life is a source of weakness to the church. This fact is often ignored. Some ministers and churches are so desirous of securing an increase of numbers that they do not bear faithful testimony against unchristian habits and practices. Those who accept the truth are not taught that they cannot safely be worldlings in conduct while they are Christians in name. Heretofore they were Satan's subjects; henceforth they are to be subjects of Christ. The life must testify to the change of leaders. Public opinion favors a profession of Christianity. Little self-denial or self-sacrifice is required in order to put on a form of godliness and to have one's name enrolled upon the church book. Hence many join the church without first becoming united to Christ. In this Satan triumphs. Such converts are his most efficient agents. They serve as decoys to other souls. They are false lights, luring the unwary to perdition. It is in vain that men seek to make the Christian's path broad and pleasant for worldlings. God has not smoothed or widened the rugged, narrow way. If we would enter into life, we must follow the same path which Jesus and His disciples trod—the path of humility, self-denial, and sacrifice.

Ministers should see that their own hearts are sanctified

through the truth, and then labor to secure these results for their converts. It is pure religion that ministers and people need. Those who put away iniquity from their hearts and stretch out their hands in earnest supplication unto God will have that help which God alone can give them. A ransom has been paid for the souls of men, that they may have an opportunity to escape from the thralldom of sin and obtain pardon, purity, and heaven.

God hears the cry of the lowly and contrite. Those who frequent the throne of grace, offering up sincere, earnest petitions for divine wisdom and power, will not fail to become active, useful servants of Christ. They may not possess great talents, but with humility of heart and firm reliance upon Jesus they may do a good work in bringing souls to Christ. They can reach men through God.

Ministers of Christ should ever feel that a sacred work engages all their souls; their efforts should be for the edification of the body of Christ, and not to exalt themselves before the people. And while Christians should esteem the faithful minister as Christ's ambassador, they should avoid all praise of the man.

"Be ye therefore followers of God, as dear children; and walk in love, as Christ also hath loved us, and hath given Himself for us an offering and a sacrifice to God for a sweet-smelling savor." Man by wicked works alienated himself from God, but Christ gave His life that all who would, might be freed from sin and reinstated in the favor of the Creator. It was the anticipation of a redeemed, holy universe that prompted Christ to make this great sacrifice. Have we accepted the privileges so dearly purchased? Are we followers of God as dear children, or are we servants of the prince of darkness? Are we worshipers of Jehovah, or of Baal? of the living God, or of idols?

No outward shrines may be visible, there may be no image for the eye to rest upon, yet we may be practicing idolatry. It is as easy to make an idol of cherished ideas or objects as to fashion gods of wood or stone. Thousands have a false conception of God and His attributes. They are as verily serving a false god as were the servants of Baal. Are we worshiping the true God as He is revealed in His word, in Christ, in nature, or are we adoring some philosophical idol enshrined in His place? God is a God of truth. Justice and mercy are the attributes of His throne. He is a God of love, of pity and tender compassion. Thus He is represented in His Son, our Saviour. He is a God of patience and long-suffering. If such is the being whom we adore and to whose character we are seeking to assimilate, we are worshiping the true God.

If we are following Christ, His merits, imputed to us, come up before the Father as sweet odor. And the graces of our Saviour's character, implanted in our hearts, will shed around us a precious fragrance. The spirit of love, meekness, and forbearance pervading our life will have power to soften and subdue hard hearts and win to Christ bitter opposers of the faith.

"Let nothing be done through strife or vainglory; but in lowliness of mind let each esteem other better than themselves. Look not every man on his own things, but every man also on the things of others." "Do all things without murmurings and disputings: that ye may be blameless and harmless, the sons of God, without rebuke, in the midst of a crooked and perverse nation, among whom ye shine as lights in the world."

Vainglory, selfish ambition, is the rock upon which many souls have been wrecked and many churches rendered powerless. Those who know least of devotion, who are least connected with God, are the ones who will most eagerly seek the highest place. They have no sense of their weakness and their deficiencies of character. Unless many of our young ministers shall feel the converting power of God, their labors will be a hindrance rather than a help to the church. They may have learned the doctrines of Christ, but they have not learned

Christ. The soul that is constantly looking unto Jesus will see His self-denying love and deep humility, and will copy His example. Pride, ambition, deceit, hatred, selfishness, must be cleansed from the heart. With many these evil traits are partially subdued, but not thoroughly uprooted from the heart. Under favorable circumstances they spring up anew and ripen into rebellion against God. Here lies a terrible danger. To spare any sin is to cherish a foe that only awaits an unguarded moment to cause our ruin.

"Who is a wise man and endued with knowledge among you? let him show out of a good conversation his works with meekness of wisdom." My brethren and sisters, how are you employing the gift of speech? Have you learned so to control the tongue that it shall ever obey the dictates of an enlightened conscience and holy affections? Is your conversation free from levity, pride and malice, deceit and impurity? Are you without guile before God? Words exert a telling power. Satan will, if possible, keep the tongue active in his service. Of ourselves we cannot control the unruly member. Divine grace is our only hope.

Those who are eagerly studying how they may secure the pre-eminence should study rather how they may gain that wisdom which is "first pure, then peaceable, gentle, and easy to be entreated, full of mercy and good fruits, without partiality, and without hypocrisy." I have been shown that many ministers need to have these words imprinted on the tablets of the soul. He who has Christ formed within, the hope of glory, will "show out of a good conversation his works with meekness of wisdom."

Peter exhorts the believers: "Be ye all of one mind, having compassion one of another, love as brethren, be pitiful, be courteous: not rendering evil for evil, or railing for railing: but contrariwise blessing; knowing that ye are thereunto called, that ye should inherit a blessing. For he that will love life, and see good days, let him refrain his tongue from evil, and his lips that they speak no guile: let him eschew evil, and do good; let him seek peace, and ensue it. For the eyes of the Lord are over the righteous, and His ears are open unto their prayers: but the face of the Lord is against them that do evil."

When the right way is so plainly marked out, why do not the professed people of God walk in it? Why do they not study and pray and labor earnestly to be of one mind? Why do they not seek to cherish compassion for one another, to love as brethren, instead of rendering evil for evil and railing for railing? Who does not love life and desire good days? yet how few comply with the conditions, to refrain the tongue from evil and the lips from speaking guile. Few are willing to follow the Saviour's example of meekness and humility. Many ask the Lord to humble them, but are unwilling to submit to the needful discipline. When the test comes, when trials or even annoyances occur, the heart rebels, and the tongue utters words that are like poisoned arrows or blasting hail.

Evilspeaking is a twofold curse, falling more heavily upon the speaker than upon the hearer. He who scatters the seeds of dissension and strife reaps in his own soul the deadly fruits. How miserable is the talebearer, the surmiser of evil! He is a stranger to true happiness.

"Blessed are the peacemakers." Grace and peace rest upon those who refuse to join in the strife of tongues. When vendors of scandal are passing from family to family, those who fear God will be chaste keepers at home. The time that is so often worse than wasted in idle, frivolous, and malicious gossip should be given to higher and nobler objects. If our brethren and sisters would become missionaries for God, visiting the sick and afflicted, and laboring patiently and kindly for the erring,—in short, if they would copy the Pattern,—the church would have prosperity in all her borders.

The sin of evilspeaking begins with the cherishing of evil thoughts. Guile includes impurity in all its forms. An impure thought tolerated, an unholy desire cherished, and the soul is contaminated, its integrity compromised. "Then when lust hath conceived, it bringeth forth sin: and sin, when it is finished, bringeth forth death." If we would not commit sin, we must shun its very beginnings. Every emotion and desire must be held in subjection to reason and conscience. Every unholy thought must be instantly repelled. To your closet, followers of Christ. Pray in faith and with all the heart. Satan is watching to ensnare your feet. You must have help from above if you would escape his devices.

By faith and prayer all may meet the requirements of the gospel. No man can be forced to transgress. His own consent must be first gained; the soul must purpose the sinful act before passion can dominate over reason or iniquity triumph over conscience. Temptation, however strong, is never an excuse for sin. "The eyes of the Lord are over the righteous, and His ears are open unto their cry." Cry unto the Lord, tempted soul. Cast yourself, helpless, unworthy, upon Jesus, and claim His very promise. The Lord will hear. He knows how strong are the inclinations of the natural heart, and He will help in every time of temptation.

Have you fallen into sin? Then without delay seek God for mercy and pardon. When David was convicted of his sin, he poured out his soul in penitence and humiliation before God. He felt that he could endure the loss of his crown, but he could not be deprived of the favor of God. Mercy is still extended to the sinner. The Lord is calling to us in all our wanderings: "Return, ye backsliding children, and I will heal your backslidings." The blessing of God may be ours if we will heed the pleading voice of His Spirit. "Like as a father pitieth his children, so the Lord pitieth them that fear Him."

DILIGENCE IN BUSINESS

Seest thou a man diligent in his business? he shall stand before kings; he shall not stand before mean men." "He becometh poor that dealeth with a slack hand: but the hand of the diligent maketh rich." "Be kindly affectioned one to another with brotherly love; in honor preferring one another; not slothful in business; fervent in spirit; serving the Lord."

The many admonitions to diligence found in both the Old and the New Testament plainly indicate the intimate relation existing between our habits of life and our religious feelings and practices. The human mind and body are so constituted that plenty of exercise is necessary in order to a proper development of all the faculties. While many are too much engaged in worldly business, others go to the opposite extreme and do not labor sufficiently to support themselves or those dependent upon them. Brother _____ is one of this class. While he occupies the position of house band to his family he is not this in reality. The heaviest responsibilities and burdens he allows to rest upon his wife, while he indulges in careless indolence or busies himself about small matters that tell little for the support of his family. He will sit for hours and chat with his sons or his neighbors upon matters of no great consequence. He takes things easy and enjoys himself while the wife and mother does the work which must be done to prepare food to eat and clothes to wear.

This brother is a poor man and always will be a burden to society unless he asserts his God-given privilege and becomes a man. Anyone can find work of some kind to do if he really desires it; but if he is careless and inattentive, the positions which he might have secured he will find filled by those who had greater activity and business tact.

God never designed that you, my brother, should be in the

position of poverty that you are now in. Why did He give you that physical frame? You are just as responsible for your physical powers as your brethren are for their means. Some of these would today be gainers could they exchange their property for your physical strength. But if placed in your position, they would, by a diligent use of both mental and physical powers, soon be above want and owe no man anything. It is not because God owes you a grudge that circumstances appear to be against you, but because you do not use the strength He has given you. He did not intend that your powers should rust by inaction, but that they should strengthen by use.

The religion you profess makes it as much your duty to employ your time during the six working days as to attend church on the Sabbath. You are not diligent in business. You let hours, days, and even weeks pass without accomplishing anything. The very best sermon you could preach to the world would be to show a decided reformation in your life, and provide for your own family. Says the apostle: "If any provide not for his own, and specially for those of his own house, he hath denied the faith, and is worse than an infidel."

You bring a reproach upon the cause by locating in a place, where you indulge indolence for a time and then are obliged to run in debt for provision for your family. These your honest debts you are not always particular to pay, but, instead, move to another place. This is defrauding your neighbor. The world has a right to expect strict integrity in those who profess to be Bible Christians. By one man's indifference in regard to paying his just dues, all our people are in danger of being regarded as unreliable.

"Whatsoever ye would that men should do to you, do ye even so to them." This refers to those who labor with their hands as well as to those who have gifts to bestow. God has given you strength and skill, but you have not used them.

Your strength is sufficient to abundantly support your family. Rise in the morning, even while the stars are shining, if need be. Lay your plans to do something, and then accomplish it. Redeem every pledge unless sickness lays you prostrate. Better deny yourself food and sleep than be guilty of keeping from others their just dues.

The hill of progress is not to be climbed without effort. No one need expect to be carried along to the prize, either in religious or secular matters, independently of his own exertions. The race is not always to the swift, nor the battle to the strong, yet he that dealeth with a slack hand will become poor. The persevering and industrious are not only happy themselves, but they contribute largely to the happiness of others. Competency and comfort are not ordinarily attained except at the price of earnest industry. Pharaoh showed his appreciation of this trait of character when he said to Joseph: If thou knowest any men of activity among them [Joseph's brethren], then make them rulers over my cattle."

There is no excuse for Brother _____, unless love of ease and inability to plan and set himself to work is an excuse. The best course for him now to pursue is to go from home and work under someone who shall plan for him. He has so long been a careless, indolent master over himself that he accomplishes but little, and his example before his children is bad. They have his stamp of character. They let mother bear the burdens. When asked to do anything, they will do it; but they do not cultivate, as all children should, the faculty of seeing what needs to be done and doing it without being told.

A woman does herself and her family a serious wrong when she does her work and theirs too—when she brings the wood and water, and even takes the ax to prepare the wood, while her husband and sons sit about the fire having a social, easy time. God never designed that wives and mothers should be slaves to their families. Many a mother is overburdened with care while her children are not educated to share the domestic burdens. As the result, she grows old and dies prematurely, leaving her children just when a mother is most needed to guide their inexperienced feet. Who is to blame?

Husbands should do all they can to save the wife care and keep her spirit cheerful. Never should idleness be fostered or permitted in children, for it soon becomes a habit. When not engaged in useful employment, the faculties either depreciate or become active in an evil work.

What you need, my brother, is active exercise. Every feature of your countenance, every faculty of your mind, is indicative of this. You do not love hard work nor to earn your bread by the sweat of your brow. But this is God's ordained plan in the economy of life.

You fail to carry through what you undertake. You have not disciplined yourself to regularity. System is everything. Do but one thing at a time, and do that well, finishing it before you begin a second piece of work. You should have regular hours for rising, for praying, and for eating. Many waste hours of precious time in bed because it gratifies the natural inclination and to do otherwise requires an exertion. One hour wasted in the morning is lost never to be recovered. Says the wise man: "I went by the field of the slothful, and by the vineyard of the man void of understanding; and, lo, it was all grown over with thorns, and nettles had covered the face thereof, and the stone wall thereof was broken down. Then I saw, and considered it well: I looked upon it, and received instruction. Yet a little sleep, a little slumber, a little folding of the hands to sleep: so shall thy poverty come as one that traveleth; and thy want as an armed man."

Those who make any pretensions to godliness should adorn the doctrine they profess and not give occasion for the truth to be reviled through their inconsiderate course of action. "Owe no man anything," says the apostle. You ought now, my brother, to take hold earnestly to correct your habits of indolence, redeeming the time. Let the world see that the truth has wrought a reformation in your life.

MOVING TO BATTLE CREEK

Our Saviour represents Himself as a man taking his journey into a far country, who left his house in charge of chosen servants, giving to every man his work. Every Christian has something to do in the service of his Master. We are not to seek our own ease or convenience, but rather to make the upbuilding of Christ's kingdom our first consideration. Unselfish efforts to help and bless our fellow men will not only evince our love for Jesus, but will keep us near Him in dependence and faith, and our own souls will be constantly growing in grace and in a knowledge of the truth.

God has scattered His children in various communities that the light of truth may be kept shining amid the moral darkness that enshrouds the earth. The deeper the darkness around us, the greater the need that our light should shine for God. We may be placed in circumstances of great difficulty and trial, but this does not prove that we are not in the very position assigned us by Providence. Among the Christians at Rome in Paul's day the apostle mentions them "that are of Caesar's household." Nowhere could the moral atmosphere be more unfavorable to Christianity than at that Roman court under the cruel and profligate Nero. Yet those who had, while in the emperor's service, accepted Christ did not feel at liberty, after their conversion, to leave their post of duty. In the face of seductive temptations, fierce opposition, and appalling dangers they were faithful witnesses for Christ.

Whoever will rely wholly upon divine grace may make his life a constant testimony for the truth. No one is so situated that he cannot be a true and faithful Christian. However great the obstacles, all who are determined to obey God will find the way opening as they go forward.

Those who maintain their fidelity to God in the midst of opposing influences are gaining an experience of the highest value. Their strength increases with every obstacle surmounted, every temptation overcome. This fact is often overlooked. When a person has received the truth, mistaken friends fear to expose him to any test or trial, and they immediately endeavor to secure for him an easier position. He goes to some place where all are in harmony with him. But is his spiritual strength increased thereby? In many cases not. He comes to have as little real stamina as a hothouse plant. He ceases to watch; his faith becomes weak; he is neither growing in grace himself nor aiding others.

Do any shrink from maintaining the truth in the midst of unbelief and opposition? I ask them to call to mind the believers in Nero's household; consider the depravity and persecution which they encountered, and gather from their example a lesson of courage, fortitude, and faith.

It may at times be advisable for those who are young in the faith to be withdrawn from great temptations or opposition and to be placed where they can enjoy the care and counsel of experienced Christians. But it should be ever kept before their minds that the Christian life is a constant warfare; that the indulgence of sloth or indolence will be fatal to success.

We should not, after accepting the truth, unite with those who oppose it, nor in any manner place ourselves where it will be difficult for us to live out our faith. But should anyone while thus situated receive the truth, he should weigh the matter carefully before leaving his position. It may be the design of Providence that his influence and example shall bring others to the knowledge of the truth.

Many are connected in family relations with opposers of the faith. These believers are often subjected to great trials, but by divine grace they may glorify God by obedience to the truth.

As servants of Christ we should be faithful in the position where God sees that we can render most efficient service. If opportunities of greater usefulness are presented to us, we should accept them at the Master's bidding, and His approving smile will be upon us. But we should fear to leave our appointed work unless the Lord clearly indicates our duty to serve Him in another field.

Different qualifications are needed for different departments of the work. The carpenter is not fitted to work at the anvil, nor the blacksmith to use the plane. The merchant would be out of place beside the sickbed, and the doctor in the counting room. Those who become weary with the work which God has committed to them, and place themselves in positions where they cannot or will not work, will be accounted slothful servants. "To every man his work." Not one is excused.

Our duty to act as missionaries for God in the very position where He has placed us has been greatly overlooked by us as a people. Many are eagerly turning from present duties and opportunities to some wider field; many imagine that in some other position they would find it less difficult to obey the truth. Our larger churches are looked upon as enjoying great advantages, and there is among our people a growing tendency to leave their special post of duty and move to Battle Creek or to the vicinity of some other large church. This practice not only threatens the prosperity and even the life of our smaller churches, but it is preventing us from doing the very work which God has given us to do, and is destroying our spirituality and usefulness as a people.

From nearly all our churches in Michigan, and, to some extent, from other states, our brethren and sisters have been crowding into Battle Creek. Many of them were efficient helpers in smaller churches, and their removal has greatly weakened those little companies; in some cases the church has thus been completely disorganized.

Have those who moved to Battle Creek proved a help to the church? As the matter was presented before me, I looked to see who were bearing a living testimony for God, who were feeling a burden for the youth, who were visiting from house to house, praying with families and laboring for their spiritual interests. I saw that this work had been neglected. On coming to this large church, many feel that they have no part to act. Hence they fold their hands and shun all responsibility and effort.

There are some who come here merely to secure financial benefit. This class are a heavy burden to the church. They are cumberers of the ground, their unproductive boughs shutting from other trees the glory of heaven's sunlight.

It is not pleasing to God that so many of our ministers should settle at Battle Creek. If their families were scattered in different parts of the field, they might be far more useful. It is true that the minister spends but a short time at home, yet there are many places where that time would be of far greater benefit to the cause of God.

The Lord says to many at Battle Creek: What doest thou here? What account can you render for leaving your appointed work and becoming a hindrance rather than a help to the church?

Brethren, I entreat you to compare your own spiritual state as it now is with what it was when you were actively engaged in the cause of Christ. While helping and encouraging the church you were gaining a useful experience and keeping your own souls in the love of God. As you have ceased to work for others, has not your own love grown cold and your zeal languid? And how is it with your children? Are they more firmly established in the truth and more devoted to God than before coming to this large church?

The influence exerted by some who have long been connected with the work of God is fatal to spirituality and devotion. These gospel-hardened youth have surrounded themselves with an atmosphere of worldliness, irreverence, and infidelity. Dare you risk the effect of such associations upon your children? It would be better for them never to obtain an education than to acquire it at the sacrifice of principle and the blessing of God.

Among the youth who come to Battle Creek there are some who maintain their fidelity to God in the midst of temptation, but the number is small. Many who come here with confidence in the truth, in the Bible, and in religion have been led astray by irreligious associates and have returned to their homes doubting every truth which we as a people hold dear.

Let all our brethren who contemplate removing to Battle Creek, or sending their children here, consider the matter well before taking this step. Unless the forces at this great center are keeping the fort, unless the faith and devotion of the church are proportioned to her privileges and opportunities, this is the most dangerous position which you can choose. I have seen the condition of this church as angels look upon it. There is a spiritual deception upon both the people and the watchmen. They maintain the forms of religion, but lack the abiding principles of righteousness. Unless there is a decided change, a marked transformation in this church, the school here should be removed to some other locality.

Had the youth who have lived here for years improved their privileges, several who are now skeptics would have devoted themselves to the work of the ministry. But they have considered it an evidence of intellectual superiority to doubt the truth and have been proud of their independence in cherishing infidelity. They have done despite to the Spirit of grace and have trampled upon the blood of Christ.

Where are the missionaries who should be raised up at the heart of the work? From twenty to fifty should be sent out from Battle Creek every year to carry the truth to those who sit in darkness. But piety is at so low an ebb, the spirit of devotion is so weak, worldliness and selfishness so prevalent, that the moral atmosphere begets a lethargy fatal to missionary zeal.

We need not go to foreign lands to become missionaries for God. All around us are fields "white already to harvest," and whoever will may gather "fruit unto life eternal." God calls upon many in Battle Creek who are dying of spiritual sloth to go where their labor is needed in His cause. Move out of Battle Creek, even if it requires a pecuniary sacrifice. Go somewhere to be a blessing to others. Go where you can strengthen some weak church. Put to use the powers which God has given you.

Shake off your spiritual lethargy. Work with all your might to save your own souls and the souls of others. It is no time now to cry, "Peace and safety." It is not silver-tongued orators that are needed to give this message. The truth in all its pointed severity must be spoken. Men of action are needed —men who will labor with earnest, ceaseless energy for the purifying of the church and the warning of the world.

A great work is to be accomplished; broader plans must be laid; a voice must go forth to arouse the nations. Men whose faith is weak and wavering are not the ones to carry forward the work at this important crisis. We need the courage of heroes and the faith of martyrs.

WORLDLINESS IN THE CHURCH

It is recorded of the holy men of old that God was not ashamed to be called their God. The reason assigned is that instead of coveting earthly possessions or seeking happiness in worldly plans or aspirations they placed their all upon the altar of God and made disposition of it to build up His kingdom. They lived only for God's glory and declared plainly that they were strangers and pilgrims on earth, seeking a better country, that is, an heavenly. Their conduct proclaimed their faith. God could entrust to them His truth and could leave the world to receive from them a knowledge of His will.

But how are the professed people of God today maintaining the honor of His name? How could the world infer that they are a peculiar people? What evidence do they give of citizenship in heaven? Their self-indulgent, ease-loving course falsifies the character of Christ. He could not honor them in any marked manner before the world without endorsing their false representation of His character.

I speak to the church at Battle Creek: What testimony are you bearing to the world? As your course was presented before me, I was pointed to the dwellings recently erected by our people in that city. These buildings are so many monuments of your unbelief of the doctrines which you profess to hold. They are preaching sermons more effective than any delivered from the pulpit. I saw worldlings point to them with jesting and ridicule, as a denial of our faith. They proclaimed that which the owners have been saying in their hearts: "My Lord delayeth His coming."

I looked upon the dress and listened to the conversation of many who profess the truth. Both were opposed to the principles of truth. Dress and conversation reveal that which is most treasured by those who claim to be pilgrims and strangers on the earth. "They are of the world: therefore speak they of the world, and the world heareth them." Puritan plainness and simplicity should mark the dwellings and apparel of all who believe the solemn truths for this time. All means needlessly expended in dress or in the adorning of our houses is a waste of our Lord's money. It is defrauding the cause of God for the gratification of pride. Our institutions are burdened with debt, and how can we expect the Lord to answer our prayers for their prosperity when we are not doing what we can do to relieve them from embarrassment?

I would address you as Christ addressed Nicodemus: "Ye must be born again." Those who have Christ ruling within will feel no desire to imitate the world's display. They will carry everywhere the standard of the cross, ever bearing witness of higher aims and nobler themes than those in which worldlings are absorbed. Our dress, our dwellings, our conversation, should testify of our consecration to God. What power would attend those who thus evinced that they had given up all for Christ. God would not be ashamed to acknowledge them as His children. He would bless His devoted people, and the unbelieving world would fear Him.

Christ longs to work mightily by His Spirit for the conviction and conversion of sinners. But, according to His divine plan, the work must be performed through the instrumentality of His church; and her members have so far departed from Him that He cannot accomplish His will through them. He chooses to work by means, yet the means employed must be in harmony with His character.

Who are there in Battle Creek that are faithful and true? Let them come over on the Lord's side. If we would be in a position where God can use us, we must have an individual faith and an individual experience. Only those who trust wholly in God are safe now. We must not follow any human example or lean upon any human support. Many are constantly taking wrong positions and making wrong moves; if we trust to their guidance we shall be misled.

Some who profess to be spokesmen for God are in their daily life denying the faith. They present to the people important truths; but who are impressed by these truths? who are convicted of sin? The hearers know that those who are preaching today will tomorrow be the first to join in pleasure, mirth, and frivolity. Their influence out of the pulpit soothes the conscience of the impenitent and causes the ministry to be despised. They are themselves asleep upon the very verge of the eternal world. The blood of souls is upon their garments.

How are the faithful servants of Christ employed? "Praying always with all prayer and supplication in the Spirit," praying in the closet, in the family, in the congregation, everywhere; "and watching thereunto with all perseverance." They feel that souls are in peril, and with earnest, humble faith they plead the promises of God in their behalf. The ransom paid by Christ—the atonement on the cross—is ever before them. They will have souls as seals of their ministry.

The rebuke of the Lord is upon His people for their pride and unbelief. He will not restore unto them the joys of His salvation while they are departing from the instructions of His word and His Spirit. He will give grace to those who fear Him and walk in the truth, and He will withdraw His blessing from all that assimilate to the world. Mercy and truth are promised to the humble and penitent, and judgments are denounced against the rebellious.

The church at Battle Creek might have stood free from idolatry, and her faithfulness would have been an example to other churches. But she is more willing to depart from God's commandments than to renounce the friendship of the world. She is joined to the idols which she has chosen, and because temporal prosperity and the favor of a wicked world are hers, she believes herself to be rich toward God. This will prove to many a fatal delusion. Her divine character and spiritual strength have departed from her.

I counsel this church to give heed to the Saviour's admonition: "Remember therefore from whence thou art fallen, and repent, and do the first works; or else I will come unto thee quickly, and will remove thy candlestick out of his place, except thou repent."

SHALL WE CONSULT SPIRITUALIST PHYSICIANS?

"Ahaziah fell down through a lattice in his upper chamber that was in Samaria, and was sick: and he sent messengers, and said unto them, Go, inquire of Baalzebub the god of Ekron whether I shall recover of this disease. But the angel of the Lord said to Elijah the Tishbite, Arise, go up to meet the messengers of the king of Samaria, and say unto them, Is it not because there is not a God in Israel, that ye go to inquire of Baalzebub the god of Ekron? Now therefore thus saith the Lord, Thou shalt not come down from that bed on which thou art gone up, but shalt surely die."

This narrative most strikingly displays the divine displeasure against those who turn from God to satanic agencies. A short time previous to the events above recorded the kingdom of Israel had changed rulers. Ahab had fallen under the judgment of God and had been succeeded by his son Ahaziah, a worthless character, who did only evil in the sight of the Lord, walking in the ways of his father and mother, and causing Israel to sin. He served Baal and worshiped him and provoked the Lord God of Israel to anger, as his father Ahab had done. But judgments followed close upon the sins of the rebellious king. A war with Moab, and then the accident by which his own life was threatened, attested the wrath of God against Ahaziah.

How much had the king of Israel heard and seen in his father's time of the wondrous works of the Most High! What terrible evidence of His severity and jealousy had God given apostate Israel! Of all this, Ahaziah was cognizant; yet he acted as though these awful realities, and even the fearful end of his own father, were only an idle tale. Instead of humbling his heart before the Lord he ventured upon the most daring act of impiety which marked his life. He commanded his servants: "Go, inquire of Baalzebub the god of Ekron whether I shall recover of this disease."

The idol of Ekron was supposed to give information, through the medium of its priests, concerning future events. It had obtained such general credence that it was resorted to by large numbers from a considerable distance. The predictions there uttered and the information given proceeded directly from the prince of darkness. It is Satan who created and who maintains the worship of idols, to divert the minds of men from God. It is by his agency that the kingdom of darkness and falsehood is supported.

The history of King Ahaziah's sin and punishment has a lesson of warning which none can disregard with impunity. Though we do not pay homage to heathen gods, yet thousands are worshiping at Satan's shrine as verily as did the king of Israel. The very spirit of heathen idolatry is rife today, though under the influence of science and education it has assumed a more refined and attractive form. Every day adds sorrowful evidence that faith in the sure word of prophecy is fast decreasing, and that in its stead superstition and satanic witchery are captivating the minds of men. All who do not earnestly search the Scriptures and submit every desire and purpose of life to that unerring test, all who do not seek God in prayer for a knowledge of His will, will surely wander from the right path and fall under the deception of Satan.

The heathen oracles have their counterpart in the spiritualistic mediums, the clairvoyants, and fortunetellers of today. The mystic voices that spoke at Ekron and En-dor are still by their lying words misleading the children of men. The prince of darkness has but appeared under a new guise. The mysteries of heathen worship are replaced by the secret associations and séances, the obscurities and wonders, of the sorcerers of our time. Their disclosures are eagerly received by thousands who refuse to accept light from God's word or from His Spirit. While they speak with scorn of the magicians of old, the great deceiver laughs in triumph as they yield to his arts under a different form.

His agents still claim to cure disease. They attribute their power to electricity, magnetism, or the so-called "sympathetic remedies." In truth, they are but channels for Satan's electric currents. By this means he casts his spell over the bodies and souls of men.

I have from time to time received letters both from ministers and lay members of the church, inquiring if I think it wrong to consult spiritualist and clairvoyant physicians. I have not answered these letters for want of time. But just now the subject is again urged upon my attention. So numerous are these agents of Satan becoming, and so general is the practice of seeking counsel from them, that it seems needful to utter words of warning.

God has placed it in our power to obtain a knowledge of the laws of health. He has made it our duty to preserve our physical powers in the best possible condition, that we may render to Him acceptable service. Those who refuse to improve the light and knowledge that has been mercifully placed within their reach are rejecting one of the means which God has granted them to promote spiritual as well as physical life. They are placing themselves where they will be exposed to the delusions of Satan.

Not a few in this Christian age and Christian nation resort

to evil spirits rather than trust to the power of the living God. The mother, watching by the sickbed of her child, exclaims: "I can do no more. Is there no physician who has power to restore my child?" She is told of the wonderful cures performed by some clairvoyant or magnetic healer, and she trusts her dear one to his charge, placing it as verily in the hands of Satan as if he were standing by her side. In many instances the future life of the child is controlled by a satanic power which it seems impossible to break.

Many are unwilling to put forth the needed effort to obtain a knowledge of the laws of life and the simple means to be employed for the restoration of health. They do not place themselves in right relation to life. When sickness is the result of their transgression of natural law, they do not seek to correct their errors and then ask the blessing of God, but they resort to the physicians. If they recover health they give to drugs and doctors all the honor. They are ever ready to idolize human power and wisdom, seeming to know no other God than the creature—dust and ashes.

I have heard a mother pleading with some infidel physician to save the life of her child; but when I entreated her to seek help from the Great Physician who is able to save to the uttermost all who come unto Him in faith, she turned away with impatience. Here we see the same spirit that was manifested by Ahaziah.

It is not safe to trust to physicians who have not the fear of God before them. Without the influence of divine grace the hearts of men are "deceitful above all things, and desperately wicked." Self-aggrandizement is their aim. Under the cover of the medical profession what iniquities have been concealed, what delusions supported! The physician may claim to possess great wisdom and marvelous skill, when his character is abandoned and his practice contrary to the laws of life. The Lord our God assures us that He is waiting to be gracious; He invites us to call upon Him in the day of trouble. How can we turn from Him to trust in an arm of flesh?

Go with me to yonder sickroom. There lies a husband and father, a man who is a blessing to society and to the cause of God. He has been suddenly stricken down by disease. The fire of fever seems consuming him. He longs for pure water to moisten the parched lips, to quench the raging thirst, and cool the fevered brow. But, no; the doctor has forbidden water. The stimulus of strong drink is given and adds fuel to the fire. The blessed, heaven-sent water, skillfully applied, would quench the devouring flame; but it is set aside for poisonous drugs.

For a time nature wrestles for her rights; but at last, overcome, she gives up the contest, and death sets the sufferer free. God desired that man to live, to be a blessing to the world; Satan determined to destroy him, and through the agency of the physician he succeeded. How long shall we permit our most precious lights to be thus extinguished?

Ahaziah sent his servants to inquire of Baalzebub, at Ekron; but instead of a message from the idol, he heard the awful denunciation from the God of Israel: "Thou shalt not come down from that bed on which thou art gone up, but shalt surely die." It was Christ that bade Elijah speak these words to the apostate king. Jehovah Immanuel had cause to be greatly displeased at Ahaziah's impiety. What had Christ not done to win the hearts of sinners and to inspire them with unwavering confidence in Himself? For ages He had visited His people with manifestations of the most condescending kindness and unexampled love. From the times of the patriarchs He had shown how His "delights were with the sons of men." He had been a very present help to all who sought Him in sincerity. "In all their affliction He was afflicted, and the angel of His presence saved them: in His love and in His pity He redeemed them." Yet Israel had revolted from God and turned for help to the Lord's worst enemy.

The Hebrews were the only nation favored with a knowledge of the true God. When the king of Israel sent to inquire of a pagan oracle, he proclaimed to the heathen that he had more confidence in their idols than in the God of his people, the Creator of the heavens and the earth. In the same manner do those who profess to have a knowledge of God's word dishonor Him when they turn from the Source of strength and wisdom to ask help or counsel from the powers of darkness. If God's wrath was kindled by such a course on the part of a wicked, idolatrous king, how can He regard a similar course pursued by those who profess to be His servants?

Why is it that men are so unwilling to trust Him who created man, and who can by a touch, a word, a look, heal all manner of disease? Who is more worthy of our confidence than the One who made so great a sacrifice for our redemption? Our Lord has given us definite instruction through the apostle James as to our duty in case of sickness. When human help fails, God will be the helper of His people. "Is any sick among you? let him call for the elders of the church; and let them pray over him, anointing him with oil in the name of the Lord: and the prayer of faith shall save the sick, and the Lord shall raise him up." If the professed followers of Christ would, with purity of heart, exercise as much faith in the promises of God as they repose in satanic agencies, they would realize in soul and body the life-giving power of the Holy Spirit.

God has granted to this people great light, yet we are not placed beyond the reach of temptation. Who among us are seeking help from the gods of Ekron? Look on this picture—not drawn from imagination. In how many, even among Seventh-day Adventists, may its leading characteristics be seen? An invalid—apparently very conscientious, yet bigoted and self-sufficient—freely avows his contempt for the laws of health and life, which divine mercy has led us as a people to accept. His food must be prepared in a manner to satisfy his morbid cravings. Rather than sit at a table where wholesome food is provided, he will patronize restaurants, because he can there indulge appetite without restraint. A fluent advocate of temperance, he disregards its foundation principles. He wants relief, but refuses to obtain it at the price of self-denial. That man is worshiping at the shrine of perverted appetite. He is an idolater. The powers which, sanctified and ennobled, might be employed to honor God, are weakened and rendered of little service. An irritable temper, a confused brain, and unstrung nerves are among the results of his disregard of nature's laws. He is inefficient, unreliable.

Whoever has the courage and honesty to warn him of danger thereby incurs his displeasure. The slightest remonstrance or opposition is sufficient to rouse his combative spirit. But now an opportunity is presented to seek help from one whose power comes through the medium of witchcraft. To this source he applies with eagerness, freely expending time and money in hope of securing the proffered boon. He is deceived, infatuated. The sorcerer's power is made the theme of praise, and others are influenced to seek his aid. Thus the God of Israel is dishonored, while Satan's power is revered and exalted.

In the name of Christ I would address His professed followers: Abide in the faith which you have received from the beginning. Shun profane and vain babblings. Instead of putting your trust in witchcraft, have faith in the living God. Cursed is the path that leads to En-dor or to Ekron. The feet will stumble and fall that venture upon the forbidden ground. There is a God in Israel, with whom is deliverance for all that are oppressed. Righteousness is the habitation of His throne.

There is danger in departing in the least from the Lord's

instruction. When we deviate from the plain path of duty, a train of circumstances will arise that seems irresistibly to draw us further and further from the right. Needless intimacies with those who have no respect for God will seduce us ere we are aware. Fear to offend worldly friends will deter us from expressing our gratitude to God or acknowledging our dependence upon Him. We must keep close to the word of God. We need its warnings and encouragement, its threatenings and promises. We need the perfect example given only in the life and character of our Saviour.

Angels of God will preserve His people while they walk in the path of duty, but there is no assurance of such protection for those who deliberately venture upon Satan's ground. An agent of the great deceiver will say and do anything to gain his object. It matters little whether he calls himself a spiritualist, an "electric physician," or a "magnetic healer." By specious pretenses he wins the confidence of the unwary. He pretends to read the life history and to understand all the difficulties and afflictions of those who resort to him. Disguising himself as an angel of light, while the blackness of the pit is in his heart, he manifests great interest in women who seek his counsel. He tells them that all their troubles are due to an unhappy marriage. This may be too true, but such a counselor does not better their condition. He tells them that they need love and sympathy. Pretending great interest in their welfare, he casts a spell over his unsuspecting victims, charming them as the serpent charms the trembling bird. Soon they are completely in his power; sin, disgrace, and ruin are the terrible sequel.

These workers of iniquity are not few. Their path is marked by desolated homes, blasted reputations, and broken hearts. But of all this the world knows little; still they go on making fresh victims, and Satan exults in the ruin he has wrought.

The visible and the invisible world are in close contact. Could the veil be lifted, we would see evil angels pressing their darkness around us and working with all their power to deceive and destroy. Wicked men are surrounded, influenced, and aided by evil spirits. The man of faith and prayer has yielded his soul to divine guidance, and angels of God bring to him light and strength from heaven.

No man can serve two masters. Light and darkness are no more opposites than are the service of God and the service of Satan. The prophet Elijah presented the matter in the true light when he fearlessly appealed to apostate Israel: "If the Lord be God, follow Him: but if Baal, then follow him."

Those who give themselves up to the sorcery of Satan may boast of great benefit received thereby, but does this prove their course to be wise or safe? What if life should be prolonged? What if temporal gain should be secured? Will it pay in the end to disregard the will of God? All such apparent gain will prove at last an irrecoverable loss. We cannot with impunity break down a single barrier which God has erected to guard His people from Satan's power.

Our only safety is in preserving the ancient landmarks. "To the law and to the testimony: if they speak not according to this word, it is because there is no light in them."

LOOKING UNTO JESUS

Many make a serious mistake in their religious life by keeping the attention fixed upon their feelings and thus judging of their advancement or decline. Feelings are not a safe criterion. We are not to look within for evidence of our acceptance with God. We shall find there nothing but that which will discourage us. Our only hope is in "looking unto Jesus the Author and Finisher of our faith." There is everything in Him to inspire with hope, with faith, and with courage. He is our righteousness, our consolation and rejoicing.

Those who look within for comfort will become weary and disappointed. A sense of our weakness and unworthiness should lead us with humility of heart to plead the atoning sacrifice of Christ. As we rely upon His merits we shall find rest and peace and joy. He saves to the uttermost all who come unto God by Him.

We need to trust in Jesus daily, hourly. He has promised that as our day is, our strength shall be. By His grace we may bear all the burdens of the present and perform its duties. But many are weighed down by the anticipation of future troubles. They are constantly seeking to bring tomorrow's burdens into today. Thus a large share of all their trials are imaginary. For these, Jesus has made no provision. He promises grace only for the day. He bids us not to burden ourselves with the cares and troubles of tomorrow; for "sufficient unto the day is the evil thereof."

The habit of brooding over anticipated evils is unwise and unchristian. In thus doing we fail to enjoy the blessings and to improve the opportunities of the present. The Lord requires us to perform the duties of today and to endure its trials. We are today to watch that we offend not in word or deed. We must today praise and honor God. By the exercise of living faith today we are to conquer the enemy. We must today seek God and be determined that we will not rest satisfied without His presence. We should watch and work and pray as though this were the last day that would be granted us. How intensely earnest, then, would be our life. How closely would we follow Jesus in all our words and deeds.

There are few who rightly appreciate or improve the precious privilege of prayer. We should go to Jesus and tell Him all our needs. We may bring Him our little cares and perplexities as well as our greater troubles. Whatever arises to disturb or distress us, we should take it to the Lord in prayer. When we feel that we need the presence of Christ at every step, Satan will have little opportunity to intrude his temptations. It is his studied effort to keep us away from our best and most sympathizing friend. We should make no one our confidant but Jesus. We can safely commune with Him of all that is in our hearts.

Brethren and sisters, when you assemble for social worship, believe that Jesus meets with you; believe that He is willing to bless you. Turn the eye away from self; look unto Jesus, talk of His matchless love. By beholding Him you will become changed into His likeness. When you pray, be brief, come right to the point. Do not preach the Lord a sermon in your long prayers. Ask for the bread of life as a hungry child asks bread of his earthly father. God will bestow upon us every needed blessing if we ask Him in simplicity and faith.

The prayers offered by ministers previous to their discourses are frequently long and inappropriate. They embrace a whole round of subjects that have no reference to the necessities of the occasion or the wants of the people. Such prayers are suitable for the closet, but should not be offered in public. The hearers become weary and long for the minister to close. Brethren, carry the people with you in your prayers. Go to your Saviour in faith, tell Him what you need on that occasion. Let the soul go out after God with intense longing for the blessing needed at that time.

Prayer is the most holy exercise of the soul. It should be sincere, humble, earnest—the desires of a renewed heart breathed in the presence of a holy God. When the suppliant feels that he is in the divine presence, self will be forgotten. He will have no desire to display human talent; he will not seek to please the ear of men, but to obtain the blessing which the soul craves.

If we would only take the Lord at His word, what blessings might be ours! Would that there were more fervent, effectual prayer. Christ will be the helper of all who seek Him in faith.

CALLS FOR LABORERS

A spirit of worldliness and selfishness has deprived the church of many a blessing. We have no right to suppose an arbitrary withholding from the church of the divine light and power, to account for its limited usefulness. The measure of success which in the past has followed well-directed effort contradicts such an idea. Success has ever been granted proportionate to the labor performed. It is the limitation of labors and sacrifices alone which has restricted the usefulness of the church. The missionary spirit is feeble; devotion is weak; selfishness and cupidity, covetousness and fraud, exist in its members.

Does not God care for these things? Can He not read the intents and purposes of the heart? Earnest, fervent, contrite prayer would open to them the windows of heaven and bring down showers of grace. A clear, steady view of the cross of Christ would counteract their worldliness and fill their souls with humility, penitence, and gratitude. They would then feel that they are not their own, but that they are the purchase of Christ's blood.

A deadly spiritual malady is upon the church. Its members are wounded by Satan; but they will not look to the cross of Christ, as the Israelites looked to the brazen serpent, that they may live. The world has so many claims upon them that they have not time to look to the cross of Calvary long enough to see its glory or to feel its power. When they now and then catch a glimpse of the self-denial and self-dedication which the truth demands, it is unwelcome, and they turn their attention in another direction, that they may the sooner forget it. The Lord cannot make His people useful and efficient while they are not careful to comply with the conditions He has laid down.

Great demands are everywhere made for the light which God has given to His people; but these calls are for the most part in vain. Who feels the burden of consecrating himself to God and to His work? Where are the young men who are qualifying themselves to answer these calls? Vast territories are opened before us where the light of truth has never penetrated. Whichever way we look we see rich harvests ready to be gathered, but there are none to do the reaping. Prayers are offered for the triumph of the truth. What do your prayers mean, brethren? What kind of success do you desire?—a success to suit your indolence, your selfish indulgence?—a success that will sustain and support itself without any effort on your part?

There must be a decided change in the church which will inconvenience those who are reclining on their lees, before laborers who are fitted for their solemn work can be sent into the field. There must be an awakening, a spiritual renovation. The temperature of Christian piety must be raised. Plans must be devised and executed for the spread of truth to all nations of the earth. Satan is lulling Christ's professed followers to sleep while souls are perishing all around them, and what excuse can they give to the Master for their negligence?

The words of Christ apply to the church: "Why stand ye here all the day idle?" Why are you not at work in some capacity in His vineyard? Again and again He has bidden you: "Go ye also into the vineyard; and whatsoever is right, that shall ye receive." But this gracious call from heaven has been disregarded by the large majority. Is it not high time that you obey the commands of God? There is work for every individual who names the name of Christ. A voice from heaven is solemnly calling you to duty. Heed this voice, and go to work at once in any place, in any capacity. Why stand ye here all the day idle? There is work for you to do, a work that demands your best energies. Every precious moment of life is related to some duty which you owe to God or to your fellow men, and yet you are idle!

A great work of saving souls remains yet to be done. Every angel in glory is engaged in this work, while every demon of darkness is opposing it. Christ has demonstrated to us the great value of souls in that He came to the world with the hoarded love of eternity in His heart, offering to make man heir to all His wealth. He unveils before us the love of the Father for the guilty race and presents Him as just and the justifier of him that believeth.

"Christ pleased not Himself." He did nothing for Himself; His work was in behalf of fallen man. Selfishness stood abashed in His presence. He assumed our nature that He might suffer in our stead. Selfishness, the sin of the world, has become the prevailing sin of the church. In sacrificing Himself for the good of men, Christ strikes at the root of all selfishness. He withheld nothing, not even His own honor and heavenly glory. He expects corresponding self-denial and sacrifice on the part of those whom He came to bless and save. Everyone is required to work to the extent of his ability. Every worldly consideration should be laid aside for the glory of God. The only desire for worldly advantages should be that we may the better advance the cause of God.

Christ's interests and those of His followers should be one; but the world would judge that they are separate and distinct, for those who claim to be Christ's pursue their own ends as eagerly, and waste their substance as selfishly, as nonprofessors. Worldly prosperity comes first; nothing is made equal to this. The cause of Christ must wait till they gather a certain portion for themselves. They must increase their gains at all hazards. Souls must perish without a knowledge of the truth. Of what value is a soul for whom Christ died in comparison with their gains, their merchandise, their houses and lands? Souls must wait till they get prepared to do something. God calls these servers of Mammon slothful and unfaithful servants, but Mammon boasts of them as among his most diligent and devoted servants. They sacrifice their Lord's goods to ease and enjoyment. Self is their idol.

Doing nothing to bring souls to Jesus, who sacrificed everything to bring salvation within our reach! Selfishness is driving benevolence and the love of Christ from the church. Millions of the Lord's money are squandered in the gratification of worldly lust, while His treasury is left empty. I know not how to present this matter before you as it was presented to me. Thousands of dollars are spent every year in gratifying pride of dress. That very means should be used in our missions. I was shown families who load their tables with almost every luxury and gratify almost every desire for fine clothes. They are engaged in a prosperous business, or are earning good wages, but nearly every dollar is expended upon themselves or their families. Is this imitating Christ? What burden do these feel to carefully economize and deny inclination that they may do more to advance the work of God on earth? Should Elder Andrews have the advantage of some of the means thus needlessly expended, it would be a great blessing to him and give him advantages which would prolong his life. The missionary work might be enlarged a hundredfold if there were more means to employ in carrying out larger plans. But the means which God designed should be used for this very purpose is expended for articles which are thought necessary to comfort and happiness, and which there might be no sin in possessing were not means so greatly needed in extending the truth. How many of you, my brethren, are seeking your own and not the things which are Jesus Christ's!

Suppose Christ should abide in every heart and selfishness in all its forms should be banished from the church, what would be the result? Harmony, unity, and brotherly love would be seen as verily as in the church which Christ first established. Christian activity would be seen everywhere. The whole church would be kindled into a sacrificial flame for the glory of God. Every Christian would cast in the fruit of his self-denial to be consumed upon the altar. There would be far greater activity in devising fresh methods of usefulness and in studying how to come close to poor sinners to save them from eternal ruin.

Should we dress in plain, modest apparel, without reference to the fashions; should our tables at all times be set with simple, healthful food, avoiding all luxuries, all extravagance; should our houses be built with becoming plainness and furnished in the same manner, it would show the sanctifying power of the truth and would have a telling influence upon unbelievers. But while we conform to the world in these matters, in some cases apparently seeking to excel worldlings in fanciful arrangement, the preaching of the truth will have but little or no effect. Who will believe the solemn truth for this time when those who already profess to believe it contradict their faith by their works? It is not God who has closed the windows of heaven to us, but it is our own conformity to the customs and practices of the world.

The third angel of Revelation 14 is represented as flying swiftly through the midst of heaven crying: "Here are they that keep the commandments of God, and the faith of Jesus." Here is shown the nature of the work of the people of God. They have a message of so great importance that they are represented as flying in the presentation of it to the world. They are holding in their hands the bread of life for a famishing world. The love of Christ constraineth them. This is the last message. There are no more to follow, no more invitations of mercy to be given after this message shall have done its work. What a trust! What a responsibility is resting upon all to carry the words of gracious invitation: "And the Spirit and the bride say, Come. And let him that heareth say, Come. And let him that is athirst come. And whosoever will, let him take the water of life freely."

Everyone who heareth is to say: Come. Not only ministers, but the people. All are to join in the invitation. Not only by their profession, but by their character and dress, all are to have a winning influence. They are made trustees for the world, executors of the will of One who has bequeathed sacred truth to men. Would that all could feel the dignity and glory of their God-given trust.

THE SEAL OF GOD

"He cried also in mine ears with a loud voice, saying, Cause them that have charge over the city to draw near, even every man with his destroying weapon in his hand."

"And he called to the man clothed with linen, which had the writer's inkhorn by his side; and the Lord said unto him, Go through the midst of the city, through the midst of Jerusalem, and set a mark on the foreheads of the men that sigh and that cry for all the abominations that be done in the midst thereof. And to the others he said in mine hearing, Go ye after him through the city, and smite: let not your eye spare, neither have ye pity: slay utterly old and young, both maids, and little children, and women: but come not near any man upon whom is the mark; and begin at My sanctuary. Then they began at the ancient men which were before the house."

Jesus is about to leave the mercy seat of the heavenly sanctuary to put on garments of vengeance and pour out His wrath in judgments upon those who have not responded to the light God has given them. "Because sentence against an evil work is not executed speedily, therefore the heart of the sons of men is fully set in them to do evil." Instead of being softened by the patience and long forbearance that the Lord has exercised toward them, those who fear not God and love not the truth strengthen their hearts in their evil course. But there are limits even to the forbearance of God, and many are exceeding these boundaries. They have overrun the limits of grace, and therefore God must interfere and vindicate His own honor.

Of the Amorites the Lord said: "In the fourth generation they shall come hither again: for the iniquity of the Amorites is not yet full." Although this nation was conspicuous because of its idolatry and corruption, it had not yet filled up the cup of its iniquity, and God would not give command for its utter destruction. The people were to see the divine power manifested in a marked manner, that they might be left without excuse. The compassionate Creator was willing to bear with their iniquity until the fourth generation. Then, if no change was seen for the better, His judgments were to fall upon them.

With unerring accuracy the Infinite One still keeps an account with all nations. While His mercy is tendered with calls to repentance, this account will remain open; but when the figures reach a certain amount which God has fixed, the ministry of His wrath commences. The account is closed. Divine patience ceases. There is no more pleading of mercy in their behalf.

The prophet, looking down the ages, had this time presented before his vision. The nations of this age have been the recipients of unprecedented mercies. The choicest of heaven's blessings have been given them, but increased pride, covetousness, idolatry, contempt of God, and base ingratitude are written against them. They are fast closing up their account with God.

But that which causes me to tremble is the fact that those who have had the greatest light and privileges have become contaminated by the prevailing iniquity. Influenced by the unrighteous around them, many, even of those who profess the truth, have grown cold and are borne down by the strong current of evil. The universal scorn thrown upon true piety and holiness leads those who do not connect closely with God to lose their reverence for His law. If they were following the light and obeying the truth from the heart, this holy law would seem even more precious to them when thus despised and set aside. As the disrespect for God's law becomes more manifest, the line of demarcation between its observers and the world becomes more distinct. Love for the divine precepts increases with one class according as contempt for them increases with another class.

The crisis is fast approaching. The rapidly swelling figures show that the time for God's visitation has about come. Although loath to punish, nevertheless He will punish, and that speedily. Those who walk in the light will see signs of the approaching peril; but they are not to sit in quiet, unconcerned expectancy of the ruin, comforting themselves with the belief that God will shelter His people in the day of visitation. Far from it. They should realize that it is their duty to labor diligently to save others, looking with strong faith to God for help. "The effectual fervent prayer of a righteous man availeth much."

The leaven of godliness has not entirely lost its power. At the time when the danger and depression of the church are greatest, the little company who are standing in the light will be sighing and crying for the abominations that are done in the land. But more especially will their prayers arise in behalf of the church because its members are doing after the manner of the world.

The earnest prayers of this faithful few will not be in vain. When the Lord comes forth as an avenger, He will also come as a protector of all those who have preserved the faith in its purity and kept themselves unspotted from the world. It is at this time that God has promised to avenge His own elect which cry day and night unto Him, though He bear long with them.

The command is: "Go through the midst of the city, through the midst of Jerusalem, and set a mark upon the foreheads of the men that sigh and that cry for all the abominations that be done in the midst thereof." These sighing, crying ones had been holding forth the words of life; they had reproved, counseled, and entreated. Some who had been dishonoring God repented and humbled their hearts before Him. But the glory of the Lord had departed from Israel; although many still continued the forms of religion, His power and presence were lacking.

In the time when His wrath shall go forth in judgments, these humble, devoted followers of Christ will be distinguished from the rest of the world by their soul anguish, which is expressed in lamentation and weeping, reproofs and warnings. While others try to throw a cloak over the existing evil, and excuse the great wickedness everywhere prevalent, those who have a zeal for God's honor and a love for souls will not hold their peace to obtain favor of any. Their righteous souls are vexed day by day with the unholy works and conversation of the unrighteous. They are powerless to stop the rushing torrent of iniquity, and hence they are filled with grief and alarm. They mourn before God to see religion despised in the very homes of those who have had great light. They lament and afflict their souls because pride, avarice, selfishness, and deception of almost every kind are in the church. The Spirit of God, which prompts to reproof, is trampled underfoot, while the servants of Satan triumph. God is dishonored, the truth made of none effect.

The class who do not feel grieved over their own spiritual declension, nor mourn over the sins of others, will be left without the seal of God. The Lord commissions His messengers, the men with slaughtering weapons in their hands: "Go ye after him through the city, and smite: let not your eye spare, neither have ye pity: slay utterly old and young, both maids, and little children, and women: but come not near any man upon whom is the mark; and begin at My sanctuary. Then they began at the ancient men which were before the house."

Here we see that the church—the Lord's sanctuary—was the first to feel the stroke of the wrath of God. The ancient men, those to whom God had given great light and who had stood as guardians of the spiritual interests of the people, had betrayed their trust. They had taken the position that we need not look for miracles and the marked manifestation of God's power as in former days. Times have changed. These words strengthen their unbelief, and they say: The Lord will not do good, neither will He do evil. He is too merciful to visit His people in judgment. Thus "Peace and safety" is the cry from men who will never again lift up their voice like a trumpet to show God's people their transgressions and the house of Jacob their sins. These dumb dogs that would not bark are the ones who feel the just vengeance of an offended God. Men, maidens, and little children all perish together.

The abominations for which the faithful ones were sighing and crying were all that could be discerned by finite eyes, but by far the worst sins, those which provoked the jealousy of the pure and holy God, were unrevealed. The great Searcher of hearts knoweth every sin committed in secret by the workers of iniquity. These persons come to feel secure in their deceptions and, because of His long-suffering, say that the Lord seeth not, and then act as though He had forsaken the earth. But He will detect their hypocrisy and will open before others those sins which they were so careful to hide.

No superiority of rank, dignity, or worldly wisdom, no position in sacred office, will preserve men from sacrificing principle when left to their own deceitful hearts. Those who have been regarded as worthy and righteous prove to be ringleaders in apostasy and examples in indifference and in the abuse of God's mercies. Their wicked course He will tolerate no longer, and in His wrath He deals with them without mercy.

It is with reluctance that the Lord withdraws His presence from those who have been blessed with great light and who have felt the power of the word in ministering to others. They were once His faithful servants, favored with His presence and guidance; but they departed from Him and led others into error, and therefore are brought under the divine displeasure.

The day of God's vengeance is just upon us. The seal of God will be placed upon the foreheads of those only who sigh and cry for the abominations done in the land. Those who link in sympathy with the world are eating and drinking with the drunken and will surely be destroyed with the workers of iniquity. "The eyes of the Lord are upon the righteous, and His ears are open unto their cry," but "the face of the Lord is against them that do evil."

Our own course of action will determine whether we shall receive the seal of the living God or be cut down by the destroying weapons. Already a few drops of God's wrath have fallen upon the earth; but when the seven last plagues shall be poured out without mixture into the cup of His indignation, then it will be forever too late to repent and find shelter. No atoning blood will then wash away the stains of sin.

"And at that time shall Michael stand up, the great prince

which standeth for the children of thy people: and there shall be a time of trouble, such as never was since there was a nation even to that same time: and at that time thy people shall be delivered, everyone that shall be found written in the book." When this time of trouble comes, every case is decided; there is no longer probation, no longer mercy for the impenitent. The seal of the living God is upon His people. This small remnant, unable to defend themselves in the deadly conflict with the powers of earth that are marshaled by the dragon host, make God their defense. The decree has been passed by the highest earthly authority that they shall worship the beast and receive his mark under pain of persecution and death. May God help His people now, for what can they then do in such a fearful conflict without His assistance!

Courage, fortitude, faith, and implicit trust in God's power to save do not come in a moment. These heavenly graces are acquired by the experience of years. By a life of holy endeavor and firm adherence to the right the children of God were sealing their destiny. Beset with temptations without number, they knew they must resist firmly or be conquered. They felt that they had a great work to do, and at any hour they might be called to lay off their armor; and should they come to the close of life with their work undone, it would be an eternal loss. They eagerly accepted the light from heaven, as did the first disciples from the lips of Jesus. When those early Christians were exiled to mountains and deserts, when left in dungeons to die with hunger, cold, and torture, when martyrdom seemed the only way out of their distress, they rejoiced that they were counted worthy to suffer for Christ, who was crucified for them. Their worthy example will be a comfort and encouragement to the people of God who will be brought into the time of trouble such as never was.

Not all who profess to keep the Sabbath will be sealed.

There are many even among those who teach the truth to others who will not receive the seal of God in their foreheads. They had the light of truth, they knew their Master's will, they understood every point of our faith, but they had not corresponding works. These who were so familiar with prophecy and the treasures of divine wisdom should have acted their faith. They should have commanded their households after them, that by a well-ordered family they might present to the world the influence of the truth upon the human heart.

By their lack of devotion and piety, and their failure to reach a high religious standard, they make other souls contented with their position. Men of finite judgment cannot see that in patterning after these men who have so often opened to them the treasures of God's word, they will surely endanger their souls. Jesus is the only true pattern. Everyone must now search the Bible for himself upon his knees before God, with the humble, teachable heart of a child, if he would know what the Lord requires of him. However high any minister may have stood in the favor of God, if he neglects to follow out the light given him of God, if he refuses to be taught as a little child, he will go into darkness and satanic delusions and will lead others in the same path.

Not one of us will ever receive the seal of God while our characters have one spot or stain upon them. It is left with us to remedy the defects in our characters, to cleanse the soul temple of every defilement. Then the latter rain will fall upon us as the early rain fell upon the disciples on the Day of Pentecost.

We are too easily satisfied with our attainments. We feel rich and increased with goods and know not that we are "wretched, and miserable, and poor, and blind, and naked." Now is the time to heed the admonition of the True Witness: "I counsel thee to buy of Me gold tried in the fire, that thou mayest be rich; and white raiment, that thou mayest be clothed, and that the shame of thy nakedness do not appear; and anoint thine eyes with eyesalve, that thou mayest see."

In this life we must meet fiery trials and make costly sacrifices, but the peace of Christ is the reward. There has been so little self-denial, so little suffering for Christ's sake, that the cross is almost entirely forgotten. We must be partakers with Christ of His sufferings if we would sit down in triumph with Him on His throne. So long as we choose the easy path of self-indulgence and are frightened at self-denial, our faith will never become firm, and we cannot know the peace of Jesus nor the joy that comes through conscious victory. The most exalted of the redeemed host that stand before the throne of God and the Lamb, clad in white, know the conflict of overcoming, for they have come up through great tribulation. Those who have yielded to circumstances rather than engage in this conflict will not know how to stand in that day when anguish will be upon every soul, when, though Noah, Job, and Daniel were in the land, they could save neither son nor daughter, for everyone must deliver his soul by his own righteousness.

No one need say that his case is hopeless, that he cannot live the life of a Christian. Ample provision is made by the death of Christ for every soul. Jesus is our ever-present help in time of need. Only call upon Him in faith, and He has promised to hear and answer your petitions.

Oh, for a living, active faith! We need it; we must have it, or we shall faint and fail in the day of trial. The darkness that will then rest upon our path must not discourage us or drive us to despair. It is the veil with which God covers His glory when He comes to impart rich blessings. We should know this by our past experience. In that day when God has a controversy with His people this experience will be a source of comfort and hope.

It is now that we must keep ourselves and our children unspotted from the world. It is now that we must wash our robes of character and make them white in the blood of the Lamb. It is now that we must overcome pride, passion, and spiritual slothfulness. It is now that we must awake and make determined effort for symmetry of character. "Today if ye will hear His voice, harden not your hearts." We are in a most trying position, waiting, watching for our Lord's appearing. The world is in darkness. "But ye, brethren," says Paul, "are not in darkness, that that day should overtake you as a thief." It is ever God's purpose to bring light out of darkness, joy out of sorrow, and rest out of weariness for the waiting, longing soul.

What are you doing, brethren, in the great work of preparation? Those who are uniting with the world are receiving the worldly mold and preparing for the mark of the beast. Those who are distrustful of self, who are humbling themselves before God and purifying their souls by obeying the truth—these are receiving the heavenly mold and preparing for the seal of God in their foreheads. When the decree goes forth and the stamp is impressed, their character will remain pure and spotless for eternity.

Now is the time to prepare. The seal of God will never be placed upon the forehead of an impure man or woman. It will never be placed upon the forehead of the ambitious, world-loving man or woman. It will never be placed upon the forehead of men or women of false tongues or deceitful hearts. All who receive the seal must be without spot before God— candidates for heaven. Go forward, my brethren and sisters. I can only write briefly upon these points at this time, merely calling your attention to the necessity of preparation. Search the Scriptures for yourselves, that you may understand the fearful solemnity of the present hour.

AN APPEAL*

I am filled with sadness when I think of our condition as a people. The Lord has not closed heaven to us, but our own course of continual backsliding has separated us from God. Pride, covetousness, and love of the world have lived in the heart without fear of banishment or condemnation. Grievous and presumptuous sins have dwelt among us. And yet the general opinion is that the church is flourishing and that peace and spiritual prosperity are in all her borders.

The church has turned back from following Christ her Leader and is steadily retreating toward Egypt. Yet few are alarmed or astonished at their want of spiritual power. Doubt, and even disbelief of the testimonies of the Spirit of God, is leavening our churches everywhere. Satan would have it thus. Ministers who preach self instead of Christ would have it thus. The testimonies are unread and unappreciated. God has spoken to you. Light has been shining from His word and from the testimonies, and both have been slighted and disregarded. The result is apparent in the lack of purity and devotion and earnest faith among us.

Let each put the question to his own heart: "How have we fallen into this state of spiritual feebleness and dissension? Have we not brought upon ourselves the frown of God because our actions do not correspond with our faith? Have we not been seeking the friendship and applause of the world

*This appeal was written at Healdsburg, California, May 30, 1882, to be read at the camp meetings. It presents warnings and instruction which the writer, being absent in person, felt urged to give to the church. For the benefit of those who were not present at those meetings, and also for all who may desire to preserve it in permanent form, it is inserted here.

rather than the presence of Christ and a deeper knowledge of His will?" Examine your own hearts, judge your own course. Consider what associates you are choosing. Do you seek the company of the wise, or are you willing to choose worldly associates, companions who fear not God and obey not the gospel?

Are your recreations such as to impart moral and spiritual vigor? Will they lead to purity of thought and action? Impurity is today widespread, even among the professed followers of Christ. Passion is unrestrained; the animal propensities are gaining strength by indulgence, while the moral powers are constantly becoming weaker. Many are eagerly participating in worldly, demoralizing amusements which God's word forbids. Thus they sever their connection with God and rank themselves with the pleasure lovers of the world. The sins that destroyed the antediluvians and the cities of the plain exist today—not merely in heathen lands, not only among popular professors of Christianity, but with some who profess to be looking for the coming of the Son of man. If God should present these sins before you as they appear in His sight, you would be filled with shame and terror.

And what has caused this alarming condition? Many have accepted the theory of the truth who have had no true conversion. I know whereof I speak. There are few who feel true sorrow for sin, who have deep, pungent convictions of the depravity of the unregenerate nature. The heart of stone is not exchanged for a heart of flesh. Few are willing to fall upon the Rock and be broken.

No matter who you are or what your life has been, you can be saved only in God's appointed way. You must repent; you must fall helpless on the Rock, Christ Jesus. You must feel your need of a physician and of the one only remedy for sin, the blood of Christ. This remedy can be secured only by repentance toward God and faith toward our Lord Jesus Christ.

Here the work is yet to be begun by many who profess to be Christians and even to be ministers of Christ. Like the Pharisees of old many of you feel no need of a Saviour. You are self-sufficient, self-exalted. Said Christ: "I came not to call the righteous, but sinners to repentance." The blood of Christ will avail for none but those who feel their need of its cleansing power.

What surpassing love and condescension, that when we had no claim upon divine mercy, Christ was willing to undertake our redemption! But our great Physician requires of every soul unquestioning submission. We are never to prescribe for our own case. Christ must have the entire management of will and action.

Many are not sensible of their condition and their danger; and there is much in the nature and manner of Christ's work averse to every worldly principle and opposed to the pride of the human heart. Jesus requires us to trust ourselves wholly to His hands and confide in His love and wisdom.

We may flatter ourselves, as did Nicodemus, that our moral character has been correct and we need not humble ourselves before God like the common sinner. But we must be content to enter into life in the very same way as the chief of sinners. We must renounce our own righteousness and plead for the righteousness of Christ to be imputed to us. We must depend wholly upon Christ for our strength. Self must die. We must acknowledge that all we have is from the exceeding riches of divine grace. Let this be the language of our hearts: "Not unto us, O Lord, not unto us, but unto Thy name give glory, for Thy mercy, and for Thy truth's sake."

Genuine faith is followed by love, and love by obedience. All the powers and passions of the converted man are brought under the control of Christ. His Spirit is a renewing power, transforming to the divine image all who will receive it. It makes me sad to say that this experience is understood by but few who profess the truth. Very many follow on in their own ways and indulge their sinful desires and yet profess to be disciples of Christ. They have never submitted their hearts to God. Like the foolish virgins they have neglected to obtain the oil of grace in their vessels with their lamps. I tell you, my brethren, that a large number who profess to believe and even to teach the truth are under the bondage of sin. Base passions defile the mind and corrupt the soul. Some who are in the vilest iniquity have borrowed the livery of heaven, that they may serve Satan more effectively.

"Whosoever is born of God doth not commit sin." He feels that he is the purchase of the blood of Christ and bound by the most solemn vows to glorify God in his body and in his spirit, which are God's. The love of sin and the love of self are subdued in him. He daily asks: "What shall I render unto the Lord for all His benefits toward me?" "Lord, what wilt Thou have me to do?" The true Christian will never complain that the yoke of Christ is galling to the neck. He accounts the service of Jesus as the truest freedom. The law of God is his delight. Instead of seeking to bring down the divine commands, to accord with his deficiencies, he is constantly striving to rise to the level of their perfection.

Such an experience must be ours if we would be prepared to stand in the day of God. Now, while probation lingers, while mercy's voice is still heard, is the time for us to put away our sins. While moral darkness covers the earth like a funeral pall, the light of God's standard-bearers must shine the more brightly, showing the contrast between heaven's light and Satan's darkness.

God has made ample provision that we may stand perfect in His grace, wanting in nothing, waiting for the appearing of our Lord. Are you ready? Have you the wedding garment on? That garment will never cover deceit, impurity, corruption, or hypocrisy. The eye of God is upon you. It is a discerner of the thoughts and intents of the heart. We may conceal our sins from the eyes of men, but we can hide nothing from our Maker.

God spared not His own Son, but delivered Him to death for our offenses and raised Him again for our justification. Through Christ we may present our petitions at the throne of grace. Through Him, unworthy as we are, we may obtain all spiritual blessings. Do we come to Him, that we may have life?

How shall we know for ourselves God's goodness and His love? The psalmist tells us—not, hear and know, read and know, or believe and know; but—*"Taste* and see that the Lord is good."* Instead of relying upon the word of another, taste for yourself.

Experience is knowledge derived from experiment. Experimental religion is what is needed now. "Taste and see that the Lord is good." Some—yes, a large number—have a theoretical knowledge of religious truth, but have never felt the renewing power of divine grace upon their own hearts. These persons are ever slow to heed the testimonies of warning, reproof, and instruction indited by the Holy Spirit. They believe in the wrath of God, but put forth no earnest efforts to escape it. They believe in heaven, but make no sacrifice to obtain it. They believe in the value of the soul and that erelong its redemption ceaseth forever. Yet they neglect the most precious opportunities to make their peace with God.

They may read the Bible, but its threatenings do not alarm or its promises win them. They approve things that are excellent, yet they follow the way in which God has forbidden them to go. They know a refuge, but do not avail themselves of it. They know a remedy for sin, but do not use it. They know the right, but have no relish for it. All their knowledge will but increase their condemnation. They have never tasted and learned by experience that the Lord is good.

To become a disciple of Christ is to deny self and follow Jesus through evil as well as good report. Few are doing this now. Many prophesy falsely, and the people love to have it so; but what will be done in the end thereof? What will be the decision when their work, with all its results, shall be brought in review before God?

The Christian life is a warfare. The apostle Paul speaks of wrestling against principalities and powers as he fought the good fight of faith. Again, he declares: "Ye have not yet resisted unto blood, striving against sin." Ah, no. Today sin is cherished and excused. The sharp sword of the Spirit, the word of God, does not cut to the soul. Has religion changed? Has Satan's enmity to God abated? A religious life once presented difficulties and demanded self-denial. All is made very easy now. And why is this? The professed people of God have compromised with the power of darkness.

There must be a revival of the strait testimony. The path to heaven is no smoother now than in the days of our Saviour. All our sins must be put away. Every darling indulgence that hinders our religious life must be cut off. The right eye or the right hand must be sacrificed if it cause us to offend. Are we willing to renounce our own wisdom and to receive the kingdom of heaven as a little child? Are we willing to part with self-righteousness? Are we willing to give up our chosen worldly associates? Are we willing to sacrifice the approbation of men? The prize of eternal life is of infinite value. Will we put forth efforts and make sacrifices proportionate to the worth of the object to be attained?

Every association we form, however limited, exerts some influence upon us. The extent to which we yield to that influence will be determined by the degree of intimacy, the constancy of the intercourse, and our love and veneration for the one with whom we associate. Thus by acquaintance and association with Christ we may become like Him, the one faultless Example.

Communion with Christ — how unspeakably precious! Such communion it is our privilege to enjoy if we will seek it, if we will make any sacrifice to secure it. When the early disciples heard the words of Christ, they felt their need of Him. They sought, they found, they followed Him. They were with Him in the house, at the table, in the closet, in the field. They were with Him as pupils with a teacher, daily receiving from His lips lessons of holy truth. They looked to Him as servants to their master, to learn their duty. They served Him cheerfully, gladly. They followed Him, as soldiers follow their commander, fighting the good fight of faith. "And they that are with Him are called, and chosen, and faithful."

"He that saith he abideth in Him ought himself also so to walk, even as He walked." "Now if any man have not the spirit of Christ, he is none of His." This conformity to Jesus will not be unobserved by the world. It is a subject of notice and comment. The Christian may not be conscious of the great change; for the more closely he resembles Christ in character the more humble will be his opinion of himself; but it will be seen and felt by all around him. Those who have had the deepest experience in the things of God are the farthest removed from pride or self-exaltation. They have the humblest thoughts of self, and the most exalted conceptions of the glory and excellence of Christ. They feel that the lowest place in His service is too honorable for them.

Moses did not know that his face shone with a brightness painful and terrifying to those who had not, like himself, communed with God. Paul had a very humble opinion of his own advancement in the Christian life. He says: "Not as though I had already attained, either were already perfect." He speaks of himself as the "chief" of sinners. Yet Paul had been highly honored of the Lord. He had been taken in holy vision to the third heaven and had there received revelations of divine glory which he could not be permitted to make known.

John the Baptist was pronounced by our Saviour the greatest of prophets. Yet what a contrast between the language of this man of God and that of many who profess to be ministers of the cross. When asked if he was the Christ, John declares himself unworthy even to unloose his Master's sandals. When his disciples came with the complaint that the attention of the people was turned to the new Teacher, John reminded them that he himself had claimed to be only the forerunner of the Promised One. To Christ, as the bridegroom, belongs the first place in the affections of His people. "The friend of the bridegroom, which standeth and heareth him, rejoiceth greatly because of the bridegroom's voice: this my joy therefore is fulfilled. He must increase, but I must decrease. He that cometh from above is above all." "He that hath received His testimony hath set to his seal that God is true."

It is such workers that are needed in the cause of God today. The self-sufficient, the envious and jealous, the critical and faultfinding, can well be spared from His sacred work. They should not be tolerated in the ministry, even though they may apparently have accomplished some good. God is not straitened for men or means. He calls for workers who are true and faithful, pure and holy; for those who have felt their need of the atoning blood of Christ and the sanctifying grace of His Spirit.

My brethren, God is grieved with your envying and jealousies, your bitterness and dissension. In all these things you are yielding obedience to Satan and not to Christ. When we see men firm in principle, fearless in duty, zealous in the cause of God, yet humble and lowly, gentle and tender, patient toward all, ready to forgive, manifesting love for souls for whom Christ died, we do not need to inquire: Are they Christians? They give unmistakable evidence that they have been with Jesus and learned of Him. When men reveal the opposite traits, when they are proud, vain, frivolous, worldly-minded, avaricious, unkind, censorious, we need not be told with whom they are associating, who is their most intimate friend. They may not believe in witchcraft; but, notwithstanding this, they are holding communion with an evil spirit.

To this class I would say: "Glory not, and lie not against the truth. This wisdom descendeth not from above, but is earthly, sensual, devilish. For where envying and strife is, there is confusion and every evil work. But the wisdom that is from above is first pure, then peaceable, gentle, and easy to be entreated, full of mercy and good fruits, without partiality, and without hypocrisy. And the fruit of righteousness is sown in peace of them that make peace."

When the Pharisees and Sadducees flocked to the baptism of John, that fearless preacher of righteousness addressed them: "O generation of vipers, who hath warned you to flee from the wrath to come? Bring forth therefore fruits meet for repentance." These men were actuated by unworthy motives in coming to John. They were men of poisonous principles and corrupt practices. Yet they had no sense of their true condition. Filled with pride and ambition, they would not hesitate at any means to exalt themselves and strengthen their influence with the people. They came to receive baptism at the hand of John that they might better carry out these designs.

John read their motives, and met them with the searching inquiry: "Who hath warned you to flee from the wrath to come?" Had they heard the voice of God speaking to their hearts they would have given evidence of the fact by bringing forth fruit meet for repentance. No such fruit was seen. They had heard the warning as merely the voice of man. They were charmed with the power and boldness with which John spoke, but the Spirit of God did not send conviction to their hearts and as the sure result bring forth fruit unto eternal life. They gave no evidence of a change of heart. Without the transforming power of the Holy Spirit, John would have them understand that no outward ceremony could benefit them.

The reproof of the prophet is applicable to many in our day. They cannot gainsay the clear and convincing arguments that sustain the truth, but they accept it more as the result of human reasoning than of divine revelation. They have no true sense of their condition as sinners, they manifest no real brokenness of heart; but, like the Pharisees, they feel that it is a great condescension for them to accept the truth.

None are further from the kingdom of heaven than self-righteous formalists, filled with pride at their own attainments, while they are wholly destitute of the spirit of Christ, while envy, jealousy, or love of praise and popularity controls them. They belong to the same class that John addressed as a generation of vipers, children of the wicked one. Such persons are among us, unseen, unsuspected. They serve the cause of Satan more effectively than the vilest profligate; for the latter does not disguise his true character; he appears what he is.

God requires fruit meet for repentance. Without such fruit our profession of faith is of no value. The Lord is able to raise up true believers among those who have never heard His name. "Think not to say within yourselves, We have Abraham to our father: for I say unto you, that God is able of these stones to raise up children unto Abraham."

God is not dependent upon men who are unconverted in heart and life. He will never favor any man who practices iniquity. "And now also the ax is laid unto the root of the trees: therefore every tree which bringeth not forth good fruit is hewn down, and cast into the fire."

Those who laud and flatter the minister, while they neglect the works of righteousness, give unmistakable evidence that they are converted to the minister and not to God. We inquire: "Who hath warned you to flee from the wrath to come?" Was it the voice of the Holy Spirit or merely the voice of man which you heard in the message sent from God? The fruit borne will testify to the character of the tree.

No outward forms can make us clean; no ordinance, administered by the saintliest of men, can take the place of the baptism of the Holy Ghost. The Spirit of God must do its work upon the heart. All who have not experienced its regenerating power are chaff among the wheat. Our Lord has His fan in His hand, and He will thoroughly purge His floor. In the coming day He will discern "between him that serveth God and him that serveth Him not."

The spirit of Christ will be revealed in all who are born of God. Strife and contention cannot arise among those who are controlled by His Spirit. "Be ye clean, that bear the vessels of the Lord." The church will rarely take a higher stand than is taken by her ministers. We need a converted ministry and a converted people. Shepherds who watch for souls as they that must give account will lead the flock on in paths of peace and holiness. Their success in this work will be in proportion to their own growth in grace and knowledge of the truth. When the teachers are sanctified, soul, body, and spirit, they can impress upon the people the importance of such sanctification.

To talk of religious things in a casual way, to pray for spiritual blessings without real soul hunger and living faith, avails little. The wondering crowd that pressed close about Christ realized no vital power from the contact. But when the poor, suffering woman, in her great need, put forth her hand and touched the hem of Jesus' garment, she felt the healing virtue. Hers was the touch of faith. Christ recognized that touch, and He determined there to give a lesson for all

His followers to the close of time. He knew that virtue had gone out of Him, and turning about in the throng He said: "Who touched My clothes?" Surprised at such a question His disciples answered: "Thou seest the multitude thronging Thee, and sayest thou, Who touched Me?"

Jesus fixed His eyes upon her who had done this. She was filled with fear. Great joy was hers, but had she overstepped her duty? Knowing what was done in her, she came trembling and fell at His feet and told Him all the truth. Christ did not reproach her. He gently said: "Go in peace, and be whole of thy plague."

Here was distinguished the casual contact from the touch of faith. Prayer and preaching, without the exercise of living faith in God, will be in vain. But the touch of faith opens to us the divine treasure house of power and wisdom; and thus, through instruments of clay, God accomplishes the wonders of His grace.

This living faith is our great need today. We must know that Jesus is indeed ours, that His spirit is purifying and refining our hearts. If the ministers of Christ had genuine faith, with meekness and love, what a work they might accomplish! What fruit would be seen to the glory of God!

What can I say to you, my brethren, that shall arouse you from your carnal security? I have been shown your perils. There are both believers and unbelievers in the church. Christ represents these two classes in His parable of the vine and its branches. He exhorts His followers: "Abide in Me, and I in you. As the branch cannot bear fruit of itself, except it abide in the vine; no more can ye, except ye abide in Me. I am the Vine, ye are the branches: He that abideth in Me, and I in him, the same bringeth forth much fruit: for without Me ye can do nothing."

There is a wide difference between a pretended union and a real connection with Christ by faith. A profession of the truth places men in the church, but this does not prove that they have a vital connection with the living Vine. A rule is given by which the true disciple may be distinguished from those who claim to follow Christ but have not faith in Him. The one class are fruit bearing, the other, fruitless. The one are often subjected to the pruning knife of God that they may bring forth more fruit; the other, as withered branches, are erelong to be severed from the living Vine.

I am deeply solicitous that our people should preserve the living testimony among them, and that the church should be kept pure from the unbelieving element. Can we conceive of a closer, more intimate relation to Christ than is set forth in the words: "I am the Vine, ye are the branches"? The fibers of the branch are almost identical with those of the vine. The communication of life, strength, and fruitfulness from the trunk to the branches is unobstructed and constant. The root sends its nourishment through the branch. Such is the true believer's relation to Christ. He abides in Christ and draws his nourishment from Him.

This spiritual relation can be established only by the exercise of personal faith. This faith must express on our part supreme preference, perfect reliance, entire consecration. Our will must be wholly yielded to the divine will, our feelings, desires, interests, and honor identified with the prosperity of Christ's kingdom and the honor of His cause, we constantly receiving grace from Him, and Christ accepting gratitude from us.

When this intimacy of connection and communion is formed, our sins are laid upon Christ; His righteousness is imputed to us. He was made sin for us that we might be made the righteousness of God in Him. We have access to God through Him; we are accepted in the Beloved. Whoever by word or deed injures a believer thereby wounds Jesus. Whoever gives a cup of cold water to a disciple because he is a child of God will be regarded by Christ as giving to Him.

It was when Christ was about to take leave of His disciples that He gave them the beautiful emblem of His relation to believers. He had been presenting before them the close union with Himself by which they could maintain spiritual life when His visible presence was withdrawn. To impress it upon their minds He gave them the vine as its most striking and appropriate symbol.

The Jews had always regarded the vine as the most noble of plants and a type of all that was powerful, excellent, and fruitful. "The vine," our Lord would seem to say, "which you prize so highly, is a symbol. I am the reality; I am the True Vine. As a nation you prize the vine; as sinners you should prize Me above all things earthly. The branch cannot live separated from the vine; no more can you live unless you are abiding in Me."

All Christ's followers have as deep an interest in this lesson as had the disciples who listened to His words. In the apostasy, man alienated himself from God. The separation is wide and fearful; but Christ has made provision again to connect us with Himself. The power of evil is so identified with human nature that no man can overcome except by union with Christ. Through this union we receive moral and spiritual power. If we have the spirit of Christ we shall bring forth the fruit of righteousness, fruit that will honor and bless men, and glorify God.

The Father is the vinedresser. He skillfully and mercifully prunes every fruit-bearing branch. Those who share Christ's suffering and reproach now will share His glory hereafter. He "is not ashamed to call them brethren." His angels minister to them. His second appearing will be as the Son of man, thus even in His glory identifying Himself with humanity. To those who have united themselves to Him, He declares: "Though a mother may forget her child, 'yet will not I forget thee. Behold, I have graven thee upon the palms of My hands.' Thou art continually before Me."

Oh, what amazing privileges are proffered us!

Will we put forth most earnest efforts to form this alliance with Christ, through which alone these blessings are attained? Will we break off our sins by righteousness and our iniquities by turning unto the Lord? Skepticism and infidelity are widespread. Christ asked the question: "When the Son of man cometh, shall He find faith on the earth?" We must cherish a living, active faith. The permanence of our faith is the condition of our union.

A union with Christ by living faith is enduring; every other union must perish. Christ first chose us, paying an infinite price for our redemption; and the true believer chooses Christ as first and last and best in everything. But this union costs us something. It is a union of utter dependence, to be entered into by a proud being. All who form this union must feel their need of the atoning blood of Christ. They must have a change of heart. They must submit their own will to the will of God. There will be a struggle with outward and internal obstacles. There must be a painful work of detachment as well as a work of attachment. Pride, selfishness, vanity, worldliness—sin in all its forms—must be overcome if we would enter into a union with Christ. The reason why many find the Christian life so deplorably hard, why they are so fickle, so variable, is that they try to attach themselves to Christ without first detaching themselves from these cherished idols.

After the union with Christ has been formed, it can be preserved only by earnest prayer and untiring effort. We must resist, we must deny, we must conquer self. Through the grace of Christ, by courage, by faith, by watchfulness, we may gain the victory.

Believers become one in Christ, but one branch cannot be sustained by another. The nourishment must be obtained through the vital connection with the vine. We must feel our utter dependence on Christ. We must live by faith on the

Son of God. That is the meaning of the injunction: "Abide in Me." The life we live in the flesh is not to the will of men, not to please our Lord's enemies, but to serve and honor Him who loved us and gave Himself for us. A mere assent to this union, while the affections are not detached from the world, its pleasures and its dissipations, only emboldens the heart in disobedience.

As a people we are sadly destitute of faith and love. Our efforts are altogether too feeble for the time of peril in which we live. The pride and self-indulgence, the impiety and iniquity, by which we are surrounded have an influence upon us. Few realize the importance of shunning, so far as possible, all associations unfriendly to religious life. In choosing their surroundings, few make their spiritual prosperity the first consideration.

Parents flock with their families to the cities because they fancy it easier to obtain a livelihood there than in the country. The children, having nothing to do when not in school, obtain a street education. From evil associates they acquire habits of vice and dissipation. The parents see all this; but it will require a sacrifice to correct their error, and they stay where they are until Satan gains full control of their children. Better sacrifice any and every worldly consideration than to imperil the precious souls committed to your care. They will be assailed by temptations, and should be taught to meet them; but it is your duty to cut off every influence, to break up every habit, to sunder every tie, that keeps you from the most free, open, and hearty committal of yourselves and your family to God.

Instead of the crowded city seek some retired situation where your children will be, so far as possible, shielded from temptation, and there train and educate them for usefulness. The prophet Ezekiel thus enumerates the causes that led to Sodom's sin and destruction: "Pride, fullness of bread, and abundance of idleness was in her and in her daughters, neither did she strengthen the hand of the poor and needy." All who would escape the doom of Sodom must shun the course that brought God's judgments upon that wicked city.

My brethren, you are disregarding the most sacred claims of God by your neglect to consecrate yourselves and your children to Him. Many of you are reposing in false security, absorbed in selfish interests, and attracted by earthly treasures. You fear no evil. Danger seems a great way off. You will be deceived, deluded, to your eternal ruin unless you arouse and with penitence and deep humiliation return unto the Lord.

Again and again has the voice from heaven addressed you. Will you obey this voice? Will you heed the counsel of the True Witness to seek the gold tried in the fire, the white raiment, and the eyesalve? The gold is faith and love, the white raiment is the righteousness of Christ, the eyesalve is that spiritual discernment which will enable you to see the wiles of Satan and shun them, to detect sin and abhor it, to see truth and obey it.

The deadly lethargy of the world is paralyzing your senses. Sin no longer appears repulsive because you are blinded by Satan. The judgments of God are soon to be poured out upon the earth. "Escape for thy life" is the warning from the angels of God. Other voices are heard saying: "Do not become excited; there is no cause for special alarm." Those who are at ease in Zion cry "Peace and safety," while heaven declares that swift destruction is about to come upon the transgressor. The young, the frivolous, the pleasure loving, consider these warnings as idle tales and turn from them with a jest. Parents are inclined to think their children about right in the matter, and all sleep on at ease. Thus it was at the destruction of the old world and when Sodom and Gomorrah were consumed by fire. On the night prior to their destruction the cities of the plain rioted in pleasure. Lot was derided for his fears and warnings. But it was these scoffers that perished in the flames. That very night the door of mercy was forever closed to the wicked, careless inhabitants of Sodom.

It is God who holds in His hands the destiny of souls. He will not always be mocked; He will not always be trifled with. Already His judgments are in the land. Fierce and awful tempests leave destruction and death in their wake. The devouring fire lays low the desolate forest and the crowded city. Storm and shipwreck await those who journey upon the deep. Accident and calamity threaten all who travel upon the land. Hurricanes, earthquakes, sword and famine, follow in quick succession. Yet the hearts of men are hardened. They recognize not the warning voice of God. They will not flee to the only refuge from the gathering storm.

Many who have been placed upon the walls of Zion, to watch with eagle eye for the approach of danger and lift the voice of warning, are themselves asleep. The very ones who should be most active and vigilant in this hour of peril are neglecting their duty and bringing upon themselves the blood of souls.

My brethren, beware of the evil heart of unbelief. The word of God is plain and close in its restrictions; it interferes with your selfish indulgence; therefore you do not obey it. The testimonies of His Spirit call your attention to the Scriptures, point out your defects of character, and rebuke your sins; therefore you do not heed them. And to justify your carnal, ease-loving course you begin to doubt whether the testimonies are from God. If you would obey their teachings you would be assured of their divine origin. Remember, your unbelief does not affect their truthfulness. If they are from God they will stand. Those who seek to lessen the faith of God's people in these testimonies, which have been in the church for the last thirty-six years, are fighting against God.

It is not the instrument whom you slight and insult, but God, who has spoken to you in these warnings and reproofs.

In the instruction given by our Saviour to His disciples are words of admonition especially applicable to us: "Take heed to yourselves, lest at any time your hearts be overcharged with surfeiting, and drunkenness, and cares of this life, and so that day come upon you unawares." Watch, pray, work—this is the true life of faith. "Pray always;" that is, be ever in the spirit of prayer, and then you will be in readiness for your Lord's coming.

The watchmen are responsible for the condition of the people. While you open the door to pride, envy, doubt, and other sins, there will be strife, hatred, and every evil work. Jesus, the meek and lowly One, asks an entrance as your guest; but you are afraid to bid Him enter. He has spoken to us in both the Old and the New Testament; He is speaking to us still by His Spirit and His providences. His instructions are designed to make men true to God and true to themselves.

Jesus took upon Himself man's nature, that He might leave a pattern for humanity, complete, perfect. He proposes to make us like Himself, true in every purpose, feeling, and thought—true in heart, soul, and life. This is Christianity. Our fallen nature must be purified, ennobled, consecrated by obedience to the truth. Christian faith will never harmonize with worldly principles; Christian integrity is opposed to all deception and pretense. The man who cherishes the most of Christ's love in the soul, who reflects the Saviour's image most perfectly, is in the sight of God the truest, most noble, most honorable man upon the earth.

CHRISTIAN UNITY

"I beseech you, brethren, by the name of our Lord Jesus Christ, that ye all speak the same thing, and that there be no divisions among you; but that ye be perfectly joined together in the same mind and in the same judgment."

Union is strength; division is weakness. When those who believe present truth are united, they exert a telling influence. Satan well understands this. Never was he more determined than now to make of none effect the truth of God by causing bitterness and dissension among the Lord's people.

The world is against us, the popular churches are against us, the laws of the land will soon be against us. If there was ever a time when the people of God should press together, it is now. God has committed to us the special truths for this time to make known to the world. The last message of mercy is now going forth. We are dealing with men and women who are judgment bound. How careful should we be in every word and act to follow closely the Pattern, that our example may lead men to Christ. With what care should we seek so to present the truth that others by beholding its beauty and simplicity may be led to receive it. If our characters testify of its sanctifying power, we shall be a continual light to others— living epistles, known and read of all men. We cannot afford now to give place to Satan by cherishing disunion, discord, and strife.

That union and love might exist among His disciples was the burden of our Saviour's last prayer for them prior to His crucifixion. With the agony of the cross before Him, His solicitude was not for Himself, but for those whom He should leave to carry forward His work in the earth. The severest trials awaited them, but Jesus saw that their greatest danger would be from a spirit of bitterness and division. Hence He prayed:

(236)

"Sanctify them through Thy truth: Thy word is truth. As Thou hast sent Me into the world, even so have I also sent them into the world. And for their sakes I sanctify Myself, that they also might be sanctified through the truth. Neither pray I for these alone, but for them also which shall believe on Me through their word; that they all may be one; as Thou, Father, art in Me, and I in Thee, that they also may be one in Us: that the world may believe that Thou hast sent Me."

That prayer of Christ embraces all His followers to the close of time. Our Saviour foresaw the trials and dangers of His people; He is not unmindful of the dissensions and divisions that distract and weaken His church. He is looking upon us with deeper interest and more tender compassion than moves an earthly parent's heart toward a wayward, afflicted child. He bids us learn of Him. He invites our confidence. He bids us open our hearts to receive His love. He has pledged Himself to be our helper.

When Christ ascended to heaven, He left the work on earth in the hands of His servants, the undershepherds. "And He gave some, apostles; and some, prophets; and some, evangelists; and some, pastors and teachers; for the perfecting of the saints, for the work of the ministry, for the edifying of the body of Christ: till we all come in the unity of the faith, and of the knowledge of the Son of God, unto a perfect man, unto the measure of the stature of the fullness of Christ."

In sending forth His ministers our Saviour gave gifts unto men, for through them He communicates to the world the words of eternal life. This is the means which God has ordained for the perfecting of the saints in knowledge and true holiness. The work of Christ's servants is not merely to preach the truth; they are to watch for souls as they that must render account to God. They are to reprove, rebuke, exhort with long-suffering and doctrine.

All who have been benefited by the labors of God's servant should, according to their ability, unite with him in working for the salvation of souls. This is the work of all true believers, ministers and people. They should keep the grand object ever in view, each seeking to fill his proper position in the church, and all working together in order, harmony, and love.

There is nothing selfish or narrow in the religion of Christ. Its principles are diffusive and aggressive. It is represented by Christ as the bright light, as the saving salt, as the transforming leaven. With zeal, earnestness, and devotion the servants of God will seek to spread far and near the knowledge of the truth; yet they will not neglect to labor for the strength and unity of the church. They will watch carefully lest opportunity be given for diversity and division to creep in.

There have of late arisen among us men who profess to be the servants of Christ, but whose work is opposed to that unity which our Lord established in the church. They have original plans and methods of labor. They desire to introduce changes into the church to suit their ideas of progress and imagine that grand results are thus to be secured. These men need to be learners rather than teachers in the school of Christ. They are ever restless, aspiring to accomplish some great work, to do something that will bring honor to themselves. They need to learn that most profitable of all lessons, humility and faith in Jesus. Some are watching their fellow laborers and anxiously endeavoring to point out their errors, when they should rather be earnestly seeking to prepare their own souls for the great conflict before them. The Saviour bids them: "Learn of Me; for I am meek and lowly in heart: and ye shall find rest unto your souls."

Teachers of the truth, missionaries, officers in the church, can do a good work for the Master if they will but purify their own souls by obeying the truth. Every living Christian will be a disinterested worker for God. The Lord has given us a knowledge of His will that we may become channels of light to others. If Christ is abiding in us, we cannot help working for Him. It is impossible to retain the favor of God and enjoy the blessing of a Saviour's love, and yet be indifferent to the danger of those who are perishing in their sins. "Herein is My Father glorified, that ye bear much fruit."

Paul urges the Ephesians to preserve unity and love: "I therefore, the prisoner of the Lord, beseech you that ye walk worthy of the vocation wherewith ye are called, with all lowliness and meekness, with long-suffering, forbearing one another in love; endeavoring to keep the unity of the Spirit in the bond of peace. There is one body, and one Spirit, even as ye are called in one hope of your calling; one Lord, one faith, one baptism, one God and Father of all, who is above all, and through all, and in you all."

The apostle exhorts his brethren to manifest in their lives the power of the truth which he had presented to them. By meekness and gentleness, forbearance and love, they were to exemplify the character of Christ and the blessings of His salvation. There is but one body, and one Spirit, one Lord, one faith. As members of the body of Christ all believers are animated by the same spirit and the same hope. Divisions in the church dishonor the religion of Christ before the world and give occasion to the enemies of truth to justify their course. Paul's instructions were not written alone for the church in his day. God designed that they should be sent down to us. What are we doing to preserve unity in the bonds of peace?

When the Holy Spirit was poured out upon the early church, the brethren loved one another. "They . . . did eat their meat with gladness and singleness of heart, praising God, and having favor with all the people: and the Lord added to the church daily such as should be saved." Those primitive

Christians were few in numbers, without wealth or honor, yet they exerted a mighty influence. The light of the world shone out from them. They were a terror to evildoers wherever their character and their doctrines were known. For this cause they were hated by the wicked and persecuted even unto death.

The standard of holiness is the same today as in the days of the apostles. Neither the promises nor the requirements of God have lost aught of their force. But what is the state of the Lord's professed people as compared with the early church? Where is the Spirit and power of God which then attended the preaching of the gospel? Alas, "how is the gold become dim! how is the most fine gold changed!"

The Lord planted His church as a vine in a fruitful field. With tenderest care He nourished and cherished it, that it might bring forth the fruits of righteousness. His language is: "What could have been done more to My vineyard, that I have not done in it?" But this vine of God's planting has inclined to the earth and entwined its tendrils about human supports. Its branches are extended far and wide, but it bears the fruit of a degenerate vine. The Master of the vineyard declares: "When I looked that it should bring forth grapes, brought it forth wild grapes?"

The Lord has bestowed great blessings upon His church. Justice demands that she return these talents with usury. As the treasures of truth committed to her keeping have increased, her obligations have increased. But instead of improving upon these gifts and going forward unto perfection, she has fallen away from that which she had attained in her earlier experience. The change in her spiritual state has come gradually and almost imperceptibly. As she began to seek the praise and friendship of the world, her faith diminished, her zeal grew languid, her fervent devotion gave place to dead formality. Every advance step toward the world was a step away from God. As pride and worldly ambition have been cherished, the spirit of Christ has departed, and emulation, dissension, and strife have come in to distract and weaken the church.

Paul writes to his Corinthian brethren: "Ye are yet carnal: for whereas there is among you envying, and strife, and divisions, are ye not carnal, and walk as men?" It is impossible for minds distracted by envy and strife to comprehend the deep spiritual truths of God's word. "The natural man receiveth not the things of the Spirit of God: for they are foolishness unto him: neither can he know them, because they are spiritually discerned." We cannot rightly understand or appreciate divine revelation without the aid of that Spirit by whom the word was given.

Those who are appointed to guard the spiritual interests of the church should be careful to set a right example, giving no occasion for envy, jealousy, or suspicion, ever manifesting that same spirit of love, respect, and courtesy which they desire to encourage in their brethren. Diligent heed should be given to the instructions of God's word. Let every manifestation of animosity or unkindness be checked; let every root of bitterness be removed. When trouble arises between brethren, the Saviour's rule should be strictly followed. All possible effort should be made to effect a reconciliation; but if the parties stubbornly persist in remaining at variance, they should be suspended till they can harmonize.

Upon the occurrence of trials in the church let every member examine his own heart to see if the cause of trouble does not exist within. By spiritual pride, a desire to dictate, an ambitious longing for honor or position, a lack of self-control, by the indulgence of passion or prejudice, by instability or lack of judgment, the church may be disturbed and her peace sacrificed.

Difficulties are often caused by the vendors of gossip, whose whispered hints and suggestions poison unsuspecting minds and separate the closest friends. Mischiefmakers are seconded in their evil work by the many who stand with open ears and evil heart, saying: "Report, . . . and we will report it." This sin should not be tolerated among the followers of Christ. No Christian parent should permit gossip to be repeated in the family circle or remarks to be made disparaging the members of the church.

Christians should regard it as a religious duty to repress a spirit of envy or emulation. They should rejoice in the superior reputation or prosperity of their brethren, even when their own character or achievements seem to be cast in the shade. It was the pride and ambition cherished in the heart of Satan that banished him from heaven. These evils are deeply rooted in our fallen nature, and if not removed they will overshadow every good and noble quality and bring forth envy and strife as their baleful fruits.

We should seek for true goodness rather than greatness. Those who possess the mind of Christ will have humble views of themselves. They will labor for the purity and prosperity of the church, and be ready to sacrifice their own interests and desires rather than to cause dissension among their brethren.

Satan is constantly seeking to cause distrust, alienation, and malice among God's people. We shall be often tempted to feel that our rights are invaded, when there is no real cause for such feelings. Those whose love for self is stronger than their love for Christ and His cause will place their own interests first and resort to almost any expedient to guard and maintain them. When they consider themselves injured by their brethren, some will even go to law instead of following the Savior's rule. Even many who appear to be conscientious Christians are hindered by pride and self-esteem from going privately to those they think in error, that they may talk the matter over in the spirit of Christ and pray for one another. Contentions strife, and lawsuits between brethren are a disgrace to the cause of truth. Those who take such a course expose the church to the ridicule of her enemies and cause the powers of darkness to triumph. They are piercing the wounds of Christ afresh and putting Him to an open shame. By ignoring the authority of the church they show contempt for God, who gave to the church its authority.

Paul writes to the Galatians: "I would they were even cut off which trouble you. For, brethren, ye have been called unto liberty; only use not liberty for an occasion to the flesh, but by love serve one another. For all the law is fulfilled in one word, even in this; Thou shalt love thy neighbor as thyself. But if ye bite and devour one another, take heed that ye be not consumed one of another. This I say then, Walk in the Spirit, and ye shall not fulfill the lust of the flesh."

False teachers had brought to the Galatians doctrines that were opposed to the gospel of Christ. Paul sought to expose and correct these errors. He greatly desired that the false teachers might be separated from the church, but their influence had affected so many of the believers that it seemed hazardous to take action against them. There was danger of causing strife and division which would be ruinous to the spiritual interests of the church. He therefore sought to impress upon his brethren the importance of trying to help one another in love. He declared that all the requirements of the law setting forth our duty to our fellow men are fulfilled in love to one another. He warned them that if they indulged hatred and strife, dividing into parties, and like the brutes biting and devouring one another, they would bring upon themselves present unhappiness and future ruin. There was but one way to prevent these terrible evils and that was, as the apostle enjoined upon them, to "walk in the Spirit." They must by constant prayer seek the guidance of the Holy Spirit, which would lead them to love and unity.

A house divided against itself cannot stand. When Christians contend, Satan comes in to take control. How often has he succeeded in destroying the peace and harmony of churches. What fierce controversies, what bitterness, what hatred, has a very little matter started! What hopes have been blasted, how many families have been rent asunder by discord and contention!

Paul charged his brethren to beware lest in trying to correct the faults of others they should commit sins equally great themselves. He warns them that hatred, emulation, wrath, strife, seditions, heresies, and envyings are as truly the works of the flesh as are lasciviousness, adultery, drunkenness, and murder, and will as surely close the gate of heaven against the guilty.

Christ declares: "Whosoever shall offend one of these little ones that believe in Me, it is better for him that a millstone were hanged about his neck, and he were cast into the sea." Whoever by willful deception or by a wrong example misleads a disciple of Christ is guilty of a great sin. Whoever would make him an object of slander or ridicule is insulting Jesus. Our Saviour marks every wrong done to His followers.

How were those punished who in olden time made light of what God had chosen as sacred to Himself? Belshazzar and his thousand lords profaned the golden vessels of Jehovah and praised the idols of Babylon. But the God whom they defied was a witness of the unholy scene. In the midst of their sacrilegious mirth a bloodless hand was seen tracing mysterious characters upon the palace wall. Filled with terror, king and courtiers heard their doom pronounced by the servant of the Most High.

Let those who delight to trace words of calumny and falsehood against the servants of Christ remember that God is a witness of their deeds. Their slanderous touch is not profaning soulless vessels but the characters of those whom Christ has purchased by His blood. The hand which traced the characters upon the walls of Belshazzar's palace keeps faithful record of every act of injustice or oppression committed against God's people.

Sacred history presents striking examples of the Lord's jealous care for the weakest of His children. During the journeying of Israel in the wilderness the weary and feeble ones who had fallen behind the body of the people were attacked and slain by the cowardly and cruel Amalekites. Afterward Israel made war with the Amalekites and defeated them. "And the Lord said unto Moses, Write this for a memorial in a book, and rehearse it in the ears of Joshua: for I will utterly put out the remembrance of Amalek from under heaven." Again the charge was repeated by Moses just before his death, that it might not be forgotten by his posterity: "Remember what Amalek did unto thee by the way, when ye were come forth out of Egypt; how he met thee by the way, and smote the hindmost of thee, even all that were feeble behind thee, when thou wast faint and weary; and he feared not God. . . . Thou shalt blot out the remembrance of Amalek from under heaven; thou shalt not forget it."

If God thus punished the cruelty of a heathen nation, how must He regard those who, professing to be His people, will make war upon their own brethren who are worn and wearied laborers in His cause? Satan has great power over those who yield to his control. It was the chief priests and elders—the religious teachers of the people—that urged on the murderous throng from the judgment hall to Calvary. There are hearts today among the professed followers of Christ inspired by the same spirit that clamored for the crucifixion of our Saviour. Let the workers of evil remember that to all their acts there is one witness, a holy, sin-hating God. He will bring all their works into judgment, with every secret thing.

"We then that are strong ought to bear the infirmities of

the weak, and not to please ourselves. Let every one of us please his neighbor for his good to edification. For even Christ pleased not Himself." As Christ has pitied and helped us in our weakness and sinfulness, so should we pity and help others. Many are perplexed with doubt, burdened with infirmities, weak in faith, and unable to grasp the unseen; but a friend whom they can see, coming to them in Christ's stead, can be as a connecting link to fasten their trembling faith upon God. Oh, this is a blessed work! Let not pride and selfishness prevent us from doing the good which we may do if we will work in Christ's name and with a loving, tender spirit.

"Brethren, if a man be overtaken in a fault, ye which are spiritual, restore such an one in the spirit of meekness; considering thyself, lest thou also be tempted. Bear ye one another's burdens, and so fulfill the law of Christ." Here, again, our duty is plainly set before us. How can the professed followers of Christ so lightly regard these inspired injunctions? Not long since I received a letter describing a circumstance in which a brother had manifested indiscretion. Although it occurred years ago, and was a very small matter, hardly worthy of a second thought, the writer stated that it had forever destroyed her confidence in that brother. If that sister's life should show upon review no greater errors, it would be indeed a marvel, for human nature is very weak. I have been and am still fellowshiping as brethren and sisters those who have been guilty of grave sins and who even now do not see their sins as God sees them. But the Lord bears with these persons, and why should not I? He will yet cause His Spirit so to impress their hearts that sin will appear to them as it appeared to Paul, exceedingly sinful.

We know but little of our own hearts and have but little sense of our own need of the mercy of God. This is why we cherish so little of that sweet compassion which Jesus manifests toward us and which we should manifest toward one another. We should remember that our brethren are weak, erring mortals like ourselves. Suppose that a brother has through unwatchfulness been overborne by temptation and contrary to his general conduct has committed some error, what course shall be pursued toward him? We learn from the Bible that men whom God had used to do a great and good work committed grave sins. The Lord did not pass these by unrebuked, neither did He cast off His servants. When they repented, He graciously forgave them and revealed to them His presence and wrought through them. Let poor, weak mortals consider how great is their own need of pity and forbearance from God and from their brethren. Let them beware how they judge and condemn others. We should give heed to the instruction of the apostle: "Ye which are spiritual, restore such an one in the spirit of meekness; considering thyself, lest thou also be tempted." We may fall under temptation and need all the forbearance which we are called to exercise toward the offender. "With what judgment ye judge, ye shall be judged and with what measure ye mete, it shall be measured to you again."

The apostle adds a caution to the independent and self-confident: "If a man think himself to be something, when he is nothing, he deceiveth himself. . . . Every man shall bear his own burden." He who considers himself superior in judgment and experience to his brethren and despises their counsel and admonition, evinces that he is in a dangerous delusion. The heart is deceitful. He should test his character and life by the Bible standard. God's word sheds an unerring light upon the pathway of man's life. Notwithstanding the many influences which arise to divert and distract the mind, those who honestly seek God for wisdom will be guided into the right course. Every man must at last stand or fall for himself, not according to the opinion of the party that sustains or opposes him, not according to the judgment of any man, but according to his real character in the sight of God. The church may warn, counsel, and admonish, but it cannot compel any to take a right course. Whoever persists in disregarding the word of God must bear his own burden, answer to God for himself, and suffer the consequences of his own course.

The Lord has given us in His word definite, unmistakable instructions, by obedience to which we may preserve union and harmony in the church. Brethren and sisters, are you giving heed to these inspired injunctions? Are you Bible readers and doers of the word? Are you striving to fulfill the prayer of Christ that His followers might be one? "The God of patience and consolation grant you to be like-minded one toward another according to Christ Jesus: that ye may with one mind and one mouth glorify God." "Be perfect, be of good comfort, be of one mind, live in peace; and the God or love and peace shall be with you."

TESTIMONY FOR THE CHURCH

THE WORK OF THE GOSPEL MINISTER

There are many things that need to be corrected in the Upper Columbia and North Pacific Conferences.* The Creator expected the brethren there to bear fruit according to the light and privileges bestowed upon them, but in this He has been disappointed. He has given them every advantage; but they have not improved in meekness, godliness, benevolence. They have not pursued that course of life, have not revealed that character nor exercised that influence, which would tend most to honor their Creator, ennoble themselves, and make them a blessing to their fellow men. Selfishness exists in their hearts. They love to have their own way and seek their own ease, honor, and wealth, and their own pleasure in its grosser or more refined forms. If we pursue the course of the world and follow the bent of our own minds, will that work for our best good? Does not God, who formed man, look for something better from us?

"Be ye therefore followers of God, as dear children." Christians must be like Christ. They should have the same spirit, exert the same influence, and have the same moral excellence that He possessed. The idolatrous and corrupt in heart must repent and turn to God. Those who are proud and self-righteous must abase self and become penitent and meek and lowly in heart. The worldly-minded must have the tendrils of the heart removed from the rubbish of the world, around which they are clinging, and entwined about God; they must

---

*These were local conferences in what is now the North Pacific Union Conference.—*Trustees of Ellen G. White*.

become spiritually minded. The dishonest and untruthful must become just and true. The ambitious and covetous must be hid in Jesus and seek His glory, not their own. They must despise their own holiness and lay up their treasure above. The prayerless must feel the need of both secret and family prayer, and must make their supplications to God with great earnestness.

As the worshipers of the true and living God we should bear fruit corresponding to the light and privileges we enjoy. Many are worshiping idols instead of the Lord of heaven and earth. Anything that men love and trust in instead of loving the Lord and trusting wholly in Him becomes an idol and is thus registered in the books of heaven. Even blessings are often turned into a curse. The sympathies of the human heart, strengthened by exercise, are sometimes perverted until they become a snare. If one is reproved, there are always some who will sympathize with him. They entirely overlook the harm that has been done to God's cause by the wrong influence of one whose life and character do not in any way resemble those of the pattern. God sends His servants with a message to the people professing to be followers of Christ; but some are children of God only in name, and they reject the warning.

God has in a wonderful manner endowed man with reasoning powers. He who fitted the tree to bear its burden of goodly fruit has made man capable of bearing the precious fruits of righteousness. He has planted man in His garden and tenderly cared for him, and He expects him to bear fruit. In the parable of the fig tree Christ says: "Behold, these three years I come seeking fruit." For more than two years has the Owner looked for the fruit that He has a right to expect from these conferences, but how has His search been rewarded? How anxiously we watch a favorite tree or plant, expecting it to reward our care by producing buds, blossoms, and fruit; and how disappointed we are to find upon it nothing but leaves. With how much more anxiety and tender interest does the heavenly Father watch the spiritual growth of those whom He has made in His own image and for whom He condescended to give His Son that they may be elevated, ennobled, and glorified.

The Lord has His appointed agencies to meet men in their errors and backslidings. His messengers are sent to bear a plain testimony to arouse them from their sleepy condition and to open the precious words of life, the Holy Scriptures, to their understanding. These men are not to be preachers merely, but ministers, light bearers, faithful watchmen, who will see the threatened danger and warn the people. They must resemble Christ in their earnest zeal, in their thoughtful tact, in their personal efforts—in short, in all their ministry. They are to have a vital connection with God, and are to become so familiar with the prophecies and the practical lessons of the Old and the New Testament that they may bring from the treasure house of God's word things new and old.

Some of these ministers make a mistake in the preparation of their discourses. They arrange every minutia with such exactness that they give the Lord no room to lead and impress their minds. Every point is fixed, stereotyped as it were, and they cannot depart from the plan marked out. This course, if continued, will cause them to become narrow-minded, circumscribed in their views, and will soon leave them as destitute of life and energy as are the hills of Gilboa of dew and rain. They must throw the soul open and let the Holy Spirit take possession to impress the mind. When everything is laid out beforehand, and they feel that they cannot vary from these set discourses, the effect is little better than that produced by reading a sermon.

God would have His ministers wholly dependent upon Him, but at the same time they should be thoroughly furnished unto every good work. No subject can be treated before all congregations in the same manner. The Spirit of God, if allowed to do its work, will impress the mind with ideas calculated to meet the cases of those who need help. But the tame, formal discourses of many who enter the desk have very little of the vitalizing power of the Holy Spirit in them. The habit of preaching such discourses will effectually destroy a minister's usefulness and ability. This is one reason why the efforts of the workers in _____ and _____ have not been more successful. God has had too little to do with impressing the mind in the desk.

Another cause of failure in these conferences is that the people to whom God's messenger is sent wish to mold his ideas to theirs and to put into his mouth the words that he should speak. God's watchmen must not study how they shall please the people, nor listen to their words and utter them; but they must listen to hear what saith the Lord, what is His word for the people. If they rely upon discourses prepared years before they may fail to meet the necessities of the occasion. Their hearts should be laid open so that the Lord may impress their minds, and then they will be able to give the people the precious truth warm from heaven. God is not pleased with those narrow-minded ministers who devote their God-given powers to matters of little moment and fail to grow in divine knowledge to the full stature of men in Christ Jesus. He would have His ministers possess breadth of mind and true moral courage. Such men will be prepared to meet opposition and surmount difficulties, and will lead the flock of God instead of being led by them.

There is altogether too little of the Spirit and power of God in the labor of the watchmen. The Spirit which characterized that wonderful meeting on the Day of Pentecost is waiting to manifest its power upon the men who are now standing between the living and the dead as ambassadors for God. The power which stirred the people so mightily in the 1844 movement will again be revealed. The third angel's message will go forth, not in whispered tones, but with a loud voice.

Many who profess to have great light are walking in sparks of their own kindling. They need to have their lips touched with a live coal from off the altar, that they may pour forth the truth like men who are inspired. Too many go into the desk with mechanical discourses that have no light from heaven in them.

There is too much of self and too little of Jesus in the ministry of all denominations. The Lord uses humble men to proclaim His messages. Had Christ come in the majesty of a king, with the pomp which attends the great men of earth, many would have accepted Him. But Jesus of Nazareth did not dazzle the senses with a display of outward glory and make this the foundation of their reverence. He came as a humble man to be the Teacher and Exemplar as well as the Redeemer of the race. Had He encouraged pomp, had He come followed by a retinue of the great men of earth, how could He have taught humility? how could He have presented such burning truths as in His Sermon upon the Mount? His example was such as He wished all His followers to imitate. Where would have been the hope of the lowly in life had He come in exaltation and dwelt as a king upon the earth? Jesus knew the needs of the world better than they themselves knew. He did not come as an angel, clothed with the panoply of heaven, but as a man. Yet combined with His humility was an inherent power and grandeur that awed men while they loved Him. Although possessing such loveliness, such an unassuming appearance, He moved among them with the dignity and power of a heaven-born king. The people were amazed, confounded. They tried to reason the matter out; but, unwilling to renounce their own ideas, they yielded to doubts, clinging to the old expectation of a Saviour to come in earthly grandeur.

When Jesus delivered the Sermon on the Mount, His disciples were gathered close about Him, and the multitude, filled with intense curiosity, also pressed as near as possible. Something more than usual was expected. Eager faces and listening attitudes gave evidence of the deep interest. The attention of all seemed riveted upon the speaker. His eyes were lighted up with unutterable love, and the heavenly expression upon His countenance gave meaning to every word uttered. Angels of heaven were in that listening throng. There, too, was the adversary of souls with his evil angels, prepared to counteract, as far as possible, the influence of the heavenly Teacher. The truths there uttered have come down through the ages and have been a light amid the general darkness of error. Many have found in them that which the soul most needed—a sure foundation of faith and practice. But in these words spoken by the greatest Teacher the world has ever known there is no parade of human eloquence. The language is plain, and the thoughts and sentiments are marked with the greatest simplicity. The poor, the unlearned, the most simple-minded, can understand them. The Lord of heaven was in mercy and kindness addressing the souls He came to save. He taught them as one having authority, speaking the words of eternal life.

All should copy the Pattern as closely as possible. While they cannot possess the consciousness of power which Jesus had, they can so connect with the Source of strength that Jesus can abide in them and they in Him, and so His spirit and His power will be revealed in them.

"Walk in the light, as He is in the light." It is earthliness and selfishness that separate from God. The messages from heaven are of a character to arouse opposition. The faithful witnesses for Christ and the truth will reprove sin. Their words will be like a hammer to break the flinty heart, like a fire to consume the dross. There is constant need of earnest, decided messages of warning. God will have men who are true to duty. At the right time He sends His faithful messengers to do a work similar to that of Elijah.

MINISTERS AS EDUCATORS

The state of things in _____ is a matter of deep regret. That which the Lord has been pleased to present before me has been of a character to give me pain. Whoever shall labor here or in _____ hereafter will have uphill work and must carry a heavy load because the work has not been faithfully bound off, but has been left in an unfinished state. And this is the more grievous because the failure is not wholly chargeable to worldliness and want of love for Jesus and the truth on the part of the people; but much of it lies at the door of the ministers, who, while laboring among them, have signally failed in their duty. They have not had the missionary spirit; they have not felt the great need of thoroughly educating the people in all branches of the work, in all places where the truth has gained a foothold. The work done thoroughly for one soul is done for many. But the ministers have not realized this and have failed to educate persons who in their turn should stand steadfast in defense of the truth and educate others. This loose, slack, halfway manner of working is displeasing to God.

A minister may enjoy sermonizing, for it is the pleasant part of the work and is comparatively easy; but no minister should be measured by his ability as a speaker. The harder part comes after he leaves the desk, in watering the seed sown. The interest awakened should be followed up by personal labor,—visiting, holding Bible readings, teaching how to search the Scriptures, praying with families and interested ones, seeking to deepen the impression made upon hearts and consciences.

There are many who have no desire to become acquainted with their unbelieving neighbors and those with whom they come in contact, and they do not feel it their duty to overcome this reluctance. The truth they teach and the love of Jesus should have great power to help them to overcome this feeling. They should remember that they must meet these very men and women in the judgment. Have they left words unsaid that should have been spoken? Have they felt interest enough for souls, to warn, to entreat, to pray for them, to make every effort to win them to Christ? Have they united discrimination with zeal, heeding the direction of the apostle: "Of some have compassion, making a difference: and others save with fear, pulling them out of the fire; hating even the garment spotted by the flesh"?

There is earnest work to be done by all who would be successful in their ministry. I entreat you, dear brethren, ministers of Christ, not to fail in your appointed duty to educate the people to work intelligently to sustain the cause of God in all its varied interests. Christ was an educator, and His ministers, who represent Him, should be educators. When they neglect to teach the people their obligation to God in tithes and offerings, they neglect one important part of the work which their Master has left them to do, and "Unfaithful servant" is written against their names in the books of heaven. The church come to the conclusion that if these things were essential, the minister, whom God has sent to present the truth to them, would tell them so; and they feel secure and at ease while neglecting their duty. They go contrary to the express requirements of God and as the result become lifeless and inefficient. They do not exert a saving influence upon the world, and they are represented by Christ as salt without savor.

Companies of Sabbathkeepers may be raised up in many places. Often they will not be large companies; but they must not be neglected, they must not be left to die for want of proper personal effort and training. The work should not be left prematurely. See that all are intelligent in the truth, established in the faith, and interested in every branch of the work, before leaving them for another field. And then, like the apostle Paul, visit them often to see how they do. Oh, the slack work that is done by many who claim to be commissioned of God to preach His word, makes angels weep.

The cause might be in a healthful condition in every field, and it would be if ministers would trust in God and allow nothing to come between them and their work. Laborers are needed much more than mere preachers, but the two offices must be united. It has been proved in the missionary field that, whatever may be the preaching talent, if the laboring part is neglected, if the people are not taught how to work, how to conduct meetings, how to act their part in missionary labor, how to reach people successfully, the work will be nearly a failure. There is much to be done in the Sabbath school work also in bringing the people to realize their obligation and to act their part. God calls them to work for Him, and the ministers should guide their efforts.

The sad fact is apparent that the work in these fields ought to be years in advance of what it now is. The negligence on the part of the ministers has discouraged the people, and the lack of interest, self-sacrifice, and appreciation of the work on the part of the people has discouraged the ministers. "Two years behind" stands recorded in the Ledger of Heaven. This people might have done much to advance the cause of truth and to bring souls to Christ in different localities, and at the same time might themselves have been growing in grace and in the knowledge of the truth, had they improved their opportunities and made the most of their privileges, walking, not with murmuring and complaining, but in faith and courage. Eternity alone can reveal how much has been lost during these years—how many souls have been left to perish through this state of things. The loss is too great to be computed. God has been insulted. The course pursued has brought upon the cause a wound which will be years in healing; and if the mistakes that have been made are not seen and repented of, they will surely be repeated.

A realization of these facts has brought unspeakable burdens upon me, driving sleep from my eyes. At times it has seemed that my heart would break, and I could only pray, while giving vent to my anguish in weeping aloud. Oh, I felt so sorry for my Saviour! His searching for fruit amid the leaf-covered branches of the fig tree and His disappointment in finding "nothing but leaves" seemed so vivid before my eyes. I felt that I could not have it so. I could in no way be reconciled to the past years of neglect of duty on the part of ministers and people. I feared that the withering curse passed upon the fig tree might be the fate of these careless ones. The terrible neglect of doing the work and fulfilling the mission which God has entrusted to them incurs a loss which none of us can afford to sustain. It is running a risk too fearful to contemplate and too terrible to be ventured at any time in our religious history, but especially now, when time is so short and so much is to be done in this day of God's preparation. All heaven is earnestly engaged for the salvation of men; light is coming from God to His people, defining their duty, so that none need err from the right path. But God does not send His light and truth to be lightly esteemed and trifled with. If the people are inattentive, they are doubly guilty before Him.

As Christ was riding into Jerusalem, on the crest of Olivet He broke forth in uncontrollable grief, exclaiming in broken utterances as He looked upon Jerusalem: "If thou hadst known, even thou, at least in this thy day, the things which belong unto thy peace! but now they are hid from thine eyes." He wept not for Himself, but for the despisers of His mercy, long-suffering, and forbearance. The course taken by the hard-hearted and impenitent inhabitants of the doomed city is similar to the attitude of churches and individuals toward Christ at the present time. They neglect His requirements and despise His forbearance. There is a form of godliness, there is ceremonial worship, there are complimentary prayers, but the real power is wanting. The heart is not softened by grace, but is cold and unimpressible. Many, like the Jews, are blinded by unbelief and know not the time of their visitation. So far as the truth is concerned, they have had every advantage, God has been appealing to them for years in warnings, reproofs, corrections, and instruction in righteousness; but special directions have been given only to be disregarded and placed on a level with common things.

DUTY TO REPROVE MONEY LOVERS

Many who are numbered with the believers are not really with them in faith and principle. They are doing exactly that which Jesus told them not to do—seeking to lay up treasures upon the earth. Christ said: "Lay not up for yourselves treasures upon earth: . . . but lay up for yourselves treasures in heaven: . . . for where your treasure is, there will your heart be also." Here is one danger which threatens Christians. They are not obedient to Christ's positive directions. They show no real faith and confidence in God. In order to gain riches they accumulate burdens and cares until their minds are almost wholly engrossed with them. They are eager for gains and always anxious for fear of losses. "The more money and lands they possess the more eager are they for more." They are drunken, but not with wine; they stagger, but not with strong drink." They are surfeited with the cares of this life, which affect them as strong drink does the drunkard. They are so blinded by selfishness that they work night and day to secure perishable treasures. Their eternal interests are neglected; they have no time to attend to these things. The great matters of truth are not kept in mind, as is evidenced by their words, their plans, and their course of action. What if souls around them perish in their sins? This is not of so much consequence to them as their earthly treasures. Let souls for whom Christ died sink to ruin; they have no time to save them. In laying plans for earthly gain they show skill and talent; but these precious qualities are not devoted to winning souls to Christ, to the upbuilding of the Redeemer's kingdom. Are not the senses of such persons perverted? Are they not drunken with the intoxicating cup of worldliness? Is not reason laid aside, and have not selfish aims and purposes become the ruling power? The work of preparing themselves to stand in the day of the Lord, and employing their God-given abilities in helping to prepare a people for that day, is considered too tame and unsatisfying.

The Saviour of the world has presented a most profitable business in which rich and poor, learned and unlearned, may engage. All may safely lay up for themselves "a treasure in the heavens that faileth not." This is investing their powers on the right side. It is putting out their talents to the exchangers.

Jesus illustrated His teaching by the case of a substantial farmer whom the Lord had greatly favored. The Lord had blessed his grounds, causing them to produce plentifully, thus placing it in his power to exercise liberality to others not so greatly blessed. But when he found that his grounds had produced so abundantly, far beyond his expectation, instead of planning how to relieve the poor in their necessities, he began to devise means to secure all to himself. As he saw the gifts of heaven rolling into his garners he poured not out his soul in thanksgiving to the bounteous Giver, neither did he consider that this great blessing had brought additional responsibility. In the pure selfishness of his nature he inquires: "What shall I do, because I have no room where to bestow my fruits?" Taking counsel with his own covetous heart, he said: "This will I do: I will pull down my barns, and build greater; and there will I bestow all my fruits and my goods. And I will say to my soul, Soul, thou hast much goods laid up for many years; take thine ease, eat, drink, and be merry." The means of real enjoyment and elevation of soul are activity, self-control, holy purposes; but all that this man proposed to do with the bounties God had given him was to degrade the soul. And what was the result? "God said unto him, Thou fool, this night thy soul shall be required of thee: then whose shall those things be, which thou hast provided? So is he that layeth up treasure for himself, and is not rich toward God."

This poor rich man possessed great earthly treasure, but was destitute of the true riches. How many today are under condemnation for a similar reason. Streams of salvation are poured in upon us from the throne of God. Temporal blessings are given, but they are not improved to bless humanity or to glorify God. The Lord is our gracious benefactor. He has brought light and immortality to light through Jesus Christ. Yes, through Jesus all our blessings come. Oh, that every tongue would acknowledge the great Giver! Let every voice, in clear and joyful strains, proclaim the glad tidings that through Jesus the future, immortal life is opened to us; and invitations are given for all to accept this great boon. All the treasures of heaven are brought within our reach, waiting our demand. Can we be surprised that this poor rich man was called a fool because he turned away from eternal riches, the priceless gift of immortal life, the eternal weight of glory, and was satisfied with perishable, earthly treasures?

God tests men, some in one way, and some in another. He tests some by bestowing upon them His rich bounties, and others by withholding His favors. He proves the rich to see if they will love God, the Giver, and their neighbor as themselves. When man makes a right use of these bounties, God is pleased; He can then trust him with greater responsibilities. The Lord reveals man's relative estimate of time and eternity, of earth and heaven. He has admonished us: "If riches increase, set not your heart upon them." They have a value when used for the good of others and the glory of God; but no earthly treasure is to be your portion, your god, or your savior.

My brethren, the world will never believe that you are in earnest in your faith until you have less to say about temporal things and more about the realities of the eternal world. The Lord is coming, but many who profess the faith do not realize that that event is nigh. They cannot fasten their faith upon the revealed purposes of God. With some, the passion for money-making has become all-absorbing, and earthly riches have eclipsed the heavenly treasure. Eternal things have faded from the mind as of minor consequence, while worldliness has come in like a flood. The great question is: How can I make money? Men are alive to every hope of gain. They try a thousand plans and devices, among them various inventions and patent rights. Some dig in the earth for the precious metals, others deal in bank stock, still others till the soil; but all have the one object in view of making money. They become bewildered and even insane in the pursuit of wealth, yet they refuse to see the advantage of securing an immortal inheritance.

When Christ was on earth, He was brought in contact with some whose imaginations were fevered with the hope of worldly gain. They were never at rest, but were constantly trying something new, and their extravagant expectations were aroused only to be disappointed. Jesus knew the wants of the human heart, which are the same in all ages; and He called their attention to the only permanent riches. "The kingdom of heaven," said He, "is like unto treasure hid in a field; the which when a man hath found, he hideth, and for joy thereof goeth and selleth all that he hath, and buyeth that field." He tells men of treasure beyond estimate, which is within the reach of all. He came to earth to guide their minds in their search for this treasure. The way is marked out; the very poorest who will follow Him will be made richer than the most wealthy upon earth who know not Jesus, and they will be made increasingly rich by sharing their happiness with others.

"Lay not up for yourselves treasures upon earth, where moth and rust doth corrupt, and where thieves break through and steal: but lay up for yourselves treasures in heaven, where neither moth nor rust doth corrupt, and where thieves do not break through nor steal." Those who do this will meet with no loss. The treasure laid up in heaven is secure; and it is put to our account, for Jesus said: "Lay up for *yourselves* treasures in heaven." Men may sow here, but they reap in eternity.

It is this eternal treasure that ministers of Christ are to present wherever they may go. They are to urge the people to become wise unto salvation. They are not to allow world-loving, timeserving professed believers to influence their course and weaken their faith. It is not their mission to help individuals or churches to contrive how they can save money by narrow plans and circumscribed efforts in the cause of God. Instead of this they are to teach men how to work disinterestedly and thus become rich toward God. They should educate minds to place the right estimate on eternal things and to make the kingdom of heaven first.

Calebs are wanted in these two fields. There must be in these conferences, not children, but men who will move understandingly and bear burdens, letting their voice be heard above the voices of the unfaithful, who present objections, doubts, and criticism. Great interests are not to be managed by children. An undeveloped Christian, dwarfed in religious growth, destitute of wisdom from above, is unprepared to meet the fierce conflicts through which the church is often called to pass. "I have set watchmen upon thy walls, O Jerusalem, which shall never hold their peace day nor night." Unless the minister shall fearlessly declare the whole truth, unless he shall have an eye single to the glory of God and shall work under the direction of the great Captain of his salvation, unless he shall move to the front, irrespective of censure and uncontaminated by applause, he will be accounted an unfaithful watchman.

There are some in _____ who ought to be men instead of boys and heavenly minded instead of earthly and sensual; but their spiritual vision has become obscured; the Saviour's great love has not ravished their souls. He has many things to say unto you, but you cannot bear them now. You are children in growth and cannot comprehend the mysteries of God. When God raises up men to do His work, they are false to their trust if they allow their testimony to be shaped to please the minds of the unconsecrated. He will prepare men for the times. They will be humble, God-fearing men, not conservative, not policy men; but men who have moral independence and will move forward in the fear of the Lord. They will be kind, noble, courteous; yet they will not be swayed from the right path, but will proclaim the truth in righteousness whether men will hear or whether they will forbear.

CHRISTIAN GROWTH

I have been shown that those who have a knowledge of the truth, and yet allow all their powers to be absorbed in worldly interests, are unfaithful. They are not, by their good works, letting the light of truth shine to others. Nearly all their ability is devoted to becoming sharp, skillful men of the world. They forget that their talents were given them of God to be used in advancing His cause. If they were faithful to their duty, the result would be great gain of souls to the Master, but many are lost through their neglect.

God calls upon those who know His will to be doers of

His word. Weakness, halfheartedness, and indecision provoke the assaults of Satan; and those who permit these traits to grow will be borne helplessly down by the surging waves of temptation. Everyone who professes the name of Christ is required to grow up to the full stature of Christ, the Christian's living head.

We all need a guide through the many strait places in life as much as the sailor needs a pilot over the sandy bar or up the rocky river, and where is this guide to be found? We point you, dear brethren, to the Bible. Inspired of God, written by holy men, it points out with great clearness and precision the duties of both old and young. It elevates the mind, softens the heart, and imparts gladness and holy joy to the spirit. The Bible presents a perfect standard of character; it is an infallible guide under all circumstances, even to the end of the journey of life. Take it as the man of your counsel, the rule of your daily life.

Every means of grace should be diligently improved that the love of God may abound in the soul more and more, "that ye may approve things that are excellent; that ye may be sincere and without offense till the day of Christ; being filled with the fruits of righteousness." Your Christian life must take on vigorous and stalwart forms. You can attain to the high standard set before you in the Scriptures, and you must if you would be children of God. You cannot stand still; you must either advance or retrograde. You must have spiritual knowledge, that you "may be able to comprehend with all saints what is the breadth, and length, and depth, and height; and to know the love of Christ," that you may "be filled with all the fullness of God."

Many who have an intelligent knowledge of the truth, and are able to defend it by arguments, are doing nothing for the upbuilding of Christ's kingdom. We meet them from time to time, but they bear no fresh testimonies of personal experience in the Christian life; they relate no new victories gained in the holy warfare. Instead of this you notice the same old routine, the same expressions in prayer and exhortation. Their prayers have no new note; they express no greater intelligence in the things of God, no more earnest, living faith. Such persons are not living plants in the garden of the Lord, sending forth fresh shoots and new foliage, and the grateful fragrance of a holy life. They are not growing Christians. They have limited views and plans, and there is no expansion of mind, no valuable additions to the treasures of Christian knowledge. Their powers have not been taxed in this direction. They have not learned to view men and things as God views them, and in many cases unsanctified sympathy has injured souls and greatly crippled the cause of God. The spiritual stagnation that prevails is terrible. Many lead a formal Christian life and claim that their sins have been forgiven, when they are as destitute of any real knowledge of Christ as is the sinner.

Brethren, will you have a stinted Christian growth, or will you make healthy progress in the divine life? Where there is spiritual health there is growth. The child of God grows up to the full stature of a man or woman in Christ. There is no limit to his improvement. When the love of God is a living principle in the soul, there are no narrow, confined views; there is love and faithfulness in warnings and reproofs; there is earnest work and a disposition to bear burdens and take responsibilities.

Some are not willing to do self-denying work. They show real impatience when urged to take some responsibility. "What need is there," say they, "of an increase of knowledge and experience? This explains it all. They feel that they are "rich, and increased with goods, and have need of nothing," while heaven pronounces them poor, miserable, blind, and naked. To these the True Witness says: "I counsel thee to buy of Me gold tried in the fire, that thou mayest be rich; and white raiment, that thou mayest be clothed, and that the shame of thy nakedness do not appear; and anoint thine eyes with eyesalve, that thou mayest see." Your very self-complacency shows you to be in need of everything. You are spiritually sick and need Jesus as your physician.

In the Scriptures thousands of gems of truth lie hidden from the surface seeker. The mine of truth is never exhausted. The more you search the Scriptures with humble hearts, the greater will be your interest, and the more you will feel like exclaiming with Paul: "O the depth of the riches both of the wisdom and knowledge of God! how unsearchable are His judgments, and His ways past finding out!" Every day you should learn something new from the Scriptures. Search them as for hid treasures, for they contain the words of eternal life. Pray for wisdom and understanding to comprehend these holy writings. If you would do this you would find new glories in the word of God; you would feel that you had received new and precious light on subjects connected with the truth, and the Scriptures would be constantly receiving a new value in your estimation.

"The great day of the Lord is near, it is near, and hasteth greatly." Jesus says: "Behold, I come quickly." We should keep these words ever in mind, and act as though we do indeed believe that the coming of the Lord is nigh, and that we are pilgrims and strangers upon the earth. The vital energies of the church of God must be brought into active exercise for the great object of self-renovation; every member must be an active agent for God. "For through Him we both have access by one Spirit unto the Father. Now therefore ye are no more strangers and foreigners, but fellow citizens with the saints, and of the household of God; and are built upon the foundation of the apostles and prophets, Jesus Christ Himself being the chief Cornerstone; in whom all the building fitly framed together groweth unto an holy temple in the Lord: in whom ye also are builded together for an habitation of God through the Spirit." This is a particular work, which must be carried forward in all harmony, in unity of Spirit, and in the bonds of peace. No place should be given to criticisms, doubts, and unbelief.

The Upper Columbia and North Pacific Conferences* are years behind. Some who ought to be strong and established in Christ are as babes in understanding and experimental

*See footnote on page 249.

knowledge of the workings of the Spirit of God. After years of experience they are able to comprehend only the first principles of that grand system of faith and doctrine that constitutes the Christian religion. They do not comprehend that perfection of character which will receive the commendation: "Well done."

Brethren, your duty, happiness, future usefulness, and final salvation call upon you to sever the tendrils of your affections from everything earthly and corruptible. There is an unsanctified sympathy that partakes of the nature of lovesick sentimentalism and is earthly, sensual. It will require no feeble effort for some of you to overcome this and change the course of your life, for you have not placed yourselves in connection with the Strength of Israel and have become enfeebled in all your faculties. Now you are loudly called upon to be diligent in the use of every means of grace, that you may be transformed in character and may grow to the full stature of men and women in Christ Jesus.

We have great victories to gain, and a heaven to lose if we do not gain them. The carnal heart must be crucified; for its tendency is to moral corruption, and the end thereof is death. Nothing but the life-giving influences of the gospel can help the soul. Pray that the mighty energies of the Holy Spirit, with all their quickening, recuperative, and transforming power, may fall like an electric shock on the palsy-stricken soul, causing every nerve to thrill with new life, restoring the whole man from his dead, earthly, sensual state to spiritual soundness. You will thus become partakers of the divine nature, having escaped the corruption that is in the world through lust; and in your souls will be reflected the image of Him by whose stripes you are healed.

TITHES AND OFFERINGS

The Lord requires that we return to Him in tithes and offerings a portion of the goods He has lent us. He accepts these offerings as an act of humble obedience on our part and a grateful acknowledgment of our indebtedness to Him for all the blessings we enjoy. Then let us offer willingly, saying with David: "All things come of Thee, and of Thine own have we given Thee." Withholding more than is meet tends to poverty. God will bear long with some, He will test and prove all, but His curse will surely follow the selfish, world-loving professor of truth. God knows the heart; every thought and every purpose is open to His eye. He says: "Them that honor Me I will honor, and they that despise Me shall be lightly esteemed." He knows whom to bless and who are deserving of His curse. He makes no mistakes, for angels are keeping a record of all our works and words.

When the people of God were about to build the sanctuary in the wilderness, extensive preparations were necessary. Costly materials were collected, and among them was much gold and silver. As the rightful owner of all their treasures, the Lord called for these offerings from the people; but He accepted only those that were given freely. The people offered willingly, until word was brought to Moses: "The people bring much more than enough for the service of the work, which the Lord commanded to make." And the proclamation was made to all the congregation: "Let neither man nor woman make any more work for the offering of the sanctuary. So the people were restrained from bringing. For the stuff they had was sufficient for all the work to make it, and too much."

Had some men of limited ideas been on the ground they would have opened their eyes in horror. Like Judas they would have asked: "To what purpose is this waste?" "Why not make everything in the cheapest manner?" But the sanctuary was not designed to honor man, but the God of heaven. He had given specific directions how everything was to be done. The people were to be taught that He was a being of greatness and majesty, and that He was to be worshiped with reverence and awe.

The house where God is worshiped should be in accordance with His character and majesty. There are small churches that ever will be small because they place their own interests above the interests of God's cause. While they have large, convenient houses for themselves, and are constantly improving their premises, they are content to have a most unsuitable place for the worship of God, where His holy presence is to dwell. They wonder that Joseph and Mary were obliged to find shelter in a stable, and that there the Saviour was born, but they are willing to expend upon themselves a large part of their means, while the house of worship is shamefully neglected. How often they say: "The time is not come, the time that the Lord's house should be built." But the word of the Lord to them is: "Is it time for you, O ye, to dwell in your ceiled houses, and this house lie waste?"

The house where Jesus is to meet with His people should be neat and attractive. If there are but few believers in a place, put up a neat but humble house, and by dedicating it to God invite Jesus to come as your guest. How does He look upon His people when they have every convenience that heart could wish, but are willing to meet for His worship in a barn, some miserable, out-of-the-way building, or some cheap, forsaken apartment? You work for your friends, you expend means to make everything around them as attractive as possible; but Jesus, the One who gave everything for you, even His precious life,—He who is the Majesty of heaven, the King of kings and Lord of lords,—is favored with a place on earth but little better than the stable which was His first home. Shall we not look at these things as God looks at them? Shall we not test our motives and see what kind of faith we possess?

"God loveth a cheerful giver," and those who love Him will give freely and cheerfully when by so doing they can advance His cause and promote His glory. The Lord never requires His people to offer more than they are able, but according to their ability He is pleased to accept and bless their thank offerings. Let willing obedience and pure love bind upon the altar every offering that is made to God; for with such sacrifices He is well pleased, while those that are offered grudgingly are an offense to Him. When churches or individuals have no heart in their offerings, but would limit the cost of carrying forward the work of God, and gauge it by their own narrow views, they show decidedly that they have no living connection with God. They are at variance with His plan and manner of working, and He will not bless them.

We are builders for God, and we must build upon the foundation which He has prepared for us. No man is to build upon his own foundation, independent of the plan which God has devised. There are men whom God has raised up as counselors, men whom He has taught, and whose heart and soul and life are in the work. These men are to be highly esteemed for their work's sake. There are some who will wish to follow their own crude notions; but they must learn to receive advice and to work in harmony with their brethren, or they will sow doubt and discord that they will not care to harvest. It is the will of God that those who engage in His work shall be subject to one another. His worship must be conducted with consistency, unity, and sound judgment. God is our only sufficient helper. The laws which govern His people, their principles of thought and action, are received from Him through His word and Spirit. When His word is loved and obeyed, His children walk in the light, and there is no occasion of stumbling in them. They do not accept the world's low standard, but work from the Bible standpoint.

The selfishness which exists among God's people is very offensive to Him. The Scriptures denounce covetousness as idolatry. No "covetous man," says Paul, "who is an idolater, hath any inheritance in the kingdom of Christ and of God." The trouble with many is that they have too little faith. Like the rich man in the parable they want to see their supplies piled up in their granaries. The world is to be warned, and God wants us wholly engaged in His work; but men have so much to do to forward their money-making projects that they have no time to push the triumphs of the cross of Christ. They have neither time nor disposition to put their intellect, tact, and energy into the cause of God.

Brethren and sisters, I wish to excite in your minds disgust for your present limited ideas of God's cause and work. I want you to comprehend the great sacrifice that Christ made for you when He became poor, that through His poverty you might come into possession of eternal riches. Oh! do not, by your indifference to the eternal weight of glory which is within your reach, cause angels to weep and hide their faces in shame and disgust. Arouse from your lethargy; arouse every God-given faculty, and work for precious souls for whom Christ died. These souls, if brought to the fold of Christ, will live through the ceaseless ages of eternity; and will you plan to do as little as possible for their salvation, while, like the man with the one talent, you invest your means in the earth? Like that unfaithful servant, are you charging God with reaping where He has not sown, and gathering where He has not strewed?

All that you have and are belongs to God. Then will you not say from the heart: "All things come of Thee, and of Thine own have we given Thee"? "Honor the Lord with thy substance, and with the first fruits of all thine increase." Paul thus exhorts his Corinthian brethren to Christian beneficence: "As ye abound in everything, in faith, and utterance, and knowledge, and in all diligence, and in your love to us, see that ye abound in this grace also." In his epistle to Timothy he says: "Charge them that are rich in this world, that they be not high-minded, nor trust in uncertain riches, but in the living God, who giveth us richly all things to enjoy; that they do good, that they be rich in good works, ready to distribute, willing to communicate; laying up in store for themselves a good foundation against the time to come, that they may lay hold on eternal life."

Liberality is not so natural to us that we gain this virtue by accident. It must be cultivated. We must deliberately resolve that we will honor God with our substance; and then we must let nothing tempt us to rob Him of the tithes and offerings that are His due. We must be intelligent, systematic, and continuous in our acts of charity to men and our expressions of gratitude to God for His bounties to us. This is too sacred a duty to be left to chance or to be controlled by impulse or feeling. We should regularly reserve something for God's cause, that He may not be robbed of the portion which He claims. When we rob God we rob ourselves also. We give up the heavenly treasure for the sake of having more of this earth. This is a loss that we cannot afford to sustain. If we live so that we can have the blessing of God we shall have His prospering hand with us in our temporal affairs, but if His hand is against us He can defeat all our plans and scatter faster than we can gather.

I was shown that the situation of things in these two conferences is sad indeed, but God has many precious souls here over whom He has a jealous care, and He will not leave them to be deceived and misled.

FAITHFULNESS IN THE WORK OF GOD

There is precious talent in the churches in Oregon and Washington Territory, and had it been developed by well-directed labor, there might now be efficient workers in these conferences. A live church is always a working church. The truth is a power, and those who see its force will stand boldly and fearlessly in its defense. Truth must be apprehended by the intellect, received into the heart, and its principles incorporated into the character, and then there must be a constant effort to win others to accept it, for God holds men responsible for the use they make of the light He imparts to them.

The Lord calls upon all His people to improve the ability He has given them. The mental powers should be developed to the utmost; they should be strengthened and ennobled by dwelling upon spiritual truths. If the mind is allowed to run almost entirely upon trifling things and the common business of everyday life, it will, in accordance with one of its unvarying laws, become weak and frivolous, and deficient in spiritual power.

Times that will try men's souls are just before us, and those who are weak in the faith will not stand the test of those days of peril. The great truths of revelation are to be carefully studied, for we shall all want an intelligent knowledge of the word of God. By Bible study and daily communion with Jesus we shall gain clear, well-defined views of individual responsibility and strength to stand in the day of trial and temptation. He whose life is united to Christ by hidden links will be kept by the power of God through faith unto salvation.

More thought should be given to the things of God, and less to temporal matters. The world-loving professor, if he will exercise his mind in that direction, may become as familiar with the word of God as he now is with worldly business. "Search the Scriptures," said Christ; "for in them ye think ye have eternal life: and they are they which testify of Me." The Christian is required to be diligent in searching the Scriptures, to read over and over again the truths of God's word. Willful ignorance on this subject endangers the Christian life and character. It blinds the understanding and corrupts the noblest powers. It is this that brings confusion into our lives. Our people need to understand the oracles of God; they need to have a systematic knowledge of the principles of revealed truth, which will fit them for what is coming upon the earth and prevent them from being carried about by every wind of doctrine.

Great changes are soon to take place in the world, and everyone will need an experimental knowledge of the things of God. It is the work of Satan to dishearten the people of God and to unsettle their faith. He tries in every way to insinuate doubts and questionings in regard to the position, the faith, the plans, of the men upon whom God has laid the burden of a special work and who are zealously doing that work. Although he may be baffled again and again, yet he renews his attacks, working through those who profess to be humble and God-fearing, and who are apparently interested in, or believers of, present truth. The advocates of truth expect fierce and cruel opposition from their open enemies, but this is far less dangerous than the secret doubts expressed by those who feel at liberty to question and find fault with what God's servants are doing. These may appear to be humble men; but they are self-deceived, and they deceive others. In their hearts are envy and evil surmisings. They unsettle the faith of the people in those in whom they should have confidence, those whom God has chosen to do His work; and when they are reproved for their course they take it as personal abuse. While professing to be doing God's work they are in reality aiding the enemy.

Brethren, never allow anyone's ideas to unsettle your faith in regard to the order and harmony which should exist in the church. Many of you do not see all things clearly. The directions in regard to order in the tabernacle service were recorded that lessons might be drawn from it by all who should live upon the earth. Men were selected to do various parts of the work of setting up and taking down the tabernacle, and if one strayed in carelessly and put his hands to the work assigned to another, he was to be put to death. We serve the same God today. But the death penalty has been abolished; had it not been, there would not now be so much careless, disorderly work in His cause. The God of heaven is a God of order, and He requires all His followers to have rules and regulations, and to preserve order. All should have a perfect understanding of God's work.

It is unsafe to cherish doubt in the heart even for a moment. The seeds of doubt which Pharaoh sowed when he rejected the first miracle were allowed to grow, and they produced such an abundant harvest that all subsequent miracles could not persuade him that his position was wrong. He continued to venture on in his own course, going from one degree of questioning to another, and his heart became more and more hardened until he was called to look upon the cold, dead faces of the first-born.

God is at work, and we are not doing one half that must be done to prepare a people to stand in the day when the Son of man shall be revealed. Woe be to the man that shall in the least degree seek to hinder the work which God is doing. We must labor for others; we must try to weaken the hold of our brethren upon their earthly treasures; for many will sell their birthright to eternal life for worldly advantages. How much better to encourage them to lay up their treasure in heaven than complainingly to drop the words: "It is money, money, that these men are continually calling for; and they are getting rich by it." How sweet are words like these to the world-loving professor! How they strengthen his courage to withhold from God the proportion which belongs to Him and which should be returned to Him in tithes and offerings! The curse of the Lord will rest upon those who fail to render to Him His own. Let us work in harmony with God. His servants have a message to bear to money lovers; why should they not bear a close testimony in regard to bringing all the tithes into the storehouse, when the Lord Himself has set them the example?

The religion of Christ subdues the selfish spirit and transforms the mind and the affections; it lays low the pride of men, that God alone may be exalted. This is what Brother A wants. He needs a practical faith in God. He needs to see and feel the glory of serving Christ; he needs to exalt principle and elevate the Christian standard; he needs to store his mind with the rich promises, the warnings, the counsels and threatenings, of God's word; he needs to see the importance of having faith and corresponding works, that he may fairly represent, at home, in the church, and in his business, the purity and elevated character of religion. He should place himself in connection with Christ, that he may have spiritual power. His connection with the world, and with influences adverse to the spirit of truth, have greater power over him than the Spirit of Christ. Here is his danger, and he will eventually make shipwreck of faith unless he changes his course of action and firmly connects with the Source of light.

If his interest in spiritual things were as great as it is in the things of the world, his consecration to God would be entire; he would show himself a true disciple of Christ, and God would accept and use the talents which are now wholly devoted to the service of the world. The very same ability is required in the cause of God that is now given to the accumulation of property. Managers are needed in every branch of His work, that it may be carried on with energy and system. If a man has tact, industry, and enthusiasm, he will make a success in temporal business, and the same qualities, consecrated to the work of God, will prove even doubly efficient; for divine power will be combined with human effort. The best of plans, either in temporal or spiritual matters, will prove a failure if their execution is entrusted to inexperienced, incapable hands.

Those who bury their talents in this world are not pleasing God. All their powers are devoted to the accumulation of property, and the desire to accumulate becomes a passion. Brother A is an active man, and he takes pride in carrying out worldly projects. If the same interest, tact, and ambition were exercised in trading for the Lord, how much grander, nobler results would he realize! The education obtained in worldly business will not be of the least advantage in the future life, for no such business will be carried on in heaven; but if the faculties which God has given are used to His glory, to the upbuilding of His kingdom, an education is received which will be taken into heaven.

What is our position in the world? We are in the waiting time. But this period is not to be spent in abstract devotion. Waiting, watching, and vigilant working are to be combined. Our life should not be all bustle and drive and planning about the things of the world, to the neglect of personal piety and of the service that God requires. While we should not be slothful in business, we should be fervent in spirit, serving the Lord. The lamp of the soul must be trimmed, and we must have the oil of grace in our vessels with our lamps. Every precaution must be used to prevent spiritual declension, lest the day of the Lord overtake us as a thief. That day is not to be put far off; it is near, and no man should say, even in his heart, much less by his works, "My Lord delayeth His coming," lest for so doing his portion be appointed with hypocrites and unbelievers.

I saw that God's people are in great peril; many are dwellers upon the earth, their interest and affections are centered in the world. Their example is not right. The world is deceived by the course pursued by many who profess great and noble truths. Our responsibility is in accordance with the light given, the graces and gifts bestowed. On the workers whose talents, whose means, whose opportunities and abilities, are greatest rests the heaviest responsibility. God calls upon Brother A to change his course of action, to use his ability to God's glory instead of debasing it to sordid worldly interests. Now is his day of trust; soon will come his day of reckoning.

Brother A was presented before me to represent a class who are in a similar position. They have never been indifferent to the smallest worldly advantage. By diligent business tact and successful investments, by trading, not on pounds, but on pence and farthings, they have accumulated property. But in doing this they have educated faculties inconsistent with the development of Christian character. Their lives in no way represent Christ; for they love the world and its gain better than they love God or the truth. "If any man love the world, the love of the Father is not in him."

All the abilities which men possess belong to God. Worldly conformity and attachments are emphatically forbidden in His word. When the power of the transforming grace of God is felt upon the heart, it will send a man, hitherto worldly, into every pathway of beneficence. He who has in his heart a determination to lay up treasure in the world, will "fall into temptation and a snare, and into many foolish and hurtful lusts, which drown men in destruction and perdition. For the love of money is the root of all evil [the foundation of all avarice and worldliness]: which while some coveted after, they have erred from the faith, and pierced themselves through with many sorrows."

Each member of the church should feel under sacred obligations to guard strictly the interests of the cause of God. The individual members of the church are responsible for its distracted, discouraged state, by which the most sacred truths ever committed to man are dishonored. There is no excuse for this condition of things. Jesus has opened to everyone a way by which wisdom, grace, and power may be obtained. He is our example in all things, and nothing should divert the mind from the main object in life, which is to have Christ in the soul, melting and subduing the heart. When this is the case, every member of the church, every professor of the truth, will be Christlike in character, in words, in actions.

Some who have been channels of light, whose hearts have been made glad by the precious light of truth, have denied that truth by assimilating to the world. They have thus lost the spirit of self-sacrifice and the power of the truth, and have depended for happiness upon unstable things of earth. They are in great peril. Having once rejoiced in the light, they will be left in total darkness unless they speedily gather up the rays that are still shining upon them and return to the Lord with repentance and confession. We are in a day of peril, when error and deception are captivating the people. Who will warn the world, who will show them the better way, unless those who have had the light of truth are sanctified through it and shall let their light so shine that others may see their good works and glorify God? I wish I could impress upon all the danger they are in of losing heaven. Joining the church is one thing, and connecting with Christ is quite another. Not all the names registered in the church books are registered in the Lamb's book of life. Many, though apparently sincere believers, do not keep up a living connection with Christ. They have enlisted, they have entered their names on the register; but the inner work of grace is not wrought in the heart. As the result they are not happy, and they make hard work of serving God.

"With what judgment ye judge, ye shall be judged." Remember that your brethren are fallible creatures like yourself, and regard their mistakes and errors with the same mercy and forbearance that you wish them to exercise toward you. They should not be watched and their defects paraded to the front for the world to exult over. Those who dare to do this have climbed upon the judgment seat and made themselves judges, while they have neglected the garden of their own hearts and have allowed poisonous weeds to obtain a rank growth.

We individually have a case pending in the court of heaven. Character is being weighed in the balances of the sanctuary, and it should be the earnest desire of all to walk humbly and carefully, lest, neglecting to let their light shine forth to the world, they fail of the grace of God and lose everything that is valuable. All dissension, all differences and faultfinding, should be put away, with all evil speaking and bitterness; kindness, love, and compassion for one another should be cherished, that the prayer of Christ that His disciples might be one as He is one with the Father may be answered. The harmony and unity of the church are the credentials that they present to the world that Jesus is the Son of God. Genuine conversion will ever lead to genuine love for Jesus and for all those for whom He died.

Everyone who does what he can for God, who is true and earnest to do good to those around him, will receive the blessing of God upon his efforts. A man may render effective service for God although he is not the head or the heart of the body of Christ. The service represented in the word of God by that of the hand or the foot, though lowly, is nevertheless important. It is not the greatness of the work, but the love with which it is done, the motive underlying the action, that determines its worth. There is work to be done for our neighbors and for those with whom we associate. We have no liberty to cease our patient, prayerful labors for souls as long as any are out of the ark of safety. There is no release in this war. We are soldiers of Christ, and are under obligation to watch lest the enemy gain the advantage and secure to his service souls that we might win to Christ.

The day of trust and responsibility is ours; we have a work to do for God. The church in _____ has been gradually growing cold and irreligious. There is much to be done for its individual members. Great light has shone upon their pathway. For this they will be held accountable. Said Christ: "Ye are the light of the world," "ye are the salt of the earth." They need a deeper work of grace in their hearts. There must be a reformation before God can bless them. There are plenty of formal professors. A selfish grasping for gain eclipses the heavenly inheritance. If the kingdom of heaven is made first, noble integrity will shine forth in the life and character. This is what Brother A needs if he would exert an influence for good. He loves to handle money, and to see it accumulate by turning it one way and another. His mind and affections are absorbed in worldly enterprises. He is drunken with the cares of this life; that is, he is so swallowed up in his business that he cannot think rationally and intelligently of the things of God; his vision is obscured by love of money. The truth should reach down deep into his heart and develop fruit in his private and public life.

Brother A has excused himself for not making the Scriptures his study because he was a businessman. But to one pressed with business cares the Scriptures will be a source of strength and safety. Such a man has greater need of light from the word of God, of its counsels and warnings, than if he were not placed in such a dangerous position. If Brother A would exercise the same forethought and business tact in the things of God that he has given to worldly matters, he would realize blessed results. If he thinks that God is satisfied with him while giving his talent and energy almost entirely to the service of mammon, he is fearfully deceived. Said Christ: "No man can serve two masters: for either he will hate the one, and love the other; or else he will hold to the one, and despise the other. Ye cannot serve God and mammon." If Brother A continues to make eternal things subordinate to his worldly interests, his passion for accumulating will steadily increase until it will overrule principle, and he will be so blinded by the god of this world that he will be unable to discern between the sacred and the common.

Brother A has a strong influence upon the minds of his brethren; they view things largely from his standpoint. He needs to improve in spiritual soundness and be wise in the things of God. He should begin to show an interest in and devotion to heavenly things and to so educate his powers that they may be of service in the cause of God. He needs the armor of righteousness with which to ward off the darts of the enemy. It is impossible for him to obtain salvation unless there is a decided change in the objects and pursuits of his life, unless he exercises himself continually in spiritual things.

God calls upon the individual members of the churches in these two conferences to arouse and be converted. Brethren, your worldliness, your distrust, your murmuring, have placed you in such a position that it will be exceedingly difficult for anyone to labor among you. While your president neglected his work and failed in his duty, your attitude was not such as to give him any encouragement. The one in authority should have acquitted himself as a man of God, reproving, exhorting, encouraging, as the case demanded, whether you would receive or reject his testimony. But he was easily discouraged, and left you without the help that a faithful minister of Christ should have given. He failed in not keeping up with the opening providence of God, and in not showing you your duty and educating you up to the demands of the time; but the minister's neglect should not dishearten you and lead you to excuse yourselves for neglecting duty. There is the more need of energy and fidelity on your part.

VOWING AND NOT PAYING

Some of you have been stumbling over your pledges. The Spirit of the Lord came into the _____ meeting in answer to prayer, and while your hearts were softened under its influence, you pledged. While the streams of salvation were pouring upon your hearts, you felt that you must follow the example of Him who went about doing good and who cheerfully gave His life to ransom man from sin and degradation. Under the heavenly, inspiring influence you saw that selfishness and worldliness were not consistent with Christian character and that you could not live for yourselves and be Christlike. But when the influence of His abundant love and mercy was not felt in so marked a manner in your hearts, you withdrew your offerings, and God withdrew His blessing from you.

Adversity came upon some. There was a failure in their crops, so that they could not redeem their pledges; and some were even brought into straitened circumstances. Then, of course, they could not be expected to pay. But had they not murmured and withdrawn their hearts from their pledges, God would have worked for them and would have opened ways whereby every one could have paid what he had promised. They did not wait in faith, trusting God to open the way so that they could redeem their pledges. Some had means at their command; and had they possessed the same willing mind as when they pledged, and had they heartily rendered to God in tithes and offerings that which He had lent them for this purpose, they would have been greatly blessed. But Satan came in with his temptations and led some to question the motives and the spirit which actuated the servant of God in presenting the call for means. Some felt that they had been deceived and defrauded. In spirit they repudiated their vows, and whatever they did afterward was with reluctance, and therefore they received no blessing.

In the parable of the talents the man to whom was entrusted one talent manifested a grudging spirit and hid his money so that his lord could not be benefited by it. When his master required him to give an account of his stewardship, he excused his neglect by laying blame upon his lord. "I knew thee [he professes to be acquainted with his lord] that thou art an hard man, reaping where thou hast not sown, and gathering where thou hast not strewed: and I was afraid [that all my improvements would not be mine, but that you would claim them], and went and hid thy talent in the earth:

lo, there thou hast that is thine. His lord answered and said unto him, Thou wicked and slothful servant, thou knewest that I reap where I sowed not, and gather where I have not strewed: thou oughtest therefore to have put my money to the exchangers, and then at my coming I should have received mine own with usury. Take therefore the talent from him, and give it unto him which hath ten talents. For unto everyone that hath [made a right use of my goods] shall be given, and he shall have abundance [for I can trust him, knowing that he will make right improvement of what is lent him]: but from him that hath not [who has been fearful to trust me] shall be taken away even that which he hath. [I shall deprive him of what he claims as his; he shall forfeit all right of trust; I will take away his talents and give them to one who will improve them.] And cast ye the unprofitable servant into outer darkness: there shall be weeping and gnashing of teeth."

The spirit manifested by the brethren in regard to their pledges has been very offensive to God. Had they seen the cause prospering in the fields already entered they would have felt differently. There was no deception practiced upon them, and the charge of deception which they made was against the Spirit of God and not against the servant He sent. Had Brother A occupied the right position in this matter, had he cherished the spirit which influenced him to make the pledge, he would not have felt such an unwillingness to invest in the cause of God. But he thought how much he could do with his means by investing it in worldly enterprises. Avarice, worldliness, and covetousness are defects in character which are opposed to the exercise of the Christian graces. Said the apostle: "Let your conversation [your very deportment and habits of life] be without covetousness; and be content with such things as ye have: for He hath said, I will never leave thee, nor forsake thee."

It was evident that many who vowed had no faith and believed themselves wronged. They talked of it and dwelt upon it until it seemed a reality to them. They felt that they ought not to have aided the General Conference, and urged that they ought to have had the means to use in their own field. The Lord worked for them according to their limited faith. Satan, who had been holding their minds in deception, caused them to think that they had done a liberal thing in sending means to the General Conference, when, upon investigation, the facts showed that they still lacked a considerable of returning to the conference the amount that had been paid out in sending them laborers and in helping them in various ways to start the work and carry it forward. Yet these persons have been grieved, dissatisfied, unhappy, and have backslidden from God, because they thought they were doing such great things. This only shows what a terrible deception can come upon minds when they are not under the special control of the Spirit of God. Their doubting, their suspicions, their prejudice in regard to the General Conference, were all prompted by Satan. The cause of God is one the world over. Every branch of the work centers in Christ. No one portion of the field is independent of the rest.

Dear brethren, you have let Satan into your hearts, and he will never be fully vanquished until you repent of your wicked doubts and the withdrawal of your pledges. The Lord's messenger was despised and charged with bringing an undue pressure upon the people. God was displeased with Brother B because he did not bear a decided testimony against everything of that sort and show you your sin as it really was.

"When thou vowest a vow unto God, defer not to pay it; for He hath no pleasure in fools: pay that which thou hast vowed. Better is it that thou shouldest not vow, than that thou shouldest vow and not pay. Suffer not thy mouth to cause thy flesh to sin; neither say thou before the angel, that it was an error; wherefore should God be angry at thy voice, and destroy the work of thine hands?"

Here the matter is presented in its true light. Your work was done before the angel of God. Your words were not only heard by men, but the angel of God listened to them, and can you be surprised that God was angry with you? Can you wonder that He has not blessed you and made you able to pay your pledges? When you have grumbled and murmured and withdrawn your pledges and felt that God's servants had deceived you and extorted from you pledges that were not just, the enemy has exulted. Could you see your course as it is you would never make one semblance of an excuse for it.

Be careful how you speak one word to lessen the influence of God's messengers. There may sometimes have been too much urging for means. But when the light and love of Jesus illuminates the hearts of His followers, there will be no occasion for urging or begging their money or their service. When they become one with Jesus, and realize that they are not their own, that they are bought with a price and are therefore the Lord's property, and that all they have is simply entrusted to them as His stewards, they will with cheerful heart and unswerving fidelity render to God the things that are His. The Lord will not accept an offering that is made unwillingly, grudgingly. With your present feelings there would be no virtue in making more pledges. When you recover from this snare of the enemy, when you heal the breach that you have made, and realize that the wants of God's cause are as continual as are His gifts to the children of men, your works will correspond with your faith, and you will receive a rich blessing from the Lord.

INFLUENCE OF UNBELIEF

The church in ____ ____ has greatly backslidden from God. It is no longer in a state of healthful prosperity. Each individual member of the church has had burdens and discouragements of his own to bear, but these he should have borne and kept his soul alive before God without weakening others in the church. He should have added to the strength of the church instead of diminishing it. Brother C has not taken a position to strengthen his own faith or that of the church. He has been acting on the side of the enemy to dishearten and discourage. Satan is constantly encouraging unbelief. He notes the mistakes and failings of Christ's professed followers, and taunts the angels of God with them. He is an accuser of the brethren, and he will influence as many as possible to do the same work. Those who take it upon themselves to watch their neighbor's garden instead of weeding their own plot of ground will surely find their own gardens so grown up to weeds that every precious plant will be crowded out.

Brother C is not in a position to be a light to the world. Oh, no; he is a body of darkness. Eternity will reveal the fact that his inconsiderate words have planted the seeds of questioning, doubt, and faultfinding in many minds and that his influence has turned many souls from the truth. He has consented to make himself a channel of darkness, to communicate suspicion and bring discouragement upon minds. God is not pleased with him. His own soul is becoming less and less susceptible to the influence of the Spirit of God. He has but little faith; and how could it be otherwise, when by his words he is constantly strengthening unbelief? While he suggests doubts instead of letting beams of precious light shine upon others, he is aiding the enemy in his work. This spirit makes him almost an infidel, and unless he turns square about he will yet become one.

Brother C is thoughtless of his words and actions. Idle words, for which he must render an account in the day of God, are almost continually falling from his lips. He places himself upon the enemy's ground and, as the result, has not the Spirit of Christ. He will sometime see that he has made a great mistake, that he has been losing precious, golden moments which he might have employed in purifying his own heart. He has been picking flaws in others, living on their mistakes; and this is spiritual starvation. Every revival is liable to bring persons into the church who are not really converted. They hold the truth nominally, but are not sanctified by its sweet influence. Being destitute of grace, they are selfish, hard, and unyielding. Such persons are always unreliable. They will ever be doing and saying things contrary to our faith. The church that has such a burden inflicted upon it deserves pity. The world is in opposition to the church, and Satan and his angels are constantly at war with it. Therefore the defects of these unworthy members are held up before those who are sound in the faith.

Those who believe the truth should be determined to help and not to hinder the few in ____ ____ who are struggling under discouragements. The members of the church should each have a jealous care that the enemies of our faith have no occasion to triumph over their lifeless, backslidden state. Some have wasted their influence, when with a little self-denial, earnestness, and zeal, they might have been a power on the side of good. This zeal will not come without effort, without earnest struggles. If only three faithful souls were left in the ____ ____ church, they would, if connected with God, be living channels of light, and He would add to their numbers. God has raised up standard-bearers in ____ ____. Some have moved away, some have died, and some have become spiritually dead; their services are given to Satan. They do not realize that a by-and-by is coming when their account in the heavenly records will be balanced and when every man's work will be revealed of what sort it is.

Remember that everyone must be judged according to his work. When, in the great day of final reckoning, the record of your life shall be opened before you, my doubting, questioning, accusing brother, how will it stand? "Your words have been stout against Me, saith the Lord. Yet ye say, What have we spoken so much against Thee? Ye have said, It is vain to serve God: and what profit is it that we have kept His ordinance, and that we have walked mournfully before the Lord of hosts?" This has been the language of your heart; and "out of the abundance of the heart the mouth speaketh." By your words you are to be justified or condemned. Accusing the brethren is the very work that Satan has been engaged in since his fall. You have disheartened the church who had little enough courage at best. You have presented the truth in almost every objectionable light. This is the work Satan is doing. You have no occasion to be proud of your words; for they will bring confusion of face, shame and despair, in the day when every man shall receive according to the deeds done in the body.

Your wife has heard your expressions of darkness until she is molded in a great degree to your ideas. The fear of the Lord is almost entirely removed from you both. You are now sowing seeds of unbelief, and they will produce a plentiful harvest by and by, in the reaping of which you will take no satisfaction. You have lent yourself to the enemy to be his agent to lead souls to doubt and unbelief. Your whole work has been to scatter from Christ. You glory in your sharpness, your aptness in confusing minds. You think it a mark of intelligence; but it is the same kind of intelligence that the prince of darkness possesses, and will receive the same reward that he is winning by his intense activity and shrewdness. The tendency of this age is to unbelief, to making light of godliness and true religion. This is Satan's plan, and when you yield your powers to unbelief you are led captive by his devices to do his work.

Your wife will have a hard fight to conquer the devices of the enemy, to overcome her own defects of character, and bring all her powers into subjection to the will of God, planting her feet firmly upon the platform of eternal truth. She is not naturally devotional, and you have placed things before her in such an uncertain light that she is left to drift without anchorage. She takes no real comfort in faith and hope, for she has not an intelligent knowledge of the truth. She is greatly affected by the atmosphere of unbelief she breathes, and if she is lost, the blood of her soul will be found on your garments.

You are just as surely doing the work of Satan as is any one of his open agents. The doubts which you have introduced into many minds will bear fruit. Your harvest is ripening for the final gathering. Will you be proud of it then?

You may turn to the Lord; you may find rest in Him. But you have so long educated yourself to criticize, to turn and twist everything in a false light, that it will require earnest prayer and constant watchfulness to break the habit which has become second nature. My heart yearns over you and your family. The Lord is displeased with you; He is grieved every day. You must be a thoroughly converted, transformed man, or you will never have the precious gift of everlasting life.

DECEITFULNESS OF SIN

Brother D was presented before me as doing a work which in the judgment he will wish undone. He is not correct in all points of doctrine, and he obstinately maintains his erroneous positions. He is an accuser of the brethren. He has not only thought evil of those whom God has chosen as laborers in His cause, but he has spoken this evil to others. He has not conformed to the Bible rule and conferred with the leading brethren, and yet he finds fault with them all.

The excuse made for him is: "Oh, Brother D is such a good man. He is a pattern of amiability and kindheartedness, and is a ready helper anywhere." Brother D has many excellent traits of character. He has no great ability as a preacher, but may become an earnest, faithful worker. The enemy has come in through his estimation of himself. Had he not esteemed himself more highly than he should, he would never have dared to use the reputation of his brethren as he has done. By his freedom in gathering up and repeating false reports, he has come in between the people and the message which God has given His ministers to bear to them to fit them to stand in the day of the Lord. His good traits have made him all the more dangerous; for they have given him influence. People have thought that what he said must be so. Had he been an immoral or quarrelsome person, he could not have succeeded in winning the confidence of so many.

Brother D's manner of working also makes his course more deserving of censure and a greater offense to God. Had he shown his feelings undisguised, had he said in public the things he talked in private, no one would have thought for a moment of sending him out to labor in the conference. While he is laboring under its sanction, his brethren have a right to suppose that his views are correct. And with this sanction his influence has been a power for evil. There are some who would never have entertained suspicion of their brethren or thought evil of them had it not been for his words. He has started minds on a track which, if pursued, will end in rebellion and the loss of the soul. Stripped of its disguise, this is the work which our good brother has been doing.

God has presented this matter before me in its true light. Brother D's heart is not right. It is defiled with bitterness, wrath, envy, jealousy, and evil surmising, and it needs to be purified. Unless he changes his course entirely, he will soon be a fallen man. Charity, or love, "suffereth long, and is kind; charity envieth not; charity vaunteth not itself, is not puffed up, doth not behave itself unseemly, seeketh not her own, is not easily provoked, thinketh no evil; rejoiceth not in iniquity, but rejoiceth in the truth; beareth all things, believeth all things, hopeth all things, endureth all things."

Suppose that Brother D leads the people to question and reject the testimonies that God has been giving to His people during the past thirty-eight years; suppose he makes them believe that the leaders in this work are designing, dishonest men, engaged in deceiving the people; what great and good work has he done? It is a work exactly similar to that of Korah, Dathan, and Abiram; and with all whom he has influenced the result will be disastrous. He has thought that he could not be in error; but does this work bear the signet of heaven? No; Brother D has indulged a self-righteous spirit, which has almost ruined him. Let him come upon an equality with his brethren; if he has difficulties with them in regard to their course of action, let him show wherein their sin lies.

When Satan became disaffected in heaven, he did not lay his complaint before God and Christ, but he went among the angels who thought him perfect and represented that God had done him injustice in preferring Christ to himself. The result of this misrepresentation was that through their sympathy with him one third of the angels lost their innocence, their high estate, and their happy home. Satan is instigating men to continue on earth the same work of jealousy and evil surmising that he commenced in heaven.

When Jesus was upon earth, the Jews were ever acting as spies on His track. They gathered up every false report and charged Him with one crime after another. They were constantly endeavoring to turn the people away from Him. Was their course right? If it was, then Brother D has not sinned, for he is doing a similar work. He may now break the snare of the enemy; he may conquer this spirit which leads him to exalt himself above his brethren. Let him seek meekness, and learn to esteem others better than himself. If he will work in fidelity and in harmony with God's plan he will hear the sweet words, "Well done," from the lips of the Master. But if he rejects the labors of God's servants, if he chooses his own way and leans to his own understanding, he will surely make shipwreck of faith. God has not passed His people by and chosen one solitary man here and another there as the only ones worthy to be entrusted with His truth. He does not give one man new light contrary to the established faith of the body. In every reform men have arisen making this claim. Paul warned the church in his day: "Of your own selves shall men arise, speaking perverse things, to draw away disciples after them." The greatest harm to God's people comes through those who go out from among them speaking perverse things. Through them the way of truth is evil spoken of.

Let none be self-confident, as though God had given them special light above their brethren. Christ is represented as dwelling in His people. Believers are represented as "built upon the foundation of the apostles and prophets, Jesus Christ Himself being the chief Cornerstone; in whom all the building fitly framed together groweth unto an holy temple in the Lord: in whom ye also are builded together for an habitation of God through the Spirit." "I therefore, the prisoner of the Lord," says Paul, "beseech you that ye walk worthy of the vocation wherewith ye are called, with all lowliness and meekness, with long-suffering, forbearing one another in love; endeavoring to keep the unity of the Spirit in the bond of peace. There is one body, and one Spirit, even as ye are called in one hope of your calling; one Lord, one faith, one baptism, one God and Father of all, who is above all, and through all, and in you all."

That which Brother D calls light is apparently harmless; it does not look as though anyone could be injured by it. But, brethren, it is Satan's device, his entering wedge. This has been tried again and again. One accepts some new and original idea which does not seem to conflict with the truth. He talks of it and dwells upon it until it seems to him to be clothed with beauty and importance, for Satan has power to give this false appearance. At last it becomes the all-absorbing theme, the one great point around which everything centers; and the truth is uprooted from the heart.

No sooner are erratic ideas started in his mind than Brother D begins to lose faith and to question the work of the Spirit which has been manifested among us for so many years. He is not a man who will entertain what he believes to be special light without imparting it to others; therefore it is not safe to give him influence that will enable him to unsettle other minds. It is opening a door through which Satan will rush in many errors to divert the mind from the importance of the truth for this time. Brethren, as an ambassador of Christ I warn you to beware of these side issues, whose tendency is to divert the mind from the truth. Error is never harmless. It never sanctifies, but always brings confusion and dissension. It is always dangerous. The enemy has great power over minds that are not thoroughly fortified by prayer and established in Bible truth.

There are a thousand temptations in disguise prepared for those who have the light of truth; and the only safety for any of us is in receiving no new doctrine, no new interpretation of the Scriptures, without first submitting it to brethren of experience. Lay it before them in a humble, teachable spirit, with earnest prayer; and if they see no light in it, yield to their judgment; for "in the multitude of counselors there is safety."

Satan saw in Brother D traits that would enable him to gain an advantage. "The prince of this world cometh," said Christ, "and hath nothing in Me." But while appearing to possess great humility, Brother D has placed too high an estimate upon himself. For years he has entertained the feeling that his brethren did not appreciate him, and he has expressed this feeling to others, and Satan found in him a self-conceit to which he could successfully appeal.

This is a time of extreme peril to Brother D, and to many others. Angels of God are watching these souls with intense interest, and Satan and his angels are very anxious to see how their plans will succeed. This is a crisis in Brother D's life. He will here make decisions for time and for eternity. God loves him, and this experience may be one of great value to him. If he fully yields his heart to God and accepts all the truth he will be a tireless laborer; God will work through him, and he may do much good. But he must work in harmony with his brethren. He must overcome sensitiveness and learn to endure hardness as a good soldier of the cross of Christ.

Satan is constantly at work, but few have any idea of his activity and subtlety. The people of God must be prepared to withstand the wily foe. It is this resistance that Satan dreads. He knows better than we do the limit of his power and how easily he can be overcome if we resist and face him. Through divine strength the weakest saint is more than a match for him and all his angels, and if brought to the test he would be able to prove his superior power. Therefore Satan's step is noiseless, his movements stealthy, and his batteries masked. He does not venture to show himself openly, lest he arouse the Christian's dormant energies and send him to God in prayer.

The enemy is preparing for his last campaign against the church. He has so concealed himself from view that many can hardly believe that he exists, much less can they be convinced of his amazing activity and power. They have to a great extent forgotten his past record; and when he makes another advance move, they will not recognize him as their enemy, that old serpent, but they will consider him a friend, one who is doing a good work. Boasting of their independence they will, under his specious, bewitching influence, obey the worst impulses of the human heart and yet believe that God is leading them. Could their eyes be opened to distinguish their captain, they would see that they are not serving God, but the enemy of all righteousness. They would see that their boasted independence is one of the heaviest fetters Satan can rivet on unbalanced minds.

Man is Satan's captive and is naturally inclined to follow his suggestions and do his bidding. He has in himself no power to oppose effectual resistance to evil. It is only as Christ abides in him by living faith, influencing his desires and strengthening him with strength from above, that man may venture to face so terrible a foe. Every other means of defense is utterly vain. It is only through Christ that Satan's power is limited. This is a momentous truth that all should understand. Satan is busy every moment, going to and fro, walking up and down in the earth, seeking whom he may devour. But the earnest prayer of faith will baffle his strongest efforts. Then take "the shield of faith," brethren, "wherewith ye shall be able to quench all the fiery darts of the wicked."

The worst enemies we have are those who are trying to destroy the influence of the watchmen upon the walls of Zion. Satan works through agents. He is making an earnest effort here. He works according to a definite plan, and his agents act in concert. A line of unbelief stretches across the continent and is in communication with the church of God. Its influence has been exerted to undermine confidence in the work of the Spirit of God. This element is here and is silently working. Be careful lest you be found aiding the enemy of God and man by spreading false reports and by criticisms and decided opposition.

Through deceptive means and unseen channels, Satan is working to strengthen his authority and to place obstacles in the way of God's people, that souls may not be freed from his power and gathered under the banner of Christ. By his deceptions he is seeking to allure souls from Christ, and those who are not established upon the truth will surely be taken in his snare. And those whom he cannot lead into sin he will persecute, as the Jews did Christ.

Satan's object is to dishonor God, and he works with every element that is unsanctified to accomplish this design. The men whom he makes his instruments in doing this work are blinded and do not see what they are doing until they are so deeply involved in guilt that they think it would be useless to try to recover themselves, and they risk all and continue in their course of transgression to the bitter end.

Satan hopes to involve the remnant people of God in the general ruin that is coming upon the earth. As the coming of Christ draws nigh, he will be more determined and decisive in his efforts to overthrow them. Men and women will arise professing to have some new light or some new revelation whose tendency is to unsettle faith in the old landmarks. Their doctrines will not bear the test of God's word, yet souls will be deceived. False reports will be circulated, and some will be taken in this snare. They will believe these rumors and in their turn will repeat them, and thus a link will be formed connecting them with the archdeceiver. This spirit will not always be manifested in an open defiance of the messages that God sends, but a settled unbelief is expressed in many ways. Every false statement that is made feeds and strengthens this unbelief, and through this means many souls will be balanced in the wrong direction.

We cannot be too watchful against every form of error, for Satan is constantly seeking to draw men from the truth. He fills them with notions of their own sufficiency, and persuades them, as he has Brother D, that originality is a gift much to be coveted. Brother D needs to learn the truth more perfectly. Satan has taken advantage of his ignorance in this direction, and here comes the danger. One man has been drawn aside who is hard to be persuaded when once he has set his feet in a wrong track, and many who thought they were only following the man as he followed Christ are betrayed into following him when he has turned his back upon his Saviour.

Pride dwells in the heart of Brother D, and it will be exceedingly difficult for him to yield; but unless he makes a full surrender to Christ, the enemy will continue to work through him. And if he does not at once take a decided stand, I fear he never will.

The _____ and _____ churches have taken a heavy responsibility. The full result of the work they have done will not be known until the judgment. You need heavenly wisdom, brethren, for sin has many disguises. The want of spiritual vision makes you stumble like blind men. Had you had singleness of purpose, it would have been in your conference an element of tremendous power. But the very things I feared have come. There was work to be done that has been left undone. The companies that I saw would have been raised up as the result of well-directed effort, and the meetinghouses that would have been built,—where are they? Your unbelief has held the work. You have done comparatively nothing yourselves, and when one would work, you hedged the way so that he could not labor to any advantage.

Some are slow, very slow, and they pride themselves in it. But this indolent sluggishness is a defect of character of which no man should boast. Make a firm resolve to be prompt, and with divine help you will succeed. Let your consecration be complete; bind property and friends on the altar of God, and when the heart is prepared to receive the heavenly influence, bright beams from the throne of God will flash into your soul, quickening all its dormant energies.

Some men have no firmness of character. They are like a ball of putty and can be pressed into any conceivable shape. They are of no definite form and consistency, and are of no practical use in the world. This weakness, indecision, and inefficiency must be overcome. There is an indomitableness about true Christian character which cannot be molded or subdued by adverse circumstances. Men must have moral backbone, an integrity which cannot be flattered, bribed, or terrified.

I greatly fear for the church. As Paul expressed it: "I fear lest by any means, as the serpent beguiled Eve through his subtlety, so your minds should be corrupted from the simplicity that is in Christ." Paul then explains that it is by means of corrupt teachers that the enemy will assail the faith of the church. "For such are false apostles," he says, "deceitful workers, transforming themselves into the apostles of Christ. And no marvel; for Satan himself is transformed into an angel of light. Therefore it is no great thing if his ministers also be transformed as the ministers of righteousness."

The more we learn in reference to the early days of the Christian church, and see with what subtlety Satan worked to weaken and destroy, the better we shall be prepared to resist his devices and meet coming perils. We are in the time when tribulations such as the world has never yet seen will prevail. "Woe to the inhabiters off the earth and of the sea! for the devil is come down unto you, having great wrath, because he knoweth that he hath but a short time." But God has set bounds that Satan cannot pass. Our most holy faith is this barrier; and if we build ourselves up in the faith, we shall be safe in the keeping of the Mighty One. "Because thou hast kept the word of My patience, I also will keep thee from the hour of temptation, which shall come upon all the world, to try them that dwell upon the earth."

CRITICIZING MINISTERS

One mistake leads to another. Our brethren must learn to move intelligently and not from impulse. Feeling must not be the criterion. A neglect of duty, the indulgence of undue sympathy, will be followed by a neglect to properly estimate those who are laboring to build up the cause of God. Jesus said: "I am come in My Father's name, and ye receive Me not: if another shall come in his own name, him ye will receive."

Many do not look upon preaching as Christ's appointed means of instructing His people and therefore always to be highly prized. They do not feel that the sermon is the word of the Lord to them and estimate it by the value of the truths spoken; but they judge it as they would the speech of a lawyer at the bar—by the argumentative skill displayed and the power and beauty of the language. The minister is not infallible, but God has honored him by making him His messenger. If you listen to him as though he were not commissioned from above you will not respect his words nor receive them as the message of God. Your souls will not feed upon the heavenly manna; doubts will arise concerning some things that are not pleasing to the natural heart, and you will sit in judgment upon the sermon as you would upon the remarks of a lecturer or a political speaker. As soon as the meeting closes you will be ready with some complaint or sarcastic remark, thus showing that the message, however true and needful, has not profited you. You esteem it not; you have learned the habit of criticizing and finding fault, and you pick and choose, and perhaps reject the very things that you most need.

There is very little reverence for sacred things in either the Upper Columbia or the North Pacific Conference.* The ordained instrumentalities of God are almost entirely lost sight of. God has instituted no new method of reaching the children of men. If they cut themselves off from heaven's appointed agencies to reprove their sins, correct their errors, and point out the path of duty, there is no way to reach them with any heavenly communication. They are left in darkness and are ensnared and taken by the adversary.

The minister of God is commanded: "Cry aloud, spare not, lift up thy voice like a trumpet, and show My people their transgression, and the house of Jacob their sins." The Lord says of these people: "They seek Me daily, and delight to know My ways, as a nation that did righteousness." Here is a people who are self-deceived, self-righteous, self-complacent, and the minister is commanded to cry aloud and show them their transgressions. In all ages this work has been done for God's people, and it is needed now more than ever before.

The word of the Lord came to Elijah; he did not seek to be the Lord's messenger, but the word came to him. God always has men to whom He entrusts His message. His Spirit moves upon their hearts and constrains them to speak. Stimulated by holy zeal, and with the divine impulse strong upon them, they enter upon the performance of their duty without coldly calculating the consequences of speaking to the people the word which the Lord has given them. But the servant of God is soon made aware that he has risked something. He finds himself and his message made the subject of criticism. His manners, his life, his property, are all inspected and commented upon. His message is picked to pieces and rejected in the most illiberal and unsanctified spirit, as men in their finite judgment see fit. Has that message done the work that God designed it should accomplish? No, it has signally failed because the hearts of the hearers were unsanctified.

If the minister's face is not flint, if he has not indomitable faith and courage, if his heart is not made strong by constant communion with God, he will begin to shape his testimony to please the unsanctified ears and hearts of those he is addressing. In endeavoring to avoid the criticism to which he is exposed, he separates from God and loses the sense of divine favor, and his testimony becomes tame and lifeless. He finds that his courage and faith are gone and his labors powerless. The world is full of flatterers and dissemblers who have yielded to the desire to please; but the faithful men, who do not study self-interest, but love their brethren too well to suffer sin upon them, are few indeed.

It is Satan's settled purpose to cut off all communication between God and His people, that he may practice his deceptive wiles with no voice to warn them of their danger. If he can lead men to distrust the messenger or to attach no sacredness to the message, he knows that they will feel under no obligation to heed the word of God to them. And when light is set aside as darkness, Satan has things his own way.

Our God is a jealous God; He is not to be trifled with. He who does all things according to the counsel of His own will has been pleased to place men under various circumstances, and to enjoin upon them duties and observances peculiar to the times in which they live and the conditions under which they are placed. If they would prize the light given them, their faculties would be greatly enlarged and ennobled, and broader views of truth would be opened before them. The mysteries of eternal things, and especially the wonderful grace of God as manifested in the plan of redemption, would be unfolded to their minds; for spiritual things are spiritually discerned.

We are never to forget that Christ teaches through His servants. There may be conversions without the instrumentality of a sermon. Where persons are so situated that they are deprived of every means of grace, they are wrought upon by the Spirit of God and convinced of the truth through reading the word; but God's appointed means of saving souls is through "the foolishness of preaching." Though human, and compassed with the frailties of humanity, men are God's messengers; and the dear Saviour is grieved when so little is effected by their labors. Every minister who goes out into the great harvest field should magnify his office. He should not only seek to bring men to the knowledge of the truth, but he should labor, as did Paul, "warning every man, and teaching every man in all wisdom," that he may "present every man perfect in Christ Jesus."

The man is to be regarded and honored only as God's ambassador. To praise the man is not pleasing to God. The message he brings is to be brought to the test of the Bible. "To the law and to the testimony: if they speak not according to this word, it is because there is no light in them." But the word of the Lord is not to be judged by a human standard. It will be seen that those whose minds have the mold of earthliness, those who have a limited Christian experience and know but little of the things of God, are the ones who have the least respect for God's servants and the least reverence for the message He bids them bear. They listen to a searching discourse and go to their homes prepared to sit in judgment on it, and the impression disappears from their minds like the morning dew before the sun. If the preaching is of an emotional character, it will affect the feelings, but not the heart and conscience. Such preaching results in no lasting good, but it often wins the hearts of the people and calls out their affections for the man who pleases them. They forget that God has said: "Cease ye from man, whose breath is in his nostrils."

Jesus is waiting with longing desire to open before His people the glory that will attend His second advent, and to carry them forward to a contemplation of the landscapes of bliss. There are wonders to be revealed. A long lifetime of prayer and research will leave much unexplored and unexplained. But what we know not now will be revealed hereafter. The work of instruction begun here will be carried on to all eternity. The Lamb, as He leads the hosts of the redeemed to the Fountain of living waters, will impart rich stores of knowledge; He will unravel mysteries in the works and providence of God that have never before been understood.

We can never by searching find out God. He does not lay open His plans to prying, inquisitive minds. We must not attempt to lift with presumptuous hand the curtain behind which He veils His majesty. The apostle exclaims: "How unsearchable are His judgments, and His ways past finding out!" It is a proof of His mercy that there is the hiding of His power, that He is enshrouded in the awful clouds of mystery and obscurity; for to lift the curtain that conceals the divine presence is death. No mortal mind can penetrate the secrecy in which the Mighty One dwells and works. We can comprehend no more of His dealings with us and the motives that actuate Him than He sees fit to reveal. He orders everything in righteousness, and we are not to be dissatisfied and distrustful, but to bow in reverent submission. He will reveal to us as much of His purposes as it is for our good to know; and beyond that we must trust the hand that is omnipotent, the heart that is full of love.

FIDELITY AND PERSEVERANCE NEEDED

The state of the church in _____ is far from what it should be. Unless there is a decided change, it will wither and die. There is much faultfinding; many are giving way to doubt and unbelief. Those who talk faith and cultivate faith will have faith, but those who cherish and express doubts will have doubts.

There has been a neglect on the part of the ministers. They have not urged home to the hearts of their hearers the necessity of faithfulness. They have not educated the church on all points of truth and duty nor labored with zeal to bring them into working order and to get them interested in every branch of the cause of God. I have been shown that had the church been properly educated, they would have been far in advance of their present position. The neglect on the part of the ministers has made the people careless and unfaithful. They have not felt their individual responsibility, but have excused themselves on account of the failure of the ministers to do the work of a pastor. But God does not hold them excused. Had they no Bible, had they no warnings, reproofs, and entreaties from heaven to bring duty to their minds, there would be less condemnation. But the Lord has given counsel and instruction;

the duty of each individual has been made so plain that he need make no mistake.

God gives light to guide those who honestly desire light and truth; but it is not His purpose to remove all cause for questioning and doubt. He gives sufficient evidence to found faith upon, and then requires men to accept that evidence and exercise faith.

He who will study the Bible with a humble and teachable spirit will find it a sure guide, pointing out the way of life with unfailing accuracy. But what does your study of the Bible avail, brethren and sisters, unless you practice the truths it teaches? That holy book contains nothing that is nonessential; nothing is revealed that has not a bearing upon our actual lives. The deeper our love for Jesus, the more highly we shall regard that word as the voice of God directly to us.

The church in _____ is standing on Satan's enchanted ground, and there is necessity for a thorough conversion. Individual effort is needed. The rich promises of the Bible are for those who take up their cross and deny self daily. Everyone who has a sincere desire to be a learner in the school of Christ will cultivate spiritual-mindedness and will avail himself of every means of grace, but in this church opportunities and privileges have been slighted. One may be able to say but few words in public and to do but little in the vineyard of the Lord, but he is in duty bound to say something and to be an interested worker. Every member should help to strengthen and sustain the church; but in many cases there are one or two who have the spirit of faithfulness that characterized Caleb of old, and these are permitted to bear the burdens and take the responsibilities, while the rest shirk all care.

Caleb was faithful and steadfast. He was not boastful, he made no parade of his merits and good deeds; but his influence was always on the side of right. And what was his reward? When the Lord denounced judgments against the men who refused to hearken to His voice, He said: "But My servant Caleb, because he had another spirit with him, and hath followed Me fully, him will I bring into the land whereinto he went; and his seed shall possess it." While the cowards and murmurers perished in the wilderness, faithful Caleb had a home in the promised Canaan. "Them that honor Me I will honor," saith the Lord.

Hannah prayed and trusted; and in her son Samuel she gave to the Israel of God a most precious treasure—a useful man, with a well-formed character, one who was as firm as a rock where principle was concerned.

In Joppa there was a Dorcas, whose skillful fingers were more active than her tongue. She knew who needed comfortable clothing and who needed sympathy, and she freely ministered to the wants of both classes. And when Dorcas died, the church in Joppa realized their loss. It is no wonder that they mourned and lamented, nor that warm teardrops fell upon the inanimate clay. She was of so great value that by the power of God she was brought back from the land of the enemy, that her skill and energy might still be a blessing to others.

Such patient, prayerful, and persevering fidelity as was possessed by these saints of God is rare; yet the church cannot prosper without it. It is needed in the church, in the Sabbath school, and in society. Many come together in church relationship with their natural traits of character unsubdued; and in a crisis, when strong, hopeful spirits are needed, they give up to discouragement and bring burdens on the church; and they do not see that this is wrong. The cause does not need such persons, for they are unreliable; but there is always a call for steadfast, God-fearing workers, who will not faint in the day of adversity.

There are some in the church in ＿＿＿ who will cause trouble, for their wills have never been brought into harmony with the will of Christ. Brother E will be a great hindrance to this church. When he can have the supremacy he is satisfied, but when he cannot stand first he is always upon the wrong side. He moves from impulse. He will not draw in even cords, but questions and takes opposite views, because it is his nature to be faultfinding and an accuser of his brethren. While he claims to be very zealous for the truth, he is drawing away from the body; he is not strong in moral power, rooted and grounded in the faith. The holy principles of truth are not made a part of his nature. He cannot be trusted; God is not pleased with him.

Brother and Sister E have not regarded the directions of God's word in the training of their children. These children have been allowed to control at home to a very great degree and have come and gone as they pleased. Unless they are placed under entirely different influences they will be found in the enemy's ranks, warring against order, discipline, and subordination. Children thus left to have their own way are not happy; and where parental authority is lightly regarded, the authority of God will not be respected.

The work of the parent is solemn and sacred; but many do not realize this because their eyes are blinded by the enemy of all righteousness. Their children are allowed to grow up undisciplined, uncourteous, forward, self-confident, unthankful, and unholy, when a firm, decided, even course, in which justice and mercy are blended with patience and self-control, would produce wonderful results.

Brother E must have transforming grace. There is no safety for him while he retains his natural defects of character, and he must war against them continually. Unless he will live a watchful, prayerful life he will not be well balanced, and there is danger that the truth will be hindered, misrepresented, and brought into disrepute through his influence. Let him be careful lest he awaken in unbelievers prejudices that can never be removed.

There is in human nature a tendency to run to extremes and from one extreme to another entirely opposite. Many are fanatics. They are consumed by a fiery zeal which is mistaken for religion, but character is the true test of discipleship. Have they the meekness of Christ? have they His humility and sweet benevolence? Is the soul-temple emptied of pride, arrogance, selfishness, and censoriousness? If not, they know not what manner of spirit they are of. They do not realize that true Christianity consists in bearing much fruit to the glory of God.

Others go to an extreme in their conformity to the world. There is no clear, distinct line of separation between them and the worldling. If in one case men are driven away from the truth by a harsh, censorious, condemnatory spirit, in this they are led to conclude that the professed Christian is destitute of principle and knows nothing of a change of heart or character. "Let your light so shine before men, that they may see your good works, and glorify your Father which is in heaven," are the words of Christ.

There are many who have not a correct knowledge of what constitutes a Christian character, and their lives are a reproach to the cause of truth. If they were thoroughly converted they would not bear briers and thorns, but rich clusters of the precious fruits of the Spirit,— "love, joy, peace, long-suffering, gentleness, goodness, faith, meekness, temperance." The great danger is in neglecting a heartwork. Many feel well pleased with themselves; they think that a nominal observance of the divine law is sufficient, while they are unacquainted with the grace of Christ, and He is not abiding in the heart by living faith.

"Without Me," says Christ, "ye can do nothing;" but with His divine grace working through our human efforts, we can do all things. His patience and meekness will pervade the character, diffusing a precious radiance which makes bright and clear the pathway to heaven. By beholding and imitating His life we shall become renewed in His image. The glory of heaven will shine in our lives and be reflected upon others. At the throne of grace we are to find the help we need to enable us to live thus. This is genuine sanctification, and what more exalted position can mortals desire than to be connected with Christ as a branch is joined to the vine?

I have seen a device representing a bullock standing between a plow and an altar, with the inscription, "Ready for either"—willing to swelter in the weary furrow or to bleed on the altar of sacrifice. This is the position the child of God should ever be in—willing to go where duty calls, to deny self, and to sacrifice for the cause of truth. The Christian church was founded upon the principle of sacrifice. "If any man will come after Me," says Christ, "let him deny himself, and take up his cross daily, and follow Me." He requires the whole heart, the entire affections. The exhibitions of zeal, earnestness, and unselfish labor which His devoted followers have given to the world should kindle our ardor and lead us to emulate their example. Genuine religion gives an earnestness and fixedness of purpose which molds the character to the divine image and enables us to count all things but loss for the excellency of Christ. This singleness of purpose will prove an element of tremendous power.

We have a greater and more solemn truth than was ever before committed to mortals, and we are responsible for the way we treat that truth. Every one of us should be intent on saving souls. We should show the power of the truth upon our own hearts and characters, while doing all we can to win others to love it. To bring a sinner to Christ is to elevate, dignify, and ennoble his whole character, and make him a blessing in the home, in society, and in the church. Is not this a work that is worthy of our noblest powers?

Persons of little talent, if faithful in keeping their hearts in the love of God, may win many souls to Christ. Harlan Page was a poor mechanic of ordinary ability and limited education; but he made it his chief business to seek to advance the cause of God, and his efforts were crowned with marked success. He labored for the salvation of his fellow men in private conversation and in earnest prayer. He established prayer meetings, organized Sunday schools, and distributed tracts and other religious reading. And on his deathbed, with the shadow of eternity resting upon his countenance, he was able to say: "I know that it is all of God's grace, and not through any merit of anything that I have done, but I think I have evidence that more than one hundred souls have been converted to God through my personal instrumentality."

Every member of the church should be instructed in a regular system of labor. All are required to do something for the Lord. They may interest persons to read; they may converse and pray with them. The minister who shall educate, discipline, and lead an army of efficient workers will have glorious conquests here, and a rich reward awaits him when, around the great white throne, he shall meet those saved through his influence.

> Do something, do it soon, with all thy might;
> An angel's wing would droop if long at rest;
> And God Himself, inactive, were no longer blest.

After the church in _____ came to the knowledge of the truth, they would have been fruitful in good works, and would have had an influence that would make them a power on the side of right, had they manifested becoming earnestness, zeal, and love. But they have been indifferent, and have been growing cold and dead. Some have attended social meetings when they have carried with them the atmosphere of earth rather than that of heaven. The church has not been ready to respond to the efforts that have been made for them. In their present state they cannot see or realize the need of co-operation on their part; and their lack of earnestness and consecration has discouraged the ministers. Instead of this carelessness, there should have been a feeling of individual responsibility. This church will never prosper until the members commence the work of reform in their own hearts. Many who profess the faith are easily satisfied; if they come up to a few points of self-denial and reform they do not see the necessity of going further. Why is there such a resting on the lees? There is no halting place for us this side of heaven. None of us should be content with our present spiritual attainments. No one is living up to his opportunities unless he can show continual progress. He must be climbing, still climbing. It is the privilege of every Christian to grow up until he shall reach the full stature of a man in Christ Jesus.

How much the dear people in _____ need instruction in personal godliness; how much they need pastoral labor. But they do not do as well as they know. God will test you, brethren, and some will prove to be chaff and some precious grains of wheat. Yield not to the power of the tempter. He will come as a strong man armed, but give him no advantage. Nerve yourselves for duty, and dispute every inch of ground. Instead of retreating, advance; instead of becoming weak and nerveless, brace yourselves for the conflict. God calls on you to engage with all your powers against sin in every form. Put on the whole armor of God, and keep your eye steadily fixed on the Captain of your salvation; for there is danger ahead. Follow no false colors, but watch the banner of our holy faith, and be found where that waves, even though it be in the thickest of the fight. Soon the warfare will be over and the victory won, and if you are faithful you will come off more than conquerors through Him that has loved you. The glorious prize, the eternal weight of glory, will then be yours.

SINFULNESS OF REPINING

Dear Friends: I have been shown that as a family you experience much needless unhappiness. God has not designed that you should be miserable; but you have taken your minds from Jesus and centered them too much upon yourselves. The great sin of your family is that of needless repining over God's providences; your unsubmissiveness in this respect is indeed alarming. You have magnified small difficulties and have talked discouragements too much. You have a habit of draping everything about you in mourning and have made yourselves unhappy without cause. Your continued murmurings are separating you from God.

You should keep off from Satan's enchanted ground and not allow your minds to be swayed from allegiance to God. Through Christ you may and should be happy and should acquire habits of self-control. Even your thoughts must be brought into subjection to the will of God and your feelings under the control of reason and religion. Your imagination was not given you to be allowed to run riot and have its own way without any effort at restraint or discipline. If the thoughts are wrong the feelings will be wrong, and the thoughts and feelings combined make up the moral character. When you decide that as Christians you are not required to restrain your thoughts and feelings you are brought under the influence of evil angels and invite their presence and their control. If you yield to your impressions and allow your thoughts to run in a channel of suspicion, doubt, and repining you will be among the most unhappy of mortals, and your lives will prove a failure.

Dear Sister F, you have a diseased imagination; and you dishonor God by allowing your feelings to have complete control of your reason and judgment. You have a determined will, which causes the mind to react upon the body, unbalancing the circulation and producing congestion in certain organs; and you are sacrificing health to your feelings.

You are making a mistake, which, if not corrected, will not end with wrecking your own happiness merely. You are doing positive injury, not only to yourself, but to the other members of your family, and especially your mother. She is very nervous and highly sensitive. If one of her children is suffering, she becomes confused and almost distracted. Her mind is becoming unbalanced by the frequent fits of hysteria which she is compelled to witness, and great unhappiness is brought upon all around you. And yet you are capable of controlling your imagination and overcoming these nervous attacks. You have will power, and you should bring it to your aid. You have not done this, but have let your highly wrought imagination control reason. In this you have grieved the Spirit of God. Had you no power over your feelings, this would not be sin; but it will not answer thus to yield to the enemy. Your will needs to be sanctified and subdued instead of being arrayed in opposition to that of God.

My dear friends, instead of taking a course to baffle disease, you are petting it and yielding to its power. You should avoid the use of drugs and carefully observe the laws of health. If you regard your life you should eat plain food, prepared in the simplest manner, and take more physical exercise. Each member of the family needs the benefits of health reform. But drugging should be forever abandoned; for while it does not cure any malady, it enfeebles the system, making it more susceptible to disease.

Man has been placed in a world of sorrow, care, and perplexity. He is placed here to be tested and proved, as were Adam and Eve, that he may develop a right character and bring harmony out of discord and confusion. There is much for us to do that is essential to our own happiness and that of others. And there is much for us to enjoy. Through Christ we are brought into connection with God. His mercies place us under continual obligation; feeling unworthy of His favors, we are to appreciate even the least of them.

For all that you have and are, dear friends, you are indebted to God. He has given you powers that, to a certain extent, are similar to those which He Himself possesses; and you should labor earnestly to develop these powers, not to please and exalt self, but to glorify Him. You have not improved your privileges to the best advantage. You should educate yourselves to bear responsibilities. Intellect must be cultivated; if left to rust from inaction it will become debased.

This earth is the Lord's. Here it may be seen that nature, animate and inanimate, obeys His will. God created man a superior being; he alone is formed in the image of God and is capable of partaking of the divine nature, of cooperating with his Creator and executing His plans; and he alone is found at war with God's purposes.

How wonderfully, with what marvelous beauty, has everything in nature been fashioned. Everywhere we see the perfect works of the great Master Artist. The heavens declare His glory, and the earth which is formed for the happiness of man, speaks to us of His matchless love. Its surface is not a monotonous plain, but grand old mountains rise to diversify the landscape. There are sparkling streams and fertile valleys, beautiful lakes, broad rivers, and the boundless ocean. God sends the dew and the rain to refresh the thirsty earth. The breezes, that promote health by purifying and cooling the atmosphere, are controlled by His wisdom. He has placed the sun in the heavens to mark the periods of day and night, and by its genial beams give light and warmth to the earth, causing vegetation to flourish.

I call your attention to these blessings from the bounteous hand of God. Let the fresh glories of each new morning awaken praise in your hearts for these tokens of His loving care. But while our kind heavenly Father has given us so many things to promote our happiness, He has given us also blessings in disguise. He understands the necessities of fallen man; and while He has given us advantages on the one hand, on the other there are inconveniences which are designed to stimulate us to use the ability He has given us. These develop patient industry, perseverance, and courage.

There are evils which man may lessen but can never remove. He is to overcome obstacles and make his surroundings instead of being molded by them. He has room to exercise his talents in bringing order and harmony out of confusion. In this work he may have divine aid if he will claim it. He is not left to battle with temptations and trials in his own strength. Help has been laid upon One who is mighty. Jesus left the royal courts of heaven and suffered and died in a world degraded by sin, that He might teach man how to pass through the trials of life and overcome its temptations. Here is a pattern for us.

As the benefits conferred upon His creatures by our heavenly Father are recounted, do you not feel reproved for your ungrateful repinings? For a number of years He lent you a daughter and sister, until you began to regard her as yours and felt that you had a right to this good gift. God heard your murmurings. If there was a cloud in sight, you seemed to forget that the sun ever shone; and clouds and darkness were ever about you. God sent you affliction; He removed your treasure from you that you might discern between prosperity and real sorrow. But you did not subdue your hearts before Him and repent of the great sin of ingratitude which had separated you from His love. Like Job, you felt that you had cause for grief, and would not be comforted. Was this reasonable? You know that death is a power that none can resist; but you have made your lives nearly useless by your unavailing grief. Your feelings have been little less than rebellion against God. I saw you all dwelling upon your bereavement, and giving way to your excitable feelings, until your noisy demonstrations of grief caused angels to hide their faces and withdraw from the scene.

While thus giving way to your feelings, did you remember that you had a Father in heaven who gave His only Son to die for us that death might not be an eternal sleep? Did you remember that the Lord of life and glory passed through the tomb and brightened it with His own presence? Said the beloved disciple: "Write, Blessed are the dead which die in the Lord from henceforth: Yea, saith the Spirit, that they may rest from their labors; and their works do follow them." The apostle well knew what he was talking about when he wrote these words; but when you give way to uncontrollable grief, is your conduct consistent with the comfort which they express?

The Lord is gracious, merciful, and true. He has permitted the one of your household band who was the most innocent and the best prepared to rest through the perils of the last days. Oh! do not shut up your souls against melody and joy, mourning as though there were to be no resurrection of the dead, but praise God that for her there is no more death, no more trial, no more sorrow. She rests in Jesus until the Life-giver shall call forth His sleeping saints to a glorious immortality.

F has a work to do, through the grace of God, to control her feelings. She knows that she is not in heaven, but in a world where death reigns and where our loved ones may be removed from us at any moment. She should feel that the great burden of life is to prepare for a better world. If she has a right hold on eternal life, it will not disqualify her for living in this world and nobly bearing life's burdens, but it will help her in the performance of self-denying, self-sacrificing duties.

As a family you have talked darkness and complaining until you are changed into the same image. You seem to work upon one another's sympathies and to arouse nervous excitability until you have a dark, sad, dismal time by yourselves. You have held mourning services, but these do not attract angels around you. If you do not change your course, God will come a little closer and deal with you in judgment. Is it not time that you hold thanksgiving services in your home and recount with rejoicing the blessings that have been bestowed upon you?

The power of the truth should be sufficient to sustain and console in every adversity. It is in enabling its possessor to triumph over affliction that the religion of Christ reveals its true value. It brings the appetites, the passions, and the emotions under the control of reason and conscience, and disciplines the thoughts to flow in a healthful channel. And then the tongue will not be left to dishonor God by expressions of sinful repining.

Our Creator justly claims the right to do as He chooses with the creatures of His hand. He has a right to govern as He will, and not as man chooses. But He is not a severe judge, a harsh, exacting creditor. He is the very fountain of love, the giver of blessings innumerable. It should cause you the deepest grief that you have disregarded such love, and have not let gratitude and praise well up in your hearts for the marvelous goodness of God. We do not deserve all His benefits; but they are continued to us, notwithstanding our unworthiness and cruel ingratitude. Then cease to complain as though you were bond servants under a hard taskmaster. Jesus is good. Praise Him. Praise Him who is the health of your countenance, and your God.

"PRAISE YE THE LORD"

"Let everything that hath breath praise the Lord." Have any of us duly considered how much we have to be thankful for? Do we remember that the mercies of the Lord are new every morning and that His faithfulness faileth not? Do we acknowledge our dependence upon Him and express gratitude for all His favors? On the contrary, we too often forget that "every good gift and every perfect gift is from above, and cometh down from the Father of lights."

How often those who are in health forget the wonderful mercies that are continued to them day by day, year after year. They render no tribute of praise to God for all His benefits. But when sickness comes, God is remembered. The strong desire for recovery leads to earnest prayer, and this is right. God is our refuge in sickness as in health. But many do not leave their cases with Him; they encourage weakness and disease by worrying about themselves. If they would cease repining and rise above depression and gloom, their recovery would be more sure. They should remember with gratitude how long they enjoyed the blessing of health; and should this precious boon be restored to them, they should not forget that they are under renewed obligations to their Creator. When the ten lepers were healed, only one returned to find Jesus and give Him glory. Let us not be like the unthinking nine, whose hearts were untouched by the mercy of God.

God is love. He has a care for the creatures He has formed. "Like as a father pitieth his children, so the Lord pitieth them that fear Him." "Behold, what manner of love the Father hath bestowed upon us, that we should be called the sons of God." What a precious privilege is this, that we may be sons and daughters of the Most High, heirs of God and joint heirs with Jesus Christ. Then let us not mourn and grieve because in this life we are not free from disappointments and afflictions. If in the providence of God we are called upon to endure trials, let us accept the cross and drink the bitter cup, remembering that it is a Father's hand that holds it to our lips. Let us trust Him in the darkness as well as in the day. Can we not believe that He will give us everything that is for our good? "He that spared not His own Son, but delivered Him up for us all, how shall He not with Him also freely give us all things?" Even in the night of affliction how can we refuse to lift heart and voice in grateful praise, when we remember the love to us expressed by the cross of Calvary?

What a theme for meditation is the sacrifice that Jesus made for lost sinners! "He was wounded for our transgressions, He was bruised for our iniquities: the chastisement of our peace was upon Him; and with His stripes we are healed." How shall we estimate the blessings thus brought within our reach? Could Jesus have suffered more? Could He have purchased for us richer blessings? Should it not melt the hardest heart when we remember that for our sakes He left the happiness and glory of heaven and suffered poverty and shame, cruel affliction and a terrible death? Had He not by His death and resurrection opened for us the door of hope, we should have known nothing but the horrors of darkness and the miseries of despair. In our present state, favored and blessed as we are, we cannot realize from what depths we have been rescued. We cannot measure how much deeper our afflictions would have been, how much greater our woes, had not Jesus encircled us with His human arm of sympathy and love, and lifted us up.

We may rejoice in hope. Our Advocate is in the heavenly sanctuary, pleading in our behalf. Through His merits we have pardon and peace. He died that He might wash away our sins, clothe us with His righteousness, and fit us for the society of heaven, where we may dwell in light forever. Dear brother, dear sister, when Satan would fill your mind with despondency, gloom, and doubt, resist his suggestions. Tell him of the blood of Jesus, that cleanses from all sin. You cannot save yourself from the tempter's power, but he trembles and flees when the merits of that precious blood are urged. Then will you not gratefully accept the blessings Jesus bestows? Will you not take the cup of salvation that He presents, and call on the name of the Lord? Do not show distrust of Him who has called you out of darkness into His marvelous light. Do not for a moment pain the heart of the pitying Saviour by your unbelief. He watches with the most intense interest your progress in the heavenly way; He sees your earnest efforts; He notes your declensions and your recoveries, your hopes and your fears, your conflicts and your victories.

Shall all our devotional exercises consist in asking and receiving? Shall we be always thinking of our wants and never of the benefits we receive? Shall we be recipients of His mercies and never express our gratitude to God, never praise Him for what He has done for us? We do not pray any too much, but we are too sparing of giving thanks. If the loving-kindness of God called forth more thanksgiving and praise, we would have far more power in prayer. We would abound more and more in the love of God and have more bestowed to praise Him for. You who complain that God does not hear your prayers, change your present order and mingle praise with your petitions. When you consider His goodness and mercies you will find that He will consider your wants.

Pray, pray earnestly and without ceasing, but do not forget to praise. It becomes every child of God to vindicate His character. You can magnify the Lord; you can show the power of sustaining grace. There are multitudes who do not appreciate the great love of God nor the divine compassion of Jesus. Thousands even regard with disdain the matchless grace shown in the plan of redemption. All who are partakers of this great salvation are not clear in this matter. They do not cultivate grateful hearts. But the theme of redemption is one that the angels desire to look into; it will be the science and the song of the ransomed throughout the ceaseless ages of eternity. Is it not worthy of careful thought and study now? Should we not praise God with heart and soul and voice "for His wonderful works to the children of men"?

Praise the Lord in the congregation of His people. When the word of the Lord was spoken to the Hebrews anciently, the command was: "And let all the people say, Amen." When the ark of the covenant was brought into the city of David, and a psalm of joy and triumph was chanted, "all the people said, Amen, and praised the Lord." This fervent response was an evidence that they understood the word spoken and joined in the worship of God.

There is too much formality in our religious services. The Lord would have His ministers who preach the word energized by His Holy Spirit; and the people who hear should not sit in drowsy indifference, or stare vacantly about, making no responses to what is said. The impression that is thus given to the unbeliever is anything but favorable for the religion of Christ. These dull, careless professed Christians are not destitute of ambition and zeal when engaged in worldly business; but things of eternal importance do not move them deeply. The voice of God through His messengers may be a pleasant song; but its sacred warnings, reproofs, and encouragements are all unheeded. The spirit of the world has paralyzed them. The truths of God's word are spoken to leaden ears and hard, unimpressible hearts. There should be wide-awake, active churches to encourage and uphold the ministers of Christ and to aid them in the work of saving souls. Where the church is walking in the light, there will ever be cheerful, hearty responses and words of joyful praise.

Our God, the Creator of the heavens and the earth, declares: "Whoso offereth praise glorifieth Me." All heaven unite in praising God. Let us learn the song of the angels now, that we may sing it when we join their shining ranks. Let us say with the psalmist: "While I live will I praise the Lord: I will sing praises unto my God while I have any being." "Let the people praise Thee, O God; let all the people praise Thee."

PARENTAL RESPONSIBILITY

Parents are in a great degree responsible for the mold given to the characters of their children. They should aim at symmetry and proportion. There are few well-balanced minds, because parents are wickedly negligent of their duty to stimulate weak traits and repress wrong ones. They do not remember that they are under the most solemn obligation to watch the tendencies of each child, that it is their duty to train their children to right habits and right ways of thinking.

Sometimes parents wait for the Lord to do the very work that He has given them to do. Instead of restraining and controlling their children as they should, they pet and indulge them, and gratify their whims and desires. When these children go out from their early homes, it is with characters deformed by selfishness, with ungoverned appetites, with strong self-will; they are destitute of courtesy or respect for their parents, and do not love religious truth or the worship of God. They have grown up with traits that are a lifelong curse to themselves and to others. Home is made anything but happy if the evil weeds of dissension, selfishness, envy, passion, and sullen stubbornness are left to flourish in the neglected garden of the soul.

Parents should show no partiality, but should treat all their children with tenderness, remembering that they are the purchase of Christ's blood. Children imitate their parents; hence great care should be taken to give them correct models. Parents who are kind and polite at home, while at the same time they are firm and decided, will see the same traits manifested in their children. If they are upright, honest, and honorable, their children will be quite likely to resemble them in these particulars. If they reverence and worship God, their children, trained in the same way, will not forget to serve Him also.

It is often the case that parents are not careful to surround their children with right influences. In choosing a home they think more of their worldly interests than of the moral and social atmosphere, and the children form associations that are unfavorable to the development of piety and the formation of right characters. Then parents allow the world to engross their time, strength, and thought, and when the Sabbath comes, it finds them so utterly exhausted that they have nought to render to God on His holy day, no sweet piety to grace the home and make the Sabbath a delight to their children. They are seldom visited by a minister, for they have placed themselves out of reach of religious privileges. An apathy steals over the soul. The children are contaminated by evil communications, and the tenderness of soul that they once felt dies away and is forgotten.

Parents who denounce the Canaanites for offering their children to Moloch, what are you doing? You are making a most costly offering to your mammon god; and then, when your children grow up unloved and unlovely in character, when they show decided impiety and a tendency to infidelity, you blame the faith you profess because it was unable to save them. You are reaping that which you have sown—the result of your selfish love of the world and neglect of the means of grace. You moved your families into places of temptation, and the ark of God, your glory and defense, you did not consider essential; and the Lord has not worked a miracle to deliver your children from temptation.

You who profess to love God, take Jesus with you wherever you go, and, like the patriarchs of old, erect an altar to the Lord wherever you pitch your tent. A reformation in this respect is needed, a reformation that shall be deep and broad. Parents need to reform; ministers need to reform. They need God in their households. They need to build the waste places of Zion, to set up her gates and make strong her walls for a defense of the people.

There is earnest work to be done in this age, and parents should educate their children to share in it. The words of Mordecai to Esther may apply to the men and youth of today: "Who knoweth whether thou art come to the kingdom for such a time as this?" Young men should be gaining solidity of character, that they may be fitted for usefulness. Daniel and Joseph were youth of firm principle, whom God could use to carry out His purposes. Mark their history, and see how God wrought for them. Joseph met with a variety of experiences, experiences that tested his courage and uprightness to the fullest extent. After being sold into Egypt he was at first favored and entrusted with great responsibilities; but suddenly, without any fault on his part, he was unjustly accused and cast into prison. But he is not discouraged. He trusts in God; and the purpose of his heart, the purity of his motive, is made manifest. The eye of God is upon him, a divine hand leads him, and soon we see him come forth from prison to share the throne of Egypt.

Joseph's checkered life was not an accident; it was ordered of Providence. But how was he enabled to make such a record of firmness of character, uprightness, and wisdom? It was the result of careful training in his early years. He had consulted duty rather than inclination; and the purity and simple trust of the boy bore fruit in the deeds of the man. The most brilliant talents are of no value unless they are improved; industrious habits and force of character must be gained by cultivation. A high moral character and fine mental qualities are not the result of accident. God gives opportunities; success depends upon the use made of them. The openings of Providence must be quickly discerned and eagerly seized upon.

Young men, if you would be strong, if you would have the

integrity and wisdom of a Joseph or a Daniel, study the Scriptures. Parents, if you would educate your children to serve God and do good in the world, make the Bible your textbook. It exposes the wiles of Satan. It is the great elevator of the race, the reprover and corrector of moral evils, the detector which enables us to distinguish between the true and the false. Whatever else is taught in the home or at school, the Bible, as the great educator, should stand first. If it is given this place, God is honored, and He will work for you in the conversion of your children. There is a rich mine of truth and beauty in this Holy Book, and parents have themselves to blame if they do not make it intensely interesting to their children.

To many, education means a knowledge of books; but "the fear of the Lord is the beginning of wisdom." The true object of education is to restore the image of God in the soul. The first and most precious knowledge is the knowledge of Christ; and wise parents will keep this fact ever before the minds of their children. Should a limb be broken or fractured, parents will try every means that love or wisdom can suggest to restore the affected member to comeliness and soundness. This is right; it is their duty. But the Lord requires that still greater tact, patience, and persevering effort be employed to remedy blemishes of the soul. That father is unworthy of the name who is not to his children a Christian teacher, ruler, and friend, binding them to his heart by the strong ties of sanctified love—a love which has its foundation in duty faithfully performed.

Parents have a great and responsible work to do, and they may well inquire: "Who is sufficient for these things?" But God has promised to give wisdom to those that ask in faith, and He will do just as He said He would. He is pleased with the faith that takes Him at His word. The mother of Augustine prayed for her son's conversion. She saw no evidence that the Spirit of God was impressing his heart, but she was not discouraged. She laid her finger upon the texts, presenting before God His own words, and pleaded as only a mother can.

Her deep humiliation, her earnest importunities, her unwavering faith, prevailed, and the Lord gave her the desire of her heart. Today He is just as ready to listen to the petitions of His people. His "hand is not shortened, that it cannot save; neither His ear heavy, that it cannot hear;" and if Christian parents seek Him earnestly, He will fill their mouths with arguments, and for His name's sake will work mightily in their behalf in the conversion of their children.

THE TRAINING OF CHILDREN

Dear Brother and Sister G: I am troubled in reference to your case. I see dangers that you seem never to have realized. Have you thoughtfully and prayerfully considered your duty to the children you have taken the responsibility of bringing into the world? Have you thought whether these children are receiving from you an education and discipline that will lead them to honor their Creator in the days of their youth? Have you considered that if you fail to teach them to respect you, their father and mother, and to yield to your authority, you are educating them to dishonor God? Every time you allow them to trample on your authority, and their will to control yours, you are fostering a defect which will be carried with them into all their experience should they become religiously inclined, and will teach them to disregard and trample upon divine authority.

The question to be settled by you is: "Am I raising a family of children to strengthen the influence and swell the ranks of the powers of darkness, or am I bringing up children for Christ?" If you do not govern your children and mold their characters to meet the requirements of God, then the fewer children there are to suffer from your defective training the better it will be for you, their parents, and the better it will be for society. Unless children can be trained and disciplined from their babyhood by a wise and judicious mother, who is conscientious and intelligent, and who rules her household in the fear of the Lord, molding and shaping their characters to meet the standard of righteousness, it is a sin to increase your family. God has given you reason, and He requires you to use it.

You should feel under obligation, by patient, painstaking effort and by earnest, fervent prayer, to so form the characters of your children as to make them a blessing in the home, a blessing in the church, and a blessing in society. You will receive no credit for your work if you allow your children to be controlled by the enemy of all righteousness; the reward is promised for conscientiously forming their characters after the divine Pattern. If you neglect this work, which is so far-reaching in its results, because for the present it is more agreeable for you to do so, and your children grow up morally deformed, their feet in the broad road to death, can God pronounce your work well done? Those who cannot inform themselves, and work intelligently with all their powers to bring their children to Jesus, should decide not to take upon themselves the responsibility of becoming parents.

Mothers must be willing and even anxious to qualify themselves for their important work of developing the characters of their children, guiding, instructing, and restraining their tender charge. Fathers and mothers should be united in this work. Weakness in requiring obedience, and false love and sympathy—the false notion that to indulge and not to restrain is wisdom—constitute a system of training that grieves angels; but it delights Satan, for it brings hundreds and thousands of children into his ranks. This is why he blinds the eyes of parents, benumbs their sensibilities, and confuses their minds. They see that their sons and daughters are not pleasant, lovely, obedient, and care-taking; yet children accumulate in their homes, to poison their lives, fill their hearts with grief, and add to the number whom Satan is using to allure souls to destruction.

Oh! when will parents be wise? When will they see and realize the character of their work in neglecting to require obedience and respect according to the instructions of God's word? The results of this lax training are seen in the children as they go out into the world and take their place at the head of families of their own. They perpetuate the mistakes of their parents. Their defective traits have full scope; and they transmit to others the wrong tastes, habits, and tempers that were permitted to develop in their own characters. Thus they become a curse instead of a blessing to society.

Because men and women do not obey God, but choose their own way and follow their own perverted imagination, Satan is permitted to set up his hellish banner in their families and make his power felt through babes, children, and youth. His voice and will are expressed in the unsubdued will and warped characters of the children, and through them he exerts a controlling power and carries out his plans. God is dishonored by the exhibition of perverse tempers, which exclude reverence for Him and induce obedience to Satan's suggestions. The sin committed by parents in thus permitting Satan to bear sway is beyond conception. They are sowing seed which will produce briers and thorns, and choke out every plant of heavenly growth; and the harvest that will be gathered the judgment alone will reveal. But how sad is the thought that when life and its mistakes are viewed in the light of eternity, it will be too late for this aftersight to be of any avail.

The utter neglect of training children for God has perpetuated evil and thrown into the ranks of the enemy many who with judicious care might have been co-laborers with Christ. False ideas and a foolish, misdirected affection have nurtured traits which have made the children unlovely and unhappy, have embittered the lives of the parents, and have extended their baleful influence from generation to generation. Any child that is permitted to have his own way will dishonor God and bring his father and mother to shame. Light has been shining from the word of God and the testimonies of His Spirit so that none need err in regard to their duty. God requires parents to bring up their children to know Him and to respect His claims; they are to train their little ones, as the younger members of the Lord's family, to have beautiful characters and lovely tempers, that they may be fitted to shine in the heavenly courts. By neglecting their duty and indulging their children in wrong, parents close to them the gates of the city of God.

These facts must be pressed home upon parents; they must arouse, and take up their long-neglected work. Parents who profess to love God are not doing His will. Because they do not properly restrain and direct their children, thousands are coming up with deformed characters, with lax morals, and with little education in the practical duties of life. They are left to do as they please with their impulses, their time, and their mental powers. The loss to the cause of God in these neglected talents lies at the door of fathers and mothers; and what excuse will they render to Him whose stewards they are, entrusted with the sacred duty of fitting the souls under their charge to improve all their powers to the glory of their Creator?

My dear brother and sister, may the Lord open your eyes and quicken your minds, that you may see and redeem your failures. You are neither of you living with an eye single to the glory of God. You show but little power to stand up for Jesus and in defense of the faith once delivered to the saints. You have neglected your duty in the family and have proved that youth entrusted to your care are not safe. Thus God looks upon your work in the home; thus it stands registered in the books of heaven. You might have brought many to Jesus; but your want of moral courage has made you unfaithful in every position.

The errors in your lax system of family government are revealed in the characters of your children. You have not educated yourselves to follow the instructions given in the word of God. The evils resulting from your failures in duty are becoming serious and deep. Sister G does not have the right influence. She has yielded to the strong wills of her wrong-minded children, and has indulged them to their hurt.

Both of you should have taught your children from their very babyhood that they could not control you, but that your will was to be obeyed. Had Sister G received the proper training in her childhood, had she been disciplined and educated according to the word of God, she would have a different mold of character herself and would better understand the duties that devolve upon her. She would know how to train her children so as to make their ways pleasing to God. But the defects that have resulted from her own wrong training are reproduced in her children, and what will be the nature of their work should they ever stand at the head of families of their own? The oldest may have some knowledge of domestic duties; but, further than this, she is a mere novice.

With wise, firm government these children might have been useful members of society; as it is, they are a curse, a reproach to our faith. They are vain, frivolous, willful, extravagant. They have but little reverence for their parents, and their consciences are far from sensitive. They have had their own way, and their wishes have governed their parents, until it is almost impossible to arouse their moral sensibilities. The natural tendencies of the parents, particularly those that are objectionable, are strongly developed in the children. The whole family, parents and children, are under divine censure; and none of them can hope to enter the peaceful abodes of bliss unless they will take up their long-neglected duties and, in the spirit of Christ, build up characters that God can approve.

Parents are responsible for the work coming from their hands. They should have wisdom and firmness to do their work faithfully and in the right spirit. They are to train their children for usefulness by developing their God-given talents. A failure to do this should not be winked at, but should be made a matter of church discipline, for it will bring the curse of God on the parents and a reproach and grievous trials and difficulties on the church. A moral leprosy that is contagious, polluting the bodies and souls of the youth, often results from a failure to discipline and restrain the young; and it is time that something was done to check its ravages.

The Bible gives explicit directions concerning the important work of educating children: "Hear, O Israel: The Lord our God is one Lord: and thou shalt love the Lord thy God with all thine heart, and with all thy soul, and with all thy might. And these words, which I command thee this day, shall be in thine heart." The parents are themselves to be connected with God; they are to have His fear before them and to have a knowledge of His will. Then comes their work: "And thou shalt teach them diligently unto thy children, and shalt talk of them when thou sittest in thine house, and when thou walkest by the way, and when thou liest down, and when thou risest up. And thou shalt bind them for a sign upon thine hand, and they shall be as frontlets between thine eyes. And thou shalt write them upon the posts of thy house, and on thy gates."

The Lord commanded Israel not to make marriages with the idolatrous nations around them. "Thy daughter thou shalt not give unto his son, nor his daughter shalt thou take unto thy son. For they will turn away thy son from following Me, that they may serve other gods: so will the anger of the Lord be kindled against you, and destroy thee suddenly." "For thou art an holy people unto the Lord thy God: the Lord thy God hath chosen thee to be a special people unto Himself, above all people that are upon the face of the earth. The Lord did not set His love upon you, nor choose you, because ye were more in number than any people; for ye were the fewest of all people: but because the Lord loved you, and because He would keep the oath which He had sworn unto your fathers."

Here are positive directions that reach down to our time. God is speaking to us in these last days, and He will be understood and obeyed. God spoke to Israel through His servants. "This book of the law shall not depart out of thy mouth; but thou shalt meditate therein day and night, that thou mayest observe to do according to all that is written therein: for then thou shalt make thy way prosperous, and then thou shalt have good success.'' ''The law of the Lord is perfect, converting the soul: the testimony of the Lord is sure, making wise the simple.'' ''The entrance of Thy words giveth light; it giveth understanding unto the simple.'' ''Thy word is a lamp unto my feet, and a light unto my path.''

Here the duties of parents are clearly set forth. The word of God is to be their daily monitor. It gives such instruction that parents need not err in regard to the education of their children; but it admits of no indifference or negligence. The law of God is to be kept before the minds of the children as the great moral standard. When they rise up, and when they sit down, when they go out, and when they come in, this law is to be taught them as the great rule of life, and its principles are to be interwoven with all their experience. They are to be taught to be honest, truthful, temperate, economical, and industrious, and to love God with the whole heart. This is bringing them up in the nurture and admonition of the Lord. This is setting their feet in the path of duty and safety.

Youth are ignorant and inexperienced, and the love of the Bible and its sacred truths will not come naturally. Unless great pains are taken to build up around them barriers to shield them from Satan's devices, they are subject to his temptations and are led captive by him at his will. In their early years children are to be taught the claims of God's law and faith in Jesus our Redeemer to cleanse from the stains of sin. This faith must be taught day by day, by precept and example.

A solemn responsibility rests upon parents, and how can the Lord bless them in the positive neglect of their duty? Children can be molded when they are young. But years pass when their hearts are tender and susceptible to the impressions of truth, and but little time is devoted to their moral culture. The precious lessons of truth and duty should be instilled into their hearts daily. They should have a knowledge of God in His created works; this will be of greater value to them than any knowledge of books.

"Man shall not live by bread alone, but by every word that proceedeth out of the mouth of God," are the words of our Saviour. Errors in doctrine are multiplying and twining themselves with serpentlike subtlety around the affections of the people. There is not a doctrine of the Bible that has not been denied. The great truths of prophecy, showing our position in the history of the world, have been shorn of their beauty and power by the clergy, who seek to make these all-important truths dark and incomprehensible. In many cases the children are drifting away from the old landmarks. The Lord commanded His people Israel: "When thy son asketh thee in time to come, saying, What mean the testimonies, and the statutes, and the judgments, which the Lord our God hath commanded you? then thou shalt say unto thy son, We were pharaoh's bondmen in Egypt; and the Lord brought us out of Egypt with a mighty hand: and the Lord showed signs and wonders, great and sore, upon Egypt, upon Pharaoh, and upon all his household, before our eyes: and He brought us out from thence, that He might bring us in, to give us the land which He sware unto our fathers. And the Lord commanded us to do all these statutes, to fear the Lord our God, for our good always, that He might preserve us alive, as it is at this day. And it shall be our righteousness, if we observe to do all these commandments before the Lord our God, as He hath commanded us."

Here are principles that we are not to regard with indifference. Those who have seen the truth and felt its importance, and have had an experience in the things of God, are to teach sound doctrine to their children. They should make them acquainted with the great pillars of our faith, the reasons why we are Seventh-day Adventists,—why we are called, as were the children of Israel, to be a peculiar people, a holy nation, separate and distinct from all other people on the face of the earth. These things should be explained to the children in simple language, easy to be understood; and as they grow in years, the lessons imparted should be suited to their increasing capacity, until the foundations of truth have been laid broad and deep.

Parents, you profess to be children of God; are you obedient children? Are you doing the will of your heavenly Father? Are you following His directions, or are you walking in the light of sparks of your own kindling? Are you daily working to outgeneral the enemy and save your children from his devices? Are you opening to them the precious truths of the word of God, explaining to them the reasons of our faith, that their young feet may be planted on the platform of truth?

The Bible with its precious gems of truth was not written for the scholar alone. On the contrary, it was designed for the common people; and the interpretation given by the common people, when aided by the Holy Spirit, accords best with the truth as it is in Jesus. The great truths necessary for salvation are made clear as the noonday, and none will mistake and lose their way except those who follow their own judgment instead of the plainly revealed will of God.

CHRISTIAN FORBEARANCE

Dear Brother and Sister H: In regard to your present relations with the church I would advise that you do all that can be done on your part to come into harmony with your brethren. Cultivate a kind, conciliatory spirit, and let no feeling of retaliation come into your minds and hearts. We have but a little time in this world, and let us work for time and for eternity. Be diligent to make your calling and election sure. See that you make no mistake in regard to your title to a home in Christ's kingdom. If your name is registered in the Lamb's book of life, then all will be well with you. Be ready and anxious to confess your faults and forsake them, that your mistakes and sins may go beforehand to judgment and be blotted out.

I believe that you are making improvement; but let the work be deeper, more thorough, more earnest. Leave nothing undone that you can do. Walk humbly with God, set your heart in order, overcome self, and watch to avoid every device of Satan. When the heart is in harmony with Jesus, when in words, in spirit, and in deportment, you copy the Pattern, the manners will be refined and elevated, convincing all that there has been in you a radical change. You will then be numbered among the virtuous, God-fearing followers of Jesus.

My brother, you have a very spotted record. God and your own soul know this. But no one will be more rejoiced than I to see you setting your feet in the way that Christ has walked, and to meet you in the kingdom of God. It is difficult for us to understand ourselves, to have a correct knowledge of our own characters. The word of God is plain, but often there is an error in applying it to one's self. There is liability to self-deception and to think its warnings and reproofs do not mean me. "The heart is deceitful above all things, and desperately wicked: who can know it?" Self-flattery may be construed into Christian emotion and zeal. Self-love and confidence may give us assurance that we are right when we are far from meeting the requirements of God's word.

The Bible is full, clear, and explicit; the character of the true disciple of Christ is marked out with exactness. We must search the Scriptures with humble hearts, trembling at the word of the Lord, if we would not be in any way deceived in regard to our true character. There must be persevering effort to overcome selfishness and self-confidence. Self-examination must be thorough, that there be no danger of self-deception. A little catechizing of self on special occasions is not sufficient. Daily examine the foundation of your hope, and see whether you are indeed in the love of Christ. Deal truly with your own hearts, for you cannot afford to run any risk here. Count the cost of being a wholehearted Christian, and then gird on the armor. Study the Pattern; look to Jesus, and be like Him. Your peace of mind, your hope of eternal salvation, depend on faithfulness in this work. As Christians we are less thorough in self-examination than in anything else; it is no wonder, then, that we make such slow advancement in understanding self.

I am writing these things to you because I want you to be saved. I do not want to discourage you, but to urge you to more earnest, vigorous effort. Self-love will prompt you to make a superficial work of self-examination; but let no vain confidence cheat you out of eternal life. Do not build yourself up on the mistakes and errors of others, but between God and your own soul settle the important question upon which hangs your eternal destiny.

"Man looketh on the outward appearance, but the Lord looketh on the heart," —the human heart, with its conflicting emotions of joy and sorrow,—the wandering, wayward heart, which is the abode of so much impurity and deceit. He knows its motives, its very intents and purposes. Go to Him with your soul all stained as it is. Like the psalmist, throw its chambers open to the all-seeing Eye, exclaiming: "Search me, O God, and know my heart: try me, and know my thoughts: and see if there be any wicked way in me, and lead me in the way everlasting." Submit your heart to be refined and purified; then you will become a partaker of the divine nature, having escaped the corruption that is in the world through lust. Then you will "be ready always to give an answer to every man that asketh you a reason of the hope that is in you with meekness and fear." The peace of Christ will be yours. Your name will stand registered in the book of life; your title to the heavenly inheritance will bear the royal signet, which none on earth dare question. No one can bar your way to the portals of the city of God, but you will have free access to the royal presence and to the temple of God on high.

A few words more press upon my mind. I want you to be united with the church, not because I regard all the church members perfect nor because I regard you perfect. God has precious ones in His church; there are also men and women who are as tares among the wheat. But the Lord does not give you or anyone else the office of saying who are tares and who are wheat. We may see and condemn the faults of others, while we have greater faults which we have never realized, but which are distinctly seen by others. God requires you to give to the world and the church a good example, a life that represents Jesus. There are duties to be performed and responsibilities to be borne. The world has not enough true Christians; the church has need of them; society cannot spare them. Christ's prayer for His disciples was: "I pray not that Thou shouldest take them out of the world, but that Thou shouldest keep them from the evil." Jesus knows we are in the world, exposed to its temptations, but He loves us and will give us grace to triumph over its corrupting influences. He would have us perfect in character, that our waywardness may not occasion moral deformity in others.

You see that your brethren do not come up to the Bible standard, that there are defects in them; and you dwell upon these defects. You feed upon them instead of feeding upon Christ, and by beholding you become changed into the same image. But criticize no one; do not contrast your own exact course with the deficiencies of others. You may be in danger of wanting to correct others and make them feel their wrongs. Do not do this. This is not the work God has given you to do. He has not made you a church tinker. There are many things which you view in the light of the Bible. But though you may be in the right on some points, do not get the impression that your positions are always correct; for on many points your ideas are distorted and will not bear criticism.

Do not seek to exalt self, but learn in the school of Christ meekness and lowliness of heart. You know what Peter's character was, how strikingly his peculiar traits were developed. Before his great fall he was always forward and dictatorial, speaking unadvisedly from the impulse of the moment. He was always ready to correct others and to express his mind before he had a clear comprehension of himself or of what he had to say. But Peter was converted, and the converted Peter was very different from the rash, impetuous

Peter. While he retained his former fervor, the grace of Christ regulated his zeal. Instead of being impetuous, self-confident, and self-exalted, he was calm, self-possessed, and teachable. He could then feed the lambs as well as the sheep of Christ's flock.

You, my brother, have a great work to do for yourself day by day. You must make constant effort to curb bad tempers and evil propensities. These have grown with your growth, and Jesus alone can strengthen you to fully overcome them. You should regard yourself as a servant of Christ and seek to be like Him in character. Try to make yourself agreeable to others. Even in your business relations, be courteous, kind, and forbearing, showing the meekness of Jesus and that His spirit is ruling you. You are related to humanity, and you must be patient, kind, and pitiful. You need to cherish thoughtfulness and subdue selfishness. Let your inquiry be: "What can I do to bless others?" If your heart is yearning to do them good, even at inconvenience to yourself, you will have the blessing of God. Love, lifted out of the realm of passion and impulse, becomes spiritualized and is revealed in words and acts. A Christian must have a sanctified tenderness and love, in which there is no impatience or fretfulness; the rude, harsh manners must be softened by the grace of Christ.

O my brother, my sister, educate yourselves in the school of Christ. Let the spirit of controversy cease at home and in the church. Let your hearts be drawn out in love for the people of God. Hearts that are filled with the love of Christ can never get very far apart. Religion is love, and a Christian home is one where love reigns and finds expression in words and acts of thoughtful kindness and gentle courtesy. Let no harsh words be spoken. Let the family worship be made pleasant and interesting. Be a Christian gentleman, my brother; for the very same principles that characterize the home life will be carried into the church. A lack of courtesy, a moment of petulance, a single rough, thoughtless word, will mar your reputation and may close the door to hearts so that you can never reach them.

Now I have set before you your dangers, and I tell you there are precious victories that you may gain. We can never see the kingdom of heaven unless we have the mind and spirit of Christ. Then copy the pattern at home, at your work, and in the church. Do not try to teach others nor to see how widely you can differ from your brethren, but try to see how near you can come to them, how fully you can be in harmony with them. While doing all that you can on your part to perfect Christian character, give your heart to God for Him to mold according to His pleasure. He will help you; I know He will. May God bless you and your dear children; and may I meet you all around the great white throne, is my prayer.

WORLDLY AMBITION

My Dear Brother I: Since meeting you at the Maine camp meeting I have felt that it is not too late for you to set your heart and house in order. I know that you have been impressed by the Spirit of God; and now the question is: Will you, in response to this invitation to repent, gladly surrender your heart to God? Your case has been presented to me in vision; but while you were so completely under the control of the enemy of souls, I had no courage to send you the message given me of the Lord. I feared that you would make light of it and that the Holy Spirit would be grieved away for the last time. But now I feel urged to send you this testimony, which will prove to you a savor of life unto life or death unto death.

Do not read this if you are decided to choose darkness rather than light, to serve mammon rather than Christ. But if you really want to do the will of God, and are willing to be saved in His own appointed way, then read the testimony; but do not read it to cavil, nor to pervert, ridicule, and despise it; for in that case it will be to you a savor of death unto death, and will witness against you in the judgment. Before reading this warning message, go alone before God and ask Him to remove from you the spirit of defiance, rebellion, and unbelief, and to melt and subdue your stony heart.

We do not understand the greatness and majesty of God nor remember the immeasurable distance between the Creator and the creatures formed by His hand. He who sitteth in the heavens, swaying the scepter of the universe, does not judge according to our finite standard, nor reckon according to our computation. We are in error if we think that that which is great to us must be great to God, and that which is small to us must be small to Him. He would be no more exalted than ourselves if He possessed only the same faculties.

God does not regard all sins as of equal magnitude; there are degrees of guilt in His estimation as well as in that of finite man. But however trifling this or that wrong in their course may seem in the eyes of men, no sin is small in the sight of God. The sins which man is disposed to look upon as small may be the very ones which God accounts as great crimes. The drunkard is despised and is told that his sin will exclude him from heaven, while pride, selfishness, and covetousness go unrebuked. But these are sins that are especially offensive to God. He "resisteth the proud," and Paul tells us that covetousness is idolatry. Those who are familiar with the denunciations against idolatry in the word of God will at once see how grave an offense this sin is.

God speaks through His prophet: "Let the wicked forsake his way, and the unrighteous man his thoughts: and let him return unto the Lord, and He will have mercy upon him; and to our God, for He will abundantly pardon. For My thoughts are not your thoughts, neither are your ways, My ways, saith the Lord. For as the heavens are higher than the earth, so are My ways higher than your ways, and My thoughts than your thoughts." We need clear discernment, that we may measure sin by the Lord's standard and not by our own. Let us take for our rule, not human opinions, but the divine word.

We are on the great battlefield of life, and let it never be forgotten that we are individually responsible for the issue of the struggle; that though Noah, Job, and Daniel were in the land, yet should they deliver neither son nor daughter by their righteousness. You, my brother, have not thought of this. But you have justified your own course because you thought that your brethren did not do right. Sometimes you have acted like a petted, spoiled child and have talked unbelief and doubt to spite others; but will it pay? Is there anything in your family, in the church, or in the world to justify your indifference to the claims of God? Will any of your excuses avail when you stand face to face with the Judge of all the earth? How foolish and sinful will your selfish, avaricious course then appear. How unaccountable it will seem to you that you could let worldly opinions and worldly gain eclipse the reward to be given to the faithful,—an eternity of bliss in the Paradise of God.

When you were in great physical suffering and there was no hope for you in human skill, the Lord pitied you and mercifully removed disease from you. Satan has sought to afflict and ruin you, and even to take your life; but your Saviour has shielded you again and again, lest you should be cut down when your heart was filled with a satanic frenzy, your tongue uttering words of bitterness and unbelief against the Bible and against the truth you once advocated. When Satan has clamored for you, claiming you as his own, Christ has repulsed your cruel and malignant foe with the words: "I have not yet withdrawn My Spirit from him. He has two more steps to take before he will pass the boundary of My mercy and love. Souls are the purchase of My blood. The Lord rebuke thee, O Satan; the Lord rebuke thee."

I was then carried back in your life, and you were shown to me when the truth found a response in your heart. The Spirit of God convicted you of the course you should pursue, and you had quite a struggle with self. You had been a sharp, scheming man. You had not done by others as you would wish them to do by you, but had taken advantage of them whenever you could. You had a close, stern battle to fight to subdue self and mortify pride; and it was only through the grace of God that this work could be accomplished. Instead of effecting a thorough reformation, you joined the truth to a patched-up character, which would not stand the test of temptation. You did not begin by seeking God with a broken and contrite heart, and making wrongs right. Had you done this, you would not have stumbled and fallen into the snare of the enemy. There was a mixture of selfishness in your motives, which you yourself did not clearly see. Arguments drawn from worldly interest, social position, and comparative respectability influenced you and decided you not to make earnest, thorough work before God and men. Reaching after the worldly standard marred the sincerity and purity of your Christian character; and you failed to bring forth fruits meet for repentance.

Zacchaeus declared: "If I have taken anything from any man by false accusation, I restore him fourfold." You could at least have made efforts to correct your acts of injustice to your fellow men. You cannot make every case right, for some whom you have injured have gone into their graves, and the account stands registered against you. In these cases the best you can do is to bring a trespass offering to the altar of the Lord, and He will accept and pardon you. But where you can, you should make reparation to the wronged ones.

Had the unbelievers with whom you have associated seen in you the transforming power of the truth, they would have had an argument in favor of Christianity which they could not controvert. You might thus have reflected a clear, sharp light to the world; but instead of this you have mingled with the world and imbibed its spirit. My brother, you must be born again. A mere form of Christianity is not of the least value. It is destitute of saving power, having in it no reformative energy. A religion which is confined to Sabbath worship emits no rays of light to others. I entreat you to examine your own heart closely. You have a combative, contentious spirit, and you are cultivating instead of repressing that spirit. You should make a decided change, and cultivate meekness, faith, humility, and love. Your soul is in peril; you will surely be subject to the strong delusions of Satan unless you stop where you are and press against the current of worldliness and ambition. Your relations with the world must be changed, and a decided separation must take place. The positions which you occupy, which are continually opening to you doors of temptation, must be given up. Avoid politics; shun contention. Keep clear of every office which would encourage those traits in your character that need to be battled down and overcome.

My brother, you must make a strong, decided effort, or you will never be able to cast off the works of darkness. Satan looks upon you as his own. When you listen to the testimonies of God's servants, as at the late camp meeting, you are deeply convicted. But you do not respond to the impressions of the Spirit of God; and as you mingle with worldlings you drink in their spirit and are borne down by the worldly current, having no moral power to resist its influence. You become one with the world-loving, and your spirit is worse than theirs, for your choice is voluntary. You love the praise of men, and you love worldly possessions above Jesus. The love of mammon has been woven into every fiber of your being and has become all-absorbing. To eradicate it will be like plucking out the right eye or cutting off the right arm. But I speak to you as one who knows: Unless you overcome this intense love of money, it will cost you your soul's salvation, and then it would have been better for you had you never been born.

"Ye cannot serve God and mammon." Just as far as you love and cherish the spirit of the world you will have a spirit of defiance and will question and find fault with those who bring you the message of truth. You will deride the truth, and will become a false witness, an accuser of the brethren. The talents given you of God to be improved to His glory will be actively employed against His work and cause. There is no concord between Christ and Belial. You have already chosen the friendship of the world, therefore you are decidedly on the side of Satan. The natural heart is at enmity against God, and will resist the clearest evidence of truth. The wicked will not endure the light that condemns their wrong course of action.

You have opened your heart to doubt and skepticism, but you will never be able to be an honest infidel. You may boast that you do not believe the Bible, but you will be perjuring yourself all the time, for you know better.

I entreat you to make earnest work for eternal life. Break the snare of Satan; work against his devices. Let this be the language of your soul. "There is nothing in the universe that I fear so much as that I shall not know all my duty, or that, knowing, I shall fail to do it." "Stand up for Jesus" were the words of a dying saint. Yes, Brother I, stand up for Jesus. It will take all to do this. You may have to change your position in the world; but a name, distinction, office, are to you a snare, imperiling your soul. A calculating, worldly wisdom is continually seeking to turn you away from the Saviour. A bold, defiant, blasphemous infidelity will attempt to crush His gospel, not only out of your own soul, but out of the world. But stand up for Jesus. In the presence of your relatives and friends, in all your business relations, in your associations with the world,—anywhere and everywhere, under all circumstances,—stand up for Jesus.

LOVE AMONG BRETHREN

Dear Brethren and Sisters in _____: My mind has been exceedingly troubled in regard to your condition. I have not been able to sleep, and I arise at twelve o'clock to write to J, and to you as a church. I do not know what might have been the condition of J at the present time had you pursued a righteous, Christian course toward him—such a course as every child of God should pursue in such a case. Some of you will not be able to comprehend my words, for your own course has placed you where you have not sanctified discernment. You have allowed strong, hard feelings against him to come into your hearts, and have justified yourselves in treating him with indifference and even contempt. You have reasoned that by his unbelief and his wrong course he was certainly injuring the church and endangering souls, and you must have no fellowship with him. But will you, in the light of God's great standard of righteousness, critically examine every word and act of your own that you can call to mind and compare these with the life of Christ? If you have been doing the will of God, then His light and His approval will second your efforts, and prosperity will attend you. I wish the members of this once prosperous church would each begin to build over against his own house. When they see their course in its true light they will know that they have made a very great mistake in allowing their own critical, pharisaical spirit to control their tongues and develop itself in their treatment of their brethren. This unchristian harshness has excluded Jesus from the church and has brought in a spirit of dissension. It has fostered a disposition to judge and condemn, a hatred of those who do not see things as you see them. Even if your brethren say and do many things that really injure you, will you push them to one side, and say: "I am holier than thou"?

"By their fruits ye shall know them." Christ has not been revealed in your deportment toward some who were much nearer the kingdom of heaven than yourselves. The Lord has opened before you your wrong toward His children—your want of mercy and love, your determination to control minds and make them see things just as you see them. And when light came to you, what course did you take? Did you merely admit that you were wrong, or did you heartily confess your error and humble your proud hearts before God? Did you cast aside your ways and accept God's teachings? Did you go to the very ones you had bruised and wounded, and say:

"I have been wrong; I have sinned against you. Forgive me. I have failed; I have worked in my own spirit. I had a zeal, but not according to knowledge. It was the spirit of Jehu, rather than the meekness and lowliness of Christ. The word of God directs: 'Confess your faults one to another, and pray one for another, that ye may be healed.' Will you pray for me that God will forgive me for the distress and anguish I have caused you?"

If you who have engaged in this work of bruising and condemning have not heartily repented, then light, peace, and joy will not come into your souls. When you are careful, kind, and tender to your brethren in the same degree that you have been hard, unforgiving, and oppressive, you will confess your faults and make restitution as far as possible; and when you have done all on your part you may ask the Lord to do that which it is impossible for you to do—heal the wounds you have made, forgive you, and blot out your transgression. When there is so great reluctance to confess a wrong which is laid open and plain before the erring, it shows that they are controlled by their own untamable, unsanctified natures rather than by the spirit of the gospel of Christ.

If God has ever spoken by me, you have most earnest work to do in zealous repentance for showing to the erring the satanic element in your character, not in coldness and indifference merely, but in neglect and contempt. If they are indeed in darkness and doing things that imperil their souls, you should manifest the greater interest in them. Show them that while you will be true to principle and will not swerve from the right, you love their souls. Let them know by your words and actions that you have not a spirit of revenge and retaliation, but that for their sakes you will sacrifice feeling and subdue self. Represent Jesus, our pattern; manifest His spirit at all times and under all circumstances, and let that mind be in you which was in Christ Jesus. Your ways have not been God's ways; your will has not been God's will. The precious plant of love has not been cultivated, and watered by

the dews of grace. Self-love, self-righteousness, self-complacency, have exerted a controlling power.

What has Jesus done for you, and what is He continually
doing for us individually? What have you that you have not
received? Said Christ: "I am the Vine, ye are the branches."
"Every branch in Me that beareth not fruit He taketh away:
and every branch that beareth fruit, He purgeth it, that it may
bring forth more fruit." The branches do not sustain the vine,
but the vine supports and nourishes the branches. The church
does not support Christ, but Christ, by His vital power, supports the church. It is not enough to be a branch; we are to be
fruitful branches. "He that abideth in Me," said Jesus, "and
I in him, the same bringeth forth much fruit." But if the fruit
produced be that of the thornbush, it is evident that we are not
branches of the living Vine.

Life is disciplinary. While in the world, the Christian will
meet with adverse influences. There will be provocations to
test the temper; and it is by meeting these in a right spirit that
the Christian graces are developed. If injuries and insults are
meekly borne, if insulting words are responded to by gentle
answers, and oppressive acts by kindness, this is evidence
that the Spirit of Christ dwells in the heart, that sap from the
living Vine is flowing to the branches. We are in the school of
Christ in this life, where we are to learn to be meek and lowly
of heart; and in the day of final accounts we shall see that all
the obstacles we meet, all the hardships and annoyances that
we are called to bear, are practical lessons in the application
of principles of Christian life. If well endured, they develop
the Christlike in the character and distinguish the Christian
from the worldling.

There is a high standard to which we are to attain if we
would be children of God, noble, pure, holy, and undefiled;
and a pruning process is necessary if we would reach this
standard. How would this pruning be accomplished if there
were no difficulties to meet, no obstacles to surmount, nothing to call out patience and endurance? These trials are not the

smallest blessings in our experience. They are designed to nerve us to determination to succeed. We are to use them as God's means to gain decided victories over self instead of allowing them to hinder, oppress, and destroy us.

Character will be tested. Christ will be revealed in us if we are indeed branches of the living Vine. We shall be patient, kind, and forbearing, cheerful amid frets and irritations. Day by day and year by year we shall conquer self and grow into a noble heroism. This is our allotted task; but it cannot be accomplished without continual help from Jesus, resolute decision, unwavering purpose, continual watchfulness, and unceasing prayer. Each one has a personal battle to fight. Each must win his own way through struggles and discouragements. Those who decline the struggle lose the strength and joy of victory. No one, not even God, can carry us to heaven unless we make the necessary effort on our part. We must put features of beauty into our lives. We must expel the unlovely natural traits that make us unlike Jesus. While God works in us to will and to do of His own good pleasure, we must work in harmony with Him. The religion of Christ transforms the heart. It makes the worldly-minded man heavenly-minded. Under its influence the selfish man becomes unselfish because this is the character of Christ. The dishonest, scheming man becomes upright, so that it is second nature to him to do unto others as he would have others do unto him. The profligate is changed from impurity to purity. He forms correct habits, for the gospel of Christ has become to him a savor of life unto life.

Now, while probation lingers, it does not become one to pronounce sentence upon others and look to himself as a model man. Christ is our model; imitate Him, plant your feet in His steps. You may professedly believe every point of present truth, but unless you practice these truths it will avail you nothing. We are not to condemn others; this is not our work; but we should love one another and pray for one another. When we see one err from the truth, then we may weep over him as Christ wept over Jerusalem. Let us see what our heavenly Father in His word says about the erring: "If a man be overtaken in a fault, ye which are spiritual, restore such an one in the spirit of meekness; considering thyself, lest thou also be tempted." "If any of you do err from the truth, and one convert him; let him know, that he which converteth the sinner from the error of his way shall save a soul from death, and shall hide a multitude of sins." What a great missionary work is this! how much more Christlike than for poor, fallible mortals to be ever accusing and condemning those who do not exactly meet their minds. Let us remember that Jesus knows us individually and is touched with the feeling of our infirmities. He knows the wants of each of His creatures and reads the hidden, unspoken grief of every heart. If one of the little ones for whom He died is injured, He sees it and calls the offender to account. Jesus is the Good Shepherd. He cares for His feeble, sickly, wandering sheep. He knows them all by name. The distress of every sheep and every lamb of His flock touches His heart of sympathizing love, and the cry for aid reaches His ear. One of the greatest sins of the shepherds of Israel is thus pointed out by the prophet: "The diseased have ye not strengthened, neither have ye healed that which was sick, neither have ye bound up that which was broken, neither have ye brought again that which was driven away, neither have ye sought that which was lost; but with force and with cruelty have ye ruled them. And they were scattered, because there is no shepherd: and they became meat to all the beasts of the field, when they were scattered. My sheep wandered through all the mountains, and upon every high hill: yea, My flock was scattered upon all the face of the earth, and none did search or seek after them."

Jesus cares for each one as though there were not another individual on the face of the earth. As Deity He exerts mighty power in our behalf, while as our Elder Brother He feels for all our woes. The Majesty of heaven held not Himself aloof from degraded, sinful humanity. We have not a high priest who is so high, so lifted up, that He cannot notice us or sympathize with us, but one who was in all points tempted like as we are, yet without sin.

How different from this spirit is the feeling of indifference and contempt that has been manifested by some in _____ toward J and those who have been affected by his influence. If ever the transforming grace of God was needed, it is needed in this church. In judging and condemning a brother, they have undertaken to do a work that God never put into their hands. A hardness of heart, a censorious, condemnatory spirit that would destroy individuality and independence, has been woven into their Christian experience, and they have lost the love of Jesus out of their hearts. Make haste, brethren, to get these things off your soul before it shall be said in heaven: "He that is unjust, let him be unjust still: and he which is filthy, let him be filthy still: and he that is righteous, let him be righteous still and he that is holy, let him be holy still."

You will have many perplexities to meet in your Christian life in connection with the church, but do not try too hard to mold your brethren. If you see that they do not meet the requirements of God's word, do not condemn; if they provoke, do not retaliate. When things are said that would exasperate, quietly keep your soul from fretting. You see many things which appear wrong in others, and you want to correct these wrongs. You commence in your own strength to work for a reform, but you do not go about it in the right way. You must labor for the erring with a heart subdued, softened by the Spirit of God, and let the Lord work through you, the agent. Roll your burden on Jesus. You feel that the Lord must take up the case where Satan is striving for the mastery over some soul; but you are to do what you can in humility and meekness, and put the tangled work, the complicated matters, into the hands of God. Follow the directions in His word, and leave the outcome of the matter to His wisdom. Having done all you can to save your brother, cease worrying, and go calmly about other pressing duties. It is no longer your matter, but God's.

Do not, through impatience, cut the knot of difficulty, making matters hopeless. Let God untangle the snarled-up threads for you. He is wise enough to manage the complications of our lives. He has skill and tact. We cannot always see His plans; we must wait patiently their unfolding and not mar and destroy them. He will reveal them to us in His own good time. Seek for unity; cultivate love and conformity to Christ in all things. He is the source of unity and strength; but you have not sought for Christian unity that you might knit hearts together in love.

There is work for you to do in the church and out of the church. "Herein is My Father glorified, that ye bear much fruit." The fruit we bear is the only test of the character of the tree before the world. This is the proof of our discipleship. If our works are of such a character that as branches of the living Vine we bear rich clusters of precious fruit, then we wear before the world God's own badge as His sons and daughters. We are living epistles, known and read of all men.

Now, I fear that you will fail in doing the work you must do to redeem the past and become living, fruit-bearing branches. If you do as God would have you, His blessing will come into the church. You have not yet been humble enough to make thorough work and meet the mind of the Spirit of God. There has been self-justification, self-pleasing, self-vindication, when there should have been humiliation, contrition, and repentance. You should remove every stumbling block and make "straight paths for your feet, lest that which is lame be turned out of the way." It is not too late for wrongs to be righted; but you must not feel that you are whole and have no need of a physician, for you need help. When you come to Jesus with a broken heart, He will help and bless you, and you will go forth in the Master's work with courage and energy. The best evidence that you are in Christ is the fruit you bear. If you are not truly united to Him, your light and privileges will condemn and ruin you.

REDEEMING THE TIME

Dear Brother J: I have arisen at twelve o'clock to write to you because my mind is burdened. I am troubled on your account; for I know that we are near the close of earth's history, and your life record is not such a one as you will be pleased to meet in the great day when every man will receive as his works have been.

You may feel that others have done wrong, and I know as well as you do that a Christlike spirit has not been manifested in the church. But will this avail you in the judgment? Will two wrongs make one right? Though one, two, or three in the church have done wrong, this will not blot out or excuse your sin. Whatever course others may take, your work is to set your own heart in order. God has claims upon you which no circumstances should lead you to forget or neglect, for every soul is precious in His sight.

My heart is drawn out after those who have stumbled on the dark mountains of unbelief, and I want to help them. There is good material in the church in _____; but the members have not been transformed by the Spirit of God, and brought into a position where they can let their light shine to the world. Some, with the best of motives, and possessing capabilities for great usefulness, utterly fail in times of trial in the church, for want of the love and mercy that dwelt so richly in the heart of Christ. They see one in error; and instead of helping him they hold themselves aloof. They are inclined to make unpleasant allusions, and to touch sensitive spots when they might avoid them. Self comes up and bears sway, and they give pain and stir up wrong feelings. However pure their intentions, their efforts to do good nearly always result in failure, if not in actual harm, because the tenderness and compassion of Christ are wanting. They would make very good surgeons, but they are poor nurses. They have not the tact that is born of love. If they had this they would know how to speak the right word and do the right thing at the right time and in the right place. Others may have no more sincere desires to do right, no deeper interest in the cause of God; they may be no more true and loyal, their sympathies no deeper, their love no warmer; yet because of their gentleness and tact they are far more successful in winning back the erring.

The Lord would be pleased to have His people more considerate than they now are, more merciful and more helpful to one another. When the love of Christ is in the heart, each will be tenderly regardful of the interests of others. Brother will not take advantage of brother in business transactions. One will not charge exorbitant interest because he sees his brother in a close place where he must have help. Those who will take advantage of the necessities of another prove conclusively that they are not governed by the principles of the gospel of Christ. Their course is recorded in the books of heaven as fraud and dishonesty; and wherever these principles rule, the blessing of the Lord will not come into the heart. Such persons are receiving the impress of the great adversary rather than that of the Spirit of God. But those who shall finally inherit the heavenly kingdom must be transformed by divine grace. They must be pure in heart and life and possess symmetrical characters.

I regard you, my brother, as in great peril. Your treasure is laid up on the earth, and your heart is upon your treasure. But all the means you may accumulate, even though it should be millions, will not be sufficient to pay a ransom for your soul. Then do not remain in impenitence and unbelief, and in your case defeat the gracious purposes of God; do not force from His reluctant hand destruction of your property or affliction of your person.

How many there are who are now taking a course which must erelong lead to just such visitations of judgment. They live on day by day, week by week, year by year, for their own selfish interest. Their influence and means, accumulated through God-given skill and tact, are used upon themselves and their families without thought of their gracious Benefactor. Nothing is allowed to flow back to the Giver. Indeed, they come to regard life and its entrusted talents as their own; and if they render back to God that portion which He justly claims, they think that they have placed their Creator under obligation to them. At last His patience with these unfaithful stewards is exhausted; and He brings all their selfish, worldly schemes to an abrupt termination, showing them that as they have gathered for their own glory, He can scatter; and they are helpless to resist His power.

Brother J, I address you today as a prisoner of hope. But will you consider that your sun passed its meridian some time ago and is now rapidly declining? The evening has come. Do you not discern the lengthening shadows? You have but a little time left in which to work for yourself, for humanity, and for your Master. There is a special work to be done for your own soul if you are ever to be numbered with the overcomers. How stands your life record? Is Jesus pleading in your behalf in vain? Shall He be disappointed in you? Some of your companions, who stood side by side with you, have already been summoned away. Eternity will reveal whether they were bankrupt in faith and failed to secure eternal life, or whether they were rich toward God and heirs of the "far more exceeding and eternal weight of glory." Will you not consider that the long forbearance of God toward you calls for repentance and humiliation of soul before Him?

There are other weighty considerations aside from your own personal salvation which demand your attention. Late as it now is, with your sun about to sink behind the western hills, you have still a great work to do for your children, who have allowed the love of the world to separate them from God. You have also unsaved relatives, neighbors, and friends. Had your example been consistent with the light given you; had you been as diligent to save these precious souls as you have been to gather earthly treasure; had you used your means and influence, your wisdom and tact, in an effort to gather these straying ones into the fold of Christ—had this been your lifework, you would have secured a harvest of souls and would have ensured a rich reward in the day of God. You would thus have been building upon the true foundation valuable and imperishable material; but instead of this you have been building wood, hay, and stubble, to be consumed when every man's work shall be tried, of what sort it is.

Your life has been a failure. You have been a stumbling block to sinners. They have said of you: "If the religion which this man professes is indeed genuine, why is he so eager after this world? Why does he not in his own conduct show the spirit of Christ?" Hasten, my brother, before it is forever too late, to remove this stumbling block from the way of sinners. Can you look with pleasure upon your life or upon the influence you have exerted? Will you now consider your ways? Will you now make efforts to come into right relations with God? I do not believe your heart is unimpressible, and I know that the loving-kindness and tender mercy of God are marvelous. You have a little time of probation; will you improve it now while Jesus is pleading His blood before the Father? He has graciously spared your life; but it has been like the barren fig tree upon which year after year there appeared no fruit, nothing but leaves. How long will you continue to disappoint the Master? Will you compel Him to say: "Let no fruit grow on thee henceforward forever;" or, "Cut it down; why cumbereth it the ground"? Oh, wait not for the Lord to put His hand against you and scatter the property which you have accumulated. Remember that all your wealth will not give you one moment of sweet assurance and peace upon your dying bed.

I earnestly urge upon you the necessity of returning to the Lord at once. I entreat you to disappoint the enemy. Break from off you his cruel power. Seek, during the remainder of your life, to make an entirely different record in heaven, one of which you will not be ashamed when the books shall be opened and the Judge shall pronounce sentence upon those who have neglected this great salvation.

Paul exhorts his Ephesian brethren to redeem the time because the days are evil. This exhortation is very applicable to you. In one sense it is impossible to redeem the time; for once gone, it is gone forever. But you are called upon to reform, to be zealous of good works in the same degree that you have been negligent of duty. Turn square about. Double your diligence to make your calling and election sure. Keep God's commandments, and live, and His law as the apple of your eye. Tax every moment to the utmost in laboring for your own eternal interest and for the salvation of souls around you. By so doing you may save both yourself and those who are more or less controlled by your example. These are motives which should be duly considered.

Wake up! wake up! You have work to do, and your sun is fast hastening to its setting. Your powers are becoming enfeebled; but all there is of you, every particle of your ability, belongs to God, and should be used earnestly and disinterestedly in His service. Work while the sun still lingers in the heavens; for the "night cometh, when no man can work."

Come, my brother, come just as you are, sinful and polluted. Lay your burden of guilt on Jesus, and by faith claim His merits. Come now, while mercy lingers; come with confession, come with contrition of soul, and God will abundantly pardon. Do not dare to slight another opportunity. Listen to the voice of mercy that now pleads with you to arise from the dead that Christ may give you light. Every moment now seems to connect itself directly with the destinies of the unseen world. Then let not your pride and unbelief lead you to still further reject offered mercy. If you do you will be left to lament at the last: "The harvest is past, the summer is ended, and we are not saved."

Wait in deep humiliation before God. From this hour resolve to be the Lord's, doing your whole duty, trusting implicitly in the great atonement. Do this and you will have nothing to fear. The remainder of your life journey will be tranquil and happy, and you will secure to yourself that life which shall continue as long as God shall live.

I have written this because I felt urged to do so by the Spirit of God, and because I have a deep interest for you. Do not for one moment let your feelings rise against me; for I have been influenced by love for your soul. We have enjoyed many precious seasons in worshiping God, when our hearts were made joyful by His sweet blessing. Are these seasons forever past? We may never meet again in this life, but shall we not meet when the ransomed are gathered around the great white throne?

THE MANUFACTURE OF WINE AND CIDER

Dear Brethren and Sisters of the Church at _____: I have been shown that as a church you are not growing in grace and in the knowledge of the truth. There is not that consecration to God, that devotion to His service, and that disinterested labor for the upbuilding of His cause which would make you a prosperous and healthy church. You are not subject one to another. There are too many among you who have their own ideas to maintain and their own selfish plans to carry out, and some who occupy prominent places in the church are of this number.

Brother K has not an eye single to the glory of God; he does not view things from a right standpoint. He is giving heed to suggestions of Satan and taking counsel of his own unsanctified judgment, and he grasps at every word that can be framed into a justification of his wrong course. He is self-deceived; he does not see that he is shutting himself away from the Spirit of God. When he entered upon this path he did not know its dangers nor realize where it would lead him. All who are walking in the same way would do well to turn their feet at once into the path of safety.

We are living in an age of intemperance, and catering to the appetite of the cider bibber is an offense against God. With others you have engaged in this work because you have not followed the light. Had you stood in the light, you would not, you could not, have done this. Every one of you who has acted a part in this work will come under the condemnation of God unless you make an entire change in your business. You need to be in earnest. You need to commence the work at once to clear your souls from condemnation.

Some of you in _____ developed wonderful zeal in denouncing the red-ribbon clubs. So far as you were actuated by a desire to condemn the evil in these societies, you were right; but when you acted as though it were a crime to speak at all in their favor, or to show them the least good will, you carried matters to extremes. You should be consistent in all things. You have cherished a hatred for the very name "red-ribbon club" that savors not of the Spirit of Christ, and your feelings of bitterness have not helped you or anyone else.

You have taken the testimonies given in reference to our people's mingling with the temperance societies to the detriment of their spiritual interest, and by perverting them have used them to oppress and burden souls. By this treatment of the light given you have brought my work into disrepute. There was not the least necessity for this, and some of you have a work to do to make this matter right. You would make an iron bedstead for others; if too short, they must be stretched; if too long, they must be cut off. "Judge not, that ye be not judged."

After you had taken a decided stand in opposition to active participation in the work of the temperance societies, you might still have retained an influence over others for good, had you acted conscientiously in accordance with the holy faith which you profess; but by engaging in the manufacture of cider you have hurt your influence very much; and what is worse, you have brought reproach upon the truth, and your own souls have been injured. You have been building up a barrier between yourselves and the temperance cause. Your course led unbelievers to question your principles. You are not making straight paths for your feet, and the lame are halting and stumbling over you to perdition.

I cannot see how, in the light of the law of God, Christians can conscientiously engage in the raising of hops or in the manufacture of wine or cider for the market. All these articles may be put to a good use and prove a blessing, or they may be put to a wrong use and prove a temptation and a curse. Cider and wine may be canned when fresh and kept sweet a long time, and if used in an unfermented state they will not dethrone reason. But those who manufacture apples into cider for the market are not careful as to the condition of the fruit used, and in many cases the juice of decayed apples is expressed. Those who would not think of using the poisonous rotten apples in any other way will drink the cider made from them and call it a luxury; but the microscope would reveal the fact that this pleasant beverage is often unfit for the human stomach, even when fresh from the press. If it is boiled, and care is taken to remove the impurities, it is less objectionable.

I have often heard people say: "Oh! this is only sweet cider; it is perfectly harmless, and even healthful." Several quarts, perhaps gallons, are carried home. For a few days it is sweet; then fermentation begins. The sharp flavor makes it all the more acceptable to many palates, and the lover of sweet wine or cider is loath to admit that his favorite beverage ever becomes hard or sour. Persons may become just as really intoxicated on wine and cider as on stronger drinks, and the worst kind of inebriation is produced by these so-called milder drinks. The passions are more perverse; the transformation of character is greater, more determined and obstinate. A few quarts of cider or wine may awaken a taste for stronger drinks, and in many cases those who have become confirmed drunkards have thus laid the foundation of the drinking habit. For some persons it is by no means safe to have wine or cider in the house. They have inherited an appetite for stimulants, which Satan is continually soliciting them to indulge. If they yield to his temptations they do not stop; appetite clamors for indulgence and is gratified to their ruin. The brain is benumbed and clouded; reason no longer holds the reins, but they are laid on the neck of lust. Licentiousness, adultery, and vices of almost every type are committed as the result of indulging the appetite for wine and cider. A professor of religion who loves these stimulants, and accustoms himself to their use, never grows in grace. He becomes gross and sensual; the animal passions control the higher powers of the mind, and virtue is not cherished.

Moderate drinking is the school in which men are receiving an education for the drunkard's career. So gradually does Satan lead away from the strongholds of temperance, so insidiously do the harmless wine and cider exert their influence upon the taste, that the highway to drunkenness is entered upon all unsuspectingly. The taste for stimulants is cultivated; the nervous system is disordered; Satan keeps the mind in a fever of unrest; and the poor victim, imagining himself perfectly secure, goes on and on, until every barrier is broken down, every principle sacrificed. The strongest resolutions are undermined; and eternal interests are not strong enough to keep the debased appetite under the control of reason.

Some are never really drunk, but are always under the influence of cider or fermented wine. They are feverish, unbalanced in mind, not really delirious, but in fully as bad a condition; for all the noble powers of the mind are perverted. A tendency to disease of various kinds, as dropsy, liver complaint, trembling nerves, and a determination of blood to the head, results from the habitual use of sour cider. By its use many bring upon themselves permanent disease. Some die of consumption or fall under the power of apoplexy from this cause alone. Some suffer from dyspepsia. Every vital function is deadened and the physicians tell them that they have liver complaint, when if they would break open the cider barrel and never replace it, their abused life forces would recover their vigor.

Cider drinking leads to the use of stronger drinks. The

stomach loses its natural vigor, and something stronger is needed to arouse it to action. On one occasion, when my husband and myself were traveling, we were obliged to spend several hours waiting for the train. While we were in the depot, a red-faced, bloated farmer came into the restaurant connected with it, and in a loud, rough voice asked: "Have you first-class brandy?" He was answered in the affirmative, and ordered half a tumbler. "Have you pepper sauce?" "Yes," was the answer. "Well, put in two large spoonfuls." He next ordered two spoonfuls of alcohol added, and concluded by calling for "a good dose of black pepper." The man who was preparing it asked: "What will you do with such a mixture?" He replied: "I guess that will take hold," and, placing the full glass to his lips, drank the whole of this fiery compound. That man had used stimulants until he had deadened the tender coats of the stomach.

Many, as they read this, will laugh at the warning of danger. They will say: "Surely the little wine or cider that I use cannot hurt me." Satan has marked such as his prey; he leads them on step by step, and they perceive it not until the chains of habit and appetite are too strong to be broken. We see the power that appetite for strong drink has over men; we see how many of all professions and of heavy responsibilities, men of exalted station, of eminent talents, of great attainments, of fine feeling, of strong nerves, and of good reasoning powers, sacrifice everything for the indulgence of appetite, until they are reduced to the level of the brutes; and in very many cases their downward course commenced with the use of wine or cider.

When intelligent men and women who are professedly Christians plead that there is no harm in making wine or cider for the market because when unfermented it will not intoxicate, I feel sad at heart. I know there is another side to this subject that they refuse to look upon; for selfishness has closed their eyes to the terrible evils that may result from the use of these stimulants. I do not see how our brethren can abstain from all appearance of evil and engage largely in the business of hop raising, knowing to what use the hops are put. Those who help to produce these beverages that encourage and educate the appetite for stronger stimulants will be rewarded as their works have been. They are transgressors of the law of God, and they will be punished for the sins which they commit and for those which they have influenced others to commit through the temptations which they have placed in their way.

Let all who profess to believe the truth for this time, and to be reformers, act in accordance with their faith. If one whose name is on the church book manufactures wine or cider for the market, he should be faithfully labored with, and, if he continues the practice, he should be placed under censure of the church. Those who will not be dissuaded from doing this work are unworthy of a place and a name among the people of God. We are to be followers of Christ, to set our hearts and our influence against every evil practice. How should we feel in the day when God's judgments are poured out, to meet men who have become drunkards through our influence? We are living in the antitypical day of atonement, and our cases must soon come in review before God. How shall we stand in the courts of heaven if our course of action has encouraged the use of stimulants that pervert reason and are destructive of virtue, purity, and the love of God?

The lawyer asked Christ: "Master, what shall I do to inherit eternal life? He said unto him, What is written in the law? how readest thou? And he answering said, Thou shalt love the Lord thy God with all thy heart, and with all thy soul, and with all thy strength, and with all thy mind; and thy neighbor as thyself. And He said unto him, Thou hast answered right: this do, and thou shalt live." Eternal life is the prize at stake, and Christ tells us how we may gain it. He directs us to the written word: "How readest thou?" The way is there pointed out; we are to love God supremely and our neighbor as ourselves. But if we love our neighbor as ourselves we shall not throw upon the market anything that will be a snare to him.

To love God and man is the Christian's whole duty. The

law of love is written upon the tablets of the soul, the Spirit of God dwells in him, and his character appears in good works. Jesus became poor that through His poverty we might be made rich. What sacrifices are we willing to make for His sake? Have we His love enshrined in our hearts? Do we love our neighbor as Christ loved us? If we have this love for souls, it will lead us to consider carefully whether by our words, our acts, our influence in any way, we are placing temptation before those who have little moral power. We shall not censure the weak and suffering, as the Pharisees were continually doing, but we shall endeavor to remove every stone of stumbling from our brother's path lest the lame be turned out of the way.

As a people we profess to be reformers, to be light bearers in the world, to be faithful sentinels for God, guarding every avenue whereby Satan could come in with his temptations to pervert the appetite. Our example and influence must be a power on the side of reform. We must abstain from any practice which will blunt the conscience or encourage temptation. We must open no door that will give Satan access to the mind of one human being formed in the image of God. If all would be vigilant and faithful in guarding the little openings made by the moderate use of the so-called harmless wine and cider, the highway to drunkenness would be closed up. What is needed in every community is firm purpose, and a will to touch not, taste not, handle not; then the temperance reformation will be strong, permanent, and thorough.

The love of money will lead men to violate conscience. Perhaps that very money may be brought to the Lord's treasury, but He will not accept any such offering; it is an offense to Him. It was obtained by transgressing His law, which requires that a man love his neighbor as himself. It is no excuse for the transgressor to say that if he had not made wine or cider, somebody else would, and his neighbor might have become a drunkard just the same. Because some will place the bottle to their neighbor's lips, will Christians venture to stain their garments with the blood of souls,—to incur the curse pronounced upon these who place this temptation in the way of erring men? Jesus calls upon His followers to stand under His banner and aid in destroying the works of the devil.

The world's Redeemer, who knows well the state of society in the last days, represents eating and drinking as the sins that condemn this age. He tells us that as it was in the days of Noah, so shall it be when the Son of man is revealed. "They were eating and drinking, marrying and giving in marriage, until the day that Noah entered into the ark, and knew not until the Flood came, and took them all away." Just such a state of things will exist in the last days, and those who believe these warnings will use the utmost caution not to take a course that will bring them under condemnation.

Brethren, let us look at this matter in the light of the Scriptures and exert a decided influence on the side of temperance in all things. Apples and grapes are God's gifts; they may be put to excellent use as healthful articles of food, or they may be abused by being put to a wrong use. Already God is blighting the grapevine and the apple crop because of men's sinful practices. We stand before the world as reformers; let us give no occasion for infidels or unbelievers to reproach our faith. Said Christ: "Ye are the salt of the earth," "the light of the world." Let us show that our hearts and consciences are under the transforming influence of divine grace, and that our lives are governed by the pure principles of the law of God, even though these principles may require the sacrifice of temporal interests.

MARRIAGE WITH UNBELIEVERS

Dear Sister L: I have learned of your contemplated marriage with one who is not united with you in religious faith, and I fear that you have not carefully weighed this important matter. Before taking a step which is to exert an influence upon all your future life, I urge you to give the subject careful and prayerful deliberation. Will this new relationship prove a source of true happiness? Will it be a help to you in the Christian life? Will it be pleasing to God? Will your example be a safe one for others to follow?

Before giving her hand in marriage, every woman should inquire whether he with whom she is about to unite her destiny is worthy. What has been his past record? Is his life pure? Is the love which he expresses of a noble, elevated character, or is it a mere emotional fondness? Has he the traits of character that will make her happy? Can she find true peace and joy in his affection? Will she be allowed to preserve her individuality, or must her judgment and conscience be surrendered to the control of her husband? As a disciple of Christ, she is not her own; she has been bought with a price. Can she honor the Saviour's claims as supreme? Will body and soul, thoughts and purposes, be preserved pure and holy? These questions have a vital bearing upon the well-being of every woman who enters the marriage relation.

Religion is needed in the home. Only this can prevent the grievous wrongs which so often embitter married life. Only where Christ reigns can there be deep, true, unselfish love. Then soul will be knit with soul, and the two lives will blend in harmony. Angels of God will be guests in the home, and their holy vigils will hallow the marriage chamber. Debasing sensuality will be banished. Upward to God will the thoughts be directed; to Him will the heart's devotion ascend.

The heart yearns for human love, but this love is not strong enough, or pure enough, or precious enough, to supply the place of the love of Jesus. Only in her Saviour can the wife find wisdom, strength, and grace to meet the cares, responsibilities, and sorrows of life. She should make Him her strength and her guide. Let woman give herself to Christ before giving herself to any earthly friend, and enter into no relation which shall conflict with this. Those who would find true happiness must have the blessing of heaven upon all that they possess and all that they do. It is disobedience to God that fills so many hearts and homes with misery. My sister, unless you would have a home where the shadows are never lifted, do not unite yourself with one who is an enemy of God.

As one who expects to meet these words in the judgment, I entreat you to ponder the step you contemplate taking. Ask yourself: "Will not an unbelieving husband lead my thoughts away from Jesus? He is a lover of pleasure more than a lover of God; will he not lead me to enjoy the things that he enjoys?" The path to eternal life is steep and rugged. Take no additional weights to retard your progress. You have too little spiritual strength, and you need help instead of hindrance.

The Lord commanded ancient Israel not to intermarry with the idolatrous nations around them: "Neither shalt thou make marriages with them; thy daughter thou shalt not give unto his son, nor his daughter shalt thou take unto thy son." The reason is given. Infinite Wisdom, foreseeing the result of such unions, declares: "For they will turn away thy son from following Me, that they may serve other gods: so will the anger of the Lord be kindled against you, and destroy thee suddenly." "For thou art an holy people unto the Lord thy God: the Lord thy God hath chosen thee to be a special people unto Himself, above all people that are upon the face of the earth." "Know therefore that the Lord thy God, He is God, the faithful God, which keepeth covenant and mercy with them that love Him and keep His commandments to a thousand generations; and repayeth them that hate Him to their face, to destroy them: He will not be slack to him that hateth Him, He will repay him to his face."

In the New Testament are similar prohibitions concerning the marriage of Christians with the ungodly. The apostle Paul, in his first letter to the Corinthians, declares: "The wife is bound by the law as long as her husband liveth; but if her husband be dead, she is at liberty to be married to whom she will; *only in the Lord.*" Again, in his second epistle, he writes: "Be ye not unequally yoked together with unbelievers: for what fellowship hath righteousness with unrighteousness? and what communion hath light with darkness? and what concord hath Christ with Belial? or what part hath he that believeth with an infidel? and what agreement hath the temple of God with idols? for ye are the temple of the living God; as God hath said, I will dwell in them, and walk in them; and I will be their God, and they shall be My people. Wherefore come out from among them, and be ye separate, saith the Lord, and touch not the unclean thing; and I will receive you, and will be a Father unto you, and ye shall be My sons and daughters, saith the Lord Almighty."

My sister, dare you disregard these plain and positive directions? As a child of God, a subject of Christ's kingdom, the purchase of His blood, how can you connect yourself with one who does not acknowledge His claims, who is not controlled by His Spirit? The commands I have quoted are not the word of man, but of God. Though the companion of your choice were in all other respects worthy (which he is not), yet he has not accepted the truth for this time; he is an unbeliever, and you are forbidden of heaven to unite yourself with him. You cannot, without peril to your soul, disregard this divine injunction.

I would warn you of your danger before it shall be too late. You listen to smooth, pleasant words and are led to believe that all will be well; but you do not read the motives that prompt these fair speeches. You cannot see the depths of wickedness hidden in the heart. You cannot look behind the scenes and discern the snares that Satan is laying for your soul. He would lead you to pursue such a course that he can obtain easy access to aim his shafts of temptation against you. Do not give him the least advantage. While God moves upon the minds of His servants, Satan works through the children of disobedience. There is no concord between Christ and Belial. The two cannot harmonize. To connect with an unbeliever is to place yourself on Satan's ground. You grieve the Spirit of God and forfeit His protection. Can you afford to have such terrible odds against you in fighting the battle for everlasting life?

You may say: "But I have given my promise, and shall I now retract it?" I answer: If you have made a promise contrary to the Scriptures, by all means retract it without delay, and in humility before God repent of the infatuation that led you to make so rash a pledge. Far better take back such a promise, in the fear of God, than keep it and thereby dishonor your Maker.

Remember, you have a heaven to gain, an open path to perdition to shun. God means what He says. When He prohibited our first parents from eating the fruit of the tree of knowledge, their disobedience opened the floodgates of woe to the whole world. If we walk contrary to God, He will walk contrary to us. Our only safe course is to render obedience to all His requirements, at whatever cost. All are founded in infinite love and wisdom.

The spirit of intense worldliness that now exists, the disposition to acknowledge no higher claim than that of self-gratification, constitutes one of the signs of the last days. "As it was in the days of Noah," said Christ, "so shall it be also in the days of the Son of man. They did eat, they drank, they married wives, they were given in marriage, until the day that Noah entered into the ark, and the Flood came, and destroyed them all." The people of this generation are marrying and giving in marriage with the same reckless disregard of God's requirements as was manifested in the days of Noah. There is in the Christian world an astonishing, alarming indifference to the teaching of God's word in regard to the marriage of Christians with unbelievers. Many who profess to love and fear God choose to follow the bent of their own minds rather than take counsel of Infinite Wisdom. In a matter which vitally concerns the happiness and well-being of both parties for this world and the next, reason, judgment, and the fear of God are set aside, and blind impulse, stubborn determination, is allowed to control. Men and women who are otherwise sensible and conscientious close their ears to counsel; they are deaf to the appeals and entreaties of friends and kindred and of the servants of God. The expression of a caution or warning is regarded as impertinent meddling, and the friend who is faithful enough to utter a remonstrance is treated as an enemy. All this is as Satan would have it. He weaves his spell about the soul, and it becomes bewitched, infatuated. Reason lets fall the reins of self-control upon the neck of lust, unsanctified passion bears sway, until, too late, the victim awakens to a life of misery and bondage. This is not a picture drawn by the imagination, but a recital of facts. God's sanction is not given to unions which He has expressly forbidden. For years I have been receiving letters from different persons who have formed unhappy marriages, and the revolting histories opened before me are enough to make the heart ache. It is no easy thing to decide what advice can be given to these unfortunate ones, or how their hard lot can be lightened; but their sad experience should be a warning to others.

In this age of the world, as the scenes of earth's history are soon to close and we are about to enter upon the time of trouble such as never was, the fewer the marriages contracted, the better for all, both men and women. Above all, when Satan is working with all deceivableness of unrighteousness in them that perish, let Christians beware of connecting themselves with unbelievers. God has spoken. All who fear Him will submit to His wise injunctions. Our feelings, impulses, and affections must flow heavenward, not earthward, not in the low, base channel of sensual thought and indulgence. It is time now that every soul should stand as in the sight of the heart-searching God.

My dear sister, as a disciple of Jesus you should inquire what will be the influence of the step you are about to take, not only upon yourself, but upon others. The followers of Christ are to be co-workers with their Master; they must be "blameless and harmless, the sons of God, without rebuke, in the midst of a crooked and perverse nation, among whom," says Paul, "ye shine as lights in the world." We are to receive the bright beams from the Sun of Righteousness, and by our good works let them shine forth to others in clear, steady rays, never fitful, never growing dim. We cannot be sure that we are doing no harm to those about us unless we are exerting a positive influence to lead them heavenward.

"Ye are My witnesses," said Jesus, and in each act of our lives we should inquire: How will our course affect the interests of the Redeemer's kingdom? If you are indeed Christ's disciple, you will choose to walk in His footsteps, however painful this may be to your natural feelings. Said Paul: "God forbid that I should glory, save in the cross of our Lord Jesus Christ, by whom the world is crucified unto me, and I unto the world." You, Sister L, need to sit at the feet of Jesus and learn of Him, as did Mary of old. God requires of you an entire surrender of your will, your plans and purposes. Jesus is your leader; to Him you must look, in Him you must trust, and you must permit nothing to deter you from the life of consecration which you owe to God. Your conversation must be in heaven, from whence you look for your Saviour. Your piety must be of a character to make itself felt by all within the sphere of your influence. God requires you in every act of life to shun the very appearance of evil. Are you doing this? You are under the most sacred obligation not to belittle or compromise your holy faith by uniting with the Lord's enemies. If you are tempted to disregard the injunctions of His word because others have done so, remember that your example also will exert an influence. Others will do as you do, and thus the evil will be extended. While you profess to be a child of God, a departure on your part from His requirements will result in infinite harm to those who look to you for guidance.

The salvation of souls will be the constant aim of those who are abiding in Christ. But what have you done to show forth the praises of Him who has called you out of darkness? "Awake, thou that sleepest, and arise from the dead, and

Christ shall give thee light." Shake off this fatal infatuation that benumbs your senses and palsies the energies of the soul.

The very strongest incentives to faithfulness are set before us, the highest motives, the most glorious rewards. Christians are to be Christ's representatives, sons and daughters of God. They are His jewels, His peculiar treasures. Of all who will maintain their steadfastness He declares: "They shall walk with Me in white: for they are worthy." Those who reach the portals of eternal bliss will not count that any sacrifice which they have made was too great.

May God help you to stand the test and preserve your integrity. Cling by faith to Jesus. Disappoint not your Redeemer.

St. Helena, California, Feb. 13, 1885.

THE SUPPORT OF CITY MISSIONS

Dear Brother M: A few days ago I received a letter written by you to Elder N, in which you raise very serious objections to leaving the _____ mission to be supported by your conference, and say that other conferences all over the field should have an equal interest in this mission. But if these conferences do not now have important missions to sustain in cities in their own borders, are there not places where such missions should be established? If your conference is asked to take the _____ mission under its care and carry it on under the supervision of the General Conference, the responsible men should feel that this is an evidence that their brethren have confidence in them, and they should say: "Yes; we accept the sacred trust. We will do all in our power to make the mission a success and to show that the confidence of our brethren is not misplaced. We will ask wisdom of God and will practice self-denial and rigid economy if necessary." God will sustain you in the cheerful performance of this duty and will make it a blessing to you rather than a burden, a hindrance to the cause in your state.

That great city is in darkness and error, and we have left it so thus long. Will God pardon this negligence on our part? What account shall we give for the men and women who have died without hearing the sound of present truth, who would have received it had the light been brought to them? My spirit is stirred that the work in _____ has been delayed so long. The work that is now being done there might have been done years ago and could then have been accomplished with far less expenditure of money, time, and labor. Nevertheless it must not be left undone now. A small beginning has been made on a very economical plan, and much more has been accomplished than could have been expected considering the facilities that have been provided. But better facilities must be furnished. There must be a place where people can hear the truth. There must be means to support the workers in this mission field, not in ease and luxury, but in a plain, comfortable manner. They are God's instruments, and nothing should be said or done to discourage them. On the contrary, let their hands be strengthened and their hearts encouraged.

There is enough wealth in your conference to carry forward this work successfully; and shall the prince of darkness be left in undisputed possession of our great cities because it costs something to sustain missions? Let those who would follow Christ fully come up to the work, even if it be over the heads of ministers and president. Those who in such a work as this will say, "I pray thee have me excused," should beware lest they receive their discharge for time and for eternity. Let Christians who love duty lift every ounce they can and then look to God for further strength. He will work through the efforts of thoroughgoing men and women and will do what they cannot do. New light and power will be given them as they use what they have. New fervor and zeal will stir the church as they see something accomplished.

We rejoice in spirit as we contemplate what may be done; but we blush before our Maker at the thought of the little that has been accomplished. Shepherds have neglected their God-given responsibilities; they have become narrow and faithless, and have encouraged unpardonable cowardice, slothfulness, and covetousness. They have not realized the magnitude and importance of the work. Men are wanted whose eyes are anointed to see and understand heaven's designs. Then the standard of piety will be raised, and there will be real missionaries who will be ready to sacrifice for the truth's sake. There is no room in the church of God for the selfish and ease-loving; but men and women are called for who will make exertions to plant the standard of truth in our large cities, in the great thoroughfares of travel.

A world is to be warned, and in humility we should work as God has given us ability. Let every state come up to the work. What right have those with narrow and unconsecrated ideas to say what their conference will do and what it will not do? The _____ mission will not be left wholly to your state; but if your conference had a heart to work, it could sustain two such missions and not feel the burden. Come, brethren, arouse to action. Time lost through your unbelief and want of courage is lost forever. Let the ministers act as though something were to be done, and the largehearted men who love God and keep His commandments will come up to the help of the Lord. In this way the church will be disciplined for future efforts; for their beneficence is never to cease.

Elder M, as president of the _____ Conference; you have shown by your general management that you are unworthy of the trust reposed in you. You have shown that you are conservative, and that your ideas are narrow. You have not done one half what you might have done had you had the true spirit of the work. You might have been far more capable and experienced than you now are; you might have been far better prepared to manage successfully this sacred and important mission—a work which would have given you the strongest claim to the general confidence of our people. But, like the other ministering brethren in your state, you have failed to advance with the opening providence of God; you have not shown that the Holy Spirit was deeply impressing your heart, so that God could speak through you to His people. If in this crisis you do anything to strengthen doubt and distrust in the churches of your state, anything that will prevent the people from engaging heartily in this work, God will hold you responsible. Has God given you unmistakable evidence that the brethren of your state are excused from the responsibility of putting their arms about the city of _____ as Christ has put His arms about them? If you were standing in the light, you would encourage this mission by your faith.

You need to drink deep of the streams of grace and salvation before you can lead others to the Fountain of living waters. Holding the office of president of a conference, with the experience and influence that this office gives, instead of discouraging the people you should have urged them to new exertion, to bear weightier responsibilities. There are special duties devolving upon men in responsible positions; there are laborious efforts to be made which it would be convenient to neglect. But when the shepherds are negligent of duty, may the Lord pity the poor sheep.

Your work, my brother, does not show that you have realized that your obligations are sacred and weighty. I have been shown that you are capable of doing much better work than you have done, and that God requires more and better work at your hands. He requires integrity and faithfulness. The work of saving souls is the highest and noblest ever entrusted to mortal man; and you should allow nothing to come in between you and this sacred work to absorb your mind and confuse your judgment. One standing in the responsible position that you occupy should make eternal interests first, and temporal matters of secondary importance. You are an ambassador for Christ; and you should encourage those under your charge to seek for higher spiritual attainments, to live holier and purer lives. In your efforts to save souls from perdition and to build up the church in truth and righteousness, you should use tact, wisdom, and the power that it is your privilege to have through constant communion with God. God requires this of you and of every other minister engaged in His work. You should show your loyalty to your crucified Redeemer by acting as though you realized that you have a solemn charge to present every man perfect in Christ Jesus, wanting in nothing.

In your case very much more might have been accomplished by holy living, by fervent prayer, and by a careful, painstaking discharge of every duty. You might have done much by faithful warnings and reproofs and by affectionate appeals. It is not brain power alone that is needed, but heart power. The truth presented as it is in Jesus will have an effect. You lack ardent, active home religion. Selfish interests have clouded your mind and perverted your judgment, and the claims of God have not been realized. You need to unburden your soul of worldly cares and business, and to have an eye single to the glory of God.

The eternal destiny of all is soon to be decided. From Illinois, Wisconsin, Iowa, and other conferences scores of ministers should go forth with burning zeal to proclaim the last message of warning. And at such a time as this will the presidents of our conferences lie back in the harness and refuse to draw the heavy load? Will they by voice or pen exert an influence to discourage those who have a mind to work? Any course on their part that would encourage indolence and unbelief is criminal in the highest degree. They should encourage the people to diligence in the cause of God, to make every exertion for the salvation of souls; but they should never leave even the slightest impression on their minds that they are sacrificing too much for the cause of God, or that more is required of them than is reasonable. In the heavenly warfare something must be ventured. Now is our time to work, to encounter difficulties and dangers. The providence of God says, "Go forward," not back into Egypt; and instead of framing a testimony to please the people, ministers should seek to arouse those who are asleep.

I discern in your letter, Elder M, a vein of unbelief, a lack of judgment and discernment. Your position confirms the testimony I have had that you are giving the conference a narrow mold and have stood in the way of its advancement because you have not elevated the standard of truth. I will here quote a few paragraphs from this testimony, which was written during the General Conference at Battle Creek, in November, 1883:

"Our conversation in regard to the _____ mission has left a disagreeable impression on my mind. Do not think me severe in my remarks in regard to this mission. You spoke with great satisfaction of the way this work had been carried forward. You said that Brother O and those associated with him were willing to do any way to get along; that they had a small room in a loft, where they prepared their food; and that they were doing a good work in the most economical way. Your ideas on this subject are not correct. The light which God has given us, precious above the price of silver and gold, is to go forth in a way to give character to the work. The brethren connected with this mission are not free from the infirmities of humanity; and unless attention is given to their health, their work must be greatly embarrassed. Those who stand at the head of the work in the conference should not permit such a state of things to exist. They should educate the people to give of their means, that no pinched want may be experienced by the workers. As the stewards of God the responsibility rests upon them to see that one or two do not have all the sacrificing to do while others are taking their ease, eating, drinking, and dressing, without a thought of our sacred missions or of their duty with reference to them.

"I have been shown, Elder M, that you do not take a correct view of the work, that you do not realize its importance. You have failed to educate the people in the true spirit of self-sacrifice and devotion. You have feared to urge duty upon wealthy men; and when you have made a feeble effort in the right direction, and they have begun to make excuses and to find a little fault with someone in regard to the management of the work, you have thought perhaps they were right. This subterfuge, which has developed in them doubt and unbelief, has taken effect in your own heart, and they have turned this to account and have learned just how to treat your efforts. When they have encouraged doubt in regard to the *Testimonies,* you have not done what you should to uproot this feeling. You should have shown them that Satan is always picking flaws, questioning, accusing, and laying reproach upon the brethren, and that it is unsafe to be in any such position."

"My brother, you have not taken a course to encourage men to give themselves to the ministry. Instead of bringing the expense of the work down to a low figure, it is your duty to bring the minds of the people to understand that 'the laborer is worthy of his hire.' " "The churches need to be impressed with the fact that it is their duty to deal honestly with the cause of God, not allowing the guilt of the worst kind of robbery to rest upon them, that of robbing God in tithes and offerings. When settlements are made with the laborers in His cause, they should not be forced to accept small remuneration because there is a lack of money in the treasury. Many have been defrauded of their just dues in this way, and it is just as criminal in the sight of God as for one to keep back the wages of those who are employed in any other regular business.

"There are men of ability who would like to go out and labor in our several conferences; but they have no courage, for they must have means to support their families. It is the worst kind of generalship to allow a conference to stand still or to fail to settle its honest debts. There is a great deal of this done; and whenever it is done, God is displeased.

"If the presidents and other laborers in our conferences impress upon the minds of the people the character of the crime of robbing God, and if they have a true spirit of devotion and a burden of the work, God will make their labors a blessing to the people, and fruit will be seen as the result of their efforts. Ministers have failed greatly in their duty to so labor with the churches. There is important work to be done aside from that of preaching. Had this been done, as God designed it should be, there would have been many more laborers in the field than there now are. And had the ministers done their duty in educating every member, whether rich or poor, to give as God has prospered him, there would be a full treasury from which to pay the honest debts to the workers; and this would greatly advance missionary work in all their borders. God has shown me that many souls are in danger of eternal ruin through selfishness and worldliness; and the watchmen are guilty, for they have neglected their duty. This is a state of things that Satan exults to see.

"All branches of the work belong to the ministers. It is not God's order that someone should follow after them and bind off their unfinished work. It is not the duty of the conference to be at the expense of employing other laborers to follow after and pick up the stitches dropped by negligent workers. It is the duty of the president of the conference to have an oversight of the laborers and their work, and to teach them to be faithful in these things; for no church can prosper that is robbing God. The spiritual dearth in our churches is frequently the result of an alarming prevalence of selfishness. Selfish, worldly pursuits and schemes interpose between the soul and God. Men cling to the world, seeming to fear that should they let go their hold upon it, God would not care for them. And so they attempt to take care of themselves; they are anxious, troubled, distressed, holding on to their large farms and adding to their possessions.

"The word of God speaks of 'the hire of the laborers, . . . which is of you kept back by fraud.' This is generally understood to apply to wealthy men who employ servants and do not pay them for their labor, but it has a broader meaning than this. It applies with great force to those who have been enlightened by the Spirit of God and yet in any degree work upon the same principle that these men do in hiring servants, grinding them down to the lowest price."

I solemnly warn you not to stand in an attitude similar to that of the unfaithful spies, who went up to view the land of promise. When these spies returned from their search, the congregation of Israel were cherishing high hopes and were waiting in eager expectancy. The news of their return is carried from tribe to tribe and is hailed with rejoicing. The people rush out to meet the messengers, who have endured the fatigue of travel in the dusty highways and under a burning sun. These messengers bring specimens of the fruit, showing the fertility of the soil. The congregation rejoice that they are to come into possession of so goodly a land; and they listen intently as the report is brought to Moses, that not a word shall escape them. "We came unto the land whither thou sentest us," the spies begin, "and surely it floweth with milk and honey; and this is the fruit of it." The people are enthusiastic; they would eagerly obey the voice of the Lord and go up at once to possess the land.

But the spies continue: "Nevertheless the people be strong that dwell in the land, and the cities are walled, and very great: and moreover we saw the children of Anak there." Now the scene changes. Hope and courage give place to cowardly despair as the spies utter the sentiments of their unbelieving hearts, which are filled with discouragement prompted by Satan. Their unbelief casts a gloomy shadow over the congregation, and the mighty power of God, so often manifested in behalf of the chosen nation, is forgotten.

The people are desperate in their disappointment and despair. A wail of agony arises and mingles with the confused murmur of voices. Caleb comprehends the situation and, bold to stand in defense of the word of God, does all in his power to counteract the evil influence of his unfaithful associates. For an instant the people are stilled to listen to his words of hope and courage respecting the goodly land. He does not contradict what has already been said; the walls are high and the Canaanites strong. "Let us go up at once, and possess it," he urges; "for we are well able to overcome it." But the ten interrupt him and picture the obstacles in darker colors than at first. "We be not able to go up against the people," they declare, "for they are stronger than we." "All the people that we saw in it are men of a great stature. And there we saw the giants, the sons of Anak, which come of the giants: and we were in our own sight as grasshoppers, and so we were in their sight."

"And all the congregation lifted up their voice, and cried; and the people wept that night." The men who have so long borne with the perversity of Israel know too well what the next scene will be. Revolt and open mutiny quickly follow; for Satan has had full sway, and the people seem bereft of reason. They curse Moses and Aaron, forgetting that God hears their wicked speeches, and that, enshrouded in the cloudy pillar, the Angel of His presence is witnessing their terrible outburst of wrath. In bitterness they cry out: "Would God that we had died in the land of Egypt! or would God we had died in this wilderness! And wherefore hath the Lord brought us unto this land, to fall by the sword, that our wives and our children should be a prey? Were it not better for us to return into Egypt? And they said one to another, Let us make a captain, and let us return into Egypt."

In humiliation and distress, Moses and Aaron fall on "their faces before all the assembly of the congregation of the children of Israel," not knowing what to do to turn them from their rash and passionate purpose. Caleb and Joshua attempt to quiet the tumult. With their garments rent in token of grief and indignation, they rush in among the people, and their ringing voices are heard above the tempest of lamentation and rebellious grief: "The land, which we passed through to search it, is an exceeding good land. If the Lord delight in us, then He will bring us into this land, and give it us; a land which floweth with milk and honey. Only rebel not ye against the Lord, neither fear ye the people of the land; for they are bread for us: their defense is departed from them, and the Lord is with us: fear them not."

The false report of the unfaithful spies was fully accepted, and through it the whole congregation were deluded, just as Satan meant that they should be; and the voice of God through His faithful servants was disregarded. The traitors had done their work. All the assembly, as with one voice, cried out in favor of stoning Caleb and Joshua.

And now the mighty God reveals Himself, to the confusion of His disobedient, murmuring people. "And the glory of the Lord appeared in the tabernacle of the congregation before all the children of Israel." What a burden was brought upon Moses and Aaron, and how earnest were their entreaties that God would not destroy His people! Moses pleads before the Lord the wonderful manifestations of divine power that have made the name of Israel's God a terror to their enemies, and entreats that the enemies of God and of His people may have no occasion to triumph, saying: "Because the Lord was not able to bring this people into the land which He sware unto them, therefore He hath slain them in the wilderness." The Lord hearkened unto the prayer of Moses; but he declared that those who had rebelled against Him, after having witnessed His power and glory, should fall in the wilderness; they should never see the land which was their promised inheritance. But of Caleb He said: "My servant Caleb, because he had another spirit with him, and hath followed Me fully, him will I bring into the land whereinto he went; and his seed shall possess it."

It was Caleb's faith in God that gave him courage; that kept him from the fear of man, even the mighty giants, the sons of Anak, and enabled him to stand boldly and unflinchingly in defense of the right. From the same exalted source, the mighty General of the armies of heaven, every true soldier of the cross of Christ must receive strength and courage to overcome obstacles that often seem insurmountable. The law of God is made void; and those who would do their duty must be ever ready to speak the words that God gives them, and not the words of doubt, discouragement, and despair.

Elder M, although you may be sustained by many, as were the unfaithful spies, yet the sentiments of your letter are not prompted by the Spirit of the Lord. Beware lest your words and your spirit be like theirs, and your work of the same baleful character. At such a time as this we must not harbor a thought nor breathe a word of unbelief, nor encourage an act of self-serving. This has been done in the Upper Columbia and North Pacific Conferences; and while there we felt in some measure the sorrow, mortification, and discouragement that Moses and Aaron, Caleb and Joshua, experienced. We tried to set the current flowing in an opposite direction; but it was at the cost of much severe labor and great anxiety and distress of mind. And the work of reform in these conferences has but just commenced. It is the work of time to overcome the unbelief, distrust, and suspicion of years. Satan has been to a great extent successful in carrying out his purposes in these conferences because he has found persons whom he could use as his agents.

For Christ's sake and the truth's sake, Brother M, do not leave the work in your conference in such a shape that it will be impossible for the one that succeeds you to set things in order. The people have received narrow and limited views of the work; selfishness has been encouraged, and worldliness has been unrebuked. I call upon you to do all in your power to efface the wrong mold you have given to this conference, to remedy the sad effects of your neglect of duty, and thus to prepare the field for another laborer. Unless you do this, may God pity the workman who shall follow you.

Presidents of conferences should be men who can be fully trusted with God's work. They should be men of integrity, unselfish, devoted, working Christians. If they are deficient in these respects, the churches under their care will not prosper. They, even more than other ministers of Christ, should set an example of holy living and of unselfish devotion to the interests of God's cause, that those looking to them for an example may not be misled. But in some instances they are trying to serve both God and mammon. They are not self-denying; they do not carry a burden for souls. Their consciences are not sensitive; when the cause of God is wounded, they are not bruised in spirit. In their hearts they question and doubt the *Testimonies* of the Spirit of God. They do not themselves bear the cross of Christ; they know not the fervent love of Jesus. And they are not faithful shepherds of the flock over which they have been made overseers; their record is not one that they will rejoice to meet in the day of God.

How much is required of the minister in his work of watching for souls as they that must give an account! What devotion, what singleness of purpose, what elevated piety, should be seen in his life and character! How much is lost through a want of tact and skill in presenting the truth to others, how much through a carelessness of deportment, a roughness of speech, and a worldliness that in no way represents Jesus or savors of heaven. Our work is about to close up. Soon it will be said in heaven: "He that is unjust, let him be unjust still: and he which is filthy, let him be filthy still: and he that is righteous, let him be righteous still: and he that is holy, let him be holy still." At this solemn time the church is called upon to be vigilant because of the intense activity of Satan. His agency is seen on every hand, and yet ministers and people act as though they were ignorant of his devices and paralyzed by his power. Let each member of the church awake. Let each laborer remember that the vineyard he tills is not his own, but belongs to his Lord, who has gone on a long journey and in His absence has commissioned His servants to look after His interests; and let him remember that if he is unfaithful to his trust he must give an account to his Lord when He shall return.

While the doubting ones talk of impossibilities, while they tremble at the thought of high walls and strong giants, let the faithful Calebs, who have "another spirit," come to the front. The truth of God, which bringeth salvation, will go forth to the people if ministers and professed believers will not hedge up its way, as did the unfaithful spies. Our work is aggressive. Something must be done to warn the world; and let no voice be heard that will encourage selfish interests to the neglect of missionary fields. We must engage in the work with heart and soul and voice; both mental and physical powers must be aroused. All heaven is interested in our work, and angels of God are ashamed of our weak efforts.

I am alarmed at the indifference of our churches. Like Meroz, they have failed to come up to the help of the Lord. The laymen have been at ease. They have folded their hands, feeling that the responsibility rested upon the ministers. But to every man God has appointed his work; not work in his fields of corn and wheat, but earnest, persevering work for the salvation of souls. God forbid, Elder M, that you or any other minister should quench one particle of the spirit of labor that now exists. Will you not rather stimulate it by your words of burning zeal? The Lord has made us the depositaries of His law; He has committed to us sacred and eternal truth, which is to be given to others in faithful warnings, reproofs, and encouragement. By means of railroads and steamboat lines we are connected with every part of the world and given access to every nation with our message of truth. Let us sow the seed of gospel truth beside all waters; for we know not which shall prosper, this or that, or whether both shall be alike fruitful. Paul may plant, and Apollos water; but it is God who giveth the increase.

"Let your light so shine before men, that they may see your good works, and glorify your Father which is in heaven." Do not put your light under a bushel, but on a candlestick, that it may give light to all that are in the house. "Ye are not your own; for ye are bought with a price," even the precious blood of the Son of God. We have no right to live to ourselves. Every minister should be a consecrated missionary; every layman a worker, using his talents of influence and means in his Lord's service, for active benevolence is a vital principle of Christianity. It is the exercise of this principle that is to bring sheaves to the Lord of the harvest, while a want of it hinders the work of God and bars the way for the salvation or souls.

Ministers have neglected to enforce gospel beneficence. The subject of tithes and offerings has not been dwelt upon as it should have been. Men are not naturally inclined to be benevolent, but to be sordid and avaricious, and to live for self. And Satan is ever ready to present the advantages to be gained by using all their means for selfish, worldly purposes; he is glad when he can influence them to shirk duty and rob God in tithes and offerings. But not one is excused in this matter. "Let every one of you lay by him in store, as God hath prospered him." The poor and the rich, the young men and the young women who earn wages—all are to lay by a portion; for God claims it. The spiritual prosperity of every member of the church depends on personal effort and strict fidelity to God. Says the apostle Paul: "Charge them that are rich in this world, that they be not high-minded, nor trust in uncertain riches, but in the living God, who giveth us richly all things to enjoy; that they do good, that they be rich in good works, ready to distribute, willing to communicate; laying up in store for themselves a good foundation against the time to come, that they may lay hold on eternal life." All are required to show a deep interest in the cause of God in its various branches, and close and unexpected tests will be brought to bear upon them to see who are worthy to receive the seal of the living God.

All should feel that they an not proprietors, but stewards, and that the time is coming when they must give an account for the use they have made of their Lord's money. Means will be needed in the cause of God. With David they should say: "All things come of Thee, and of Thine own have we given Thee." Schools are to be established in various places, publications are to be multiplied, churches are to be built in the large cities, and laborers are to be sent forth, not only into the cities, but into the highways and hedges. And now, my brethren who believe the truth, is your opportunity. We are standing, as it were, on the borders of the eternal world. We are looking for the glorious appearing of our Lord; the night is far spent; the day is at hand. When we realize the great-

ness of the plan of redemption we shall be far more courageous, self-sacrificing, and devotional than we now are.

There is a great work for us to do before success will crown
our efforts. There must be decided reforms in our homes and
in our churches. Parents must labor for the salvation of their
children. God will work with our efforts when we do on our
part all that He has enjoined upon us and qualified us to do;
but because of our unbelief, worldliness, and indolence,
blood-bought souls in the very shadow of our homes are dying
in their sins, and dying unwarned. Is Satan always thus to
triumph? Oh, no! The light reflected from the cross of Calvary indicates that a greater work is to be done than our eyes
have yet witnessed.

The third angel, flying in the midst of heaven and heralding
the commandments of God and the testimony of Jesus, represents our work. The message loses none of its force in the
angel's onward flight, for John sees it increasing in strength
and power until the whole earth is lightened with its glory.
The course of God's commandment-keeping people is onward, ever onward. The message of truth that we bear must
go to nations, tongues, and peoples. Soon it will go with a
loud voice, and the earth will be lightened with its glory. Are
we preparing for this great outpouring of the Spirit of God?

Human agencies are to be employed in this work. Zeal and
energy must be intensified; talents that are rusting from inaction must be pressed into service. The voice that would say,
"Wait; do not allow yourself to have burdens imposed upon
you," is the voice of the cowardly spies. We want Calebs
now who will press to the front—chieftains in Israel who with
courageous words will make a strong report in favor of immediate action. When the selfish, ease-loving, panic-stricken
people, fearing tall giants and inaccessible walls, clamor for
retreat, let the voice of the Calebs be heard, even though the
cowardly ones stand with stones in their hands, ready to beat
them down for their faithful testimony.

Can we not discern the signs of the times? Can we not

see how earnestly Satan is at work binding the tares in bundles, uniting the elements of his kingdom, that he may gain control of the world? This work of binding up the tares is going forward far more rapidly than we imagine. Satan is opposing every obstacle to the advancement of the truth. He is seeking to create diversity of opinion and to encourage worldliness and avarice. He works with the subtlety of the serpent and, when he sees it will do, with the ferocity of the lion. The ruin of souls is his only delight, their destruction his only employment; and shall we act as though we were paralyzed? Will those who profess to believe the truth listen to the temptations of the wily foe and allow themselves to become selfish and narrow, and their worldly interests to interfere with efforts for the salvation of souls?

All who ever enter heaven's gates will enter as conquerors. When the redeemed throng surround the throne of God, with palm branches in their hands and crowns on their heads, it will be known what victories have been won. It will be seen how Satan's power has been exercised over minds, how he has linked with himself souls who flattered themselves that they were doing God's will. It will then be seen that his power and subtlety could not have been successfully resisted had not divine power been combined with human effort. Man must also be victor over himself; his temper, inclinations, and spirit must be brought into subjection to the will of God. But the righteousness and strength of Christ avail for all who will claim His merits.

Then let earnest and determined effort be made to beat back the terrible foe. We want on the whole armor of righteousness. Time is passing, and we are fast approaching the close of our probation. Will our names stand registered in the Lamb's book of life, or shall we be found with the unfaithful? Are we of the number who shall gather around the great white throne, singing the song of the redeemed? There are no cold, formal ones in that throng. Every soul is in earnest, every heart full of thanksgiving for the marvelous love of God and the overcoming grace that has enabled His people to conquer in the warfare against sin. And with a loud voice they swell the song: "Salvation to our God which sitteth upon the throne, and unto the Lamb."

THE TRUE MISSIONARY SPIRIT

The true missionary spirit is the spirit of Christ. The world's Redeemer was the great model missionary. Many of His followers have labored earnestly and unselfishly in the cause of human salvation; but no man's labor can bear comparison with the self-denial, the sacrifice, the benevolence, of our Exemplar.

The love which Christ has evinced for us is without a parallel. How earnestly He labored! How often was He alone in fervent prayer, on the mountainside or in the retirement of the garden, pouring out His supplications with strong crying and tears. How perseveringly He urged His petitions in behalf of sinners! Even on the cross He forgot His own sufferings in His deep love for those whom He came to save. How cold our love, how feeble our interest, when compared with the love and interest manifested by our Saviour! Jesus gave Himself to redeem our race; and yet how ready are we to excuse ourselves from giving all that we have for Jesus. Our Saviour submitted to wearing labor, ignominy, and suffering. He was repulsed, mocked, derided, while engaged in the great work which He came to earth to do.

Do you, my brethren and sisters, inquire: What model shall we copy? I do not point you to great and good men, but to the world's Redeemer. If we would have the true missionary spirit we must be imbued with the love of Christ; we must look to the Author and Finisher of our faith, study His character, cultivate His spirit of meekness and humility, and walk in His footsteps.

Many suppose that the missionary spirit, the qualification for missionary work, is a special gift or endowment bestowed upon the ministers and a few members of the church and that all others are to be mere spectators. Never was there a greater mistake. Every true Christian will possess a missionary spirit, for to be a Christian is to be Christlike. No man liveth to himself, and "if any man have not the Spirit of Christ, he is none of His." Everyone who has tasted of the powers of the world to come, whether he be young or old, learned or unlearned, will be stirred with the spirit which actuated Christ. The very first impulse of the renewed heart is to bring others also to the Saviour. Those who do not possess this desire give evidence that they have lost their first love; they should closely examine their own hearts in the light of God's word, and earnestly seek a fresh baptism of the Spirit of Christ; they should pray for a deeper comprehension of that wondrous love which Jesus manifested for us in leaving the realms of glory and coming to a fallen world to save the perishing.

There is work for every one of us in the vineyard of the Lord. We are not to seek that position which will yield us the most enjoyment or the greatest gain. True religion is free from selfishness. The missionary spirit is a spirit of personal sacrifice. We are to work anywhere and everywhere, to the utmost of our ability, for the cause of our Master.

Just as soon as a person is really converted to the truth there springs up in his heart an earnest desire to go and tell some friend or neighbor of the precious light shining forth from the sacred pages. In his unselfish labor to save others he is a living epistle, known and read of all men. His life shows that he has been converted to Christ and has become a colaborer with Him.

As a class, Seventh-day Adventists are a generous and warmhearted people. In the proclamation of the truth for this time we can rely upon their strong and ready sympathy. When a proper object for their liberality is presented, appealing to their judgment and conscience, it calls forth a hearty response. Their gifts in support of the cause testify that they believe it to be the cause of truth. There are, indeed, exceptions among us. Not all who profess to accept the faith are earnest and true-hearted believers. But the same was true in the days of Christ. Even among the apostles there was a Judas; but that did not prove all to be of the same character. We have no reason for discouragement while we know that there are so many who are devoted to the cause of truth, and are ready to make noble sacrifices for its advancement. But there is still a great lack, a great need among us. There is too little of the true missionary spirit. All missionary workers should possess that deep interest for the souls of their fellow men that will unite heart to heart in sympathy and in the love of Jesus. They should plead earnestly for divine aid and should work wisely to win souls to Christ. A cold, spiritless effort will accomplish nothing. There is need that the spirit of Christ fall upon the sons of the prophets. Then will they manifest such love for the souls of men as Jesus exemplified in His life.

The reason why there is no deeper religious fervor and no more earnest love for one another in the church is that the missionary spirit has been dying out. Little is now said concerning Christ's coming, which was once the theme of thought and of conversation. There is an unaccountable reluctance, a growing disrelish for religious conversation; and in its stead, idle, frivolous chitchat is indulged in, even by the professed followers of Christ.

My brethren and sisters, do you desire to break the spell that holds you? Would you arouse from this sluggishness that resembles the torpor of death? Go to work, whether you feel like it or not. Engage in personal effort to bring souls to Jesus and the knowledge of the truth. In such labor you will find both a stimulus and a tonic; it will both arouse and strengthen. By exercise your spiritual powers will become more vigorous, so that you can with better success work out your own salvation. The stupor of death is upon many who profess Christ. Make every effort to arouse them. Warn, entreat, expostulate. Pray that the melting love of God may warm and soften their icebound natures. Though they may refuse to hear, your labor will not be lost. In the effort to bless others your own souls will be blessed.

We have the theory of the truth, and now we need to seek most earnestly for its sanctifying power. I dare not hold my peace in this time of peril. It is a time of temptation, of despondency. Everyone is beset by the wiles of Satan, and we should press together to resist his power. We should be of one mind, speaking the same things, and with one mouth glorifying God. Then may we successfully enlarge our plans and by vigilant missionary effort take advantage of every talent we can use in the various departments of the work.

The light of truth is shedding its bright beams upon the world through missionary effort. The press is an instrumentality by which many are reached whom it would be impossible to reach by ministerial effort. A great work can be done by presenting to the people the Bible just as it reads. Carry the word of God to every man's door, urge its plain statements upon every man's conscience, repeat to all the Saviour's command: "Search the Scriptures." Admonish them to take the Bible as it is, to implore divine enlightenment, and then, when the light shines, to gladly accept each precious ray and fearlessly abide the consequences.

The downtrodden law of God is to be exalted before the people; as soon as they turn with earnestness and reverence to the Holy Scriptures, light from heaven will reveal to them wondrous things out of God's law. Great truths that have long been obscured by superstition and false doctrine will blaze forth from the illuminated pages of the Sacred Word. The living oracles pour forth their treasures new and old, bringing light and joy to all who will receive them. Many are roused from their slumber. They rise as it were from the dead and receive the light and life which Christ alone can give. Truths which have proved an overmatch for giant intellects are understood by babes in Christ. To these is plainly revealed that which has clouded the spiritual perception of the most learned expositors of the word, because, like the Sadducees of old, they were ignorant of the Scriptures and of the power of God.

Those who study the Bible with a sincere desire to know and do the will of God will become wise unto salvation. The Sabbath school is an important branch of the missionary work, not only because it gives to young and old a knowledge of God's word, but because it awakens in them a love for its sacred truths and a desire to study it for themselves; above all, it teaches them to regulate their lives by its holy teachings.

All who take the word of God as their rule of life are brought into close relationship with one another. The Bible is their bond of union. But their companionship will not be sought or desired by those who do not bow to the Sacred Word as the one unerring guide. They will be at variance, both in faith and practice. There can be no harmony between them; they are unreconcilable. As Seventh-day Adventists we appeal from custom and tradition to the plain "Thus saith the Lord;" and for this reason we are not, and cannot be, in harmony with the multitudes who teach and follow the doctrines and commandments of men.

All who are born of God will become co-workers with Christ. Such are the salt of the earth. "But if the salt have lost his savor, wherewith shall it be salted?" If the religion we profess fails to renew our hearts and sanctify our lives, how shall it exert a saving power upon unbelievers? "It is thenceforth good for nothing, but to be cast out, and to be trodden underfoot of men." That religion which will not exert a regenerating power upon the world is of no value. We cannot trust it for our own salvation. The sooner we cast it away the better, for it is powerless and spurious.

We are to serve under our great Leader, to press against every opposing influence, to be laborers together with God. The work appointed us is to sow the gospel seed beside all waters. In this work everyone must act a part. The manifold grace of Christ imparted to us constitutes us stewards of talents which we must increase by putting them out to the exchangers, that when the Master calls for them, He may receive His own with usury.

YOUNG MEN AS MISSIONARIES

Young men who desire to enter the field as ministers, colporteurs, or canvassers should first receive a suitable degree of mental training, as well as a special preparation for their calling. Those who are uneducated, untrained, and unrefined are not prepared to enter a field in which the powerful influences of talent and education combat the truths of God's word. Neither can they successfully meet the strange forms of error, religious and philosophical combined, to expose which requires a knowledge of scientific as well as Scriptural truth.

Those especially who have the ministry in view should feel the importance of the Scriptural method of ministerial training. They should enter heartily into the work, and while they study in the schools they should learn of the Great Teacher the meekness and humility of Christ. A covenant-keeping God has promised that in answer to prayer His Spirit shall be poured out upon these learners in the school of Christ, that they may become ministers of righteousness.

There is hard work to be done in dislodging error and false doctrine from the head, that Bible truth and Bible religion may find a place in the heart. It was as a means ordained of God to educate young men and women for the various departments of missionary labor that colleges were established among us. It is God's will that they send forth not merely a few, but many laborers. But Satan, determined to overthrow this purpose, has often secured the very ones whom God would qualify for places of usefulness in His work. There are many who would work if urged into service, and who would save their souls by thus working. The church should feel her great responsibility in shutting up the light of truth and restraining the grace of God within her own narrow limits when money and influence should be freely employed in bringing competent persons into the missionary field.

Hundreds of young men should have been preparing to act a part in the work of scattering the seeds of truth beside all waters. We want men who will push the triumphs of the cross; men who will persevere under discouragements and privations; who will have the zeal and resolution and faith that are indispensable in the missionary field.

Our churches are called upon to take hold of this work with far greater earnestness than has yet been manifested. Every church should make special provision for the training of its missionaries, thus aiding the fulfillment of the great command: "Go ye into all the world, and preach the gospel to every creature." My brethren, we have erred and sinned in attempting too little. There should be more laborers in the foreign missionary field. There are among us those who, without the toil and delay of learning a foreign language, might qualify themselves to proclaim the truth to other nations. In the primitive church, missionaries were miraculously endowed with a knowledge of the languages in which they were called to preach the unsearchable riches of Christ. And if God was willing thus to help His servants then, can we doubt that His blessing will rest upon our efforts to qualify those who naturally possess a knowledge of foreign tongues, and who with proper encouragement would bear to their own countrymen the message of truth? We might have had more laborers in foreign missionary fields had those who entered these fields availed themselves of every talent within their reach. But some have had a disposition to refuse help if it did not come just according to their ideas and plans. And what is the result? If our missionaries were to be removed by sickness or death from their fields of labor, where are the men whom they have educated to fill their places?

Not one of our missionaries has secured the co-operation of every available talent. Much time has thus been lost. We rejoice in the good work which has been done in foreign lands; but had different plans of labor been adopted, tenfold, yes, twentyfold, more might have been accomplished; an acceptable offering would have been presented to Jesus in many souls rescued from the bondage of error.

Everyone who receives the light of truth should be taught to bear the light to others. Our missionaries in foreign lands should gratefully accept every help, every facility, offered them. They must be willing to run some risk, to venture something. It is not pleasing to God that we defer present opportunities for doing good, in hope of accomplishing a greater work in the future. Each should follow the leadings of Providence, not consulting self-interest, and not trusting wholly to his own judgment. Some may be so constituted as to see failure where God intends success; they may see only giants and walled cities, where others, with clearer vision, see also God and angels ready to give victory to His truth.

It may in some cases be necessary that young men learn foreign languages. This they can do with most success by associating with the people, at the same time devoting a portion of each day to studying the language. This should be done, however, only as a necessary step preparatory to educating such as are found in the missionary field themselves, and who with proper training can become workers. It is essential that those be urged into the service who can speak in their mother tongue to the people of different nations. It is a great undertaking for a man of middle age to learn a foreign language, and with all his efforts it will be next to impossible for him to speak it so readily and correctly as to render him an efficient laborer.

We cannot afford to deprive our home missions of the influence of middle-aged and aged ministers to send them into distant fields, to engage in a work for which they are not qualified, and to which no amount of training will enable them to adapt themselves. The men thus sent out leave vacancies which inexperienced laborers cannot supply.

But the church may inquire whether young men can be trusted with the grave responsibilities involved in establishing and superintending a foreign mission. I answer: God designed that they should be so trained in our colleges and by association in labor with men of experience that they would be prepared for departments of usefulness in this cause. We must manifest confidence in our young men. They should be pioneers in every enterprise involving toil and sacrifice, while the overtaxed servants of Christ should be cherished as counselors, to encourage and bless those who strike the heaviest blows for God. Providence thrust these experienced fathers into trying, responsible positions at an early age, when neither physical nor intellectual powers were fully developed. The magnitude of the trust committed to them aroused their energies, and their active labor in the work aided both mental and physical development.

Young men are wanted. God calls them to missionary fields. Being comparatively free from care and responsibilities, they are more favorably situated to engage in the work than are those who must provide for the training and support of a large family. Furthermore, young men can more readily adapt themselves to new climates and new society, and can better endure inconveniences and hardships. By tact and perseverance they can reach the people where they are.

Strength comes by exercise. All who put to use the ability which God has given them will have increased ability to devote to His service. Those who do nothing in the cause of God will fail to grow in grace and in the knowledge of the truth. A man who would lie down and refuse to exercise his limbs would soon lose all power to use them. Thus the Christian who will not exercise his God-given powers not only fails to grow up into Christ, but he loses the strength which he already has; he becomes a spiritual paralytic. It is those who, with love for God and their fellow men, are striving to help others that become established, strengthened, settled, in the truth. The true Christian works for God, not from impulse, but from principle; not for a day or a month, but during the entire period of life.

How is our light to shine forth to the world unless it be

by our consistent Christian life? How is the world to know that we belong to Christ, if we do nothing for Him? Said our Saviour: "Ye shall know them by their fruits." And again: "He that is not with Me is against Me." There is no neutral ground between those who work to the utmost of their ability for Christ and those who work for the adversary of souls. Everyone who stands as an idler in the vineyard of the Lord is not merely doing nothing himself, but he is a hindrance to those who are trying to work. Satan finds employment for all who are not earnestly striving to secure their own salvation and the salvation of others.

The church of Christ may be fitly compared to an army. The life of every soldier is one of toil, hardship, and danger. On every hand are vigilant foes, led on by the prince of the powers of darkness, who never slumbers and never deserts his post. Whenever a Christian is off his guard, this powerful adversary makes a sudden and violent attack. Unless the members of the church are active and vigilant, they will be overcome by his devices.

What if half the soldiers in an army were idling or asleep when ordered to be on duty; the result would be defeat, captivity, or death. Should any escape from the hands of the enemy, would they be thought worthy of a reward? No; they would speedily receive the sentence of death. And is the church of Christ careless or unfaithful, far more important consequences are involved. A sleeping army of Christian soldiers—what could be more terrible! What advance could be made against the world, who are under the control of the prince of darkness? Those who stand back indifferently in the day of battle, as though they had no interest and felt no responsibility as to the issue of the contest, might better change their course or leave the ranks at once.

The Master calls for gospel workers. Who will respond? All who enter the army are not to be generals, captains, sergeants, or even corporals. All have not the care and responsibility of leaders. There is hard work of other kinds to be done. Some must dig trenches and build fortifications; some are to stand as sentinels, some to carry messages. While there are but few officers, it requires many soldiers to form the rank and file of the army; yet its success depends upon the fidelity of every soldier. One man's cowardice or treachery may bring disaster upon the entire army.

There is earnest work to be done by us individually if we would fight the good fight of faith. Eternal interests are at stake. We must put on the whole armor of righteousness, we must resist the devil, and we have the sure promise that he will be put to flight. The church is to conduct an aggressive warfare, to make conquests for Christ, to rescue souls from the power of the enemy. God and holy angels are engaged in this warfare. Let us please Him who has called us to be soldiers.

All can do something in the work. None will be pronounced guiltless before God unless they have worked earnestly and unselfishly for the salvation of souls. The church should teach the youth, both by precept and example, to be workers for Christ. There are many who complain of their doubts, who lament that they have no assurance of their connection with God. This is often attributable to the fact that they are doing nothing in God's cause. Let them seek earnestly to help and bless others, and their doubts and despondency will disappear.

Many who profess to be followers of Christ speak and act as though their names were a great honor to the cause of God, while they bear no burdens and win no souls to the truth. Such persons live as though God had no claims upon them. If they continue in this course they will find at last that they have no claims upon God.

He who has appointed "to every man his work," according to his ability, will never let the faithful performance of duty go unrewarded. Every act of loyalty and faith will be crowned with special tokens of God's favor and approbation. To every worker is given the promise: "He that goeth forth and weepeth, bearing precious seed, shall doubtless come again with rejoicing, bringing his sheaves with him."

IMPORTANCE OF THE CANVASSING WORK

Very much more efficient work can be done in the canvassing field than has yet been done. The canvasser should not rest satisfied unless he is constantly improving. He should make thorough preparation, but should not be content with a set form of words; he should give the Lord a chance to work with his efforts and impress his mind. The love of Jesus abiding in his heart will enable him to devise means to gain access to individuals and families.

Canvassers need self-culture and polished manners, not the affected and artificial manners of the world, but the agreeable manners that are the natural result of kindness of heart and a desire to copy the example of Christ. They should cultivate thoughtful, care-taking habits,—habits of industry and discretion,—and should seek to honor God by making of themselves all that it is possible for them to become. Jesus made an infinite sacrifice to place them in right relations to God and to their fellow men, and divine aid combined with human effort will enable them to reach a high standard of excellence. The canvasser should be chaste like Joseph, meek like Moses, and temperate like Daniel; then a power will attend him wherever he goes.

If the canvasser pursues a wrong course, if he utters falsehood or practices deception, he loses his own self-respect. He may not be conscious that God sees him and is acquainted with every business transaction, that holy angels are weighing his motives and listening to his words, and that his reward will be according to his works; but if it were possible to conceal his wrongdoing from human and divine inspection, the fact that he himself knows it, is degrading to his mind and character. One act does not determine the character, but it breaks down the barrier, and the next temptation is more readily entertained, until finally a habit of prevarication and dishonesty in business is formed, and the man cannot be trusted.

There are too many in families and in the church who

make little account of glaring inconsistencies. There are young men who appear what they are not. They seem honest and true; but they are like whited sepulchers, fair without, but corrupt to the core. The heart is spotted, stained with sin; and thus the record stands in the heavenly courts. A process has been going on in the mind that has made them callous, past feeling. But if their characters, weighed in the balances of the sanctuary, are pronounced wanting in the great day of God, it will be a calamity that they do not now comprehend. Truth, precious, untarnished truth, is to be a part of the character.

Whatever way is chosen, the path of life is beset with perils. If the workers in any branch of the cause become careless and inattentive to their eternal interests, they are meeting with great loss. The tempter will find access to them. He will spread nets for their feet, and will lead them in uncertain paths. Those only are safe whose hearts are garrisoned with pure principles. Like David they will pray: "Hold up my goings in Thy paths, that my footsteps slip not." A constant battle must be kept up with the selfishness and corruption of the human heart. Often the wicked seem to be prospered in their way; but those who forget God, even for an hour or a moment, are in a dangerous path. They may not realize its perils; but ere they are aware, habit, like an iron band, holds them in subjection to the evil with which they have tampered. God despises their course, and His blessing will not attend them.

I have seen that young men undertake this work without connecting themselves with heaven. They place themselves in the way of temptation to show their bravery. They laugh at the folly of others. They know the right way; they know how to conduct themselves. How easily they can resist temptation! how vain to think of their falling! But they make not God their defense. Satan has an insidious snare prepared for them, and they themselves become the sport of fools.

Our great adversary has agents that are constantly hunting

for an opportunity to destroy souls, as a lion hunts his prey. Shun them, young man; for, while they appear to be your friends, they will slyly introduce evil ways and practices. They flatter you with their lips, and offer to help and guide you; but their steps take hold on hell. If you listen to their counsel, it may be the turning point in your life. One safeguard removed from conscience, the indulgence of one evil habit, a single neglect of the high claims of duty, may be the beginning of a course of deception that will pass you into the ranks of those who are serving Satan, while you are all the time professing to love God and His cause. A moment of thoughtlessness, a single misstep, may turn the whole current of your lives in the wrong direction. And you may never know what caused your ruin until the sentence is pronounced: "Depart from Me, ye that work iniquity."

Some young men know that what I have said fairly describes their course. Their ways are not hidden from the Lord, although they may be hidden from their best friends, even their fathers and mothers. I have little hope that some of these will ever change their course of hypocrisy and deception. Others who have erred are seeking to redeem themselves. May the dear Jesus help them to set their faces as a flint against all falsehoods and the flatteries of those who would weaken their purpose to do right or who would insinuate doubts or infidel sentiments to shake their faith in the truth. Young friends, do not spend an hour in the company of those who would unfit you for the pure and sacred work of God. Do nothing before strangers that you would not do before your father and mother, or that you would be ashamed of before Christ and the holy angels.

Some may think these cautions are not needed by Sabbathkeepers, but those to whom they apply know what I mean. I tell you, young men, to beware; for you can do nothing that is not open to the eyes of angels and of God. You cannot do an evil work and others not be affected by it. While your course of action reveals what kind of material is used in your own character building, it also has a powerful influence over others. Never lose sight of the fact that you belong to God, that He has bought you with a price, and you must render an account to Him for all His entrusted talents. No one should have any part in the work of the canvasser or colporteur whose hand is defiled with sin or whose heart is not right with God, for such persons will surely dishonor the cause of truth. Those who are workers in the missionary field need God to guide them. They should be careful to start right and then keep quietly and firmly on in the path of rectitude. They should be decided, for Satan is determined and persevering in his efforts to overthrow them.

A mistake has been made in soliciting subscriptions for our periodicals for only a few weeks, when by a proper effort much longer subscriptions might have been obtained. One yearly subscription is of more value than many for a short time. When the paper is taken for only a few months, the interest often ends with the short subscription. Few renew their subscriptions for a longer period, and thus there is a large outlay of time that brings small returns, when, with a little more tact and perseverance, yearly subscriptions might have been obtained. You strike too low, brethren; you are too narrow in your plans. You do not put into your work all the tact and perseverance that it deserves. There are more difficulties in this work than in some other branches of business; but the lessons that will be learned, the tact and discipline that will be acquired, will fit you for other fields of usefulness, where you may minister to souls. Those who poorly learn their lesson, and are careless and abrupt in approaching persons, would show the same defects of manner, the same want of tact and skill in dealing with minds, should they enter the ministry.

While short subscriptions are accepted, some will not make the effort necessary to obtain them for a longer time. Canvassers should not go over the ground in a careless, unconcerned manner. They should feel that they are God's workmen, and the love of souls should lead them to make every effort to enlighten men and women in regard to the truth. Providence and grace, means and ends, are closely connected. When His laborers do the very best they can, God does for them that which they cannot do themselves; but no one need expect to succeed independently and by his own exertions. There must be activity united with firm trust in God.

Economy is needed in every department of the Lord's work. The natural turn of youth in this age is to neglect and despise economy, and to confound it with stinginess and narrowness. But economy is consistent with the most broad and liberal views and feelings; there can be no true generosity where it is not practiced. No one should think it beneath him to study economy and the best means of taking care of the fragments. Said Christ, after He had performed a notable miracle: "Gather up the fragments that remain, that nothing be lost."

Quite a sum may be expended in hotel bills that are not at all necessary. The cause of God lay so near the heart of the pioneers in this message that they seldom took a meal at a hotel, even though the cost was but twenty-five cents each. But young men and women generally are not educated to economize, and waste follows waste everywhere. In some families there is a wicked waste of enough to support another family if reasonable economy were used. If, while traveling, our youth will keep an exact account of the money they expend, item by item, their eyes will be opened to see the leaks. While they may not be called upon to deprive themselves of warm meals, as the early workers did in their itinerant life, they may learn to supply their real wants with less expense than they now think necessary. There are persons who practice self-denial in order to give means to the cause of God; then let the workers in the cause also practice self-denial by limiting their expenses as far as possible. It would be well for all our workers to study the history of the Waldensian missionaries and to imitate their example of sacrifice and self-denial.

We have a grand work to do for the Master, to open the word of God to those who are in the darkness of error. Young friends, act as though you had a sacred charge. You should be Bible students, ever ready to give to every man that asketh you a reason of the hope that is in you. By your true Christian dignity give evidence that you know you have a truth that it is for the interest of the people to hear. If this truth is inwrought in the soul, it will manifest itself in the countenance and demeanor, in a calm, noble self-possession and peace which the Christian alone can possess.

Those who have genuine humility, and whose minds have been expanded by the truths unfolded in the gospel, will have an influence that will be felt. They will make an impression upon minds and hearts, and they will be respected by the larger number, even of those who have no sympathy with their faith. With the truths of the Bible and our valuable papers they will have success, for the Lord will open the way before them. But to urge our papers upon the people by means of gifts and premiums does not have a permanent influence for good. If our workers would go forth relying upon the truths of the Bible, with the love of Christ and of souls in their hearts, they would accomplish more in obtaining permanent subscribers than by depending upon premiums or low prices. The prominence given to these inducements to take the paper gives the impression that it cannot possess real merit in itself. The results would be better if the paper were made prominent and the money spent for premiums were reserved to distribute a few copies free. When premiums are offered, some may be induced to take the paper who otherwise would not, but others will refuse to subscribe because they think it a speculation. If the canvasser would present the merits of the paper itself, with his heart uplifted to God for success, and would depend less upon premiums, more would be accomplished.

In this age the trivial is praised and magnified. There is a call for anything that will create a sensation and make sales.

The country is flooded with utterly worthless publications, which were written for the sake of making money, while really valuable books are unsold and unread. Those who handle this sensational literature because by so doing they can make higher wages are missing a precious opportunity to do good. There are battles to be fought to arrest the attention of men and women, and interest them in really valuable books that have the Bible for their foundation; and it will be a still greater task to find conscientious, God-fearing workers who will enter the field to canvass for these books for the purpose of diffusing light.

The worker who has the cause of God at heart will not insist on receiving the highest wages. He will not plead, as some of our youth have done, that unless he can make a stylish and elegant appearance, and board at the best hotels, he will not be patronized. What the canvasser needs is not the faultless apparel, or the address of the dandy or the clown, but that honesty and integrity of character which is reflected in the countenance. Kindness and gentleness leave their impress upon the face, and the practiced eye sees no deception, detects no pomposity of manner.

A large number have entered the field as canvassers with whom premiums are the only means of success. They have no real merit as workers. They have no experience in practical religion; they have the same faults, the same tastes and self-indulgences, that characterized them before they claimed to be Christians. Of them it may be said that God is not in their thoughts; He has no abiding place in their hearts. There is a littleness, an earthliness, a debasement in their character and deportment, that testifies against them that they are walking in the way of their own hearts and in the sight of their own eyes. They will not practice self-denial, but are determined to enjoy life. The heavenly treasure has no attractions for them; all their tastes are downward, not upward. Friends and relatives cannot elevate such persons, for they have not a mind to despise the evil and choose the good.

The less we trust these persons, who are not few but many, the better will the work of present truth stand in the eyes of the world. Our brethren should show discretion in selecting canvassers and colporteurs, unless they have made up their minds to have the truth misapprehended and misrepresented. They should give all real workers good wages; but the sum should not be increased to buy canvassers, for this course hurts them. It makes them selfish and spendthrifts. Seek to impress them with the spirit of true missionary work and with the qualifications necessary to ensure success. The love of Jesus in the soul will lead the canvasser to feel it a privilege to labor to diffuse light. He will study, plan, and pray over the matter.

Young men are wanted who are men in understanding, who appreciate the intellectual faculties that God has given them, and who cultivate them with the utmost care. Exercise enlarges these faculties, and if heart culture is not neglected, the character will be well balanced. The means of improvement are within the reach of all. Then let none disappoint the Master, when He comes seeking for fruit, by presenting nothing but leaves. A resolute purpose, sanctified by the grace of Christ, will do wonders. Jesus and holy angels will give success to the efforts of intelligent, God-fearing men who do all in their power to save souls. Quietly, modestly, with a heart overflowing with love, let them seek to win minds to investigate the truth, engaging in Bible readings when they can. By so doing they will be sowing the seed of truth beside all waters, showing forth the praises of Him who hath called them out of darkness into His marvelous light. Those who are doing this work from right motives are doing an important work of ministering. They will manifest no feeble, undecided character. Their minds are enlarging, their manners are becoming more refined. They should place no bounds to their improvement, but every day be better fitted to do good work.

Many of the workers in the canvassing field are making no sacrifices. As a class they have less of the missionary spirit than the workers in any other denomination. When the way is all prepared for them, when they can command the highest wages, then they are willing to enter the field. Many inducements are presented to canvassers to handle popular books; large wages are offered them; and many refuse to work for less wages to circulate books treating on present truth. Therefore the inducements have been increased to correspond with those offered by other publishers, and as a consequence the expense of getting our publications before the people is large; many of the canvassers obtain their money easily and spend it freely.

Among the people professing present truth there is not a missionary spirit corresponding with our faith. The ring of the true gold in character is wanting. Christian life is more than they take it to be. It does not consist in mere gentleness, patience, meekness, and kindliness. These graces are essential; but there is need of courage, force, energy, and perseverance also. Many who engage in the work of canvassing are weak, nerveless, spiritless, easily discouraged. They lack push. They have not those positive traits of character that give men power to do something,—the spirit and energy that kindle enthusiasm. The canvasser is engaged in an honorable business, and he should not act as though he were ashamed of it. If he would have success attend his efforts he must be courageous and hopeful.

The active virtues must be cultivated as well as the passive. The Christian, while he is ever ready to give the soft answer that turneth away wrath, must possess the courage of a hero to resist evil. With the charity that endureth all things, he must have the force of character which will make his influence a positive power for good. Faith must be wrought into his character. His principles must be firm; he must be noble-spirited, above all suspicion of meanness. The canvasser must not be self-inflated. As he associates with men he must not make himself conspicuous, talking of himself in a boastful way; for by this course he would disgust intelligent, sensible people. He must not be selfish in his habits nor overbearing and domineering in his manners. Very many have settled it in their minds that they cannot find time to read one in ten thousand of the books that are published and put upon the market. And in many cases when the canvasser makes known his business, the door of the heart closes firmly; hence the great need of doing his work with tact and in a humble, prayerful spirit. He should be familiar with the word of God and have words at his command to unfold the precious truth and to show the great value of the pure reading matter he carries.

Well may everyone feel an individual responsibility in this work. Well may he consider how he may best arrest the attention, for his manner of presenting the truth may decide the destiny of a soul. If he makes a favorable impression, his influence may be to that soul a savor of life unto life; and that one person, enlightened in regard to the truth, may enlighten many others. Therefore it is dangerous to do careless work in dealing with minds.

The canvassing work is God's means of reaching many that would not otherwise be impressed with the truth. The work is a good one, the object high and elevating; and there should be a corresponding dignity of deportment. The canvasser will meet men of varied minds. He will meet those who are ignorant and debased and can appreciate nothing that does not bring them money. These will be abusive, but he should not heed them. His good nature should never fail; he should take a cheerful, hopeful view of every perplexity. He will meet those who are bereaved, disheartened, and sore and wounded in spirit. He will have many opportunities of speaking to these kind words and words of courage, hope, and faith. He may be a wellspring to refresh others if he will; but, in order to do this, he must himself draw from the Fountain of living truth.

The canvassing work is more important than many have regarded it, and as much care and wisdom must be used in selecting the workers as in selecting men for the ministry. Young men can be trained to do much better work than has been done and on much less pay than many have received.

Lift up the standard, and let the self-denying and the self-sacrificing, the lovers of God and of humanity, join the army of workers. Let them come, not expecting ease, but to be brave and of good courage under rebuffs and hardships. Let those come who can give a good report of our publications because they themselves appreciate their value.

May the Lord help everyone to improve to the utmost the talents committed to his trust. Those who work in this cause do not study their Bibles as they should. If they did, its practical teachings would have a positive bearing upon their lives. Whatever your work may be, dear brethren and sisters, do it as for the Master, and do your best. Do not overlook present golden opportunities and let your life prove a failure while you sit idly dreaming of ease and success in a work for which God has never fitted you. Do the work that is nearest you. Do it, even though it may be amid perils and hardships in the missionary field; but do not, I beg of you, complain of hardships and self-sacrifices. Look at the Waldenses. See what plans they devised that the light of the gospel might shine into benighted minds. We should not labor with the expectation of receiving our reward in this life, but with our eyes fixed steadfastly upon the prize at the end of the race. Men and women are wanted now who are as true to duty as the needle to the pole, men and women who will work without having their way smoothed and every obstacle removed.

I have described what canvassers ought to be; and may the Lord open their minds to comprehend this subject in its length and breadth, and may they realize their duty to represent the character of Christ by their patience, courage, and steadfast integrity. Let them remember that they can deny Him by a loose, lax, undecided character. Young men, if you take these principles with you into the canvassing field you will be respected; and many will believe the truth you advocate, because you live your faith, because your daily life is as a bright light set upon a candlestick, which giveth light to all that are in the house. Even your enemies, as much as they war against your doctrines, will respect you; and when you have gained this much, your simple words will have a power and will carry conviction to hearts.

THE PUBLISHING WORK

There are and ever will be many perplexities connected with the publishing office at Battle Creek. The institutions established there are God's instrumentalities for accomplishing His work in the earth. For this reason Satan is on the ground, exercising his ingenuity to embarrass and hinder. He comes with his temptations to men and women connected with these institutions, whether in responsible positions or doing the humblest work, and if possible he so ensnares them with his devices that they lose their connection with God, become confused in judgment, and are unable to discern between right and wrong. He knows that the time will surely come when the spirit that has controlled the life will be made manifest, and he is glad to have the lives of these persons testify against them that they are not co-workers with Christ.

Many who have grown to the years and stature of manhood are deficient in the elements that constitute a noble, manly character. God does not regard them as men. They are not reliable. Some of these are connected with our institutions. They have influence; but it is of a pernicious character, for it is seldom on the side of right. While they profess godliness, their example constantly tends to encourage unrighteousness. Skepticism is interwoven with their thoughts and expressed in their words, and their powers are used for the perversion of righteousness, truth, and justice. Their minds are controlled by Satan, and he works through them to demoralize and bring in confusion. The more pleasing and attractive their manners, the more richly they are endowed with brilliant talents, the more effectual agents are they in the hands of the enemy of all righteousness to demoralize all who come under their influence. It will be found a hard and thankless task to keep these from becoming a ruling power and carrying out their own purposes in encouraging disorder and loose, lax principles.

The youth exposed to their influence are never safe unless those under whose care they are placed exercise the greatest vigilance and they themselves have right principles firmly established. But it is a sad fact that in this age many of the young yield readily to the influence of Satan, but resist the Spirit of God; and in many cases wrong habits have become so firmly fixed that the greatest effort on the part of the managers would not result in molding their characters in the right direction.

Those who stand in positions of trust in the publishing house have weighty responsibilities to bear, and they are not fitted for these places unless they are day by day gaining a deeper and more reliable Christian experience. Eternal interests should be made the first consideration, and every influence which would help in the divine life should be welcomed. Men to whom the Lord has given the charge of business matters connected with His cause should be spiritually minded. They should not neglect to attend religious meetings nor consider it a task to speak often one to another of their religious life and experience. God will listen to their testimonies; they will be recorded in His book of remembrance; and He will favor His faithful ones and "will spare them, as a man spareth his own son that serveth him."

Those standing at the head of the publishing work should remember that they are an example to many; and they should be faithful in the public worship of God, just as they would have every workman in every department of the office faithful. If they are seen in the house of worship only occasionally, others will excuse themselves on account of their neglect. These businessmen can at any time talk fluently and intelligently on business matters, showing that they have not exercised their powers in this direction in vain. They have put tact and skill and knowledge into their work, but how important it is that their hearts, their minds, and all their powers be also trained for faithful service in the cause and worship of God; that they be able to point out the way of salvation through Christ in language eloquent in its simplicity. They should be men of earnest prayer and firm reliance upon God; men who, like Abraham, will order their households after them and will manifest a special interest in the spiritual welfare of all connected with the office.

Those who make Christ first in everything can be trusted. They will not be self-confident, nor will they sink their religious interest in their business. Has God entrusted men with sacred responsibilities? then He would have them feel their own weakness and their dependence upon Him. It is unsafe for men to lean to their own understanding; therefore they should daily seek strength and wisdom from above. God should be in all their thoughts; then all the wiles and subtleties of the old serpent cannot betray them into sinful neglect of duty. They will meet the adversary with the simple weapon that Christ used, "It is written," or will repulse him with, "Get thee behind Me, Satan."

In the warning to "watch and pray," Jesus has indicated the only safe course. There is need of watchfulness. Our own hearts are deceitful; we are compassed with the weaknesses and frailties of humanity, and Satan is intent to destroy. We may be off our guard, but our adversary is never idle. Knowing his tireless vigilance, let us not sleep, as do others, but "watch and be sober." The spirit and influence of the world must be met, but they must not be allowed to take possession of the mind and heart.

The active man of business, as he is brought in contact with the world, will have trials, perplexity, and anxious care. He will find that there is a tendency to let worldly thoughts and plans take the lead, and that it will require effort, and discipline of mind and soul, to maintain a devotional spirit.

But divine grace waits his demand, and his great need is the mighty argument that will prevail with God. For these men Jesus has made special provision. He invites them: "Come unto Me, all ye that labor and are heavy-laden, and I will give you rest. Take My yoke upon you, and learn of Me; for I am meek and lowly in heart: and ye shall find rest unto your souls. For My yoke is easy, and My burden is light." Those who have fellowship with Christ have constant rest and peace. Then why do we walk alone, disdaining His companionship? Why do we not take Him into all our counsels? Why do we not come to Him in all our perplexities and prove the strength of His promises?

The Holy Spirit illumines our darkness, informs our ignorance, and understands and helps us in our manifold necessities. But the mind must be constantly going out after God. If coldness and worldliness are allowed to come in, we shall have no heart to pray, no courage to look up to Him who is the source of strength and wisdom. Then pray always, dear brethren and sisters, "lifting up holy hands, without wrath and doubting." Urge your requests to the throne of grace, and rely upon God hour by hour and moment by moment. The service of Christ will regulate all your relations with your fellow men and make your life fruitful in good works.

Let none imagine that selfishness, self-esteem, and self-indulgence are compatible with the Spirit of Christ. Upon every truly converted man or woman there rests a responsibility that we cannot rightly estimate. The maxims and ways of the world are not to be adopted by the sons and daughters of the heavenly King. "Beloved, now are we the sons of God, and it doth not yet appear what we shall be: but we know that, when He shall appear, we shall be like Him; for we shall see Him as He is. And every man that hath this hope in Him purifieth himself, even as He is pure." But the world know us not, because they knew not Christ, our Master.

Business managers are needed in the Review office who will correctly represent Jesus and the plan of salvation. God is displeased when they use all their powers in worldly enterprises, or even in business relating to the publishing work, and do nothing for the strengthening of His church, the upbuilding of His kingdom. To labor for God and for the salvation of souls is the highest and noblest calling that men ever had or ever can have. The losses and gains in this business are of great importance; for the results do not end with this life, but reach over into eternity.

Brethren, whatever business you engage in, whatever department of the work is allotted to you, carry your religion with you. God and heaven should not be left out of the experience and the lifework. The workers in this cause should guard against becoming one-sided men and letting only the worldly element in their characters appear. In the past there have been decided failures on the part of men connected with the office. They have not been spiritually minded; and their influence has not tended to lead toward the heavenly Canaan, but backward toward Egypt.

Brother P has been blessed with abilities which, if consecrated to God, would enable him to do great good. He has a quick mind. He understands the theory of the truth and the claims of God's law; but he has not learned in the school of Christ the meekness and lowliness that would make him a safe man to stand in a position of trust. He has been weighed in the balances of the sanctuary and found wanting. He has had great light in warnings and reproofs; but he has not given heed to them; he has not even seen the necessity of changing his course of action. His example before those laboring in the office has not been consistent with his profession. He has not manifested a steadfast purpose; he has been a boyish man, and his influence has had a tendency to lead away from Christ toward conformity to the world.

The cross of Christ has been presented to Brother P; but he has turned away from it, for it involves shame and reproach rather than the honor and praise of the world. Again and again Jesus has called: Take up the cross and follow Me, so shall ye be My disciple. But other voices have been calling in the direction of worldly pride and ambition; and he has listened to these voices because their spirit is more pleasing to the natural heart. He has turned from Jesus, divorced himself from God, and embraced the world. He was called to represent Christ, and to be a bright light in the world; but he has betrayed his sacred trust. The world interposes between his soul and Jesus, and he has had a worldly experience when he should have been gaining one of an entirely opposite character. He has been decidedly worldly in his tastes and opinions, and consequently has been unable to comprehend spiritual things.

Brother P's success in the ministry, and also in his position of trust in the office, depended upon the character he should maintain. Painstaking, persevering effort was needed that in going out and coming in before his fellow laborers no wrong example should be set. The plan he should have adopted, the course of action he should have pursued, is plainly marked out in the word of God. Had he taken heed to that word, it would have been a light to his path, guiding his inexperienced feet into a safe way. Testimonies of the Spirit of God have been sent to him again and again, showing him where he was diverging from the highway cast up for the ransomed of the Lord to walk in and warning and entreating him to change his course of action. But his own ways have seemed right in his eyes; and he has followed inclination, not heeding the light given him. He was not a safe counselor. He was not a safe man in the office; neither was he a safe shepherd, for he would lead the sheep astray. He has preached excellent discourses; but out of the desk he has not carried out the principles he has preached. This kind of work is an offense to God.

Brother P's union with the world has proved a snare to himself and to others. Oh, how many stumble over such lives as his. They get the impression that when they take the first steps in conversion,—repentance, faith, and baptism,—this is all that is required of them. But this is a fatal error. The arduous struggle for conquest over self, for holiness and heaven, is a lifelong struggle. There is no release in this war; the effort must be continuous and persevering. Christian integrity must be sought with resistless energy and maintained with a resolute fixedness of purpose.

A genuine religious experience unfolds and intensifies. Continual advancement, increasing knowledge and power in the word of God, is the natural result of a vital connection with God. The light of holy love will grow brighter and brighter unto the perfect day. It was Brother P's privilege to have such an experience as this; but he has not had the oil of grace in his vessel with his lamp, and his light has been growing dim. If he does not make a decided change soon, he will be where no warnings or entreaties will ever reach him. His light will go out in darkness, and he will be left in despair.

IMPORTANCE OF ECONOMY

Brother R has good business ability for some branches of the work, which would enable him to serve the office acceptably; but he has not educated and disciplined himself to be a thorough, efficient manager. Under his charge there have been grave neglects; a disorderly, disorganized state of things has existed, which should be promptly corrected. There are many little matters connected with his work that have not received attention, and as a consequence there are leaks. Losses and wastes are allowed that might be avoided.

I have passed through the office and have been shown how the angels of God look upon the work done in the various rooms. In some the condition of things is better than in others; but in all there are wrongs that might be remedied. Loss, loss, is seen in many departments. The reckless way that many work results in loss to the office and is an offense to God. It is sad that it should be thus. Jesus has given us lessons in economy. "Gather up the fragments," He says, "that nothing be lost." It would have been better not to undertake so many large enterprises if by this means so many small matters must be left without attention, for the little things are like small screws that keep the machinery from falling to pieces. The word of God explains duty; it gives the rule of faithful service: "He that is faithful in that which is least is faithful also in much: and he that is unjust in the least is unjust also in much."

I have been shown that, in addition to the help now in the office, competent men should be employed to assist in the management of the different departments of the work. Men should be employed who have experience in business and who are wise managers. It would have been better years ago to have employed men who were thorough managers,—men who would have taught thoroughness, promptness, and economy,—even if double the wages that has been paid to foremen had been necessary. Brother R is deficient here; he has not a happy way of correcting evils. He undertakes to do this, but very many things are entirely neglected that ought to be reformed at once. The office has lacked a care-taking economist, a thorough businessman. There is three times as much lost as would be required to pay for the very best talent and experience in this work.

Very much is lost for want of a competent person, one who is efficient, apt, and practical, to oversee the different departments of the work. One is needed who is a practical printer and is acquainted with every part of the work. There are some who understand printing, but utterly fail in generalship. Others do the best they can, but they are yet inexperienced and do not understand the publishing work. Their ideas are often narrow. They do not know how to meet the demands of the cause; and, as a consequence, they are unable to estimate the advantages and disadvantages of enlarging their work. They are also liable to misjudge, to make wrong calculations, and to estimate incorrectly. There have been losses in consequence of a failure to make proper estimates and to improve opportunities of pushing the publishing work. In such an institution as this, thousands of dollars may be lost through the calculations of incompetent persons. Brother P had ability in some respects to understand and properly estimate the interests of the publishing work, but his influence was an injury to the office.

There should be someone to see that the youth, as they enter the office to learn trades, have prompt and proper attention. A man should be employed for this work who is apt to teach, patient, kind, and discerning. If one man is not sufficient for this work, let others be employed. If it is done faithfully it will save to the office the wages of three men. These youth are forming habits that will affect their entire experience. They are, as it were, in a school; and if they are left to pick up their knowledge as best they can, marked defects will be seen all through their future work. The basis of thoroughness, honesty, and integrity must be laid in youth. The formation of correct habits in youth is of the utmost importance. If instead of being trained to obedience to rules and regulations, and to habits of punctuality, thoroughness, neatness, order, and economy, they are allowed to form loose, lax habits, they will be liable to retain these bad habits all through life. They may have talent to make a success in their business, and they should be taught the importance of making a right use of their powers. They should also be taught to be economical, to gather up the fragments that nothing be lost.

Men in responsible positions should undertake no more than they can do thoroughly, promptly, and well; for if they would have those under their care form right habits they must set a right example. A great responsibility rests upon these leading men as to the mold of character that by their principles and their manner of working they are giving to the youth. They should consider that, by the instruction they are giving, both in regard to their work and in the way of religious education, they are helping these youth to form character. Progress is the watchword. The youth should be taught to aim at perfection in whatever branch of labor they undertake. If there are persons at the head of any of the rooms who are not thorough, who are not economists, who are not diligent in the use of their time and careful of their influence, they mold others in the same way. If these do not change after being admonished, they should be removed and more competent persons secured, even if it is necessary to try again and again. The workers ought to be far more efficient and faithful than they are at the present time.

The first impressions, the first discipline, of these youthful workers should be of the very highest order, for their characters are being molded for time and for eternity. Let those who have charge of them remember that they have a great and solemn responsibility. Let them mold the plastic clay before it becomes hardened and insensible to impressions; let them train the sapling ere it becomes a gnarled and tangled oak; let them direct the course of the rivulet ere it becomes a swollen river. If they are left to choose their own boardinghouse and their own companions, some will choose those that are good, and others will choose improper associations. If the religious element is not mingled with their education, they will become easy subjects of temptation, and their characters will be liable to become warped and one-sided. The youth who show respect for sacred and holy things learn these lessons under the home roof, before the world has placed upon the soul its mark,—the image of sin, deceit, and dishonesty. Love to God is learned at the family altar, of the father and mother in very babyhood.

The want of a religious influence is sadly felt in the office; there should be greater devotion, more spirituality, more practical religion. Missionary work done here by God-fearing men and women would be attended with the very best results. Brother R's course is not well-pleasing to God. A man in his position should be a man of devotion; he should be among the first in religious matters. His only safety is in maintaining a living connection with God and feeling his dependence upon Him. Without this, he will not do justice to his position, neither will he exert a right influence in the office and over those with whom his business brings him in contact.

I have also seen that there should be a close investigation of the manner of dealing in the office, both with brethren and with unbelievers. Benevolence, purity, truth, and peace are the fruits that should be seen there. Motives and actions should be closely examined and compared with the law of God; for this law is the only infallible rule by which to regulate the conduct, the only reliable code of honor between man and man.

UNITY OF THE WORK

The Lord would have union among those who manage His work in different parts of the field. Those who manage His work on the Pacific Coast, and those who are engaged in His work on the east side of the Rocky Mountains, should be of the same mind and judgment,—one in heart, in plans, and in action. He would not have those at either office think it a virtue to differ with their brethren at the other publishing house. There should be a comparing of notes, an interchange of plans and ideas; and if any improvements are suggested in either office, let the managers consider the proposition, and adopt improved plans and methods. In both publishing houses there are very great improvements to be made, and the managers have much to learn. And the lesson which will bear its mark most decidedly and happily in the advancement of the work is to lean less to their own understanding, and to learn more of the meekness and lowliness of Christ. Let not those at either office be so egotistical, so unlike Christ, as to maintain their own plans for the gratification of having their own way, irrespective of consequences.

Those connected with our office of publication at Battle Creek are not what they should be nor what they might be. They think their tastes, habits, and opinions are correct. They are in constant danger of becoming narrow in their ideas and jealous of the Pacific Press, and of standing in an attitude to criticize and have feelings of superiority. This feeling is suffered to grow and to mar and hinder their own interests and also the interests of the work on the Pacific Coast, all because selfish feelings control and prevent clear discernment as to what is for their own good and for the advancement and upbuilding of the cause of God. This sectional feeling is contrary to the spirit of Christ. God is displeased with it; He would have every particle of it overcome. The cause is one, the vineyard is one great field, with God's servants employed in various parts of the work. There should be no aim but to work disinterestedly to warn the careless and to save the lost.

The men connected with the work of God in the office, the sanitarium, and the college can be accounted safe men only so far as they assimilate to the character of Christ. But many have inherited traits of character that in no way represent the divine Model. There are many who have some defect of character received as a birthright, which they have not overcome, but have cherished as though it were fine gold, and brought with them into their religious experience. In many cases these traits are retained through the entire life. For a time no particular harm may be seen to result from them; but the leaven is at work, and when a favorable opportunity arrives, the evil manifests itself.

Some of these men who have marked deformities of character have strong, decided opinions and are unyielding when it would be Christlike to yield to others whose love for the cause of truth is just as deep as their own. Such persons need to cultivate opposite traits of character and to learn to esteem others better than themselves. When they become connected with an important enterprise, where great designs are to be worked out, they should be careful lest their own peculiar ideas and special traits of character have an unfavorable influence on its development. The Lord saw the danger that would result from one man's mind and judgment controlling decisions and working out plans, and in His Inspired Word we are commanded to be subject one to another and to esteem others better than ourselves. When plans are to be laid that will affect the cause of God, they should be brought before a council composed of chosen men of experience; for harmony of effort is essential in all these enterprises.

Men of various temperaments and defective characters can

see the faults of others, but do not seem to have a knowledge of their own errors; and if left to carry out their own plans without consultation with others, they would make sad mistakes. Their ideas must become broader. With ordinary humanity there is a selfishness, an ambition, that mars the work of God. Self-interest must be lost sight of. There should be no aiming to be first, no standing aloof from God's workmen, speaking and writing in a bigoted manner of things that have not been critically and prayerfully investigated and humbly brought before the council.

The future world is close at hand, with its unalterable and solemn issues—so near, so very near, and such a great work to be done, so many important decisions to be made; yet in your councils the preconceived opinions, the selfish ideas and plans, the wrong traits of character received by birth, are lugged in and allowed to have an influence. You should ever feel that it is a sin to move from impulse. You should not abuse your power, using it to carry out your own ends regardless of the consequences to others, because you are in a position that makes this possible; but you should use the power that is given you as a sacred, solemn trust, remembering that you are servants of the most high God and must meet in the judgment every decision that you make. If your acts are unselfish and for the glory of God, they will bear the trying test. Ambition is death to spiritual advancement, genius is erring, slothful indolence is criminal; but a life where every just principle is respected must be a successful one.

Many of your councils do not bear the stamp of heaven. You do not come to them as men who have been communing with God and who have His mind and His merciful compassion, but as men having a firm purpose to carry out your own plans and to settle questions according to your own minds. In every department of the work it is essential to have the mind and spirit of Christ. You are God's workmen; and you must possess courtesy and grace, else you cannot represent Jesus.

All who are employed in our institutions should realize

that they will be a blessing or a curse. If they would be a blessing they must renew their spiritual strength daily; they must be partakers of the divine nature, having escaped the corruption that is in the world through lust.

Amid the cares of active life it is sometimes difficult to discern our own motives, but progress is made daily either for good or evil. Likes or dislikes, an uprising of personal feelings, will come in to control our actions; the things of sense will blind our vision. I have been shown that Jesus loves us; but He is grieved to see such a want of wise discrimination, of adaptability to the work, and of wisdom to reach human hearts and enter into the feelings of others. While we are to guard against the constant danger of forming an alliance with the enemies of Christ and being corrupted by them, we must guard against holding ourselves aloof from those whom our Lord claims as His. "Inasmuch as ye have done it unto one of the least of these My brethren," He says, "ye have done it unto Me." If with an earnest, loving purpose we improve every opportunity to help to their feet those who have stumbled and fallen, we shall not have lived in vain. Our manners will not be harsh, overbearing, and dictatorial, but our lives will be fragrant with the hidden grace of Christ.

Our heavenly Father requires of His servants according to that which He has entrusted to them, and His requirements are reasonable and just. He will not accept less of us than He claims; all His righteous demands must be fully met, or they will testify against us that we are weighed in the balances and found wanting. But Jesus watches our efforts with the deepest interest. He knows that men with all the infirmities of humanity are doing His work, and He notes their failures and discouragements with the tenderest pity. But the failures and defects might be far less than they are. If we will move in harmony with heaven, ministering angels will work with us and crown our efforts with success.

This is the great day of preparation, and the solemn work going on in the sanctuary above should be kept constantly before the minds of those employed in our various institutions. Business cares should not be allowed to absorb the mind to such a degree that the work in heaven, which concerns every individual, will be lightly regarded. The solemn scenes of the judgment, the great day of atonement, should be kept before the people, and urged upon their consciences with earnestness and power. The subject of the sanctuary will give us correct views of the importance of the work for this time. A proper appreciation of it will lead the workers in the publishing houses to manifest greater energy and zeal to make the work a success. None should become careless, blinded to the wants of the cause and the perils that attend every soul; but each should seek to be a channel of light.

In all our institutions there is too much of self, and too little of Christ. All eyes should turn to our Redeemer, all characters should become like His. He is the model to copy, if we would have well-balanced minds and symmetrical characters. His life was as the garden of the Lord, in which grew every tree that is pleasant to the sight and good for food. While embracing in His soul every lovely trait of character, His sensibility, courtesy, and love brought Him into close sympathy with humanity. He was the creator of all things, sustaining worlds by His infinite power. Angels were ready to do Him homage and to obey His will. Yet He could listen to the prattle of the infant and accept its lisping praise. He took little children in His arms and pressed them to His great heart of love. They felt perfectly at home in His presence and reluctant to leave His arms. He did not look upon the disappointments and woes of the race as a mere trifle, but His heart was ever touched by the sufferings of those He came to save.

The world had lost the original pattern of goodness and had sunk into universal apostasy and moral corruption; and the life of Jesus was one of laborious, self-denying effort to bring man back to his first estate by imbuing him with the spirit of divine benevolence and unselfish love. While in the world, He was not of the world. It was a continual pain to Him to be brought in contact with the enmity, depravity, and impurity which Satan had brought in; but He had a work to do to bring man into harmony with the divine plan, and earth in connection with heaven, and He counted no sacrifice too great for the accomplishment of the object. He "was in all points tempted like as we are." Satan stood ready to assail Him at every step, hurling at Him his fiercest temptations; yet He "did no sin, neither was guile found in His mouth." "He . . . suffered being tempted," suffered in proportion to the perfection of His holiness. But the prince of darkness found nothing in Him; not a single thought or feeling responded to temptation.

His doctrine dropped as the rain; His speech distilled as the dew. In the character of Christ was blended such majesty as God had never before displayed to fallen man and such meekness as man had never developed. Never before had there walked among men one so noble, so pure, so benevolent, so conscious of His godlike nature; yet so simple, so full of plans and purposes to do good to humanity. While abhorring sin, He wept with compassion over the sinner. He pleased not Himself. The Majesty of heaven clothed Himself with the humility of a child. This is the character of Christ. Are we walking in His footsteps? O my Saviour, how poorly art Thou represented by Thy professed followers!

BUSINESS AND RELIGION

Those employed in our various institutions—our publishing houses, our schools, and our health institutions—should have a living connection with God. Especially is it very important that those who have the management of these great branches of the work be men who make the kingdom of God and His righteousness the first consideration. They are not fit for their positions of trust unless they take counsel of God and bear fruit to His glory. They should pursue a course of life that will honor their Creator, ennoble themselves, and bless their fellow men. All have natural traits which must be cultivated or repressed, as they shall help or hinder in obtaining a growth in grace, a depth of religious experience.

Those engaged in the work of God cannot serve His cause acceptably unless they make the best use possible of the religious privileges they enjoy. We are as trees planted in the garden of the Lord; and He comes to us seeking the fruit He has a right to expect. His eye is upon each of us; He reads our hearts and understands our lives. This is a solemn search, for it has reference to duty and to destiny; and with what interest is it prosecuted. Let each of those to whom are committed sacred trusts inquire: "How do I meet the inspecting eye of God? Is my heart cleansed from its defilement? or have its temple courts become so desecrated, so occupied with buyers and sellers, that Christ finds no room?" The bustle of business, if continuous, will dry up spirituality and leave the soul Christless. Although they may profess the truth, yet if men pass along day by day with no living connection with God, they will be led to do strange things; decisions will be made not in accordance with the will of God. There is no safety for our leading brethren while they shall go forward according to their own impulses. They will not be yoked up with Christ, and so will not move in harmony with Him. They will be unable to see and realize the wants of the cause, and Satan will move upon them to take positions that will embarrass and hinder.

My brethren, are you cultivating devotion? Is love of religious things prominent? Are you living by faith and overcoming the world? Do you attend the public worship of God? and are your voices heard in the prayer and social meeting? Is the family altar established? Do you gather your children together morning and evening, and present their cases to God? Do you instruct them how to become followers of the Lamb? Your families, if irreligious, testify to your neglect and unfaithfulness. If, while you are connected with the sacred cause of God, your children are careless, irreverent, and have no love for religious meetings or sacred truth, it is a sad thing. Such a family exerts an influence against Christ and against the truth; and "he that is not with Me is against Me," says Christ. The neglect of home religion, the neglect to train your children, is most displeasing to God. If one of your children were in the river, battling with the waves and in imminent danger of drowning, what a stir there would be! What efforts would be made, what prayers offered, what enthusiasm manifested, to save the human life! But here are your children out of Christ, their souls unsaved. Perhaps they are even rude and uncourteous, a reproach to the Adventist name. They are perishing without hope and without God in the world, and you are careless and unconcerned.

What example do you give your children? What order do you have at home? Your children should be educated to be kind, thoughtful of others, gentle, easy to be entreated, and, above everything else, to respect religious things and feel the importance of the claims of God. They should be taught to respect the hour of prayer; they should be required to rise in the morning so as to be present at family worship.

Fathers and mothers who make God first in their households, who teach their children that the fear of the Lord is the beginning of wisdom, glorify God before angels and before men by presenting to the world a well-ordered, well-disciplined family, a family that love and obey God instead of rebelling against Him. Christ is not a stranger in their homes; His name is a household name, revered and glorified. Angels delight in a home where God reigns supreme, and the children are taught to reverence religion, the Bible, and their Creator. Such families can claim the promise: "Them that honor Me I will honor." As from such a home the father goes forth to his daily duties, it is with a spirit softened and subdued by converse with God. He is a Christian, not only in his profession, but in trade, in all his business relations. He does his work with fidelity, knowing that the eye of God is upon him.

In the church his voice is not silent. He has words of gratitude and encouragement to utter; for he is a growing Christian, with a fresh experience every day. He is a helpful, active worker in the church, laboring for the glory of God and the salvation of his fellow men. He would feel condemned and guilty before God were he to neglect to attend public worship, thus failing to improve the privileges that would enable him to do better and more effective service in the cause of truth.

God is not glorified when influential men make themselves mere businessmen, ignoring their eternal interests, that are so much more enduring, so much more noble and elevated, than the temporal. Where should the greatest tact and skill be exercised, if not upon those things that are imperishable, as enduring as eternity? Brethren, develop your talent in the direction of serving the Lord; manifest as much tact and ability in working for the upbuilding of the cause of Christ as you do in worldly enterprises.

There is, I am sorry to say, a great want of earnestness and interest in spiritual things on the part of the heads of many families. There are some who are seldom found in the house of worship. They make one excuse, then another, and still another, for their absence; but the real reason is that their hearts are not religiously inclined. A spirit of devotion is not cultivated in the family. The children are not brought up in the nurture and admonition of the Lord. These men are not what God would have them. They have no living connection with Him; they are purely businessmen. They have not a conciliatory spirit; there is such a lack of meekness, kindness, and courtesy in their deportment that their motives are misconstrued, and the good they really do possess is evil spoken of. If they could realize how offensive their course is in the sight of God, they would make a change.

The work of God should be carried forward by men who have a daily, living experience in the religion of Christ. "Without Me," says Christ, "ye can do nothing." None of us are beyond the power of temptation. All who are connected with our institutions, our conferences, and our missionary enterprises may ever have the assurance that they have a powerful foe, whose constant aim is to separate them from Christ, their strength. The more responsible the position they occupy, the more fierce will be Satan's attacks; for he knows that if he can move them to take an objectionable course, others will follow their example. But those who are continually learning in the school of Christ will be able to pursue the even tenor of their way, and Satan's efforts to throw them off their balance will be signally defeated. Temptation is not sin. Jesus was holy and pure; yet He was tempted in all points as we are, but with a strength and power that man will never be called upon to endure. In His successful resistance He has left us a bright example, that we should follow His steps. If we are self-confident or self-righteous we shall be left to fall under the power of temptation; but if we look to Jesus and trust in Him we call to our aid a power that has conquered the foe on the field of battle, and with every temptation He will make a way of escape. When Satan comes in like a flood, we must meet his temptations with the sword of the Spirit, and Jesus will be our helper and will lift up for us a standard against him. The father of lies quakes and trembles when the truth of God, in burning power, is thrown in his face.

Satan makes every effort to lead people away from God; and he is successful in his purpose when the religious life is drowned in business cares, when he can so absorb their minds in business that they will not take time to read their Bibles, to pray in secret, and to keep the offering of praise and thanksgiving burning on the altar of sacrifice morning and evening. How few realize the wiles of the archdeceiver! how many are ignorant of his devices! When our brethren voluntarily absent themselves from religious meetings, when God is not thought of and reverenced, when He is not chosen as their counselor and their strong tower of defense, how soon secular thoughts and wicked unbelief come in, and vain confidence and philosophy take the place of humble, trusting faith. Often temptations are cherished as the voice of the True Shepherd because men have separated themselves from Jesus. They cannot be safe a moment unless right principles are cherished in the heart and carried into every business transaction.

"If any of you lack wisdom, let him ask of God, that giveth to all men liberally, and upbraideth not; and it shall be given him." Such a promise is of more value than gold or silver. If with a humble heart you seek divine guidance in every trouble and perplexity, His word is pledged that a gracious answer will be given you. And His word can never fail. Heaven and earth may pass away, but His word will never pass away. Trust in the Lord, and you will never be confounded or ashamed. "It is better to trust in the Lord than to put confidence in man. It is better to trust in the Lord than to put confidence in princes."

Whatever position in life we may occupy, whatever our business, we must be humble enough to feel our need of help; we must lean implicitly on the teachings of God's word, acknowledge His providence in all things, and be faithful in pouring out our souls in prayer. Lean to your own understanding, dear brethren, as you make your way through the world, and you will reap sorrow and disappointment. Trust in the Lord with all your heart, and He will guide your steps in wisdom, and your interests will be safe for this world and for the next. You need light and knowledge. You will take counsel either of God or your own heart; you will walk in the sparks of your own kindling, or will gather to yourself divine light from the Sun of Righteousness.

Do not act from motives of policy. The great danger of our businessmen and those in responsible positions is that they will be turned from Christ to secure some help aside from Him. Peter would not have been left to show such weakness and folly had he not sought by the use of policy to avoid reproach and scorn, persecution and abuse. His highest hopes centered in Christ; but when he saw Him in humiliation, unbelief came in and was entertained. He fell under the power of temptation, and, instead of showing his fidelity in a crisis, he wickedly denied his Lord.

For the sake of making money, many divorce themselves from God and ignore their eternal interests. They pursue the same course as the scheming, worldly man, but God is not in this; it is an offense to Him. He would have them prompt to devise and execute plans; but all business matters should be transacted in harmony with the great moral law of God. The principles of love to God and our neighbor must be carried out in all the acts of the daily life, the least as well as the greatest. There must be a spirit to do more than pay tithes on mint, anise, and cummin; the weightier matters of the law, judgment, mercy, and the love of God, must not be neglected; for the personal character of each one connected with the work leaves its impress upon it.

There are men and women who have left all for Christ's sake. Their own temporal interests, their own enjoyment of society and of family and friends, are made of less importance than the interests of the kingdom of God. They have not made houses and lands, and relatives and friends however dear, first in their affections, and God's cause second. And those who do this, who devote their lives to the advancement of the truth, to bringing many sons and daughters to God, have the promise that they shall have a hundredfold in this life and in the world to come life everlasting. Those who work from a noble standpoint and with unselfish motives will be consecrated to God, body, soul, and spirit. They will not exalt self; they will not feel competent to take responsibilities; but they will not refuse to bear burdens, for they will have a desire to do all that they are capable of doing. These will not study their own convenience; the question with them will be: What is duty?

The more responsible the position, the more essential that the influence be right. Every man whom God has chosen to do a special work becomes a target for Satan. Temptations press thick and fast upon him; for our vigilant foe knows that his course of action has a molding influence upon others.

We are amid the perils of the last days, and Satan has come down in great wrath, knowing that he has but a short time. He works with all deceivableness of unrighteousness; but heaven is open to everyone who makes God his trust. The only safety for any of us is in clinging to Jesus and letting nothing separate the soul from the mighty Helper.

Those who have merely a form of godliness, and yet are connected with the cause in business relations, are to be feared. They will surely betray their trust. They will be overcome by the devices of the tempter and will imperil the cause of God. There will be temptations to allow self to control; an overbearing, critical spirit will arise, and in many cases compassion and consideration for those who need to be dealt with in thoughtful tenderness will be wanting.

"Whatsoever a man soweth, that shall he also reap." What seed are we scattering? What will be our harvest for time and for eternity? To every man the Master has assigned his work in accordance with his ability. Are we sowing the seed of truth and righteousness, or that of unbelief, disaffection, evil surmising, and love of the world? The one who scatters evil seed may discern the nature of his work, and repent and be forgiven. But the pardon of the Master does not change the character of the seed sown, and make of briers and thistles precious wheat. He himself may be saved so as by fire; but when the time of harvest comes, there will be only poisonous weeds where there should be fields of waving grain. That which was sown in wicked heedlessness will do its work of death. This thought pains my heart and fills me with sadness. If all who profess to believe the truth would sow the precious seeds of kindness, love, faith, and courage, they would make melody to God in their hearts as they travel the upward way, rejoicing in the bright beams of the Sun of Righteousness, and in the great gathering day they would receive an eternal reward.

WORLDLY-MINDEDNESS A SNARE

Dear Brother and Sister P: My soul is exceedingly sorrowful as I review your cases. Last night my mind was heavily burdened. In dreams I was conversing with you, Brother P. Your separation from God was so evident, and you were so blind in regard to your true condition, that it seemed like saying to a blind man, "See," to try to make you discern your true standing.

I have not been able to sleep since three o'clock, and have been pleading with God for a larger measure of His Spirit. I inquire over and over again: Who is sufficient for these things? I dare not hold my peace when light has been given me of God. I must speak; and yet it is with trembling, fearing that the message will be rejected, and the souls to whom it is addressed will be enshrouded in darkness more dense than before the light came to them. I must come close to Jesus. I have laid my hand in His, with the earnest prayer: "Lead me, guide me; I have not wisdom to go alone." Jesus seems very near; and I am deeply impressed that He is about to do a special work for His people, particularly for those that labor in word and doctrine. He is willing to help you both if you will receive help in His own appointed way, but I cannot speak one word of encouragement to you while you remain in your present position. The words of Christ to the Pharisees, "Ye will not come to Me, that ye might have life," are applicable to you.

I wish we could do something to help you; but while you remain in the worldly channel in which you have placed yourselves, what can be done for you? You love the world, and the world loves you, because, so far as practical godliness is concerned, there is no separation between yourselves and worldlings. In their eyes you are agreeable, smart, and good; they find in you both that which pleases them. They have praised you and spoken to you smooth things, and thus have had an influence to soothe and comfort you; and you, in your turn, have soothed and comforted them in their careless indifference to the claims of God. You have encouraged them in their pride and love of pleasure; for your actions have said to the sinner: "It shall be well with thee." By mingling with worldlings, your judgment has become perverted; and sins which God abhors are tame and harmless in your sight.

I greatly fear that by your self-righteousness you are building around your souls barriers that nothing can break down. You have been no nearer to God, no more working His works, no more imbued with His Spirit, than the professors in the nominal churches. You have had no real sense of the sacredness of the Sabbath, and God has not accepted your observance of His holy day. You have had no true consecration, no sincere devotion. God has not been honored by either of you; you have not known Him experimentally. You have walked apart from Him so long that He is nearly a stranger to you. Spiritual things are spiritually discerned; but you have so long cultivated worldly tastes and habits that it will not be easy for you to bend your mind in an opposite direction.

You will feel: "This is an hard saying; who can hear it?" But the world cannot understand the people of God. There is no harmony between the children of light and the children of darkness. Paul asks: "And what concord hath Christ with Belial? or what part hath he that believeth with an infidel? And what agreement hath the temple of God with idols? for ye are the temple of the living God; as God hath said, I will dwell in them, and walk in them, and I will be their God, and they shall be My people. Wherefore come out from among them, and be ye separate, saith the Lord, and touch not the unclean thing; and I will receive you, and will be a Father unto you, and ye shall be My sons and daughters, saith the Lord Almighty." John testifies: "Beloved, now are we the sons of God, and it doth not yet appear what we shall be: But we know that, when He shall appear, we shall be like Him; for we shall see Him as He is. And every man that hath this hope in Him purifieth himself, even as He is pure." "Know ye not that the friendship of the world is enmity with God?"

asks James. "Whosoever therefore will be a friend of the world is the enemy of God."

Jesus said to His disciples: "If ye love Me, keep My Commandments. And I will pray the Father, and He shall give you another Comforter, that He may abide with you forever [not a profession of the truth, not a form of godliness, but]; even the Spirit of truth; whom the world cannot receive, because it seeth Him not, neither knoweth Him: but ye know Him; for He dwelleth with you, and shall be in you." "He that hath My commandments, and keepeth them, he it is that loveth Me: and he that loveth Me shall be loved of My Father, and I will love him, and will manifest Myself to him. Judas saith unto Him, not Iscariot, Lord how is it that Thou wilt manifest Thyself unto us, and not unto the world? Jesus answered and said unto him, If a man love Me, he will keep My words: and My Father will love him, and We will come unto him, and make Our abode with him. He that loveth Me not keepeth not My sayings."

The words of Christ find no response in your hearts, for you have blinded your eyes and hardened your hearts. In the books of heaven you are both accounted as of the world. Your hearts are sometimes troubled, but not enough to lead you to repent and change your course of action. The world holds your affections, and its customs are more agreeable to you than obedience to the heavenly Teacher.

Your example before your children is not at all in accordance with the truth you profess to love. The truth does not sanctify you or them. You love selfish enjoyment; and the lessons taught your children, both by precept and example, have not been of a character to foster in them humility, meekness, and a Christlike disposition. You are molding them after the world's standard. When Jesus shall open before you the book of records, where day by day your words and actions have been faithfully registered, you will see that with both of you life has been a terrible failure.

What your recent affliction may have done for you, I am unable to say; but if it has had power to open your eyes and convict your souls, you will certainly take a course to make this evident. Without a thorough conversion, you can never receive the crown of everlasting life; and your children will never have part with the blood-washed throng unless they first unlearn the lessons you have taught them, which have become a part of their life and character. Your example has led them to think that religion is like a garment that may be worn or laid off as occasion requires or convenience dictates; and unless there is an entire change in the influences brought to bear upon them, these lax ideas of the claims of God will cling to them. They do not know what constitutes the Christian life; they have not learned what it is to live the truth and bear the cross.

"If the world hate you," said Christ, "ye know that it hated Me before it hated you." You have entertained the opinion that the reason why the world is so much opposed to us as a people is that we are too unsocial, too plain in our dress, and too strict in regard to amusements, withdrawing ourselves from them too much in practice as well as in precept. You have thought that if we would be less exclusive and would mingle more with the world, their opinions and impressions of us would be greatly modified. But no greater mistake could affect the human mind. Said Christ: "If ye were of the world, the world would love his own: but because ye are not of the world, but I have chosen you out of the world, therefore the world hateth you. Remember the word that I said unto you, The servant is not greater than his lord. If they have persecuted Me, they will also persecute you; if they have kept My saying, they will keep yours also. But all these things will they do unto you for My name's sake, because they know not Him that sent Me."

These are the words of One of whom even His enemies were forced to admit: "Never man spake like this Man." The words of men express their own human thoughts; but those of Christ are spirit and life. "If ye continue in My word," He says, "then are ye My disciples indeed." "He that is of God heareth God's words," but these divine utterances find no place in the heart of one who is of the world and loves its pleasures.

God has given us specific directions so that no one need err. "Man shall not live by bread alone," He says, "but by every word that proceedeth out of the mouth of God." The truth given by inspiration "is profitable for doctrine, for reproof, for correction, for instruction in righteousness." Not by one word, not by many words, but by *every word* that God has spoken, shall man live. You cannot disregard one word, a single injunction that He has given, however trifling it may seem to you, and be safe. "Whosoever therefore shall break one of these least commandments, and shall teach men so, he shall be called the least in the kingdom of heaven: but whosoever shall do and teach them, the same shall be called great in the kingdom of heaven." Whosoever will willfully break one command cannot in spirit and in truth keep any of them. He may claim that, with the exception of what he may regard as slight deviations, he keeps them all; yet if he willingly offends in one point he is guilty of all.

Brother and Sister P, while you have been making a profession of Christianity you have been keeping back part of the price. You have robbed God of thought and devotion; you have robbed Him of your talents and influence. Your inclinations have been a snare to you. You have not followed the light that God has graciously given you in testimonies; and you have done things that without repentance and reformation on your part will exclude you from heaven. Had you heeded the reproofs sent to you by the Holy Spirit you would now be strong in God and far advanced in Christian experience, and you would have had an entirely different record in the books of heaven.

"He that rejecteth Me," says Christ, "and receiveth not My words, hath One that judgeth him: the word that I have spoken, the same shall judge him in the last day." In that day what shame and confusion of face will cover those who have had such light and privileges, who have had salvation brought within their reach by the infinite sacrifice of the Son of God, and yet have not availed themselves of these precious gifts. Through His word God is constantly pointing out to us the right path, even the high and glorious path of the just. The travelers in this path do not walk in darkness, for it is illuminated by the Sun of Righteousness; but you have rejected it because it was too far separated from the world. Self-love and selfish ambition cannot pass the strait gate and walk the narrow, upward way.

It will be found in the day of final settlement that God was acquainted with everyone by name. There is an unseen witness to every action of the life. "I know thy works," says He that "walketh in the midst of the seven golden candlesticks." It is known what opportunities have been slighted, how untiring have been the efforts of the Good Shepherd to search out those who were wandering in crooked ways, and to bring them back to the path of safety and peace. Again and again God has called after the pleasure lovers; again and again He has flashed the light of His word across their path, that they might see their peril, and escape. But on and on they go, jesting and joking as they travel the broad road, until at length their probation is ended. God's ways are just and equal; and when sentence is pronounced against those who are found wanting, every mouth will be stopped.

How different it would now be with you both had you regarded in their true light the praise and honor that come from men. You both thirst more for the praise of the world than for the waters of life. The idea of being thought of importance among men of the world has intoxicated you; their words of esteem have deceived you. When you place a right estimate on eternal things, the friendship and esteem of the rich and the learned will have no influence over you. Pride, in whatever form it may manifest itself, will no longer live in your heart. But you have so long drunk of the turbid stream of worldliness that you see no better way to live.

Again and again God has stretched out His hand to save you by showing you your duties and obligations. These duties change in character with the increase of light. When the light shines, making manifest and reproving the errors that were undiscovered, there must be a corresponding change in the life and character. The mistakes that are the natural result of blindness of mind are, when pointed out, no longer sins of ignorance or errors of judgment, but unless there are decided reforms in accordance with the light given, they then become presumptuous sins. The moral darkness that surrounds you will become more dense; your heart will become harder and harder, and you will be more offensive in the sight of God. You do not realize the great peril you are in, the danger there is that in your case the light will become entirely obscured, veiled in complete darkness. When the light is received and acted upon, you will be crucified to sin, being dead indeed unto the world, but alive to God. Your idols will be abandoned, and your example will be on the side of self-denial rather than that of self-indulgence.

Brother and Sister P, had you heeded the *Testimonies* of the Spirit of God, you would now be walking in the light, in harmony with the people of God; but your unbelief has shut you away from great good. Sister P has not risen up against the *Testimonies,* neither has she shown confidence in them as from the Lord by obeying them. She loves to have her husband praised and honored by the world; it gratifies her pride, which is by no means small. You may each appropriately inquire: "Why am I so slow to come out from the world and take Christ for my portion? Why should I love and honor those whom I know do not love God nor respect His claims? Why should I wish to retain the friendship of my Lord's enemies? Why should I follow their customs or be influenced by their opinions?" You cannot, my dear friends, serve both God and mammon. You must make an unreserved surrender, or in the near future the light that shines upon your pathway will go out in the darkness of despair. You are on the enemy's ground. You have voluntarily placed yourselves there, and the Lord will not protect you against his assaults.

In your present state you are doing far more harm than good; for you have a form of godliness and profess to believe the truth, while your words and actions say: "Wide is the gate, and broad is the way" that leads to life, "and many there be which go in thereat." If your life is a confession of Christ, then we may truly say that the world has gone after Him. Your profession may be right; but have you humility and love, meekness and devotion? "Whosoever shall confess Me before men," by a holy life and godly conversation, "him shall the Son of man also confess before the angels of God." No one can confess Christ unless he has the mind and spirit of Christ; he cannot communicate that which he does not possess. The daily life must be an expression of the sanctifying power of the truth, and evidence that Christ is abiding in the soul by faith. Whatever is opposed to the fruits of the Spirit, or to the work of God in separating His people from the world, is a denial of Christ; and His words are: "He that denieth Me before men shall be denied before the angels of God."

We may deny Christ by our worldly conversation and by our pride of apparel. You have a circle of friends who are a snare to you and to your children. You love their companionship. Through association with them, you are led to dress yourselves and your children after the fashions followed by those who have no fear of God before their eyes. You thus show that you have friendship with the world. "In the multitude of words there wanteth not sin." Does your intercourse with these friends incline you to visit the closet and ask divine love and grace, or does it estrange your mind from God? And your dear children—what is your neglect of their eternal interests doing for them? Your example has encouraged them to hurry on the life journey with heedless presumption or with blind self-confidence, having no fixed religious principles to guide them. They have no conscientious regard for the Sabbath, or for the claims of God in any respect; they do not love Christian duties, and are straying further and further from the Source of light, peace, and joy.

Without faith it is impossible to please God; "for whatsoever is not of faith is sin." The faith that is required is not a mere assent to doctrines; it is the faith that works by love and purifies the soul. Humility, meekness, and obedience are not faith; but they are the effects, or fruit, of faith. These graces you have yet to attain by learning in the school of Christ. You do not know the sentiments and principles of heaven; its language is almost a strange language to you both. The Spirit of God still pleads in your behalf; but I have serious, painful doubts whether you will heed that voice that has been appealing to you for years. I hope you will, and that you will turn and live.

Do you feel that it is too great a sacrifice to give your poor unworthy selves to Jesus? Will you choose the hopeless bondage of sin and death rather than to have your life severed from the world and united to Christ by bonds of love? Jesus still lives to intercede for us. This should daily call out the gratitude of our hearts. He that realizes his guilt and helplessness may come just as he is and receive the blessing of God. The promise belongs to him if he will grasp it by faith. But he that in his own eyes is rich, and honorable, and righteous, who sees as the world sees, and calls evil good and good evil, cannot ask and receive, because he feels no need. He feels that he is full; therefore he must go away empty.

Should you become alarmed for your own souls, should you seek God diligently, He will be found of you; but He will accept no halfhearted repentance. If you will forsake your sins, He is ever ready to forgive. Will you just now surrender to Him? Will you look to Calvary and inquire: "Did Jesus make this sacrifice for me? Did He endure humiliation, shame, and reproach, and suffer the cruel death of the cross because He desired to save me from the sufferings of guilt and the horror of despair, and make me unspeakably happy in His kingdom?" Look upon Him whom your sins have pierced, and resolve: "The Lord shall have the service of my life. I will no longer unite with His enemies; I will no longer lend my influence to the rebels against His government. All I have and am is too little to devote to Him who so loved me that He gave His life for me—His whole divine self for one so sinful and erring." Separate from the world, be wholly on the Lord's side, press the battle to the gates, and you will win glorious victories.

Blessed is he who heeds the words of eternal life. Guided by "the Spirit of truth," he will be led into all truth. He will not be loved, honored, and praised by the world, but he will be precious in the sight of heaven. "Behold, what manner of love the Father hath bestowed upon us, that we should be called the sons of God: therefore the world knoweth us not because it knew Him not."

RESPONSIBILITIES OF THE PHYSICIAN

"The fear of the Lord is the beginning of wisdom." Professional men, whatever their calling, need divine wisdom. But the physician is in special need of this wisdom in dealing with all classes of minds and diseases. He occupies a position even more responsible than that of the minister of the gospel. He is called to be a colaborer with Christ, and he needs stanch religious principles and a firm connection with the God of wisdom. If he takes counsel of God he will have the Great Healer to work with his efforts, and he will move with the greatest caution lest by his mismanagement he injure one of God's creatures. He will be firm as a rock to principle, yet kind and courteous to all. He will feel the responsibility of his position, and his practice will show that he is actuated by pure, unselfish motives and a desire to adorn the doctrine of Christ in all things. Such a physician will possess a heaven-born dignity and will be a powerful agent for good in the world. Although he may not be appreciated by those who have no connection with God, yet he will be honored of heaven. In God's sight he will be more precious than gold, even the gold of Ophir.

The physician should be a strictly temperate man. The physical ailments of humanity are numberless, and he has to deal with disease in all its varied forms. He knows that much of the suffering he seeks to relieve is the result of intemperance and other forms of selfish indulgence. He is called to attend young men, and men in the prime of life and in mature age, who have brought disease upon themselves by the use of the narcotic tobacco. If he is an intelligent physician he will be able to trace disease to its cause, but unless he is free from the use of tobacco himself he will hesitate to put his finger upon the plague spot and faithfully unfold to his patients the cause of their sickness. He will fail to urge upon the young the necessity of overcoming the habit before it becomes fixed. If he uses the weed himself, how can he present to the inexperienced youth its injurious effects, not only upon themselves, but upon those around them?

In this age of the world the use of tobacco is almost universal. Women and children suffer from having to breathe the atmosphere that has been polluted by the pipe, the cigar, or the foul breath of the tobacco user. Those who live in this atmosphere will always be ailing, and the smoking physician is always prescribing some drug to cure ailments which could be best remedied by throwing away tobacco.

Physicians cannot perform their duties with fidelity to God or to their fellow men while they are worshiping an idol in the form of tobacco. How offensive to the sick is the breath of the tobacco user! How they shrink from him! How inconsistent for men who have graduated from medical colleges and claim to be capable of ministering to suffering humanity, to constantly carry a poisonous narcotic with them into the sickrooms of their patients. And yet many chew and smoke until the blood is corrupted and the nervous system undermined. It is especially offensive in the sight of God for physicians who are capable of doing great good, and who profess to believe the truth of God for this time, to indulge in this disgusting habit. The words of the apostle Paul are applicable to them: "Having therefore these promises, dearly beloved, let us cleanse ourselves from all filthiness of the flesh and spirit, perfecting holiness in the fear of God." "I beseech you therefore, brethren, by the mercies of God, that ye present your bodies a living sacrifice, holy, acceptable unto God, which is your reasonable service."

Tobacco users cannot be acceptable workers in the temperance cause, for there is no consistency in their profession to be temperance men. How can they talk to the man who is destroying reason and life by liquor drinking, when their pockets are filled with tobacco, and they long to be free to chew and smoke and spit all they please? How can they with any degree of consistency plead for moral reforms before boards of health and from temperance platforms while they themselves are under the stimulus of tobacco? If they would have power to influence the people to overcome their love for stimulants, their words must come forth with pure breath and from clean lips.

Of all men in the world, the physician and the minister should have strictly temperate habits. The welfare of society demands total abstinence of them, for their influence is constantly telling for or against moral reform and the improvement of society. It is willful sin in them to be ignorant of the laws of health or indifferent to them, for they are looked up to as wise above other men. This is especially true of the physician, who is entrusted with human life. He is expected to indulge in no habit that will weaken the life forces.

How can a tobacco-using minister or doctor bring up his children in the nurture and admonition of the Lord? How can he discountenance in his child that which he allows in himself? If he does the work enjoined upon him by the Ruler of the universe he will protest against iniquity in every form and in every degree; he will exert his authority and influence on the side of self-denial, and strict, undeviating obedience to the just requirements of God. It will be his object to place his children in the most favorable conditions to secure happiness in this life and a home in the city of God. How can he do this while yielding to the indulgence of appetite? How can he place the feet of others on the ladder of progress while he himself is treading the downward way?

Our Saviour set an example of self-denial. In His prayer for His disciples He said: "For their sakes I sanctify Myself, that they also might be sanctified through the truth." If a man who assumes so grave a responsibility as that of a physician sins against himself in not conforming to nature's laws, he will reap the consequences of his own doings and abide her righteous decision, from which there can be no appeal. The cause produces the effect; and in many cases the physician, who should have a clear, sharp mind and steady nerves, that he may be able to discern quickly and execute with precision, has disordered nerves and a brain clouded by narcotics. His capabilities for doing good are lessened. He will lead others in the path his own feet are traveling. Hundreds will follow the example of one intemperate physician, feeling that they are safe in doing what the doctor does. And in the day of God he will meet the record of his course and be called to give an account for all the good he might have done, but did not do because by his own voluntary act he weakened his physical and mental powers by selfish indulgence.

The question is not, What is the world doing? but, What are professional men doing in regard to the widespread and prevailing curse of tobacco using? Will men to whom God has given intelligence, and who are in positions of sacred trust, be true to follow intelligent reason? Will these responsible men, having under their care persons whom their influence will lead in a right or a wrong direction, be pattern men? Will they, by precept and example, teach obedience to the laws which govern the physical system? If they do not put to a practical use the knowledge they have of the laws that govern their own being, if they prefer present gratification to soundness of mind and body, they are not fit to be entrusted with the lives of others. They are in duty bound to stand in the dignity of their God-given manhood, free from the bondage of any appetite or passion. The man who chews and smokes is doing injury not only to himself but to all who come within the sphere of his influence. If a physician must be called, the tobacco devotee should be passed by. He will not be a safe counselor. If the disease has its origin in the use of tobacco, he will be tempted to prevaricate and assign some other than the true cause; for how can he condemn himself in his own daily practice?

There are many ways of practicing the healing art, but there is only one way that Heaven approves. God's remedies are the simple agencies of nature that will not tax or debilitate the system through their powerful properties. Pure air and water, cleanliness, a proper diet, purity of life, and a firm trust in God are remedies for the want of which thousands are dying; yet these remedies are going out of date because their skillful use requires work that the people do not appreciate. Fresh air, exercise, pure water, and clean, sweet premises are within the reach of all with but little expense, but drugs are expensive, both in the outlay of means and in the effect produced upon the system.

The work of the Christian physician does not end with healing the maladies of the body; his efforts should extend to the diseases of the mind, to the saving of the soul. It may not be his duty, unless asked, to present any theoretical points of truth; but he may point his patients to Christ. The lessons of the divine Teacher are ever appropriate. He should call the attention of the repining to the ever-fresh tokens of the love and care of God, to His wisdom and goodness as manifested in His created works. The mind can then be led through nature up to nature's God and centered on the heaven which He has prepared for those that love Him.

The physician should know how to pray. In many cases he must increase suffering in order to save life; and whether the patient is a Christian or not, he feels greater security if he knows that his physician fears God. Prayer will give the sick an abiding confidence; and many times if their cases are borne to the Great Physician in humble trust, it will do more for them than all the drugs that can be administered.

Satan is the originator of disease; and the physician is warring against his work and power. Sickness of the mind prevails everywhere. Nine tenths of the diseases from which men suffer have their foundation here. Perhaps some living home trouble is, like a canker, eating to the very soul and weakening the life forces. Remorse for sin sometimes undermines the constitution and unbalances the mind. There are erroneous doctrines also, as that of an eternally burning hell and the endless torment of the wicked, that, by giving exaggerated and distorted views of the character of God, have produced the same result upon sensitive minds. Infidels have made the most of these unfortunate cases, attributing insanity to religion; but this is a gross libel and one which they will not be pleased to meet by and by. The religion of Christ, so far from being the cause of insanity, is one of its most effectual remedies; for it is a potent soother of the nerves.

The physician needs more than human wisdom and power that he may know how to minister to the many perplexing cases of disease of the mind and heart with which he is called to deal. If he is ignorant of the power of divine grace he cannot help the afflicted one, but will aggravate the difficulty; but if he has a firm hold upon God he will be able to help the diseased, distracted mind. He will be able to point his patients to Christ and teach them to carry all their cares and perplexities to the great Burden Bearer.

There is a divinely appointed connection between sin and disease. No physician can practice for a month without seeing this illustrated. He may ignore the fact; his mind may be so occupied with other matters that his attention will not be called to it; but if he will be observing and honest he cannot help acknowledging that sin and disease bear to each other the relationship of cause and effect. The physician should be quick to see this and to act accordingly. When he has gained the confidence of the afflicted by relieving their sufferings and bringing them back from the verge of the grave, he may teach them that disease is the result of sin and that it is the fallen foe who seeks to allure them to health-and-soul-destroying practices. He may impress their minds with the necessity of denying self and obeying the laws of life and health. In the minds of the young especially he may instill right principles. God loves His creatures with a love that is both tender and strong. He has established the laws of nature, but His laws are not arbitrary exactions. Every "Thou shalt not," whether in physical or moral law, contains or implies a promise. If it is obeyed, blessings will attend our steps; if it is disobeyed, the result is danger and unhappiness. The laws of God are designed to bring His people closer to Himself. He will save them from the evil and lead them to the good if they will be led, but force them He never will. We cannot discern God's plans, but we must trust Him and show our faith by our works.

Physicians who love and fear God are few compared with those who are infidels or openly irreligious, and these should be patronized in preference to the latter class. We may well distrust the ungodly physician. A door of temptation is open to him, a wily devil will suggest base thoughts and actions, and it is only the power of divine grace that can quell tumultuous passion and fortify against sin. To those who are morally corrupt, opportunities to corrupt pure minds are not wanting. But how will the licentious physician appear in the day of God? While professing to care for the sick, he has betrayed sacred trusts. He has degraded both the soul and the body of God's creatures, and has set their feet in the path that leads to perdition. How terrible to trust our loved ones in the hands of an impure man, who may poison the morals and ruin the soul! How out of place is the godless physician at the bedside of the dying!

The physician is almost daily brought face to face with death. He is, as it were, treading upon the verge of the grave. In many instances familiarity with scenes of suffering and death results in carelessness and indifference to human woe, and recklessness in the treatment of the sick. Such physicians seem to have no tender sympathy. They are harsh and abrupt, and the sick dread their approach. Such men, however great their knowledge and skill, can do the suffering little good; but if the love and sympathy that Jesus manifested for the sick is combined with the physician's knowledge, his very presence will be a blessing. He will not look upon his patient as a mere piece of human mechanism, but as a soul to be saved or lost.

The duties of the physician are arduous. Few realize the mental and physical strain to which he is subjected. Every energy and capability must be enlisted with the most intense anxiety in the battle with disease and death. Often he knows that one unskillful movement of the hand, even but a hairbreadth in the wrong direction, may send a soul unprepared into eternity. How much the faithful physician needs the sympathy and prayers of the people of God. His claims in this direction are not inferior to those of the most devoted minister or missionary worker. Deprived, as he often is, of needed rest and sleep, and even of religious privileges on the Sabbath, he needs a double portion of grace, a fresh supply daily, or he will lose his hold on God and will be in danger of sinking deeper in spiritual darkness than men of other callings. And yet often he is made to bear unmerited reproaches and is left to stand alone, the subject of Satan's fiercest temptations, feeling himself misunderstood, betrayed by his friends.

Many, knowing how trying are the duties of the physician and how few opportunities physicians have for release from care, even upon the Sabbath, will not choose this for their lifework. But the great enemy is constantly seeking to destroy the workmanship of God's hands, and men of culture and intelligence are called upon to combat his cruel power. More of the right kind of men are needed to devote themselves to this profession. Painstaking effort should be made to induce suitable men to qualify themselves for this work. They should be men whose characters are based upon the broad principles of the word of God—men who possess a natural energy, force, and perseverance that will enable them to reach a high standard of excellence. It is not everyone who can make a successful physician. Many have entered upon the duties of this profession every way unprepared. They have not the requisite knowledge; neither have they the skill and tact, the carefulness and intelligence, necessary to ensure success.

A physician can do much better work if he has physical strength. If he is feeble he cannot endure the wearing labor incident to his calling. A man who has a weak constitution, who is a dyspeptic, or who has not perfect self-control, cannot become qualified to deal with all classes of disease. Great care should be taken not to encourage persons who might be useful in some less responsible position, to study medicine at a great outlay of time and means, when there is no reasonable hope that they will succeed.

Some have been singled out as men who might be useful as physicians, and they have been encouraged to take a medical course. But some who commenced their studies in the medical colleges as Christians did not keep the divine law prominent; they sacrificed principle and lost their hold on God. They felt that singlehanded they could not keep the fourth commandment and meet the jeers and ridicule of the ambitious, the world-loving, the superficial, the skeptic, and the infidel. This kind of persecution they were not prepared to meet. They were ambitious to climb higher in the world, and they stumbled on the dark mountains of unbelief and became untrustworthy. Temptations of every kind opened before them, and they had no strength to resist. Some of these have become dishonest, scheming policy men and are guilty of grave sins.

In this age there is danger for everyone who shall enter upon the study of medicine. Often his instructors are worldly-wise men and his fellow students infidels, who have no thought of God, and he is in danger of being influenced by these irreligious associations. Nevertheless, some have gone through the medical course and have remained true to principle. They would not continue their studies on the Sabbath, and they have proved that men may become qualified for the duties of a physician and not disappoint the expectations of those who furnish them means to obtain an education. Like Daniel they have honored God, and He has kept them. Daniel purposed in his heart that he would not adopt the customs of kingly courts; he would not eat of the king's meat nor drink of his wine. He looked to God for strength and grace, and God gave him wisdom and skill and knowledge above that of the astrologers, the soothsayers, and the magicians of the kingdom. To him the promise was verified: "Them that honor Me I will honor."

The young physician has access to the God of Daniel. Through divine grace and power he may become as efficient in his calling as Daniel was in his exalted position. But it is a mistake to make a scientific preparation the all-important thing, while religious principles, that lie at the very foundation of a successful practice, are neglected. Many are lauded as skillful men in their profession who scorn the thought that they need to rely upon Jesus for wisdom in their work. But if these men who trust in their knowledge of science were illuminated by the light of heaven, to how much greater excellence might they attain! How much stronger would be their powers, with how much greater confidence could they undertake difficult cases! The man who is closely connected with the Great Physician of soul and body has the resources of heaven and earth at his command, and he can work with a wisdom, an unerring precision, that the godless man cannot possess.

Those to whom the care of the sick is entrusted, whether as physicians or nurses, should remember that their work must stand the scrutiny of the piercing eye of Jehovah. There is no missionary field more important than that occupied by the faithful, God-fearing physician. There is no field where a man may accomplish greater good or win more jewels to shine in the crown of his rejoicing. He may carry the grace of Christ, as a sweet perfume, into all the sickrooms he enters; he may carry the true healing balm to the sin-sick soul. He can point the sick and dying to the

Lamb of God that taketh away the sin of the world. He should not listen to the suggestion that it is dangerous to speak of their eternal interests to those whose lives are in peril, lest it should make them worse; for in nine cases out of ten the knowledge of a sin-pardoning Saviour would make them better both in mind and body. Jesus can limit the power of Satan. He is the physician in whom the sin-sick soul may trust to heal the maladies of the body as well as of the soul.

The superficial and the evil-minded in the profession will seek to arouse prejudice against the man who faithfully discharges the duties of his profession, and to strew his path with obstacles; but these trials will only reveal the pure gold of character. Christ will be his refuge from the strife of tongues. Though his life may be hard and self-denying, and in the estimation of the world may be a failure, in the sight of heaven it will be a success, and he will be ranked as one of God's noblemen. "They that be wise shall shine as the brightness of the firmament; and they that turn many to righteousness as the stars for ever and ever."

THE COMING CRISIS

"And the dragon was wroth with the woman, and went to make war with the remnant of her seed, which keep the commandments of God, and have the testimony of Jesus Christ." In the near future we shall see these words fulfilled as the Protestant churches unite with the world and with the papal power against commandment keepers. The same spirit which actuated papists in ages past will lead Protestants to pursue a similar course toward those who will maintain their loyalty to God.

Church and state are now making preparations for the future conflict. Protestants are working in disguise to bring Sunday to the front, as did the Romanists. Throughout the land the papacy is piling up her lofty and massive structures, in the secret recesses of which her former persecutions are to be repeated. And the way is preparing for the manifestation, on a grand scale, of those lying wonders by which, if it were possible, Satan would deceive even the elect.

The decree which is to go forth against the people of God will be very similar to that issued by Ahasuerus against the Jews in the time of Esther. The Persian edict sprang from the malice of Haman toward Mordecai. Not that Mordecai had done him harm, but he had refused to show him reverence which belongs only to God. The king's decision against the Jews was secured under false pretenses through misrepresentation of that peculiar people. Satan instigated the scheme in order to rid the earth of those who preserved the knowledge of the true God. But his plots were defeated by a counterpower that reigns among the children of men. Angels that excel in strength were commissioned to protect the people of God, and the plots of their adversaries returned upon their own heads. The Protestant world today see in the little company keeping the Sabbath a Mordecai in the gate. His character and conduct, expressing reverence for the law of God, are a constant rebuke to those who have cast off the fear of the Lord and are trampling upon His Sabbath; the unwelcome intruder must by some means be put out of the way.

The same masterful mind that plotted against the faithful in ages past is still seeking to rid the earth of those who fear God and obey His law. Satan will excite indignation against the humble minority who conscientiously refuse to accept popular customs and traditions. Men of position and reputation will join with the lawless and the vile to take counsel against the people of God. Wealth, genius, education, will combine to cover them with contempt. Persecuting rulers, ministers, and church members will conspire against them. With voice and pen, by boasts, threats, and ridicule, they will seek to overthrow their faith. By false representations and angry appeals they will stir up the passions of the people. Not having a "Thus saith the Scriptures" to bring against the advocates of the Bible Sabbath, they will resort to oppressive enactments to supply the lack. To secure popularity and patronage, legislators will yield to the demand for a Sunday law. Those who fear God cannot accept an institution that violates a precept of the Decalogue. On this battlefield comes the last great conflict of the controversy between truth and error. And we are not left in doubt as to the issue. Now, as in the days of Mordecai, the Lord will vindicate His truth and His people.

By the decree enforcing the institution of the papacy in violation of the law of God, our nation will disconnect herself fully from righteousness. When Protestantism shall stretch her hand across the gulf to grasp the hand of the Roman power, when she shall reach over the abyss to clasp hands with spiritualism, when, under the influence of this threefold union, our country shall repudiate every principle of its Constitution as a Protestant and republican government, and shall make provision for the propagation of papal falsehoods and delusions, then we may know that the time has come for the marvelous working of Satan and that the end is near.

As the approach of the Roman armies was a sign to the disciples of the impending destruction of Jerusalem, so may this apostasy be a sign to us that the limit of God's forbearance is reached, that the measure of our nation's iniquity is full, and that the angel of mercy is about to take her flight, never to return. The people of God will then be plunged into those scenes of affliction and distress which prophets have described as the time of Jacob's trouble. The cries of the faithful, persecuted ones ascend to heaven. And as the blood of Abel cried from the ground, there are voices also crying to God from martyrs' graves, from the sepulchers of the sea, from mountain caverns, from convent vaults: "How long, O Lord, holy and true, dost Thou not judge and avenge our blood on them that dwell on the earth?"

The Lord is doing His work. All heaven is astir. The Judge of all the earth is soon to arise and vindicate His insulted authority. The mark of deliverance will be set upon the men who keep God's commandments, who revere His law, and who refuse the mark of the beast or of his image.

God has revealed what is to take place in the last days, that His people may be prepared to stand against the tempest of opposition and wrath. Those who have been warned of the events before them are not to sit in calm expectation of the coming storm, comforting themselves that the Lord will shelter His faithful ones in the day of trouble. We are to be as men waiting for their Lord, not in idle expectancy, but in earnest work, with unwavering faith. It is no time now to allow our minds to be engrossed with things of minor importance. While men are sleeping, Satan is actively arranging matters so that the Lord's people may not have mercy or justice. The Sunday movement is now making its way in darkness. The leaders are concealing the true issue, and many who unite in the movement do not themselves see whither the undercurrent as tending. Its professions are mild and apparently Christian, but when it shall speak it will reveal the spirit of the dragon. It is our duty to do all in our power to avert the threatened danger. We should endeavor to disarm prejudice by placing ourselves in a proper light before the people. We should bring before them the real question at issue, thus interposing the most effectual protest against measures to restrict liberty of conscience. We should search the Scriptures and be able to give the reason for our faith. Says the prophet: "The wicked shall do wickedly: and none of the wicked shall understand; but the wise shall understand."

Those who have access to God through Christ have important work before them. Now is the time to lay hold of the arm of our strength. The prayer of David should be the prayer of pastors and laymen: "It is time for Thee, Lord, to work: for they have made void Thy law." Let the servants of the Lord weep between the porch and the altar, crying: "Spare Thy people, O Lord, and give not Thine heritage to reproach." God has always wrought for His people in their greatest extremity, when there seemed the least hope that ruin could be averted. The designs of wicked men, the enemies of the church, are subject to His power and overruling providence. He can move upon the hearts of states-men; the wrath of the turbulent and disaffected, the haters of God, His truth, and His people can be turned aside, even as the rivers of water are turned, if He orders it thus. Prayer moves the arm of Omnipotence. He who marshals the stars in order in the heavens, whose word controls the waves of the great deep, the same infinite Creator will work in behalf of His people if they call upon Him in faith. He will restrain the forces of darkness until the warning is given to the world and all who will heed it are prepared for the conflict.

"The wrath of man shall praise Thee," says the psalmist; "the remainder of wrath shalt Thou restrain." God means that testing truth shall be brought to the front and become a subject of examination and discussion, even if it is through the contempt placed upon it. The minds of the people must be agitated. Every controversy, every reproach, every slander, will be God's means of provoking inquiry and awakening minds that otherwise would slumber.

Thus it has been in the past history of God's people. For refusing to worship the great golden image which Nebuchad-nezzar had set up, the three Hebrews were cast into the fiery furnace. But God preserved His servants in the midst of the flames, and the attempt to enforce idolatry resulted in bring-ing the knowledge of the true God before the assembled princes and great men of the vast kingdom of Babylon.

So when the decree went forth forbidding prayer to any god save the king. As Daniel, according to his custom, made his supplications three times a day to the God of heaven, the at-tention of the princes and rulers was called to his case. He had an opportunity to speak for himself, to show who is the true God, and to present the reason why He alone should receive worship, and the duty of rendering Him praise and homage. And the deliverance of Daniel from the den of lions was an-other evidence that the Being whom he worshiped was the true and living God.

So the imprisonment of Paul brought the gospel before

kings, princes, and rulers who otherwise would not have had this light. The efforts made to retard the progress of truth will serve to extend it. The excellence of truth is more clearly seen from every successive point from which it may be viewed. Error requires disguise and concealment. It clothes itself in angel robes, and every manifestation of its real character lessens its chance of success.

The people whom God has made the depositaries of His law are not to permit their light to be hidden. The truth must be proclaimed in the dark places of the earth. Obstacles must be met and surmounted. A great work is to be done, and this work has been entrusted to those who know the truth. They should make mighty intercession with God for help now. The love of Christ must be diffused in their own hearts. The Spirit of Christ must be poured out upon them, and they must be making ready to stand in the judgment. While they are consecrating themselves to God, a convincing power will attend their efforts to present the truth to others, and its light will find access to many hearts. We must sleep no longer on Satan's enchanted ground, but call into requisition all our resources and avail ourselves of every facility with which Providence has furnished us. The last warning is to be proclaimed "before many peoples, and nations, and tongues, and kings;" and the promise is given, "Lo, I am with you alway, even unto the end of the world."

THE CHURCH THE LIGHT OF THE WORLD

The Lord called out His people Israel and separated them from the world that He might commit to them a sacred trust. He made them the depositaries of His law, and He designed, through them, to preserve among men the knowledge of Himself. Through them the light of heaven was to shine out to the dark places of the earth, and a voice was to be heard appealing to all peoples to turn from their idolatry to serve the living and true God. Had the Hebrews been true to their trust, they would have been a power in the world. God would have been their defense, and He would have exalted them above all other nations. His light and truth would have been revealed through them, and they would have stood forth under His wise and holy rule as an example of the superiority of His government over every form of idolatry.

But they did not keep their covenant with God. They followed after the idolatrous practices of other nations, and instead of making their Creator's name a praise in the earth their course held it up to the contempt of the heathen. Yet the purpose of God must be accomplished. The knowledge of His will must be spread abroad in the earth. God brought the hand of the oppressor upon His people and scattered them as captives among the nations. In affliction many of them repented of their transgressions and sought the Lord. Scattered throughout the countries of the heathen, they spread abroad the knowledge of the true God. The principles of the divine law came in conflict with the customs and practices of the nations. Idolaters endeavored to crush out the true faith. The Lord in His providence brought His servants, Daniel, Nehemiah, Ezra, face to face with kings and rulers, that these idolaters might have an opportunity to receive the light. Thus the work which God had given His people to do in prosperity, in their own borders, but which had been neglected through their unfaithfulness, was done by them in captivity, under great trial and embarrassment.

God has called His church in this day, as He called ancient Israel, to stand as a light in the earth. By the mighty cleaver of truth, the messages of the first, second, and third angels, He has separated them from the churches and from the world to bring them into a sacred nearness to Himself. He has made them the depositaries of His law and has committed to them the great truths of prophecy for this time. Like the holy oracles committed to ancient Israel, these are a sacred trust to be communicated to the world. The three angels of Revelation 14 represent the people who accept the light of God's messages and go forth as His agents to sound the warning throughout the length and breadth of the earth. Christ declares to His followers: "Ye are the light of the world." To every soul that accepts Jesus the cross of Calvary speaks: "Behold the worth of the soul: 'Go ye into all the world, and preach the gospel to every creature.' " Nothing is to be permitted to hinder this work. It is the all-important work for time; it is to be far-reaching as eternity. The love that Jesus manifested for the souls of men in the sacrifice which He made for their redemption, will actuate all His followers.

But very few of those who have received the light are doing the work entrusted to their hands. There are a few men of unswerving fidelity who do not study ease, convenience, or life itself, who push their way wherever they can find an opening to press the light of truth and vindicate the holy law of God. But the sins that control the world have come into the churches, and into the hearts of those who claim to be God's peculiar people. Many who have received the light exert an influence to quiet the fears of worldlings and formal professors. There are lovers of the world even among those who profess to be waiting for the Lord. There is ambition for riches and honor. Christ describes this class when He declares that the day of God is to come as a snare upon all that dwell upon the earth. This world is their home. They make it their business to secure earthly treasures. They erect costly dwellings and furnish them with every good thing; they find pleasure in dress and the indulgence of appetite. The things of the world are their idols. These interpose between the soul and Christ, and the solemn and awful realities that are crowding upon us are but dimly seen and faintly realized. The same disobedience and failure which were seen in the Jewish church have characterized in a greater degree the people who have had this great light from heaven in the last messages of warning. Shall we, like them, squander our opportunities and privileges until God shall permit oppression and persecution to come upon us? Will the work which might be performed in peace and comparative prosperity be left undone until it must be performed in days of darkness, under the pressure of trial and persecution?

There is a terrible amount of guilt for which the church is responsible. Why are not those who have the light putting forth earnest efforts to give that light to others? They see that the end is near. They see multitudes daily transgressing God's law; and they know that these souls cannot be saved in transgression. Yet they have more interest in their trades, their farms, their houses, their merchandise, their dress, their tables, than in the souls of men and women whom they must meet face to face in the judgment. The people who claim to obey the truth are asleep. They could not be at ease as they are if they were awake. The love of the truth is dying out of their hearts. Their example is not such as to convince the world that they have truth in advance of every other people upon the earth. At the very time when they should be strong in God, having a daily, living experience, they are feeble, hesitating, relying upon the preachers for support, when they should be ministering to others with mind and soul and voice and pen and time and money.

Brethren and sisters, many of you excuse yourselves from labor on the plea of inability to work for others. But did God make you so incapable? Was not this inability produced by your own inactivity and perpetuated by your own deliberate choice? Did not God give you at least one talent to improve, not for your own convenience and gratification, but for Him? Have you realized your obligation, as His hired servant, to bring a revenue to Him by the wise and skillful use of this entrusted capital? Have you not neglected opportunities to improve your powers to this end? It is too true that few have felt any real sense of their responsibility to God. Love, judgment, memory, foresight, tact, energy, and every other faculty have been devoted to self. You have displayed greater wisdom in the service of evil than in the cause of God. You have perverted, disabled, nay, even besotted your powers, by your intense activity in worldly pursuits to the neglect of God's work.

Still you soothe your conscience by saying that you cannot undo the past, and gain the vigor, the strength, and the skill which you might have had if you had employed your powers as God required. But remember that He holds you responsible for the work negligently done or left undone through your unfaithfulness. The more you exercise your powers for the Master, the more apt and skillful you will become. The more closely you connect yourself with the Source of light and power, the greater light will be shed upon you, and the greater power will be yours to use for God. And for all that you might have had, but failed to obtain through your devotion to the world, you are responsible. When you became a follower of Christ you pledged yourself to serve Him and Him alone, and He promised to be with you and bless you, to refresh you with His light, to grant you His peace, and to make you joyful in His work. Have you failed to experience these blessings? be sure it is the result of your own course.

In order to escape the draft during the war, there were men who induced disease, others maimed themselves that they might be rendered unfit for service. Here is an illustration of the course which many have been pursuing in relation to the cause of God. They have crippled their powers, both physical and mental, so that they are unable to do the work which is so greatly needed.

Suppose that a sum of money were placed in your hands to invest for a certain purpose; would you throw it away and declare that you were not now responsible for its use? would you feel that you had saved yourself a great care? Yet this is what you have been doing with the gifts of God. To excuse yourself from working for others on the plea of inability, while you are all absorbed in worldly pursuits, is mockery of God. Multitudes are going down to ruin; the people who have received light and truth are but as a handful to withstand all the host of evil; and yet this little company are devoting their energies to anything and everything but to learning how they may rescue souls from death. Is it any marvel that the church is weak and inefficient, that God can do but little for His professed people? They place themselves where it is impossible for Him to work with them and for them. Dare you continue thus to disregard His claims? Will you still trifle with heaven's most sacred trusts? Will you say with Cain: "Am I my brother's keeper?"

Remember that your responsibility is measured, not by your present resources and capacities, but by the powers originally bestowed and the possibilities for improvement. The question which each one should ask himself is not whether he is now inexperienced and unfit to labor in God's cause, but how and why he is in this condition, and how it can be remedied. God will not supernaturally endow us with the qualifications which we lack; but while we exert the ability we have, He will work with us to increase and strengthen every faculty; our dormant energies will be aroused, and powers which have long been palsied will receive new life.

So long as we are in the world, we must have to do with the things of the world. There will ever be a necessity for the transaction of temporal, secular business; but this should never become all-absorbing. The apostle Paul has given a safe rule: "Not slothful in business; fervent in spirit; serving the Lord." The humble, common duties of life are all to be performed with fidelity; "heartily," says the apostle, "as to the Lord." Whatever our department of labor, be it housework or field work or intellectual pursuits, we may perform it to the glory of God so long as we make Christ first and last and best in everything. But aside from these worldly employments there is given to every follower of Christ a special work for the upbuilding of His kingdom—a work which requires personal effort for the salvation of men. It is not a work to be performed once a week merely, at the place of worship, but at all times and all places.

Everyone who connects himself with the church makes in that act a solemn vow to work for the interest of the church and to hold that interest above every worldly consideration. It is his work to preserve a living connection with God, to engage with heart and soul in the great scheme of redemption, and to show, in his life and character, the excellency of God's commandments in contrast with the customs and precepts of the world. Every soul that has made a profession of Christ has pledged himself to be all that it is possible for him to be as a spiritual worker, to be active, zealous, and efficient in his Master's service. Christ expects every man to do his duty; let this be the watchword throughout the ranks of His followers.

We are not to wait to be solicited to give light, to be importuned for counsel or instruction. Everyone who receives the rays of the Sun of Righteousness is to reflect its brightness to all about him. His religion should have a positive and decided influence. His prayers and entreaties should be so imbued with the Holy Spirit that they will melt and subdue the soul. Said Jesus: "Let your light so shine before men, that they may see your good works, and glorify your Father which is in heaven." It would be better for a worldling never to have seen a professor of religion than to come under the influence of one who is ignorant of the power of godliness. If Christ were our pattern, His life our rule, what zeal would be manifested, what efforts put forth, what liberality exercised, what self-denial practiced! How untiringly should we labor, what fervent petitions for power and wisdom would ascend to God! If all the professed children of God would feel that it is the chief business of life to do the work which He has bidden them to do, if they would labor unselfishly in His cause, what a change would be seen in hearts and homes, in churches, yea, in the world itself!

Vigilance and fidelity have been required of Christ's followers in every age; but now that we are standing upon the very verge of the eternal world, holding the truths we do, having so great light, so important a work, we must double our diligence. Everyone is to do to the very utmost of his ability. My brother, you endanger your own salvation if you hold back now. God will call you to account if you fail in the work He has assigned you. Have you a knowledge of the truth? give it to others.

What can I say to arouse our churches? What can I say to those who have acted a prominent part in the proclamation of the last message? "The Lord is coming," should be the testimony borne, not only by the lips, but by the life and character; but many to whom God has given light and knowledge, talents of influence and means, are men who do not love the truth and do not practice it. They have drunk so deeply from the intoxicating cup of selfishness and worldliness that they have become drunken with the cares of this life. Brethren, if you continue to be as idle, as worldly, as selfish as you have been, God will surely pass you by, and take those who are less self-caring, less ambitious for worldly honor, and who will not hesitate to go, as did their Master, without the camp, bearing the reproach. The work will be given to those who will take it, those who prize it, who weave its principles into their everyday experience. God will choose humble men who are seeking to glorify His name and advance His cause rather than to honor and advance themselves. He will raise up men who have not so much worldly wisdom, but who are connected with Him, and who will seek strength and counsel from above.

Some of our leading men are inclined to indulge the spirit manifested by the apostle John when he said: "Master, we saw one casting out devils in Thy name; and we forbade him, because he followeth not with us." Organization and discipline are essential, but there is now very great danger of a departure from the simplicity of the gospel of Christ. What we need is less dependence upon mere form and ceremony, and far more of the power of true godliness. If their life and character are exemplary, let all work who will, in any capacity. Although they may not conform exactly to your methods, not a word should be spoken to condemn or discourage them. When the Pharisees desired Jesus to silence the children who sang His praise, the Saviour said: "If these should hold their peace, the stones would immediately cry out." Prophecy must be fulfilled. So in these days, the work must be done. There are many departments of labor; let everyone act a part as best he can. The man with one talent is not to bury that in the earth. God has given to every man his work according to his ability. Those to whom larger trusts and capabilities have been committed should not endeavor to silence others who are less able or experienced. Men with one talent may reach a class that those with two or five talents cannot approach. Great and small alike are chosen vessels to bear the water of life to thirsting souls. Let not those who preach the word lay their hands upon the humblest worker and say: "You must labor in this channel or not work at all." Hands off, brethren. Let everyone work in his own sphere, with his own armor on, doing whatever he can do in his humble way. Strengthen his hands in the work. This is no time for pharisaism to control. Let God work through whom He will. The message must go.

All are to show their fidelity to God by the wise use of His entrusted capital, not in means alone, but in any endowment that will tend to the upbuilding of His kingdom. Satan will employ every possible device to prevent the truth from reaching those who are buried in error; but the voice of warning and entreaty must come to them. And while only a few are engaged in this work, thousands ought to be as much interested as they. God never designed that the lay members of the church should be excused from labor in His cause. "Go, labor in My vineyard," is the Master's command to each of His followers. As long as there are unconverted souls in the world, there should be the most active, earnest, zealous, determined effort for their salvation. Those who have received the light should seek to enlighten those who have it not. If the church members do not individually take hold of this work, then they show that they have no living connection with God. Their names are registered as slothful servants. Can you not discern the reason why there is no more spirituality in our churches? It is because you are not colaborers with Christ.

God has given to every man his work. Let us each wait on God, and He will teach us how to work and what work we are best adapted to perform. Yet none are to start out in an independent spirit to promulgate new theories. The workers should be in harmony with the truth and with their brethren. There should be counsel and cooperation. But they are not to feel that at every step they must wait to ask some higher officer if they may do this or that. Look not to man for guidance, but to the God of Israel.

The work which the church has failed to do in a time of peace and prosperity she will have to do in a terrible crisis under most discouraging, forbidding circumstances. The warnings that worldly conformity has silenced or withheld must be given under the fiercest opposition from enemies of the faith. And at that time the superficial, conservative class, whose influence has steadily retarded the progress of the work, will renounce the faith and take their stand with its avowed enemies, toward whom their sympathies have long been tending. These apostates will then manifest the most bitter enmity, doing all in their power to oppress and malign their former brethren and to excite indignation against them. This day is just before us. The members of the church will individually be tested and proved. They will be placed in circumstances where they will be forced to bear witness for the truth. Many will be called to speak before councils and in courts of justice, perhaps separately and alone. The experience which would have helped them in this emergency they have neglected to obtain, and their souls are burdened with remorse for wasted opportunities and neglected privileges.

My brother, my sister, ponder these things, I beseech you. You have each a work to do. Your unfaithfulness and neglect are registered against you in the Ledger of Heaven. You have diminished your powers and lessened your capabilities. You lack the experience and efficiency which you might have had. But before it is forever too late, I urge you to arouse. Delay no longer. The day is almost spent. The westering sun is about sinking forever from your sight. Yet while the blood of Christ is pleading, you may find pardon. Summon every energy of the soul, employ the few remaining hours in earnest labor for God and for your fellow men.

My heart is stirred to the very depths. Words are inadequate to express my feelings as I plead for perishing souls. Must I plead in vain? As Christ's ambassador I would arouse you to labor as you never labored before. Your duty cannot be shifted upon another. No one but yourself can do your work. If you withhold your light, someone must be left in darkness through your neglect.

Eternity stretches before us. The curtain is about to be lifted. We who occupy this solemn, responsible position, what are we doing, what are we thinking about, that we cling to our selfish love of ease, while souls are perishing around us? Have our hearts become utterly callous? Cannot we feel or understand that we have a work to do for the salvation of others? Brethren, are you of the class who having eyes see not, and having ears hear not? Is it in vain that God has given you a knowledge of His will? Is it in vain that He has sent you warning after warning? Do you believe the declarations of eternal truth concerning what is about to come upon the earth, do you believe that God's judgments are hanging over the people, and can you still sit at ease, indolent, careless, pleasure loving?

It is no time now for God's people to be fixing their affections or laying up their treasure in the world. The time is not far distant, when, like the early disciples, we shall be forced to seek a refuge in desolate and solitary places. As the siege of Jerusalem by the Roman armies was the signal for flight to the Judean Christians, so the assumption of power on the part of our nation in the decree enforcing the papal sabbath will be a warning to us. It will then be time to leave the large cities, preparatory to leaving the smaller ones for retired homes in secluded places among the mountains. And now, instead of seeking expensive dwellings here, we should be preparing to move to a better country, even a heavenly. Instead of spending our means in self-gratification, we should be studying to economize. Every talent lent of God should be used to His glory in giving the warning to the world. God has a work for His colaborers to do in the cities. Our missions must be sustained; new missions must be opened. To carry forward this work successfully will require no small outlay. Houses of worship are needed, where the people may be invited to hear the truths for this time. For this very purpose, God has entrusted a capital to His stewards. Let not your property be tied up in worldly enterprises, so that this work shall be hindered. Get your means where you can handle it for the benefit of the cause of God. Send your treasures before you into heaven.

The members of the church should individually hold themselves and all their possessions upon the altar of God. Now, as never before, the Saviour's admonition is applicable: "Sell that ye have, and give alms; provide yourselves bags which wax not old, a treasure in the heavens that faileth not, where no thief approacheth, neither moth corrupteth. For where your treasure is, there will your heart be also." Those who are fastening their means in large houses, in lands, in worldly enterprises, are saying by their actions: "God cannot have it; I want it for myself." They have bound up their one talent in a napkin and hid it in the earth. There is cause for such to be alarmed. Brethren, God has not entrusted means to you to lie idle nor to be covetously retained or hid away, but to be used to advance His cause, to save the souls of the perishing. It is not the time now to bind up the Lord's money in your expensive buildings and your large enterprises, while His cause is crippled and left to beg its way, the treasury half-supplied. The Lord is not in this way of working. Remember, the day is fast approaching when it will be said: "Give an account of thy stewardship." Can you not discern the signs of the times?

Every day that passes brings us nearer the last great important day. We are one year nearer the judgment, nearer eternity, than we were at the beginning of 1884. Are we also drawing nearer to God? Are we watching unto prayer? Another year of our time to labor has rolled into eternity. Every day we have been associating with men and women who are judgment bound. Each day may have been the dividing line to some soul; someone may have made the decision which shall determine his future destiny. What has been our influence over these fellow travelers? What efforts have we put forth to bring them to Christ?

It is a solemn thing to die, but a far more solemn thing to live. Every thought and word and deed of our lives will meet us again. What we make of ourselves in probationary time, that we must remain to all eternity. Death brings dissolution to the body, but makes no change in the character. The coming of Christ does not change our characters; it only fixes them forever beyond all change.

Again I appeal to the members of the church to be Christians, to be Christlike. Jesus was a worker, not for Himself, but for others. He labored to bless and save the lost. If you are Christians you will imitate His example. He has laid the foundation, and we are builders together with Him. But what material are we bringing to lay on this foundation? "Every man's work shall be made manifest: for the day shall declare it, because it shall be revealed by fire; and the fire shall try every man's work of what sort it is." If you are devoting all your strength and talent to the things of this world, your life-work is represented by wood, hay, and stubble, to be consumed by the fires of the last day. But unselfish labor for Christ and the future life will be as gold, silver, and precious stones; it is imperishable.

My brethren and sisters, awake, I beseech you, from the sleep of death. It is too late to devote the strength of brain, bone, and muscle to self-serving. Let not the last day find you destitute of heavenly treasure. Seek to push the triumphs of the cross, seek to enlighten souls, labor for the salvation of your fellow beings, and your work will abide the trying test of fire.

"If any man's work abide, . . . he shall receive a reward." Glorious will be the reward bestowed when the faithful workers are gathered about the throne of God and the Lamb. When John in his mortal state beheld the glory of God, he fell as one dead; he was not able to endure the sight. But when mortal shall have put on immortality, the ransomed ones are like Jesus, for they see Him as He is. They stand before the throne, signifying that they are accepted. All their sins are blotted out, all their transgressions borne away. Now they can look upon the undimmed glory from the throne of God. They have been partakers with Christ of His sufferings, they have been workers together with Him in the plan of redemption, and they are partakers with Him in the joy of beholding souls saved through their instrumentality to praise God through all eternity.

JOSHUA AND THE ANGEL

If the veil which separates the visible from the invisible world could be lifted, and the people of God could behold the great controversy that is going on between Christ and holy angels and Satan and his evil hosts concerning the redemption of man; if they could understand the wonderful work of God for the rescue of souls from the bondage of sin, and the constant exercise of His power for their protection from the malice of the evil one, they would be better prepared to withstand the devices of Satan. Their minds would be solemnized in view of the vast extent and importance of the plan of redemption and the greatness of the work before them as colaborers with Christ. They would be humbled, yet encouraged, knowing that all heaven is interested in their salvation.

A most forcible and impressive illustration of the work of Satan and the work of Christ, and the power of our Mediator to vanquish the accuser of His people, is given in the prophecy of Zechariah. In holy vision the prophet beholds Joshua the high priest, "clothed with filthy garments," standing before the Angel of the Lord, entreating the mercy of God in behalf of his people who are in deep affliction. Satan stands at his right hand to resist him. Because Israel had been chosen to preserve the knowledge of God in the earth, they had been, from their first existence as a nation, the special objects of Satan's enmity, and he had determined to cause their destruction. He could do them no harm while they were obedient to God; therefore he had bent all his power and cunning to enticing them into sin. Ensnared by his temptations they had transgressed the law of God and thus separated from the Source of their strength, and had been left to become the prey of their heathen enemies. They were carried into captivity to Babylon, and there remained for many years. Yet they were not forsaken of the Lord. His prophets were sent to them with reproofs and warnings. The people were awakened to see their guilt, they humbled themselves before God, and returned to Him with true repentance. Then the Lord sent them messages of encouragement, declaring that He would deliver them from their captivity and restore them to His favor. It was this that Satan was determined to prevent. A remnant of Israel had already returned to their own land, and Satan was seeking to move upon the heathen nations, who were his agents, to utterly destroy them.

As Joshua humbly pleads for the fulfillment of God's promises, Satan stands up boldly to resist him. He points to the transgressions of Israel as a reason why that people should not be restored to the favor of God. He claims them as his prey and demands that they be given into his hands to be destroyed.

The high priest cannot defend himself or his people from Satan's accusations. He does not claim that Israel are free from fault. In his filthy garments, symbolizing the sins of the people, which he bears as their representative, he stands before the Angel, confessing their guilt, yet pointing to their repentance and humiliation, relying upon the mercy of a sin-pardoning Redeemer and in faith claiming the promises of God.

Then the Angel, who is Christ Himself, the Saviour of sinners, puts to silence the accuser of His people, declaring: "The Lord rebuke thee, O Satan; even the Lord that hath chosen Jerusalem rebuke thee: is not this a brand plucked out of the fire?" Israel had long remained in the furnace of affliction. Because of their sins they had been well-nigh consumed in the flame kindled by Satan and his agents for their destruction, but God had now set His hand to bring them forth. In their penitence and humiliation the compassionate Saviour will not leave His people to the cruel power of the heathen. "A bruised reed shall He not break, and the smoking flax shall He not quench."

As the intercession of Joshua is accepted, the command is given, "Take away the filthy garments from him," and to Joshua the Angel declares, "Behold, I have caused thine iniquity to pass from thee, and I will clothe thee with change of raiment." "So they set a fair miter upon his head, and clothed him with garments." His own sins and those of his people were pardoned. Israel were clothed with "change of raiment"—the righteousness of Christ imputed to them. The miter placed upon Joshua's head was such as was worn by the priests and bore the inscription, "Holiness to the Lord," signifying that, notwithstanding his former transgressions, he was now qualified to minister before God in His sanctuary.

After thus solemnly investing him with the dignity of the priesthood the Angel declared: "Thus saith the Lord of hosts; If thou wilt walk in My ways, and if thou wilt keep My charge, then thou shalt also judge My house, and shalt also keep My courts, and I will give thee places to walk among these that stand by." He would be honored as the judge or ruler over the temple and all its services; he should walk among attending angels, even in this life, and should at last join the glorified throng around the throne of God.

"Hear now, O Joshua the high priest, thou, and thy fellows that sit before thee: for they are men wondered at: for, behold, I will bring forth My servant the Branch." Here is revealed the hope of Israel. It was by faith in the coming Saviour that Joshua and his people received pardon. Through faith in Christ they were restored to God's favor. By virtue of His merits, if they walked in His ways and kept His statutes, they would be "men wondered at," honored as the chosen of heaven among the nations of the earth. Christ was their hope, their defense, their justification and redemption, as He is the hope of His church today.

As Satan accused Joshua and his people, so in all ages he accuses those who are seeking the mercy and favor of God. In the Revelation he is declared to be the "accuser of our brethren," "which accused them before our God day and night." The controversy is repeated over every soul that is rescued from the power of evil and whose name is registered in the Lamb's book of life. Never is one received from the family of Satan into the family of God without exciting the determined resistance of the wicked one. Satan's accusations against those who seek the Lord are not prompted by displeasure at their sins. He exults in their defective characters. Only through their transgression of God's law can he obtain power over them. His accusations arise solely from his enmity to Christ. Through the plan of salvation, Jesus is breaking Satan's hold upon the human family and rescuing souls from his power. All the hatred and malignity of the archrebel is stirred as he beholds the evidence of Christ's supremacy, and with fiendish power and cunning he works to wrest from Him the remnant of the children of men who have accepted His salvation.

He leads men into skepticism, causing them to lose confidence in God and to separate from His love; he tempts them to break His law, and then he claims them as his captives and contests the right of Christ to take them from him. He knows that those who seek God earnestly for pardon and grace will obtain it; therefore he presents their sins before them to discourage them. He is constantly seeking occasion against those who are trying to obey God. Even their best and most accept-able services he seeks to make appear corrupt. By countless devices, the most subtle and the most cruel, he endeavors to secure their condemnation. Man cannot meet these charges himself. In his sin-stained garments, confessing his guilt, he stands before God. But Jesus our Advocate presents an effec-tual plea in behalf of all who by repentance and faith have committed the keeping of their souls to Him. He pleads their cause and vanquishes their accuser by the mighty arguments of Calvary. His perfect obedience to God's law, even unto the death of the cross, has given Him all power in heaven and in earth, and He claims of His Father mercy and reconciliation for guilty man. To the accuser of His people He declares: " 'The Lord rebuke thee, O Satan.' These are the purchase of My blood, brands plucked from the burning." Those who rely upon Him in faith receive the comforting assurance: "Be-hold, I have caused thine iniquity to pass from thee, and I will clothe thee with change of raiment." All that have put on the robe of Christ's righteousness will stand before Him as cho-sen and faithful and true. Satan has no power to pluck them out of the hand of Christ. Not one soul that in penitence and faith has claimed His protection will Christ permit to pass un-der the enemy's power. His word is pledged: "Let him take hold of My strength, that he may make peace with Me; and he shall make peace with Me." The promise given to Joshua is made to all: "If thou wilt keep My charge, . . . I will give thee places to walk among these that stand by." Angels of God will walk on either side of them, even in this world, and they will stand at last among the angels that surround the throne of God.

The fact that the acknowledged people of God are repre-sented as standing before the Lord in filthy garments should lead to humility and deep searching of heart on the part of all who profess His name. Those who are indeed purifying their souls by obeying the truth will have a most humble opinion of themselves. The more closely they view the spotless char-

acter of Christ, the stronger will be their desire to be conformed to His image, and the less will they see of purity or
holiness in themselves. But while we should realize our sinful
condition, we are to rely upon Christ as our righteousness, our
sanctification, and our redemption. We cannot answer the
charges of Satan against us. Christ alone can make an effectual plea in our behalf. He is able to silence the accuser with
arguments founded not upon our merits, but on His own.

Yet we should never be content with a sinful life. It is a
thought that should arouse Christians to greater zeal and
earnestness in overcoming evil, that every defect in character, every point in which they fail to meet the divine standard, is an open door by which Satan can enter to tempt and
destroy them; and, furthermore, that every failure and defect on their part gives occasion to the tempter and his
agents to reproach Christ. We are to exert every energy of
the soul in the work of overcoming, and to look to Jesus for
strength to do what we cannot do of ourselves. No sin can
be tolerated in those who shall walk with Christ in white.
The filthy garments are to be removed, and Christ's robe of
righteousness is to be placed upon us. By repentance and
faith we are enabled to render obedience to all the commandments of God, and are found without blame before
Him. Those who shall meet the approval of God are now
afflicting their souls, confessing their sins, and earnestly
pleading for pardon through Jesus their Advocate. Their attention is fixed upon Him, their hopes, their faith, are centered on Him, and when the command is given, "Take
away the filthy garments, and clothe him with change of
raiment, and set a fair miter upon his head," they are prepared to give Him all the glory of their salvation.

Zechariah's vision of Joshua and the Angel applies with
peculiar force to the experience of God's people in the closing
up of the great day of atonement. The remnant church will be
brought into great trial and distress. Those who keep the commandments of God and the faith of Jesus will feel the ire of
the dragon and his hosts. Satan numbers the world as his

subjects, he has gained control of the apostate churches; but here is a little company that are resisting his supremacy. If he could blot them from the earth, his triumph would be complete. As he influenced the heathen nations to destroy Israel, so in the near future he will stir up the wicked powers of earth to destroy the people of God. All will be required to render obedience to human edicts in violation of the divine law. Those who will be true to God and to duty will be menaced, denounced, and proscribed. They will "be betrayed both by parents, and brethren, and kinsfolks, and friends."

Their only hope is in the mercy of God; their only defense will be prayer. As Joshua was pleading before the Angel, so the remnant church, with brokenness of heart and earnest faith, will plead for pardon and deliverance through Jesus their Advocate. They are fully conscious of the sinfulness of their lives, they see their weakness and unworthiness, and as they look upon themselves they are ready to despair. The tempter stands by to accuse them, as he stood by to resist Joshua. He points to their filthy garments, their defective characters. He presents their weakness and folly, their sins of ingratitude, their unlikeness to Christ, which has dishonored their Redeemer. He endeavors to affright the soul with the thought that their case is hopeless, that the stain of their defilement will never be washed away. He hopes to so destroy their faith that they will yield to his temptations, turn from their allegiance to God, and receive the mark of the beast.

Satan urges before God his accusations against them, declaring that they have by their sins forfeited the divine protection, and claiming the right to destroy them as transgressors. He pronounces them just as deserving as himself of exclusion from the favor of God. "Are these," he says, "the people who are to take my place in heaven and the place of the angels who united with me? While they profess to obey the law of God, have they kept its precepts? Have they not been lovers of self more than of God? Have they not placed their own interests above His service? Have they not loved the things of the world? Look at the sins which have marked their lives. Behold their selfishness, their malice, their hatred toward one another."

The people of God have been in many respects very faulty. Satan has an accurate knowledge of the sins which he has tempted them to commit, and he presents these in the most exaggerated light, declaring: "Will God banish me and my angels from His presence, and yet reward those who have been guilty of the same sins? Thou canst not do this, O Lord, in justice. Thy throne will not stand in righteousness and judgment. Justice demands that sentence be pronounced against them."

But while the followers of Christ have sinned, they have not given themselves to the control of evil. They have put away their sins, and have sought the Lord in humility and contrition, and the divine Advocate pleads in their behalf. He who has been most abused by their ingratitude, who knows their sin, and also their repentance, declares: " 'The Lord rebuke thee, O Satan.' I gave My life for these souls. They are graven upon the palms of My hands."

The assaults of Satan are strong, his delusions are terrible; but the Lord's eye is upon His people. Their affliction is great, the flames of the furnace seem about to consume them; but Jesus will bring them forth as gold tried in the fire. Their earthliness must be removed that the image of Christ may be perfectly reflected; unbelief must be overcome; faith, hope, and patience are to be developed.

The people of God are sighing and crying for the abominations done in the land. With tears they warn the wicked of their danger in trampling upon the divine law, and with unutterable sorrow they humble themselves before the Lord on account of their own transgressions. The wicked mock their sorrow, ridicule their solenm appeals, and sneer at what they term their weakness. But the anguish and humiliation of God's people is unmistakable evidence that they are regaining the strength and nobility of character lost in consequence of sin. It is because they are drawing nearer to Christ, and their eyes are fixed upon His perfect purity, that they so clearly discern the exceeding sinfulness of sin. Their contrition and self-abasement are infinitely more acceptable in the sight of God than is the self-sufficient, haughty spirit of those who see no cause to lament, who scorn the humility of Christ, and who claim perfection while transgressing God's holy law. Meekness and lowliness of heart are the conditions for strength and victory. The crown of glory awaits those who bow at the foot of the cross. Blessed are these mourners, for they shall be comforted.

The faithful, praying ones are, as it were, shut in with God. They themselves know not how securely they are shielded. Urged on by Satan, the rulers of this world are seeking to destroy them; but could their eyes be opened, as were the eyes of Elisha's servant at Dothan, they would see the angels of God encamped about them, by their brightness and glory holding in check the hosts of darkness.

As the people of God afflict their souls before Him, pleading for purity of heart, the command is given, "Take away the filthy garments" from them, and the encouraging words are spoken, "Behold, I have caused thine iniquity to pass from thee, and I will clothe thee with change of raiment." The spotless robe of Christ's righteousness is placed upon the tried, tempted, yet faithful children of God. The despised remnant are clothed in glorious apparel, nevermore to be defiled by the corruptions of the world. Their names are retained in the Lamb's book of life, enrolled among the faithful of all ages. They have resisted the wiles of the deceiver; they have not been turned from their loyalty by the dragon's roar. Now they are eternally secure from the tempter's devices. Their sins are transferred to the originator of sin. And the remnant are not only pardoned and accepted, but honored. "A fair miter" is set upon their heads. They are to be as kings and priests unto God. While Satan was urging his accusations and seeking to destroy this company, holy angels, unseen, were passing to and fro, placing upon them the seal of the living God. These are they that stand upon Mount Zion with the Lamb, having the Father's name written in their foreheads. They sing the new song before the throne, that song which no man can learn save the hundred and forty and four thousand, which were redeemed from the earth. "These are they which follow the Lamb whithersoever He goeth. These were redeemed from among men, being the first fruits unto God and to the Lamb. And in their mouth was found no guile: for they are without fault before the throne of God."

Now is reached the complete fulfillment of those words of the Angel: "Hear now, O Joshua the high priest, thou, and thy fellows that sit before thee: for they are men wondered at: for, behold, I will bring forth My servant the Branch." Christ is revealed as the Redeemer and Deliverer of His people. Now indeed are the remnant "men wondered at," as the tears and humiliation of their pilgrimage give place to joy and honor in the presence of God and the Lamb. "In that day shall the branch of the Lord be beautiful and glorious, and the fruit of the earth shall be excellent and comely for them that are escaped of Israel. And it shall come to pass, that he that is left in Zion, and he that remaineth in Jerusalem, shall be called holy, even everyone that is written among the living in Jerusalem."

TESTIMONY FOR THE CHURCH

UNITY AND LOVE IN THE CHURCH

Dear Brethren and Sisters in Healdsburg: Do not forget that the most dangerous snares which Satan has prepared for the church will come through its own members who do not love God supremely or their neighbor as themselves. Satan is continually striving to wedge himself in between brethren. He seeks to gain control of those who claim to believe the truth, but who are unconverted; and when he can influence these, through their own carnal nature, to unite with him in trying to thwart the purposes of God, then he is exultant.

The Health Institute, the college, the ministry, and the missionary societies, are all instrumentalities which God employs for the accomplishment of His work. If Satan can in any way invent something which will divert talent and means from these instrumentalities into another channel, he will do it. There are some who are deceived in themselves. While flattering themselves that they are doing God's work, they are playing into the hands of the great deceiver and rendering him effectual service. Beware of these deceptions. Ever remember what is due to our Christian profession as God's peculiar people; and beware lest, in the exercise of personal independence, your influence may work against the purposes of God, and you, through Satan's devices, become a stumbling block, directly in the way of those who are weak

(477)

and halting. There is danger of giving our enemies occasion to blaspheme God and heap scorn upon believers in the truth.

Be especially guarded against becoming a tool in the hands of the enemy to divert the minds of any—men and women, or children—from an entire surrender of themselves to God and to the great work for this time. Beware of flattering the young by holding out to them the prospect of financial gain, wonderful educational advantages, or great personal achievements. Flattering words are sweet to the unconsecrated heart, and some who think they are standing firm, are dazed, allured, and intoxicated with hopes that will never be realized. A great wrong has been done in this way. All should think and speak modestly of their own capabilities, and should be careful not to encourage pride and self-esteem in others. Men and women, unless consecrated to God, are weak in moral power and may be entirely mistaken in their estimate of human ability and of what constitutes Christian fidelity. Present no inducements which will lessen the interest of any in building up an institution which God has said should be built up.

Brother A does not manifest good judgment upon all occasions and in all matters. He is not well-balanced, and unless he walks in humility before God, he will make dangerous mistakes. He lacks discernment, and therefore misjudges character, using such extravagant words of flattery to some as will hurt their souls. He will lead them to think that they can do some great thing, and thus they will neglect the little duties lying directly in their path.

I do not plead for inactivity, but I plead for this selfish, worldly spirit to be overcome. Any enterprise which will unite the interests of church members, and will bring harmony and unity of effort into the work of God, may be safely entered into. But never, never forget that you are either servants of Jesus Christ, working strenuously for that unity of believers which Christ prayed might exist, or you are working against this unity and against Christ.

Those who seek to lessen the interest of any in the school at Healdsburg, or in the missionary work in any of its branches, are not working together with God, but are working under another captain, whose aim is to weaken and destroy. Your usefulness, brethren and sisters of the Healdsburg church, requires that you be straightforward in all your dealings; that you be humble, holy, and undefiled. There should be less proud self-seeking, less self-importance. When the members of the church are clothed with humility, when they put from them self-esteem and self-seeking, when they seek constantly to do God's will—then they will work together in harmony. God's Spirit is one. . . .

The crisis is just before us when each will need much strength from God in order to stand against the wiles of Satan, for his deceptions will come in every conceivable form. Those who have allowed themselves to be the sport of Satan's temptations will be unprepared then to take the right side. Their ideas will be confused so that they cannot discern between the divine and the satanic.

There will come a crisis in every one of our institutions. Influences will be at work against them from both believers and unbelievers. There must be no betraying of confidence or holy trust now to benefit or exalt self. We should constantly watch our life with jealous care lest we leave wrong impressions upon the world. Say it, act it: "I am a Christian. I cannot act upon the world's maxims. I must love God supremely and my neighbor as myself. I cannot enter into or connive at any arrangement which will interfere in the slightest manner with my usefulness or weaken my influence or destroy the confidence of anyone in God's instrumentalities." . . .

Remember that God's people are but a little flock compared with the professedly Christian world and the myriads of world-adoring men and women. They are to be Bible Christians, examples to our youth of righteousness and exactness in all things. Every influence surrounding the young should be of a holy character, and this influence should begin in our own families. The sacred and the common should not be commingled.

GUARDING THE INTERESTS OF BRETHREN

By his baptismal vows every member of the church has solemnly pledged himself to guard the interests of his brethren. All will be tempted to cling to their own cherished plans and ideas, which appear sound to them; but they should watch and pray, and endeavor, to the utmost of their ability, to build up the kingdom of Jesus in the world. Every Christian is required by God, as far as it is in his power, to ward off from his brethren and sisters every influence which will have the least tendency to divide them or to separate their interests from the work for this present time. He should not only have a regard for his own spiritual interests, but should manifest a burden for the souls of those to whom he stands related; and he should, through Christ, have a constraining power over other members of the church. His words and deportment should have an influence to lead them to follow Christ's example in self-denial, self-sacrifice, and love for others.

If there are any in the church who exert an influence contrary to the love and disinterested benevolence which Jesus manifested for us, if they draw apart from their brethren, faithful men should deal with these cases in wisdom, laboring for their souls, yet being careful that their influence shall not leaven others, and that the church shall not be led astray by their disaffection and false reports. Some are filled with self-sufficiency. There are a few who they think are right, but they question and find fault with every act of others. These persons must not be allowed to imperil the interests of the church. In order to raise the moral tone of the church, each should feel it his duty to seek personal spiritual culture, through the practice of strict Bible principles, as in the sight of a holy God.

Let each church member feel that he himself must be right with God, that he must be sanctified through the truth. Then he can represent Christian character to others and can set an example of unselfishness. If each will do this, the church will increase in spirituality and in favor with God.

Every church member should feel under obligation to consecrate his tithe to God. None are to follow the sight of their eyes or the inclination of their selfish hearts and thus rob God. They should not use their means to gratify vanity or for any other selfish indulgence, for in so doing they entangle themselves in Satan's snares. God is the giver of tact, of ability to accumulate wealth, and therefore all is to be laid upon His altar. The requirement is: "Honor the Lord with thy substance." The tendency to covetousness must be constantly restrained, else it will eat into the hearts of men and women, and they will run greedily after gain.

In the wilderness of temptation, Satan, the adversary of souls, presented before Christ the glories of this world and said: "If Thou therefore wilt worship me, all shall be Thine." The Saviour repulsed Satan; but how easily is man seduced by the representations of the great enemy! Many are charmed with the attractions of the world; they serve mammon rather than God, and so lose their souls.

In a little while we are to meet our Lord; and what account shall we have to give Him of the use we have made of our time, our talents of influence, and our possessions? Our joy should be in the work of saving souls. I solemnly inquire of the Healdsburg church: Is God among you of a truth? Says the True Witness: "Thou hast a few names even in Sardis which have not defiled their garments; and they shall walk with Me in white: for they are worthy." Are you of this number? Have you held fast your integrity? As drowning men, have you clung to Jesus, who is your refuge? Are you obeying Him, living for Him, loving Him? Is each member pure and holy and undefiled, one in whose mouth there is no guile? If so, you are most happy; for you are, in the sight of God, "more precious than fine gold; even . . . than the golden wedge of Ophir." While multitudes are devoted to mammon, and serve not the Holy One of Israel, there are a few who have not defiled their garments, but have kept them unspotted from the world; and these few will be a power. This class will have that faith which works by love and purifies the soul. They will exemplify lofty Christian principles. They will seek for personal connection with the Source of light and will endeavor to make constant improvement, cultivating every faculty to its fullest extent. God would have you bring into your life the most unbending uprightness and integrity; this will distinguish you before the world as children of the most high God. Jesus was calm and gentle, not losing His self-command, even when in stormy conflict, amid fiercest elements of opposition.

God says to you who have had great light: "Come up higher." Draw nearer to God and heaven. Go forward. You need faith, an unfeigned love for your brethren, and a deeper interest in them. God has entrusted you with sacred responsibilities. There is a mission field for every member of the church, where he may exert an influence for good.

Our college is not what it should be nor what it will be if our brethren and sisters will feel that it is a sacred trust committed to them. If they will elevate the standard of spirituality in the church, if they will set an example of integrity in all their dealings, if all will cultivate godliness and Christian dignity, then the influence of the college will be wide spread, and a light will go forth from it with rich blessings. I have seen that if the college is properly conducted, many youth will go forth from it to be active laborers in the cause of God. But let all take heed lest in word or action they cast an influence against it or against the truth by an unconsecrated life, by evil surmising, or by evil report; for God will surely mark it against them. The college will always be obliged to struggle against difficulties because some men lack faith and are not controlled by the mind of Christ. If Satan can find persons among us who will watch for evil and speak disparagingly of our institutions, picking up every little unpleasant thing that happens, he is well pleased. He will not cease his efforts to lead persons to depreciate the college because it does not in every particular meet their ideas. If he sees that youth can be benefited he will press every influence into the church to discourage rather than to strengthen and build up.

That these elements are in Healdsburg as well as in other places none will deny; and if Satan did not use them, he would use some other influence to the same end. But "woe to that man by whom the offense cometh;" for it were "better for him that a millstone were hanged about his neck, and he were cast into the sea." God has His means of working. Men cannot always discern them, and by attaching so much importance to their own efforts they not only give the Lord no room to work, but are found working against Him. "Let him that thinketh he standeth take heed lest he fall." "Ye therefore, beloved, seeing ye know these things before, beware lest ye also, being led away with the error of the wicked, fall from your own steadfastness. But grow in grace, and in the knowledge of our Lord and Saviour Jesus Christ."

We are nearing the end of time. Trials will be abundant from without, but let them not come from within the church. Let God's professed people deny self for the truth's sake, for Christ's sake. "For we must all appear before the judgment seat of Christ; that everyone may receive the things done in his body, according to that he hath done, whether it be good or bad." Everyone who truly loves God will have the spirit of Christ and a fervent love for his brethren. The more a person's heart is in communion with God, and the more his affections are centered in Christ, the less will he be disturbed by the roughness and hardships he meets in this life. Those who are growing up to the full stature of men and women in Christ Jesus, will become more and more like Christ in character, rising above the disposition to murmur and be discontented. They will despise to be faultfinders.

The church at this time should have the faith once delivered to the saints, which will enable them to say boldly: "God is mine helper;" "I can do all things through Christ which strengtheneth me." The Lord bids us arise and go forward. Whenever the church at any period have forsaken their sins, and believed and walked in the truth, they have been honored of God. There is in faith and humble obedience a power that the world cannot withstand. The order of God's providence in relation to His people is progression—continual advancement in the perfection of Christian character, in the way of holiness, rising higher and higher in the clear light and knowledge and love of God, to the very close of time. Oh! why are we ever learning only the first principles of the doctrine of Christ?

The Lord has rich blessings for the church if its members will seek earnestly to arouse from this perilous lukewarmness. A religion of vanity, words devoid of vitality, a charter destitute of moral strength,—these are pointed out in the solemn message addressed by the True Witness to the churches, warning them against pride, worldliness, formalism, and self-sufficiency. To him that says, "I am rich, and increased with goods, and have need of nothing," the Lord of heaven declares, Thou "knowest not that thou art wretched, and miserable, and poor, and blind, and naked." But to the lowly, the suffering, the faithful, the patient, who are alive to their weakness and insufficiency, are given words of encouragement: "Behold, I stand at the door, and knock: if any man hear My voice, and open the door, I will come in to him, and will sup with him, and he with Me." The True Witness says to all: "I know thy works." This close scrutiny is over the churches in California. Nothing escapes His searching gaze; their faults and errors, their neglects and failures, their sinful departure from the truth, their declensions and short-comings—all are "opened unto the eyes of Him with whom we have to do."

I hope and pray that you may walk in all lowliness of mind, that you may be a blessing to one another. "Yet a little while, and He that shall come will come, and will not tarry." The bridal lamps must be kept trimmed and burning. Our Lord delays because of His long-suffering to usward, "not willing that any should perish, but that all should come to repent-ance." But when we, with all the redeemed, shall stand upon the sea of glass, with harps of gold and crowns of glory, and before us the immensity of eternity, then we shall see how short was the waiting period of probation. "Blessed are those servants, whom the Lord when He cometh shall find watching."

We are living in an age when all should especially give heed to the injunction of the Saviour: "Watch and pray, that ye enter not into temptation." Let everyone bear in mind that he should be true and loyal to God, believing the truth, growing in grace and in the knowledge of Jesus Christ. The Saviour's invitation is: "Learn of Me; for I am meek and lowly in heart: and ye shall find rest unto your souls." The Lord is willing to help us, to strengthen and bless us; but we must pass through the refining process until all the impurities in our character are burned away. Every member of the church will be subjected to the furnace, not to consume, but to purify.

The Lord has wrought among you, but Satan has also in-truded himself, to bring in fanaticism. There are other evils also to be avoided. Some are in danger of being satisfied with the glimpses they have had of the light and love of God, and so ceasing to advance. Watchfulness and prayer have not been maintained. At the very time when the acclamation is made, "The temple of the Lord, The temple of the Lord, are these," temptations come in, and darkness gathers about the soul—earthliness, selfishness, and self-glorification. There is a necessity for the Lord Himself to communicate His own ideas to the soul. What a thought!—that instead of our poor, earthly, contracted ideas and plans the Lord will communicate to us His own ideas, His own thought, noble, broad, far-reaching, always leading heavenward!

Here is your danger, in failing to press forward "toward the mark for the prize of the high calling of God in Christ Jesus." Has the Lord given you light? Then you are responsible for that light; not merely while its rays are shining upon you, but for all which it has revealed to you in the past. You are to surrender your will to God daily; you are to walk in the light, and to expect more; for the light from the dear Saviour is to shine forth in clearer, more distinct rays amid the moral darkness, increasing in brightness more and more unto the perfect day.

Are all the members of your church seeking to gather fresh manna every morning and evening? Are you seeking divine enlightenment? or are you devising means whereby you can glorify yourselves? Are you, with your whole soul, might, mind, and strength, loving and serving God in blessing others around you by leading them to the Light of the world? Are you satisfied with past blessings? or are you walking as Christ walked, working as He worked, revealing Him to the world in your words and actions? Are you, as obedient children, living a pure and holy life? Christ must be brought into your life. He alone can cure you of envy, of evil surmising against your brethren; He alone can take away from you the self-sufficient spirit that some of you cherish to your own spiritual detriment. Jesus alone can make you feel your weakness, your ignorance, your corrupt nature. He alone can make you pure, refine you, fit you for the mansions of the blessed.

"Through God we shall do valiantly." What an amount of good you can do by being loyal to God and to your brethren, by repressing every unkind thought, every feeling of envy or self-importance! Let your life be filled with the ministry of kindness to others. How soon you may be called to lay off the armor, you know not. Death may claim you suddenly, giving you no time to prepare for your last change, no physical strength or mental power to fix your thoughts on God and make your peace with Him. Some, erelong, will know by experience how vain is the help of man, how worthless is the self-important, self-sufficient righteousness which has satisfied them.

I feel urged by the Spirit of the Lord to tell you that now is your day of privilege, of trust, of blessing. Will you improve it? Are you working for the glory of God, or for selfish interests? Are you keeping before your mind's eye brilliant prospects of worldly success, whereby you may obtain self-gratification and financial gain? If so, you will be most bitterly disappointed. But if you seek to live a pure and holy life, to learn daily in the school of Christ the lessons that He has invited you to learn, to be meek and lowly in heart, then you have a peace which no worldly circumstances can change.

A life in Christ is a life of restfulness. Uneasiness, dissatisfaction, and restlessness reveal the absence of the Saviour. If Jesus is brought into the life, that life will be filled with good and noble works for the Master. You will forget to be self-serving, and will live closer and still closer to the dear Saviour; your character will become Christlike, and all around you will take knowledge that you have been with Jesus and learned of Him. Each one possesses in himself the source of his own happiness or wretchedness. If he will, he may rise above the low, sentimental feeling which makes up the experience of many; but so long as he is self-inflated, the Lord can do nothing for him. Satan will present ambitious projects to daze the senses, but we must ever keep before us "the mark for the prize of the high calling of God in Christ Jesus." Crowd all the good works you possibly can into this life. "They that be wise shall shine as the brightness of the firmament; and they that turn many to righteousness as the stars for ever and ever."

If our lives are filled with holy fragrance, if we honor God by having good thoughts toward others, and doing good deeds to bless others, it matters not whether we live in a cottage or a palace. Circumstances have but little to do with the experiences of the soul. It is the spirit cherished which gives coloring to all our actions. A man at peace with God and his fellow men cannot be made miserable. Envy will not be in his heart; evil surmising will find no room there; hatred cannot exist. The heart in harmony with God is lifted above the annoyances and trials of this life. But a heart where the peace of Christ is not, is unhappy, full of discontent; the person sees defects in everything, and he would bring discord into the most heavenly music. A life of selfishness is a life of evil. Those whose hearts are filled with love of self will store away evil thoughts of their brethren and will talk against God's instrumentalities. Passions kept warm and fierce by Satan's promptings are a bitter fountain, ever sending forth bitter streams to poison the life of others. . . .

Let each one who claims to follow Christ esteem himself less and others more. Press together, press together! In union there is strength and victory; in discord and division there is weakness and defeat. These words have been spoken to me from heaven. As God's ambassador I speak them to you.

Let everyone seek to answer the prayer of Christ: "That they all may be one; as Thou, Father, art in Me, and I in

Thee." Oh, what unity is this! and says Christ: "By this shall all men know that ye are My disciples, if ye have love one to another."

When death claims one of our number, what are our memories of the treatment he has received? Are the pictures upon memory's walls pleasant to reflect upon? Are they memories of kind words spoken, of sympathy given at the right time? Have his brethren turned away the evil surmisings of indiscreet meddlers? Have they vindicated his cause? Have they been faithful to the inspired injunction: "Comfort the feeble-minded, support the weak"? "Behold, thou hast instructed many, and thou hast strengthened the weak hands." "Strengthen ye the weak hands, and confirm the feeble knees. Say to them that are of a fearful heart, Be strong, fear not."

When he with whom we have associated in the church is dead, when we know that his account in the books of heaven is fixed, and that he must meet that record in the judgment, what are the reflections of his brethren as to the course they have pursued toward him? What has been their influence upon him? How clearly now every harsh word, every unadvised act, is called to mind! How differently they would conduct themselves if they had another trial!

The apostle Paul thanked God for the comfort given him in sorrow, saying: "Blessed be . . . the God of all comfort; who comforteth us in all our tribulation, that we may be able to comfort them which are in any trouble, by the comfort wherewith we ourselves are comforted of God." As Paul felt the comfort and warmth of God's love breaking into his soul, he reflected the blessing upon others. Let us so order our conduct that the pictures hung upon the walls of our memory may not be of such a character that we cannot endure to reflect upon them.

After those with whom we associate are dead, there will

never be an opportunity to recall any word spoken to them, or to wipe from the memory any painful impression. Then let us take heed to our ways, that we do not offend God with our lips. Let all coldness and variance be put away. Let the heart melt into tenderness before God, as we recall His merciful dealings with us. Let the Spirit of God, like a holy flame, burn away the rubbish that is piled up at the door of the heart, and let Jesus in; then His love will flow out to others through us, in tender words and thoughts and acts. Then if death parts us from our friends, to meet no more till we stand at the bar of God, we shall not be ashamed to have the record of our words appear.

When death closes the eyes, when the hands are folded upon the silent breast, how quickly feelings of variance change! There is no grudging, no bitterness; slights and wrongs are forgiven, forgotten. How many loving words are spoken of the dead! How many good things in their life are brought to mind! Praise and commendation are now freely expressed; but they fall upon ears that hear not, hearts that feel not. Had these words been spoken when the weary spirit needed them so much, when the ear could hear and the heart could feel, what a pleasant picture would have been left in the memory! How many, as they stand awed and silent beside the dead, recall with shame and sorrow the words and acts that brought sadness to the heart now forever still! Let us now bring all the beauty, love, and kindness we can into our life. Let us be thoughtful, grateful, patient, and forbearing in our intercourse with one another. Let the thoughts and feelings which find expression around the dying and the dead be brought into the daily association with our brethren and sisters in life.

BEHAVIOR IN THE HOUSE OF GOD

To the humble, believing soul, the house of God on earth is the gate of heaven. The song of praise, the prayer, the words spoken by Christ's representatives, are God's appointed agencies to prepare a people for the church above, for that loftier worship into which there can enter nothing that defileth.

From the sacredness which was attached to the earthly sanctuary, Christians may learn how they should regard the place where the Lord meets with His people. There has been a great change, not for the better, but for the worse, in the habits and customs of the people in reference to religious worship. The precious, the sacred, things which connect us with God are fast losing their hold upon our minds and hearts, and are being brought down to the level of common things. The reverence which the people had anciently for the sanctuary where they met with God in sacred service has largely passed away. Nevertheless, God Himself gave the order of His service, exalting it high above everything of a temporal nature.

The house is the sanctuary for the family, and the closet or the grove the most retired place for individual worship; but the church is the sanctuary for the congregation. There should be rules in regard to the time, the place, and the manner of worshiping. Nothing that is sacred, nothing that pertains to the worship of God, should be treated with carelessness or indifference. In order that men may do their best work in showing forth the praises of God, their associations must be such as will keep the sacred distinct from the common, in their minds. Those who have broad ideas, noble thoughts and aspirations, are those who have associations that strengthen all thoughts of divine things. Happy are those who have a sanctuary, be it high or low, in the city or among the rugged mountain caves, in the lowly cabin or in the wilder-

(491)

ness. If it is the best they can secure for the Master, He will hallow the place with His presence, and it will be holy unto the Lord of hosts.

When the worshipers enter the place of meeting, they should do so with decorum, passing quietly to their seats. If there is a stove in the room, it is not proper to crowd about it in an indolent, careless attitude. Common talking, whispering, and laughing should not be permitted in the house of worship, either before or after the service. Ardent, active piety should characterize the worshipers.

If some have to wait a few minutes before the meeting begins, let them maintain a true spirit of devotion by silent meditation, keeping the heart uplifted to God in prayer that the service may be of special benefit to their own hearts and lead to the conviction and conversion of other souls. They should remember that heavenly messengers are in the house. We all lose much sweet communion with God by our restlessness, by not encouraging moments of reflection and prayer. The spiritual condition needs to be often reviewed and the mind and heart drawn toward the Sun of Righteousness. If when the people come into the house of worship, they have genuine reverence for the Lord and bear in mind that they are in His presence, there will be a sweet eloquence in silence. The whispering and laughing and talking which might be without sin in a common business place should find no sanction in the house where God is worshiped. The mind should be prepared to hear the word of God, that it may have due weight and suitably impress the heart.

When the minister enters, it should be with dignified, solemn mien. He should bow down in silent prayer as soon as he steps into the pulpit, and earnestly ask help of God. What an impression this will make! There will be solemnity and awe upon the people. Their minister is communing with God; he is committing himself to God before he dares to stand before the people. Solemnity rests upon all, and angels of God are brought very near. Every one of the congregation, also, who fears God should with bowed head unite in silent prayer with him that God may grace the meeting with His presence and give power to His truth proclaimed from human lips. When the meeting is opened by prayer, every knee should bow in the presence of the Holy One, and every heart should ascend to God in silent devotion. The prayers of faithful worshipers will be heard, and the ministry of the word will prove effectual. The lifeless attitude of the worshipers in the house of God is one great reason why the ministry is not more productive of good. The melody of song, poured forth from many hearts in clear, distinct utterance, is one of God's instrumentalities in the work of saving souls. All the service should be conducted with solemnity and awe, as if in the visible presence of the Master of assemblies.

When the word is spoken, you should remember, brethren, that you are listening to the voice of God through His delegated servant. Listen attentively. Sleep not for one instant, because by this slumber you may lose the very words that you need most—the very words which, if heeded, would save your feet from straying into wrong paths. Satan and his angels are busy creating a paralyzed condition of the senses so that cautions, warnings, and reproofs shall not be heard; or if heard, that they shall not take effect upon the heart and reform the life. Sometimes a little child may so attract the attention of the hearers that the precious seed does not fall into good ground and bring forth fruit. Sometimes young men and women have so little reverence for the house and worship of God that they keep up a continual communication with each other during the sermon. Could these see the angels of God looking upon them and marking their doings, they would be filled with shame, with abhorrence of themselves. God wants attentive hearers. It was while men slept that Satan sowed his tares.

When the benediction is pronounced, all should still be

quiet, as if fearful of losing the peace of Christ. Let all pass out without jostling or loud talking, feeling that they are in the presence of God, that His eye is resting upon them, and that they must act as in His visible presence. Let there be no stopping in the aisles to visit or gossip, thus blocking them up so that others cannot pass out. The precincts of the church should be invested with a sacred reverence. It should not be made a place to meet old friends and visit and introduce common thoughts and worldly business transactions. These should be left outside the church. God and angels have been dishonored by the careless, noisy laughing and shuffling of feet heard in some places.

Parents, elevate the standard of Christianity in the minds of your children; help them to weave Jesus into their experience; teach them to have the highest reverence for the house of God and to understand that when they enter the Lord's house it should be with hearts that are softened and subdued by such thoughts as these: "God is here; this is His house. I must have pure thoughts and the holiest motives. I must have no pride, envy, jealousy, evil surmising, hatred, or deception in my heart, for I am coming into the presence of the holy God. This is the place where God meets with and blesses His people. The high and holy One who inhabiteth eternity looks upon me, searches my heart, and reads the most secret thoughts and acts of my life."

Brethren, will you not devote a little thought to this subject and notice how you conduct yourselves in the house of God and what efforts you are making by precept and example to cultivate reverence in your children? You roll vast responsibilities upon the preacher and hold him accountable for the souls of your children; but you do not sense your own responsibility as parents and as instructors and, like Abraham, command your household after you, that they may keep the statutes of the Lord. Your sons and daughters are corrupted by your own example and lax precepts; and, notwithstanding this lack of domestic training, you expect the minister to counteract your daily work and accomplish the wonderful achievement of training their hearts and lives to virtue and piety. After the minister has done all he can do for the church by faithful, affectionate admonition, patient discipline, and fervent prayer to reclaim and save the soul, yet is not successful, the fathers and mothers often blame him because their children are not converted, when it may be because of their own neglect. The burden rests with the parents; and will they take up the work that God has entrusted to them, and with fidelity perform it? Will they move onward and upward, working in a humble, patient, persevering way to reach the exalted standard themselves and to bring their children up with them? No wonder our churches are feeble and do not have that deep, earnest piety in their borders that they should have. Our present habits and customs, which dishonor God and bring the sacred and heavenly down to the level of the common, are against us. We have a sacred, testing, sanctifying truth; and if our habits and practices are not in accordance with the truth, we are sinners against great light, and are proportionately guilty. It will be far more tolerable for the heathen in the day of God's retributive justice than for us.

A much greater work might be done than we are now doing in reflecting the light of truth. God expects us to bear much fruit. He expects greater zeal and faithfulness, more affectionate and earnest efforts, by the individual members of the church for their neighbors and for those who are out of Christ. Parents must begin their work on a high plane of action. All who name the name of Christ must put on the whole armor and entreat, warn, and seek to win souls from sin. Lead all you can to listen to the truth in the house of God. We must do much more than we are doing to snatch souls from the burning.

It is too true that reverence for the house of God has become almost extinct. Sacred things and places are not discerned; the holy and exalted are not appreciated. Is there not a cause for the want of fervent piety in our families? Is it not because the high standard of religion is left to trail in the dust? God gave rules of order, perfect and exact, to His ancient people. Has His character changed? Is He not the great and mighty God who rules in the heaven of heavens? Would it not be well for us often to read the directions given by God Himself to the Hebrews, that we who have the light of the glorious truth shining upon us may imitate their reverence for the house of God? We have abundant reason to maintain a fervent, devoted spirit in the worship of God. We have reason even to be more thoughtful and reverential in our worship than had the Jews. But an enemy has been at work to destroy our faith in the sacredness of Christian worship.

The place dedicated to God should not be a room where worldly business is transacted. If the children assemble to worship God in a room that is used during the week for a school or a storeroom, they will be more than human if, mingled with their devotional thoughts, they do not also have thoughts of their studies or of things that have happened during the week. The education and training of the youth should be of a character that would exalt sacred things and encourage pure devotion for God in His house. Many who profess to be children of the heavenly King have no true appreciation of the sacredness of eternal things. Nearly all need to be taught how to conduct themselves in the house of God. Parents should not only teach, but command, their children to enter the sanctuary with sobriety and reverence.

The moral taste of the worshipers in God's holy sanctuary must be elevated, refined, sanctified. This matter has been sadly neglected. Its importance has been overlooked, and as the result, disorder and irreverence have become prevalent, and God has been dishonored. When the leaders in the church, ministers and people, father and mothers, have not had elevated views of this matter, what could be expected of the inexperienced children? They are too often found in groups, away from the parents, who should have charge of them. Notwithstanding they are in the presence of God, and His eye is looking upon them, they are light and trifling, they whisper and laugh, are careless, irreverent, and inattentive. They are seldom instructed that the minister is God's ambassador, that the message he brings is one of God's appointed agencies in the salvation of souls, and that to all who have the privilege brought within their reach it will be a savor of life unto life or of death unto death.

The delicate and susceptible minds of the youth obtain their estimate of the labors of God's servants by the way their parents treat the matter. Many heads of families make the service a subject of criticism at home, approving a few things and condemning others. Thus the message of God to men is criticized and questioned, and made a subject of levity. What impressions are thus made upon the young by these careless, irreverent remarks the books of heaven alone will reveal. The children see and understand these things very much quicker than parents are apt to think. Their moral senses receive a wrong bias that time will never fully change. The parents mourn over the hardness of heart in their children and the difficulty in arousing their moral sensibility to answer to the claims of God. But the books of heavenly record trace with unerring pen the true cause. The parents were unconverted. They were not in harmony with heaven or with heaven's work. Their low, common ideas of the sacredness of the ministry and of the sanctuary of God were woven into the education of their children. It is a question whether anyone who has for years been under this blighting influence of home instruction will ever have a sensitive reverence and high regard for God's ministry and the agencies He has appointed for the salvation of souls. These things should be spoken of with reverence, with propriety of language, and with fine susceptibility, that you may reveal to all you associate with that you regard the message from God's servants as a message to you from God Himself.

Parents, be careful what example and what ideas you give your children. Their minds are plastic, and impressions are easily made. In regard to the service of the sanctuary, if the speaker has a blemish, be afraid to mention it. Talk only of the good work he is doing, of the good ideas he presented, which you should heed as coming through God's agent. It may be readily seen why children are so little impressed with the ministry of the word and why they have so little reverence for the house of God. Their education has been defective in this respect. Their parents need daily communion with God. Their own ideas need to be refined and ennobled; their lips need to be touched with a live coal from off the altar; then their habits, their practices at home, will make a good impression on the minds and characters of their children. The standard of religion will be greatly elevated. Such parents will do a great work for God. They will have less earthliness, less sensuality, and more refinement and fidelity at home. Life will be invested with a solemnity of which they have scarcely conceived. Nothing will be made common that pertains to the service and worship of God.

I am often pained as I enter the house where God is worshiped, to see the untidy dress of both men and women. If the heart and character were indicated by the outward apparel, then certainly nothing could be heavenly about them. They have no true idea of the order, the neatness, and the refined deportment that God requires of all who come into His presence to worship Him. What impressions do these things give to unbelievers and to the youth, who are keen to discern and to draw their conclusions?

In the minds of many there are no more sacred thoughts

connected with the house of God than with the most common place. Some will enter the place of worship with their hats on, in soiled, dirty clothes. Such do not realize that they are to meet with God and holy angels. There should be a radical change in this matter all through our churches. Ministers themselves need to elevate their ideas, to have finer susceptibilities in regard to it. It is a feature of the work that has been sadly neglected. Because of the irreverence in attitude, dress, and deportment, and lack of a worshipful frame of mind, God has often turned His face away from those assembled for His worship.

All should be taught to be neat, clean, and orderly in their dress, but not to indulge in that external adorning which is wholly inappropriate for the sanctuary. There should be no display of the apparel; for this encourages irreverence. The attention of the people is often called to this or that fine article of dress, and thus thoughts are intruded that should have no place in the hearts of the worshipers. God is to be the subject of thought, the object of worship; and anything that attracts the mind from the solemn, sacred service is an offense to Him. The parading of bows and ribbons, ruffles and feathers, and gold and silver ornaments is a species of idolatry and is wholly inappropriate for the sacred service of God, where the eye of every worshiper should be single to His glory. All matters of dress should be strictly guarded, following closely the Bible rule. Fashion has been the goddess who has ruled the outside world, and she often insinuates herself into the church. The church should make the word of God her standard, and parents should think intelligently upon this subject. When they see their children inclined to follow worldly fashions, they should, like Abraham, resolutely command their households after them. Instead of uniting them with the world, connect them with God. Let none dishonor God's sanctuary by their showy apparel. God and angels are there. The Holy One of Israel has spoken through His apostle: "Whose adorning let it not be that outward adorning of plaiting the hair, and of wearing of gold, or of putting on of apparel; but let it be the hidden man of the heart, in that which is not corruptible, even the ornament of a meek and quiet spirit, which is in the sight of God of great price."

When a church has been raised up and left uninstructed on these points, the minister has neglected his duty and will have to give an account to God for the impressions he allowed to prevail. Unless correct ideas of true worship and true reverence are impressed upon the people, there will be a growing tendency to place the sacred and eternal on a level with common things, and those professing the truth will be an offense to God and a disgrace to religion. They can never, with their uncultivated ideas, appreciate a pure and holy heaven, and be prepared to join with the worshipers in the heavenly courts above, where all is purity and perfection, where every being has perfect reverence for God and His holiness.

Paul describes the work of God's ambassadors as that by which every man shall be presented perfect in Christ Jesus. Those who embrace the truth of heavenly origin should be refined, ennobled, sanctified through it. It will require much painstaking effort to reach God's standard of true manhood. The irregular stones hewed from the quarry must be chiseled, their rough sides must be polished. This is an age famous for surface work, for easy methods, for boasted holiness aside from the standard of character that God has erected. All short routes, all cutoff tracks, all teaching which fails to exalt the law of God as the standard of religious character, is spurious. Perfection of character is a lifelong work, unattainable by those who are not willing to strive for it in God's appointed way, by slow and toilsome steps. We cannot afford to make any mistake in this matter, but we want day by day to be growing up into Christ, our living Head.

RELIGION AND SCIENTIFIC EDUCATION

Dear Brother and Sister B: You have both been presented before me as in danger spiritually. You were leaving the right path and were placing your feet in a broader road. Sister B was saying many things, in jots and tittles, here a little and there a little, which were as seed sown, and the harvest will surely come. She was encouraging unbelief and telling her husband that the road they had been traveling was altogether too narrow and lowly. She thought that her husband's qualifications were of a high order and should be exercised in a broader and more influential manner. Brother B was of the very same mind; in fact, he had led her into this train of thought. You both held the banner upon which was inscribed, "The commandments of God, and the faith of Jesus;" but as you met in your way with people whom you thought were popular, down came the banner, and you put it behind your backs, saying: "If we let it be known that we are Seventh-day Adventists, then our influence will be at an end, and we shall lose many advantages." I saw the banner of truth trailing behind you. Then the question arose: "Why carry it at all? We can believe that which we see to be truth, but we need not let the educators and students know that we bear this unpopular banner." There were those in your company who were not pleased or satisfied with these suggestions, but they weakly followed your influence in place of letting their light shine by holding aloft their standard. They hid their banners and marched on, fearing to let the light which was given them of heaven shine before all.

I saw one approaching you with firm tread and grieved countenance. He said: "Let no man take your crown." Have you forgotten the humiliation endured by the Son of God in coming to our world, how He suffered abuse, reproach, insult, hatred, mockery, and betrayal, how He endured the shameful trial in the judgment hall after having suffered the superhuman assaults of Satan in the Garden of Gethsemane? Have you forgotten the wild cry from the mob, "Crucify Him, crucify Him," and how He died as a malefactor? Is the servant greater than his Lord? The followers of Jesus will not be popular, but will be like their Master, meek and lowly of heart. You are seeking to climb to the highest seat, but will find yourselves at last in the lowest. If you seek to deal justly, to love mercy, to walk humbly with God, you will be partakers with Christ of His sufferings and sharers with Him of His glory in His kingdom. The Lord has blessed you, but how little have you appreciated His loving-kindness! How little praise He has received from your lips! You may do a good work for the Master, but not with *your* ideas as supreme. You must learn in the school of Christ, else you can never be qualified to enter the higher grade, receive the seal of the living God, enter in through the gates into the city of God, and be crowned with glory, honor, and immortality.

Satan works in many ways where he is not discerned, even through men and women who are in positions of trust. He will suggest to their minds plausible errors of thought and action and speech that will create doubt and work distrust where they think there is assurance of safety. He will work upon dissatisfied elements to put them in active operation. There will be a desire for greatness and honor. Envy will be excited in minds where it is not supposed to exist, and circumstances will not be wanting to call it into action. Doubts will be raised, and flattering promises of gain will be offered if the cross is not made so prominent. Satan will tempt some to think that our faith stands as a barrier to great advancement and bars the way to reaching a high worldly position and being called remarkable men and women.

In his first display of disaffection Satan was very cunning. All he claimed was that he wanted to bring in a better order of things, to make great improvements. He led the holy pair away from God, away from their allegiance to His commandments, on the same point where thousands are tempted today and where thousands fall; that is, by their vain imaginings. True knowledge is divine. Satan insinuated into the minds of our first parents a desire for a speculative knowledge, whereby he declared they would greatly improve their condition; but in order to gain this, they must take a course contrary to God's holy will; for God would not lead them to the greatest heights. It was not God's purpose that they should obtain knowledge that had its foundation in disobedience. This was a broad field into which Satan was seeking to lead Adam and Eve, and it is the same field that he opens for the world today by his temptations.

You were presenting the idea that education must stand as an independent work. This mixing of religious matters and Bible doctrines with scientific education you considered as a drawback in our educational work and as a hindrance in the work of carrying the students to the higher degrees of scientific knowledge.

The great reason why so few of the world's great men and those having a college education are led to obey the commandments of God is that they have separated education from religion, thinking that each should occupy a field by itself. God presented a field large enough to perfect the knowledge of all who should enter it. This knowledge was obtained under divine supervision; it was bound about with the immutable law of Jehovah, and the result would have been perfect blessedness.

God did not create evil, He only made the good, which was like Himself. But Satan would not be content to know the will of God and do it. His curiosity was on the stretch to know that which God had not designed he should know. Evil, sin, and death were not created by God; they are the result of disobedience, which originated in Satan. But the knowledge of evil now in the world was brought in through the cunning of Satan. These are very hard and expensive lessons; but men will learn them, and many will never be convinced that it is bliss to be ignorant of a certain kind of knowledge, which arises from unsatisfied desires and unholy aims. The sons and daughters of Adam are fully as inquisitive and presumptuous as was Eve in seeking forbidden knowledge. They gain an experience, a knowledge, which God never designed they should have, and the result will be, as it was to our first parents, the loss of their Eden home. When will human beings learn that which is demonstrated so thoroughly before them?

The history of the past shows an active, working devil. He can no more be idle than harmless. Satan was found in only one tree to endanger the safety of Adam and Eve. He planned to attract the holy pair to that one tree, that they might do the very thing God had said they should not do—eat of the tree of knowledge. There was no danger to them in approaching any other tree. How plausible his speech! He laid hold of the very arguments which he uses today,—flattery, envy, distrust, questioning, and unbelief. If Satan was so cunning at first, what must he be now after gaining an experience of many thousands of years? Yet God and holy angels, and all those who abide in obedience to all the Lord's expressed will, are wiser than he. The subtlety of Satan will not decrease, but the wisdom given to men through a living connection with the Source of all light and divine knowledge will be proportionate to his arts and wiles.

If men would stand the test which Adam failed to endure, and would, in the strength of Jesus, obey all the requirements of God, because they are righteousness, then they would never become acquainted with the objectionable knowledge. God never designed that men should have this knowledge which comes of disobedience, and which, carried into practice, ends in eternal death. When men almost invariably choose the knowledge that Satan presents; when their taste is so perverted that it craves that knowledge as though it were a fountain of supreme wisdom, then they give evidence that they are separated from God and are in rebellion against Christ.

THE EDUCATION OF OUR CHILDREN

Dear Sister C: If God in His providence has established a school among our own people in _____, and if in place of sending your daughter where she would be in the society and under the influence of those who love the truth, you place her in _____ Seminary, where she will be associated with a worldly class who have no respect for God or His law, I ask you how you expect the Lord will work to counteract the evil influence that must surround her and which you have voluntarily chosen. Will He commission His angels to do the work which He has left for you to do? God does not work in that way; He expects us to follow the light He has given in His word.

When God was about to smite the first-born of Egypt, He commanded the Israelites to gather their children from among the Egyptians into their own dwellings and strike their doorposts with blood, that the destroying angel might see it and pass over their homes. It was the work of parents to gather in their children. This is your work, this is my work, and the work of every mother who believes the truth. The angel is to place a mark upon the forehead of all who are separated from sin and sinners, and the destroying angel will follow, to slay utterly both old and young.

God is not pleased with our inattention and trifling with His blessings placed within our reach. Neither is He pleased to have us place our children in worldly society, because this best suits their tastes and inclinations. If the souls of your children are saved, you must do your work with fidelity. God has not been wholly pleased with your course in regard to worldly associations, and now the peril is revealed. You have also encouraged the reading of storybooks; these, and papers with continued stories, lying upon your table, have educated the taste of your daughter until she is a mental inebriate and needs a stronger power, a firmer will than her own, to control her.

The enemy has had his way with your daughter until his toils have bound her about like bands of steel, and it will require a strong, persevering effort to save her soul. If you have success in this case, there must be no halfway work. The habits of years cannot easily be broken. She should be placed where a steady, firm, abiding influence is constantly exercised. I would advise you to put her in the college at _____; let her have the discipline of the boardinghouse. It is where she ought to have been years ago. The boardinghouse is conducted upon a plan that makes it a good home. This home may not suit the inclinations of some, but it is because they have been educated to false theories, to self-indulgence and self-gratification, and all their habits and customs have been in a wrong channel. But, my dear sister, we are nearing the end of time, and we want now, not to meet the world's tastes and practices, but to meet the mind of God; to see what saith the Scriptures, and then to walk according to the light which God has given us. Our inclinations, our customs and practices, are not to have the preference. God's word is our standard.

So far as your daughter's health is concerned, right habits will secure to her health, while wrong habits will ruin her for this life and for the future, immortal life. There is a heaven to gain, a perdition to shun; and when you in the fear of God have done all that you can do on your part, then you may expect that the Lord will do His part. Decisive action now may save a soul from death.

Your daughter needs a strong influence to counteract that of the society she loves. It will take just as decided efforts to cure her of this mental disorder as it does to cure the drunkard of his craving for liquor. You have a work to do which no other can do for you, and will you fail to do it? Will you in the name of the Lord deal with your child as with a soul in danger of eternal ruin? Were she a girl who loved God, one who could exercise self-control, her peril would not be so great. But she does not love to think of God, of her duty, or of heaven. She persists in having her own way. She does not daily seek strength from God, that she may resist temptation. Will you, then, place her in connection with influences calculated to lead her thoughts away from God, away from the truth, and from righteousness? If so, you place her on the enemy's battleground, with no strength to resist his power or to overcome his temptations.

If she were situated where there were heavenly and divine influences, her moral sensibilities, which are now paralyzed, might be aroused, and her thoughts and purposes, by the blessing of God, might be changed to flow in the heavenly channel, and she be restored. But she is now in danger through inward corruption and outward temptation. Satan is playing the game of life for her soul, and he has every advantage for winning the game.

In my dreams I have been talking to you as I have here written. My heart yearns over you with intensity. Trying as your case now is, do not despond. You need cheerfulness and decision. Seek for help from God. God is your friend. You are never alone. The Bible is your counselor. It is a light to them who are in darkness. Be steadfast in the hour of trial, for you will have new trials to meet. But cling to Jesus, and make Him your strength.

DANGERS OF THE YOUNG

Brother D: My prayers are ascending to God for you, and my love for your soul leads me to write to you again. I feel deeply grieved over your case, not that I look upon you as persecuted, but as a deceived, misguided man, who has not Christ's likeness in his soul, and who is deceiving himself to his certain ruin.

If you had the cause of God at heart you would see that your brethren have done only their duty in their action toward you. You speak of going to _____ and showing that you can be a man. All that is asked of you by those in responsible places at the office is that you show yourself a man just where you are; that you do not degrade yourself by associating with sinners; and that you do not unite with them in evil practices. Cease sympathizing with yourself, and remember the world's Redeemer. Consider the infinite sacrifice He has made in behalf of man, and then think of His disappointment that, after He has made such a sacrifice in man's behalf, man should choose to ally himself with those who hate Christ and righteousness, and should become one with them in the indulgence of perverted appetite, thus bringing eternal ruin to his soul.

But you have heard me say all these things; you have read them, as I have written to you, and yet they have not affected your heart and life. You have set your heart against good and opened it to evil. You have placed yourself in the enemy's way and have had no hold upon God to enable you to resist his temptations. Suppose you do sever all connection with _____ through a revengeful spirit, because your brethren have told you the truth; whom will it injure, you or them? You will grieve them by so doing, but the work will go on just the same. God is raising up workers on every hand; He is not dependent on you or any other man to do His work. If your heart is not pure, if your hands are not clean in His sight, He cannot work with you. He wants you to have truth in your heart and life, interwoven with your character.

I counsel you to humble your heart and confess your wrongs. Consider the solemn charge David gave to Solomon on his dying bed: "I go the way of all the earth: be thou strong therefore, and show thyself a man; and keep the charge of the Lord thy God, to walk in His ways, to keep His statutes, and His commandments, and His judgments, and His testimonies, as it is written in the law of Moses, that thou mayest prosper in all that thou doest, and whithersoever thou turnest thyself." Take this charge to your own heart. Let no one flatter you in wrongdoing. While it is a disgrace to sin, it is no disgrace, but rather an honor, to confess one's sins. Maintain true individuality, and cultivate manly dignity. Put away pride, self-conceit, and false dignity; for these can be maintained only at the most terrible consequences to yourself.

It is not the boisterous song, the merry company, or the stimulating drink that can make you a man in the sight of God, or cheer your heart in sickness and sorrow. True religion alone can be your solace and comfort in trouble. The discipline you received at the office has not been more close and severe than God's word has imposed upon you. Will you call God unjust? Will you tell Him to His face that He is arbitrary because He declares that the wrongdoer shall be separated from His presence?

How plainly the picture is drawn in the word of God of His dealing with the man who accepted His invitation to the wedding, but who did not put on the wedding garment which had been purchased for him, the robe of Christ's righteousness! He thought his own defiled garments good enough to come into the presence of Christ, but he was cast out as one who had insulted his Lord and abused His gracious benevolence.

My brother, your righteousness will not be sufficient. You must put on the robe of Christ's righteousness. You must be like Christ. Consider the severe test that Christ endured in the wilderness of temptation on the point of appetite. He was emaciated by that long abstinence on your account and on mine; He fought and conquered Satan, that He might give us vantage ground, bringing us divine strength to conquer appetite and every unholy passion.

I ask you to look at this matter as it is. When you unite with the despisers of God in drinking beer or wine or stronger drink, imagine Jesus before you, suffering the keenest pangs of hunger that He may break the power of Satan and make it possible for man to conquer in his own behalf. Remember, when, with the godless who reject the truth and refuse salvation, you are lifting the mug of foaming beer, that Jesus is there looking on, even that Jesus whom you claim as your Saviour, in whom your hopes of eternal life are centered. Oh, how can you, how can you be so weak in moral perception as not to see the influence of these things upon yourself and others! You violate the most solemn pledge and then talk of being persecuted!

When those who feel compelled to do something to break the power that Satan is exerting over our youth tell you in sorrow that if you do not change your habits they cannot retain you in connection with the work of God as a translator, how can you stand before them defiantly, without any evidence of sorrow for your course? How does that Saviour who gave His life for you regard your attitude? And yet you think you are persecuted. "For we must all appear before the judgment seat of Christ; that every one may receive the things done in his body, according to that he hath done, whether it be good or bad." When you stand before this grand and awful tribunal, from whose decisions there will be no appeal and where there will be no misinterpretation, no misconception, then you will be silent. You will not have one word to say in vindication of your course. You will stand guilty, condemned, and hopeless, unless you now put way your sins, make diligent work of repentance, and clothe yourself in the robe of Christ's righteousness.

What other course could have been pursued toward you than has been taken? I have the tenderest feelings of pity and love for your soul, but false words of sympathy to sustain you in rebellion and in defiance of those whom God has placed in responsible positions in His work shall never be uttered by me. I have too much regard for you to tell you, as some will surely do, that it will be well with you when you are taking such a course, disgracing your manhood, defacing the moral image of God in your soul, deceiving your own heart, and dishonoring Him who redeemed you with the price of His own blood.

Christ has said: "To him that overcometh will I grant to sit with Me in My throne, even as I also overcame, and am set down with My Father in His throne." Are you overcoming? or are you being overcome by your own lusts and appetites and passions?

In order to be safely trusted with the translation of our most important works, to handle sacred things, ought you not to have the fullest connection with God and complete consecration to His service? Ought you not to be where you can have the holy angels to minister to you, to give you wisdom and knowledge as God gave to Daniel, to inspire you to give the correct ideas, in order that you may do the work of translating correctly? If you choose to open your heart to Satan's suggestions, if you choose the society of those who are the enemies of Christ, do you expect God to work a miracle to keep you from yielding to Satan's power? Evil angels are gathering about your soul, but they are invited guests. They make propositions, and you accept them. Until you have the resolution to obey God's will you cannot have His guidance.

Jesus expects all who claim to be His soldiers to do service for Him. He expects you to recognize the enemy and to resist him, not to invite him to your confidence and thus betray sacred trust. The Lord has placed you in a position where you may be elevated and ennobled, and be constantly gaining fitness for His work. If you do not obtain these qualifications you alone are to blame.

There are three ways in which the Lord reveals His will to us, to guide us, and to fit us to guide others. How may we know His voice from that of a stranger? How shall we distinguish it from the voice of a false shepherd? God reveals His will to us in His word, the Holy Scriptures. His voice is also revealed in His providential workings; and it will be recognized if we do not separate our souls from Him by walking in our own ways, doing according to our own wills, and following the promptings of an unsanctified heart, until the senses have become so confused that eternal things are not discerned, and the voice of Satan is so disguised that it is accepted as the voice of God.

Another way in which God's voice is heard is through the appeals of His Holy Spirit, making impressions upon the heart, which will be wrought out in the character. If you are in doubt upon any subject you must first consult the Scriptures. If you have truly begun the life of faith you have given yourself to the Lord to be wholly His, and He has taken you to mold and fashion according to His purpose, that you may be a vessel unto honor. You should have an earnest desire to be pliable in His hands and to follow whithersoever He may lead you. You are then trusting Him to work out His designs, while at the same time you are cooperating with Him by working out your own salvation with fear and trembling. You, my brother, will find difficulty here because you have not yet learned by experience to know the voice of the Good Shepherd, and this places you in doubt and peril. You ought to be able to distinguish His voice.

THE EXERCISE OF THE WILL

Pure religion has to do with the will. The will is the governing power in the nature of man, bringing all the other faculties under its sway. The will is not the taste or the inclination, but it is the deciding power which works in the children of men unto obedience to God or unto disobedience.

You are a young man of intelligence; you desire to make your life such as will fit you for heaven at last. You are often discouraged at finding yourself weak in moral power, in slavery to doubt, and controlled by the habits and customs of your old life in sin. You find your emotional nature untrue to yourself, to your best resolutions, and to your most solemn pledges. Nothing seems real. Your own instability leads you to doubt the sincerity of those who would do you good. The more you struggle in doubt, the more unreal everything looks to you, until it seems that there is no solid ground for you anywhere. Your promises are like ropes of sand, and you regard in the same unreal light the words and works of those in whom you should trust.

You will be in constant peril until you understand the true force of the will. You may believe and promise all things, but your promises or your faith are of no value until you put your will on the side of faith and action. If you fight the fight of faith with all your will power, you will conquer. Your feelings, your impressions, your emotions, are not to be trusted, for they are not reliable, especially with your perverted ideas; and the knowledge of your broken promises and your forfeited pledges weakens your confidence in yourself, and the faith of others in you.

But you need not despair. You must be determined to believe, although nothing seems true and real to you. I need not tell you it is you yourself that has brought you into this unenviable position. You must win back your confidence in

God and in your brethren. It is for you to yield up your will to the will of Jesus Christ; and as you do this, God will immediately take possession and work in you to will and to do of His good pleasure. Your whole nature will then be brought under the control of the Spirit of Christ, and even your thoughts will be subject to Him. You cannot control your impulses, your emotions, as you may desire, but you can control the will, and you can make an entire change in your life. By yielding up your will to Christ, your life will be hid with Christ in God and allied to the power which is above all principalities and powers. You will have strength from God that will hold you fast to His strength; and a new life, even the life of living faith will be possible to you. But your will must co-operate with God's will, not with the will of associates through whom Satan is constantly working to ensnare and destroy you.

Will you not without delay place yourself in right relation to God? Will you not say, "I will give my will to Jesus, and I will do it now," and from this moment be wholly on the Lord's side? Disregard custom and the strong clamoring of appetite and passion. Give Satan no chance to say: "You are a wretched hypocrite." Close the door so that Satan will not thus accuse and dishearten you. Say, "I will believe, I do believe that God is my helper," and you will find that you are triumphant in God. By steadfastly keeping the will on the Lord's side, every emotion will be brought into captivity to the will of Jesus. You will then find your feet on solid rock. It will take, at times, every particle of will power which you possess; but it is God that is working for you, and you will come forth from the molding process a vessel unto honor.

Talk faith. Keep on God's side of the line. Set not your foot on the enemy's side, and the Lord will be your helper. He will do for you that which it is not possible for you to do for yourself. The result will be that you will become "like a cedar in Lebanon." Your life will be noble, and your works will be wrought in God. There will be in you a power, an earnestness, and a simplicity that will make you a polished instrument in the hands of God.

You need to drink daily at the fountain of truth, that you may understand the secret of pleasure and joy in the Lord. But you must remember that your will is the spring of all your actions. This will, that forms so important a factor in the character of man, was at the Fall given into the control of Satan; and he has ever since been working in man to will and to do of his own pleasure, but to the utter ruin and misery of man. But the infinite sacrifice of God in giving Jesus, His beloved Son, to become a sacrifice for sin, enables Him to say, without violating one principle of His government: "Yield yourself up to Me; give Me that will; take it from the control of Satan, and I will take possession of it; then I can work in you to will and to do of My good pleasure." When He gives you the mind of Christ, your will becomes as His will, and your character is transformed to be like Christ's character. Is it your purpose to do God's will? Do you wish to obey the Scriptures? "If any man will come after Me, let him deny himself, and take up his cross, and follow Me."

There is no such thing as following Christ unless you refuse to gratify inclination and determine to obey God. It is not your feelings, your emotions, that make you a child of God, but the doing of God's will. A life of usefulness is before you if your will becomes God's will. Then you may stand in your God-given manhood, an example of good works. You will then help to maintain rules of discipline instead of helping to break them down. You will then help to maintain order instead of despising it and inciting to irregularity of life by your own course of action. I tell you in the fear of God: I know what you may be if your will is placed on the side of God. "We are laborers together with God." You may be doing your work for time and eternity in such a manner that it will stand the test of the judgment. Will you try? Will you now turn square about? You are the object of Christ's love and intercession. Will you now surrender to God and help those who are placed as sentinels to guard the interests of His work, instead of causing them grief and discouragement?

SUITABLE READING FOR CHILDREN

Dear Brother E: I have just read the *Review and Herald* and have seen your article giving a list of good books for our youth. I was much surprised to read your recommendation of *Uncle Tom's Cabin, Robinson Crusoe,* and such books. You are in danger of becoming somewhat careless in your writing. It would be well to give thought and careful study to whatever is to be immortalized in print. I am really alarmed to see that your spiritual eyesight is not more clear in the matter of selecting and recommending reading for our youth. I know that the recommendation in our papers of such infatuating books as *Uncle Tom's Cabin* will in many minds justify the reading of other books which are nothing but fiction. . . . This recommendation will make taxing work for those who are laboring to persuade the youth to discard fictitious reading. I have repeatedly seen the evil of reading such books as you recommend, and have an article all prepared, cautioning our youth in this very matter.

Be sure, my brother, not to lead away from the searching of the Scriptures. It has been revealed to me that the purchase and sale by our brethren of storybooks such as are commonly circulated in Sunday schools is a snare to our people, especially to our children. It leads them to expend money for that class of reading which fevers the imagination and unfits them for the real duties of practical life. You may be assured that this recommendation of yours will be acted upon. The youth need no such sanction or liberty, for their taste and inclination are all in this direction. But I hope no more such recommendations will appear. You must be getting away from Jesus and His teachings and do not realize it.

It is Satan's work to present to our youth newspaper stories and storybooks that fascinate the senses and thus destroy their relish for the word of God. Do not, my dear brother, throw everything that comes into your mind into the *Review and Herald,* but write guardedly. If the Spirit of Christ moves you to write, then use your pen, feeling the burden of souls, weeping between the porch and the altar, crying: "Spare Thy people, O Lord, and give not Thine heritage to reproach." But if it is only your own feelings and active mind that prompt you to write, then refrain until the Lord's Spirit presses and moves you. Do not think that because you pursue a certain course and do certain things it is an evidence that they are right and that you must present them to others as a rule or guide. It is not best for you to feel at liberty to speak your mind upon such matters as concern the welfare of our youth, recommending books which do not tend to spirituality or piety. If you fancy that such reading will develop firm, unspotted principle you are mistaken. May the Lord help you to move cautiously and humbly, and not throw out misleading statements in the papers; for they will be considered as having been sanctioned by our people. You are putting a burden upon others to counteract the influence of these sentiments.

My brother, your safety is in walking humbly with God. I tremble when I read your many articles, giving counsel and rules for other ministers. It is hardly proper for you to have so much to say in this direction. If you become self-sufficient and self-confident, the Lord will certainly leave you to make some mistake. You need carefully to guard your own soul and to seek a daily, living experience in the things of God. You should keep self out of sight and let Jesus appear. Christ is your strength, your shield; you are a weak, erring man and need to be very cautious, lest you stumble. I entreat you to be on your guard that you do not in word or in deed mar the sacred work of God.

I have felt so thankful for you that you could act a part in this great work. Jesus loves you, and He will work with your efforts if you have a living connection with God. But you must live a life of watchfulness and prayer. Do not become careless. Do not separate from Jesus, but bring Him into your everyday life. Do not make work for yourself and others by careless admissions and counsels; but know that unless Christ is taken into your heart, unless your eye is single to the glory of God, pride will come into your heart, self-esteem will prevail, and you will, ere you are aware, be walking carelessly. "Make straight paths for your feet, lest that which is lame be turned out of the way."

There are many of our youth whom God has endowed with superior capabilities. He has given them the very best of talents; but their powers have been enervated, their minds confused and enfeebled, and for years they have made no growth in grace and in a knowledge of the reasons of our faith, because they have gratified a taste for story reading. They have as much difficulty to control the appetite for such superficial reading as the drunkard has to control his appetite for intoxicating drink. These might today be connected with our publishing houses and be efficient workers to keep books, prepare copy for the press, or to read proof; but their talents have been perverted until they are mental dyspeptics, and consequently are unfitted for a responsible position anywhere. The imagination is diseased. They live an unreal life. They are unfitted for the practical duties of life; and that which is the most sad and discouraging is that they have lost all relish for solid reading. They have become infatuated and charmed with just such food for the mind as the intensely exciting stories contained in *Uncle Tom's Cabin.* That book did good in its day to those who needed an awakening in regard to their false ideas of slavery; but we are standing upon the very borders of the eternal world, where such stories are not needed in the preparation for eternal life.

The only safety for any of us is to be thoroughly converted and to be conversant with the truth as it is revealed in the word of God, that we may be able to give to every man that asks us, a reason of the hope that is in us, with meekness and fear.

The special effort of ministers and of workers all through our ranks for this time should be to turn away the attention of the youth from all exciting stories to the sure word of prophecy. The attention of every soul striving for eternal life should center upon the Bible.

It seems wonderfully strange to me, considering all I have written in regard to the reading of exciting stories, to see a recommendation from your pen to read *Robinson Crusoe, Uncle Tom's Cabin,* and *Aesop's Fables.* My brother, you made a mistake in writing that article. If these books are among those which you have for sale, I beg of you never to offer them again to our youth. It is your duty to call their attention to the Bible; do not become their tempter by offering to them attractive storybooks, which will divert their minds from the study of the Scriptures. We must ourselves be drinking of the water of life, else we will be constantly hewing out for ourselves broken cisterns which can hold no water.

There are a thousand ways and plans that Satan has of creeping in to unsettle the minds of youth; and unless the soul is firmly and fully stayed upon God, and conscientiously guarded upon the very point of keeping the mind employed in searching the Scriptures and becoming grounded in our faith, they will surely be ensnared. We cannot be off guard for a moment. We cannot allow ourselves to move from impulse. We must set a guard about our minds and the minds of our children, that they may not be allured by Satan's temptations.

We are in the great day of atonement, and the sacred work of Christ for the people of God that is going on at the present time in the heavenly sanctuary should be our constant study. We should teach our children what the typical Day of Atonement signified and that it was a special season of great humiliation and confession of sins before God. The antitypical day of atonement is to be of the same character. Everyone who teaches the truth by precept and example will give the trumpet a certain sound. You need ever to cultivate spirituality, because it is not natural for you to be heavenly-minded. The great work is before us of leading the people away from worldly customs and practices, up higher and higher, to spirituality, piety, and earnest work for God. It is your work to proclaim the message of the third angel, to sound the last note of warning to the world. May the Lord bless you with spiritual eyesight. I write this in love, seeing your danger. Please consider these things carefully and prayerfully.

ADVICE TO THE YOUNG

To the students of South Lancaster Academy I would say: "Draw nigh to God, and He will draw nigh to you." Never be ashamed of your faith; never be found on the side of the enemy. "Ye are the light of the world." Your faith is to be revealed as precious truth, truth which all should have and all must have if they are saved. As a people, we are in the minority. We are not popular. Our enemies will be watching us for evil, to betray us and to ruin our souls. They will not appreciate our motives. They will misinterpret our earnest zeal and our intense desire to have others see and understand the truth, that they may do the will of God by obeying all His commandments. But we should fight the good fight of faith, and be found "steadfast, unmovable, always abounding in the work of the Lord."

It is with feelings of inexpressible sadness, and sometimes almost with despair, that I contemplate the condition of the young and see how difficult it is to encourage those to obtain an education to whom I know God has liberally entrusted capabilities. Without education they will be crippled and inefficient in any position. Yet in gaining this education they will be exposed to dangers and temptations. Satan will try to employ their cultivated abilities in his service.

Some employ their powers to evil purposes. The subtle poison of sensuality courses through their veins, and it finds little obstruction in its way. It is fascinating, bewitching. The mind, which, with due regard for moral integrity, is capable of the highest degree of cultivation and literary excellence, is often degraded to administer to lust. Elevated morals and practical godliness have no charms for these deluded souls, and it is almost impossible to bring to bear upon them any influence, either by precept or example, that shall counteract the efforts of Satan to corrupt and ruin their souls. Unless these young men and women are willing to learn, willing to be counseled by those of experience, they will surely be led astray by the wiles of Satan. And unless those who teach them are steadily growing in grace and in a knowledge of the truth, and in real spiritual discernment, they will be in danger, by their example and by advancing erroneous ideas, of unconsciously aiding the enemy in his work, leading souls to regard that as best for them which will bring the least good and be of the least benefit to their souls.

The plans devised and carried out for the education of

our youth are none too broad. They should not have a one-sided education, but all their powers should receive equal attention. Moral philosophy, the study of the Scriptures, and physical training should be combined with the studies usually pursued in schools. Every power—physical, mental, and moral—needs to be trained, disciplined, and developed, that it may render its highest service; for unless all are equally developed, one faculty cannot do its work thoroughly without overtaxing some part of the human machinery.

Much has been said and written in regard to the importance of training the mind for its highest service. This has sometimes led to the opinion that if the intellect is educated to put forth its highest powers, it will strengthen the physical and moral nature, for the development of the whole man. Time and experience have proved this to be an error. We have seen men and women go forth as graduates from college who were in no way qualified to make a proper use of the wonderful physical organism with which God had provided them. The whole body is designed for action, not for inaction. If the physical powers are not taxed equally with the mental, too much strain is brought upon the latter. Unless every part of the human machinery performs its allotted tasks, the mental powers cannot be used to their highest capability for any length of time. Natural powers must be governed by natural laws, and the faculties must be educated to work harmoniously and in accord with these laws. The teachers in our schools can disregard none of these particulars without shirking responsibility. Pride may lead them to seek for a high worldly standard of intellectual attainment, that students may make a brilliant show; but when it comes to solid acquirements,—those which are essential to fit men and women for any and every emergency in practical life,—such students are only partially prepared to make life a success. Their defective education often leads to failure in whatever branch of business they undertake.

Gymnasium exercises may in some instances be an advantage. They were brought in to supply the want of useful physical training, and have become popular with educational institutions, but they are not without drawbacks. Unless carefully regulated, they are productive of more harm than good. Some have suffered lifelong physical injury through these gymnasium sports. The manual training connected with our schools, if rightly conducted, will largely take the place of the gymnasium.

Teachers should give far more attention to the physical, mental, and moral influences in our schools. Although the study of the sciences may carry the students to high literary attainments, it does not give a full, perfect education. When special attention is given to the thorough development of every physical and moral power which God has given, then students will not leave our colleges calling themselves educated while they are ignorant of that knowledge which they must have for practical life and for the fullest development of character.

My heart aches as I see these deficiencies; for the result must be loss of health, a lack of care-taking ability, and a want of adaptation to that kind of labor which is most essential to success in life. The newspapers abound in sensational records of frauds and embezzlements, of misery in families, husbands eloping with other men's wives, and wives eloping with other women's husbands—all because these parties were not trained to habits of industry and never learned how to economize time or to employ their faculties in the best way to make a happy home.

Would that I could arouse every teacher in our land on this subject. There is a work for them to do to broaden and elevate their educational work. There is a period of time just before us when the condition of the world will become desperate, when that true religion which yields obedience to a "Thus saith the Lord" will become almost extinct. Our youth should be taught that wicked deeds are not forgotten or overlooked because God does not immediately punish the perpetrators with extreme indignation. God keeps a reckoning with the nations. Through every century of this world's history evil workers have been treasuring up wrath against the day of wrath; and when the time fully comes that iniquity shall have reached the stated boundary of God's mercy, His forbearance will cease. When the accumulated figures in heaven's record books shall mark the sum of transgression complete, wrath will come, unmixed with mercy, and then it will be seen what a tremendous thing it is to have worn out the divine patience. This crisis will be reached when the nations shall unite in making void God's law.

The days will come when the righteous will be stirred to zeal for God because of the abounding iniquity. None but divine power can stay the arrogance of Satan united with evil men; but in the hour of the church's greatest danger most fervent prayer will be offered in her behalf by the faithful remnant, and God will hear and answer at the very time when the guilt of the transgressor has reached its height. He will "avenge His own elect, which cry day and night unto Him, though He bear long with them." They will be jealous for the honor of God. They will be zealous in prayer, and their faith will grow strong.

There is too little zeal among the students. They should make more earnest efforts. It requires much study to know how to study. Each student must cultivate the habit of industry. He should see that no second-class work comes forth from his hand. He should take to himself the words Paul addressed to Timothy: "Give attendance to reading, to exhortation, to doctrine. Neglect not the gift that is in thee, which was given thee by prophecy, with the laying on of the hands of the presbytery. Meditate upon these things; give thyself wholly to them; that thy profiting may appear to all. Take heed unto thyself, and unto the doctrine; continue in them: for in doing this thou shalt both save thyself, and them that hear thee."

The duty of old and young must be set forth in simple, positive language because our lot is cast in perilous times when it seems that truth must be overborne by falsehood and satanic delusions. In the time of testing and trial the shield of Omnipotence will be spread over those whom God has made the depositaries of His law. When legislators shall abjure the principles of Protestantism, so as to give countenance and the right hand of fellowship to Romanism, then God will interpose in a special manner in behalf of His own honor and the salvation of His people.

The principles necessary for our youth to cultivate must be kept before them in their daily education, that when the decree shall go forth requiring all to worship the beast and his image, they may make the right decisions, and have strength to declare, without wavering, their confidence in the commandments of God and the faith of Jesus, even at the very time when the law of God is made void by the religious world. Those who waver now and are tempted to follow in the wake of apostates who have departed from the faith, "giving heed to seducing spirits, and doctrines of devils," will surely be found on the side of those who make void the law of God, unless they repent and plant their feet firmly upon the faith once delivered to the saints.

If we are living amid those fearful perils described in the word of God, should we not be awake to the realities of the situation? Why keep so silent? Why make of the least importance the things that are of the greatest interest to every one of us? The Bible should be our dearest treasure and should be earnestly studied and zealously taught to others. How can this marvelous indifference continue upon those who have had light and knowledge?

Prophecy and history should form a part of the studies in our schools, and all who accept positions as educators should prize more and more the revealed will of God. They should in simplicity, instruct the students. They should unfold the

Scriptures and show by their own life and character the preciousness of Bible religion and the beauty of holiness; but never, for one moment, let the impression be left upon anyone that it would be for his profit to hide his faith and doctrines from the unbelieving people of the world, fearing that he might not be so highly honored if his principles were known.

It is no time to be ashamed of our faith. We are a spectacle to the world, to angels, and to men. The whole universe is looking with inexpressible interest to see the closing work of the great controversy between Christ and Satan. At such a time as this, just as the great work of judging the living is to begin, shall we allow unsanctified ambition to take possession of the heart? What can be of any worth to us now except to be found loyal and true to the God of heaven? What is there of any real value in this world when we are on the very borders of the eternal world? What education can we give to the students in our schools that is so necessary as a knowledge of "What saith the Scripture"?

EXAMPLES OF HEROIC FIDELITY TO GOD

Joseph, when honored by the Egyptians, did not conceal his loyalty to God.

Elijah, amid the general apostasy, did not seek to hide the fact that he served the God of heaven. Baal's prophets numbered four hundred and fifty, his priests, four hundred, and his worshipers were thousands; yet Elijah did not try to make it appear that he was on the popular side. He grandly stood alone. The mountain was covered with people full of eager expectation. The king came in great pomp, and the idolaters, confident of triumph, shouted his welcome. But God had been greatly dishonored. One man, and only one man, appeared to vindicate the honor of God. With clear, trumpetlike tones Elijah addressed the vast multitude: "How long halt ye between two opinions? if the Lord be God, follow Him: but if

Baal, then follow him." The result was that the Lord God, who ruleth in the heavens, was vindicated, and the Baal worshipers were slain. Where are the Elijahs of today?

Daniel's history is a remarkable one. He carried out his faith and principles against great opposition. He was condemned to death because he would not abate one jot of his allegiance to God even in the face of the king's decree. It might, at this day, be called overrighteousness to go, as was his wont, three times a day and kneel before the open window for prayer while he knew that prying eyes were observing him and that his enemies were ready to accuse him of disloyalty to the king; but Daniel would allow no earthly power to come in between him and his God, even with the prospect of death in the den of lions. Although God did not prevent Daniel from being cast into a den of lions, an angel went in with him and closed their mouths, so that no harm befell him; and in the morning, when the king called him, he responded: "My God hath sent His angel, and hath shut the lions' mouths, that they have not hurt me: forasmuch as before Him innocency was found in me; and also before thee, O king, have I done no hurt." He was a noble, steadfast servant of God.

Nothing is gained by cowardice or by fearing to let it be known that we are God's commandment-keeping people. Hiding our light, as if ashamed of our faith, will result only in disaster. God will leave us to our own weakness. May the Lord forbid that we should refuse to let our light shine forth in any place to which He may call us. If we venture to go forth of ourselves, following our own ideas, our own plans, and leave Jesus behind, we need not expect to gain fortitude, courage, or spiritual strength. God has had moral heroes, and He has them now,—those who are not ashamed of being His peculiar people. Their wills and plans are all subordinate to the law of God. The love of Jesus has led them not to count their lives dear unto themselves. Their work has been to catch the light from the word of God and to let it shine forth in clear, steady rays to the world. "Fidelity to God" is their motto.

AN EDUCATED MINISTRY

The merchant, the carpenter, the farmer, and the lawyer all have to learn their trade or profession. At first, for want of knowledge, they do imperfect work; but as they continue patiently at their vocations they become masters of their several callings. Without close application of mind and heart, and all the powers of the being, the minister will prove a failure. He may be a preacher, but he must also be fitted to act as a pastor. Study must never cease; it must be continued all through the period of his labor, no matter how well qualified for the labor he may think himself to be.

The times demand an intelligent, educated ministry, not novices. False doctrines are being multiplied. The world is becoming educated to a high standard of literary attainment; and sin, unbelief, and infidelity are becoming more bold and defiant, as intellectual knowledge and acuteness are acquired. This state of things calls for the use of every power of the intellect; for it is keen minds, under the control of Satan, that the minister will have to meet. He should be well balanced by religious principles, growing in grace and in the knowledge of our Lord Jesus Christ. Too much haphazard work has been done, and minds have not been exercised to their fullest capacity. Our ministers will have to defend the truth against base apostates, as well as to measure Scripture evidence with those who advocate specious errors. Truth must be placed in contrast with bold assertions. Our ministers must be men who are wholly consecrated to God, men of no mean culture; but their minds must be all aglow with religious fervor, gathering divine rays of light from heaven and flashing them amid the darkness that covers the earth and the gross darkness that surrounds the people.

Vice and crime, and iniquity of all kinds, are steadily on the increase. The penetrating power of Bible truth must show the contrast between truth and error. A higher grade of preparation is required in order to do good service for the Master. But if the minister leans upon the knowledge he acquires, and does not feel the great necessity of divine enlightenment daily, the education gained is only a stumbling block to sinners. We want the God of all wisdom to be brought into all our labor, into all our experiences; then every iota of knowledge obtained is a power for good and will aid in developing capacity and Christlike earnestness. This is religion.

WORLDLY-MINDEDNESS

Dear Brother F: It is time that we were closely examining our hearts to see whether or not we are in the faith and in the love of God. If there is not an awakening among us who have had so great light and so many privileges, we shall sink to ruin, and our fate will be worse than that of Chorazin and Bethsaida; "for," as Christ said of those cities, "if the mighty works, which were done in you, had been done in Tyre and Sidon, they would have repented long ago in sackcloth and ashes."

It is high time that you were deeply in earnest for your own soul and for the souls of your children. Your calling in Christ requires this. My soul is weighed down with grief, my heart is sick and sad, as I contemplate your condition; for I know that unless you are a transformed man, your anchorage will be continually shifting. Oh, "seek ye the Lord while He may be found, call ye upon Him while He is near." I entreat of you to humble your heart before God and never, never give over the effort till you are a different man. I feel a deep interest in your spiritual condition and want to see you striving earnestly for your own salvation and for that of your dear children, who I know are managed very much as Eli managed his children. Let all your influence be on the Lord's side. Let your children see that you are not a creature of impulse, but a man of unwavering principle. They will copy the pattern you give them. Until I see a change in you for the better I shall continue to plead with you and exhort you.

We are nearing the close of time. We want not only to teach present truth in the pulpit, but to live it out of the pulpit. Examine closely the foundation of your hope of salvation. While you stand in the position of a herald of truth, a watchman upon the walls of Zion, you cannot have your interest interwoven with mining or real-estate business and at the same time do effectually the sacred work committed to your hands. Where the souls of men are at stake, where eternal things are involved, the interest cannot safely be divided. This is especially so in your case. While engaged in this business, you have not been cultivating heartfelt piety. You have had a feverish desire to obtain means. You have talked to many about the financial advantages to be gained by investing in lands in _____. Again and again you have been engaged in picturing the advantages of these enterprises; and this while you were an ordained minister of Christ, pledged to give your soul, body, and spirit to the work of the salvation of souls. At the same time you were receiving money from the treasury to support yourself and your family. Your talk was calculated to draw the attention and money of our people away from our institutions and from the business of promoting the Redeemer's kingdom on the earth. Its tendency was to beget in them a desire to invest their means where you assured them that it would be doubled in a short time, and to flatter them with the prospect that they could help the cause a great deal more by so doing. You may not knowingly have advised them to withdraw their means from the cause of God; but some had no money to handle except that invested in our institutions, and it has been withdrawn from them to invest according to your suggestions.

We are in a certain sense our brother's keeper. We are individually related to souls who may, through the merits of Jesus Christ, seek for glory, honor, and immortality. Their purity, sincerity, zeal, consistency, and piety are affected by our words, our works, our deportment, our prayers, and our faithful discharge of duty. Christ said to His disciples: "Ye are the light of the world." The ministers of Jesus Christ must teach, both in the church and to individuals, the fact that a profession of faith, even by Seventh-day Adventists, unless it proceeds from heartfelt piety, is powerless for good. Religious light is to shine forth from the church, and especially from the ministers, in clear, steady rays. It is not to flame up on special occasions, and then grow dim, and flicker, as if about to go out. The excellence of Jesus Christ will ever shine in the character of true believers, and they will adorn the doctrine of our Saviour. Thus the excellency and the power of the gospel are revealed. Each member of the church is required to be in living connection with the Source of all light, and to be a spiritual worker, doing his part by good works to reflect light to the world.

Especially should the minister keep himself from every worldly entanglement and bind himself to the Source of all power, that he may represent correctly what it means to be a Christian. He should cut loose from everything that would in any way divert his mind from God and the great work for this time. Christ expects him, as His employed servant, to be like Himself in mind, in thought, in word, in action. He expects every man who opens the Scriptures to others to work carefully and intelligently, not exercising his powers unwisely, in a way to injure or overtask them, but so that he may be fitted to do good work for the Lord. Every soul is called into active labor in some one of the various departments of the work, and the Shepherd will lead and guide His flock.

The tongue of the minister is not to be employed in telling men the best way to bury their means in the earth; he should tell them how to invest safely in the bank of heaven. May the Lord impart to you spiritual discernment, is my prayer; for you will surely make shipwreck of faith unless you get into a different condition spiritually. You need the converting power of God, and unless you are changed you will surely let go your hold of the truth. But although you should gain the whole world, it would be a poor return for the loss of your soul. May the Lord help you, my brother, to come speedily to your senses and move like a man who has a well-balanced mind. May you take up your work with heart and lips sanctified, and walk humbly with your God.

PRACTICAL GODLINESS

Dear Brethren and Sisters at Oakland: My mind is drawn out to write to you. Again and again I find myself talking to you in my dreams, and in every case you are in trouble. But whatever comes, let it not enfeeble your moral courage and cause your religion to degenerate into a heartless form. The loving Jesus is ready to bless abundantly; but we need to obtain an experience in faith, in earnest prayer, and in rejoicing in the love of God. Shall any of us be weighed in the balances and be found wanting? We must watch ourselves, watch the least unholy promptings of our nature, lest we become traitors to the high responsibilities God has bestowed upon us as His human agencies.

We must study the warnings and corrections He has given His people in past ages. We do not lack light. We know what works we should avoid and what requirements He has given us to observe; so if we do not seek to know and do that which is right, it is because wrongdoing suits the carnal heart better than rightdoing.

There will always be faithless ones, who wait to be carried forward by the faith of others. They have not an experimental knowledge of the truth and consequently have not felt its sanctifying power on their own souls. It should be the work of every member of the church quietly and diligently to search his own heart and see if his life and character are in harmony with God's great standard of righteousness.

The Lord has done great things for you in California, particularly in Oakland; but there is much more that He would be well pleased to do if you would make your works correspond with your faith. God never honors unbelief with rich blessings. Review what God has done, and then know that it is only the beginning of what He is willing to do.

We must place a higher value than we have upon the Scriptures, for therein is the revealed will of God to men. It is not enough merely to assent to the truthfulness of God's word, but we must search the Scriptures to learn what they contain. Do we receive the Bible as "the oracle of God"? It is as really a divine communication as though its words came to us in an audible voice. We do not know its preciousness because we do not obey its instructions.

There are evil angels at work all around us, but because we do not discern their presence with our natural vision we do not consider as we should the reality of their existence as set forth in the word of God. If there was nothing in the Scriptures hard to be understood, man, in searching its pages, would become lifted up in pride and self-sufficiency. It is never best for one to think that he understands every phase of truth, for he does not. Then let no man flatter himself that he has a correct understanding of all portions of Scripture and feel it his duty to make everybody else understand them just as he does. Let intellectual pride be banished. I lift my voice in warning against every species of spiritual pride. There is an abundance of it in the church today.

When the truth we now cherish was first seen to be Bible truth, how very strange it appeared, and how strong was the opposition we had to meet in presenting it to the people for the first time; but how earnest and sincere were the obedient, truth-loving laborers! We were indeed a peculiar people. We were few in numbers, without wealth, without worldly wisdom or worldly honors; and yet we believed God and were strong and successful, a terror to evildoers. Our love for one another was steadfast, it was not easily shaken. Then the power of God was manifested among us, the sick were healed, and there was much calm, sweet, holy joy. But while the light has continued to increase, the church has not advanced proportionately. The fine gold has gradually become dim, and deadness and formality have come in to cripple the energies of the church. Their abundant privileges and opportunities have not led God's people onward and upward to purity and holiness. A faithful improvement of the talents God has entrusted to them would greatly increase those talents. Where much is given, much will be required. Those only who faithfully accept and appreciate the light God has given us, and who take a high, noble stand in self-denial and self-sacrifice, will be channels of light to the world. Those who do not advance will retrograde, even on the very borders of the heavenly Canaan. It has been revealed to me that our faith and our works in no way correspond to the light of truth bestowed. We must not have a halfhearted faith, but that perfect faith which works by love and purifies the soul. God calls upon you in California to come into close relationship with Him.

One point will have to be guarded, and that is individual independence. As soldiers in Christ's army, there should be concert of action in the various departments of the work. No one has the right to start out on his own responsibility and advance ideas in our papers on Bible doctrines when it is known that others among us hold different opinions on the subject and that it will create controversy. The first-day Adventists have done this. Each has followed his own independent judgment and sought to present original ideas, until there is no concerted action among them, except, perhaps, in opposing Seventh-day Adventists. We should not follow their example. Each laborer should act with reference to the others. Followers of Jesus Christ will not act independently one of another. Our strength must be in God, and it must be husbanded, to be put forth in noble, concentrated action. It must not be wasted in meaningless movements.

In union there is strength. There should be union between our publishing houses and our other institutions. If this unity existed, they would be a power. No strife or variance should exist among the workers. The work is one, superintended by one Leader. Occasional and spasmodic efforts have done harm. However energetic they may be, they are of little value; for the reaction will surely come. We must cultivate a steady perseverance, continually searching to know and do God's will.

We should know what we must do to be saved. We should not, my brethren and sisters, float along with the popular current. Our present work is to come out from the world and be separate. This is the only way we can walk with God, as did Enoch. Divine influences were constantly working with his human efforts. Like him, we are called upon to have a strong, living, working faith, and this is the only way we can be laborers together with God. We must meet the conditions laid down in the word of God or die in our sins. We must know what moral changes are essential to be made in our characters, through the grace of Christ, in order to be fitted for the mansions above. I tell you in the fear of God: We are in danger of living like the Jews—destitute of the love of God and ignorant of His power, while the blazing light of truth is shining all around us.

Ten thousand times ten thousand may profess to obey the law and the gospel, and yet be living in transgression. Men may present in a clear manner the claims of truth upon others and yet their own hearts be carnal. Sin may be loved and practiced in secret. The truth of God may be no truth to them, because their hearts have not been sanctified by it. The love of the Saviour may exercise no constraining power over their base passions. We know by the history of the past that men may stand in sacred positions and yet handle the truth of God deceitfully. They cannot lift up holy hands to God, "without wrath and doubting." This is because God has no control over their minds. The truth was never stamped upon their hearts. "With the heart man believeth unto righteousness." "Thou shalt love the Lord thy God with all thy heart, and with all thy soul, and with all thy mind, and with all thy strength." Are you doing this? Many are not, and never have done it. Their conversion has been only superficial.

"If ye then," says the apostle, "be risen with Christ, seek those things which are above, where Christ sitteth on the right hand of God. Set your affection on things above, not on things on the earth." The heart is the citadel of the man. From it are the issues of life or death. Until the heart is purified, a person is unfit to have any part in the fellowship of the saints. Does not the Heart Searcher know who are lingering in sin, regardless of their souls? Has there not been a witness to the most secret things in the life of everyone? I was compelled to hear the words spoken by some men to women and girls—words of flattery, words that would deceive and infatuate. Satan uses all these means to destroy souls. Some of you may thus have been his agents; and if so, you will have to meet these things in the judgment. The angel said of this class: "Their hearts have never been given to God. Christ is not in them. Truth is not there. Its place is occupied by sin, deception, and falsehood. The word of God is not believed and acted upon."

The present activity of Satan in working upon hearts, and upon churches and nations, should startle every student of prophecy. The end is near. Let our churches arise. Let the converting power of God be experienced in the hearts of the individual members, and then we shall see the deep movings of the Spirit of God. The forgiveness of sins is not the sole result of the death of Jesus. He made the infinite sacrifice, not only that sin might be removed, but that human nature might be restored, rebeautified, reconstructed from its ruins, and made fit for the presence of God.

We should show our faith by our works. A greater anxiety should be manifested to have a large measure of the spirit of Christ; for in this will be the strength of the church. It is Satan who is striving to have God's children draw apart. Love, oh, how little love we have—love for God and for one another! The word and spirit of truth, dwelling in our hearts, will separate us from the world. The immutable principles of truth and love will bind heart to heart, and the strength of the union will be according to the measure of grace and truth enjoyed. Well would it be for us each to hold up the mirror, God's royal law, and see in it the reflection of His own character. Let us be careful not to neglect the danger signals and the warnings given in His word. Unless heed is given to these warnings, and defects of character are overcome, these defects will overcome those who possess them, and they will fall into error, apostasy, and open sin. The mind that is not elevated to the highest standard will in time lose its power to retain that which it had once gained. "Let him that thinketh he standeth take heed lest he fall." "Ye therefore, beloved, seeing ye know these things before, beware lest ye also, being led away with the error of the wicked, fall from your own steadfastness. But grow in grace, and in the knowledge of our Lord and Saviour Jesus Christ."

God has selected a people in these last days whom He has made the depositaries of His law, and this people will ever have disagreeable tasks to perform. "I know thy works, and thy labor, and thy patience, and how thou canst not bear them which are evil: and thou hast tried them which say they are apostles, and are not, and hast found them liars: and hast borne, and hast patience, and for My name's sake hast labored, and hast not fainted." It will require much diligence and a continual struggle to keep evil out of our churches. There must be rigid, impartial discipline exercised; for some who have a semblance of religion will seek to undermine the faith of others and will privily work to exalt themselves.

The Lord Jesus, on the Mount of Olives, plainly stated that "because iniquity shall abound, the love of many shall wax cold." He speaks of a class who have fallen from a high state of spirituality. Let such utterances as these come home with solemn, searching power to our hearts. Where is the fervor, the devotion to God, that corresponds to the greatness of the truth which we claim to believe? The love of the world, the love of some darling sin, has weaned the heart from the love of prayer and of meditation on sacred things. A formal round of religious services is kept up; but where is the love of Jesus? Spirituality is dying. Is this torpor, this mournful deterioration, to be perpetuated? Is the lamp of truth to flicker and go out in darkness because it is not replenished by the oil of grace?

I wish that every minister and every one of our workers could see this matter as it has been presented to me. Self-esteem and self-sufficiency are killing spiritual life. Self is lifted up; self is talked about. Oh, that self might die! "I die daily," said the apostle Paul. When this proud, boasting self-sufficiency and this complacent self-righteousness permeate the soul, there is no room for Jesus. He is given an inferior place, while self swells into importance and fills the whole temple of the soul. This is the reason why the Lord can do so little for us. Should He work with our efforts, the instrument would appropriate all the glory to his own smartness, his wisdom, his ability, and he would congratulate himself, as did the Pharisee: "I fast twice in the week, I give tithes of all that I possess." When self shall be hidden in Christ, it will not be brought to the surface so frequently. Shall we meet the mind of the Spirit of God? Shall we dwell more upon practical godliness, and far less upon mechanical arrangements?

The servants of Christ should live as in His sight and as in the sight of angels. They should seek to understand the requirements of our time and prepare to meet them. Satan is constantly attacking us in new and untried ways, and why should the officers in God's army be inefficient? Why should they leave any faculty of their nature uncultivated? There is a great work to be done, and if there is any want of harmonious action in doing it, it is because of self-love and self-esteem. It is only when we are careful to carry out the Master's orders without leaving our stamp and identity upon the work that we work efficiently and harmoniously. "Press together," said the angel, "press together."

I urge upon you who minister in sacred things to dwell more upon practical religion. How rarely are seen the tender conscience, and true, heartfelt sorrow of soul and conviction of sin. It is because there are no deep movings of the Spirit of God among us. Our Saviour is the ladder which Jacob saw, whose base rested on the earth and whose topmost rounds reached the highest heavens. This shows the appointed method of salvation. If any of us are finally saved, it will be by clinging to Jesus as to the rounds of a ladder. To the believer, Christ is made wisdom and righteousness, sanctification and redemption. Let no one imagine that it is an easy thing to overcome the enemy and that he can be borne aloft to an incorruptible inheritance without effort on his part. To look back is to grow dizzy; to let go the hold is to perish. Few appreciate the importance of striving constantly to overcome. They relax their diligence and, as a result, become selfish and self-indulgent. Spiritual vigilance is not thought to be essential. Earnestness in human effort is not brought into the Christian life.

There will be some terrible falls by those who think they stand firm because they have the truth, but they have it not as it is in Jesus. A moment's carelessness may plunge a soul into irretrievable ruin. One sin leads to the second, and the second prepares the way for the third, and so on. We must, as faithful messengers of God, plead with Him constantly to be kept by His power. If we swerve a single inch from duty, we are in danger of following on in a course of sin that will end in perdition. There is hope for every one of us, but only in one way, and that is by binding ourselves to Christ, and exerting every energy to attain to the perfection of His character.

That religion which makes of sin a light matter, dwelling upon the love of God to the sinner regardless of his actions, only encourages the sinner to believe that God will receive him while he continues in that which he knows to be sin. This is what some are doing who profess to believe present truth. The truth is kept apart from the life, and that is the reason it has no power to convict and convert the soul.

God has shown me that the truth as it is in Jesus has never been brought into the lives of some in California. They do not have the religion of the Bible. They have never been converted; and unless their hearts are sanctified through the truth which they have accepted, they will be bound up with the tares; for they bear no clusters of precious fruit to show that they are branches of the living Vine.

"Seek ye the Lord while He may be found, call ye upon Him while He is near: let the wicked forsake his way, and the unrighteous man his thoughts: and let him return unto the Lord, and He will have mercy upon him; and to our God, for He will abundantly pardon." The lives of many show that they have no living connection with God. They are drifting into the channel of the world. They have, in reality, no part or lot with Christ. They love amusement and are filled with selfish ideas, plans, hopes, and ambitions. They serve the enemy under the pretense of serving God. They are in bondage to a taskmaster, and this bondage they choose, making themselves willing slaves of Satan.

The false idea entertained by many, that the restraining of children is an injury, is ruining thousands upon thousands. Satan will surely take possession of the children if you are not on your guard. Do not encourage their association with the ungodly. Draw them away. Come out from among such yourselves, and show them that you are on the Lord's side.

Will those who claim to be the children of the Most High elevate the standard, not simply while assembled in your meeting, but as long as time shall last? Will you not be on the Lord's side and serve Him with full purpose of heart? If you do as did the children of Israel in forsaking God's express requirements you will surely receive of His judgments; but if you put away sin and exercise living faith, the richest of heaven's blessings will be yours.

Basel, Switzerland, March 1, 1887.

"YOUR REASONABLE SERVICE"

"Present your bodies a living sacrifice, holy, acceptable unto God, which is your reasonable service."

In the time of ancient Israel the priests critically examined every offering that was brought as a sacrifice. If any defect was discovered, the animal was refused; for the Lord had commanded that the offering should be "without blemish." We are to present our bodies a living sacrifice to God, and should we not seek to make the offering as perfect as possible? God has given us every instruction necessary for our physical, mental, and moral well-being; and it is the duty of every one of us to bring our habits of life into conformity with the divine standard in every particular. Will the Lord be pleased with anything less than the best we can offer? "Thou shalt love the Lord thy God with all thy heart." If you do love Him with all your heart you will desire to give Him the best service of your life, and you will seek to bring every power of your being into harmony with the laws that will promote your ability to do His will.

Every faculty of our being was given us that we might render acceptable service to our Maker. When, through sin, we perverted the gifts of God and sold our powers to the prince of darkness, Christ paid a ransom for us, even His own precious blood. "He died for all, that they which live should not henceforth live unto themselves, but unto Him which died for them." You are not to follow the customs of the world. "Be not conformed to this world: but be ye transformed by the renewing of your mind."

WORLDLY INFLUENCES

Dear Sister G: My heart is drawn out in love and sympathy for you. The present state of things in your family is the sure result of following out your mistaken ideas, and the end is not yet. You have not seen the danger of associating so freely with your relatives. They have had a far greater influence over you and yours than you have had over them. Their being your relatives makes them no less a hindrance to your spiritual welfare and no less transgressors of God's holy law. Their course is fully as offensive to God as that of any others who refuse light and truth, and will not listen to any evidence in its favor. Injurious impressions have been made upon your mind and have influenced your course of action. God has made every provision to bring salvation within our reach, but He will not thrust it upon us against our will. He has laid down conditions in His word, and we should diligently, interestedly, with heart and mind, set about the task of learning these conditions, lest we make some mistake and fail to secure our title to the mansions above.

We cannot serve God and the world at the same time. We must not center our affections on worldly relatives, who have no desire to learn the truth. We may seek in every way, while associated with them, to let our light shine; but our words, our deportment, our customs and practices, should not in any sense be molded by their ideas and customs. We are to show forth the truth in all our intercourse with them. If we cannot do this, the less association we have with them, the better it will be for our spirituality. If we place ourselves among associates whose influence has a tendency to make us forgetful of the high claims the Lord has upon us we invite temptation and become too weak in moral power to resist it. We come to partake of the spirit and cherish the ideas of our associates and to place sacred and eternal things lower than the ideas of our friends. We are, in short, leavened just as the enemy of all righteousness designed we should be.

The young, if brought under this influence, are more easily affected by it than those who are older. Everything leaves its impress upon their minds, the countenances they look upon, the voices they hear, the places they visit, the company they keep, and the books they read. It is impossible to overestimate the importance for this world and the next of the associations we choose for ourselves and, more especially, for our children.

The first years of life are more important than any other period. Decided progress will be made either in a right direction or a wrong one. On one hand, any amount of frivolous attainment may be gained; and on the other, any amount of solid, valuable knowledge for practical life, in becoming acquainted with God, and in learning how to strengthen every faculty that God has entrusted to us. Most important and essential for our present and eternal good is the knowledge of divine truth as revealed in the word of God.

We are living in a time when everything that is false and superficial is exalted above the real, the natural, and the enduring. The mind must be kept free from everything that would lead it in a wrong direction. It should not be encumbered with trashy stories, which do not add strength to the mental powers. The thoughts will be of the same character as the food we provide for the mind. The time devoted to needless, unimportant things would better be spent in contemplating the wonderful mysteries of the plan of salvation and in using every God-given power to learn the ways of the Lord, that our feet may not stumble upon the dark mountain of unbelief or stray from the path of holiness which was cast up by infinite sacrifice for the ransomed of the Lord to walk in. The strength of intellect, the substantial knowledge gained, are acquisitions which the gold of Ophir could not buy. Their price is above gold and silver. This kind of education the young do not usually choose. They urge their desires, their likes and dislikes, their preferences and inclinations; but if the parents have correct views of God, of the truth, and of the influences and associations which should surround their children, they will feel their God-given responsibility to firmly guide the inexperienced youth in the right way, knowing that what they sow they will also reap.

Could my voice reach the parents all through the land, I would warn them not to yield to the desires of their children in choosing their companions or associates. Little do parents consider that injurious impressions are far more readily received by the young than are divine impressions; therefore their associations should be the most favorable for the growth of grace and for the truth revealed in the word of God to be established in the heart. If children are with those whose conversation is upon unimportant, earthly things, their minds will come to the same level. If they hear the principles of religion slurred and our faith belittled, if sly objections to the truth are dropped in their hearing, these things will fasten in their minds and mold their characters. If their minds are filled with stories, be they true or fictitious, there is no room for the useful information and scientific knowledge which should occupy them. What havoc has this love for light reading wrought with the mind! How it has destroyed the principles of sincerity and true godliness, which lie at the foundation of a symmetrical character. It is like a slow poison taken into the system, which will sooner or later reveal its bitter effects. When a wrong impression is left upon the mind in youth, a mark is made, not on sand, but on enduring rock.

The associations of your children are of a character to draw them away from every influence that would interfere with, or break up, their health-destroying habits. They are impatient if they cannot have their own way. The advice of Christians is distasteful to them. They are traveling the road to ruin, and any influence which seeks to lead them in an opposite direction stirs the worst impulses of their hearts. They are creatures of circumstance. The formation of these early ties which are unfavorable to religious impressions has had a powerful, controlling influence over them at every subsequent step. Let the youth be placed in the most favorable circumstances possible; for the company they keep, the principles they adopt, the habits they form, will settle the question of their usefulness here, and of their future, eternal interests, with a certainty that is infallible. The parents should not concede to the inclinations of their children, but should follow the plain path of duty which God has marked out, restraining them in kindness, denying with firmness and determination, yet with love, their wrong desires, and with earnest, prayerful, persevering effort leading their steps away from the world upward to heaven. Children should not be left to drift into whatever way they are inclined, and to go into avenues which are open on every side, leading away from the right path. None are in so great danger as those who apprehend no danger and are impatient of caution and counsel.

It is because I see your danger, my sister, that I write you now as I do. While there may be many to flatter you and enjoy your hospitality without seeking to impart a blessing by right counsel, I must warn you of unseen danger, which will imperil your present and eternal happiness. We are approaching stormy times, and we want to study the true foundation of our faith. We need to search the Lawbook to see if our title to the immortal inheritance is without a flaw.

Our people have been regarded as too insignificant to be worthy of notice, but a change will come. The Christian world is now making movements which will necessarily bring commandment-keeping people into prominence. There is a constant supplanting of God's truth by the theories and false doctrines of human origin. Movements are being set on foot to enslave the consciences of those who would be loyal to God. The lawmaking powers will be against God's people. Every soul will be tested. Oh, that we would, as a people, be wise for ourselves, and by precept and example impart that wisdom to our children! Every position of our faith will be searched into; and if we are not thorough Bible students, established, strengthened, and settled, the wisdom of the world's great men will lead us astray.

The world is busy, anxious, and devoted. Evil is eagerly followed as though it were righteousness, error as though it were truth, and sin as though it were holiness. Darkness is covering the earth, and gross darkness the people. And shall God's people be asleep at such a time as this? Shall those who hold the truth be silent, as if paralyzed? Infidels declare that if they believed what Christians profess to believe, they would be far more in earnest than they. If we believe that the end of all things is at hand, "what manner of persons ought ye to be in all holy conversation and godliness?"

Every soul who truly believes the truth will have corresponding works. All will be earnest and solemn, and unwearied in their efforts to win souls to Christ. If the truth is first planted deep in their own souls, then they will seek to plant it in the hearts of others. The truth is kept altogether too much in the outer court. Bring it into the inner temple of the soul, enthrone it in the heart, and let it control the life. The word of God should be studied and obeyed, then the heart will find rest and peace and joy, and the aspirations will tend heavenward; but when truth is kept apart from the life, in the outer court, the heart is not warmed with the glowing fire of God's goodness.

The religion of Jesus is, by many, reserved for certain days, or certain occasions, and at other times is laid aside and neglected. The abiding principle of truth is not merely for a few hours on the Sabbath, or for a few acts of charity, but it is to be brought into the heart, refining and sanctifying the character. If there is a moment when man is safe without this special light and strength from heaven, then he may dispense with the truth of God. The Bible, God's pure, holy word, must be his counselor and guide, the controlling power of his life. It gives forth its lessons to us if we will take them to heart.

Abraham was a man favored of God. The Lord said: "I know him, that he will command his children and his household after him, and they shall keep the way of the Lord, to do justice and judgment." Abraham was honored of God because he cultivated home religion and caused the fear of the

Lord to pervade his whole household. It is God who says: "I know him, that he will *command*"—there will be no betraying of sacred trust on his part, no yielding to anyone but God; there is a law, and Abraham will keep it; no blind affection will cloud his sense of right and interfere between God and the souls of his children; that kind of indulgence which is the veriest cruelty will not lead Abraham astray.

Parents and children alike belong to God to be ruled by Him. By affection and authority combined, Abraham ruled his house. God's word has given us rules for our guidance. These rules form the standard from which we cannot swerve if we would keep the way of the Lord. God's will must be paramount. The question for us to ask is not: What have others done? What will my relatives think? or, What will they say of me if I pursue this course? but, What has God said? Neither parent nor child can truly prosper in any course excepting in the way of the Lord.

I am thankful that you have noble sons who are seeking to walk in the ways of the Lord; but I hope you will discern more clearly the path of duty in respect to their associations. This will determine whether you are growing in spirituality, or whether you are dwarfed in your religious life. The stern dictates of conscience must be obeyed, even though it be difficult; and it will help you to gain in moral power. Duties are often crosses which we must lift. Prayer and praise to God are not always offered without a struggle. Self-denial and cross bearing lie directly in the path we must travel if we reach the gates of the city of God. Jesus has led the way; will we follow?

We must be workers together with God, not alone for our own salvation, but in doing all we can for the salvation of others. Thus we become partners in the great plan of redemption, and will be sharers in the eternal weight of glory by and by. God calls upon you to *press* your way "toward the mark for the prize of the high calling of God in Christ Jesus." May the Lord bless you, is my prayer. But remember, if you are united with Christ, you must be a co-worker with Him. Our piety and religious duties will become narrowed down to our own interests unless we are daily partakers of the spirit of Christ. Interest for the souls of others is calculated to give breadth and depth and stability to Christian character.

The Lord is coming. We are nearing home, and we want to take large inspirations of the heavenly atmosphere; then we shall become identified with the Saviour in all His plans. We shall be elevated and able to elevate others, and shall be efficient in good works.

NEEDS OF OUR INSTITUTIONS

From time to time I have felt urged by the Spirit of the Lord to bear testimony in regard to the necessity of procuring the very best talent to work in the various institutions and other departments of the cause. Heretofore there has not been sufficient care to secure the best ability for all parts of our work. Those who bear responsibilities must be men trained for the work, men whom God can teach and whom He can honor with wisdom and understanding, as He did Daniel. They must be thinking men, men who bear God's impress and who are steadily progressing in holiness, in moral dignity, and in an understanding of their work. They must be praying men, men who will come up into the mount and view the glory of God and the dignity of the heavenly beings whom He has ordained to have charge of His work. Then, like Moses, they will follow the pattern given them in the mount; and they will be on the alert to secure and bring into connection with the work the very best talent that can be obtained. If they are growing men, possessing sanctified intelligence; if they listen to the voice of God and seek to catch every ray of light from heaven, they will, like the sun, pursue an undeviating course, and they will grow in wisdom and in favor with God.

The publishing department is an important branch of God's work, and all connected with it should feel that it is ordained of God and that all heaven is interested in it. Especially should those who have a voice in the management of the work have breadth of mind and sanctified judgment. They should not waste their Lord's money by thoughtlessness or lack of business tact; neither should they make the mistake of limiting the work by the adoption of narrow plans and trusting the work to men of small ability.

It has been repeatedly represented to me that all our institutions should be managed by men who are spiritually minded and who will not weave their own defective ideas and plans into their management. This work should not be left to men who will mingle the sacred with the common and who will regard the work of God as being upon about the same level as earthly things, to be managed in about the same common way in which they have been in the habit of managing their own temporal affairs. Until those can be connected with our institutions who have breadth of mind and who can lay plans in harmony with the growth of the work and its exalted character, the tendency will be to narrow down everything that is undertaken, and God will be dishonored. Oh, that all who have responsibilities to bear in connection with the cause of God would come up into a higher, holier atmosphere, where every true Christian should be! If they would, then both they and the work which they represent would be elevated and clothed with sacred dignity, and they would command the respect of all connected with the work.

Among those employed in our institutions have been men who have not sought counsel of God, who have not conformed to the great principles of truth which God has laid down in His word, and who have consequently manifested marked defects of character. As the result the greatest work ever committed to mortals has been marred by man's defective management;

whereas, if heaven's rules had been made the governing principle, there would have been a much nearer approach to perfection in all departments of the work.

Those placed in leading positions should be men who have sufficient breadth of mind to appreciate persons of cultivated intellect and to recompense them proportionately to the responsibilities they bear. True, those who engage in the work of God should not do so merely for the wages they receive, but rather for the honor of God, for the advancement of His cause, and to obtain imperishable riches. At the same time we should not expect that those who are capable of doing with exactness and thoroughness work that requires thought and painstaking effort should receive no greater compensation than the less skillful workman. A true estimate must be placed upon talent. Those who cannot appreciate good work and true ability should not be managers in our institutions, for their influence would tend to circumscribe the work and to bring it down to a low level.

If our institutions would be as prosperous as God designs they shall be, there must be more thoughtfulness and earnest prayer, mingled with unabating zeal and spiritual ardor. To connect the right class of laborers with the work may require a greater outlay of means, but it will be economy in the end; for while it is essential that economy be exercised in everything possible, it will be found that the efforts to save means by employing those who will work for low wages, and whose labor corresponds in character with their wages, will result in loss. The work will be retarded and the cause belittled. Brethren, you may economize as much as you please in your personal affairs, in building your houses, in arranging your clothing, in providing your food, and in your general expenses; but do not bring this economy to bear upon the work of God in such a way as to hinder men of ability and true moral worth from engaging in it.

In the Olympic games to which the apostle Paul calls our attention, those engaged in the races were required to make most thorough preparations. For months they were trained by different masters in the physical exercises calculated to give strength and vigor to the body. They were restricted to such food as would keep the body in the most healthy condition, and their clothing was such as would leave every organ and muscle untrammeled. Now if those who were to engage in running a race for earthly honor were obliged to submit to such severe discipline in order to succeed, how much more necessary it is for those who are to engage in the work of the Lord to be thoroughly disciplined and prepared, if they would be successful! Their preparation should be as much more thorough, their earnestness and self-denying efforts as much greater, than were those of the aspirants for worldly honors, as heavenly things are of more value than earthly. The mind, as well as the muscles, should be trained to the most diligent and persevering efforts. The road to success is not a smooth way over which we are borne in palace cars, but it is a rugged path filled with obstacles which can be surmounted only by patient toil.

My brethren, not one half the care has been taken that there should have been to impress upon those who could labor in the cause the importance of qualifying themselves for the work. With their powers all undisciplined, they can do but imperfect work; but if they shall be trained by wise and consecrated teachers, and are led by the Spirit of God, they will not only be able to do good work themselves, but will give the right mold to others who may work with them. It should, then, be their constant study to learn how they can become more intelligent in the work in which they are engaged. None should rest in case and inaction; but all should seek to elevate and ennoble themselves, lest by their deficient understanding they fail to realize the exalted character of the work and lower it to meet their own finite standard.

I saw that there was great inefficiency in the bookkeeping in many departments of the cause. Bookkeeping is, and ever will be, an important part of the work; and those who have become expert in it are greatly needed in our institutions and in all branches of the missionary work. It is a work that requires study that it may be done with correctness and dispatch, and without worry or overtaxation; but the training of competent persons for this work has been shamefully neglected. It is a disgrace to allow a work of such magnitude as ours to be done in a defective, inaccurate way. God wants as perfect work as it is possible for human beings to do. It is a dishonor to sacred truth and its Author to do His work in any other way. I saw that unless the workers in our institutions were subject to the authority of God, there would be a lack of harmony and unity of action among them. If all will obey His directions, the Lord will stand as the invisible commander; but there must also be a visible head who fears God. The Lord will never accept a careless, disorderly company of workers; neither will He undertake to lead forward and upward to noble heights and certain victory those who are self-willed and disobedient. The upward progress of the soul indicates that Jesus bears rule in the heart. That heart through which He diffuses His peace and joy, and the blessed fruits of His love, becomes His temple and His throne. "Ye are My friends," says Christ, "if ye do whatsoever I command you."

Our institutions are far beneath what God would have them be, because many of those connected with them are not in fellowship with Him. They are not growing men. They are not constantly learning of Jesus; therefore they are not becoming more and more efficient. If they would come close to Him and seek His help, He would walk with them and talk with them; He would be their counselor in all things, and would grant to them, as He did to Daniel, heavenly wisdom and understanding.

Years ago I saw that our people were far behind in obtaining that knowledge which would qualify them for positions of trust in the cause. Every member of the church should put forth efforts to qualify himself to do work for the Master. To each has been appointed a work, according to his ability. Even now, at the eleventh hour, we should arouse to educate men of ability for the work, that they may, while occupying positions of trust themselves, be educating by precept and example all who are associated with them.

Through a selfish ambition some have kept from others the knowledge they could have imparted. Others have not cared to tax themselves by educating anyone else. Yet this would have been the very best kind of work they could have done for Jesus. Says Christ: "Ye are the light of the world," and for this reason we are to let our light shine before men.

If all that the Lord has spoken in reference to these things had been heeded, our institutions would today occupy a higher and holier position than they do. But men have been satisfied with small attainments. They have not sought with all their might to rise in mental, moral, and physical capabilities. They have not felt that God required this of them; they have not realized that Christ died that they might do this very work. As the result they are far behind what they might be in intelligence and in the ability to think and plan. They could have added virtue to virtue, and knowledge to knowledge, and thus have become strong in the Lord. But this they have failed to do. Let each go to work now with a firm determination to rise. The present need of the cause is not so much for more men as for greater skill and consecration in the laborers.

OUR INSTITUTIONS AT BATTLE CREEK

The evils arising from centering so many responsibilities in Battle Creek have not been few. The dangers are many because of the unconsecrated elements that wait only until a change of circumstances shall encourage them to put all their influence on the side of wrong. If all those connected with our institutions were only devoted and spiritually minded, relying upon God more than upon themselves, there would be far greater prosperity than we have hitherto seen. But while there is such decided lack of humble trust and entire dependence upon God, we cannot be sure of anything. Our great need today is for men who are baptized with the Holy Spirit of God—men who walk with God as did Enoch. We do not want men who are so narrow in their outlook that they will circumscribe the work instead of enlarging it, or who follow the motto: "Religion is religion; business is business." We need men who are farseeing, who can take in the situation and reason from cause to effect.

THE COLLEGE

The teachers in our college should be men and women of well-balanced minds, who have a strong moral influence, who know how to deal wisely with minds, and who possess the true missionary spirit. If all were of this character, the burdens that now rest on the president would be lightened, and the danger of his becoming prematurely worn would be obviated. But it is this wisdom that is lacking.

It is not desirable to place the tuition too low. It should be sufficient to meet the expenses, even if the college is not so largely patronized. Those who really prize the advantages to be obtained there will make extra exertions to secure them. The larger part of those who would be induced to come because of the low tuition would be of no benefit to other students or to the church. The larger the number, the more tact, skill, and vigilance is required in their management.

When the college was first started, there was a fund placed in the Review and Herald office for the benefit of those who wished to obtain an education, but had not the means. This was used by several students, who thus had a good start and could earn enough to replace the amount they had drawn, that others might be benefited by it.

Some provision should now be made for the maintenance of such a fund to loan to poor but worthy students who desire to prepare themselves for missionary work. There are among us persons of ability who might be of good service in the cause were they but looked after and encouraged. When any of these are too poor to obtain the advantages of the college, the churches should feel it a privilege to defray their expenses. The youth should have it plainly set before them that so far as possible they must work to meet their own expenses. That which costs little will be lightly appreciated; that which costs something near its true value will be estimated accordingly. But the churches in different fields should feel that a solemn responsibility rests upon them in regard to training youth and educating older persons to engage in missionary effort. When they see among them any who give promise of making useful workers, but who are not able to educate themselves, they should take the responsibility of sending them to the college to be instructed and developed.

QUALIFICATIONS OF MANAGERS

There should be a thorough reformation on the part of the men who are now connected with our important institutions. They possess some valuable traits of character, while they are sadly lacking in others. Their character needs to have a different mold, one after the likeness of Christ. They must all remember that they have not yet attained unto perfection, that the work of character building is not yet finished. If they will walk in every ray of light that God has given; if they will compare themselves with Christ's life and character, they will discern where they have failed to meet the requirements of God's holy law and will seek to make themselves perfect in their sphere, even as God in heaven is perfect in His sphere. If these men had realized the importance of these things, they would today be far in advance of their present condition, far better qualified to fill places of trust. During these hours of probation they are to seek for perfection of character. They must learn daily of Christ. They are connected with the work of God, not because they are perfect, unerring men, without defects of character, but notwithstanding these defects. God expects them, while connected with His work, to be constantly studying and learning how to copy the pattern.

Jesus connected John, Peter, and Judas with Him in His work, making them colaborers with Him; but at the same time they were to be constantly learning lessons of Christ. They were to gather from His divine teachings instructions which were to correct their wrong ideas and their erroneous views of what constitutes a Christian character. John and Peter were not perfect men, but they improved every opportunity to learn. Peter did not learn to distrust himself, to be jealous of himself, until he was overcome by the temptations of the devil and denied his Lord. Judas had the same opportunity that these disciples had to learn the lessons taught by Christ, but he did not appreciate their value. He was a hearer only and not a doer. The result was seen in his betrayal of his Lord.

The men whom God has connected with His institutions are not to feel that there is no improvement for them to make because they stand in responsible positions. If they are to be representative men, guardians of the most sacred work ever committed to mortals, they must take the position of learners. They must not feel self-sufficient or self-important. They should ever realize that they are treading on holy ground. Angels of God are ready to minister to them, and they must be continually in reception of light and heavenly influences, or they are no more fitted for the work than unbelievers.

If the character of the men connected with the office at Battle Creek were so transformed that they could have a helpful influence over those under their control, then the outlook would be more encouraging. Whatever the men employed there may think of their ability, I have reason to say that many will need to improve greatly before they are qualified to fill their positions acceptably. They may feel competent to give counsel, but they are themselves in need of counsel from Him who is unerring in wisdom. Great and important interests are in danger of being misshaped and of coming forth defective from their hands. If all felt their ignorance more, and would depend less on self, they might learn of the great Teacher meekness and lowliness of heart.

God is observing everything that transpires in the office. "Thou God seest me," should be always in mind. Everyone who bears responsibilities in the office should be courteous and kind to all. An ever-abiding sense of the presence of Christ would prevent the encroachment upon others' rights which is so common in the world's practice, but which is an offense to God. The love of Jesus must be incorporated into the lives of the workers in the several departments of the office, in order that justice may be done, not only to the work, but to one another.

The very first work, my brethren, is to secure the blessing of God in your own hearts. Then bring this blessing into your homes, put away your criticisms, overcome your exacting ways, and let the spirit of cheerfulness and kindness prevail. The atmosphere of your homes will be carried with you to the office, and heavenly peace will surround your souls. Wherever the love of Jesus reigns there is pitying tenderness and thought-fulness of others. The most precious work that my brethren can engage in is that of cultivating a Christlike character.

It was shown me that those who preside over our institutions should ever bear in mind that there is a chief director, who is the God of heaven. There should be strict honesty in all business transactions in every department of the work. There must be firmness in preserving order, but compassion, mercy, and forbearance should be mingled with the firmness. Justice has a twin sister, Love. These should stand side by side. The Bible should be our guide. There can be no greater deception than for a man to think that he can find a better guide, when in difficulty, than the word of God. The blessed word must be a lamp to our feet. Bible precepts must be carried into the everyday life.

BOARD MEETINGS

Those who compose our councils need to sit daily at the feet of Christ and learn in His school to be meek and lowly of heart. As they are only weak and erring men themselves, they should cherish feelings of kindness and pity for others who may have erred. They are not prepared to deal justly, to love mercy, and to exercise the true courtesy which characterized the life of Christ, unless they see the necessity of being in union with Him. The trustees should ever realize that they are under the divine eye, and act with a continual sense that, as finite men, they are liable to make mistakes in laying plans unless they are closely connected with God and are seeking to have every deficiency removed from their characters. The divine standard must be met.

Everyone who serves in board meetings needs to seek most earnestly the wisdom from above. The transforming grace of Christ should be felt in every meeting. Then the influence of the Spirit of Christ upon the hearts of those present will place a right mold upon their work. It will quell tumultuous actions and charm away the unhallowed effects of that worldliness which makes men sharp, critical, overbearing, and ready to accuse.

When these councils meet, a few words of formal prayer are offered; but the hearts of those present are not brought into harmony with God by earnest, importunate prayer, offered in living faith, in a humble and contrite spirit. If the trustees divorce themselves from the God of wisdom and power, they cannot preserve that high-souled integrity in dealing with their fellow men which God requires. Without divine wisdom, their own spirit will be woven into the decisions they make. If these men are not in communication with God, Satan will surely be one in their councils and will take advantage of their unconsecrated state. Acts of injustice will be done, because God is not presiding. The Spirit of Christ must be an abiding, controlling power over the heart and mind.

You should take the Lord with you into every one of your councils. If you realize His presence in your assemblies, every transaction will be conscientiously and prayerfully considered. Every unprincipled motive will be repressed, and uprightness will characterize all your transactions, in small as well as in great matters. Seek counsel of God first, for this is necessary in order that you may counsel together properly.

You need to watch, lest the busy activities of life lead you to neglect prayer when you most need the strength prayer would give. Godliness is in danger of being crowded out of the soul through overdevotion to business. It is a great evil to defraud the soul of the strength and heavenly wisdom which are waiting your demand. You need that illumination which God alone can give. No one is fitted to transact his business unless he has this wisdom.

Ever since the Publishing Association was formed, light has been given from time to time when perplexities have arisen, and the Lord has ofttimes laid down principles which should be carried out by all the workers. In the early experience of the work the grave responsibilities resting upon those in positions of trust were kept continually before us, and we sought the Lord from three to five times a day to give us heavenly wisdom, that we might sacredly guard the interests of the cause of God and of His chosen people.

It is the worst kind of folly to leave the Lord out of your councils and to put confidence in the wisdom of men. In your positions of trust you are, in a special sense, to be the light of the world. You should feel an intense desire to place yourselves in connection with the God of wisdom, light, and knowledge, that you may be channels of light. Important interests are to be considered, which relate to the advancement and prosperity of the cause of present truth. How, then, can you be competent to come to right decisions, to make wise plans, and to give wise counsel unless you are thus connected with the Source of all wisdom and righteousness? The business to be transacted in your councils has been considered altogether too lightly. Common talk, common remarks, comments made on the doings of others, have had a place in these important meetings. You should remember that the eternal God is a witness in all these gatherings. The all-seeing eye of Jehovah measures every one of your decisions, and they are compared with His holy law, His great standard of righteousness. Those in the position of counselors should be men of prayer, men of faith, men free from selfishness, men who will not dare to rely on their own human wisdom, but who will pray earnestly for light as to the best manner of conducting the business entrusted to them.

WORLDLY POLICY

The policy which worldly businessmen adopt is not the policy to be chosen and carried out by the men who are connected with our institutions. Selfish policy is not heaven-born, it is earthly. In this world the leading maxim is, "The end justifies the means;" and this may be traced in every department of business. It has a controlling influence in every class of society, in the grand councils of nations, and wherever the Spirit of Christ is not the ruling principle. Prudence and caution, tact and skill, should be cultivated by everyone who is connected with the office of publication and by those who serve in our college and sanitarium. But the laws of justice and righteousness must not be set aside, and the principle must not prevail that each one is to make his particular branch of the work a success, regardless of other branches. The interests of all should be closely guarded to see that no one's rights are invaded. In the world the god of traffic is too often the god of fraud, but it must not be thus with those who are dealing with the Lord's work. The worldly standard is not to be the standard of those who are connected with sacred things.

When the scenes of the judgment were brought before me, the books in which are registered the deeds of men revealed the fact that the dealings of some of those professing godliness in our institutions were after the worldling's standard, not in strict accordance with God's great standard of righteousness. The relation of men in their deal with one another, especially those connected with the work of God, was opened to me quite fully. I saw that there should be no close, sharp deal between brethren who represent important institutions, different, perhaps, in character, but branches of the same work. A noble, generous, Christlike spirit should ever be maintained by them. The spirit of avarice should have no place in their transactions. God's cause could not be advanced by any action on their part contrary to the spirit and character of Christ. A selfish manner of dealing in one will provoke the same disposition in others, but the manifestation of liberality and true courtesy will awaken the same spirit in return and would please our heavenly Father.

Worldly policy is not to be classed with sound discretion, although it is too often mistaken for it. It is a species of selfishness, in whatever cause it is exercised. Discretion and sound judgment are never narrow in their workings. The mind that is guided by them has comprehensive ideas and does not become narrowed down to one object. It looks at things from every point of view. But worldly policy has a short range of vision. It can see the object nearest at hand, but fails to discover those at a distance. It is ever watching for opportunities to gain advantage. Those who follow a course of worldly policy are building themselves up by pulling out the foundation from another man's building. Every structure must be built upon a right foundation, in order to stand.

ROYALTIES ON BOOKS

Brainworkers have a God-given capital. The result of their study belongs to God, not to man. If the worker faithfully gives to his employer the time for which he receives his pay, then his employer has no further claim upon him. And if by diligent and close economy of moments he prepare other matter valuable for publication, it is his to use as he thinks will best serve the cause of God. If he gives up all but a small royalty he has done a good work for those who handle the book, and he should not be asked to do more. God has not placed upon the publishing board the responsibility of being conscience for others. They should not persistently seek to force men to their terms.

The authors are responsible to God for the use which they make of their means. There will be many calls for money. Mission fields will have to be entered, and this requires much outlay. Those to whom God has entrusted talents are to trade upon these talents according to their ability, for they are to act their part in carrying forward these interests. When the members of the board take it upon themselves to urge that all the profits from our denominational books shall go to the Publishing Association and the agents, and that the authors, after being paid for the time and expense of writing a book, should relinquish their claim to a share in the profits, they are undertaking a work which they cannot carry out. These book writers have as much interest in the cause of God as do those who compose the board of trustees. Some of them have had a connection with the work almost from its infancy.

It was presented before me that there were poor men whose only means of obtaining a livelihood was their brain work; also that there are businessmen connected with our institutions who have not grown up with them and have not had the benefit of all the instruction that God has given from time to time relative to their management. They have not incorporated true religion, the spirit of Christ, into their business. The Publishing Association should not, therefore, be made an all-controlling power. Individual talent and individual rights must be respected. Should arrangements be made to invest all the results of personal talent in the Publishing Association, other important interests would be crippled.

To every man God has given his work. To some He has given talents of means and influence, and those who have the interests of God's cause at heart will understand His voice telling them what to do. They will have a burden to push the work where it needs pushing.

Several times it has been pointed out to me that there has been a close, ungenerous spirit exercised toward Brother H from the very first of his labors in Battle Creek. It makes me sad to state the reason. It was because he went there a stranger and in poverty. Because he was a poor man he has been placed in unpleasant positions and made to feel his poverty. Men connected with our institutions have thought that they could bring him to their terms, and he has had a very unpleasant time. There are sad chapters in his experience, which would not have passed into history if his brethren had been kind and had dealt with him in a Christlike manner. The Lord's cause should always be free from the slightest injustice, and no act connected with it should savor in the smallest degree of penuriousness or oppression.

The Lord guards every man's interest. He was always the poor man's friend. There is a most wonderful dearth of Christlike love in the hearts of nearly all who are handling sacred things. I would say to my brethren everywhere: Cultivate the love of Christ! It should well up from the soul of the Christian like streams in the desert, refreshing and beautifying, bringing gladness, peace, and joy into his own life and into the lives of others. "None of us liveth to himself." If there is shown the least oppression of the poor, or unjust dealing with them in either small or great things, God will hold the oppressor accountable.

Do not seek to make terms which are not just and fair with either Elder J or Professor H, or with any other brainworker. Do not urge of force them to accept the terms of those who do not know what it is to make books. These men have a conscience and are accountable to God for their entrusted capital and the use they make of it; you are not to be conscience for them. They want the privilege of investing the means which they may acquire by hard labor, when and where the Spirit of God shall indicate.

My brethren must remember that the cause of God covers more than the publishing house at Battle Creek and the other institutions there established. No one knows better than Brother J how that office came into existence. He has been connected with the publishing work from its very commencement—when it was oppressed by poverty; when the food upon our tables was hardly sufficient to meet the wants of nature, because self-denial had to be practiced in eating and in dressing and in our wages, in order that the paper might live. This was positively necessary then, and those who passed through that experience would be ready, under similar circumstances, to do the same again.

It is not becoming for those who have had no experience in these trials, but have become connected with the work in its present prosperity, to urge the early workers to submit to terms in which they can see no justice. Brother J loves the cause of God and will invest his means to advance it wherever he sees it is necessary. Then leave this burden of receiving and dispensing this means where it belongs—on the men to whom God has entrusted talents of influence and of ability. They are responsible to God for these. Neither the Publishing Association nor its chief workers should assume the stewardship of these authors.

If the board should be able to bring Brethren H and J to their terms, would not these writers feel that they had been dealt with unjustly? Would not a door of temptation be opened before them, which would interfere with sympathy and harmony of action? Should the managers grasp all the profits, it would not be well for the cause, but would produce a train of evils, disastrous to the Publishing Association. It would encourage the spirit of intolerance which is already manifest to some degree in their councils. Satan longs to have a narrow, conceited spirit, which God cannot approve, take possession of the men who are connected with the sacred message of truth.

The same principles which apply to the work in our institutions at Battle Creek apply as well to that in the field at large. The following extracts are from a letter written to Brother K, November 8, 1880:

"There is a broad field for the laborers, but many are getting above the simplicity of the work. Now is the time to labor and to do it in the wise counsel of God. If you connect unconsecrated persons with the missions and Sabbath schools, the work will become a mere form. The workers in every part of the field must study how to work economically and in the simplicity of Christ and how to plan most successfully to reach hearts."

"We are in danger of spreading over more territory and starting more enterprises than we can attend to properly. There is danger of neglecting some important parts of the work through overattention to others. To undertake so large an amount of work that nothing can be done perfectly is a bad plan. We are to move forward, but not to get so far above the simplicity of the work that it will be impossible to look after all the enterprises without sacrificing our best helpers to keep things in running order. Life and health must be regarded.

"While we should be ever ready to follow the opening providence of God, we should lay no larger plans than we have the help and means to carry out successfully. We must keep up and increase the interest in the enterprises already started."

"While larger plans and broader fields are constantly opening, there must be broader views in regard to the selection and training of workers who are to labor to bring souls into the truth. Our young ministers must be encouraged to take hold of the work with energy and be educated to carry it forward with simplicity and thoroughness. I am astonished to see how little some of our young ministers are appreciated and how little encouragement they receive. Yet some of them cling to the work and do anything and everything with unselfish interest."

"Narrowness and dishonest dealing must not come into the settlement with the workers, high or low. . . . There must be more of Christ's way, and less of self. Sharp criticisms should be repressed. Sympathy, compassion, and love should be cultivated by every worker. Unless Jesus comes in and takes possession of the heart, unless self is subdued and Christ is exalted, we shall not prosper as a people. I beseech of you, my brother, to labor wholly in God, not laying too many plans, but striving to have the work carried on circumspectly, and with such thoroughness that it will endure."

CHRISTIAN INFLUENCE IN THE HOME AND THE CHURCH

Dear Brother and Sister L: My heart is burdened on your account. What you need is the converting grace of God in your hearts. You need the spirit of Jesus. You should learn meekness and lowliness of heart in the school of Christ. You do not feel your need of deep, inward piety, and on this account you are being self-deceived. You are delaying the decisions which you ought to make at once, for your own good and for the good of others. God requires every man to do his duty. He demands the whole heart, the entire affection. He would not have us profess a knowledge of Jesus Christ and the truth, and yet bear no fruit. For small or great, learned or unlearned, rich or poor, the requirement is just the same.

Every one is called upon to act according to the ability God has given him. He must render his service faithfully or he will sully his conscience, and imperil his soul. No one can afford to lose heaven. Remember the words of Christ to all His followers: "Ye are the light of the world." God depends on those who know the way, to show it to others. He has entrusted to men the treasure of His truth. It is faith and trust and confidence in God that we need. Inward grace will be revealed in the outward actions. We need that spirit which will show to others that we have been learning in the school of Christ and that we copy the pattern given us. We want a heart that is not lifted up unto vanity, a mind not settled on self. Each should have a constant desire to bless others. God notices our humble efforts, and they are precious in His sight. You both need home piety, sweet, satisfied contentment, without faultfinding, pettishness, scolding, or severity. Let kindness and love be the rule of your household. Whoever does not let the light of truth shine in his home dishonors the Saviour.

The truth as it is in Jesus does much for the receiver, and not only for him, but for all who are brought within the sphere of his influence. The truly converted soul is illuminated from on high, and Christ is in that soul "a well of water springing up into everlasting life." His words, his motives, his actions, may be misinterpreted and falsified; but he does not mind it because he has greater interests at stake. He does not consider present convenience; he is not ambitious for display; he does not crave the praise of men. His hope is in heaven, and he keeps straight on, with his eye fixed on Jesus. He does right because it is right, and because only those who do right will have an entrance into the kingdom of God. He is kind and humble, and thoughtful of others' happiness. He never says, "Am I my brother's keeper?" but he loves his neighbor as himself. His manner is not harsh and dictatorial, like that of the godless; but he reflects light from heaven upon men. He is a true, bold soldier of the cross of Christ, holding forth the word of life. As he gains in influence, prejudice against him dies away, his piety is acknowledged, and his Bible principles are respected.

Thus it is with everyone who is truly converted. He bears precious fruit, and in so doing walks as Christ walked, talks as He talked, works as He worked, and the truth as it is in Jesus, through him, makes an impression in his home, in his neighborhood, and in the church. He is building a character for eternity, while working out his own salvation with fear and trembling. He is exemplifying before the world the valuable principles of truth, showing what the truth will do for the life and character of the genuine believer. He is unconsciously acting his part in the sublime work of Christ in the redemption of the world, a work which, in its character and influence, is far-reaching, undermining the foundation of false religion and false science.

I feel obliged to write thus because I know your brethren will never say these things to you. I do not want you or your wife to lose the heavenly mansions; for they are worth everything to us, and we should put forth energy and zeal proportionate to the value of the object of which we are in pursuit. Eternal life is worth persevering, untiring effort.

The Lord wants you and your family to be Christians in every sense of the word and to show in your characters the sanctifying power of the truth. If you had formed such characters, your works would stand the test of the judgment; should the fires of the last day kindle upon your works as they now are, they would prove to be only hay, wood, and stubble. Do not think this severe; it is true. Self has been mingled with all your labors. Will you come up to the high standard? It will be like learning the first principles of what constitutes a Christian character. Christ said to the apostle Peter: "When thou art converted, strengthen thy brethren." You, likewise, must be converted before you can do acceptable work for the Master.

My brother, if you will, you can be a strong man in God. You have talents of ability that God has entrusted to your keeping to be sanctified to His service. But if you do not yield up all to Christ, your ability will prove dangerous both to yourself and to others, leading them to walk apart from the truth and away from Christ.

The members of the church in _____ need very much done for them. They must have fervent zeal for Christ, must be more humble, more patient, more kind, more teachable, more Christlike in every respect. In their character they should manifest to the world the sanctifying power of grace. God forbid that you should, by precept or example, bar the way to this essential work. Will you work with Jesus? Will you be true to the Lord who has bought you? Will you put into the background all matters of minor importance? You must be baptized into a larger faith, a larger charity. You need greater reverence for things of eternal importance. It is impossible for me to impress upon your mind too strongly the extent and power of the influence which flows from the example of individual piety and from the exhibition, by the church, of the sanctifying influence of the truth upon the character.

A much greater ingathering could be realized in _____ if the church would come into a right position before God, each seeking to set his own heart and his own house in order. Talk less, and let true inward piety shine forth in good works. Be kind; cultivate love and gentleness. Pray more; read your Bibles more. Be diligent students in the school of Christ. Then the members of the church will not be finding fault with their brethren and sisters; this is Satan's work.

I hope you will be strengthened and established in the faith. The work will surely go forward, whether we advance with it or not. It will be victorious, but the question is: Shall we be victorious with it? May God help you both to feel the need of a deep work of grace in your hearts. Remember that Jesus has bought you with the sacrifice of His own life. "Ye are not your own; for ye are bought with a price: therefore glorify God in your body, and in your spirit, which are God's."

AN IMPRESSIVE DREAM

Dear Brother M: I had an impressive dream last night. I thought that you were on a strong vessel, sailing on very rough waters. Sometimes the waves beat over the top, and you were drenched with water. You said: "I shall get off; this vessel is going down." "No," said one who appeared to be the captain, "this vessel sails into the harbor. She will never go down." But you answered: "I shall be washed overboard. As I am neither captain or mate, who cares? I shall take my chances on that vessel you see yonder." Said the captain: "I shall not let you go there, for I know that vessel will strike the rocks before she reaches the harbor." You straightened yourself up, and said with great positiveness: "This vessel will become a wreck; I can see it just as plain as can be." The captain looked upon you with piercing eye, and said firmly: "I shall not permit you to lose your life by taking that boat. The timbers of her framework are worm-eaten, and she is a deceptive craft. If you had more knowledge you could discern between the spurious and the genuine, the holy and that appointed to utter ruin."

I awoke, but it is this dream that leads me to write to you. I was feeling deeply over some of these things when a letter came, saying that you were "under great temptation and trial." What is it, Brother M? Is Satan tempting you again? Is God permitting you to be brought to the same place where you have failed before? Will you now let unbelief take possession of your soul? Will you fail every time, as did the children of Israel? God help you to resist the devil and to come forth stronger from every trial of your faith!

Be careful how you move. Make straight paths for your feet. Close the door to unbelief and make God your strength. If perplexed, hold still; make no move in the dark. I am deeply concerned for your soul. This may be the last trial that God will grant you. Advance not one step in the downward road to perdition. Wait, and God will help you. Be patient, and the clear light will appear. If you yield to impressions you will lose your soul, and the soul is of great value with God.

I have been writing upon the first volume of *Great Controversy,* and it makes me feel very solemn as I review these important subjects—creation and the events from the fall of Satan to the fall of Adam. The Lord seems very near me as I write, and I am deeply moved as I contemplate this controversy from the beginning to the present time. The workings of the powers of darkness are laid clearly before my mind. Most trying times are before us, and Satan, clad in angel robes, will come to souls with his temptations as he came to Christ in the wilderness. He will quote Scripture; and unless our life is hid with Christ in God, he will surely bind our souls in unbelief.

Time is very short, and all that is to be done must be done quickly. The angels are holding the four winds, and Satan is taking advantage of everyone who is not fully established in the truth. Every soul is to be tested. Every defect in the character, unless it is overcome by the help of God's Spirit, will become a sure means of destruction. I feel as never before the necessity for our people to be energized by the spirit of the truth, for Satan's devices will ensnare every soul who has not made God his strength. The Lord has much work to be done; and if we do what He has appointed for us to do, He will work with our efforts.

DAILY STUDY OF THE BIBLE NECESSARY

Those who are called of God to labor in word and doctrine should ever be learners. They should constantly seek to improve, that they may be ensamples to the flock of God and do good to all with whom they are brought in contact. Those who do not feel the importance of advancement and self-improvement will not grow in grace and in the knowledge of Christ.

All heaven is interested in the work going on in this world, which is to prepare men and women for the future, immortal life. It is God's plan that human agencies shall have the high honor of acting as co-workers with Jesus Christ in the salvation of souls. The word of God plainly reveals that it is the privilege of the instrument in this great work to realize that there is One at his right hand ready to aid him in every sincere endeavor to reach the highest moral and spiritual excellence in the Master's work. This will be the case with all who feel their need of help. They should look upon the work of God as sacred and holy, and should bring to Him, every day, offerings of joy and gratitude, in return for the power of His grace, by which they are enabled to make advancement in the divine life. The worker should ever take humble views of himself, considering his many lost opportunities for want of diligence and appreciation of the work. He should not become discouraged, but should continually renew his efforts to redeem the time.

Men whom God has chosen to be His ministers should prepare themselves for the work by thorough heart searching and by close connection with the world's Redeemer. If they are not successful in winning souls to Christ, it is because their own souls are not right with God. There is altogether too much willing ignorance with a large number who are preaching the word. They are not qualified for this work by a thorough understanding of the Scriptures. They do not feel the importance of the truth for this time, and therefore the truth is not to them a living reality. It they would humble their souls before God; if they would walk according to the Scriptures, in all humility of mind, then they would have more distinct views of the Pattern which they should copy; but they fail to keep their eyes fixed upon the Author and Finisher of their faith.

It is not necessary that anyone should yield to the temptations of Satan and thus violate his conscience and grieve the Holy Spirit. Every provision has been made in the word of God whereby all may have divine help in their endeavors to overcome. If they keep Jesus before them they will become changed into His image. All who by faith have Christ abiding in them carry a power into their labor which makes them successful. They will be constantly growing more and more efficient in their work, and the blessing of God, shown in the prosperity of the work, will testify that they are indeed laborers together with Christ. But however much one may advance in spiritual life, he will never come to a point where he will not need diligently to search the Scriptures; for therein are found the evidences of our faith. All points of doctrine, even though they have been accepted as truth, should be brought to the law and to the testimony; if they cannot stand this test, "there is no light in them."

The great plan of redemption, as revealed in the closing work for these last days, should receive close examination. The scenes connected with the sanctuary above should make such an impression upon the minds and hearts of all that they may be able to impress others. All need to become more intelligent in regard to the work of the atonement, which is going on in the sanctuary above. When this grand truth is seen and understood, those who hold it will work in harmony with Christ to prepare a people to stand in the great day of God, and their efforts will be successful. By study, contemplation, and prayer God's people will be elevated above common, earthly thoughts and feelings, and will be brought into harmony with Christ and His great work of cleansing the sanctuary above from the sins of the people. Their faith will go with Him into the sanctuary, and the worshipers on earth will be carefully reviewing their lives and comparing their characters with the great standard of righteousness. They will see their own defects; they will also see that they must have the aid of the Spirit of God if they would become qualified for the great and solemn work for this time which is laid upon God's ambassadors.

Christ said: "Except ye eat the flesh of the Son of man, and drink His blood, ye have no life in you. Whoso eateth

My flesh, and drinketh My blood, hath eternal life; and I will raise him up at the last day. For My flesh is meat indeed, and My blood is drink indeed. He that eateth My flesh, and drinketh My blood, dwelleth in Me, and I in him. As the living Father hath sent Me, and I live by the Father: so he that eateth Me, even he shall live by Me." How many of those who are laboring in word and doctrine are eating Christ's flesh and drinking His blood? How many can comprehend this mystery? The Saviour Himself explains this matter: "It is the Spirit that quickeneth; the flesh profiteth nothing: the *words* that I speak unto you, they *are spirit,* and they are *life."* The word of God must be interwoven with the living character of those who believe it. The only vital faith is that faith which receives and assimilates the truth till it is a part of the being and the motive power of the life and action. Jesus is called the Word of God. He accepted His Father's law, wrought out its principles in His life, manifested its spirit, and showed its beneficent power in the heart. Says John: "The Word was made flesh, and dwelt among us, (and we beheld His glory, the glory as of the Only Begotten of the Father,) full of grace and truth." The followers of Christ must be partakers of His experience. They must assimilate the word of God. They must be changed into its likeness by the power of Christ and reflect the divine attributes. They must eat the flesh and drink the blood of the Son of God, or there is no life in them. The spirit and work of Christ must become the spirit and work of His disciples.

It is not enough to *preach* the truth; it must be carried out in the life. Christ must be abiding in us, and we in Him, in order to do the work of God. Each must have an individual experience and put forth personal efforts to reach souls. God requires each to put all his powers into the work and, through continual effort, educate himself to do that work acceptably. He expects everyone to bring the grace of Christ into his heart, that he may be a bright and shining light to the world. If God's workers train all their powers thoroughly, then they may work understandingly, in all wisdom, and God will surely respond to their efforts to uplift, refine, and save their fellow men. All the workers must use tact and bring their faculties under the controlling influence of the Spirit of God. They must make it a business to study His word and hear God's voice addressing them from His living oracles in reproof, in instruction, or in encouragement, and His Spirit will strengthen them, that they may, as God's workers, advance in religious experience. Thus they will be led on step by step to greater heights, and their joy will be full.

While engaged in the work that God has given them to do, they will find no time and have no disposition to glorify themselves; neither will they find time to murmur or complain, for their affections are centered on things above, not on earthly things. Heart, soul, and body will then be enlisted in the work of the Master. They will not labor selfishly, but will deny themselves for Christ's sake. They will lift His cross, for they are His true disciples. They will feed day by day upon the precious truths of God's word, and will thus be strengthened for duty and braced for trial. In this way they will become strong, well-developed men and women in Christ. They will then be true sons and daughters of the heavenly King. The greatness of the truth which they love and contemplate will expand the mind, strengthen the judgment, and elevate the character. They will not be novices in the great work of saving souls, for they are working with the wisdom given them of God. Neither will they be dwarfs in religious life, but will grow up in Christ, their living Head, to the full stature of men and women in Christ Jesus. The conflicts with the enemies of truth will then only strengthen their hopes, and they will have precious victories, because they call to their aid the mighty Helper, who never disappoints the humble seeker. If their efforts are successful, all the glory will be given to God. Heaven will come very near to them in sympathy and co-operation. They are made indeed a spectacle to the world, to angels, and to men. They are marked characters because of their purity of heart and life, their strength of purpose, their firmness and usefulness in the cause of God. They are God's noblemen.

In the religious life of every soul who is finally victorious there will be scenes of terrible perplexity and trial; but his knowledge of the Scriptures will enable him to bring to mind the encouraging promises of God, which will comfort his heart and strengthen his faith in the power of the Mighty One. He reads: "Cast not away therefore your confidence, which hath great recompense of reward;" "that the trial of your faith, being much more precious than of gold that perisheth, though it be tried with fire, might be found unto praise and honor and glory at the appearing of Jesus Christ: whom having not seen, ye love; in whom, though now ye see Him not, yet believing, ye rejoice with joy unspeakable and full of glory." The trial of faith is more precious than gold. All should learn that this is a part of the discipline in the school of Christ, which is essential to purify and refine them from the dross of earthliness. They must endure with fortitude the taunts and attacks of enemies, and overcome all obstacles that Satan may place in their path to hedge up the way. He will try to lead them to neglect prayer and to discourage them in the study of the Scriptures, and he will throw his hateful shadow athwart their path to hide Christ and the heavenly attractions from their view.

None should go along shrinking and trembling, under continual doubt, sowing their path with complainings; but all should look up to God and see His goodness and rejoice in His love. Summon all your powers to look up, not down at your difficulties; then you will never faint by the way. You will soon see Jesus behind the cloud, reaching out His hand to help you; and all you have to do is to give Him your hand in simple faith and let Him lead you. As you become trustful you will, through faith in Jesus, become hopeful. The light shining from the cross of Calvary will reveal to you God's estimate of the soul, and, appreciating that estimate, you will seek to reflect the light to the world. A great name among men is as letters traced in sand, but a spotless character will endure to all eternity. God gives you intelligence and a reasoning mind, whereby you may grasp His promises; and Jesus is ready to help you in forming a strong, symmetrical character. Those who possess such a character need never become discouraged because they have not success in worldly affairs. They "are the light of the world." Satan cannot destroy or make of none effect the light that shines forth from them.

God has a work for each to do. It is no part of His plan that souls shall be sustained in the battle of life by human sympathy and praise; but He means that they shall go without the camp, bearing the reproach, fighting the good fight of faith, and standing in His strength under every difficulty. God has opened to us all the treasures of heaven through the precious gift of His Son, who is fully able to uplift, ennoble, and fit us, through His perfection of character, for usefulness in this life and for a holy heaven. He came to our world and lived as He requires His followers to live. His was a life of self-denial and constant self-sacrifice. If we encourage selfishness and ease and the gratification of inclination, and do not put forth our best efforts to co-operate with God in the wonderful work of elevating, ennobling, and purifying us, that we may become sons and daughters of God, then we do not meet His requirements; we sustain a continual loss in this life, and we shall eventually lose the future, immortal life. God wants you to work, not with self-disparagement nor in discouragement, but with the strongest faith and hope, with cheerfulness and joy, representing Christ to the world. The religion of Jesus is joy, peace, and happiness. As we search the Scriptures, and see the infinite condescension of the Father in giving Jesus to the world that all who believe in Him may have everlasting life, every power of our being should be called into activity, to give praise and honor and glory to Him for His unspeakable love to the children of men.

EDUCATION OF WORKERS

We have a work to do which but few realize. It is to carry the truth to all nations. There is a broad field for laborers in foreign lands as well as in America. God calls for men who are devoted, pure, largehearted, broad-minded, and humble to enter these fields. How few have any sense of this great work! We must arouse and work from a higher standpoint than we have hitherto done.

Those who now embrace the truth have every advantage, especially in the accumulation of light and knowledge brought out in our publications. Past experiences, rich and varied, should now be appreciated in their true light. We know how hard the work moved at first, how many obstacles were arrayed against it, how few facilities were at the command of the pioneers in this cause to use in its advancement; but now all is changed, and the clear light is shining. If primitive Christianity could enter the hearts of all who claim to believe the truth, it would bring to them new life and power. The people who are in darkness would then see the contrast between truth and error, between the teachings of God's word and the fables of superstition.

Mistakes have been made in not seeking to reach ministers and the higher classes with the truth. People not of our faith have been shunned altogether too much. While we should not associate with them to receive their mold, there are honest ones everywhere for whom we should labor cautiously, wisely, and intelligently, full of love for their souls. A fund should be raised to educate men and women to labor for these higher classes, both here and in other countries. We have had altogether too much talk about coming down to the common mind. God wants men of talent and good minds, who can weigh arguments, men who will dig for the truth as for hid treasures. These men will be able to reach, not only the common, but the better classes. Such men will ever be students of the Bible, fully alive to the sacredness of the responsibilities resting upon them. They will give full proof of their ministry.

We have too little working talent in the different branches of the cause. New enterprises must be set on foot. We need ability to devise plans whereby souls who are in the darkness of error can be reached. We need the intelligence of varied minds, but we should not find fault with them because their ideas do not just fit our own. We should have broader plans for the education of workers to give the message. Those who believe and love the truth have done nobly in giving of their means to sustain its various enterprises, but there is great lack of capable workers. It is not wise to be constantly expending means to open untried fields while so little is done to prepare workers to occupy them. God's work must not be hindered for want of agents to execute it. He calls for cultivated men, who are Bible students, who love the truth that they open to others, and who bring it into their own lives and characters. We want men who love Jesus and cling to Him, and who appreciate the infinite sacrifice made in behalf of fallen humanity. We want lips touched with holy fire, hearts pure from the defilement of sin. Those whose piety is shallow, and who have great ambition to be considered first and best, are not the men for this time. Those who think more of their own way than of the work are not wanted.

Our churches are not receiving the kind of training that will lead them to walk in all humility of mind, to put away all pride of external display, and to labor for the inward adorning. The efficiency of the church is precisely what the zeal, purity, self-denial, and intelligent labor of the ministers make it. An active missionary spirit should characterize its individual members. They must have deeper piety, stronger faith, and broader views. They must make more thorough work in personal effort. What we need is a living religion. A single individual of enlarged conceptions of duty, whose soul is in communion with God and who is full of zeal for Christ, will exert a powerful influence for good. He drinks at no low, turbid, polluted stream, but from the pure, high waters at the fountainhead; and he can communicate a new spirit and power to the church. As the pressure from without increases, God would have His church vitalized by the sacred, solemn truths they believe. The Holy Spirit from heaven, working with the sons and daughters of God, will surmount obstacles and hold the vantage ground against the enemy. God has great victories in reserve for His truth-loving, commandment-keeping people. The fields are already whitening for the harvest. We have light, and rich, glorious endowments from heaven in the truth made ready to our hands; but men and women have not been educated and disciplined to work in the fast-ripening harvest fields.

God knows with what fidelity and spirit of consecration everyone fulfills his mission. There is no place for the slothful in this great work, no place for the self-indulgent or those who are incapable of making life a success in any calling, no place for halfhearted men who are not fervent in spirit, willing to endure hardness, opposition, reproach, or death for Christ's sake. The Christian ministry is no place for drones. There is a class of men attempting to preach who are slipshod, careless, and irreverent. They would better be tilling the soil than teaching the sacred truth of God.

Young men must soon bear the burdens older ones have borne. We have lost time in neglecting to bring young men to the front and give them a higher, more solid education. The work is constantly advancing, and we must obey the command: "Go forward." Much good could be done by youth who are established in the truth and are not easily influenced or swayed from the right by their surroundings, but who walk with God, who pray much, and who put forth most earnest endeavors to gather all the light they can. The worker should be prepared to put forth the highest mental and moral energies with which nature, cultivation, and the grace of God have endowed him; but his success will be proportionate to the degree of consecration and self-sacrifice in which the work is done, rather than to either natural or acquired endowments. The most earnest and continued efforts to acquire qualifications for usefulness are necessary; but unless God works with the human efforts, nothing can be accomplished. Christ says: "Without Me ye can do nothing." Divine grace is the great element of saving power; without it all human efforts are unavailing; its cooperation is needed even with the strongest and most earnest human efforts for the inculcation of truth.

The cause of God needs teachers who have high moral qualities and can be trusted with the education of others, men who are sound in the faith and have tact and patience, who walk with God and abstain from the very appearance of evil, who stand so closely connected with God that they can be channels of light—in short, Christian gentlemen. The good impressions made by such will never be effaced, and the training thus given will endure throughout eternity. What is neglected in this training process is likely to remain undone. Who will undertake this work? We would that there were strong young men, rooted and grounded in the faith, who had such a living connection with God that they could, if so counseled by our leading brethren, enter the higher colleges in our land, where they would have a wider field for study and observation. Association with different classes of minds, an acquaintance with the workings and results of popular methods of education, and a knowledge of theology as taught in the leading institutions of learning would be of great value to such workers, preparing them to labor for the educated classes and to meet the prevailing errors of our time. Such was the method pursued by the ancient Waldenses, and, if true to God, our youth, like theirs, might do a good work, even while gaining their education, in sowing the seeds of truth in other minds.

"Be strong, and quit yourselves like men." Ask of Him who suffered reproach, insult, and mockery for your sakes: "Lord, what wilt Thou have me to do?" None are too highly educated to become humble disciples of Christ. Those who feel it a privilege to give the best of their life and learning to Him from whom they received them, will shun no labor, no sacrifice, to render back to God in highest service His entrusted talents. In the great battle of life many of the workers lose sight of the solemnity and sacred character of their mission. The deadly curse of sin continues to blight and deface the moral image of God in them because they do not work as Christ worked.

We see the need of encouraging higher ideas of education and of employing more trained men in the ministry. Those who do not obtain the right kind of education before they enter upon God's work are not competent to accept this holy trust and to carry forward the work of reformation. Yet all should continue their education after they engage in the work. They must have the word of God abiding in them. We need more cultivation, refinement, and nobility of soul in our laborers. Such an improvement as this would show results in eternity.

"I have written unto you, fathers, because ye have known Him that is from the beginning. I have written unto you, young men, because ye are strong, and the word of God abideth in you, and ye have overcome the wicked one." The apostle here links the experience of the fathers with that of the young men; in like manner there is a link between the old disciples in this cause and those who are younger, who have not had an experience in the early events of this message. Those who were young when the message arose will have to be educated by the old standard-bearers. These teachers must realize that too great pains cannot be taken to fit men for their holy trust while the standard-bearers are still able to hold the standard aloft. And yet those who have so long fought in the battles may still win victories. They have been so thoroughly acquainted with the wiles of Satan that they will not be easily moved from the old paths. They remember the days of old. They know Him who is from the beginning. They may ever be light bearers, faithful witnesses for God, living epistles, known and read of all men.

Let us, then, thank God that a few are left, as was John, to relate their experience in the beginning of this message, and the reception of that which we now hold so dear. But one after another they are falling at their post, and it is only wisdom that we prepare others to take the work where they leave it.

Efforts must be made to fit young men for the work. They must come to the front, to lift burdens and responsibilities. Those who are now young must become strong men. They must be able to plan and give counsel. The word of God abiding in them will make them pure and will fill them with faith, hope, courage, and devotion. The work is now greatly retarded because men are carrying responsibilities for which they are unfitted. Shall this great want continue and increase? Shall these great responsibilities drop from the hands of old, experienced workers into the hands of those unable to manage them? Are we not neglecting a very important work by failing to educate and train our youth to fill positions of trust?

Let the workers be educated, but at the same time let them be meek and lowly of heart. Let us elevate the work to the highest possible standard, ever remembering that if we do our part, God will not fail to do His.

UNHOLY AMBITION

Dear Brother and Sister N: Although I have received from you no acknowledgment of my last letter, I feel drawn out to write to you again. I have been shown your danger, and cannot forbear to impress upon your minds the necessity of walking humbly with God. You will be safe as long as you have humble views of self. But I know that your souls are in peril. You are seeking for a broader path for your feet than the humble path of holiness, the royal way that leads to the city of God. You have too much of self and too little of the meekness and lowliness of Christ. You have much self-esteem and self-confidence, and little faith in God. The discordant elements in your nature are largely developed. Unruly passions have a controlling power. Pride and vanity seek for the supremacy. I know that the enemy is tempting you sorely. Your only safety is in entire conformity to the will of God. Submission is necessary on your part; a complete consecration of yourselves to Christ is your only hope of salvation. If you walk in humility of mind before the Lord, then He can work with your efforts, and His strength will be made perfect in your weakness. Christ is our Saviour. He has said for your benefit and for mine: "Without Me ye can do nothing." Oh, will you have more of Jesus, and less of self?

Brother N, you are not naturally devotional and hence need to make constant efforts to cultivate faith. It is easy for you to drop Christ out of your experience. The Lord has given you His blessing in the past, and how sweet it was to your soul! What comfort, what courage, it gave you! Your passion is to exalt education, but I speak the truth when I tell you that education, unless balanced by religious principles, will be a power for evil.

I am not willing to look on passively and see you go as others have gone in the fatal delusion that Seventh-day Adventists are too narrow in their ideas, are traveling in too obscure a path; that they must needs have greater notoriety and rise to greater eminence; that the teachers in our schools should give their powers more exclusively to the sciences and not weave religion into so much of their education. When this seed is dropped into the hearts of students, it will develop rapidly into a harvest which you will not covet to reap.

We are, as it were, on the very borders of the eternal world, and if you do the work in this school for which it was founded you must educate largely from the Book of all books. You must not exalt any other study above that of the Bible. Other schools in our land are not to be taken as your pattern.

I have been shown that you are charmed with that line of education from which the religious element is almost entirely excluded. There are numerous schools of this order in our land, where students can go if they desire that kind of training. But this school must be of a different character; it must have the mold of God in every department.

Jesus and His love should be interwoven with all the education given, as the very best knowledge the students can have. "The fear of the Lord is the beginning of wisdom." If the principal, in his ambitious projects, soars away from the Source of all wisdom and thinks that Bible religion will clip his wings, he will find that he amounts to no more than a soap bubble. Then for your soul's sake bring the Prince of life into every plan, every organization. You cannot have too much of Jesus or of Scripture history in your school.

Have we the truth? Are we living in the closing period of this earth's history? Is Christ at the door? These are questions for us all to settle. Education ought always to be of a high, holy order, and the need is more imperative now than ever before. The removal of the faithful from this world will soon be accomplished. Then why not bring all the energies of mind and soul into entire consecration to God?

Never hide your colors, never put your light under a bushel or under a bed, but set it on a candlestick, that it may give light to all that are in the house. Did you and the teachers who were with you at _____ watch for opportunities to enlighten others? Did you seek in wisdom to do all the good you possibly could? Did you try to call the attention of those whose acquaintance you formed, to Bible truths? Did you not drag your colors behind you because you were ashamed to be regarded as God's peculiar people? "Whosoever therefore shall be ashamed of Me and of My words; . . . of him also shall the Son of man be ashamed, when He cometh in the glory of His Father." If you would only feed on Christ daily then you could be a true educator.

My brother, there is danger of your trying to communicate too much at one time. You are not required to make lengthy speeches or to talk upon subjects that will not be understood or appreciated by common people. There is danger of your dwelling upon themes at the very top of the ladder, when those whom you are instructing need to be taught how to climb successfully its first rounds. You talk of things which those unacquainted with our faith cannot comprehend; hence your speeches are not interesting. They are not food for those whom you address.

Jesus was the greatest educator the world ever knew. In comparison with His knowledge the highest human knowledge is foolishness. But His instructions were so simple that all understood Him, both learned and unlearned. He made no effort to show His deep knowledge, for this they could not have understood. You seem to think your long talks have a special influence to mold and fashion your hearers just as you wish, but you will certainly fail in this. You would have a much better influence if you would talk less and pray more; God is your source of strength.

Your long speeches on education in the sciences are painful to the angels of God, who are constantly and intensely active in seeking to call the thoughts and affections to heavenly things. Souls are perishing while you neglect to work with your entrusted talents as Christ has given you an example. Souls will be lost under your long, Christless speeches. Your own soul is dwarfed and crippled in the knowledge of Christ. You are losing very much because you are blinded by the spirit and customs of an education which will not save the soul.

The youth need your labor. If you were a converted man, daily learning lessons in the school of Christ, then your labors would be a savor of life unto life. Then you could work with patience and love, and in the power of God, for the souls of youth who are exposed to temptation. Devote a portion of the time you consume in long addresses, to personal labor for the youth who need your help. Teach them the claims of God are upon them; pray with them. There are many who are bound in evil habits with fetters as firm as steel. The poor victims are fascinated with the charms of Satan's allurements and are unable to break away and stand in God-given freedom. They have lost years; shall they lose the year just entered upon? Will the principal of the school awaken to a sense of his responsibilities and give his mind and heart to the salvation of the students? If not, then let another take his place. Expenses should not run on and on, while nothing, or next to nothing, is done in the very line for which the school was brought into existence.

Shall the powers of mind and soul be misapplied? Shall opportunities be lost? Shall a form and routine be gone through day after day, with nothing gained? Oh, awake, awake! teachers and pupils, before it is too late. Awake before you hear from pale and agonized lips the terrible wail: "The harvest is past, the summer is ended, and we are not saved."

Are the gifts and talents of every educator improved for the very best good of the pupils? Who is watching for a favorable moment to speak words of kindness and love? Who loves to tell the story of Him who so loved the world that He gave His life to redeem lost and perishing sinners? Train the youth, mold the character, educate, educate, educate, for the future, immortal life. Pray often. Plead with God to give you a spirit of supplication. Do not feel that your work as teachers is done unless you can lead your scholars to faith in Jesus and love for Him. Let the love of Christ pervade your own souls, and then you will unconsciously teach it to others. When you as instructors commit yourselves unreservedly to Jesus, for Him to lead, to guide, to control, you will not fail. Teaching your students to be Christians is the greatest work before you. Go to God; He hears and answers prayer put from you questionings, doubts, and unbelief. Let no harshness come into your teaching. Be not too exacting, but cultivate tender sympathy and love. Be cheerful. Do not scold, do not censure too severely; be firm, be broad, be Christlike, pitiful, courteous. "Whatsoever a man soweth, that shall he also reap."

I cannot express to you the intense desire of my soul that you should all seek the Lord most earnestly while He may be found. We are in the day of God's preparation. Let nothing be regarded as of sufficient worth to draw your minds from the work of preparing for the great day of judgment. Get ready. Let not cold unbelief hold your souls away from God, but let His love burn on the altar of your hearts.

"THE APPEARANCE OF EVIL"

I feel urged to address those who are engaged in giving the last message of warning to the world. Whether those for whom they labor see and accept the truth depends very much upon the individual workers. The command from God is, "Be ye clean, that bear the vessels of the Lord;" and Paul charges Timothy, "Take heed unto thyself, and unto the doctrine." The work must commence with the worker; he must be united to Christ as the branch is united to the vine. "I am the Vine," said Christ; "ye are the branches." The closest possible connection is here represented. Engraft the leafless twig upon the flourishing vine stock, and it becomes a living branch, drawing sap and nourishment from the vine. Fiber by fiber, vein by vein, the sapling clings, until it buds and blossoms and bears fruit. The sapless twig represents the sinner. When united to Christ, soul is joined to soul, the feeble and finite to the holy and infinite, and man becomes one with Christ.

"Without Me," says Christ, "ye can do nothing." Are we who claim to be workers with Christ, united to Him? Do we abide in Christ? and are we one with Him? The message that we bear is world wide. It must come before all nations, tongues, and peoples. The Lord will not require any one of us to go forth with this message without giving us grace and power to present it to the people in a manner corresponding to its importance. The great question with us today is: Are we carrying to the world this solemn message of truth in a way to show its importance? The Lord will work with the laborers if they will make Christ their only dependence. He never designed that His missionaries should work without His grace, destitute of His power.

Christ has chosen us out of the world, that we might be a peculiar and holy people. He "gave Himself for us, that He might redeem us from all iniquity, and purify unto Himself a peculiar people, zealous of good works." God's workers must be men of prayer, diligent students of the Scriptures, hungering and thirsting after righteousness, that they may be a light and strength to others. Our God is a jealous God; and He requires us to worship Him in spirit and in truth, in the beauty of holiness. The psalmist says: "If I regard iniquity in my heart, the Lord will not hear me." As workers we must take heed to our ways. If the psalmist could not be heard if he regarded iniquity in his heart, how can the prayers of men now be heard while iniquity is regarded by them?

After the passing of the time in 1844, fanaticism came into the ranks of Adventists. God gave messages of warning to stay the incoming evil. There was too great familiarity between some men and women. I presented to them the holy standard of truth that we should reach and the purity of deportment that we should maintain in order to meet the approval of God and be without spot or wrinkle or any such thing. Most solemn denunciations from God were given to men and women whose thoughts were running in an impure channel, while they claimed to be especially favored by God; but the message which God gave was despised and rejected. They turned upon me and said: "Has God spoken only by you, and not by us?" They did not amend their ways, and the Lord suffered them to go on till defilement marked their lives.

We are not out of danger even now. Every soul who engages to give to the world the message of warning will be sorely tempted to pursue such a course in life as will deny his faith. It is Satan's studied plan to make the workers weak in prayer, weak in power, and weak in influence, because of their defects of character. We, as workers, must be united in frowning down and condemning everything that bears the least approach to evil in our associations with one another. Our faith is holy; our work is to vindicate the honor of God's law, and is not of a character to bring anyone down to a low level in thought or in deportment.

There is an exalted platform for us to stand upon. We must believe and teach the truth as it is in Jesus. Holiness of heart will never lead to impure actions. When one who claims to be teaching the truth is inclined to be much in the company of young or even married women, when he familiarly lays his hand upon them, or is often conversing with them in a familiar manner, be afraid of him; the pure principles of truth are not inwrought in his soul. Such are not in Christ, and Christ is not abiding in them. They need a thorough conversion before God can accept their labors. The truth of heavenly origin never degrades the receiver, never leads him to the least approach to undue familiarity; on the contrary, it sanctifies the believer, refines his taste, elevates and ennobles him, and brings him into a close connection with Jesus. It leads him to regard the apostle Paul's injunction to abstain from even the appearance of evil, lest his "good be evil spoken of."

This is a subject to which we must give heed. We must guard against the sins of this degenerate age. We must stand aloof from everything that savors of undue familiarity. God condemns it. It is forbidden ground, upon which it is unsafe to set the feet. Every word and action should tend to elevate, refine, and ennoble the character. There is sin in thoughtlessness about such matters. The apostle Paul exhorted Timothy to diligence and thoroughness in his ministry, and urged him to meditate upon those things that were pure and excellent, that his profiting might appear unto all. The same counsel is greatly needed by young men of the present age. Thoughtful consideration is essential. If men would only think more, and act less impulsively, they would meet with much greater success in their labors. We are handling subjects of infinite importance, and we cannot afford to weave into our work our own defects of character. We want to represent the character of Christ.

We have a great work to do to elevate men and win them to Christ, to lead them to choose and earnestly seek to be partakers of the divine nature, having escaped the corruption that is in the world through lust. Every thought, every word, and every action of the workers should be of that elevated character which is in harmony with the sacred truth they advocate. It may be that men and women will necessarily be united more or less in our important mission fields. If this is the case, they cannot be too circumspect. Let married men be reserved and guarded, that no evil may truthfully be said of them. We are living in an age when iniquity abounds, and an unguarded word or improper action may greatly injure the usefulness of the one who shows this weakness. Let the workers keep up the barriers of reserve; let not one instance occur of which the enemy can make capital. If they begin to place their affections upon one another, giving special attention to favorites and using flattering words, God will withdraw His Spirit.

If married men go into the work, leaving their wives to care for the children at home, the wife and mother is doing fully as great and important a work as the husband and father. Although one is in the missionary field, the other is a home missionary, whose cares and anxieties and burdens frequently far exceed those of the husband and father. Her work is a solemn and important one—to mold the minds and fashion the characters of her children, to train them for usefulness here and fit them for the future, immortal life. The husband in the open missionary field may receive the honors of men, while the home toiler may receive no earthly credit for her labor. But if she works for the best interest of her family, seeking to fashion their characters after the divine Model, the recording angel writes her name as one of the greatest missionaries in the world. God does not see things as man's finite vision views them. How careful should the husband and father be to maintain his loyalty to his marriage vows. How circumspect should be his character, lest he shall encourage thoughts in young girls, or even in married women, that are not in accordance with the high, holy standard,—the commandments of God. Those commandments Christ shows to be exceedingly broad, reaching even the thoughts, intents, and purposes of the heart. Here is where many are delinquent. Their heart imaginings are not of the pure, holy character which God requires; and however high their calling, however talented they may be, God will mark iniquity against them and will count them as far more guilty and deserving of His wrath than those who have less talent, less light, less influence.

I am pained when I see men praised, flattered, and petted. God has revealed to me the fact that some who receive these attentions are unworthy to take His name upon their lips; yet they are exalted to heaven in the estimation of finite beings, who read only from outward appearance. My sisters, never pet and flatter poor, fallible, erring men, either young or old, married or unmarried. You know not their weaknesses, and you know not but that these very attentions and this profuse praise may prove their ruin. I am alarmed at the shortsightedness, the want of wisdom, that many manifest in this respect.

Men who are doing God's work and who have Christ abiding in their hearts will not lower the standard of morality, but will ever seek to elevate it. They will not find pleasure in the flattery of women or in being petted by them. Let men, both single and married, say: "Hands off! I will never give the least occasion that my good should be evil spoken of. My good name is capital of far more value to me than gold or silver. Let me preserve it untarnished. If men assail that name, it shall not be because I have given them occasion to do so, but for the same reason that they spoke evil of Christ—because they hated the purity and holiness of His character, for it was a constant rebuke to them."

I wish I could impress upon every worker in God's cause the great need of continual, earnest prayer. They cannot be constantly upon their knees, but they can be uplifting their hearts to God. This is the way that Enoch walked with God. Be careful lest self-sufficiency come in and you drop Jesus out and work in your own strength rather than in the spirit and strength of the Master. Do not waste golden moments in frivolous conversation. When you return from doing missionary work, do not praise yourself, but exalt Jesus; lift up the cross of Calvary. Allow no one to praise or flatter you, or to cling to your hand as if loath to let it go. Be afraid of every such demonstration. When young or even married persons show a disposition to open their family secrets to you, beware. When they express a desire for sympathy, know that it is time to exercise great caution. Those who are imbued with the Spirit of Christ and who are walking with God will have no unholy pining for sympathy. They have a companionship that satisfies every desire of the mind and heart. Married men who accept the attention, the praise and petting, of women should be assured that the love and sympathy of this class are not worth the obtaining.

Women are too often tempters. On one pretense or another they engage the attention of men, married or unmarried, and lead them on till they transgress the law of God, till their usefulness is ruined, and their souls are in jeopardy. The history of Joseph is left on record for the benefit of all who, like him, are tempted. In principle he was firm as a rock, and he answered the tempter: "How then can I do this great wickedness, and sin against God?" Moral power like his is what is needed now. If women would only elevate their lives and become workers with Christ, there would be less danger through their influence; but with their present feelings of unconcern in regard to home responsibilities and in regard to the claims that God has upon them, their influence is often strong in the wrong direction, their powers are dwarfed, and their work does not bear the divine impress. They are not home missionaries, neither are they missionaries away from home; and frequently home, precious home, is left to desolation.

Let everyone who professes Christ seek to overcome all unmanliness, all weakness and folly. Some men never grow up to the full stature of men in Christ Jesus. They are childish and self-indulgent. Humble piety would correct all this. Pure religion possesses no characteristics of childish self-indulgence. It is honorable in the highest degree. Then let not one of those who have enlisted as soldiers of Christ be ready to faint in the day of trial. All should feel that they have earnest work to do to elevate their fellow men. Not one has a right to rest from the warfare to make virtue desirable and vice hated. There is no rest for the living Christian this side of the eternal world. To obey God's commandments is to do right and only right. This is Christian manliness. But many need to take frequent lessons from the life of Christ, who is the Author and Finisher of our faith. "Consider Him that endured such contradiction of sinners against Himself, lest ye be wearied and faint in your minds. Ye have not yet resisted unto blood, striving against sin." You are to show a growth in the Christian graces. By manifesting meekness under provocation and growing away from low earthliness you give evidence that you have an indwelling Saviour, and every thought, word, and deed attracts men to Jesus rather than to self. There is a great amount of work to be done and but little time in which to do it. Let it be your lifework to inspire all with the thought that they have a work to do for Christ. Wherever there are duties to be done which others do not understand because they do not wish to see their lifework, accept them and do them.

The standard of morality is not exalted high enough among God's people. Many who profess to be keeping God's commandments and standing in their defense are breaking them. Temptations present themselves in such a way that the tempted think they see an excuse to transgress. Those who enter the missionary field should be men and women who walk and talk with God. Those who stand as ministers in the sacred desk should be men of blameless reputation; their lives should be spotless, above everything that savors of impurity. Do not place your reputation in jeopardy by going in the way of temptation. If a woman lingeringly holds your hand, quickly withdraw it and save her from sin. If she manifests undue affection and mourns that her husband does not love her and sympathize with her, do not try to supply this lack. Your only safe and wise course in such a case is to keep your sympathy to yourself. Such cases are numerous. Point such souls to the Burden Bearer, the true and safe Counselor. If she has chosen Christ as a companion, He will give her grace to bear neglect without repining; meanwhile she should diligently do all in her power to bind her husband to herself by strictest fidelity to him and faithfulness in making his home cheerful and attractive. If all her efforts are unavailing and unappreciated, she will have the sympathy and aid of her blessed Redeemer. He will help her to bear all her burdens and comfort her in her disappointments. She shows distrust of Jesus when she reaches for human objects to supply the place that Christ is ever ready to fill. In her repining she sins against God. She would do well to examine her own heart critically to see if sin is not lurking in the soul. The heart that thus seeks human sympathy and accepts forbidden attentions from anyone is not pure and faultless before God.

The Bible affords many striking illustrations of the strong influence of evil-minded women. When Balaam was called upon to curse Israel, he was not permitted to do so; for the Lord "hath not beheld iniquity in Jacob, neither hath He seen perverseness in Israel." But Balaam, who had already yielded to temptation, now became fully the agent of Satan; and he determined to accomplish indirectly what God had not permitted him to do directly. He at once laid a snare whereby Israel should be enchanted with the beautiful Moabitish women, who would lead them to transgress God's law. Thus iniquity would be found in them, and God's blessing would not rest upon them. Their forces would be greatly weakened, and their enemies would no longer fear their power, because the presence of the Lord of hosts was not with their armies.

This is intended as a warning to the people of God living in the last days. If they follow after righteousness and true holiness, if they keep all the commandments of God, Satan and his agents will not be permitted to overcome them. All the opposition of their bitterest foes will prove powerless to destroy or uproot the vine of God's own planting. Satan understands what Balaam learned by sad experience, that there is no enchantment against Jacob, neither divination against Israel, while iniquity is not cherished among them; therefore his power and influence will ever be employed to mar their unity and defile the purity of their characters. His snares are laid in a thousand ways to weaken their power for good.

Again I urge upon you the necessity of purity in every thought, in every word, in every action. We have an individual accountability to God, an individual work, which no one can do for us; it is to make the world better by precept, by personal effort, and by example. While we should cultivate sociability, let it not be merely for amusement, but for a purpose. There are souls to save. Come near to them by personal effort. Open your doors to young men who are exposed to temptation. Evil invites them on every hand. Seek to interest them. If they are full of faults, seek to correct these errors. Do not hold yourselves aloof from them, but come close to them. Bring them to your firesides; invite them to your family altars. There is work that thousands need to have done for them. Every tree in Satan's garden is hung with tempting, poisonous fruit, and a woe is pronounced upon everyone who plucks and eats. Let us remember the claims of God upon us to make the path to heaven clear and bright and attractive, that we may win souls away from Satan's destructive enchantments.

God has given us reason to be used for a noble purpose. We are here as probationers for the next life. It is too solemn a period for any of us to be careless or to move in uncertainty. Our intercourse with others should be characterized by sobriety and heavenly-mindedness. Our conversation should be upon heavenly things. "Then they that feared the Lord spake often one to another: and the Lord hearkened and heard it, and a book of remembrance was written before Him for them that feared the Lord, and that thought upon His name. And they shall be Mine, saith the Lord of hosts, in that day when I make up My jewels; and I will spare them, as a man spareth his own son that serveth him."

What is more worthy to engross the mind than the plan of redemption? It is a subject that is exhaustless. The love of Jesus, the salvation offered to fallen man through His infinite love, holiness of heart, the precious, saving truth for these last days, the grace of Christ—these are subjects which may animate the soul and cause the pure in heart to feel that joy which the disciples felt when Jesus came and walked with them as they traveled toward Emmaus. He who has centered his affections upon Christ will relish this kind of hallowed association and will gather divine strength by such intercourse; but he who has no relish for this kind of conversation, and who is best pleased to talk sentimental nonsense, has wandered far away from God and is becoming dead to holy and noble aspirations. The sensual, the earthly, is interpreted by such to be heavenly. When the conversation is of a frivolous character and savors of a dissatisfied reaching out after human sympathy and appreciation, it springs from lovesick sentimentalism, and neither the youth nor the men with gray hairs are secure. When the truth of God is an abiding principle in the heart, it will be like a living spring. Attempts may be made to repress it, but it will gush forth in another place; it is there and cannot be repressed. The truth in the heart is a wellspring of life. It refreshes the weary and restrains vile thought and utterance.

Is there not enough taking place about us to show us the dangers that beset our path? Everywhere are seen wrecks of humanity, neglected family altars, broken-up families. There is a strange abandonment of principle, a lowering of the standard of morality; the sins are fast increasing which caused the judgments of God to be poured upon the earth in the Flood and in the destruction of Sodom by fire. We are nearing the end. God has borne long with the perversity of mankind, but their punishment is no less certain. Let those who profess to be the light of the world depart from all iniquity. We see the very same spirit manifested against the truth that was seen in Christ's day. For want of Bible arguments, those who are making void the law of God will manufacture falsehoods to stain and blacken the workers. They did this to the world's Redeemer; they will do it to His followers. Reports that have not the least foundation will be asserted as truth.

God has blessed His commandment-keeping people and all the opposition and falsehoods that may be brought against them will only strengthen those who stand firm in defense of the faith once delivered to the saints. But if those who profess to be the depositaries of God's law become transgressors of that law, His protecting care will be withdrawn, and many will fall through perverseness and licentiousness. Then we shall indeed be unable to stand before our enemies. But if His people remain separate and distinct from the world, as a nation that do righteousness, God will be their defense, and no weapons formed against them shall prosper.

In view of the danger of this time shall not we, as God's

commandment-keeping people, put away from among us all sin, all iniquity, all perverseness? Shall not the women professing the truth keep strict guard over themselves, lest the least encouragement be given to unwarrantable familiarity? They may close many a door of temptation if they will observe at all times strict reserve and propriety of deportment. Let men find an example in the life of Joseph and stand firm in principle, however strongly tempted. We want to be strong men and women for the right. There are those around us who are weak in moral power. They need to be in the company of those who are firm, and whose hearts are closely knit with the heart of Christ. Everyone's principles will be put to the test. But there are those who go into temptation like a fool to the correction of stocks. They invite the enemy to tempt them. They unnerve themselves, are weakened in moral power, and shame and confusion are the result.

How contemptible in the sight of a holy God are those who profess to stand in vindication of His law and yet violate its precepts! They bring reproach upon the precious cause and give the opposers of truth occasion to triumph. Never should the mark of distinction between the followers of Jesus and the followers of Satan be obliterated. There is a distinct line drawn by God Himself between the world and the church, between commandment keepers and commandment breakers. They do not blend together. They are as different as midday and midnight—different in their tastes, their aims, their pursuits, their characters. If we cultivate the love and fear of God we shall loathe the least approach to impurity.

May the Lord attract souls to Himself and impart to them individually a sense of their sacred responsibility to form such characters that Christ will not be ashamed to call them brethren. Elevate the standard, and then the heavenly benediction will be pronounced upon you in that day when every man will receive according to the deeds done in the body.

Workers for God must live as in His sight and be constantly developing in character, in true virtue and godliness. Their minds and hearts must be so thoroughly imbued with the Spirit of Christ and so solemnized by the sacred message they have to bear that every thought, every action, every motive, will be above the earthly and sensual. Their happiness will not be in forbidden, selfish gratifications, but in Jesus and His love.

My prayer is: "O Lord, anoint the eyes of Thy people, that they may discern between sin and holiness, between pollution and righteousness, and come off victors at last."

LOVE FOR THE ERRING

Christ came to bring salvation within the reach of all. Upon the cross of Calvary He paid the infinite redemption price for a lost world. His self-denial and self-sacrifice, His unselfish labor, His humiliation, above all, the offering up of His life, testifies to the depth of His love for fallen man. It was to seek and to save the lost that He came to earth. His mission was to sinners, sinners of every grade, of every tongue and nation. He paid the price for all, to ransom them and bring them into union and sympathy with Himself. The most erring, the most sinful, were not passed by; His labors were especially for those who most needed the salvation He came to bring. The greater their need of reform, the deeper was His interest, the greater His sympathy, and the more earnest His labors. His great heart of love was stirred to its depths for the ones whose condition was most hopeless and who most needed His transforming grace.

In the parable of the lost sheep is represented the wonderful love of Christ for the erring, wandering ones. He does not choose to remain with those who accept His salvation, bestowing all His efforts upon them and receiving their gratitude and love. The true shepherd leaves the flock that love him, and goes out into the wilderness, enduring hardship and facing danger and death, to seek and save the sheep that has wandered from the fold and that must perish if not brought back. When after diligent search the lost is found, the shepherd, though suffering from weariness, pain, and hunger, does not leave it in its weakness to follow him, he does not drive it along, but oh, wondrous love! he tenderly gathers it in his arms and, placing it upon his shoulder, bears it back to the fold. Then he calls upon his neighbors to rejoice with him over the lost that is found.

The parable of the prodigal son and that of the lost piece of silver teach the same lesson. Every soul that is especially imperiled by falling into temptation causes pain to the heart of Christ and calls forth His tenderest sympathy and most earnest labor. Over one sinner that repenteth, His joy is greater than over the ninety and nine who need no repentance.

These lessons are for our benefit. Christ has enjoined upon His disciples that they co-operate with Him in His work, that they love one another as He has loved them. The agony which He endured upon the cross testifies to the estimate He places upon the human soul. All who accept this great salvation pledge themselves to be co-workers with Him. None are to consider themselves special favorites of heaven and center their interest and attention upon self. All who have enlisted in the service of Christ are to work as He worked, and are to love those who are in ignorance and sin, even as He loved them.

But there has been among us as a people a lack of deep, earnest, soul-touching sympathy and love for the tempted and the erring. Many have manifested great coldness and sinful neglect, represented by Christ as passing by on the other side, keeping as far as possible from those who most need help. The newly converted soul often has fierce conflicts with established habits or with some special form of temptation, and, being overcome by some master passion or tendency, he is guilty of indiscretion or actual wrong. It is then that energy, tact, and wisdom are required of his brethren, that he may be restored to spiritual health. In such cases the instructions of God's word apply: "Brethren, if a man be overtaken in a fault, ye which are spiritual, restore such an one in a spirit of meekness; considering thyself, lest thou also be tempted." "We then that are strong ought to bear the infirmities of the weak, and not to please ourselves." But how little of the pitying tenderness of Christ is manifested by His professed followers! When one errs, others too often feel at liberty to make the case appear as bad as possible. Those who perhaps are guilty of fully as great sins in some other direction, will treat their brother with cruel severity. Errors committed through ignorance, thoughtlessness, or weakness are exaggerated into willful, premeditated sin. As they see souls going astray, some fold their hands and say: "I told you so. I knew there was no dependence to be placed upon them." Thus they place themselves in the attitude of Satan, exulting in spirit that their evil surmisings have proved to be correct.

We must expect to meet and bear with great imperfections in those who are young and inexperienced. Christ has bidden us seek to restore such in the spirit of meekness, and He holds us responsible for pursuing a course which will drive them to discouragement, despair, and ruin. Unless we daily cultivate the precious plant of love we are in danger of becoming narrow, unsympathetic, bigoted, and critical, esteeming ourselves righteous when we are far from being approved of God. Some are uncourteous, abrupt, and harsh. They are like chestnut burs: they prick whenever touched. These do incalculable harm by misrepresenting our loving Saviour.

We must come up to a higher standard, or we are unworthy of the Christian name. We should cultivate the spirit with which Christ labored to save the erring. They are as dear to Him as we are. They are equally capable of being trophies of His grace and heirs of the kingdom. But they are exposed to the snares of a wily foe, exposed to danger and defilement, and without the saving grace of Christ, to certain ruin. Did we view this matter in the right light, how would our zeal be quickened and our earnest, self-sacrificing efforts be multiplied, that we might come close to those who need our help, our prayers, our sympathy, and our love!

Let those who have been remiss in this work consider their duty in the light of the great commandment: "Thou shalt love thy neighbor as thyself." This obligation is resting upon all. All are required to labor to diminish the ills and multiply the blessings of their fellow creatures. If we are strong to resist temptation we are under the greater obligation to help those who are weak and yielding. Have we knowledge, we should instruct the ignorant. Has God blessed us with this world's goods, it is our duty to succor the poor. We must work for others' good. Let all within the sphere of our influence be partakers of whatever of excellence we may possess. None should be content to feed on the bread of life without sharing it with those around them.

Those only live for Christ and honor His name who are true to their Master in seeking to save that which is lost. Genuine piety will surely manifest the deep longing and earnest labor of the crucified Saviour to save those for whom He died. If our hearts are softened and subdued by the grace of Christ, and glowing with a sense of God's goodness and love, there will be a natural outflow of love, sympathy, and tenderness to others. The truth exemplified in the life will exert its power, like the hidden leaven, upon all with whom it is brought in contact.

God has ordained that in order to grow in grace and in a knowledge of Christ, men must follow His example and work as He worked. It will often require a struggle to control our own feelings and to refrain from speaking in a manner to discourage those who are laboring under temptation. A life of daily prayer and praise, a life which will shed light upon the path of others, cannot be maintained without earnest effort. But such effort will yield precious fruit, blessing not only the receiver, but the giver. The spirit of unselfish labor for others gives depth, stability, and Christlike loveliness to the character and brings peace and happiness to its possessor. The aspirations are elevated. There is no room for sloth or selfishness. Those who exercise the Christian graces will grow. They will have spiritual sinew and muscle, and will be strong to work for God. They will have clear spiritual perceptions, a steady, increasing faith, and prevailing power in prayer. Those who are watching for souls, who devote themselves most fully to the salvation of the erring, are most surely working out their own salvation.

But how has this work been neglected! If the thoughts and affections were wholly given to God, think you that souls in error, under the temptations of Satan, would be dropped as carelessly and unfeelingly as they have been? Would not greater efforts be put forth, in the love and simplicity of Christ, to save these wandering ones? All who are truly consecrated to God will engage with the greatest zeal in the work for which He has done the most, for which He has made an infinite sacrifice—the work for the salvation of souls. This is the special work to be cherished and sustained, and never allowed to flag.

God calls upon His people to arise and come out of the chilling, frosty atmosphere in which they have been living, to shake off the impressions and ideas that have frozen up the impulses of love and held them in selfish inactivity. He bids them come up from their low, earthly level and breathe in the clear, sunny atmosphere of heaven.

Our meetings for worship should be sacred, precious occasions. The prayer meeting is not a place where brethren are to censure and condemn one another, where there are to be unkind feelings and hard speeches. Christ will be driven from the assemblies where this spirit is manifested, and Satan will come in to take the lead. Nothing that savors of an unchristian, unloving spirit should be permitted to enter; for do we not assemble to seek mercy and forgiveness from the Lord? and the Saviour has plainly said: "With what judgment ye judge, ye shall be judged: and with what measure ye mete, it shall be measured to you again." Who can stand before God and plead a faultless character, a blameless life? And how, then, dare any criticize and condemn their brethren? Those who themselves can hope for salvation only through the merits of Christ, who must seek forgiveness by virtue of His blood, are under the strongest obligation to exercise love, pity, and forgiveness toward their fellow sinners.

Brethren, unless you educate yourselves to respect the place of devotion, you will receive no blessing from God. You may worship Him in form, but there will be no spiritual service. "Where two or three are gathered together in My name," says Jesus, "there am I in the midst of them." All should feel that they are in the divine presence, and instead of dwelling upon the faults and errors of others they should be diligently searching their own hearts. If you have confessions to make of your own sins, do your duty and leave others to do theirs.

When you indulge your own harshness of character by manifesting a hard, unfeeling spirit you are repulsing the very ones whom you should win. Your harshness destroys their love of assembling together and too often results in driving them from the truth. You should realize that you yourselves are under the rebuke of God. While you condemn others, the Lord condemns you. You have a duty to do to confess your own unchristian conduct. May the Lord move upon the hearts of the individual members of the church until His transforming grace shall be revealed in the life and the character. Then when you assemble together, it will not be to criticize one another, but to talk of Jesus and His love.

Our meetings should be made intensely interesting. They should be pervaded with the very atmosphere of heaven. Let there be no long, dry speeches and formal prayers merely for the sake of occupying the time. All should be ready to act their part with promptness, and when their duty is done, the meeting should be closed. Thus the interest will be kept up to the last. This is offering to God acceptable worship. His service should be made interesting and attractive and not be allowed to degenerate into a dry form. We must live for Christ minute by minute, hour by hour, and day by day; then Christ will dwell in us, and when we meet together, His love will be in our hearts, welling up like a spring in the desert, refreshing all, and making those who are ready to perish, eager to drink of the waters of life.

We are not to depend upon two or three members to do the work for the whole church. We must individually have a strong, active faith, carrying forward the work God has left us to do. There must be an intense, living interest to inquire of God: " 'What wilt Thou have me to do?' How shall I do my work for time and for eternity?" We must individually bend all our powers to search for the truth, employing every means within our reach that will aid us in a diligent, prayerful investigation of the Scriptures; and then we must be sanctified through the truth, that we may save souls.

An earnest effort should be made in every church to put away evilspeaking and a censorious spirit as among the sins productive of the greatest evils in the church. Severity and faultfinding must be rebuked as the workings of Satan. Mutual love and confidence must be encouraged and strengthened in the members of the church. Let all, in the fear of God and with love to their brethren, close their ears to gossip and censure. Direct the talebearer to the teachings of God's word.

Bid him obey the Scriptures and carry his complaints directly to those whom he thinks in error. This united action would bring a flood of light into the church and close the door to a flood of evil. Thus God would be glorified, and many souls would be saved.

The admonition of the True Witness to the Sardis church is: "Thou hast a name that thou livest, and art dead. Be watchful, and strengthen the things which remain, that are ready to die: for I have not found thy works perfect before God. Remember therefore how thou hast received and heard, and hold fast, and repent." The sin especially charged against this church is that they have not strengthened the things that remain, that are ready to die. Does this warning apply to us? Let us individually examine our hearts in the light of God's word, and let our first work be to set our hearts in order by the help of Christ.

God has done His part of the work for the salvation of men, and now He calls for the co-operation of the church. There are the blood of Christ, the word of truth, the Holy Spirit, on one hand, and there are the perishing souls on the other. Every follower of Christ has a part to act to bring men to accept the blessings heaven has provided. Let us closely examine ourselves and see if we have done this work. Let us question our motives and every action of our lives. Are there not many unpleasant pictures hanging in memory's halls? Often have you needed the forgiveness of Jesus. You have been constantly dependent upon His compassion and love. Yet have you not failed to manifest toward others the spirit which Christ has exercised toward you? Have you felt a burden for the one whom you saw venturing into forbidden paths? Have you kindly admonished him? Have you wept for him and prayed with him and for him? Have you shown by words of tenderness and kindly acts that you love him and desire to save him? As you have associated with those who were faltering and staggering under the load of their own infirmities of disposition and faulty habits, have you left them to fight the battles alone when you might have given them help? Have you not passed these sorely tempted ones by on the other side while the world has stood ready to give them sympathy and to allure them into Satan's nets? Have you not, like Cain, been ready to say: "Am I my brother's keeper?" How must the great Head of the church regard the work of your life? How does He to whom every soul is precious, as the purchase of His blood, look upon your indifference to those who stray from the right path? Are you not afraid that He will leave you just as you leave them? Be sure that He who is the true Watchman of the Lord's house has marked every neglect.

Have not Christ and His love been shut out from your life until a mechanical form has taken the place of heart service? Where is the kindling of soul you once felt at the mention of the name of Jesus? In the freshness of your early dedication, how fervent was your love for souls! how earnestly you sought to represent to them the Saviour's love! The absence of that love has made you cold, critical, exacting. Seek to win it back, and then labor to bring souls to Christ. If you refuse to do this, others who have had less light and experience and fewer opportunities will come up and take your place and do that which you have neglected; for the work must be done to save the tempted, the tried, the perishing. Christ offers the service to His church; who will accept it?

God has not been unmindful of the good deeds, the self-denying acts, of the church in the past. All are registered on high. But these are not enough. These will not save the church when she ceases to fulfill her mission. Unless the cruel neglect and indifference manifested in the past shall cease, the church, instead of going from strength to strength, will continue to degenerate into weakness and formality. Shall we let this be? Is the dull torpor, the mournful deterioration in love and spiritual zeal, to be perpetuated? Is this the condition in which Christ is to find His church?

Brethren, your own lamps will surely flicker and grow dim until they go out in darkness unless you make decided efforts to reform. "Remember therefore from whence thou art fallen, and repent, and do the first works." The opportunity now presented may be short. If this season of grace and repentance passes unimproved, the warning is given: "I will come unto thee quickly, and will remove thy candlestick out of his place." These words are uttered by the lips of the long-suffering, forbearing One. They are a solemn warning to churches and individuals that the Watcher who never slumbers is measuring their course of action. It is only by reason of His marvelous patience that they are not cut down as cumberers of the ground. But His Spirit will not always strive. His patience will wait but little longer.

Your faith must be something more than it has been, or you will be weighed in the balances and found wanting. At the last day the final decision by the Judge of all the earth will turn upon our interest in, and practical labor for, the needy, the oppressed, the tempted. You cannot always pass these by on the other side and yourselves find entrance as redeemed sinners into the city of God. "Inasmuch," says Christ, "as ye did it not to one of the least of these, ye did it not to Me."

It is not yet too late to redeem the neglects of the past. Let there be a revival of the first love, the first ardor. Search out the ones you have driven away, bind up by confession the wounds you have made. Come close to the great Heart of pitying love, and let the current of that divine compassion flow into your heart and from you to the hearts of others. Let the tenderness and mercy that Jesus has revealed in His own precious life be an example to us of the manner in which we should treat our fellow beings, especially those who are our brethren in Christ. Many have fainted and become discouraged in the great struggle of life, whom one word of kindly cheer and courage would have strengthened to overcome. Never, never become heartless, cold, unsympathetic, and censorious. Never lose an opportunity to say a word to encourage and inspire hope. We cannot tell how far-reaching may be our tender words of kindness, our Christlike efforts to lighten some burden. The erring can be restored in no other way than in the spirit of meekness, gentleness, and tender love.

Wouldst thou an erring soul redeem,
    And lead a lost one back to God?
Wouldst thou a guardian angel seem
    To one who long in guilt has trod?
Go kindly to him, take his hand,
    With gentle words, within thine own,
And by his side a brother stand,
    Till thou the demon sin dethrone.

Scorn not the guilty then, but plead
    With him in kindest, gentlest mood,
And back the lost one, thou mayst lead
    To God, humanity, and good.
Thou art thyself but man, and thou
    Art weak, perchance to fall as he;
Then mercy to the fallen show,
    That mercy may be shown to thee.

CHURCH DUTIES

Where the Spirit of the Lord is, there is meekness, patience, gentleness, and long-suffering. A true disciple of Christ will seek to imitate the Pattern. He will study to do the will of God on earth as it is done in heaven. Those whose hearts are still defiled with sin cannot be zealous of good works. They fail to keep the first four precepts of the Decalogue, defining the duty of man to God; neither do they keep the last six, defining the duty of man to his fellow men. Their hearts are filled with selfishness, and they are constantly finding fault with others who are better than themselves. They put their hands to a work which God has not given them, but leave undone the work He has left for them to do, which is to take heed to themselves, lest any root of bitterness springing up, trouble the church and defile it. They turn their eyes outward to watch lest the character of others should not be right, when their eyes should be turned inward to scan and criticize their own actions. When they empty the heart of self, envy, evil surmising, malice, they will not be climbing on the judgment seat and pronouncing sentence upon others who are in God's sight better than they.

He who would reform others must first reform himself. He must obtain the spirit of his Master and be willing, like Him, to suffer reproach and to practice self-denial. In comparison with the worth of one soul, the whole world sinks into insignificance. A desire to exercise authority, to lord it over God's heritage, will, if indulged, result in the loss of souls. Those who really love Jesus will seek to conform their own lives to the Pattern and will labor in His spirit for the salvation of others.

In order to secure man to Himself and ensure his eternal salvation, Christ left the royal courts of heaven and came to this earth, endured the agonies of sin and shame in man's stead, and died to make him free. In view of the infinite price paid for man's redemption, how dare any professing the name of Christ treat with indifference one of His little ones? How carefully should brethren and sisters in the church guard every word and action lest they hurt the oil and the wine! How patiently, kindly, and affectionately should they deal with the purchase of the blood of Christ! How faithfully and earnestly should they labor to lift up the desponding and the discouraged! How tenderly should they treat those who are trying to obey the truth and have no encouragement at home, who have constantly to breathe the atmosphere of unbelief and darkness!

TREATMENT OF THE ERRING

If a brother is supposed to have erred, his brethren and sisters should not whisper it among themselves and comment upon it, magnifying these supposed errors and faults. Much of this work is done, and the result is that the displeasure of God rests upon those who do it, and Satan exults that he can weaken and annoy those who might be strong in the Lord. The world sees their weakness and judges this class and the truth they profess to love, by the fruits manifested in them.

"Lord, who shall abide in Thy tabernacle? who shall dwell in Thy holy hill? He that walketh uprightly, and worketh righteousness, and speaketh the truth in his heart. He that backbiteth not with his tongue, nor doeth evil to his neighbor, nor taketh up a reproach against his neighbor. In whose eyes a vile person is contemned; but he honoreth them that fear the Lord. He that sweareth to his own hurt, and changeth not. He that putteth not out his money to usury, nor taketh reward against the innocent. He that doeth these things shall never be moved." Here the backbiter is excluded from abiding in the tabernacle of God and dwelling in the holy hill of Zion. He that taketh up a reproach against his neighbor cannot receive the approval of God.

How many ministers, while engaged in a good work in which souls are turning to God and to the truth, are called away to settle some church trial among brethren who were wholly wrong themselves and who had a contentious and overbearing spirit?

This work of withdrawing men from their fields of labor has been repeated again and again in the progress of this cause. It is a device of the great adversary of man to hinder the work of God. When souls that are upon the point of decid-ing in favor of the truth are thus left to unfavorable influences, they lose their interest, and it is very rarely that so powerful an impression can again be made upon them. Satan is ever seek-ing some device to call the minister from his field of labor at this critical point, that the results of his labors may be lost.

There are in the church unconsecrated, unconverted men and women who think more of maintaining their own dignity and their own opinions than they do of the salvation of their fellow creatures; and Satan works upon these to stir up diffi-culties that consume the time and labor of the minister, and many souls are lost as the result.

While the members of the church are in a divided state of feeling, their hearts are hard and unimpressible. The efforts of the minister are like blows upon cold iron, and each party becomes more set in his own way than before. The minister is placed in a most unenviable position; for, though he should decide ever so wisely, his decision must displease someone, and thus the party spirit is strengthened.

If the minister makes his home with some one family, others are sure to be jealous lest he shall receive impres-sions unfavorable to themselves. If he gives counsel, some will say, "Such a one has been talking with him," and his words have no weight with them. Thus their souls are armed with distrust and evil surmising, and the minister is left at the mercy of their prejudices and jealousies. Too of-ten he leaves the matter worse than he found it. Had he ut-terly refused to listen to the colored, one-sided statements of any, had he given words of advice in accordance with the Bible rule and said, like Nehemiah, "I am doing a great work, so that I cannot come down," that church would have been in a far better condition.

Ministers and lay members of the church displease God when they allow individuals to tell them the errors and faults of their brethren. They should not listen to these reports, but should inquire: "Have you strictly followed the injunctions of your Saviour? Have you gone to the offender and told him his faults between you and him alone? And has he refused to hear you? Have you carefully and prayerfully taken two or three others, and labored with him in tenderness, humility, and meekness, your heart throbbing with love for his soul?" If the Captain's orders, in the rules given for the erring, have been strictly followed, then an advance step is to be taken—tell it to the church, and let action be taken in the case according to the Scriptures. Then it is that heaven will ratify the decision made by the church in cutting off the offending member if he does not repent. If these steps have not been taken, close the ear to complaints, and thus refuse to take up a reproach against your neighbor. If there were no brethren and sisters to do this, evil tongues would soon cease; for they would not find so favorable a field in which to work in biting and devouring one another.

SELECTION OF LEADERS

The apostle Paul writes to Titus: "Set in order the things that are wanting, and ordain elders in every city, as I had appointed thee: if any be blameless, the husband of one wife, having faithful children not accused of riot or unruly. For a bishop must be blameless, as the steward of God." It would be well for all our ministers to give heed to these words and not to hurry men into office without due consideration and much prayer that God would designate by His Holy Spirit whom He will accept.

Said the inspired apostle: "Lay hands suddenly on no man." In some of our churches the work of organizing and of ordaining elders has been premature; the Bible rule has been disregarded, and consequently grievous trouble has been brought upon the church. There should not be so great haste in electing leaders as to ordain men who are in no way fitted for the responsible work—men who need to be converted, elevated, ennobled, and refined before they can serve the cause of God in any capacity.

The gospel net gathers both good and bad. It takes time for character to be developed; there must be time to learn what men really are. The family of the one suggested for office should be considered. Are they in subjection? Can the man rule his own house with honor? What character have his children? Will they do honor to the father's influence? If he has no tact, wisdom, or power of godliness at home in managing his own family, it is safe to conclude that the same defects will be carried into the church, and the same unsanctified management will be seen there. It will be far better to criticize the man before he is put into office than afterward, better to pray and counsel before taking the decisive step than to labor to correct the consequences of a wrong move.

In some churches the leader has not the right qualifications to educate the members of the church to be workers. Tact and judgment have not been used to keep up a living interest in the work of God. The leader is slow and tedious; he talks too much and prays too long in public; he has not that living connection with God which would give him a fresh experience.

The leaders of churches in every place should be earnest, full of zeal and unselfish interest, men of God who can give the right mold to the work. They should make their requests to God in faith. They may devote all the time they wish to secret prayer, but in public they should make their prayers and their testimonies short and to the point. Long, dry prayers and long exhortations should be avoided. If the brethren and sisters would have something to say that will refresh and edify others, it must first be in their hearts. They must daily be connected with God, drawing their supplies from His exhaustless storehouse and bringing therefrom things new and old. If their own souls have been vivified by the Spirit of God, they will cheer, strengthen, and encourage others; but if they have not drunk at the living fountain of salvation themselves, they will not know how to lead others there.

The necessity of experimental religion must be urged upon those who accept the theory of the truth. Ministers must keep their own souls in the love of God and then impress upon the people the necessity of an individual consecration, a personal conversion. All must obtain a living experience for themselves; they must have Christ enshrined in the heart, his Spirit controlling the affections, or their profession of faith is of no value, and their condition will be even worse than if they had never heard the truth.

Such arrangements should be made for the little companies accepting the truth as shall secure the prosperity of the church. One man may be appointed to lead for a week or a month, then another for a few weeks; and thus different persons may be enlisted in the work, and after a suitable trial someone should be selected by the voice of the church to be the acknowledged leader, never, however, to be chosen for more than one year. Then another may be selected, or the same one may be re-elected, if his service has proved a blessing to the church. The same principle should be followed in selecting men for other responsible positions, as in the offices of the conference. Untried men should not be elected as presidents of conferences. Many fail to exercise proper discernment in these important matters where eternal interests are involved.

We profess to be the depositaries of God's law; we claim to have greater light and to aim at a higher standard than any other people upon the earth; therefore we should show greater perfection of character and more earnest devotion. A most solemn message has been entrusted to those who have received the light of present truth. Our light should shine forth to brighten the pathway of those who are in darkness. As members of the visible church, and workers in the vineyard of the Lord, all professed Christians should do their utmost to preserve peace, harmony, and love in the church. Mark the prayer of Christ: "That they all may be one; as Thou, Father, art in Me, and I in Thee, that they also may be one in Us: that the world may believe that Thou hast sent Me." The unity of the church is the convincing evidence that God has sent Jesus into the world as its Redeemer. This is an argument which worldlings cannot controvert. Therefore Satan is constantly working to prevent this union and harmony, that unbelievers, by witnessing backsliding, dissension, and strife among professed Christians, may become disgusted with religion and be confirmed in their impenitence. God is dishonored by those who profess the truth while they are at variance and enmity with one another. Satan is the great accuser of the brethren, and all who engage in this work are enlisted in his service.

We profess to have more truth than other denominations; yet if this does not lead to greater consecration, to purer, holier lives, of what benefit is it to us? It would be better for us never to have seen the light of truth than to profess to accept it and not be sanctified through it.

In order to determine how important are the interests involved in the conversion of the soul from error to truth, we must appreciate the value of immortality; we must realize how terrible are the pains of the second death; we must comprehend the honor and glory awaiting the ransomed, and understand what it is to live in the presence of Him who died that He might elevate and ennoble man, and give to the overcomer a royal diadem.

The worth of a soul cannot be fully estimated by finite minds. How gratefully will the ransomed and glorified ones remember those who were instrumental in their salvation! No one will then regret his self-denying efforts and persevering labors, his patience, forbearance, and earnest heart yearnings for souls that might have been lost had he neglected his duty or become weary in well-doing.

Now these white-robed ones are gathered into the fold of the Great Shepherd. The faithful worker and the soul saved through his labor are greeted by the Lamb in the midst of the throne, and are led to the tree of life and to the fountain of living waters. With what joy does the servant of Christ behold these redeemed ones, who are made to share the glory of the Redeemer! How much more precious is heaven to those who have been faithful in the work of saving souls! "And they that be wise shall shine as the brightness of the firmament; and they that turn many to righteousness, as the stars for ever and ever."

A LETTER

Dear Brother O: I have received your letter, and need not express to you the sadness of my heart at the very sudden turn you have recently taken. As I review your past history I call to mind your experience in Colorado, your reflections while upon that rock where descent seemed impossible, and your subsequent partial recovery to the faith, your temptations through false and ambitious hopes to become greater away from our people than with them, your disappointment, your praiseworthy course of remaining silent, the prayers and sympathies of God's people that were ascending to heaven in your behalf, and my constant pleadings: "Do not let him alone, but make efforts to save him. He is ensnared; he has lost his hold upon God."

I remember the last time I rode out with your wife before she died. Her burden was for you and her children. She said she trembled for the future because of her children and the skepticism of her husband. "If I should die," she said, "and he should give up the faith and lead my children to give up the Sabbath, how terrible it would be after he has received so great light and so many evidences! For this reason I have clung to life. He has not that deep, inwrought work in the soul that will anchor him when temptations come. O Sister White, it is for the souls of my husband and children that I have clung to life. And I want to tell you right here that I am heartily sorry that I did not receive in a different spirit the testimony given me and my husband. I see now that the message to us was just what we needed; and had we accepted it, it would have placed us both in a better, far better, position spiritually than we have been in for some time. We were both proud in spirit, and since that time I have felt like shunning you; for I thought you had no faith or confidence in us. But during the last few months this has all disappeared, and I have felt the same confidence, the same close sympathy and love for you that I have had in my past life; but I know my husband does not feel thus, and it is of but little use for me to talk these things over with him. I am too weak to set matters before him as they are in my mind, and he is too firm in his ideas and feelings; but I wanted to tell you that I have implicit faith in the *Testimonies* and in your work, and have long been wishing for an opportunity to tell you this, and I shall now feel free. Will you forgive me for my feelings and words against you? I have grieved the Spirit of God and sometimes have felt that He had forsaken me; but I do not now have these feelings, neither have I had them for some time. I never realized the danger of talking unbelief as I have for a few weeks past. I fear greatly for any husband, for he expresses unbelief; and I fear he will give up all and become an infidel. Oh, how I wish I could help him!"

Brother O, when you told me that your wife died disbelieving the *Testimonies*, I did not contradict you; but I thought you did not tell me the truth. I afterward decided that you were greatly in the dark, for I have a letter which she sent me saying that she had the fullest confidence in the *Testimonies* and knew them to be true in regard to you and to herself. I attended the camp meeting in _____, and you were present. You then had an experience that would have proved of lasting value to you if you had remained humble before God as at that time. You then humbled your heart and upon your knees asked me to forgive you for the things you had said about me and my work. You said: "You have no idea how mean I have talked about you." I assured you I would just as freely forgive you as I hoped Jesus would forgive me my sins and errors. You stated there in the presence of several that you had said many things to my injury; all of which I assured you I freely forgave you, for it was not against me. None of these things were against me; I was only a servant bearing the message God gave me. It was not I personally that you were arrayed against; it was the message that God sent to you through the humble instrument. It was Christ that you injured, not I. "I do not want you," I said, "to confess to me. Make all straight between your soul and God, and all will be right between you and me." Some expressions that were written to you, you had taken in altogether too strong a light. And after reading them carefully again, you said they did not appear to you as they had, and everything was reconciled. You stated after this interview that you felt you had never before known what conversion was, but that you had been born again, converted for the first time. You could say you loved your brethren, your heart was light and happy; you saw the sacredness of the work as you had never seen it before; and your letters expressed the deep change wrought in you by the Spirit of God.

And yet I knew that you would be brought over the ground again and tested on the very points where you had failed before. Thus the Lord did for the children of Israel; thus He has done with His people in all ages. He will prove them where they have formerly failed; He will try them, and if they fail under the trial the second time, He will bring them around to the same test again.

My heart aches every time I think of you; my soul is sad indeed. Every soul is precious, because it has been purchased by the precious blood of Jesus Christ. I sometimes think that we do not place anything like a correct value upon the purchase of the blood of Jesus—the redemption of the soul. When I consider the infinite price paid for the redemption of individual souls, I think: "What if that soul is finally lost? What if he refuses to be a learner in the school of Christ and fails to practice meekness and lowliness, and will not wear the yoke of Christ?" This, my brother, has been your greatest failure. If you had taken less counsel of yourself and made Jesus your counselor you would now be strong in grace and in the knowledge of Jesus Christ. You have not yoked up with Christ; you have not been imbued with His Spirit. Oh, how much you need the divine mold upon your character!

We have much to answer for, considering our superior advantages and knowing that we must be judged by the light and privileges the Lord has granted us. We cannot plead that we are less favored with light than that people who have been for ages an astonishment and a reproach to the world. We cannot expect judgment to be given in our favor because, like Capernaum, we have been exalted to heaven. The Lord has wrought for His commandment-keeping people. The light that has been reflected to us from heaven was not granted to Sodom and Gomorrah, or they might have remained unto this day; and if the mighty works and knowledge and grace which have been manifested to this people had been made known to the nations in darkness, we know not how far in advance of this people they might now be. We cannot determine how much more tolerable it would be for them in the day of judgment than for those who have had the clear light of truth shining upon them as you have had, but through some inexplainable cause have turned from the holy commandment delivered to them. We can only point to your case with sorrow, as a beacon of warning. "Let him that thinketh he standeth take heed lest he fall." The

Lord seeth not as man seeth. His thoughts and ways are not what blind, selfish men believe they are or wish them to be. The Lord looks on the heart and works in and with His creatures to will and to do whatever He commands or requires of them, unless they reject His counsel and refuse to be obedient to His commandments.

The greater part of your life has been employed in presenting doctrines which, during the last part of your life, you will repudiate and condemn. Which is the genuine work? which is the false? Can we trust to your judgment? can we rely upon your interpretation of the Scriptures? We cannot. We would be in danger of being misled. You cannot now or at any future period of your life feel that your feet are standing on solid rock. I have been unable to keep from thinking of your future. The truth to me is a living reality. I know it to be truth. The word of God is sure. "To the law and to the testimony: if they speak not according to this word, it is because there is no light in them." Will your light go out in darkness?

I am writing out more fully the volume of *Great Controversy* containing the history of the fall of Satan and the introduction of sin into our world; and I can have a more vivid sense of this great controversy between Christ, the Prince of light, and Satan, the prince of darkness, than I have ever had before. As I see the various devices of Satan to compass the ruin of erring man, and make him like himself, a transgressor of God's holy law, I would that angels of God could come to earth and present this matter in its great importance. Then I feel so intensely for souls who are willfully departing from light and knowledge and obedience to God's holy law. As Adam and Eve believed the lie of Satan, "Ye shall be as gods," so these souls hope through disobedience to rise to greater heights, to gain some flattering position. I am so anxious that, while others are sleeping, I spend hours in prayer that God will work in mighty power to break the fatal deception upon human minds and lead them in simplicity to the cross of Calvary. Then I quiet myself with the thought that all these souls are purchased by the blood of the Lord Jesus. We may have love for these souls, but Calvary testifies how God loves them. This work is not ours, but the Lord's. We are only the instruments in His hands to do His will, not our own. We look at those who are doing despite to the Spirit of grace, and tremble for them. We feel sorry, and are disappointed, that they prove untrue to God and the truth; but we feel a deeper sorrow as we think of Jesus, who has purchased them with His own blood. We would give all our possessions to save one, but find we cannot do this. We would give life itself to save one soul unto life eternal, but even this sacrifice would not do the work. The one great sacrifice has been made in the life, the mission, and the death of Jesus Christ. Oh, that minds would contemplate the greatness of that sacrifice! Then might they be better able to comprehend the greatness of salvation.

And now, Brother O, you who have had so great light, such an abundance of evidence of Bible truth, go not onward and upward with those who will triumph with the truth at last. You now take the side of the first great rebel, to make void the law of God; and he will lead others in the same path of transgression of God's holy law, to ridicule our faith. When the judgment shall sit, and everyone shall be judged out of those things written in the books, how will your case then appear? You will look on this one and that one who would have walked in the way of God's commandments if you had not surrounded them with the atmosphere of unbelief, if you had not perverted the Scriptures by misinterpreting their meaning, and led them away from strict obedience to God's holy law. Can you then look on these countenances with pleasure? You will hear the voice of the great Judge saying: "Who hath required this at your hand?"

Your present wife has had no deep religious experience in self-denial, in self-sacrifice, in communion with God, in belief of the truth. She would easily be led from obedience to God to transgression. Your children will follow where their father leads the way; and unless some special providence shall rescue them, their disobedience and transgression will be laid upon your soul. The Judge of all the earth confronts you with that holy law of whose claims you are not ignorant. Your character and the characters of your wife and of your children are judged by that holy standard of righteousness. You have led them to transgress, and their ruin the holy law of God charges upon you. Through various devices, with which Satan is fully acquainted, you have worked for time and for eternity, trying to make others believe you an honest man in leaving the light of truth. Are you so? No, no. It is a deception, a terrible deception. What can you answer to God in that day? You will then have a terrible dread and fear of your Creator. You will try to frame some excuse for your course, but everything will seem to evade you. You will stand guilty and condemned. You may feel angry with me because I have thus put the case, but so it is, and so it will be with every transgressor of God's holy law.

Keep ever before you this truth: "Wherever I am, whatever I do, Thou, God, seest me." It is not possible for the least item of our conduct to escape the observation of the One who says "I know thy works." The depths of every heart are open to the inspection of God. Every action, every purpose, every word, is as distinctly marked as though there were only one individual in the whole universe and all the watchfulness and scrutiny of God were employed on his deportment. Shall we then break even one precept of His law and teach others to do so, by evasions, by assertions, by falsehoods, in the very sight of the Lawgiver? Shall we brave the sentence in the very face of the Judge? In this there is a hardihood which seems to surpass the worst human presumption. I know, my brother, whom I expect to meet in the day of judgment, that you will have no words of excuse for your late defection.

Oh, that I could present before you, and before others of my brethren, the necessity of an ever-abiding sense of God's presence, which would put such restraint on your life that your moral and religious standing before the people would be far different. We must reach a higher standard. Every soul, in going out and coming in, in all business transactions, at all times and in all places, should act with the consciousness that he is moving under the inspection of God and heavenly angels, and that the Being who will judge every man's work for eternity accompanies him at every step, observing all his actions and scrutinizing all his motives. A consciousness of the presence of God and the peril of violating His precepts would take possession of his entire being. What a change would be seen in man, what a change in society, what evils would be left undone! There would be exclamations from all ranks and among all ages: "I cannot do this great wickedness, and sin against God."

Who shall enter in through the gates into the city? "Blessed are they that do His commandments, that they may have right to the tree of life, and may enter in through the gates into the city." You know what these commandments are as well as I do. I love your soul and the soul of your wife and the souls of your innocent children, and this is why I now address you. Consider carefully the way your feet are tending. I have more to say, but not now. Will you please to answer me, and return to me the letter containing the dream, as I requested.

Yours with much sorrow and pity and love.
April 20, 1887.

GOD'S LOVE FOR SINNERS

Dear Brother P: I see by your letter that you are in a state of unbelief, questioning whether there is hope in your case. As Christ's ambassador I would say to you: "Hope thou in God." He "so loved the world, that He gave His only-begotten Son, that whosoever believeth in Him should not perish, but have everlasting life." Now cannot you take courage from this gracious promise? Satan may tell you many times that you are a sinner; but you can answer: "True, I am a sinner; but 'Christ Jesus came into the world to save sinners.' "

Said Jesus: "I came not to call the righteous, but sinners to repentance." And again: "I say unto you, that likewise joy shall be in heaven over one sinner that repenteth, more than over ninety and nine just persons, which need no repentance." Will you not believe these precious words? Will you not receive them into your heart? "Seek ye the Lord while He may be found, call ye upon Him while He is near: let the wicked forsake his way, and the unrighteous man his thoughts: and let him return unto the Lord, and He will have mercy upon him; and to our God, for He will abundantly pardon." Is not this promise broad and deep and full? Can you ask more? Will you not allow the Lord right here to erect a standard for you against the enemy? Satan is ready to steal away the blessed assurances of God. He desires to take every glimmer of hope and every ray of light from the soul; but you must not permit him to do this. Exercise faith; fight the good fight of faith; wrestle with these doubts; become acquainted with the promises.

"When I shall say to the righteous, that he shall surely live; if he trust to his own righteousness, and commit iniquity, all his righteousnesses shall not be remembered; but for his iniquity that he hath committed, he shall die for it. Again,

(629)

when I say unto the wicked, Thou shalt surely die; if he turn from his sin, and do that which is lawful and right; . . . he shall surely live, he shall not die. None of his sins that he hath committed shall be mentioned unto him; he hath done that which is lawful and right; he shall surely live."

"Wherewith shall I come before the Lord, and bow myself before the high God? shall I come before Him with burnt offerings, with calves of a year old? Will the Lord be pleased with thousands of rams, or with ten thousands of rivers of oil? shall I give my first-born for my transgression, the fruit of my body for the sin of my soul? He hath showed thee, O man, what is good; and what doth the Lord require of thee, but to do justly, and to love mercy, and to walk humbly with thy God?" When Satan comes in to tempt you to give up all hope, point him to these words. Pray with David: "Remember not the sins of my youth, nor my transgressions: according to Thy mercy remember Thou me for Thy goodness' sake, O Lord. Good and upright is the Lord: therefore will He teach sinners in the way. The meek will He guide in judgment: and the meek will He teach His way."

"Come now, and let us reason together, saith the Lord: though your sins be as scarlet, they shall be as white as snow; though they be red like crimson, they shall be as wool. If ye be willing and obedient, ye shall eat the good of the land: but if ye refuse and rebel, ye shall be devoured with the sword: for the mouth of the Lord hath spoken it." Here are the promises, plain and definite, rich and full; but they are all upon conditions. If you comply with the conditions, can you not trust the Lord to fulfill His word? Let these blessed promises, set in the framework of faith, be placed in memory's halls. Not one of them will fail. All that God hath spoken He will do. "He is faithful that promised."

The work which you have to do on your part is plainly set before you: "Wash you, make you clean; put away the evil of your doings from before Mine eyes; cease to do evil; learn to do well; seek judgment, relieve the oppressed, judge the fatherless, plead for the widow." "If the wicked restore the pledge, give again that he had robbed, walk in the statutes of life, without committing iniquity; he shall surely live, he shall not die." The Lord declares: "The children of thy people say, The way of the Lord is not equal." "Hear now, O house of Israel; Is not My way equal? are not your ways unequal?" "Have I any pleasure at all that the wicked should die? saith the Lord God; and not that he should return from his ways, and live?" "Therefore I will judge you, O house of Israel, everyone according to his ways, saith the Lord God. Repent, and turn yourselves from all your transgressions; so iniquity shall not be your ruin. Cast away from you all your transgressions, whereby ye have transgressed; and make you a new heart and a new spirit: for why will ye die, O house of Israel? For I have no pleasure in the death of him that dieth, saith the Lord God: wherefore turn yourselves, and live ye."

Here the Lord has plainly revealed His will concerning the salvation of the sinner. And the attitude which many assume in expressing doubts and unbelief as to whether the Lord will save them is a reflection upon the character of God. Those who complain of His severity are virtually saying: "The way of the Lord is not equal." But He distinctly throws back the imputation upon the sinner: " 'Are not your ways unequal?' Can I pardon your transgressions when you do not repent and turn from your sins?" The character of God is fully vindicated in the words of Scripture I have placed before you. The Lord will receive the sinner when he repents and forsakes his sins so that God can work with his efforts in seeking perfection of character. The promises are not yea and nay, but if man complies with the conditions, they are, in Christ, "yea, and in Him Amen, unto the glory of God by us." The whole purpose in giving His Son for the sins of the world is that man may be saved, not in transgression and unrighteousness, but in forsaking sin, washing his robes of character, and making them white in the blood of the Lamb. He proposes to remove from man the offensive thing that He hates, but man must cooperate with God in the work. Sin must be given up, hated, and the righteousness of Christ must be accepted by faith. Thus will the divine cooperate with the human.

We should beware that we do not give place to doubt and unbelief, and in our attitude of despair complain of God and misrepresent Him to the world. This is placing ourselves on Satan's side of the question. "Poor souls," he says, "I pity you, mourning under sin; but God has no pity. You long for some ray of hope; but God leaves you to perish, and finds satisfaction in your misery." This is a terrible deception. Do not give ear to the tempter, but say: "Jesus has died that I might live. He loves me, and wills not that I should perish. I have a compassionate heavenly Father; and although I have abused His love, though the blessings He has graciously given me have been squandered, I will arise, and go to my Father, and say: 'I have sinned, . . . and am no more worthy to be called Thy son: make me as one of Thy hired servants.' " The parable tells you how the wanderer will be received. "When *he was yet a great way off*, his father saw him, and had compassion, and ran, and fell on his neck, and kissed him." Thus the Bible represents God's willingness to receive the repentant, returning sinner.

But even this parable, tender and touching as it is, comes short of expressing the infinite compassion of the heavenly Father. The Lord declares by the prophet: "I have loved thee with an everlasting love: therefore *with loving-kindness have I drawn thee*." While the sinner is yet far from his Father's house, wasting his substance in a strange country, the Father's heart is yearning over him; and every longing awakened in the soul to return to God is but the tender pleading of His Spirit, wooing, entreating, drawing the wanderer to his Father's heart of love.

With the rich promises of the Bible before you, can you still give place to doubt? Can you believe that when the poor sinner longs to return, longs to forsake his sins, the Lord sternly withholds him from coming to His feet in repentance? Away with such thoughts! Nothing can be more dishonoring to God than these ideas. Nothing can hurt your own soul more than to entertain such thoughts of our heavenly Father. Our whole spiritual life will catch a tone of hopelessness from such conceptions of God. They discourage all effort to seek God or to serve Him. We must not think of God only as a judge ready to pronounce sentence against us. He hates sin; but from love to sinners He gave Himself, in the person of Christ, that all who would might be saved and have eternal blessedness in the kingdom of glory.

The Lord Himself declares His character that Satan has malignantly set in a false light. He has revealed Himself as "The Lord, The Lord God, merciful and gracious, long-suffering, and abundant in goodness and truth, keeping mercy for thousands, forgiving iniquity and transgression and sin." What stronger or more tender language could have been employed than He has chosen in which to express His love toward us? He declares: "Can a woman forget her sucking child, that she should not have compassion on the son of her womb? yea, they may forget, yet will I not forget thee."

In the plan of redemption, "mercy and truth are met together; righteousness and peace have kissed each other." The all-wise, all-powerful God, He who dwells in light unapproachable, is full of love, of goodness. Therefore give glory to God, ye that are doubting and trembling; for Jesus lives to make intercession for us. Give God the glory for the gift of His dear Son and that He has not died for us in vain.

Brother P, you ask if you have committed the sin which has no forgiveness in this life or in the life to come. I answer: I do not see the slightest evidence that this is the case. What constitutes the sin against the Holy Ghost? It is willfully attributing to Satan the work of the Holy Spirit. For example, suppose that one is a witness of the special work of the Spirit of God. He has convincing evidence that the work is in harmony with the Scriptures, and the Spirit witnesses with his spirit that it is of God. Afterward, however, he falls under temptation; pride, self-sufficiency, or some other evil trait, controls him; and rejecting all the evidence of its divine character, he declares that that which he had before acknowledged to be the power of the Holy Spirit was the power of Satan. It is through the medium of His Spirit that God works upon the human heart; and when men willfully reject the Spirit and declare it to be from Satan, they cut off the channel by which God can communicate with them. By denying the evidence which God has been pleased to give them, they shut out the light which had been shining in their hearts, and as the result they are left in darkness. Thus the words of Christ are verified: "If therefore the light that is in thee be darkness, how great is that darkness!" For a time, persons who have committed this sin may appear to be children of God; but when circumstances arise to develop character and show what manner of spirit they are of, it will be found that they are on the enemy's ground, standing under his black banner.

My brother, the Spirit invites you today. Come with your whole heart to Jesus. Repent of your sins, make confession to God, forsake all iniquity, and you may appropriate to yourself all His promises. "Look unto Me, and be ye saved," is His gracious invitation.

The day will come when the awful denunciation of God's wrath will be uttered against all who have persisted in their disloyalty to Him. This will be when God must speak and do terrible things in righteousness against the transgressors of His law. But you need not be among those who will come under the wrath of God. It is now the day of His salvation. The light from the cross of Calvary is now shining forth in clear, bright rays, revealing Jesus, our Sacrifice for sin. As you read the promises which I have set before you, remember they are the expression of unutterable love and pity. The great heart of infinite Love is drawn toward the sinner with boundless compassion. "We have redemption through His blood, the forgiveness of sins." Yes, only believe that God is your helper. He wants to restore His moral image in man. As you draw nigh to Him with confession and repentance, He will draw nigh to you with mercy and forgiveness. We owe the Lord everything. He is the author of our salvation. As you work out your own salvation with fear and trembling, "it is God which worketh in you both to will and to do of His good pleasure."

ACCEPTABLE CONFESSION

"He that covereth his sins shall not prosper: but whoso confesseth and forsaketh them shall have mercy."

The conditions of obtaining mercy of God are simple and just and reasonable. The Lord does not require us to do some grievous thing in order that we may have the forgiveness of sin. We need not make long and wearisome pilgrimages or perform painful penances, to commend our souls to the God of heaven or to expiate our transgression; but he that confesseth and forsaketh his sin shall have mercy. This is a precious promise, given to fallen man to encourage him to trust in the God of love and to seek for eternal life in His kingdom.

We read that Daniel, the prophet of God, was a man "greatly beloved" of heaven. He held a high position in the courts of Babylon and served and honored God alike in prosperity and trial, and yet he humbled himself and confessed his sin and the sin of his people. With deep sorrow of heart he acknowledged: "We have sinned, and have committed iniquity, and have done wickedly, and have rebelled, even by departing from Thy precepts and from Thy judgments: neither have we hearkened unto Thy servants the prophets, which spake in Thy name to our kings, our princes, and our fathers, and to all the people of the land. O Lord, righteousness belongeth unto Thee, but unto us confusion of faces, as at this day; to the men of Judah, and to the inhabitants of Jerusalem, and unto all Israel, that are near, and that are far off, through all the countries whither Thou hast driven them, because of their trespass that they have trespassed against Thee."

Daniel did not seek to excuse himself or his people before God; but in humility and contrition of soul he confessed the full extent and demerit of their transgressions, and vindicated God's dealings as just toward a nation that had set at nought His requirements and would not profit by His entreaties.

There is great need today of just such sincere, heartfelt repentance and confession. Those who have not humbled their souls before God in acknowledging their guilt have not yet fulfilled the first condition of acceptance. If we have not experienced that repentance which is not to be repented of, and have not confessed our sin with true humiliation of soul and brokenness of spirit, abhorring our iniquity, we have never sought truly for the forgiveness of sin; and if we have never sought, we have never found the peace of God. The only reason why we may not have remission of sins that are past is that we are not willing to humble our proud hearts and comply with the conditions of the word of truth. There is explicit instruction given concerning this matter. Confession of sin, whether public or private, should be heartfelt and freely expressed. It is not to be urged from the sinner. It is not to be made in a flippant and careless way or forced from those who have no realizing sense of the abhorrent character of sin. The confession that is mingled with tears and sorrow, that is the outpouring of the inmost soul, finds its way to the God of infinite pity. Says the psalmist: "The Lord is nigh unto them that are of a broken heart; and saveth such as be of a contrite spirit."

There are too many confessions like that of Pharaoh when he was suffering the judgments of God. He acknowledged his sin in order to escape further punishment, but returned to his defiance of heaven as soon as the plagues were stayed. Balaam's confession was of a similar character. Terrified by the angel standing in his pathway with drawn sword, he acknowledged his guilt, lest he should lose his life. There was no genuine repentance for sin, no contrition, no conversion of purpose, no abhorrence of evil, and no worth or virtue in his confession. Judas Iscariot, after betraying his Lord, returned to the priests, exclaiming: "I have sinned in that I have betrayed the innocent blood." But his confession was not of such a character as would commend him to the mercy of God. It was forced from his guilty soul by an awful sense of condemnation and a fearful looking for of judgment. The consequences that were to result to him drew forth this acknowledgment of his great sin. There was no deep, heartbreaking grief in his soul that he had delivered the Son of God to be mocked, scourged, and crucified; that he had betrayed the Holy One of Israel into the hands of wicked and unscrupulous men. His confession was only prompted by a selfish and darkened heart.

After Adam and Eve had partaken of the forbidden fruit, they were filled with a sense of shame and terror. At first their only thought was how to excuse their sin before God and escape the dreaded sentence of death. When the Lord inquired concerning their sin, Adam replied, laying the guilt partly upon God and partly upon his companion: "The woman whom Thou gavest to be with me, she gave me of the tree, and I did eat." The woman put the blame upon the serpent, saying: " 'The serpent beguiled me, and I did eat.' Why did You make the serpent? Why did You suffer him to come into Eden?" These were the questions implied in her excuse for her sin, thus charging God with the responsibility of their fall. The spirit of self-justification originated in the father of lies and has been exhibited by all the sons and daughters of Adam. Confessions of this order are not inspired by the divine Spirit and will not be acceptable before God. True repentance will lead a man to bear his guilt himself and acknowledge it without deception or hypocrisy. Like the poor publican, not lifting up so much as his eyes unto heaven, he will smite upon his breast, and cry, "God be merciful to me a sinner;" and those who do acknowledge their guilt will be justified; for Jesus will plead His blood in behalf of the repentant soul.

It is no degradation for man to bow down before his Maker and confess his sins, and plead for forgiveness through the merits of a crucified and risen Saviour. It is noble to acknowledge your wrong before Him whom you have wounded by transgression and rebellion. It lifts you up before men and angels; for "he that humbleth himself shall be exalted." But he who kneels before fallen man and opens in confession the secret thoughts and imaginations of his heart is dishonoring himself by debasing his manhood and degrading every noble instinct of his soul. In unfolding the sins of his life to a priest corrupted with wine and licentiousness his standard of character is lowered, and he is defiled in consequence. God is degraded in his thought to the likeness of sinful humanity, for the priest stands as a representative of God. It is this degrading confession of man to fallen man that accounts for much of the increasing evil which is defiling the world and fitting it for final destruction.

Says the apostle: "Confess your faults one to another, and pray one for another, that ye may be healed." This scripture has been interpreted to sustain the practice of going to the priest for absolution; but it has no such application. Confess your sins to God, who only can forgive them, and your faults to one another. If you have given offense to your friend or neighbor you are to acknowledge your wrong, and it is his duty freely to forgive you. Then you are to seek the forgiveness of God because the brother whom you wounded is the property of God, and in injuring him you sinned against his Creator and Redeemer. The case is not brought before the priest at all, but before the only true mediator, our great High Priest, who "was in all points tempted like as we are, yet without sin," and who is "touched with the feeling of our infirmities" and is able to cleanse from every stain of iniquity.

When David sinned against Uriah and his wife, he pleaded before God for forgiveness. He declares: "Against Thee, Thee only, have I sinned, and done this evil in Thy sight." All wrong done to others reaches back from the injured one to God. Therefore David seeks for pardon, not from a priest, but from the Creator of man. He prays: "Have mercy upon me, O God, according to Thy loving-kindness: according unto the multitude of Thy tender mercies blot out my transgressions."

True confession is always of a specific character, and acknowledges particular sins. They may be of such a nature as only to be brought before God, they may be wrongs that should be confessed before individuals who have suffered injury through them, or they may be of a general kind that should be made known in the congregation of the people. But all confession should be definite and to the point, acknowledging the very sins of which you are guilty.

When Israel was oppressed by the Ammonites, the chosen people made a plea before God that illustrates the definite character of true confession: "And the children of Israel cried unto the Lord, saying, We have sinned against Thee, both because we have forsaken our God, and also served Baalim. And the Lord said unto the children of Israel, Did not I deliver you from the Egyptians, and from the Amorites, from the children of Ammon, and from the Philistines? . . . Yet ye have forsaken Me, and served other gods: wherefore I will deliver you no more. Go and cry unto the gods which ye have chosen; let them deliver you in the time of your tribulation. And the children of Israel said unto the Lord, We have sinned: do Thou unto us whatsoever seemeth good unto Thee; deliver us only, we pray Thee, this day." Then they began to act in harmony with their confessions and prayers. "They put away the strange gods from among them, and served the Lord." And the Lord's great heart of love was grieved, "*was grieved for the misery of Israel.*"

Confession will not be acceptable to God without sincere repentance and reformation. There must be decided changes in the life; everything offensive to God must be put away. This will be the result of genuine sorrow for sin. Says Paul, speaking of the work of repentance: "Ye sorrowed after a godly sort, what carefulness it wrought in you, yea, what clearing of yourselves, yea, what indignation, yea, what fear, yea, what vehement desire, yea, what zeal, yea, what revenge! In all things ye have approved yourselves to be clear in this matter."

In the days of Samuel the Israelites wandered from God. They were suffering the consequences of sin, for they had lost their faith in God, lost their discernment of His power and wisdom to rule the nation, lost their confidence in His ability to defend and vindicate His cause. They turned from the great Ruler of the universe and desired to be governed as were the nations around them. Before they found peace they made this definite confession: "We have added unto all our sins this evil, to ask us a king." The very sin of which they were convicted had to be confessed. Their ingratitude oppressed their souls and severed them from God.

When sin has deadened the moral perceptions, the wrongdoer does not discern the defects of his character nor realize the enormity of the evil he has committed; and unless he yields to the convicting power of the Holy Spirit he remains in partial blindness to his sin. His confessions are not sincere and in earnest. To every acknowledgment of his guilt he adds an apology in excuse of his course, declaring that if it had not been for certain circumstances, he would not have done this or that for which he is reproved. But the examples in God's word of genuine repentance and humiliation reveal a spirit of confession in which there is no excuse for sin or attempt at self-justification.

Paul did not seek to shield himself; he paints his sin in its darkest hue, not attempting to lessen his guilt. He says: "Many of the saints did I shut up in prison, having received authority from the chief priests; and when they were put to death, I gave my voice against them. And I punished them oft in every synagogue, and compelled them to blaspheme; and being exceedingly mad against them, I persecuted them even unto strange cities." He does not hesitate to declare that "Christ Jesus came into the world to save sinners; of whom I am chief."

The humble and broken heart, subdued by genuine repentance, will appreciate something of the love of God and the cost of Calvary; and as a son confesses to a loving father, so will the truly penitent bring all his sins before God. And it is written: "If we confess our sins, He is faithful and just to forgive us our sins, and to cleanse us from all unrighteousness."

ERRONEOUS IDEAS OF CONFESSION

Dear Brethren and Sisters in_____: I have heard of the good work that has been going on among you, and it rejoices my heart. Since coming to Battle Creek my mind has been much exercised in regard to the church here. During the week of prayer the Lord wrought for us, and in all our institutions there has continued to be a steady, well-balanced interest.

Meetings have been held in the college with marked success. There have been several conversions among the students from the world. These conversions were the more striking because the individuals had had no religious experience before coming to the college, and some of them were determined not to put themselves in the channel of light by attending the meetings. But they did attend, were convicted by the Spirit of the Lord, and were soundly converted. They say they were never so happy in their lives as now. Several have gone home to spend the holidays. Their parents are not professors of religion, and their faith will be severely tested. But good letters come back, stating that they are taking up their new responsibilities and trying to show to their friends that the new faith they have received has not made them fanatics or extremists, but well-balanced Christians, better in every way than before their conversion; that they possess the principles of pure faith and love to God and their neighbor, and manifest them by a well-ordered life and a godly conversation. This good work in the college has been a source of great rejoicing to us all.

We have had morning meetings for the helpers at the sanitarium for three weeks, at half past five. I have spoken on these occasions with good results; I have also spoken to the patients several times.

We have had meetings with the workers in the Review office at noon. Here the Lord is manifestly at work. Men who have professed the truth for years and yet have never seemed to have any warmth of soul have been visited by the Spirit of the Lord, and you hear their heartfelt testimonies bearing witness to the precious love of God in their souls. Some of them say they were never converted before.

Meetings have been held at the Tabernacle twice each day for two weeks, and the message presented has taken hold of hearts. The testimonies borne have the right ring. I am thankful to the Lord for this good work. We have also had some special meetings at the Tabernacle. This church being large, after we had called the people forward for prayers Sabbath afternoon, the last Sabbath of the old year, we invited those who felt that they must make confession, to go into one of the vestries, and here a special opportunity was given them. I had spoken upon the last chapter of Malachi: "Will a man rob God?" "Bring ye all the tithes into the storehouse, that there may be meat in Mine house, and prove Me now herewith, saith the Lord of hosts, if I will not open you the windows of heaven, and pour you out a blessing, that there shall not be room enough to receive it." Many confessions were made upon this point.

Some had not dealt honestly with their neighbors, and they confessed these sins and have since made restitution. During the following week some of those who had not been dealing justly with God, and consequently had been separating themselves from Him, began to restore that which they had withheld. One brother had not paid tithes for two years. He gave his note to the secretary of the conference for the tithe he had withheld and the interest on it, amounting to $571.50. I thank the Lord that he had the courage to do this. Another gave his note for $300. Another man who had backslidden from God so far that but little hope was cherished that he would ever turn his feet into the path of righteousness again, gave his note for $1,000. It was proposed that these long-withheld tithes and offerings be devoted to the Central European Mission; so with these and the Christmas donations, nearly $6,000 has come into the treasury from this church to be applied to the missionary cause.

The soul that lives by faith on Christ desires no other nor greater good than to know and to do the will of God. It is God's will that faith in Christ shall be made perfect by works; He connects the salvation and eternal life of those who believe, with these works, and through them provides for the light of truth to go to all countries and peoples. This is the fruit of the working of God's Spirit.

The truth has taken hold of hearts. It is not a fitful impulse, but a true turning unto the Lord, and the perverse will of men is brought into subjection to the will of God. To rob God in tithes and offerings is a violation of the plain injunction of Jehovah and works the deepest injury to those who do it; for it deprives them of the blessing of God, which is promised to those who deal honestly with Him.

We have found in our experience that if Satan cannot keep souls bound in the ice of indifference, he will try to push them into the fire of fanaticism. When the Spirit of the Lord comes among His people, the enemy seizes the opportunity to work also, seeking to mold the work of God through the peculiar, unsanctified traits of different ones who are connected with that work. Thus there is always danger that unwise moves will be made. Many carry on a work of their own devising, a work which God has not prompted.

But, as far as the work has gone here in Battle Creek, there has been no fanaticism. We have felt the need of guarding it on every hand with the greatest care; for if the enemy can push individuals to extremes, he is well pleased. He can thus do greater harm than if there had been no religious awakening. We know that there has never yet been a religious effort made in which Satan has not tried his best to intrude himself, and in these last days he will do this as never before. He sees that his time is short, and he will work with all deceivableness of unrighteousness to mingle errors and incorrect views with the work of God and push men into false positions.

In many of our religious awakenings mistakes have been made in regard to confession. While confession is good for the soul, there is need of moving wisely.

I have been shown that many, many confessions should never be spoken in the hearing of mortals; for the result is that which the limited judgment of finite beings does not anticipate. Seeds of evil are scattered in the minds and hearts of those who hear, and when they are under temptation, these seeds will spring up and bear fruit, and the same sad experience will be repeated. For, think the tempted ones, these sins cannot be so very grievous; for did not those who have made confession, Christians of long standing, do these very things? Thus the open confession in the church of these secret sins will prove a savor of death rather than of life.

There should be no reckless, wholesale movements in this matter, for the cause of God may be made disreputable in the eyes of unbelievers. If they hear confessions of base conduct made by those who profess to be followers of Christ, a reproach is brought upon His cause. If Satan could by any means spread the impression that Seventh-day Adventists are the offscouring of all things, he would be glad to do it. God forbid that he should have occasion! God will be better glorified if we confess the secret, inbred corruption of the heart to Jesus alone than if we open its recesses to finite, erring man, who cannot judge righteously unless his heart is constantly imbued with the Spirit of God. God knows the heart, even every secret of the soul; then do not pour into human ears the story which God alone should hear.

There are confessions of a nature that should be brought before a select few and acknowledged by the sinner in deepest humility. The matter must not be conducted in such a way that vice shall be construed into virtue and the sinner made proud of his evil doings. If there are things of a disgraceful nature that should come before the church, let them be brought before a few proper persons selected to hear them, and do not put the cause of Christ to open shame by publishing abroad the hypocrisy that has existed in the church. It would cast reflections upon those who had tried to be Christlike in character. These things should be considered.

Then there are confessions that the Lord has bidden us make to one another. If you have wronged your brother by word or deed you are first to be reconciled to him before your worship will be acceptable to heaven. Confess to those whom you have injured, and make restitution, bringing forth fruit meet for repentance. If anyone has feelings of bitterness, wrath, or malice toward a brother, let him go to him personally, confess his sin, and seek forgiveness.

From Christ's manner of dealing with the erring we may learn profitable lessons which are equally applicable to this work of confession. He bids us go to the one who has fallen into temptation, and labor with him alone. If it is not possible to help him, because of the darkness of his mind and his separation from God, we are to try again with two or three others. If the wrong is not righted, then, and only then, we are to tell it to the church. It is far better if wrongs can be righted and injuries healed without bringing the matter before the whole church. The church is not to be made the receptacle for the outpouring of every complaint or confession.

I recognize, on the other hand, the danger of yielding to the temptation to conceal sin or to compromise with it, and thus act the hypocrite. Be sure that the confession fully covers the influence of the wrong committed, that no duty to God, to your neighbor, or to the church is left undone, and then you may lay hold upon Christ with confidence, expecting His blessing. But the question of how and to whom sins should be confessed is one that demands careful, prayerful study. We must consider it from all points, weighing it before God and seeking divine illumination. We should inquire whether to confess publicly the sins of which we have been guilty will do good or harm. Will it show forth the praises of Him who has called us out of darkness into His marvelous light? Will it help to purify the minds of the people, or will the open relation of the deceptions practiced in denying the truth have an after influence to contaminate other minds and destroy confidence in us?

Men have not the wisdom from God and the constant enlightenment from the Source of all power that would make it safe for them to follow impulses or impressions. In my experience I have seen this done to the destruction, not only of those who acted upon this principle, but of many others who came under their influence. The wildest extravagance was the result of this impulsive work. A declension in faith followed, and unbelief and skepticism became strong in proportion to the extreme in religious excitement. The work that is not wrought in God comes to nought as soon as the excitement is over.

There is power and permanency in what the Lord does, whether He works by human instrumentality or otherwise. The progress and perfection of the work of grace in the heart are not dependent upon excitement or extravagant demonstration. Hearts that are under the influence of the Spirit of God will be in sweet harmony with His will. I have been shown that when the Lord works by His Holy Spirit, there will be nothing in its operations which will degrade the Lord's people before the world, but it will exalt them. The religion of Christ does not make those who profess it coarse and rough. The subjects of grace are not unteachable, but ever willing to learn of Jesus and to counsel with one another.

What we learn of the Great Teacher of truth will be enduring; it will not savor of self-sufficiency, but will lead to humility and meekness, and the work that we do will be wholesome, pure, and ennobling, because wrought in God. Those who thus work will show in their home life, and in their association with men, that they have the mind of Christ. Grace and truth will reign in their hearts, inspiring and purifying their motives, and controlling their outward actions.

I hope that none will obtain the idea that they are earning the favor of God by confession of sins or that there is special virtue in confessing to human beings. There must be in the experience that faith that works by love and purifies the soul. The love of Christ will subdue the carnal propensities. The truth not only bears within itself the evidence of its heavenly origin, but proves that by the grace of God's Spirit it is effectual in the purification of the soul. The Lord would have us come to Him daily with all our troubles and confessions of sin, and He can give us rest in wearing His yoke and bearing His burden. His Holy Spirit, with its gracious influences, will fill the soul, and every thought will be brought into subjection to the obedience of Christ.

Now I am fearful that by some error on your part the blessing of God which has come to you in _____ will be turned into a curse; that some false idea will obtain, so that you will be in a worse condition in a few months than you were before this work of revival. If you do not keep your souls guarded you will appear in the worst possible light to unbelievers. God would not be glorified with this fitful kind of service. Be careful not to carry matters to extremes and bring lasting reproach upon the precious cause of God. The failure that many make is that after they have been blessed of God they do not, in the humility of Christ, seek to be a blessing to others. Now that words of eternal life have been sown in your hearts, I entreat you to walk humbly with God, do the works of Christ, and bring forth much fruit unto righteousness. I do hope and pray that you will act like sons and daughters of the Most High and not become extremists or do anything that shall grieve the Spirit of God.

Do not look to men nor hang your hopes upon them, feeling that they are infallible; but look to Jesus constantly. Say nothing that would cast a reproach upon our faith. Confess your secret sins alone before your God. Acknowledge your heart wanderings to Him who knows perfectly how to treat your case. If you have wronged your neighbor, acknowledge to him your sin and show fruit of the same by making restitution. Then claim the blessing. Come to God just as you are, and let Him heal all your infirmities. Press your case to the throne of grace; let the work be thorough. Be sincere in dealing with God and your own soul. If you come to Him with a heart truly contrite, He will give you the victory. Then you may bear a sweet testimony of freedom, showing forth the praises of Him who has called you out of darkness into His marvelous light. He will not misapprehend or misjudge you. Your fellow men cannot absolve you from sin or cleanse you from iniquity. Jesus is the only one who can give you peace. He loved you and gave Himself for you. His great heart of love is "touched with the feeling of our infirmities." What sins are too great for Him to pardon? what soul too dark and sin-oppressed for Him to save? He is gracious, not looking for merit in us, but of His own boundless goodness healing our backslidings and loving us freely, while we are yet sinners. He is "slow to anger, and of great kindness;" "long-suffering to usward, not willing that any should perish, but that all should come to repentance."

Do not seek to get wound up to a high pitch of excitement; but go to work for others, and patiently instruct them. You will be inclined now to conjecture that everyone has a load of evil to confess, and you will be in danger of making this the point of attack. You will want to bring everyone over the same ground that you have been over, and you will feel that nothing can be done until all have gone through the same work of confession. You will not be disposed to take up the labor of helping others with the Spirit of God resting upon you, your own hearts softened and subdued by the deep-wrought work of cleansing. You will be in great danger of marring the work of God by exercising your own spirit. If you work for souls with humble, trustful dependence upon God, if the radiance of His Spirit is reflected from you in a Christlike character, if sympathy, kindness, forbearance, and love are abiding principles in your life, you will be a blessing to all around you. You will not criticize others or manifest a harsh, denunciatory spirit toward them; you will not feel that their ideas must be made to meet your standard; but the love of Jesus and the peaceable fruits of righteousness will be revealed in you.

"The fruit of the Spirit is love, joy, peace, long-suffering, gentleness, goodness, faith, meekness, temperance. . . . And they that are Christ's have crucified the flesh with the affections and lusts. If we live in the Spirit, let us also walk in the Spirit. Let us not be desirous of vainglory, provoking one another, envying one another."

The enemy will seek to intrude himself even amid your religious exercises. Every avenue will need to be faithfully guarded lest selfishness and pride become interwoven with your work. If self has really been crucified, with the affections and lusts, the fruit will appear in good works to the glory of God. I entreat you, in the fear of God, not to let your works degenerate. Be consistent, symmetrical Christians. When the heart has given its affections to Christ, old things have passed away, and all things have become new.

Our religion must be intelligent. The wisdom from above must strengthen, establish, and settle us. We must go on and on, forward and upward, from light to still greater light, and God will still reveal His glory to us as He doth not unto the world.

Battle Creek, Michigan, Jan. 6, 1889.

GOD'S PRESENCE A REALITY

Dear Brother Q: I am glad you are today in _____, and if you make good your trust you will be the right man in the right place. Keep self out of sight; let it not come in to mar the work, though this will be natural. Walk humbly with God. Let us work for the Master with disinterested energy, keeping before us a sense of the constant presence of God. Think of Moses, what endurance and patience characterized his life. Paul, in his Epistle to the Hebrews, says: "For he endured, as seeing Him who is invisible." The character that Paul thus ascribes to Moses does not mean simply passive resistance of evil, but perseverance in the right. He kept the Lord ever before him, and the Lord was ever at his right hand to help him.

Moses had a deep sense of the personal presence of God. He was not only looking down through the ages for Christ to be made manifest in the flesh, but he saw Christ in a special manner accompanying the children of Israel in all their travels. God was real to him, ever present in his thoughts. When misunderstood, when called upon to face danger and to bear insult for Christ's sake, he endured without retaliation. Moses believed in God as one whom he needed and who would help him because of his need. God was to him a present help.

Much of the faith which we see is merely nominal; the real, trusting, persevering faith is rare. Moses realized in his own experience the promise that God will be a rewarder of those who diligently seek Him. He had respect unto the recompense of the reward. Here is another point in regard to faith which we wish to study: God will reward the man of faith and obedience. If this faith is brought into the life experience, it will enable everyone who fears and loves God to endure trials. Moses was full of confidence in God because he had appropriating faith. He needed help, and he prayed for it, grasped it by faith, and wove into his experience the belief that God cared for him. He believed that God ruled his life in particular. He saw and acknowledged God in every detail of his life and felt that he was under the eye of the All-seeing One, who weighs motives, who tries the heart. He looked to God and trusted in Him for strength to carry him uncorrupted through every form of temptation. He knew that a special work had been assigned to him, and he desired as far as possible to make that work thoroughly successful. But he knew that he could not do this without divine aid, for he had a perverse people to deal with. The presence of God was sufficient to carry him through the most trying situations in which a man could be placed.

Moses did not merely think of God; he saw Him. God was the constant vision before him; he never lost sight of His face. He saw Jesus as his Saviour, and he believed that the Saviour's merits would be imputed to him. This faith was to Moses no guesswork; it was a reality. This is the kind of faith we need, faith that will endure the test. Oh, how often we yield to temptation because we do not keep our eye upon Jesus! Our faith is not continuous because, through self-indulgence, we sin, and then we cannot endure "as seeing Him who is invisible."

My brother, make Christ your daily, hourly companion, and you will not complain that you have no faith. Contemplate Christ. View His character. Talk of Him. The less you exalt self, the more you will see in Jesus to exalt. God has a work for you to do. Keep the Lord ever before you. Brother and Sister Q, reach up higher and still higher for clearer views of the character of Christ. When Moses prayed, "I beseech Thee, show me Thy glory," the Lord did not rebuke him, but He granted his prayer. God declared to His servant: "I will make all My goodness pass before thee, and I will proclaim the name of the Lord before thee." We keep apart from God, and this is why we do not see the revealings of His power.

THE PRESENCE OF CHRIST IN THE SCHOOLROOM

My brother, my sister, may the Lord impart wisdom to you both, that you may know how to deal with minds. May the Lord teach you how great things He can do if you will only believe. Carry Jesus with you, as your companion, into the schoolroom. Keep Him before you when you speak, that the law of kindness may proceed from your lips. Do not permit anyone to mold you in this matter. Allow the children under your care to have an individuality, as well as yourselves. Ever try to lead them, but never drive them.

I see some things here in Switzerland that I think are worthy of imitation. The teachers of the schools often go out with their pupils while they are at play and teach them how to amuse themselves and are at hand to repress any disorder or wrong. Sometimes they take their scholars out and have a long walk with them. I like this; I think there is less opportunity for the children to yield to temptation. The teachers seem to enter into the sports of the children and to regulate them. I cannot in any way sanction the idea that children must feel that they are under a constant distrust and cannot act as children. But let the teachers join in the amusements of the children, be one with them, and show that they want them to be happy, and it will give the children confidence. They may be controlled by love, but not by following them at their meals and in their amusements with a stern, unbending severity.

Let me say here that those who have never had children of their own are not usually the best qualified to manage wisely the varied minds of children and youth. They are apt to make one law, from which there can be no appeal. Teachers must remember that they themselves were once children. They should adapt their teaching to the minds of the children, placing themselves in sympathy with them; then the children can be instructed and benefited both by precept and example.

May the spirit of Jesus come in to mold your hearts, to fashion your characters, to elevate and ennoble your souls! Christ said to His disciples: "Except ye be converted, and become as little children, ye shall not enter into the kingdom of heaven." There is need of laying aside these cast-iron rules, of coming down from these stilts, to the humbleness of the child. Oh, that some of the spirit of severity may change to a spirit of love, that happiness and sunshine may take the place of discouragement and grief!

THE NATURE AND INFLUENCE OF THE "TESTIMONIES"

As the end draws near and the work of giving the last warning to the world extends, it becomes more important for those who accept present truth to have a clear understanding of the nature and influence of the *Testimonies,* which God in His providence has linked with the work of the third angel's message from its very rise. In the following pages are given extracts from what I have written during the last forty years, relating to my own early experience in this special work, and also presenting what God has shown me concerning the nature and importance of the *Testimonies,* the manner in which they are given, and how they should be regarded.

"It was not long after the passing of the time in 1844 that my first vision was given me. I was visiting a dear sister in Christ, whose heart was knit with mine; five of us, all women, were kneeling quietly at the family altar. While we were praying, the power of God came upon me as I had never felt it before. I seemed to be surrounded with light, and to be rising higher and higher from the earth."[1] At this time I had a view of the experience of the advent believers, the coming of Christ, and the reward to be given to the faithful.

"In a second vision, which soon followed the first, I was shown the trials through which I must pass, and that it was my duty to go and relate to others what God had revealed to me. It was shown me that my labors would meet with great opposition and that my heart would be rent with anguish, but that the grace of God would be sufficient to sustain me through all. The teaching of this vision troubled me exceedingly, for it pointed out my duty to go out among the people and present the truth."

"One great fear that oppressed me was that if I obeyed the call of duty and went out declaring myself to be one favored of the Most High with visions and revelations for the people, I might yield to sinful exaltation and be lifted above the station that was right for me to occupy, bring upon myself the displeasure of God, and lose my own soul. I had before me several cases such as I have here described, and my heart shrank from the trying ordeal.

"I now entreated that if I must go and relate what the Lord had shown me, I should be preserved from undue exaltation. Said the angel: 'Your prayers are heard and shall be answered. If this evil that you dread threatens you, the hand of God will be stretched out to save you; by affliction He will draw you to Himself and preserve your humility. Deliver the message faithfully. Endure unto the end, and you shall eat the fruit of the tree of life and drink of the water of life.' "[2]

At this time there was fanaticism among some of those who had been believers in the first message. Serious errors in doctrine and practice were cherished, and some were ready to condemn all who would not accept their views. God revealed

[1] *Testimonies for the Church,* vol. 1, p. 58.   [2] Vol. 1, pp. 62, 64, 65.

these errors to me in vision and sent me to His erring children to declare them; but in performing this duty I met with bitter opposition and reproach.

"It was a great cross for me to relate to the erring what had been shown me concerning them. It caused me great distress to see others troubled or grieved. And when obliged to declare the messages I would often soften them down and make them appear as favorable for the individual as I could and then would go by myself and weep in agony of spirit. I looked upon those who had only their own souls to care for and thought if I were in their condition I would not murmur. It was hard to relate the plain, cutting testimonies given me of God. I anxiously watched the result, and if the persons reproved rose up against the reproof, and afterward opposed the truth, these queries would arise in my mind: Did I deliver the message just as I should? Could there not have been some way to save them? And then such distress pressed upon my soul that I often felt that death would be a welcome messenger, and the grave a sweet resting place.

"I did not realize the danger and sin of such a course until in vision I was taken into the presence of Jesus. He looked upon me with a frown and turned His face from me. It is not possible to describe the terror and agony I then felt. I fell upon my face before Him, but had no power to utter a word. Oh, how I longed to be covered and hid from that dreadful frown! Then could I realize, in some degree, what the feelings of the lost will be when they cry: 'Mountains and rocks, Fall on us, and hide us from the face of Him that sitteth on the throne, and from the wrath of the Lamb.'

"Presently an angel bade me rise, and the sight that met my eyes can hardly be described. Before me was a company whose hair and garments were torn, and whose countenances were the very picture of despair and horror. They came close to me and rubbed their garments upon mine. As I looked at my garments I saw that they were stained with blood. Again I fell like one dead at the feet of my accompanying angel. I could not plead one excuse and longed to be away from that holy place. The angel raised me to my feet and said: 'This is not your case now, but this scene has passed before you to let you know what your situation must be if you neglect to declare to others what the Lord has revealed to you.' "[1] With this solemn warning before me I went out to speak to the people the words of reproof and instruction given me of God.

PERSONAL TESTIMONIES

The messages given me for different individuals I often wrote out for them, in many cases doing this at their urgent request. As my work extended, this became an important and taxing part of my labors. Before the publication of *Testimony* 15 many requests for written testimonies were sent me by those whom I had counseled or reproved; but I was in a state of great exhaustion from wearing labor, and I shrank from the task, especially since I knew that many of these persons were very unworthy, and there seemed little hope that the warnings given would work any decided change in them. At that time I was greatly encouraged by the following dream:

"A person brought to me a web of white cloth, and bade me cut it into garments for persons of all sizes and all descriptions of character and circumstances in life. I was told to cut them out and hang them up all ready to be made when called for. I had the impression that many for whom I was required to cut garments were unworthy. I inquired if that was the last piece of cloth I should have to cut and was told that it was not; that as soon as I had finished this one, there were others for me to take hold of. I felt discouraged at the amount of work before me and stated that I had been engaged in cutting garments for others for more than twenty years, and my labors

[1]Vol. 1, pp. 73, 74.

had not been appreciated, neither did I see that my work had accomplished much good. I spoke to the person who brought the cloth to me, of one woman in particular, for whom he had told me to cut a garment. I stated that she would not prize the garment and that it would be a loss of time and material to present it to her. She was very poor, of inferior intellect, and untidy in her habits, and would soon soil it.

"The person replied: 'Cut out the garments. That is your duty. The loss is not yours, but mine. God sees not as man sees. He lays out the work that He would have done, and you do not know which will prosper, this or that.' . . .

"I then held up my hands, calloused as they were with long use of the shears, and stated that I could but shrink at the thought of pursuing this kind of labor. The person again repeated:

" 'Cut out the garments. Your release has not yet come.'

"With feelings of great weariness I arose to engage in the work. Before me lay new, polished shears, which I commenced using. At once my feelings of weariness and discouragement left me, the shears seemed to cut with hardly an effort on my part, and I cut out garment after garment with comparative ease."[1]

There are many dreams arising from the common things of life with which the Spirit of God has nothing to do. "There are also false dreams, as well as false visions, which are inspired by the spirit of Satan. But dreams from the Lord are classed in the word of God with visions and are as truly the fruits of the spirit of prophecy as visions. Such dreams, taking into the account the persons who have them, and the circumstances under which they are given, contain their own proofs of their genuineness."[2]

Since the warning and instruction given in testimony for individual cases applied with equal force to many others who

[1]Vol. 2, pp. 10-12 (first published in 1868).   [2]Vol. 1, p. 569 (1867).

had not been specially pointed out in this manner, it seemed to be my duty to publish the personal testimonies for the benefit of the church. In *Testimony* 15, speaking of the necessity for doing this, I said: "I know of no better way to present my views of general dangers and errors, and the duty of all who love God and keep His commandments, than by giving these testimonies. Perhaps there is no more direct and forcible way of presenting what the Lord has shown me."[1]

In a vision given me June 12, 1868, I was shown that which fully justified my course in publishing personal testimonies. "When the Lord singles out individual cases and specifies their wrongs, others, who have not been shown in vision, frequently take it for granted that they are right, or nearly so. If one is reproved for a special wrong, brethren and sisters should carefully examine themselves to see wherein they have failed and wherein they have been guilty of the same sin. They should possess the spirit of humble confession. If others think them right, it does not make them so. God looks at the heart. He is proving and testing souls in this manner. In rebuking the wrongs of one, He designs to correct many. But if they fail to take the reproof to themselves, and flatter themselves that God passes over their errors because He does not especially single them out, they deceive their own souls and will be shut up in darkness and be left to their own ways to follow the imagination of their own hearts.

"Many are dealing falsely with their own souls and are in a great deception in regard to their true condition before God. He employs ways and means to best serve His purpose and to prove what is in the hearts of His professed followers. He makes plain the wrongs of some that others may thus be warned and fear and shun those errors. By self-examination they may find that they are doing the same things which God condemns in others. If they really desire to serve God, and fear to offend Him, they will not wait for their sins to be specified

[1]Vol. 2, p. 9 (1868).

before they make confession and with humble repentance return unto the Lord. They will forsake the things which have displeased God, according to the light given to others. If, on the contrary, those who are not right see that they are guilty of the very sins that have been reproved in others, yet continue in the same unconsecrated course because they have not been specially named, they endanger their own souls, and will be led captive by Satan at his will."[1]

"I was shown that in the wisdom of God the sins and errors of all would not be revealed. . . . All who are guilty are addressed in these individual testimonies, although their names may not be attached to the special testimony borne; and if individuals pass over and cover up their own sins because their names are not especially called, they will not be prospered of God. They cannot advance in the divine life, but will become darker and darker, until the light of heaven will be entirely withdrawn."[2]

In a view given me about twenty years ago, "I was then directed to bring out general principles, in speaking and in writing, and at the same time specify the dangers, errors, and sins of some individuals, that all might be warned, reproved, and counseled. I saw that all should search their own hearts and lives closely to see if they had not made the same mistakes for which others were corrected and if the warnings given for others did not apply to their own cases. If so, they should feel that the counsel and reproofs were given especially for them and should make as practical an application of them as though they were especially addressed to themselves. . . . God designs to test the faith of all who claim to be followers of Christ. He will test the sincerity of the prayers of all those who claim to earnestly desire to know their duty. He will make duty plain. He will give all an ample opportunity to develop what is in their hearts."[3]

<hr>

[1]Vol. 2, pp. 112, 113 (1868).   [2]Vol. 2, p. 447 (1870).
[3]Vol. 2, p. 687 (1871).

OBJECT OF THE "TESTIMONIES"

"In ancient times God spoke to men by the mouth of prophets and apostles. In these days He speaks to them by the testimonies of His Spirit. There was never a time when God instructed His people more earnestly than He instructs them now concerning His will and the course that He would have them pursue."[1]

"The Lord has seen fit to give me a view of the needs and errors of His people. Painful though it has been to me, I have faithfully set before the offenders their faults and the means of remedying them. . . . Thus has the Spirit of God pronounced warnings and judgments, withholding not, however, the sweet promise of mercy. . . .

"Repentant sinners have no cause to despair because they are reminded of their transgressions and warned of their danger. These very efforts in their behalf show how much God loves them and desires to save them. They have only to follow His counsel and do His will, to inherit eternal life. God sets the sins of His erring people before them, that they may behold them in all their enormity under the light of divine truth. It is then their duty to renounce them forever." "If God's people would recognize His dealings with them and accept His teachings, they would find a straight path for their feet and a light to guide them through darkness and discouragement."[2]

"Warnings and reproofs are not given to the erring among Seventh-day Adventists because their lives are more blameworthy than are the lives of professed Christians of the nominal churches, nor because their example of their acts are worse than those of the Adventists who will not yield obedience to the claims of God's law, but because they have great light, and have by their profession taken their position as God's special, chosen people, having the law of God written in their hearts. They signify their loyalty to the God of heaven by yielding obedience to the laws of His government. They are God's representatives upon the earth. Any sin in them separates them from God and, in a special manner, dishonors His name by giving the enemies of His holy law occasion to reproach His cause and His people, whom He has called 'a chosen generation, a royal priesthood, an holy nation, a peculiar people,' that they should show forth the praises of Him that hath called them out of darkness into His marvelous light. . . .

"The Lord reproves and corrects the people who profess to keep His law. He points out their sins and lays open their iniquity because He wishes to separate all sin and wickedness from them, that they may perfect holiness in His fear. . . . God rebukes, reproves, and corrects them, that they may be refined, sanctified, elevated, and finally exalted to His own throne."[1]

"I have been looking over the *Testimonies* given for Sabbathkeepers and I am astonished at the mercy of God and His care for His people in giving them so many warnings, pointing out their dangers, and presenting before them the exalted position which He would have them occupy. If they would keep themselves in His love and separate from the world, He would cause His special blessings to rest upon them and His light to shine round about them. Their influence for good might be felt in every branch of the work and in every part of the gospel field. But if they fail to meet the mind of God, if they continue to have so little sense of the exalted character of the work as they have had in the past, their influence and example will prove a terrible curse. They will do harm and only harm. The blood of precious souls will be found upon their garments.

"Testimonies of warning have been repeated. I inquire: Who have heeded them? Who have been zealous in repent-

[1]Vol. 2, pp. 452, 453 (1870).

ing of their sins and idolatry, and have been earnestly pressing toward the mark for the prize of the high calling of God in Christ Jesus? . . . I have waited anxiously, hoping that God would put His Spirit upon some and use them as instruments of righteousness to awaken and set in order His church. I have almost despaired as I have seen, year after year, a greater departure from that simplicity which God has shown me should characterize the life of His followers. There has been less and less interest in, and devotion to, the cause of God. I ask: Wherein have those who profess confidence in the *Testimonies* sought to live according to the light given in them? Wherein have they regarded the warnings given? Wherein have they heeded the instructions they have received?"[1]

NOT TO TAKE THE PLACE OF THE BIBLE

That the *Testimonies* were not given to take the place of the Bible, the following extract from a testimony published in 1876 will show:

"Brother J would confuse the mind by seeking to make it appear that the light God has given through the *Testimonies* is an addition to the word of God, but in this he presents the matter in a false light. God has seen fit in this manner to bring the minds of His people to His word, to give them a clearer understanding of it."[2] "The word of God is sufficient to enlighten the most beclouded mind and may be understood by those who have any desire to understand it. But notwithstanding all this, some who profess to make the word of God their study are found living in direct opposition to its plainest teachings. Then, to leave men and women without excuse, God gives plain and pointed testimonies, bringing them back to the word that they have neglected to follow."[3] "The word of God abounds in general principles for

---

[1]Vol. 2, pp. 483, 484 (1870).   [2]Vol. 4, p. 246 (1876).
[3]Vol. 2, p. 455 (1870).

the formation of correct habits of living, and the testimonies, general and personal, have been calculated to call their attention more especially to these principles."[1]

April 30, 1871, this matter was presented to me in a dream. I seemed to be attending an important meeting, at which a large company were assembled. "Many were bowed before God in earnest prayer, and they seemed to be burdened. They were importuning the Lord for special light. A few seemed to be in agony of spirit; their feelings were intense; with tears they were crying aloud for help and light. Our most prominent brethren were engaged in this most impressive scene. Brother A was prostrated upon the floor, apparently in deep distress. His wife was sitting among a company of indifferent scorners. She looked as though she desired all to understand that she scorned those who were thus humiliating themselves.

"I dreamed that the Spirit of the Lord came upon me, and I arose amid cries and prayers, and said: The Spirit of the Lord God is upon me. I feel urged to say to you that you must commence to work individually for yourselves. You are looking to God and desiring Him to do the work for you which He has left for you to do. If you will do the work for yourselves which you know that you ought to do, then God will help you when you need help. You have left undone the very things which God has left for you to do. You have been calling upon God to do your work. Had you followed the light which He has given you, then He would cause more light to shine upon you; but while you neglect the counsels, warnings, and reproofs that have been given, how can you expect God to give you more light and blessings to neglect and despise? God is not as man; He will not be trifled with.

"I took the precious Bible and surrounded it with the several *Testimonies for the Church*, given for the people of God. Here, said I, the cases of nearly all are met. The sins they are to shun are pointed out. The counsel that they desire can be found here, given for other cases situated similarly to themselves. God has been pleased to give you line upon line and precept upon precept. But there are not many of you that really know what is contained in the *Testimonies*. You are not familiar with the Scriptures. If you had made God's word your study, with a desire to reach the Bible standard and attain to Christian perfection, you would not have needed the *Testimonies*. It is because you have neglected to acquaint yourselves with God's inspired Book that He has sought to reach you by simple, direct testimonies, calling your attention to the words of inspiration which you had neglected to obey, and urging you to fashion your lives in accordance with its pure and elevated teachings.

"The Lord designs to warn you, to reprove, to counsel, through the testimonies given, and to impress your minds with the importance of the truth of His word. The written testimonies are not to give new light, but to impress vividly upon the heart the truths of inspiration already revealed. Man's duty to God and to his fellow man has been distinctly specified in God's word, yet but few of you are obedient to the light given. Additional truth is not brought out; but God has through the *Testimonies* simplified the great truths already given and in His own chosen way brought them before the people to awaken and impress the mind with them, that all may be left without excuse.

"Pride, self-love, selfishness, hatred, envy, and jealousy have beclouded the perceptive powers, and the truth, which would make you wise unto salvation, has lost its power to charm and control the mind. The very essential principles of godliness are not understood because there is not a hungering and thirsting for Bible knowledge, purity of heart, and holiness of life. The *Testimonies* are not to belittle the word of God, but to exalt it and attract minds to it, that the beautiful simplicity of truth may impress all.

"I said further: As the word of God is walled in with these books and pamphlets, so has God walled you in with reproofs, counsel, warnings, and encouragements. Here you are crying before God, in the anguish of your souls, for more light. I am authorized from God to tell you that not another ray of light through the *Testimonies* will shine upon your pathway until you make a practical use of the light already given. The Lord has walled you about with light; but you have not appreciated the light; you have trampled upon it. While some have despised the light, others have neglected it or followed it but indifferently. A few have set heir hearts to obey the light which God has been pleased give them.

"Some that have received special warnings through testimony have forgotten in a few weeks the reproof given. The testimonies to some have been several times repeated, but they have not thought them of sufficient importance to be carefully heeded. They have been to them like idle tales. Had they regarded the light given they would have avoided losses and trials which they think are hard and severe. They have only themselves to censure. They have placed upon their own necks a yoke which they find grievous to be borne. It is not the yoke which Christ has bound upon them. God's care and love were exercised in their behalf; but their selfish, evil, unbelieving souls could not discern His goodness and mercy. They rush on in their own wisdom, until, overwhelmed with trials and confused with perplexity, they are ensnared by Satan. When you gather up the rays of light which God has given in the past, then will He give an increase of light.

"I referred them to ancient Israel. God gave them His law, but they would not obey it. He then gave the ceremonies and ordinances, that, in the performance of these, God might be kept in remembrance. They were so prone to forget Him and His claims upon them that it was necessary to keep their minds stirred up to realize their obligations to obey and honor their Creator. Had they been obedient and loved to keep God's commandments, the multitude of ceremonies and ordinances would not have been required.

"If the people who now profess to be God's peculiar treasure would obey His requirements, as specified in His word, special testimonies would not be given to awaken them to their duty and impress upon them their sinfulness and their fearful danger in neglecting to obey the word of God. Consciences have been blunted because light has been set aside, neglected, and despised. . . .

"One stood by my side and said: 'God has raised you up and has given you words to speak to the people and to reach hearts as He has given to no other one. He has shaped your testimonies to meet cases that are in need of help. You must be unmoved by scorn, derision, reproach, and censure. In order to be God's special instrument you should lean to no one, but hang upon Him alone and, like the clinging vine, let your tendrils entwine about Him. He will make you a means through which to communicate His light to the people. You must daily gather strength from God in order to be fortified, that your surroundings may not dim or eclipse the light that He has permitted to shine upon His people through you. It is Satan's special object to prevent this light from coming to the people of God, who so greatly need it amid the perils of these last days.

" 'Your success is in your simplicity. As soon as you depart from this and fashion your testimony to meet the minds of any, your power is gone. Almost everything in this age is glossed and unreal. The world abounds in testimonies given to please and charm for the moment and to exalt self. Your testimony is of a different character. It is to come down to the minutiae of life, keeping the feeble faith from dying and pressing home upon believers the necessity of shining as lights in the world.

" 'God has given you your testimony, to set before the backslider and the sinner his true condition and the immense loss he is sustaining by continuing a life of sin. God has impressed this upon you by opening it before your vision as He has to no other one now living, and according to the light He has given you will He hold you responsible. "Not by might, nor by power, but by My Spirit, saith the Lord of hosts." "Lift up thy voice like a trumpet, and show My people their transgression, and the house of Jacob their sins." ' "[1]

WRONG USE OF THE "TESTIMONIES"

Some who believe the *Testimonies* have erred by urging them unduly upon others. In volume 1, number 8, is a testimony bearing upon this point. "There were some in _____ who were God's children, and yet doubted the visions. Others had no opposition, yet dared not take a decided stand in regard to them. Some were skeptical, and they had sufficient cause to make them so. The false visions and fanatical exercises, and the wretched fruits following, had an influence upon the cause in _____ to make minds jealous of everything bearing the name of visions. All these things should have been taken into consideration and wisdom exercised. There should be no trial or labor with those who have never seen the individual having visions, and who have had no personal knowledge of the influence of the visions. Such should not be deprived of the benefits and privileges of the church if their Christian course is otherwise correct. . . .

"Some, I was shown, could receive the published visions, judging of the tree by its fruits. Others are like doubting Thomas; they cannot believe the published *Testimonies*, nor receive evidence through the testimony of others, but must see and have the evidence for themselves. Such must not be set aside, but long patience and brotherly love should be exercised toward them until they find their position and become established for or against. If they fight against the visions,

[1]Vol. 2, pp. 604-608 (1871).

of which they have no knowledge; if they carry their opposition so far as to oppose that in which they have had no experience, . . . the church may know that they are not right."[1]

Some of our brethren had had long experience in the truth and for years had been acquainted with me and my work. They had proved the truthfulness of the *Testimonies* and had asserted their belief in them. They had felt the powerful influence of the Spirit of God resting upon them to witness to their truthfulness. I was shown that if such, when reproved through the *Testimonies,* should rise up against them and work secretly to lessen their influence, they should be faithfully dealt with; for their course would endanger those who were lacking in experience.[2]

The first number of the *Testimonies* ever published contains a warning against the injudicious use of the light which is thus given to God's people.[3] I stated that some had taken an unwise course; when they had talked their faith to unbelievers, and the proof had been asked for, they had read from my writings instead of going to the Bible for proof. It was shown me that this course was inconsistent and would prejudice unbelievers against the truth. The *Testimonies* can have no weight with those who know nothing of their spirit. They should not be referred to in such cases.

Other warnings concerning the use of the *Testimonies* have been given from time to time, as follows:

"Some of the preachers are far behind. They profess to believe the testimony borne, and some do harm by making them an iron rule for those who have had no experience in reference to them, but they fail to carry them out themselves. They have had repeated testimonies which they have utterly disregarded. The course of such is not consistent."[4]

"I saw that many have taken advantage of what God has shown in regard to the sins and wrongs of others. They have

[1]Vol. 1, p. 328 (1862).   [2]Vol. 1, p. 382.   [3]Vol. 1, p. 119.
[4]Vol. 1, p. 369 (1863).

taken the extreme meaning of what has been shown in vision, and then have pressed it until it has a tendency to weaken the faith of many in what God has shown, and also to discourage and dishearten the church."[1]

The enemy will seize upon everything which he can use to destroy souls. "Testimonies have been borne in favor of individuals occupying important positions. They commence well to lift the burdens and act their part in connection with the work of God. But Satan pursues them with his temptations, and they are finally overcome. As others look upon their wrong course, Satan suggests to their minds that there must be a mistake in the testimonies given for these persons, else these men would not have proved themselves unworthy to bear a part in the work of God."

Thus doubts arise in regard to the light that God has given. "That which can be said of men under certain circumstances cannot be said of them under other circumstances. Men are weak in moral power and so supremely selfish, so self-sufficient, and so easily puffed up with vain conceit, that God cannot work in connection with them, and they are left to move like blind men and to manifest so great weakness and folly that many are astonished that such individuals should ever have been accepted and acknowledged as worthy of having any connection with God's work. This is just what Satan designed. This was his object from the time he first specially tempted them to reproach the cause of God and to cast reflections upon the *Testimonies*. Had they remained where their influence would not have been specially felt upon the cause of God, Satan would not have beset them so fiercely, for he could not have accomplished his purpose by using them as his instruments to do a special work."[2]

[1]Vol. 1, p. 166 (1857).   [2]Vol. 3, pp. 469, 470 (1875).

TO BE JUDGED BY THEIR FRUITS

Let the *Testimonies* be judged by their fruits. What is the spirit of their teaching? What has been the result of their influence? "All who desire to do so can acquaint themselves with the fruits of these visions. For seventeen years God has seen fit to let them survive and strengthen against the opposition of Satan's forces and the influence of human agencies that have aided Satan in his work."[1]

"God is either teaching His church, reproving their wrongs and strengthening their faith, or He is not. This work is of God, or it is not. God does nothing in partnership with Satan. My work . . . bears the stamp of God or the stamp of the enemy. There is no halfway work in the matter. The *Testimonies* are of the Spirit of God, or of the devil."[2]

As the Lord has manifested Himself through the spirit of prophecy, "past, present, and future have passed before me. I have been shown faces that I had never seen, and years afterward I knew them when I saw them. I have been aroused from my sleep with a vivid sense of subjects previously presented to my mind; and I have written, at midnight, letters that have gone across the continent and, arriving at a crisis, have saved great disaster to the cause of God. This has been my work for many years. A power has impelled me to reprove and rebuke wrongs that I had not thought of. Is this work of the last thirty-six years from above or from beneath?"[3]

Christ warned His disciples: "Beware of false prophets, which come to you in sheep's clothing, but inwardly they are ravening wolves. Ye shall know them by their fruits. Do men gather grapes of thorns, or figs of thistles? Even so every good tree bringeth forth good fruit; but a corrupt tree bringeth forth evil fruit. A good tree cannot bring forth evil fruit, neither can a corrupt tree bring forth good fruit. Every tree that bringeth

[1]Vol. 1, p. 330 (1862).   [2]Vol. 4, p. 230.   [3]Vol. 5, pp. 64, 65 (1882).

not forth good fruit is hewn down, and cast into the fire. Wherefore by their fruits ye shall know them." Here is a test, and all can apply it if they will. Those who really desire to know the truth will find sufficient evidence for belief.

DOUBTING THE "TESTIMONIES"

"It is Satan's plan to weaken the faith of God's people in the *Testimonies.*" "Satan knows how to make his attacks. He works upon minds to excite jealousy and dissatisfaction toward those at the head of the work. The gifts are next questioned; then, of course, they have but little weight, and instruction given through vision is disregarded." "Next follows skepticism in regard to the vital points of our faith, the pillars of our position, then doubt as to the Holy Scriptures, and then the downward march to perdition. When the *Testimonies,* which were once believed, are doubted and given up, Satan knows the deceived ones will not stop at this; and he redoubles his efforts till he launches them into open rebellion, which becomes incurable and ends in destruction."[1] "By giving place to doubts and unbelief in regard to the work of God, and by cherishing feelings of distrust and cruel jealousies, they are preparing themselves for complete deception. They rise up with bitter feelings against the ones who dare to speak of their errors and reprove their sins."[2]

A testimony for certain young men, first published in 1880, speaks of this point as follows: "A prevailing skepticism is continually increasing in reference to the *Testimonies* of the Spirit of God; and these youth encourage questionings and doubts instead of removing them, because they are ignorant of the spirit and power and force of the *Testimonies.*"[3]

I was shown that many had so little spirituality that they did not understand the value of the *Testimonies* or their real object. They talked flippantly of the *Testimonies* given by

God for the benefit of His people, and passed judgment upon them, giving their opinion and criticizing this and that, when they would better have placed their hands upon their lips, and prostrated themselves in the dust; for they could not appreciate the spirit of the *Testimonies,* because they knew so little of the Spirit of God.[1]

"There are some in _____ who have never fully submitted to reproof. They have taken a course of their own choosing. They have ever, to a greater or less degree, exerted an influence against those who have stood up to defend the right and reprove the wrong. The influence of these persons upon individuals who come here and who are brought in contact with them . . . is very bad. They fill the minds of these newcomers with questionings and doubts in regard to the *Testimonies* of the Spirit of God. They put false constructions upon the *Testimonies;* and instead of leading persons to become consecrated to God and to listen to the voice of the church, they teach them to be independent and not to mind the opinions and judgment of others. The influence of this class has been secretly at work. Some are unconscious of the harm they are doing; but, unconsecrated, proud, and rebellious themselves, they lead others in the wrong track. A poisonous atmosphere is inhaled from these unconsecrated ones. The blood of souls is in the garments of such, and Christ will say to them in the day of final settlement: 'Depart from Me, all ye workers of iniquity.' Astonished they will be, but their professedly Christian lives were a deception, a fraud."[2]

"Some express their views that the testimony of Sister White cannot be reliable. This is all that many unconsecrated ones want. The testimonies of reproof have checked their vanity and pride; but if they dared, they would go to almost any length in fashion and pride. God will give all such an opportunity to prove themselves and to develop their true characters."[3]

[1]Vol. 4, p. 443.   [2]Vol. 4, pp. 513, 514 (1880).   [3]Vol. 3, p. 313 (1873).

"I saw that the reason why visions had not been more frequent of late is, they have not been appreciated by the church. The church have nearly lost their spirituality and faith, and the reproofs and warnings have had but little effect upon them. Many of those who have professed faith in them have not heeded them."[1]

"If you lose confidence in the *Testimonies* you will drift away from Bible truth. I have been fearful that many would take a questioning, doubting position, and in my distress for your souls I would warn you. How many will heed the warning? As you now hold the *Testimonies,* should one be given crossing your track, corrcting your errors, would you feel at perfect liberty to acccept or reject any part or the whole? That which you will be least inclined to receive is the very part most needed."[2]

"My brethren, beware of the evil heart of unbelief. The word of God is plain and close in its restrictions; it interferes with your selfish indulgence; therefore you do not obey it. The *Testimonies* of His Spirit call your attention to the Scriptures, point out your defects of character, and rebuke your sins; therefore you do not heed them. And to justify your carnal, ease-loving course you begin to doubt whether the *Testimonies* are from God. If you would obey their teachings you would be assured of their divine origin. Remember, your unbelief does not affect their truthfulness. If they are from God they will stand."[3]

"I have been shown that unbelief in the testimonies of warning, encouragement, and reproof is shutting away the light from God's people. Unbelief is closing their eyes so that they are ignorant of their true condition." "They think the testimony of the Spirit of God in reproof is uncalled for or that it does not mean them. Such are in the greatest need of the grace

---

[1]Vol. 1, p. 119 (1855).   [2]Vol. 5, p. 98 (1882).   [3]Vol. 5, p. 234.

of God and spiritual discernment, that they may discover their deficiency in spiritual knowledge."[1]

"Many who have backslidden from the truth assign as a reason for their course that they do not have faith in the *Testimonies*. . . . The question now is: Will they yield their idol which God condemns, or will they continue in their wrong course of indulgence and reject the light God has given them reproving the very things in which they delight? The question to be settled with them is: Shall I deny myself and receive as of God the *Testimonies* which reprove my sins, or shall I reject the *Testimonies because* they reprove my sins?

"In many cases the *Testimonies* are fully received, the sin and indulgence broken off, and reformation at once commences in harmony with the light God has given. In other instances sinful indulgences are cherished, the *Testimonies* are rejected, and many excuses which are untrue are offered to others as the reason for refusing to receive them. The *true* reason is not given. It is a lack of moral courage—a will, strengthened and controlled by the Spirit of God, to renounce hurtful habits."[2]

"Satan has ability to suggest doubts and to devise objections to the pointed testimony that God sends, and many think it a virtue, a mark of intelligence in them, to be unbelieving and to question and quibble. Those who desire to doubt will have plenty of room. God does not propose to remove all occasion for unbelief. He gives evidence, which must be carefully investigated with a humble mind and a teachable spirit, and all should decide from the weight of evidence."[3] "God gives sufficient evidence for the candid mind to believe; but he who turns from the weight of evidence because there are a few things which he cannot make plain to his finite understanding

[1]Vol. 3, pp. 255, 253, 254 (1873). [2]Vol. 4, p. 32 (1876).
[3]Vol. 3, p. 255 (1873).

will be left in the cold, chilling atmosphere of unbelief and questioning doubts, and will make shipwreck of faith."[1]

DUTY TO GIVE REPROOF

"If wrongs are apparent among His people, and if the servants of God pass on indifferent to them, they virtually sustain and justify the sinner, and are alike guilty and will just as surely receive the displeasure of God; for they will be made responsible for the sins of the guilty. In vision I have been pointed to many instances where the displeasure of God has been incurred by a neglect on the part of His servants to deal with the wrongs and sins existing among them. Those who have excused these wrongs have been thought by the people to be very amiable and lovely in disposition, simply because they shunned to discharge a plain, Scriptural duty. The task was not agreeable to their feelings; therefore they avoided it."[2]

The searching testimony of the Spirit of God "will separate those from Israel who have ever been at war with the means that God has ordained to keep corruptions out of the church. Wrongs must be called wrongs. Grievous sins must be called by their right name. All of God's people should come nearer to Him. . . . Then will they see sin in the true light and will realize how offensive it is in the sight of God."[3] "The plain, straight testimony must live in the church, or the curse of God will rest upon His people as surely as it did upon ancient Israel because of their sins."[4]

"Never was there greater need of faithful warnings and reproofs . . . than at this very time. Satan has come down with great power, knowing that his time is short. He is flooding the world with pleasing fables, and the people of God love to have smooth things spoken to them. . . . I was shown that God's people must make more firm, determined efforts to press

<hr/>

[1]Vol. 4, pp. 232, 233 (1876).   [2]Vol. 3, p. 266 (1873).
[3]Vol. 3, p. 324 (1873).   [4]Vol. 3, p. 269 (1873).

back the incoming darkness. The close work of the Spirit of God is needed now as never before."[1]

When in my youth I accepted the work given me by God, I received with it a promise that I should have special aid from the mighty Helper. There was given me also the solemn charge to deliver faithfully the Lord's message, making no difference for friends or foes. There is no respect of persons with God. Whether dealing with rich or poor, high or low, the cultured or the ignorant, there must be no betrayal of sacred trusts with the Lord's messenger.

"Let none entertain the thought that I regret or take back any plain testimony I have borne to individuals or to the people. If I have erred anywhere, it is in not rebuking sin more decidedly and firmly. Some of the brethren have taken the responsibility of criticizing my work and proposing an easier way to correct wrongs. To these persons I would say: I take God's way and not yours. What I have said or written in testimony or reproof has not been too plainly expressed. . . .

"Those who would in any way lessen the force of the sharp reproofs which God has given me to speak, must meet their work at the judgment. . . . To those who have taken the responsibility to reprove me and, in their finite judgment, to propose a way which appears wiser to them I repeat: I do not accept your efforts. Leave me with God, and let Him teach me. I will take the words from the Lord and speak them to the people. I do not expect that all will accept the reproof and reform their lives, but I must discharge my duty all the same. I will walk in humility before God, doing my work for time and for eternity.

"God has not given my brethren the work that He has given me. It has been urged that my manner of giving reproof in public has led others to be sharp and critical and severe. If so, they must settle that matter with the Lord. If others take a

[1]Vol. 3, pp. 327, 328 (1873).

responsibility which God has not laid upon them; if they disregard the instructions He has given them again and again through the humble instrument of His choice, to be kind, patient, and forbearing, they alone must answer for the results. With a sorrow-burdened heart, I have performed my unpleasant duty to my dearest friends, not daring to please myself by withholding reproof, even from my husband; and I shall not be less faithful in warning others, whether they will hear or forbear. When I am speaking to the people I say much that I have not premeditated. The Spirit of the Lord frequently comes upon me. I seem to be carried out of, and away from, myself; the life and character of different persons are clearly presented before my mind. I see their errors and dangers, and feel compelled to speak of what is thus brought before me. I dare not resist the Spirit of God."[1]

REJECTION OF REPROOF

"Many now despise the faithful reproof given of God in testimony. I have been shown that some in these days have even gone so far as to burn the written words of rebuke and warning, as did the wicked king of Israel. But opposition to God's threatenings will not hinder their execution. To defy the words of the Lord, spoken through His chosen instruments, will only provoke His anger and eventually bring certain ruin upon the offender. Indignation often kindles in the heart of the sinner against the agent whom God chooses to deliver His reproofs. It has ever been thus, and the same spirit exists today that persecuted and imprisoned Jeremiah for obeying the word of the Lord."[2]

From the beginning of my work, as I have been called to bear a plain, pointed testimony, to reprove wrongs, and to spare not, there have been those who have stood in opposition to my testimony and have followed after to speak smooth

[1]Vol. 5, pp. 19, 20 (1882).   [2]Vol. 4, p. 180 (1876).

things, to daub with untempered mortar, and to destroy the influence of my labors. The Lord would move upon me to bear reproof, and then individuals would step in between me and the people to make my testimony of no effect.

"In almost every case where reproof is necessary, there will be some who entirely overlook the fact that the Spirit of the Lord has been grieved and His cause reproached. These will pity those who deserved reproof, because personal feelings have been hurt. All this unsanctified sympathy places the sympathizers where they are sharers in the guilt of the one reproved. In nine cases out of ten if the one reproved had been left under a sense of his wrongs, he might have been helped to see them and thereby have been reformed. But meddlesome, unsanctified sympathizers place altogether a wrong construction upon the motives of the reprover and the nature of the reproof given, and by sympathizing with the one reproved lead him to feel that he has been really abused; and his feelings rise up in rebellion against the one who has only done his duty. Those who faithfully discharge their unpleasant duties under a sense of their accountability to God will receive His blessing."[1]

"There are some in these last days who will cry: 'Speak unto us smooth things, prophesy deceits.' But this is not my work. God has set me as a reprover of His people; and just so surely as He has laid upon me the heavy burden, He will make those to whom this message is given responsible for the manner in which they treat it. God will not be trifled with, and those who despise His work will receive according to their deeds. I have not chosen this unpleasant labor for myself. It is not a work which will bring to me the favor or praise of men. It is a work which but few will appreciate. But those who seek to make my labor doubly hard by their misrepresentations, jealous suspicions, and unbelief, thus creating prejudice in the minds of others against the *Testimonies* God has given me, and limiting

[1]Vol. 3, p. 359 (1875).

my work, have the matter to settle with God, while I shall go forward as Providence and my brethren may open the way before me. In the name and strength of my Redeemer I shall do what I can. . . . My duty is not to please myself, but to do the will of my heavenly Father, who has given me my work."[1]

If God has given me a message to bear to His people, those who would hinder me in the work and lessen the faith of the people in its truth are not fighting against the instrument, but against God. "It is not the instrument whom you slight and insult, but God, who has spoken to you in these warnings and reproofs." "It is hardly possible for men to offer a greater insult to God than to despise and reject the instrumentalities that He has appointed to lead them."[2]

NEGLECT OF THE "TESTIMONIES"

It is not alone those who openly reject the *Testimonies,* or who cherish doubt concerning them, that are on dangerous ground. To disregard light is to reject it.

"Some of you in words acknowledge reproof, but you do not in heart accept it. You go on the same as before, only being less susceptible to the influence of the Spirit of God, becoming more and more blinded, having less wisdom, less self-control, less moral power, and less zeal and relish for religious exercises; and, unless converted, you will finally yield your hold upon God entirely. You have not made decided changes in your life when reproof has come, because you have not seen and realized your defects of character and the great contrast between your life and the life of Christ." "What do your prayers amount to while you regard iniquity in your hearts? Unless you make a thorough change, you will, not far hence, become weary of reproof, as did the children of Israel; and, like them, you will apostatize from God."[3]

[1]Vol. 4, pp. 231, 232 (1876).   [2]Vol. 5, p. 235; vol. 3, p. 355.
[3]Vol. 4, p. 332 (1879).

"Many are going directly contrary to the light which God has given to His people, because they do not read the books which contain the light and knowledge in cautions, reproofs, and warnings. The cares of the world, the love of fashion, and the lack of religion have turned the attention from the light God has so graciously given, while books and periodicals containing error are traveling all over the country. Skepticism and infidelity are increasing everywhere. Light so precious, coming from the throne of God, is hid under a bushel. God will make His people responsible for this neglect. An account must be rendered to Him for every ray of light He has let shine upon our pathway, whether it has been improved to our advancement in divine things or rejected because it was more agreeable to follow inclination."[1]

"The volumes of *Spirit of Prophecy*,[2] and also the *Testimonies,* should be introduced into every Sabbathkeeping family, and the brethren should know their value and be urged to read them. It was not the wisest plan to place these books at a low figure and have only one set in a church. They should be in the library of every family and be read again and again. Let them be kept where they can be read by many."[1]

Let ministers and people remember that gospel truth hardens when it does not save. The rejection of light leaves men captives, bound about by chains of darkness and unbelief. "The soul that refuses to listen to the invitations of mercy from day to day can soon listen to the most urgent appeals without an emotion stirring his soul. As laborers with God we need more fervent piety and less self-exaltation. The more self is exalted, the more will faith in the *Testimonies* of the Spirit of God be lessened. . . . Those who trust wholly in themselves will see less and less of God in the *Testimonies* of His Spirit."[3]

---

[1]Vol. 4, pp. 391, 390 (1880).   [2]*The Great Controversy*
[3]Vol. 5, p. 134 (1882).

HOW TO RECEIVE REPROOF

"Those who are reproved by the Spirit of God should not rise up against the humble instrument. It is God, and not an erring mortal, who has spoken to save them from ruin." It is not pleasing to human nature to receive reproof, nor is it possible for the heart of man, unenlightened by the Spirit of God, to realize the necessity of reproof or the blessing it is designed to bring. As man yields to temptation, and indulges in sin, his mind becomes darkened. The moral sense is perverted. The warnings of conscience are disregarded, and its voice is less clearly heard. He gradually loses the power to distinguish between right and wrong, until he has no true sense or his standing before God. He may observe the forms of religion and zealously maintain its doctrines, while destitute of its spirit. His condition is that described by the True Witness: "Thou sayest, I am rich, and increased with goods, and have need of nothing; and *knowest not* that thou art wretched, and miserable, and poor, and blind, and naked." When the Spirit of God, by message of reproof, declares this to be his condition, he cannot see that the message is true. Is he therefore to reject the warning? No. God has given sufficient evidence, so that all who desire to do so may satisfy themselves as to the character of the *Testimonies;* and, having acknowledged them to be from God, it is their duty to accept reproof, even though they do not themselves see the sinfulness of their course. If they fully realized their condition, what would be the need of reproof? Because they know it not, God mercifully sets it before them, so that they may repent and reform before it shall be too late. "Those who despise the warning will be left in blindness to become self-deceived; but those who heed it, and zealously go about the work of separating their sins from them in order to have the needed graces, will be opening the door of their hearts that the dear Saviour may come in and dwell with them."[1] "Those who are most closely connected with God are

[1]Vol. 3, p. 257 (1873).

the ones who know His voice when He speaks to them. Those who are spiritual discern spiritual things. Such will feel grateful that the Lord has pointed out their errors."[1]

"David learned wisdom from God's dealings with him and bowed in humility beneath the chastisement of the Most High. The faithful portrayal of his true state by the prophet Nathan made David acquainted with his own sins and aided him to put them away. He accepted counsel meekly and humiliated himself before God. 'The law of the Lord,' he exclaims, 'is perfect, converting the soul.' "[2]

"If ye be without chastisement, whereof all are partakers, then are ye . . . not sons." Our Lord has said: "As many as I love, I rebuke and chasten." "No chastening for the present seemeth to be joyous, but grievous: nevertheless afterward it yieldeth the peaceable fruit of righteousness unto them which are exercised thereby." Though bitter the discipline, it is appointed by a Father's tender love, "that we might be *partakers of His holiness.*"

AN UNWARRANTED DISTINCTION

Some have taken the position that the warnings, cautions, and reproofs given by the Lord through His servant, unless they come through special vision for each individual case, should have no more weight than counsels and warnings from other sources. In some cases it has been represented that in giving a testimony for churches or individuals I have been influenced to write as I did by letters received from members of the church. There have been those who claimed that testimonies purporting to be given by the Spirit of God were merely the expression of my own judgment, based upon information gathered from human sources. This statement is utterly false. If, however, in response to some question, statement, or appeal from churches or individuals, a testimony is written presenting the light which God has given concerning

[1]Vol. 5, p. 134.   [2]Vol. 4, pp. 14, 15 (1876).

them, the fact that it has been called forth in this manner in nowise detracts from its validity or importance. I quote from *Testimony* 31 a few paragraphs bearing directly upon this point:

"How was it with the apostle Paul? The news he received through the household of Chloe concerning the condition of the church at Corinth was what caused him to write his first epistle to that church. Private letters had come to him stating the facts as they existed, and in his answer he laid down general principles which if heeded would correct the existing evils. With great tenderness and wisdom he exhorts them to all speak the same things, that there be no divisions among them.

"Paul was an inspired apostle, yet the Lord did not reveal to him at all times just the condition of His people. Those who were interested in the prosperity of the church, and saw evils creeping in, presented the matter before him, and from the light which he had previously received he was prepared to judge of the true character of these developments. Because the Lord had not given him a new revelation for that special time, those who were really seeking light did not cast his message aside as only a common letter. No, indeed. The Lord had shown him the difficulties and dangers which would arise in the churches, that when they should develop, he might know just how to treat them.

"He was set for the defense of the church. He was to watch for souls as one that must render account to God, and should he not take notice of the reports concerning their state of anarchy and division? Most assuredly; and the reproof he sent them was written just as much under the inspiration of the Spirit of God as were any of his epistles. But when these reproofs came, some would not be corrected. They took the position that God had not spoken to them through Paul, that he had merely given them his opinion as a man, and they regarded their own judgment as good as that of Paul. So it is with many among our people who have drifted away from the old landmarks and who have followed their own understanding." [1]

When this position is taken by our people, then the special warnings and counsels of God through the Spirit of prophecy can have no influence with them to work a reformation in life and character. The Lord does not give a vision to meet each emergency which may arise in the different attitudes of His people in the development of His work. But He has shown me that it has been His way of dealing with His church in past ages, to impress the minds of His chosen servants with the needs and dangers of His cause and of individuals, and to lay upon them the burden of counsel and warning.

So in many cases God has given me light in regard to peculiar defects of character in members of the church and the dangers to the individual and the cause if these defects are not removed. Under certain circumstances, wrong tendencies are liable to become strongly developed and confirmed, and to work injury to the cause of God and ruin to the individual. Sometimes, when special dangers threaten the cause of God or particular individuals, a communication comes to me from the Lord, either in a dream or a vision of the night, and these cases are brought vividly to my mind. I hear a voice saying to me: "Arise and write; these souls are in peril." I obey the movings of the Spirit of God, and my pen traces their true condition. As I travel, and stand before the people in different places, the Spirit of the Lord brings before me clearly the cases I have been shown, reviving the matter previously given me.

For the last forty-five years the Lord has been revealing to me the needs of His cause and the cases of individuals in every phase of experience, showing where and how they have failed to perfect Christian character. The history of hundreds of cases has been presented to me, and that which God approves,

[1]Vol. 5, pp. 65, 66 (1882).

and that which He condemns, has been plainly set before me. God has shown me that a certain course, if followed, or certain traits of character, if indulged, would produce certain results. He has thus been training and disciplining me in order that I might see the dangers which threaten souls, and instruct and warn His people, line upon line, precept upon precept, that they might not be ignorant of Satan's devices, and might escape his snares.

The work which the Lord has laid out before me especially is to urge young and old, learned and unlearned, to search the Scriptures for themselves; to impress upon all that the study of God's word will expand the mind and strengthen every faculty, fitting the intellect to wrestle with problems of truth, deep and far-reaching; to assure all that the clear knowledge of the Bible outdoes all other knowledge in making man what God designed he should be. "The entrance of Thy words giveth light; it giveth understanding unto the simple." With the light communicated through the study of His word, with the special knowledge given of individual cases among His people under all circumstances and in every phase of experience, can I now be in the same ignorance, the same mental uncertainty and spiritual blindness, as at the beginning of this experience? Will my brethren say that Sister White has been so dull a scholar that her judgment in this direction is no better than before she entered Christ's school, to be trained and disciplined for a special work? Am I no more intelligent in regard to the duties and perils of God's people than are those before whom these things have never been presented? I would not dishonor my Maker by admitting that all this light, all the display of His mighty power in my work and experience, has been valueless, that it has not educated my judgment or better fitted me for His work.

When I see men and women taking the very course, or cherishing the very traits, which have imperiled other souls and wounded the cause of God, and which the Lord has reproved again and again, how can I but be alarmed? When I see timid souls, burdened with a sense of their imperfections, yet conscientiously striving to do what God has said is right, and know that the Lord looks down and smiles on their faithful efforts, shall I not speak a word of encouragement to these poor trembling hearts? Shall I hold my peace because each individual case has not been pointed out to me in direct vision?

"But if the watchman see the sword come, and blow not the trumpet, and the people be not warned; if the sword come, and take any person from among them, he is taken away in his iniquity; but his blood will I require at the watchman's hand. So thou, O son of man, I have set thee a watchman unto the house of Israel; therefore thou shalt hear the word at My mouth, and warn them from Me. When I say unto the wicked, O wicked man, thou shalt surely die; if thou dost not speak to warn the wicked from his way, that wicked man shall die in his iniquity; but his blood will I require at thine hand. Nevertheless, if thou warn the wicked of his way to turn from it; if he do not turn from his way, he shall die in his iniquity; but thou hast delivered thy soul."

In a recent dream I was brought before an assembly of people, some of whom were making efforts to remove the impression of a most solemn testimony of warning that I had given them. They said: "We believe Sister White's testimonies; but when she tells us things that she has not directly seen in vision in the particular case under consideration, her words are of no more account to us than the words of any other person." The Spirit of the Lord came upon me, and I arose and rebuked them in the name of the Lord. I repeated in substance that which I have presented above in regard to the watchman. This, I said, is appropriate to your case and to mine.

Now if those to whom these solemn warnings are addressed say, "It is only Sister White's individual opinion, I shall still follow my own judgment," and if they continue to do the very things they were warned not to do, they show that they despise the counsel of God, and the result is just what the Spirit of God has shown me it would be—injury to the cause of God and ruin to themselves. Some who wish to strengthen their own position will bring forward from the *Testimonies* statements which they think will support their views, and will put the strongest possible construction upon them; but that which questions their course of action, or which does not coincide with their views, they pronounce Sister White's opinion, denying its heavenly origin and placing it on a level with their own judgment.

If you, my brethren, who have been acquainted with me and my work for many years, take the position that my counsel is of no more value than the counsel of those who have not been specially educated for this work, then do not ask me to unite with you in labor; for while you occupy this position, you will inevitably counteract the influence of my work. If you feel just as safe in following your own impulses as in following the light given by God's delegated servant, the peril is your own; you will be condemned because you rejected the light which heaven had sent you.

While at _____, the Lord came to me in the night season and spoke precious words of encouragement concerning my work, repeating the same message that had been given me several times before. With regard to those who have turned from the light sent them, He said: "In slighting and rejecting the testimony that I have given you to bear, it is not you, but Me, your Lord, that they have slighted."

If those who are headstrong and full of self-esteem go on unchecked in their course, what will be the condition of things in the church? How are the wrongs to be corrected which exist in these strong-willed, ambitious ones? By what means will God reach them? How will He set His church in order? Differences of opinion are constantly arising, and apostasies often afflict the church. When controversy or division comes in, all parties claim to be right and to have a conscience void of offense; and they will not be instructed by those who have long borne the burden of the work and who, they have reason to know, have been guided by the Lord. Light has been sent to dispel their darkness, but they are too proud of heart to accept it, and they choose the darkness. They despise the counsel of God because it does not coincide with their views and plans, and favor their wrong traits of character. The work of the Spirit of God, which would bring them into the right position if they would accept it, has not come in a way to please them, and to flatter their self-right-eousness. The light which God has given is no light to them, and they wander in darkness. They claim that no more confidence is to be placed in the judgment of one who has had such a long experience, and whom the Lord has taught and used to do a special work, than in that of any other person. Is it God's plan that they should do thus, or is it the special working of the enemy of all righteousness to hold souls in error, to bind them in strong delusions that cannot be broken, because they have placed themselves beyond the reach of means that God has ordained to deal with His church?

The reproofs, the cautions, the corrections of the Lord, have been given to His church in all ages of the world. These warnings were despised and rejected in Christ's day by the self-righteous Pharisees, who claimed that they needed no such reproof and were unjustly dealt with. They would not receive the word of the Lord through His servants because it did not please their inclinations. Should the Lord give a vision right before this class of people in our day, pointing out their mistakes, rebuking their self-right-eousness and condemning their sins, they would rise up in rebellion, like the inhabitants of Nazareth when Christ showed them their true condition.

If these persons do not humble their hearts before God, if they harbor the suggestions of Satan, doubt and infidelity will take possession of the soul, and they will see everything in a false light. Let the seeds of doubt once be sown in their hearts and they will have an abundant harvest to reap. They will come to mistrust and disbelieve truths which are plain and full of beauty to others who have not educated themselves in unbelief. Those who train the mind to seize upon everything which they can use as a peg to hang a doubt upon, and suggest these thoughts to other minds, will always find occasion to doubt. They will question and criticize everything that arises in the unfolding of truth, criticize the work and position of others, criticize every branch of the work in which they have not themselves a part. They will feed upon the errors and mistakes and faults of others, "until," said the angel, "the Lord Jesus shall rise up from His mediatorial work in the heavenly sanctuary and shall clothe Himself with the garments of vengeance and surprise them at their unholy feast, and they will find themselves unprepared for the marriage supper of the Lamb." Their taste has been so perverted that they would be inclined to criticize even the table of the Lord in His kingdom.

Has God ever revealed to these self-deceived ones that no reproofs or corrections from Him are to have any weight with them unless they come through direct vision? I dwell upon this point because the position that many are now taking upon it is a delusion of Satan to ruin souls. When he has ensnared and weakened them through his sophistry, so that when they are reproved they persist in making of none effect the workings of God's Spirit, his triumph over them will be complete. Some who profess righteousness will, like Judas, betray their Lord into the hands of His bitterest enemies. These self-confident ones, determined to have their own way and to advocate their own ideas, will go on from bad to worse, until they will pursue any course rather than to give up their own will. They will go on blindly in the way of evil, but, like the deluded Pharisees, so self-deceived that they think they are doing God's service. Christ portrayed the course which a certain class will take when they have a chance to develop their true character: "And ye shall be betrayed both by parents, and brethren, and kinsfolks, and friends; and some of you shall they cause to be put to death."

God has given me a marked, solemn experience in connection with His work; and you may be assured that so long as my life is spared, I shall not cease to lift a warning voice as I am impressed by the Spirit of God, whether men will hear or whether they will forbear. I have no special wisdom in myself; I am only an instrument in the Lord's hands to do the work He has set for me to do. The instructions that I have given by pen or voice have been an expression of the light that God has given me. I have tried to place before you the principles that the Spirit of God has for years been impressing upon my mind and writing on my heart.

And now, brethren, I entreat you not to interpose between me and the people, and turn away the light which God would have come to them. Do not by your criticisms take out all the force, all the point and power, from the *Testimonies*. Do not feel that you can dissect them to suit your own ideas, claiming that God has given you ability to discern what is light from heaven and what is the expression of mere human wisdom. If the *Testimonies* speak not according to the word of God, reject them. Christ and Belial cannot be united. For Christ's sake do not confuse the minds of the people with human sophistry and skepticism, and make of none effect the work that the Lord would do. Do not, by your lack of spiritual discernment, make of this agency of God a rock of offense whereby many shall be caused to stumble and fall, "and be snared, and be taken."

UNFOUNDED REPORTS

Several times during the past winter[1] I have met the report that, during the Conference at Minneapolis, "Sister White was shown that the judgment, which since 1844 had been passing upon the righteous dead, had now begun upon the living." This report is not true. A similar rumor, which has been afloat for about two years, originated in this wise: In a letter written from Basel, Switzerland, to a minister in California I made a remark substantially as follows: "The judgment has been over forty years in progress on the cases of the dead, and we know not how soon it will pass to the cases of the living." The letter was read to different persons, and careless hearers reported what they thought they heard. Thus the matter started. The report from Minneapolis arose from someone's misunderstanding of a statement to the same effect as the one quoted from the letter. There is no other foundation for either report than this.

Secondly, report has it that a minister now living has been seen by me in vision as saved in the kingdom of God, thus representing that his final salvation is assured. There is no truth whatever in this statement. The word of God lays down the conditions of our salvation, and it rests wholly with ourselves whether or not we will comply with them.

Says the Revelator: "Thou hast a few names even in Sardis which have not defiled their garments; and they shall walk with Me in white: for they are worthy. *He that overcometh,* the same shall be clothed in white raiment; and I will not blot out his name out of the book of life, but I will confess his name before My Father, and before His angels."

"Nevertheless we, according to His promise, look for new heavens and a new earth, wherein dwelleth righteousness. Wherefore, beloved, seeing that ye look for such things, be diligent that ye may be found of Him in peace, without spot,

[1]1888-89.

and blameless." "Ye therefore, beloved, seeing ye know these things before, *beware lest ye also, being led away with the error of the wicked, fall from your own steadfastness."* "And the Lord make you to increase and abound in love one toward another, and toward all men, even as we do toward you: to the end He may stablish your hearts unblamable in holiness before God, even our Father, at the coming of our Lord Jesus Christ with all His saints." "Now the just shall live by faith: but *if any man draw back,* My soul shall have no pleasure in him. But we are not of them who draw back unto perdition, but of them that believe to the saving of the soul."

Here we have the Bible election plainly stated. Here are specified who shall be crowned in the city of God and who shall have no part with the just. *"Blessed are they that do His commandments,* that they may have right to the tree of life, and may enter in through the gates into the city."

The third report states that, in the Conference at Minneapolis, "Sister White confessed that in some of her remarks at that meeting she had been in error and had manifested a wrong spirit." This report also is wholly without foundation. I could not forbear giving to the Conference the light that God had given me. This I presented both in messages of warning and reproof and in words of hope and faith. But nothing spoken by me at that meeting has been taken back or confessed to be wrong. I still view matters from the same standpoint, and am of the same mind, as when at Minneapolis. All the dangers which I then saw, and which brought such a burden upon me, have been more clearly developed since that meeting. As I become more fully acquainted with the condition of our churches I see that every warning given at Minneapolis was needed.

The influence of this report from Minneapolis, tended to destroy confidence in all reproofs and warnings given by me to the people. One example of this I will here relate.

A sister connected with one of our missions had been reproved for her wrong influence over the young people with whom she was associated. She had encouraged a spirit of lightness, trifling, and frivolity, which grieved away the Spirit of God and which was demoralizing to the workers. When the report came by letter from Minneapolis concerning Sister White's wrong course which called for a confession there, the relatives of Sister T at once remarked: "Well, if Sister White was wrong in regard to matters in the Conference at Minneapolis, and had to confess this, she may have made a mistake as to the message she gave my sister and may have to confess that also." And they justified the wrongdoer in her course. Since that time, however, Sister T has acknowledged the wrong for which she was reproved. Those who originated and spread the report have exerted an influence to embolden wrongdoers in rejecting reproof, and souls have thus been imperiled. Let all who have engaged in this work beware lest the blood of these souls be found upon them in the great day of final judgment.

The cases mentioned will serve to show how little reliance can be placed upon reports concerning what I have done or taught. During my labors in connection with the work of the Lord I have not made it a practice to vindicate my own cause or to contradict reports that have been put in circulation in regard to myself. To do this would occupy my time to the neglect of the work which God has appointed me. These matters I have left to Him who has a care for His servants and His cause.

But I would say to my brethren: Beware how you give credence to such reports. The Saviour bade His disciples: "Take heed therefore how ye hear." And He speaks of a certain class that hear and will not understand lest they should be converted and be healed. Again He said: "Take heed what ye hear." "He that is of God heareth God's words."

Those who listened to the words of Christ heard and reported His teaching just according to the spirit that was in them. It is ever thus with those who hear God's word. The manner in which they understand and receive it depends upon the spirit which dwells in their hearts.

There are many who put their own construction upon what they hear, making the thought appear altogether different from that which the speaker endeavored to express. Some, hearing through the medium of their own prejudices or prepossessions, understand the matter as they desire it to be,—as will best suit their purpose,—and so report it. Following the promptings of an unsanctified heart, they construe into evil that which, rightly understood, might be a means of great good.

Again, an expression perfectly true and right in itself, may be wholly distorted by transmission through several curious, careless, or caviling minds. Well-meaning persons are often careless and make grievous mistakes, and it is not likely that others will report more correctly. One who has himself not fully understood a speaker's meaning repeats a remark or assertion, giving to it his own coloring. It makes an impression on the hearer just according to his prejudices and imaginings. He reports it to a third, who in turn adds a little more and sends it forward; and before any of them are aware of what they are doing, they have accomplished the purpose of Satan in planting the seeds of doubt, jealousy, and suspicion in many minds.

If persons listen to God's message of reproof, warning, or encouragement while their hearts are filled with prejudice, they will not understand the true import of that which was sent them to be a savor of life unto life. Satan stands by to present everything to their understanding in a false light. But the souls that are hungering and thirsting for divine knowledge will hear aright, and will obtain the precious blessings that God designs to convey to them. Their minds are under the influence of His Holy Spirit, and they hear aright.

When hearts are purified from selfishness and egotism, they are in harmony with the message God sends them. The perceptions are quickened, the sensibilities refined. Like appreciates like. "He that is of God heareth God's words."

And now to all who have a desire for truth I would say: Do not give credence to unauthenticated reports as to what Sister White has done or said or written. If you desire to know what the Lord has revealed through her, read her published works. Are there any points of interest concerning which she has not written, do not eagerly catch up and report rumors as to what she has said.

A MIRACLE COUNTERFEITED

Some have found difficulty in reconciling a statement in *Testimonies for the Church,* volume I, page 292, with one in *Great Controversy,* volume I, page 184.* These passages refer to the work of the sorcerers in counterfeiting the miracle performed by Aaron, of turning the rod to a serpent. The testimony says: "The magicians could not perform all those miracles which God wrought through Moses. Only a few of them could they do. The magicians' rods did become serpents, but Aaron's rod swallowed them up." This last sentence, which is the one in question, is substantially the same as the Bible statement: "They cast down every man his rod, and they became serpents: but Aaron's rod swallowed up their rods." The statement in volume I, of the *Controversy,* is: "The magicians seemed to perform several things with their enchantments similar to those things which God wrought by the hand of Moses and Aaron. They did not really cause their rods to become serpents, but by magic, aided by the great deceiver, made them appear like serpents,

---

*The account presented in this now-out-of-print volume was rewritten and amplified by Ellen G. White and published in 1890 as *Patriarchs and Prophets.* See page 264 of that volume for the statement paralleling the one referred to here.   [WHITE TRUSTEES.]

to counterfeit the work of God." This statement, instead of contradicting the former, is simply explanatory of it.

There is not, in the *Testimony,* a full expression of the thought which I wished to convey. On page 293 is a sentence which makes the meaning clearer: "The magicians wrought not by their own science alone, but by the power of their god, the devil, who ingeniously carried out his deceptive work of *counterfeiting* the work of God." Moses, by the power of God, had changed the rod to a living serpent. Satan, through the magicians, *counterfeited* this miracle. He could not produce living serpents, for he has not power to create or to give life. This power belongs to God alone. But all that Satan could do he did—he produced a *counterfeit.* By his power, working through the magicians, he caused the rods to assume the appearance of serpents.

The statement that they did become serpents, simply means that they were such in appearance; such they were believed to be by Pharaoh and his court. There was nothing in their appearance to distinguish them from the serpent produced by Moses and Aaron; but while one was real, the others were spurious. And the Lord caused the living serpent to swallow up the pretended ones.

Pharaoh desired to justify his stubbornness in resisting the divine command; he was seeking some excuse to disregard the miracle which God had wrought through Moses. Satan gave him just what he wanted. By the work which he wrought through the magicians he made it appear to the Egyptians that Moses and Aaron were only magicians and sorcerers, and hence that the message which they brought would not claim respect as coming from a superior being.

Even the swallowing up of the counterfeit serpents was not regarded by Pharaoh as the special work of God's power, but as accomplished by a kind of magic superior to that of his servants. Thus this counterfeit work emboldened him in his rebellion, causing him to fortify himself against conviction.

It was by the display of supernatural power, in making the serpent his medium, that Satan caused the fall of Adam and Eve in Eden. Before the close of time he will work still greater wonders. So far as his power extends, he will perform actual miracles. Says the Scripture: "He . . . deceiveth them that dwell on the earth by the means of those miracles which he had power to do," not merely those which he pretends to do. Something more than mere impostures is brought to view in this scripture. But there is a limit beyond which Satan cannot go, and here he calls deception to his aid and counterfeits the work which he has not power actually to perform. In the last days he will appear in such a manner as to make men believe him to be Christ come the second time into the world. He will indeed transform himself into an angel of light. But while he will bear the appearance of Christ in every particular, so far as mere appearance goes, it will deceive none but those who, like Pharaoh, are seeking to resist the truth.

THE MYSTERIES OF THE BIBLE A PROOF OF ITS INSPIRATION

"Canst thou by searching find out God? canst thou find out the Almighty unto perfection? It is as high as heaven; what canst thou do? deeper than hell; what canst thou know?" "My thoughts are not your thoughts, neither are your ways My ways, saith the Lord. For as the heavens are higher than the earth, so are My ways higher than your ways, and My thoughts than your thoughts." "I am God, and there is none like Me, declaring the end from the beginning, and from ancient times the things that are not yet done." It is impossible for the finite minds of men to fully comprehend the character or the works of the Infinite One. To the keenest intellect, to the most powerful and highly educated mind, that holy Being must ever remain clothed in mystery.

The apostle Paul exclaims: "O the depth of the riches both of the wisdom and knowledge of God! how unsearchable are His judgments, and His ways past finding out!" But though "clouds and darkness are round about Him: righteousness and judgment are the foundation of His throne."[1] We can so far comprehend His dealing with us, and the motives by which He is actuated, that we may discern boundless love and mercy united to infinite power. We can understand as much of His purposes as it is for our good to know; and beyond this we must still trust the might of the Omnipotent, the love and wisdom of the Father and Sovereign of all.

The word of God, like the character of its divine Author, presents mysteries which can never be fully comprehended by finite beings. It directs our minds to the Creator, who dwelleth "in the light which no man can approach unto." It presents to us His purposes, which embrace all the ages of human history, and which will reach their fulfillment only in the endless cycles of eternity. It calls our attention to subjects of infinite depth and importance relating to the government of God and the destiny of man.

The entrance of sin into the world, the incarnation of Christ, regeneration, the resurrection, and many other subjects presented in the Bible, are mysteries too deep for the human mind to explain or even to fully comprehend. But God has given us in the Scriptures sufficient evidence of their divine character, and we are not to doubt His word because we cannot understand all the mysteries of His providence.

The portions of Holy Writ presenting these great themes are not to be passed by as of no use to man. All that God has seen fit to make known we are to accept upon the authority of His word. Only a bare statement of facts may be given, with no explanation as to why or how; but though we cannot

[1]Revised Version.

comprehend it we should rest content that it is true, because God has said it. All the difficulty lies in the weakness and narrowness of the human mind.

The apostle Peter says that there are in Scripture "things hard to be understood, which they that are unlearned and unstable wrest . . . unto their own destruction." The difficulties of Scripture have been urged by skeptics as an argument against the Bible; but so far from this, they constitute a strong evidence of its divine inspiration. If it contained no account of God but that which we could easily comprehend; if His greatness and majesty could be grasped by finite minds, then the Bible would not bear the unmistakable credentials of divine authority. The very grandeur and mystery of the themes presented should inspire faith in it as the word of God.

The Bible unfolds truth with a simplicity and a perfect adaptation to the needs and longings of the human heart, that has astonished and charmed the most highly cultivated minds, while it enables the humble and uncultured to discern the way of salvation. And yet these simply stated truths lay hold upon subjects so elevated, so far-reaching, so infinitely beyond the power of human comprehension, that we can accept them only because God has declared them. Thus the plan of redemption is laid open to us so that every soul may see the steps he is to take in repentance toward God and faith toward our Lord Jesus Christ, in order to be saved in God's appointed way; yet beneath these truths, so easily understood, lie mysteries which are the hiding of His glory—mysteries which overpower the mind in its research, yet inspire the sincere seeker for truth with reverence and faith. The more he searches the Bible, the deeper is his conviction that it is the word of the living God, and human reason bows before the majesty of divine revelation.

Those are blessed with clearest light who are willing thus to accept the living oracles upon the authority of God. If asked to explain certain statements, they can only answer: "It is so presented in the Scriptures." They are obliged to acknowledge that they cannot explain the operation of divine power or the manifestation of divine wisdom. It is as the Lord intended it should be, that we find ourselves compelled to accept some things solely by faith. To acknowledge this, is only to admit that the finite mind is inadequate to grasp the infinite; that man, with his limited, human knowledge, cannot understand the purposes of Omniscience.

Because they cannot fathom all its mysteries, the skeptic and the infidel reject God's word; and not all who profess to believe the Bible are secure from temptation on this point. Says the apostle: "Take heed, brethren, lest there be in any of you an evil heart of unbelief, in departing from the living God." Minds that have been educated to criticize, to doubt and cavil because they cannot search into the purposes of God, will "fall after the same example of unbelief." It is right to study closely the teaching of the Bible, and to search into "the deep things of God," so far as they are revealed in Scripture. While "the secret things belong unto the Lord our God," "those things which are revealed belong unto us and to our children." But it is Satan's work to pervert the investigative powers of the mind. A certain pride is mingled with the consideration of Bible truth, so that men feel defeated and impatient if they cannot explain every portion of Scripture to their satisfaction. It is too humiliating to them to acknowledge that they do not understand the inspired words. They are unwilling to wait patiently until God shall see fit to reveal the truth to them. They feel that their unaided human wisdom is sufficient to enable them to comprehend the Scripture; and failing to do this, they virtually deny its authority. It is true that many theories and doctrines popularly supposed to be the teaching of the Bible have no foundation in Scripture and, indeed, are contrary to the whole tenor of inspiration. These things have been a cause of doubt and perplexity to many minds. They are not, however, chargeable to God's word, but to man's perversion of it. But the difficulties in the Bible do not reflect upon the wisdom of God; they will not cause the ruin of any who would not have been destroyed if no such difficulties had existed. Had there been no mysteries in the Bible for them to question, the same minds would, through their own lack of spiritual discernment, have found cause of stumbling in the plainest utterances of God.

Men who imagine themselves endowed with mental powers of so high an order that they can find an explanation of all the ways and works of God, are seeking to exalt human wisdom to an equality with the divine and to glorify man as God. They are only repeating that which Satan declared to Eve in Eden: "Ye shall be as gods." Satan fell because of his ambition to be equal with God. He desired to enter into the divine counsels and purposes, from which he was excluded by his own inability, as a created being, to comprehend the wisdom of the Infinite One. It was this ambitious pride that led to his rebellion, and by the same means he seeks to cause the ruin of man.

There are mysteries in the plan of redemption—the humiliation of the Son of God, that He might be found in fashion as a man, the wonderful love and condescension of the Father in yielding up His Son—that are to the heavenly angels subjects of continual amazement. The apostle Peter, speaking of the revelations given to the prophets of "the sufferings of Christ, and the glory that should follow," says that these are things which "the angels desire to look into." And these will be the study of the redeemed through eternal ages. As they contemplate the work of God in creation and redemption, new truth will continually unfold to the wondering and delighted mind. As they learn more and more of the wisdom, the love, and the power of God, their minds will be constantly expanding, and their joy will continually increase.

If it were possible for created beings to attain to a full understanding of God and His works, then, having reached this point, there would be for them no further discovery of truth, no growth in knowledge, no further development of mind or heart. God would no longer be supreme; and men, having reached the limit of knowledge and attainment, would cease to advance. Let us thank God that it is not so. God is infinite; in Him are "all the treasures of wisdom and knowledge." And to all eternity men may be ever searching, ever learning, and yet they can never exhaust the treasures of His wisdom, His goodness, and His power.

God intends that, even in this life, truth shall be ever unfolding to His people. There is only one way in which this knowledge can be obtained. We can attain to an understanding of God's word only through the illumination of that Spirit by which the word was given. "The things of God knoweth no man, but the Spirit of God;" "for the Spirit searcheth all things, yea, the deep things of God." And the Saviour's promise to His followers was: "When He, the Spirit of truth, is come, He will guide you into all truth. . . . For He shall receive of Mine, and shall show it unto you."

God desires man to exercise his reasoning powers; and the study of the Bible will strengthen and elevate the mind as no other study can do. It is the best mental as well as spiritual exercise for the human mind. Yet we are to beware of deifying reason, which is subject to the weakness and infirmity of humanity. If we would not have the Scriptures clouded to our understanding, so that the plainest truths shall not be comprehended, we must have the simplicity and faith of a little child, ready to learn, and beseeching the aid of the Holy Spirit. A sense of the power and wisdom of God, and of our inability to comprehend His greatness, should inspire us with humility, and we should open His word, as we would enter His presence, with holy awe. When we come to the Bible, reason must acknowledge an authority superior to itself, and heart and intellect must bow to the great I AM.

We shall advance in true spiritual knowledge only as we realize our own littleness and our entire dependence upon God; but all who come to the Bible with a teachable and prayerful spirit, to study its utterances as the word of God, will receive divine enlightenment. There are many things apparently difficult or obscure which God will make plain and simple to those who thus seek an understanding of them.

It is sometimes the case that men of intellectual ability, improved by education and culture, fail to comprehend certain passages of Scripture, while others who are uneducated, whose understanding seems weak and whose minds are undisciplined, will grasp the meaning, finding strength and comfort in that which the former declare to be mysterious or pass by as unimportant. Why is this? It has been explained to me that the latter class do not rely upon their own understanding. They go to the Source of light, the One who has inspired the Scriptures, and with humility of heart ask God for wisdom, and they receive it. There are mines of truth yet to be discovered by the earnest seeker. Christ represented the truth as treasure hid in a field. It does not lie right upon the surface; we must dig for it. But our success in finding it does not depend so much on our intellectual ability as on our humility of heart and the faith which will lay hold upon divine aid.

Without the guidance of the Holy Spirit we shall be continually liable to wrest the Scriptures or to misinterpret them. There is much reading of the Bible that is without profit and in many cases is a positive injury. When the word of God is opened without reverence and without prayer; when the thoughts and affections are not fixed upon God or in harmony with His will, the mind is clouded with doubt; and in the very study of the Bible, skepticism strengthens. The enemy takes control of the thoughts, and he suggests interpretations that are not correct.

Whenever men are not seeking, in word and deed, to be in harmony with God, then, however learned they may be, they are liable to err in their understanding of Scripture, and it is not safe to trust to their explanations. When we are truly seeking to do God's will, the Holy Spirit takes the precepts of His word and makes them the principles of the life, writing them on the tablets of the soul. And it is only those who are following the light already given that can hope to receive the further illumination of the Spirit. This is plainly stated in the words of Christ: "If any man will *do* His will, he shall know of the doctrine."

Those who look to the Scriptures to find discrepancies have not spiritual insight. With distorted vision they will see many causes for doubt and unbelief in things that are really plain and simple. But to those who take God's word with reverence, seeking to learn His will that they may obey it, all is changed. They are filled with awe and wonder as they contemplate the purity and exalted excellence of the truths revealed. Like attracts like. Like appreciates like. Holiness allies itself with holiness, faith with faith. To the humble heart and the sincere, inquiring mind the Bible is full of light and knowledge. Those who come to the Scriptures in this spirit are brought into fellowship with prophets and apostles. Their spirit assimilates to that of Christ, and they long to become one with Him.

Many feel that a responsibility rests upon them to explain every seeming difficulty in the Bible in order to meet the cavils of skeptics and infidels. But in trying to explain that which they but imperfectly understand, they are in danger of confusing the minds of others in reference to points that are clear and easy to be understood. This is not our work. Nor should we lament that these difficulties exist, but accept them as permitted by the wisdom of God. It is our duty to receive His word, which is plain on every point essential to the salvation of the soul, and practice its principles in our life, teaching them to others both by precept and example. Thus it will be evident to the world that we have a connection with God and implicit confidence in His word. A life of godliness, a daily example of integrity, meekness, and unselfish love, will be a living exemplification of the teaching of God's word, and it will be an argument in favor of the Bible which few will be able to resist. This will prove the most effectual check to the prevailing tendency to skepticism and infidelity.

By faith we should look to the hereafter and grasp the pledge of God of a growth of intellect, the human faculties uniting with the divine, and every power of the soul being brought into direct contact with the Source of light. We may rejoice that all that has perplexed us in the providences of God will then be made plain; things hard to be understood will find an explanation; and where our finite minds discovered only confusion and broken purposes, we shall see the most perfect and beautiful harmony. Says the apostle Paul: "Now we see through a glass, darkly; but then face to face: now I know in part; but then shall I know even as also I am known."

Peter exhorts his brethren to "grow in grace, and in the knowledge of our Lord and Saviour Jesus Christ." Whenever the people of God are growing in grace, they will be constantly obtaining a clearer understanding of His word. They will discern new light and beauty in its sacred truths. This has been true in the history of the church in all ages, and thus it will continue to the end. But as real spiritual life declines, it has ever been the tendency to cease to advance in the knowledge of the truth. Men rest satisfied with the light already received from God's word and discourage any further investigation of the Scriptures. They become conservative and seek to avoid discussion.

The fact that there is no controversy or agitation among God's people should not be regarded as conclusive evidence that they are holding fast to sound doctrine. There is reason to fear that they may not be clearly discriminating between truth and error. When no new questions are started by investigation of the Scriptures, when no difference of opinion arises which will set men to searching the Bible for themselves to make sure that they have the truth, there will be many now, as in ancient times, who will hold to tradition and worship they know not what.

I have been shown that many who profess to have a knowledge of present truth know not what they believe. They do not understand the evidences of their faith. They have no just appreciation of the work for the present time. When the time of trial shall come, there are men now preaching to others who will find, upon examining the positions they hold, that there are many things for which they can give no satisfactory reason. Until thus tested they knew not their great ignorance. And there are many in the church who take it for granted that they understand what they believe; but, until controversy arises, they do not know their own weakness. When separated from those of like faith and compelled to stand singly and alone to explain their belief, they will be surprised to see how confused are their ideas of what they had accepted as truth. Certain it is that there has been among us a departure from the living God and a turning to men, putting human in place of divine wisdom.

God will arouse His people; if other means fail, heresies will come in among them, which will sift them, separating the chaff from the wheat. The Lord calls upon all who believe His word to awake out of sleep. Precious light has come, appropriate for this time. It is Bible truth, showing the perils that are right upon us. This light should lead us to a diligent study of the Scriptures and a most critical examination of the positions which we hold. God would have all the bearings and positions of truth thoroughly and perseveringly searched, with prayer and fasting. Believers are not to rest in suppositions and ill-defined ideas of what constitutes truth. Their faith must be firmly founded upon the word of God so that when the testing time shall come and they are brought before councils to answer for their faith they may be able to give a reason for the hope that is in them, with meekness and fear.

Agitate, agitate, agitate. The subjects which we present to the world must be to us a living reality. It is important that in defending the doctrines which we consider fundamental articles of faith we should never allow ourselves to employ arguments that are not wholly sound. These may avail to silence an opposer, but they do not honor the truth. We should present sound arguments, that will not only silence our opponents, but will bear the closest and most searching scrutiny. With those who have educated themselves as debaters there is great danger that they will not handle the word of God with fairness. In meeting an opponent it should be our earnest effort to present subjects in such a manner as to awaken conviction in his mind, instead of seeking merely to give confidence to the believer.

Whatever may be man's intellectual advancement, let him not for a moment think that there is no need of thorough and continuous searching of the Scriptures for greater light. As a people we are called individually to be students of prophecy. We must watch with earnestness that we may discern any ray of light which God shall present to us. We are to catch the first gleamings of truth; and through prayerful study clearer light may be obtained, which can be brought before others.

When God's people are at ease and satisfied with their present enlightenment, we may be sure that He will not favor them. It is His will that they should be ever moving forward to receive the increased and ever-increasing light which is shining for them. The present attitude of the church is not pleasing to God. There has come in a self-confidence that has led them to feel no necessity for more truth and greater light. We are living at a time when Satan is at work on the right hand and on the left, before and behind us; and yet as a people we are asleep. God wills that a voice shall be heard arousing His people to action.

Instead of opening the soul to receive rays of light from heaven, some have been working in an opposite direction. Both through the press and from the pulpit have been presented views in regard to the inspiration of the Bible which have not the sanction of the Spirit or the word of God. Certain it is that no man or set of men should undertake to advance theories upon a subject of so great importance, without a plain "Thus saith the Lord" to sustain them. And when men, compassed with human infirmities, affected in a greater or less degree by surrounding influences, and having hereditary and cultivated tendencies which are far from making them wise or heavenly-minded, undertake to arraign the word of God, and to pass judgment upon what is divine and what is human, they are working without the counsel of God. The Lord will not prosper such a work. The effect will be disastrous, both upon the one engaged in it and upon those who accept it as a work from God. Skepticism has been aroused in many minds by the theories presented as to the nature of inspiration. Finite beings, with their narrow, short-sighted views, feel themselves competent to criticize the Scriptures, saying: "This passage is needful, and that passage is not needful, and is not inspired."

Christ gave no such instruction in regard to the Old Testament Scriptures, the only part of the Bible which the people of His time possessed. His teachings were designed to direct their minds to the Old Testament and to bring into clearer light the great themes there presented. For ages the people of

Israel had been separating themselves from God, and they had lost sight of precious truths which He had committed to them. These truths were covered up with superstitious forms and ceremonies that concealed their true significance. Christ came to remove the rubbish which had obscured their luster. He placed them, as precious gems, in a new setting. He showed that so far from disdaining the repetition of old, familiar truths, He came to make them appear in their true force and beauty, the glory of which had never been discerned by the men of His time. Himself the Author of these revealed truths, He could open to the people their true meaning, freeing them from the misinterpretations and false theories adopted by the leaders to suit their own unconsecrated condition, their destitution of spirituality and the love of God. He cast aside that which had robbed these truths of life and vital power, and gave them back to the world in all their original freshness and force.

If we have the Spirit of Christ and are laborers together with Him, it is ours to carry forward the work which He came to do. The truths of the Bible have again become obscured by custom, tradition, and false doctrine. The erroneous teachings of popular theology have made thousands upon thousands of skeptics and infidels. There are errors and inconsistencies which many denounce as the teaching of the Bible that are really false interpretations of Scripture, adopted during the ages of papal darkness. Multitudes have been led to cherish an erroneous conception of God, as the Jews, misled by the errors and traditions of their time, had a false conception of Christ. "Had they *known* it, they would not have crucified the Lord of glory." It is ours to reveal to the world the true character of God. Instead of criticizing the Bible, let us seek, by precept and example, to present to the world its sacred, life-giving truths, that we may "show forth the praises of Him who hath called you out of darkness into His marvelous light."

The evils that have been gradually creeping in among us have imperceptibly led individuals and churches away from reverence for God, and have shut away the power which He desires to give them.

My brethren, let the word of God stand just as it is. Let not human wisdom presume to lessen the force of one statement of the Scriptures. The solemn denunciation in the Revelation should warn us against taking such ground. In the name of my Master I bid you: "Put off thy shoes from off thy feet, for the place whereon thou standest is holy ground."

THE IMPENDING CONFLICT

A great crisis awaits the people of God. A crisis awaits the world. The most momentous struggle of all the ages is just before us. Events which for more than forty years we have upon the authority of the prophetic word declared to be impending are now taking place before our eyes. Already the question of an amendment to the Constitution restricting liberty of conscience has been urged upon the legislators of the nation. The question of enforcing Sunday observance has become one of national interest and importance. We well know what the result of this movement will be. But are we ready for the issue? Have we faithfully discharged the duty which God has committed to us of giving the people warning of the danger before them?

There are many, even of those engaged in this movement for Sunday enforcement, who are blinded to the results which will follow this action. They do not see that they are striking directly against religious liberty. There are many who have never understood the claims of the Bible Sabbath and the false foundation upon which the Sunday institution rests. Any movement in favor of religious legislation is really an act of concession to the papacy, which for so many ages has steadily warred against liberty of conscience. Sunday observance owes its existence as a so-called Christian institution to "the mystery of iniquity;" and its enforcement will be a virtual recognition of the principles which are the very cornerstone of Romanism. When our nation shall so abjure the principles of its government as to enact a Sunday law, Protestantism will in this act join hands with popery; it will be nothing else than giving life to the tyranny which has long been eagerly watching its opportunity to spring again into active despotism.

The National Reform movement, exercising the power of religious legislation, will, when fully developed, manifest the same intolerance and oppression that have prevailed in past ages. Human councils then assumed the prerogatives of Deity, crushing under their despotic power liberty of conscience; and imprisonment, exile, and death followed for those who opposed their dictates. If popery or its principles shall again be legislated into power, the fires of persecution will be rekindled against those who will not sacrifice conscience and the truth in deference to popular errors. This evil is on the point of realization.

When God has given us light showing the dangers before us, how can we stand clear in His sight if we neglect to put forth every effort in our power to bring it before the people? Can we be content to leave them to meet this momentous issue unwarned?

There is a prospect before us of a continued struggle, at the risk of imprisonment, loss of property, and even of life itself, to defend the law of God, which is made void by the laws of men. In this situation worldly policy will urge an outward compliance with the laws of the land, for the sake of peace and harmony. And there are some who will even urge such a course from the Scripture: "Let every soul be subject unto the higher powers. . . . The powers that be are ordained of God."

But what has been the course of God's servants in ages past? When the disciples preached Christ and Him crucified, after His resurrection, the authorities commanded them not to speak any more nor to teach in the name of Jesus. "But Peter and John answered and said unto them, Whether it be right in the sight of God to hearken unto you more than unto God, judge ye. For we cannot but speak the things which we have seen and heard." They continued to preach the good news of salvation through Christ, and the power of God witnessed to the message. The sick were healed, and thousands were added to the church. "Then the high priest rose up, and all they that were with him, (which is the sect of the Sadducees,) and were filled with indignation, and laid their hands on the apostles, and put them in the common prison."

But the God of heaven, the mighty Ruler of the universe, took this matter into His own hands; for men were warring against His work. He showed them plainly that there is a ruler above man, whose authority must be respected. The Lord sent His angel by night to open the prison doors, and he brought forth these men whom God had commissioned to do His work. The rulers said, Speak not "at all nor teach in the name of Jesus;" but the heavenly messenger sent by God said, "Go, stand and speak in the temple to the people all the words of this life."

Those who seek to compel men to observe an institution of the papacy, and trample upon God's authority, are doing a work similar to that of the Jewish leaders in the days of the apostles. When the laws of earthly rulers are brought into opposition to the laws of the Supreme Ruler of the universe, then those who are God's loyal subjects will be true to Him.

We as a people have not accomplished the work which God has committed to us. We are not ready for the issue to which the enforcement of the Sunday law will bring us. It is our duty, as we see the signs of approaching peril, to arouse to action. Let none sit in calm expectation of the evil, comforting themselves with the belief that this work must go on because prophecy has foretold it, and that the Lord will shelter His people. We are not doing the will of God if we sit in quietude, doing nothing to preserve liberty of conscience. Fervent, effectual prayer should be ascending to heaven that this calamity may be deferred until we can accomplish the work which has so long been neglected. Let there be most earnest prayer, and then let us work in harmony with our prayers. It may appear that Satan is triumphant and that truth is overborne with falsehood and error; the people over whom God has spread His shield, and the country which has been an asylum for the conscience-oppressed servants of God and defenders of His truth, may be placed in jeopardy. But God would have us recall His dealings with His people in the past to save them from their enemies. He has always chosen extremities, when there seemed no possible chance for deliverance from Satan's workings, for the manifestation of His power. Man's necessity is God's opportunity. It may be that a respite may yet be granted for God's people to awake and let their light shine. If the presence of ten righteous persons would have saved the wicked cities of the plain, is it not possible that God will yet, in answer to the prayers of His people, hold in check the workings of those who are making void His law? Shall we not humble our hearts greatly before God, flee to the mercy seat, and plead with Him to reveal His mighty power?

If our people continue in the listless attitude in which they have been, God cannot pour upon them His Spirit. They are unprepared to cooperate with Him. They are not awake to the situation and do not realize the threatened danger. They should feel now, as never before, their need of vigilance and concerted action.

The peculiar work of the third angel has not been seen in its importance. God meant that His people should be far in advance of the position which they occupy today. But now, when the time has come for them to spring into action, they have the preparation to make. When the National Reformers began to urge measures to restrict religious liberty, our leading men should have been alive to the situation and should have labored earnestly to counteract these efforts. It is not in the order of God that light has been kept from our people—the very present truth which they needed for this time. Not all our ministers who are giving the third angel's message really understand what constitutes that message. The National Reform movement has been regarded by some as of so little importance that they have not thought it necessary to give much attention to it and have even felt that in so doing they would be giving time to questions distinct from the third angel's message. May the Lord forgive our brethren for thus interpreting the very message for this time.

The people need to be aroused in regard to the dangers of the present time. The watchmen are asleep. We are years behind. Let the chief watchmen feel the urgent necessity of taking heed to themselves, lest they lose the opportunities given them to see the dangers.

If the leading men in our conferences do not now accept the message sent them by God, and fall into line for action, the churches will suffer great loss. When the watchman, seeing the sword coming, gives the trumpet a certain sound, the people along the line will echo the warning, and all will have opportunity to make ready for the conflict. But too often the leader has stood hesitating, seeming to say: "Let us not be in too great haste. There may be a mistake. We must be careful not to raise a false alarm." The very hesitancy and uncertainty on his part is crying: " 'Peace and safety.' Do not get excited. Be not alarmed. There is a great deal more made of this religious amendment question than is demanded. This agitation will all die down." Thus he virtually denies the message sent from God, and the warning which was designed to stir the churches fails to do its work. The trumpet of the watchman gives no certain sound, and the people do not prepare for the battle. Let the watchman beware lest, through his hesitancy and delay, souls shall be left to perish, and their blood shall be required at his hand.

We have been looking many years for a Sunday law to be enacted in our land, and, now that the movement is right upon us, we ask: Will our people do their duty in the matter? Can we not assist in lifting the standard and in calling to the front those who have a regard for their religious rights and privileges? The time is fast approaching when those who choose to obey God rather than man will be made to feel the hand of oppression. Shall we then dishonor God by keeping silent while His holy commandments are trodden underfoot?

While the Protestant world is by her attitude making concessions to Rome, let us arouse to comprehend the situation and view the contest before us in its true bearings. Let the watchmen now lift up their voice and give the message which is present truth for this time. Let us show the people where we are in prophetic history and seek to arouse the spirit of true Protestantism, awaking the world to a sense of the value of the privileges of religious liberty so long enjoyed.

God calls upon us to awake, for the end is near. Every passing hour is one of activity in the heavenly courts to make ready a people upon the earth to act a part in the great scenes that are soon to open upon us. These passing moments, that seem of so little value to us, are weighty with eternal interests. They are molding the destiny of souls for everlasting life or eternal death. The words we utter today in the ears of the people, the works we are doing, the spirit of the message we are bearing, will be a savor of life unto life or of death unto death.

My brethren, do you realize that your own salvation, as

well as the destiny of other souls, depends upon the preparation you now make for the trial before us? Have you that intensity of zeal, that piety and devotion, which will enable you to stand when opposition shall be brought against you? If God has ever spoken by me, the time will come when you will be brought before councils, and every position of truth which you hold will be severely criticized. The time that so many are now allowing to go to waste should be devoted to the charge that God has given us of preparing for the approaching crisis.

The law of God should be loved and honored by His true people now more than ever before. There is the most imperative necessity of urging the injunction of Christ upon the minds and hearts of all believers, men and women, youth and children: "Search the Scriptures." Study your Bible as you have never studied it before. Unless you arise to a higher, holier state in your religious life, you will not be ready for the appearing of our Lord. As great light has been given, God expects corresponding zeal, faithfulness, and devotion on the part of His people. There must be more spirituality, a deeper consecration to God, and a zeal in His work that has never yet been reached. Much time should be spent in prayer, that our garments of character may be washed and made white in the blood of the Lamb.

Especially should we, with unwavering faith, seek God for grace and power to be given to His people now. We do not believe that the time has fully come when He would have our liberties restricted. The prophet saw four angels standing on the four corners of the earth, holding the four winds of the earth, that the wind should not blow on the earth, nor on the sea, nor on any tree." Another angel, ascending from the east, cried to them, saying: "Hurt not the earth, neither the sea, nor the trees, till we have sealed the servants of our God in their foreheads." This points out the work we have now to do. A vast responsibility is devolving upon men and women of prayer throughout the land to petition that God will sweep back the cloud of evil and give a few more years of grace in which to work for the Master. Let us cry to God that the angels may hold the four winds until missionaries shall be sent to all parts of the world and shall proclaim the warning against disobeying the law of Jehovah.

―――――――

"THE AMERICAN SENTINEL" AND ITS MISSION

God employs various agencies in preparing His people to stand in the great crisis before us. He speaks by His word and by His ministers. He arouses the watchmen and sends them forth with messages of warning, of reproof, and of instruction, that the people may be enlightened. The *Sentinel* has been in God's order, one of the voices sounding the alarm, that the people might hear and realize their danger and do the work required at the present time. The Lord intends that His people shall heed whatever He sends them. When light is presented, it is their duty, not only to receive it, but to pass it along, adding their influence in its favor, that its full force may be felt in the church and the world. The *Sentinel* is like a trumpet giving a certain sound; and all our people should read it carefully and then send it to some relative or friend, thus putting to the best use the light that God has given them.

For three years, warnings have been sounding forth to the world through the columns of the *Sentinel*; but those who profess to believe present truth have not been influenced by these danger signals as they should have been. Had our brethren used the *Sentinel* as it was their privilege to do; and had all been united in recommending it in every conference and in every church, as God would have them do; had the attention of our people been called to this work, which was so essential to be done for this time; had they appreciated the light which God permitted to shine upon them in warnings, in counsels, and in the delineation of events that are taking place, we should not now, as a people, be so far behind in making preparation for the work. There have been surprising indifference and inactivity in this time of peril. Truth, present truth, is what the people need; and if the startling significance of the movements now in progress in regard to the religious amendments had been realized by our brethren in every church; if they had discerned in these movements the plain, direct fulfillment of prophecy, calling upon them to arouse to the demands of the crisis, they would not now be in such stupor and deathlike slumber.

The word of God is not silent in regard to this momentous time, and it will be understood by all who do not resist His Spirit by determining not to hear, not to receive, not to obey. The Lord's messages of light have been before us for years; but there have been influences working indirectly to make of no effect the warnings coming through the *Sentinel* and the *Testimonies,* and through other instrumentalities which the Lord sends to His people. Much more might have been done with the *Sentinel* if these counterinfluences had not been at work to hinder it. Even though nothing may be said against it, actions reveal the indifference that is felt. And so long as the watchmen do not give the trumpet a certain sound, the people are not alarmed and are not on the lookout for danger.

The rebuke of God is upon us because of our neglect of solemn responsibilities. His blessings have been withdrawn because the testimonies He has given have not been heeded by those who professed to believe them. Oh, for a religious awakening! The angels of God are going from church to church, doing their duty; and Christ is knocking at the door of your hearts for entrance. But the means that God has devised to awaken the church to a sense of their spiritual destitution have not been regarded. The voice of the True Witness has been heard in reproof, but has not been obeyed. Men have chosen to follow their own way instead of God's way because self was not crucified in them. Thus the light has had but little effect upon minds and hearts.

Will the people of God now arouse from their carnal lethargy? Will they make the most of present blessings and warnings, and let nothing come between their souls and the light God would have shine upon them? Let every worker for God comprehend the situation and place the *Sentinel* before our churches, explaining its contents and urging home the facts and warnings it contains. May the Lord help all to redeem the time. Let not unsanctified feelings lead any to resist the appeals of the Spirit of God. Stand not in the way of this light; let it not be disregarded or set aside as unworthy of attention or credence.

If you wait for light to come in a way that will please everyone, you will wait in vain. If you wait for louder calls or better opportunities, the light will be withdrawn, and you will be left in darkness. Accept every ray of light that God sends. Men who neglect to heed the calls of the Spirit and word of God, because obedience involves a cross, will lose their souls. When the books are opened, and every man's work and the motives that prompted him are scrutinized by the Judge of all the earth, they will see what a loss they have sustained. We should ever cherish the fear of the Lord and realize that, individually, we are standing before the Lord of hosts, and no thought, no word, no act in connection with the work of God, should savor of selfishness or of indifference.

WORKERS IN THE CAUSE

The fact that so large a number are associated together in the church at Battle Creek, and that so many important interests center there, makes it preeminently a missionary field. People from all parts of the country come to the sanitarium, and many youth from different states attend the college. That field demands the most devoted, faithful workers and the very best methods of labor in order that a strong influence for Christ and the truth may be constantly exerted. When the work is conducted as God would have it, the saving power of the grace of Christ will be manifest among those who believe the truth, and they will be a light to others.

But there is at Battle Creek a sad neglect of the many advantages at hand to keep the heart of the work in a healthy condition. Vigorous heartbeats from the center should be felt in all parts of the body of believers. But if the heart is sickly and weak in its action, all branches of the cause will be enfeebled. It is positively essential that there should be a sound, healthy working power at this central point in order that the truth may be carried to all the world. The knowledge of this last warning must be diffused through families and communities everywhere, and it will require wise generalship both to deviseplans and to educate men to assist in the work.

As year by year the work extends, the need of experienced and faithful workers becomes more urgent; and if the people of the Lord walk in His counsel, such workers will be developed. While we should rely firmly upon God for wisdom and power, He would have us cultivate our ability to the fullest extent.As the workers acquire mental and spiritual power, and become acquainted with the purposes and dealings of God, they will have more comprehensive views of the work for this time and will be better qualified both to devise and to execute plans for its advancement. Thus they may keep pace with the opening providence of God.

A constant effort should be put forth to enlist new workers. Talent should be discerned and recognized. Persons who possess piety and ability should be encouraged to obtain the necessary education, that they may be fitted to assist in spreading the light of truth. All who are competent to do so should be led to engage in some branch of the work according to their capabilities.

The solemn and momentous work for this time is not to be carried forward to completion solely by the efforts of a few chosen men who have heretofore borne the responsibilities in the cause. When those whom God has called to aid in the accomplishment of a certain work shall have carried it as far as they can, with the ability He has given them, the Lord will not allow the work to stop at that stage. In His providence He will call and qualify others to unite with the first, that together they may advance still further, and lift the standard higher.

But there are some minds that do not grow with the work; instead of adapting themselves to its increasing demands, they allow it to extend far beyond them, and thus they find themselves unable to comprehend or to meet the exigencies of the times. When men whom God is qualifying to bear responsibilities in the cause take hold of it in a slightly different way from that in which it has hitherto been conducted, the older laborers should be careful that their course be not such as to hinder these helpers or to circumscribe the work. Some may not realize the importance of certain measures, simply because they do not see the necessities of the work in all its bearings and do not themselves feel the burden which God has specially laid upon other men. Those who are not specially qualified to do a certain work should beware that they do not stand in the way of others and prevent them from fulfilling the purpose of God.

The case of David is to the point. He desired to build the temple of the Lord, and gathered together rich stores of material for this purpose. But the Lord told him that he was not to do that work; it must devolve upon Solomon, his son. David's large experience would enable him to counsel Solomon and encourage him, but the younger man must build the temple. The weary, worn minds of the older laborers may not always see the greatness of the work, and they may not be inclined to keep pace with the opening providence of God; therefore weighty responsibilities should not rest wholly upon them. They might not bring into the work all the elements essential to its advancement, hence it would be retarded.

For the want of wise management the work in Battle Creek and throughout the State of Michigan is far behind what it should be. While it is necessary for us to understand the situation and the needs of foreign missions, we should also be able to comprehend the needs of the work at our very doors. If rightly improved, the advantages which God has placed within our reach would enable us to send forth a much larger number of workers. There is need of vigorous work in our churches. The special message showing the important issues now pending, the duties and dangers of our time, should be presented before them, not in a tame, lifeless manner, "but in demonstration of the Spirit and of power." Responsibilities must be laid upon the members of the church. The missionary spirit should be awakened as never before, and workers should be appointed as needed, who will act as pastors to the flock, putting forth personal effort to bring the church up to that condition where spiritual life and activity will be seen in all her borders.

Much talent has been lost to the cause because men in responsible positions did not discern it. Their vision was not far-reaching enough to discover that the work was becoming altogether too extended to be carried forward by the workers then engaged. Much, very much, which should have been accomplished is still undone because men have held things in their own hands instead of distributing the work among a larger number and trusting that God would help them in their efforts. They have tried to carry forward all branches of the work, fearing that others would prove less efficient. Their will and judgment have controlled in these various departments, and because of their inability to grasp all the wants of the cause in its different parts, great losses have been sustained.

The lesson must be learned that when God appoints means for a certain work we are not to lay these aside and then pray and expect that He will work a miracle to supply the lack. If the farmer fails to plow and sow, God does not by a miracle prevent the results of his neglect. Harvesttime finds his fields barren—there is no grain to be reaped, there are no sheaves to be garnered. God provided the seed and the soil, the sun and the rain; and if the husbandman had employed the means that were at his hand, he would have received according to his sowing and his labor.

There are great laws that govern the world of nature, and spiritual things are controlled by principles equally certain. The means for an end must be employed if the desired results are to be attained. God has appointed to every man his work according to his ability. It is by education and practice that persons are to be qualified to meet any emergency which may arise, and wise planning is needed to place each one in his proper sphere, that he may obtain an experience which will fit him to bear responsibility.

But while education, training, and the counsel of those of experience are all essential, the workers should be taught that they are not to rely wholly upon any man's judgment. As God's free agents, all should ask wisdom of Him. When the learner depends wholly upon another's thoughts, and goes no further than to accept his plans, he sees only through that man's eyes and is, so far, only an echo of another. God deals with men as responsible beings. He will work by His Spirit through the mind He has put in man, if man will only give Him a chance to work and will recognize His dealings. He designs that each shall use his mind and conscience for himself. He does not intend that one man shall become the shadow of another, uttering only another's sentiments.

All should love their brethren and respect and esteem their leaders, but they should not make them their burden bearers. We are not to pour all our difficulties and perplexities into the minds of others, to wear them out. "If any of you lack wisdom, let him ask of God, that giveth to all men liberally, and upbraideth not; and it shall be given him. But let him ask in faith, nothing wavering." Jesus invites us: "Come unto Me, all ye that labor and are heavy-laden, and I will give you rest. Take My yoke upon you, and learn of Me; for I am meek and lowly in heart: and ye shall find rest unto your souls. For My yoke is easy, and My burden is light."

The foundation of Christianity is Christ our righteousness. Men are individually accountable to God, and each must act as God moves upon him, not as he is moved by the mind of another; for if this manner of labor is pursued, souls cannot be impressed and directed by the Spirit of the great I AM. They will be kept under a restraint which allows no freedom of action or of choice.

It is not the will of God that His people in Battle Creek should remain in their present condition of coldness and inaction until by some mighty miracle-working power the church shall be aroused to life and activity. If we would be wise, and use diligently, prayerfully, and thankfully the means whereby light and blessing are to come to God's people, then no power upon earth would be able to withhold these gifts from us. But if we refuse God's means we need not look for Him to work a miracle to give us light and vigor and power, for this will never be done.

The Lord has shown me that men in responsible positions are standing directly in the way of His work because they think the work must be done and the blessing must come in a certain way, and they will not recognize that which comes in any other way. My brethren, may the Lord place this matter before you as it is. God does not work as men plan, or as they wish; He "moves in a mysterious way His wonders to perform." Why reject the Lord's methods of working, because they do not coincide with our ideas? God has His appointed channels of light, but these are not necessarily the minds of any particular set of men. When all shall take their appointed place in God's work, earnestly seeking wisdom and guidance from Him, then a great advance will have been made toward letting light shine upon the world. When men shall cease to place themselves in the way, God will work among us as never before.

While extensive plans should be laid, great care must be taken that the work in each branch of the cause be harmoniously united with that in every other branch, thus making a perfect whole. But too often it has been the reverse of this; and, as the result, the work has been defective. One man who has the oversight of a certain branch of the work magnifies his responsibilities until, in his estimation, that one department is above every other. When this narrow view is taken, a strong influence is exerted to lead others to see the matter in the same light. This is human nature, but it is not the spirit of Christ. Just in proportion as this policy is followed, Christ is crowded out of the work, and self appears prominent.

The principles that should actuate us as workers in God's cause are laid down by the apostle Paul. He says: "We are laborers together with God." "Whatsoever ye do, do it heartily, *as to the Lord,* and not unto men." And Peter exhorts the believers: "As every man hath received the gift, even so minister the same one to another, as good stewards of the manifold grace of God. If any man speak, let him speak as the oracles of God; if any man minister, let him do it as of the ability which God giveth: that God in all things may be glorified through Jesus Christ."

When these principles control our hearts, we shall realize that the work is God's, not ours; that He has the same care for every part of the great whole. When Christ and His glory are made first and love of self is swallowed up in love for souls for whom Christ died, then no worker will be so entirely absorbed in one branch of the cause as to lose sight of the importance of every other. It is selfishness which leads persons to think that the particular part of the work in which they are engaged is the most important of all.

It is selfishness also that prompts the feeling, on the part of workers, that their judgment must be the most reliable and their methods of labor the best or that it is their privilege in any way to bind the conscience of another. Such was the spirit of the Jewish leaders in Christ's day. In their self-exaltation the priests and rabbis brought in such rigid rules and so many forms and ceremonies as to divert the minds of the people from God and leave Him no chance to work for them. Thus His mercy and love were lost sight of. My brethren, do not follow in the same path. Let the minds of the people be directed to God. Leave Him a chance to work for those who love Him. Do not impose upon the people rules and regulations, which, if followed, would leave them as destitute of the Spirit of God as were the hills of Gilboa of dew or rain.

There is a deplorable lack of spirituality among our people. A great work must be done for them before they can become what Christ designed they should be—the light of the world. For years I have felt deep anguish of soul as the Lord has presented before me the want in our churches of Jesus and His love. There has been a spirit of self-sufficiency and a disposition to strive for position and supremacy. I have seen that self-glorification was becoming common among Seventh-day Adventists and that unless the pride of man should be abased and Christ exalted we should, as a people, be in no better condition to receive Christ at His second advent than were the Jewish people to receive Him at His first advent.

Jews were looking for the Messiah; but He did not come as they had predicted that He would, and if He were accepted as the Promised One, their learned teachers would be forced to acknowledge that they had erred. These leaders had separated themselves from God, and Satan worked upon their minds to lead them to reject the Saviour. Rather than yield their pride of opinion, they closed their eyes to all the evidences of His Messiahship, and they not only rejected the message of salvation themselves, but they steeled the hearts of the people against Jesus. Their history should be a solemn warning to us. We need never expect that when the Lord has light for His people, Satan will stand calmly by and make no effort to prevent them from receiving it. He will work upon minds to excite distrust and jealousy and unbelief. Let us beware that we do not refuse the light God sends, because it does not come in a way to please us. Let not God's blessing be turned away from us because we know not the time of our visitation. If there are any who do not see and accept the light themselves, let them not stand in the way of others. Let it not be said of this highly favored people, as of the Jews when the good news of the kingdom was preached to them: "Ye entered not in yourselves, and them that were entering in ye hindered."

We are taught in God's word that this is the time, above all others, when we may look for light from heaven. It is now that we are to expect a refreshing from the presence of the Lord. We should watch for the movings of God's providence as the army of Israel watched for "the sound of a going in the tops of the mulberry trees"—the appointed signal that heaven would work for them.

God cannot glorify His name through His people while they are leaning upon man and making flesh their arm. Their present state of weakness will continue until Christ alone shall be exalted; until, with John the Baptist, they shall say from a humble and reverent heart: "He must increase, but I must decrease." Words have been given me to speak to the people of God: "Lift Him up, the Man of Calvary. Let humanity stand back, that all may behold Him in whom their hopes of eternal life are centered. Says the prophet Isaiah: 'Unto us a Child is born, unto us a Son is given: and the government shall be upon His shoulder: and His name shall be called Wonderful, Counselor, The mighty God, The everlasting Father, The Prince of Peace.' Let the church and the world look upon their Redeemer. Let every voice proclaim with John: 'Behold the Lamb of God, which taketh away the sin of the world.' "

It is to the thirsting soul that the fountain of living waters is open. God declares: "I will pour water upon him that is thirsty, and floods upon the dry ground." To souls that are earnestly seeking for light and that accept with gladness every ray of divine illumination from His holy word, to such alone light will be given. It is through these souls that God will reveal that light and power which will lighten the whole earth with His glory.

THE INESTIMABLE GIFT

"Blessed be the God and Father of our Lord Jesus Christ, who hath blessed us with all spiritual blessings in heavenly places in Christ: according as He hath chosen us in Him, . . . that we should be holy and without blame before Him in love: having predestinated us unto the adoption of children by Jesus Christ to Himself, . . . to the praise of the glory of His grace, wherein He hath made us accepted in the Beloved.

In whom we have redemption through His blood, the forgiveness of sins, according to the riches of His grace."

"God, who is rich in mercy, for His great love wherewith He loved us, even when we were dead in sins, hath quickened us together with Christ, . . . and hath raised us up together, and made us sit together in heavenly places in Christ Jesus: that in the ages to come He might show the *exceeding riches* of His grace in His kindness toward us through Christ Jesus."

Such are the words in which "Paul the aged," "a prisoner of Jesus Christ," writing from his prison house at Rome, endeavored to set before his brethren that which he found language inadequate to express in its fullness—"the unsearchable riches of Christ," the treasure of grace freely offered to the fallen sons of men. The plan of redemption was laid by a sacrifice, a gift. Says the apostle: "Ye know the grace of our Lord Jesus Christ, that, though He was rich, yet for your sakes He became poor, that ye through His poverty might be rich." "God so loved the world, that He *gave* His only-begotten Son." Christ *"gave Himself* for us, that He might redeem us from all iniquity." And as the crowning blessing of redemption, *"the gift of God* is eternal life through Jesus Christ our Lord."

"Eye hath not seen, nor ear heard, neither have entered into the heart of man, the things which God hath prepared for them that love Him." Surely there are none that, beholding the riches of His grace, can forbear to exclaim with the apostle. "Thanks be unto God for His unspeakable gift."

As the plan of redemption begins and ends with a gift, so it is to be carried forward. The same spirit of sacrifice which purchased salvation for us will dwell in the hearts of all who become partakers of the heavenly gift. Says the apostle Peter: "As every man hath received the gift, even so minister the same one to another, as good stewards of the manifold grace of God." Said Jesus to His disciples as He

sent them forth: "Freely ye have received, freely give." In
him who is fully in sympathy with Christ there can be nothing
selfish or exclusive. He who drinks of the living water will
find that it is "in him a well of water springing up into everlasting life." The Spirit of Christ within him is like a spring
welling up in the desert, flowing to refresh all, and making
those who are ready to perish, eager to drink of the water of
life. It was the same spirit of love and self-sacrifice which
dwelt in Christ that impelled the apostle Paul to his manifold
labors. "I am debtor," he says, "both to the Greeks, and to
the barbarians; both to the wise, and to the unwise." "Unto
me, who am less than the least of all saints, is this grace
given, that I should preach among the Gentiles the unsearchable riches of Christ."

Our Lord designed that His church should reflect to the world
the fullness and sufficiency that we find in Him. We are constantly receiving of God's bounty, and by imparting of the same
we are to represent to the world the love and beneficence of
Christ. While all heaven is astir, dispatching messengers to every part of the earth to carry forward the work of redemption, the
church of the living God are also to be co-laborers with Christ.
We are members of His mystical body. He is the head, controlling all the members of the body. Jesus Himself, in His infinite
mercy, is working on human hearts, effecting spiritual transfor-
mations so amazing that angels look on with astonishment and
joy. The same unselfish love that characterizes the Master is
seen in the character and life of His true followers. Christ expects that men will become partakers of His divine nature while
in this world, thus not only reflecting His glory to the praise of
God, but illumining the darkness of the world with the radiance
of heaven. Thus will be fulfilled the words of Christ: "Ye are
the light of the world."

"We are laborers together with God," "stewards of the
manifold grace of God." The knowledge of God's grace,

the truths of His word, and temporal gifts as well,—time and means, talents and influence,—are all a trust from God to be employed to His glory and the salvation of men. Nothing can be more offensive to God, who is constantly bestowing His gifts upon man, than to see him selfishly grasping these gifts and making no returns to the Giver. Jesus is today in heaven preparing mansions for those who love Him; yes, more than mansions, a kingdom which is to be ours. But all who shall inherit these blessings must be partakers of the self-denial and self-sacrifice of Christ for the good of others.

Never was there greater need of earnest, self-sacrificing labor in the cause of Christ than now, when the hours of probation are fast closing and the last message of mercy is to be given to the world. My soul is stirred within me as the Macedonian cry comes from every direction, from the cities and villages of our own land, from across the Atlantic and the broad Pacific, and from the islands of the sea: "Come over, . . . and help us." Brethren and sisters, will you answer the cry? saying: "We will do our best, both in sending you missionaries and money. We will deny ourselves in the embellishment of our houses, in the adornment of our persons, and in the gratification of appetite. We will give the means entrusted to us into the cause of God, and we will devote ourselves also unreservedly to His work." The wants of the cause are laid before us; the empty treasuries appeal to us most pathetically for help. One dollar now is of more value to the work than ten dollars will be at some future period.

Work, brethren, work while you have the opportunity, while the day lasts. Work, for "the night cometh, when no man can work." How soon that night may come, it is impossible for you to tell. Now is your opportunity; improve it. If there are some who cannot give personal effort in missionary work, let them live economically and give of their earnings. Thus they can contribute money to send papers and books to those who have not the light of truth; they can help pay the expenses of students who are fitting for missionary work. Let every dollar that you can spare be invested in the bank of heaven.

"Lay not up for yourselves treasures upon earth, where moth and rust doth corrupt, and where thieves break through and steal: but lay up for yourselves treasures in heaven, where neither moth nor rust doth corrupt, and where thieves do not break through nor steal: for where your treasure is, there will your heart be also."

These are the words of Jesus, who loved you so much that He gave His own life, that you might have a home with Him in His kingdom. Do not dishonor your Lord by disregarding His positive command.

God calls upon those who have possessions in lands and houses, to sell and to invest the money where it will be supplying the great want in the missionary field. When once they have experienced the real satisfaction that comes from thus doing they will keep the channel open, and the means the Lord entrusts to them will be constantly flowing into the treasury, that souls may be converted. These souls will, in their turn, practice the same self-denial, economy, and simplicity for Christ's sake, that they, too, may bring their offerings to God. Through these talents, wisely invested, still other souls may be converted; and thus the work goes on, showing that the gifts of God are appreciated. The Giver is acknowledged, and glory redounds to Him through the faithfulness of His stewards.

When we make these earnest appeals in behalf of the cause of God and present the financial wants of our missions, conscientious souls who believe the truth are deeply stirred. Like the poor widow, whom Christ commended, who gave her two mites into the treasury, they give, in their poverty, to the utmost of their ability. Such often deprive themselves even of the apparent necessities of life; while there are men and women who, possessing houses and lands, cling to their earthly treasure with selfish tenacity and do not have faith enough in the message and in God to put their means into His work. To these last are especially applicable the words of Christ: "Sell that ye have, and give alms."

There are poor men and women who are writing to me for advice as to whether they shall sell their homes and give the proceeds to the cause. They say the appeals for means stir their souls, and they want to do something for the Master who has done everything for them. I would say to such: "It may not be your duty to sell your little homes just now; but go to God for yourselves; the Lord will certainly hear your earnest prayers for wisdom to understand your duty." If there was more seeking God for heavenly wisdom and less seeking wisdom from men, there would be far greater light from heaven, and God would bless the humble seeker. But I can say to those to whom God has entrusted goods, who have lands and houses: "Commence your selling, and giving alms. Make no delay. God expects more of you than you have been willing to do." We call upon you who have means, to inquire with earnest prayer: What is the extent of the divine claim upon me and my property? There is work to be done now to make ready a people to stand in the day of the Lord. Means must be invested in the work of saving men, who, in turn, shall work for others. Be prompt in rendering to God His own. One reason why there is so great a dearth of the Spirit of God is that so many are robbing God.

There is a lesson for us in the experience of the churches of Macedonia, as described by Paul. He says that they "first gave their own selves to the Lord." Then they were eager to give their means for Christ. "In a great trial of affliction the abundance of their joy and their deep poverty abounded unto the riches of their liberality. For to their power, I bear record, yea, and beyond their power they were willing of themselves; praying us with much entreaty that we would receive the gift."

Paul lays down a rule for giving to God's cause, and tells us what the result will be both in regard to ourselves and to God. "Every man according as he purposeth in his heart, so let him give; not grudgingly, or of necessity: for God loveth a cheerful giver." "This I say, He which soweth sparingly shall reap also sparingly; and he which soweth bountifully shall reap also bountifully." "God is able to make all grace abound toward you; that ye, *always having all sufficiency in all things, may abound to every good work*: (. . . Now he that ministereth seed to the sower both minister bread for your food, and multiply your seed sown, and increase the fruits of your righteousness;) being enriched in everything to all bountifulness, which causeth through us thanksgiving to God."

We are not to feel that we can do or give anything that will entitle us to the favor of God. Says the apostle: "What hast thou that thou didst not receive? now if thou didst receive it, why dost thou glory, as if thou hadst not received it?" When David and the people of Israel had gathered together the material they had prepared for the building of the temple, the king, as he committed the treasure to the princes of the congregation, rejoiced and gave thanks to God in words that should ever dwell in the hearts of God's people. "David blessed the Lord before all the congregation: and David said, Blessed be Thou Lord God of Israel our father, for ever and ever. Thine, O Lord, is the greatness, and the power, and the glory, and the victory, and the majesty: for all that is in the heaven and in the earth is Thine. . . . And in Thine hand it is to make great, and to give strength unto all. Now therefore, our God, we thank Thee, and praise Thy glorious name. But who am I, and what is my people, that we should be able to offer so willingly after this sort? for all things come of Thee, and of Thine own have we given Thee. For we are strangers before Thee, and sojourners, as were all our fathers: our days on the earth are as a shadow, and there is none abiding. O Lord our God, all this store that we have prepared to build Thee an house for Thine holy name cometh of Thine hand, and is all Thine own. I know also, my God, that Thou triest the heart, and hast pleasure in uprightness. As for me, in the uprightness of mine heart I have willingly offered all these things: and now have I seen with joy Thy people, which are present here, to offer willingly unto Thee."

It was God who had provided the people with the riches of earth, and His Spirit had made them willing to bring their precious things for the temple. It was all of the Lord; if His divine power had not moved upon the hearts of the people, the king's efforts would have been in vain, and the temple would never have been erected.

All that men receive of God's bounty still belongs to God. Whatever He has bestowed in the valuable and beautiful things of earth is placed in our hands to test us, to sound the depths of our love for Him and our appreciation of His favors. Whether it be the treasures of wealth or of intellect, they are to be laid, a willing offering, at the feet of Jesus.

None of us can do without the blessing of God, but God can do His work without the aid of man if He so choose. But He has given to every man his work, and He trusts men with treasures of wealth or of intellect, as His stewards. Whatever we render to God is, through His mercy and generosity, placed to our account as faithful stewards. But we should ever realize that this is not a work of merit on man's part. However great the ability of man, he possesses nothing which God did not give him, and which He cannot withdraw if these precious tokens of His favor are not appreciated and rightly applied. Angels of God, whose perceptions are unclouded by sin, recognize the endowments of heaven as bestowed with the intention that they be returned in such a way as to add to the glory of the great Giver. With the sovereignty of God is bound up the well-being of man. The glory of God is the joy and the blessing of all created beings. When we seek to promote His glory we are seeking for ourselves the highest good which it is possible for us to receive. Brethren and sisters in Christ, God calls for the consecration to His service of every faculty, of every gift, you have received from Him. He wants you to say, with David: "All things come of Thee, and of Thine own have we given Thee."

THE CHARACTER OF GOD REVEALED IN CHRIST

Said the Saviour: "This is life eternal, that they might *know Thee* the only true God, and Jesus Christ, whom Thou hast sent." And God declared by the prophet: "Let not the wise man glory in his wisdom, neither let the mighty man glory in his might, let not the rich man glory in his riches: but let him that glorieth glory in this, that *he understandeth and knoweth Me,* that I am the Lord which exercise loving-kindness, judgment, and righteousness, in the earth: for in these things I delight, saith the Lord."

No man, without divine aid, can attain to this knowledge of God. The apostle says that "the world by wisdom knew not God." Christ "was in the world, and the world was made by Him, and the world knew Him not." Jesus declared to His disciples: "No man knoweth the Son, but the Father; neither knoweth any man the Father, save the Son, and he to whomsoever the Son will reveal Him." In that last prayer for His followers, before entering the shadows of Gethsemane, the Saviour lifted His eyes to heaven, and in pity for the ignorance of fallen men He said: "O righteous Father, the world hath not known Thee: but I have known Thee."

"I have manifested Thy name unto the men which Thou gavest Me out of the world."

From the beginning it has been Satan's studied plan to cause men to forget God, that he might secure them to himself. Hence he has sought to misrepresent the character of God, to lead men to cherish a false conception of Him. The Creator has been presented to their minds as clothed with the attributes of the prince of evil himself,—as arbitrary, severe, and unforgiving,—that He might be feared, shunned, and even hated by men. Satan hoped to so confuse the minds of those whom he had deceived that they would put God out of their knowledge. Then he would obliterate the divine image in man and impress his own likeness upon the soul; he would imbue men with his own spirit and make them captives according to his will.

It was by falsifying the character of God and exciting distrust of Him that Satan tempted Eve to transgress. By sin the minds of our first parents were darkened, their natures were degraded, and their conceptions of God were molded by their own narrowness and selfishness. And as men became bolder in sin, the knowledge and the love of God faded from their minds and hearts. "Because that, when they knew God, they glorified Him not as God," they "became vain in their imaginations, and their foolish heart was darkened."

At times Satan's contest for the control of the human family appeared to be crowned with success. During the ages preceding the first advent of Christ the world seemed almost wholly under the sway of the prince of darkness, and he ruled with a terrible power as though through the sin of our first parents the kingdoms of the world had become his by right. Even the covenant people, whom God had chosen to preserve in the world the knowledge of Himself, had so far departed from Him that they had lost all true conception of His character.

Christ came to reveal God to the world as a God of love,

full of mercy, tenderness, and compassion. The thick darkness with which Satan had endeavored to enshroud the throne of Deity was swept away by the world's Redeemer, and the Father was again manifest to men as the light of life.

When Philip came to Jesus with the request, "Show us the Father, and it sufficeth us," the Saviour answered him: "Have I been so long time with you, and yet hast thou not known Me, Philip? he that hath seen Me hath seen the Father; and how sayest thou then, Show us the Father?" Christ declares Himself to be sent into the world as a representative of the Father. In His nobility of character, in His mercy and tender pity, in His love and goodness, He stands before us as the embodiment of divine perfection, the image of the invisible God.

Says the apostle: "God was in Christ, reconciling the world unto Himself." Only as we contemplate the great plan of redemption can we have a just appreciation of the character of God. The work of creation was a manifestation of His love; but the gift of God to save the guilty and ruined race, alone reveals the infinite depths of divine tenderness and compassion. "God *so loved* the world, that He gave His only-begotten Son, that whosoever believeth in Him should not perish, but have everlasting life." While the law of God is maintained, and its justice vindicated, the sinner can be pardoned. The dearest gift that heaven itself had to bestow has been poured out that God "might be just, and the justifier of him which believeth in Jesus." By that gift men are uplifted from the ruin and degradation of sin to become children of God. Says Paul: "Ye have received the Spirit of adoption, whereby we cry, Abba, Father."

Brethren, with the beloved John I call upon you to "behold, what manner of love the Father hath bestowed upon us, that we should be called the sons of God." What love, what matchless love, that, sinners and aliens as we are, we may be brought back to God and adopted into His family! We may address Him by the endearing name, "Our Father," which is a sign of our affection for Him and a pledge of His tender regard and relationship to us. And the Son of God, beholding the heirs of grace, "is not ashamed to call them brethren." They have even a more sacred relationship to God than have the angels who have never fallen.

All the paternal love which has come down from generation to generation through the channel of human hearts, all the springs of tenderness which have opened in the souls of men, are but as a tiny rill to the boundless ocean when compared with the infinite, exhaustless love of God. Tongue cannot utter it; pen cannot portray it. You may meditate upon it every day of your life; you may search the Scriptures diligently in order to understand it; you may summon every power and capability that God has given you, in the endeavor to comprehend the love and compassion of the heavenly Father; and yet there is an infinity beyond. You may study that love for ages; yet you can never fully comprehend the length and the breadth, the depth and the height, of the love of God in giving His Son to die for the world. Eternity itself can never fully reveal it. Yet as we study the Bible and meditate upon the life of Christ and the plan of redemption, these great themes will open to our understanding more and more. And it will be ours to realize the blessing which Paul desired for the Ephesian church when he prayed "that the God of our Lord Jesus Christ, the Father of glory, may give unto you *the Spirit of wisdom and revelation in the knowledge of Him;* the eyes of your understanding being enlightened, that ye may know what is the hope of His calling, and what *the riches of the glory* of His inheritance in the saints, and what is *the exceeding greatness of His power* to usward who believe."

It is Satan's constant study to keep the minds of men occupied with those things which will prevent them from obtaining the knowledge of God. He seeks to keep them dwelling upon what will darken the understanding and discourage the soul. We are in a world of sin and corruption, surrounded by influences that tend to allure or dishearten the followers of Christ. The Saviour said: "Because iniquity shall abound, the love of many shall wax cold." Many fix their eyes upon the terrible wickedness existing around them, the apostasy and weakness on every side, and they talk of these things until their hearts are filled with sadness and doubt. They keep uppermost before the mind the masterly working of the archdeceiver and dwell upon the discouraging features of their experience, while they seem to lose sight of the heavenly Father's power and His matchless love. All this is as Satan would have it. It is a mistake to think of the enemy of righteousness as clothed with so great power, when we dwell so little upon the love of God and His might. We must talk of the mightiness of Christ. We are utterly powerless to rescue ourselves from the grasp of Satan; but God has appointed a way of escape. The Son of the Highest has strength to fight the battle for us, and "through Him that loved us" we may come off "more than conquerors."

There is no spiritual strength for us in constantly brooding over our weakness and backslidings, and bemoaning the power of Satan. This great truth must be established as a living principle in our minds and hearts—the efficacy of the offering made for us; that God can and does save to the uttermost all who come unto Him complying with the conditions specified in His word. Our work is to place our will on the side of God's will. Then, through the blood of the atonement, we become partakers of the divine nature; through Christ we are children of God, and we have the assurance that God loves us even as He loved His Son. We are one with Jesus. We walk where Christ leads the way; He has power to dispel the dark shadows which Satan casts across our path; and, in place of darkness and discouragement, the sunlight of His glory shines into our hearts.

Our hope is to be constantly strengthened by the knowledge that Christ is our righteousness. Let our faith rest upon this foundation, for it will stand fast forever. Instead of dwelling upon the darkness of Satan and fearing his power, we should open our hearts to receive light from Christ and to let it shine forth to the world, declaring that He is above all the power of Satan, that His sustaining arm will support all who trust in Him.

Said Jesus: "The Father Himself loveth you." If our faith is fixed upon God, through Christ, it will prove "as an anchor of the soul, both sure and steadfast, and which entereth into that within the veil; whither the Forerunner is for us entered." It is true that disappointments will come; tribulation we must expect; but we are to commit everything, great and small, to God. He does not become perplexed by the multiplicity of our grievances nor overpowered by the weight of our burdens. His watchcare extends to every household and encircles every individual; He is concerned in all our business and our sorrows. He marks every tear; He is touched with the feeling of our infirmities. All the afflictions and trials that befall us here are permitted, to work out His purposes of love toward us, "that we might be partakers of His holiness" and thus become participants in that fullness of joy which is found in His presence.

"The god of this world hath blinded the minds of them which believe not, lest the light of the glorious gospel of Christ, who is the image of God, should shine unto them." But the Bible in strongest terms sets before us the importance of obtaining a knowledge of God. Says Peter: "Grace and peace be multiplied unto you through the *knowledge of God, and of Jesus our Lord.*" "His divine power hath given unto us *all things* that pertain unto life and godliness, *through the knowledge of Him* that hath called us to glory and virtue." And the Scripture bids us: "Acquaint now thyself with Him, and be at peace."

God has commanded us, "Be ye holy; for I am holy;" and an inspired apostle declares that without holiness "no man shall see the Lord." Holiness is agreement with God. By sin the image of God in man has been marred and well-nigh obliterated; it is the work of the gospel to restore that which has been lost; and we are to cooperate with the divine agency in this work. And how can we come into harmony with God, how shall we receive His likeness, unless we obtain a knowledge of Him? It is this knowledge that Christ came into the world to reveal unto us.

The meager views which so many have had of the exalted character and office of Christ have narrowed their religious experience and have greatly hindered their progress in the divine life. Personal religion among us as a people is at a low ebb. There is much form, much machinery, much tongue religion; but something deeper and more solid must be brought into our religious experience. With all our facilities, our publishing houses, our schools, our sanitariums, and many, many other advantages, we ought to be far in advance of our present position. It is the work of the Christian in this life to represent Christ to the world, in life and character unfolding the blessed Jesus. If God has given us light, it is that we may reveal it to others. But in comparison with the light we have received, and the opportunities and privileges granted us to reach the hearts of the people, the results of our work thus far have been far too small. God designs that the truth which He has brought to our understanding shall produce more fruit than has yet been revealed. But when our minds are filled with gloom and sadness, dwelling upon the darkness and evil around us, how can we represent Christ to the world? How can our testimony have power to win souls? What we need is to know God and the power of His love, as revealed in Christ, by an experimental knowledge. We must search the Scriptures diligently, prayerfully; our understanding must be quickened by the Holy Spirit, and our hearts must be uplifted to God in faith and hope and continual praise.

Through the merits of Christ, through His righteousness, which by faith is imputed unto us, we are to attain to the perfection of Christian character. Our daily and hourly work is set forth in the words of the apostle: "Looking unto Jesus the Author and Finisher of our faith." While doing this our minds become clearer and our faith stronger, and our hope is confirmed; we are so engrossed with the view of His purity and loveliness, and the sacrifice He has made to bring us into agreement with God, that we have no disposition to speak of doubts and discouragements.

The manifestation of God's love, His mercy and His goodness, and the work of the Holy Spirit upon the heart to enlighten and renew it, place us, through faith, in so close connection with Christ that, having a clear conception of His character, we are able to discern the masterly deceptions of Satan. Looking unto Jesus and trusting in His merits we appropriate the blessings of light, of peace, of joy in the Holy Ghost. And in view of the great things which Christ has done for us, we are ready to exclaim: "Behold, what manner of love the Father hath bestowed upon us, that we should be called the sons of God."

Brethren and sisters, it is by beholding that we become changed. By dwelling upon the love of God and our Saviour, by contemplating the perfection of the divine character and claiming the righteousness of Christ as ours by faith, we are to be transformed into the same image. Then let us not gather together all the unpleasant pictures—the iniquities and corruptions and disappointments, the evidences of Satan's power—to hang in the halls of our memory, to talk over and mourn over until our souls are filled with discouragement. A discouraged soul is a body of darkness, not only failing himself to receive the light of God, but shutting it away from others. Satan loves to see the effect of the pictures of his triumphs, making human beings faithless and disheartened.

There are, thank God, brighter and more cheering pictures which the Lord has presented to us. Let us group together the blessed assurances of His love as precious treasures, that we may look upon them continually. The Son of God leaving His Father's throne, clothing His divinity with humanity, that He might rescue man from the power of Satan; His triumph in our behalf, opening heaven to man, revealing to human vision the presence chamber where Deity unveils His glory; the fallen race uplifted from the pit of ruin into which sin had plunged them, and brought again into connection with the infinite God, and, having endured the divine test through faith in our Redeemer, clothed in the righteousness of Christ and exalted to His throne—these are the pictures with which God bids us gladden the chambers of the soul. And "while we look not at the things which are seen, but at the things which are not seen," we shall prove it true that "our light affliction, which is but for a moment, worketh for us a far more exceeding and eternal weight of glory."

In heaven God is all in all. There holiness reigns supreme; there is nothing to mar the perfect harmony with God. If we are indeed journeying thither, the spirit of heaven will dwell in our hearts here. But if we find no pleasure now in the contemplation of heavenly things; if we have no interest in seeking the knowledge of God, no delight in beholding the character of Christ; if holiness has no attractions for us—then we may be sure that our hope of heaven is vain. Perfect conformity to the will of God is the high aim to be constantly before the Christian. He will love to talk of God, of Jesus, of the home of bliss and purity which Christ has prepared for them that love Him. The contemplation of these themes, when the soul feasts upon the blessed assurances of God, the apostle represents as tasting "the powers of the world to come."

Just before us is the closing struggle of the great controversy when, with "all power and signs and lying wonders, and with all deceivableness of unrighteousness," Satan is to work to misrepresent the character of God, that he may "seduce, if it were possible, even the elect." If there was ever a people in need of constantly increasing light from heaven, it is the people that, in this time of peril, God has called to be the depositaries of His holy law and to vindicate His character before the world. Those to whom has been committed a trust so sacred must be spiritualized, elevated, vitalized, by the truths they profess to believe. Never did the church more sorely need, and never was God more solicitous that she should enjoy, the experience described in Paul's letter to the Colossians when he wrote: We "do not cease to pray for you, and to desire that ye might be *filled with the knowledge of His will* in all wisdom and spiritual understanding; that ye might walk worthy of the Lord unto all pleasing, being fruitful in every good work, and increasing in the knowledge of God."

THE WORD MADE FLESH

The union of the divine with the human nature is one of the most precious and most mysterious truths of the plan of redemption. It is this of which Paul speaks when he says: "Without controversy great is the mystery of godliness: God was manifest in the flesh."

This truth has been to many a cause of doubt and unbelief. When Christ came into the world,—the Son of God and the Son of man,—He was not understood by the people of His time. Christ stooped to take upon Himself human nature, that He might reach the fallen race and lift them up. But the minds of men had become darkened by sin, their faculties were benumbed and their perceptions dulled, so that they could not discern His divine character beneath the garb of humanity. This lack of appreciation on their part was an obstacle to the work which He desired to accomplish for them; and in order to give force to His teaching he was often under the necessity of defining and defending His position. By referring to His mysterious and divine character, He sought to lead their minds into a train of thought which would be favorable to the transforming power of truth. Again, He used the things of nature with which they were familiar, to illustrate divine truth. The soil of the heart was thus prepared to receive the good seed. He made His hearers feel that His interests were identified with theirs, that His heart beat in sympathy with them in their joys and griefs. At the same time they saw in Him the manifestation of power and excellence far above that possessed by their most-honored rabbis. The teachings of Christ were marked with a simplicity, dignity, and power heretofore unknown to them, and their involuntary exclamation was: "Never man spake like this Man." The people listened to Him gladly; but the priests and rulers—themselves false to their trust as guardians of the truth—hated Christ for the very grace revealed, which had drawn the multitudes away from them to follow the Light of life. Through their influence the Jewish nation, failing to discern His divine character, rejected the Redeemer.

The union of the divine and the human, manifest in Christ, exists also in the Bible. The truths revealed are all "given by inspiration of God;" yet they are expressed in the words of men and are adapted to human needs. Thus it may be said of the Book of God, as it was of Christ, that "the Word was made flesh, and dwelt among us." And this fact, so far from being an argument against the Bible, should strengthen faith in it as the word of God. Those who pronounce upon the inspiration of the Scriptures, accepting some portions as divine while they reject other parts as human, overlook the fact that Christ, the divine, partook of our human nature, that He might reach humanity. In the work of God for man's redemption, divinity and humanity are combined.

There are many passages of Scripture which skeptical critics have declared to be uninspired, but which, in their tender adaptation to the needs of men, are God's own messages of comfort to His trusting children. A beautiful illustration of this occurs in the history of the apostle Peter. Peter was in prison, expecting to be brought forth next day to death; he was sleeping at night "between two soldiers, bound with two chains: and the keepers before the door kept the prison. And, behold, the angel of the Lord came upon him, and a light shined in the prison: and he smote Peter on the side, and raised him up, saying, Arise up quickly. And his chains fell off from his hands." Peter, suddenly awaking, was amazed at the brightness that flooded his dungeon, and the celestial beauty of the heavenly messenger. He understood not the scene, but he knew that he was free, and in his bewilderment and joy he would have gone forth from the prison unprotected from the cold night air. The angel of God, noting all the circumstances, said, with tender care for the apostle's need: "Gird thyself, and bind on thy sandals." Peter mechanically obeyed; but so entranced was he with the revelation of the glory of heaven that he did not think to take his cloak. Then the angel bade him: "Cast thy garment about thee, and follow me. And he went out, and followed him; and wist not that it was true which was done by the angel; but thought he saw a vision. When they were past the first and the second ward, they came unto the iron gate that leadeth unto the city; which opened to them of his own accord: and they went out, and passed on through one street; and forthwith the angel departed from him." The apostle found himself in the streets of Jerusalem alone. "And when Peter was come to himself, he said, Now I know of a surety,"—it was not a dream or a vision, but an actual occurrence,—"that the Lord hath sent His angel, and hath delivered me out of the hand of Herod, and from all the expectation of the people of the Jews."

Skeptics may sneer at the thought that a glorious angel from heaven should give attention to a matter so commonplace as caring for these simple human needs, and may question the inspiration of the narrative. But in the wisdom of God these things are recorded in sacred history for the benefit, not of angels, but of men, that as they should be brought into trying positions they might find comfort in the thought that heaven knows it all. Jesus declared to His disciples that not a sparrow falls to the ground without the notice of the heavenly Father, and that if God can keep in mind the wants of all the little birds of the air, He will much more care for those who may become the subjects of His kingdom and through faith in Him may be the heirs of immortality. Oh, if the human mind were only to comprehend—in such measure as the plan of redemption *can* be comprehended by finite minds—the work of Jesus in taking upon Himself human nature, and what is to be accomplished for us by this marvelous condescension, the hearts of men would be melted with gratitude for God's great love, and in humility they would adore the divine wisdom that devised the mystery of grace!

GOD'S CARE FOR HIS WORK

It was under circumstances of difficulty and discouragement that Isaiah, while yet a young man, was called to the prophetic mission. Disaster was threatening his country. By their transgression of God's law the people of Judah had forfeited His protection, and the Assyrian forces were about to come against the kingdom of Judah. But the danger from their enemies was not the greatest trouble. It was the perversity of the people that brought upon the Lord's servant the deepest depression. By their apostasy and rebellion they were inviting the judgments of God. The youthful prophet had been called to bear to them a message of warning, and he knew that he would meet with obstinate resistance. He trembled as he viewed himself and thought of the stubbornness and unbelief of the people for whom he was to labor. His task seemed to him almost hopeless. Should he in despair relinquish his mission and leave Israel undisturbed to their idolatry? Were the gods of Nineveh to rule the earth in defiance of the God of heaven?

Such thoughts as these were crowding upon his mind as he stood under the portico of the holy temple. Suddenly the gate and the inner veil of the temple seemed to be uplifted or withdrawn, and he was permitted to gaze within, upon the holy of holies, where even the prophet's feet might not enter. There rose up before him a vision of Jehovah sitting upon a throne high and lifted up, while His train filled the temple. On each side the throne hovered the seraphim, two wings bearing them up, two veiling their faces in adoration, and two covering their feet. These angel ministers lifted up their voices in solemn invocation, "Holy, holy, holy, is the Lord of hosts: the whole earth is full of His glory," until post and pillar and cedar gate seemed to tremble at the sound, and the house was filled with their praise.

Never before had Isaiah realized so fully the greatness of Jehovah or His perfect holiness; and he felt that in his human frailty and unworthiness he must perish in that divine presence. "Woe is me!" he cried; "for I am undone; because I am a man of unclean lips, and I dwell in the midst of a people of unclean lips: for mine eyes have seen the King, the Lord of hosts." But a seraph came to him to fit him for his great mission. A living coal from the altar was laid upon his lips with the words: "Lo, this hath touched thy lips; and thine iniquity is taken away, and thy sin purged." And when the voice of God was heard saying, "Whom shall I send, and who will go for us?" Isaiah with holy confidence responded, "Here am I; send me."

What though earthly powers should be arrayed against Judah? What though Isaiah should meet with opposition and resistance in his mission? He had seen the King, the Lord of hosts; he had heard the song of the seraphim, "The whole earth is full of His glory;" and the prophet was nerved for the work before him. The memory of this vision was carried with him throughout his long and arduous mission.

Ezekiel, the mourning exile prophet, in the land of the Chaldeans, was given a vision teaching the same lesson of faith in the mighty God of Israel. As he was upon the banks of the river Chebar, a whirlwind seemed to come from the north, "a great cloud, and a fire infolding itself, and a brightness was about it, and out of the midst thereof as the color of amber." A number of wheels of strange appearance, intersecting one another, were moved by four living creatures. High above all these was "the likeness of a throne, as the appearance of a sapphire stone: and upon the likeness of the throne was the likeness as the appearance of a man above upon it." "As for the likeness of the living creatures, their appearance was like burning coals of fire, and like the appearance of lamps: it went up and down among the living creatures; and the fire was bright, and out of the fire went forth lightning." "And there appeared in the cherubims the form of a man's hand under their wings."

There were wheels within wheels in an arrangement so complicated that at first sight they appeared to Ezekiel to be all in confusion. But when they moved, it was with beautiful exactness and in perfect harmony. Heavenly beings were impelling these wheels, and, above all, upon the glorious sapphire throne, was the Eternal One; while round about the throne was the encircling rainbow, emblem of grace and love. Overpowered by the terrible glory of the scene, Ezekiel fell upon his face, when a voice bade him arise and hear the word of the Lord. Then there was given him a message of warning for Israel.

This vision was given to Ezekiel at a time when his mind was filled with gloomy forebodings. He saw the land of his fathers lying desolate. The city that was once full of people was no longer inhabited. The voice of mirth and the song of praise were no more heard within her walls. The prophet himself was a stranger in a strange land, where boundless ambition and savage cruelty reigned supreme. That which he saw and heard of human tyranny and wrong distressed his soul, and he mourned bitterly day and night. But the wonderful symbols presented before him beside the river Chebar revealed an overruling power mightier than that of earthly rulers. Above the proud and cruel monarchs of Assyria and Babylon the God of mercy and truth was enthroned.

The wheellike complications that appeared to the prophet to be involved in such confusion were under the guidance of an infinite hand. The Spirit of God, revealed to him as moving and directing these wheels, brought harmony out of confusion; so the whole world was under His control. Myriads of glorified beings were ready at His word to overrule the power and policy of evil men, and bring good to His faithful ones.

In like manner, when God was about to open to the beloved John the history of the church for future ages, He gave him an assurance of the Saviour's interest and care for His people by revealing to him "One like unto the Son of man," walking among the candlesticks, which symbolized the seven churches. While John was shown the last great struggles of the church with earthly powers, he was also permitted to behold the final victory and deliverance of the faithful. He saw the church brought into deadly conflict with the beast and his image, and the worship of that beast enforced on pain of death. But looking beyond the smoke and din of the battle, he beheld a company upon Mount Zion with the Lamb, having, instead of the mark of the beast, the "Father's name written in their foreheads." And again he saw "them that had gotten the victory over the beast, and over his image, and over his mark, and over the number of his name, stand on the sea of glass, having the harps of God" and singing the song of Moses and the Lamb.

These lessons are for our benefit. We need to stay our faith upon God, for there is just before us a time that will try men's souls. Christ, upon the Mount of Olives, rehearsed the fearful judgments that were to precede His second coming: "Ye shall hear of wars and rumors of wars." "Nation shall rise against nation, and kingdom against kingdom: and there shall be famines, and pestilences, and earthquakes, in divers places. All these are the beginning of sorrows." While these prophecies received a partial fulfillment at the destruction of Jerusalem, they have a more direct application to the last days.

We are standing on the threshold of great and solemn events. Prophecy is fast fulfilling. The Lord is at the door. There is soon to open before us a period of overwhelming interest to all living. The controversies of the past are to be revived; new controversies will arise. The scenes to be enacted in our world are not yet even dreamed of. Satan is at work through human agencies. Those who are making an effort to change the Constitution and secure a law enforcing Sunday observance little realize what will be the result. A crisis is just upon us.

But God's servants are not to trust to themselves in this great emergency. In the visions given to Isaiah, to Ezekiel, and to John we see how closely heaven is connected with the events taking place upon the earth and how great is the care of God for those who are loyal to Him. The world is not without a ruler. The program of coming events is in the hands of the Lord. The Majesty of heaven has the destiny of nations, as well as the concerns of His church, in His own charge.

We permit ourselves to feel altogether too much care, trouble, and perplexity in the Lord's work. Finite men are not left to carry the burden of responsibility. We need to trust in God, believe in Him, and go forward. The tireless vigilance of the heavenly messengers, and their unceasing employment in their ministry in connection with the beings of earth, show us how God's hand is guiding the wheel within a wheel. The divine Instructor is saying to every actor in His work, as He said to Cyrus of old: "I girded thee, though thou hast not known Me."

In Ezekiel's vision God had His hand beneath the wings of the cherubim. This is to teach His servants that it is divine power that gives them success. He will work with them if they will put away iniquity and become pure in heart and life.

The bright light going among the living creatures with the swiftness of lightning represents the speed with which this work will finally go forward to completion. He who slumbers not, who is continually at work for the accomplishment of His designs, can carry forward His great work harmoniously. That which appears to finite minds entangled and compli- cated, the Lord's hand can keep in perfect order. He can de- vise ways and means to thwart the purposes of wicked men, and He will bring to confusion the counsels of them that plot mischief against His people.

Brethren, it is no time now for mourning and despair, no time to yield to doubt and unbelief. Christ is not now a Saviour in Joseph's new tomb, closed with a great stone and sealed with the Roman seal; we have a risen Saviour. He is the King, the Lord of hosts; He sitteth between the cherubim; and amid the strife and tumult of nations He guards His peo- ple still. He who ruleth in the heavens is our Saviour. He measures every trial. He watches the furnace fire that must test every soul. When the strongholds of kings shall be overthrown, when the arrows of God's wrath shall strike through the hearts of His enemies, His people will be safe in His hands.

SCRIPTURAL INDEX

GENERAL INDEX

gold will be separated from dross in 81

guilt of, in neglecting to warn sinners 457

how to waken, from carnal slumber 77

instructed to labor for souls 308

joining, though members are not perfect 333, 334

last warning and reproof to 99

live, a working church 272

members, active missionary spirit should characterize 582

    all to help sustain work 303, 304

    cherish purity of life 141-148

    failures of, blinded to sin of licentious life 141

    gather fresh manna daily 486

    must be individually right before God 481

    persistently at variance, suspension of 241

    to enlighten world with truth 454-467

    urged to cultivate love 123

    will be individually tested and proved 463

must finish in crisis the work not done in prosperity 463

officers, duties of 619

    to educate helpers 390, 391

    election of 619

    qualifications of 618, 619

    treating erring 615-617

peril of, betrayal of trust 211

purity of, dependent on members 147

reformation needed in 103-105, 202, 203

remnant, trial of 80-84

responsibility of, to reflect to world fullness of Christ 731

retrograding unless progressive 93

Satan, causes dissension in 236

lays snare for remnant 160

shortcomings and failures of, backsliding into worldliness 103, 104, 188-191, 202

    change in spiritual state has come gradually 240

    knowledge of, seems hidden 84

    lack of love and sympathy for erring 604-613

    selfishness 204

spirit of world fast leavening 75

spiritual malady upon 202

stand of, never higher than minister's 227

tinker, criticizing and correcting others 334

to be judged by opportunities given 83

trials, how to dispose of 241

    ministers called to deal with 615

    proper procedure in 616, 617

unity in 236-248, 534, 535

    arises from love 477-490

    convincing evidence of world's Redeemer 620

    essential to power in the world 119

victories of, at Pentecost 239, 240

    great, in store 582

walled in by warnings and reproofs 666

warnings to, in camp meetings of 1882 217-235

See also Israel; Missionaries; People of God.

Cider, manufacture and use of 354-361

Circumspection, we must walk with 532

Circumstances, few understand others' 55

    peace of soul not changed by 487, 488

Cities, dangers in, for children 232
  fleeing from 464, 465
  moving to, warnings against 153
City missions, support of 368, 385
Clairvoyants, modern counterparts of heathen oracles 193
Cleaver of truth 455
Clothing to be clean in presence of God 498, 499
See also Dress.
Colleges, churches to help students to attend 556
  criticism of management of 482, 483
  danger of adopting worldly standards in 27
  discipline in, to be sustained by our people 89
  God's purpose disregarded in 87
  great work to be done in 34
  higher, kind of young men who might attend 583, 584
  long courses of study at, condemned 22, 27
  not to pattern after worldly institutions 11, 59-61, 85
  object of establishing, educate for ministry, primary 12, 22, 60
    educate for missionary labor 27, 390
    Satan's purpose to prevent 22, 23
    study of Scriptures 21, 22
    to co-ordinate science and religion 21
    to meet wants of this time of demoralization 22
  range and type of training in 31-36
  teachers in 28-36, 555
  See also Teachers.
  test of prosperity of 31, 32
  tuition in 555

  workers in 84-94
  See also Schools.
Comfort from promises of Scripture 578
Command of God ever implies a promise 445
Commandment, breaking seventh while professedly keeping fourth 138
Commandment keepers, mark of deliverance on, in final crisis 451
Communication from the Lord in dreams and visions 685
Communion, with Christ, how to maintain 113
  that is not real 161
  unspeakably precious 223
  with God, humility is most essential to 50
  See also Meditation; Prayer.
Companion, making Christ our daily, hourly 652
Compensation, of, brain workers of ability 551, 565
  canvassers 402-406
  soul winners not merely money 551
  teachers and ministers 85
  See also Wages.
Complaining in home 314
  See also Murmuring.
Condemning others, confession after 342, 343
  instead of looking to Jesus 345-347
Conduct, controlled by Spirit of Christ 75
  does not escape God's observation 627
  See also Deportment.
Conference presidents, mismanagement of 281
  some unworthy of trust 370-375
  to be men of trust 379
Confession, acceptable 635-641
  erroneous ideas concerning 642-650

Deception—*continued*
great, comes through members who do not love God supremely 477
possible despite honesty 45
Deceptions in last days 80
Decisions of board, own spirit woven into 560, 566
Declension, spiritual, use every precaution to prevent 276
Decree, against, Daniel 453
buying or selling 152
Jews 450
Sabbathkeepers 450, 451
enforcing papal institution a sign that end is near 451, 464, 525
fixing God's seal in forehead 216
to worship beast 213
Deeds of kindness, crowd into this life all you possibly can 488
Defects, Christ recognizes our work in spite of 420
hard fight to overcome 288
of others, poor food for anyone 334
Defilement among professed Christians, loathe 146
Degeneration and unhappiness follow licentiousness 144
Deity, no man can fully comprehend 699
Delusions, terrible, in time of trouble 474
Demonstration, progress of experience not dependent on extravagant 647
Denial of Christ by lax, undecided character 406
Denominations, ministers ridicule other, instead of feeding flock 165
Denunciation, God's servants to shun spirit of 650
Deportment, carelessness of, in presenting truth 380

debasement of, in some canvassers 402
See also Conduct.
Depravity, contact with, a continual pain to Christ 422
moral, study of Scriptures would remedy 26
Desire, sinful, every indulgence of, strengthens soul's aversion to God 53
if cherished neutralizes whole power of gospel 53
prevalence of, shows delusion of soul 53
Despondency, caused by Satan's accusations 470, 471
causes us to pray more earnestly 134
remedy for, Jesus' blood 317
Devotion, Jesus prizes only wholehearted 73
lacking natural 288
more of, less sermonizing 104
more perfect 481-490
need of cultivating 423-425
robbing God of 434
Diet, at camp meeting, overabundant, causes lethargy 163
simple, essential 311
Difficulties, how to make use of 312
Dignity, gospel armor to be borne with 115
some would rather maintain, than save souls 616
Diligence, habits of, a blessing 180
in business 178-182
with watching and waiting 276
young men exhorted to 593
Discernment, spiritual, needed in giving financial advice 532
Disciples, Christ, revealed God as Father to 737-739
spoke accurately with tongues 391

History—*continued*
 reproves sin 46, 210, 211
 resistance of, hardens heart,
  sears conscience 103, 120
 sin against, by willfully attributing work of, to Satan 634
 stops strife and contention 227
 strives with humanity 632, 633
 Teacher 46, 82
 transforming, renewing power
  of 105, 219, 226
 See also Christ Jesus; Latter
  Rain.
Homage, outward, of professed
 Christians 73
Home, angels delight in, where
 God reigns supreme 424
 invite youth to your 599
 made happy by, cheerfulness,
  courtesy, love 335, 558,
  568
 marred by, marital union with
  non-Christian 363
  women's unconcern regarding responsibilities of 596,
   597
 where shadows are never lifted
  363
 whoever hinders truth shining
  in, dishonors Saviour 568
Honesty and policy will not work
 together in the same mind
 96
Honor, worldly, ambition for 435,
 436
Hope, and faith in Christ our righteousness 742
 cause, to spring up 613
 closely examine foundation of
  your 530
 God helps when there seems
  least 452
 hearts must be uplifted to God
  in 743, 744
 required to give reason for our
  519
 Satan seeks to destroy every
  glimmer of 629

 sources of, Christ 200, 470
  God 629
 See also Courage.
Hops, raising, for beermaking
 356, 358, 359
House, of God, gate to heaven to
 believing soul 491
 of worship, dress appropriate
  for 498, 499
  using, for business or school
   purposes 496
 sanctuary for family 491
Houses of worship, building 269
 liberality to be manifested in
  building 268, 269
 necessity of building 382
 to be built in cities 465
Household, let kindness and love
 rule your 568
Human and divine, co-operation
 of 579, 583
 united in Christ 746, 747
Humiliation, contrition, repentance, evidence of Chris-
 tianity 348
 let proud spirit bow in 17
 of Christ 501, 502
 our work must be accompanied
  with deep 134
 to elevate humanity 17
 to precede leadership 118, 134
Humility, and self-abasement
 needed 73
 acquired by, cherishing Christ
  in heart 49
  increase of knowledge 49, 50
 advancement in Christian experience characterized by 49
 example of, Christ in coming to
  earth 253, 254
 few have, as little child
  50
 God desires individual seeking
  for 51
 Lord uses men of, to proclaim
  messages 253
 most essential to communion
  with God 50

none too highly educated to possess 584

safety in walking in 517, 518, 586

to be cultivated by workers 574

See also Contrite; Repentance.

Husband, duty of, to lighten burdens of wife and mother 180, 181

to show interest in spiritual things 425

See also Father.

Hypocrisy of unsanctified persons in sacred positions 536

Hypocrites, more hope for open sinner than for 144

Hysteria caused by diseased imagination 310

ICEBOUND natures of many church members need melting 387

Ideas, limited, about God's work 271

new, not to be advanced independently 534, 535

Idlers are hindrance in Lord's vineyard 394

Idol, self is 205

Idols, of taste and appetite 197

set up in heart 164

Idolatry, among professed Christians 250

can be practiced without images 173

grave offense 337

in, Battle Creek church 190

more refined forms 192

modern, children sacrificed by 320

of human instrumentalities 75

perverted appetite is 197

Ignorance, sins of, natural result of mental blindness 436

Imagination, effect of, on health 310

Immorality among professed believers 138

See also Corruption; Impurity.

Impatience mars and destroys God's plans for us 348

Impressions, an unsafe guide 647

early, of children 416

Improvement of talents, responsible for 459

Impulse, danger of being controlled by 647

not to be creatures of 530

Impulsiveness, lesson from Peter's 334, 335

Impurity, association with 140-143

suggestion of, flee from 146, 147

widespread, creeps into church 218

Incarnation of Christ, incomprehensible mystery 702

Inclination, we must conquer 384

Inconstancy, youth lean to 115

Independence, selfish, is one of Satan's heaviest fetters on mind 294

Indifference, ice of, or fire of fanaticism 644

of church members is alarming 381, 457-461

Individual, Providence presides over each 346, 627, 742

responsibility 724, 725

Individually, Christ thinks of us 346

Industry, habits of, would abate many evils 523, 524

Inebriates, mental 507

Infancy, molding of character must begin in 323, 324

Infants, Jesus accepted praise of lisping 421

Infatuation of erring youth 110

Infidelity, caused by inability to comprehend divine mysteries 79

evils from, among medical students 447, 448

good, God wants men of 581

guard against diverting, from God and service 478

men of varied, needed 581

most cultivated, charmed and astonished by Bible truths 700

not to be allowed to sway from allegiance to God 310

of, redeemed will constantly expand 702, 703

    some in publishing houses controlled by Satan 407

physician to instill right principles in 444, 445

pure, corrupted by ungodly physicians 445

Satan diverts, from God through idol worship 192

Minister to be pastor as well as preacher 528

Ministers, all branches of work belong to 375

called to be, Christ's representatives 161

    correct representatives of Christ 531

    educators 255-257

    watchmen on walls of Zion 15, 16, 252

dangers and mistakes of, advocating plans and methods destructive of unity 238

    being influenced by world-loving professed believers 262

    being praised and flattered 133

    engaging in interests separate from soul winning 371, 372, 530-532

    leaving interests unfinished 254, 375

    making wrong use of *Testimonies* 668, 669

    neglecting instruction regarding true worship and reverence 500

    neglecting to follow God-given light 214

disqualifications of, desiring to imitate romantic style of modern revivalists 132

disbelieving *Testimonies* 61, 380, 669

familiarity with opposite sex 594, 598, 602

first to join in frivolity 190

immorality 142, 143

lacking missionary spirit 255

narrow in policies for advancement 370-374

self-sufficiency, self-importance, self-confidence, independence 16, 539

superficial knowledge of truth 715

drawn from work to attend church trials 615, 616

education of, of primary importance 528

example for, Christ in patience, courtesy 160, 161

needs of, Christ abiding in heart 576

    daily self-examination 574

    earnest study of Scriptures 576, 577

    family religion 161

    having hands upheld, not weakened 131, 132, 162

    heart preparation for labor at camp meetings 165, 166

    realization of sacredness of calling 166, 371

not, silver-tongued orators, but men of action 187

to be measured by speaking ability 255

qualifications of, men of prayer 190

    breadth of mind and true moral courage 252

    Christlike in mind, thought, word, action 531

Ministers—*continued*

    dependent upon God for message to people 251, 252

    fervent love for souls 165, 166

    free from worldly entanglements 531

    humble 165, 166

    increasing in piety, knowledge, efficiency 576, 577

    refusing to excuse or palliate evil 15, 16

    sound principle and steadfast purpose 133

    unconverted, unsanctified, assist Satan to plant his banner in our strongholds 12

    cause ministry to be despised 190

    incompetent to steer gospel ship amid icebergs and tempests 104, 105

    soothe conscience of impenitent 78, 104, 190

    wives of, as home missionaries 594

    work of, as educators in all branches of gospel work 254-258

    educate minds to make kingdom of heaven first 262

    follow up interests by personal labor 255, 256

    impress people with necessity of personal conversion 619

    in dealing with church difficulties 96, 97, 615-617

    in house-to-house work 255

    in new churches 256

    in Sabbath school work 256

    reprove, rebuke, exhort, with long-suffering and doctrine 237

    reveal Saviour to world 237, 238

    teach obligations regarding tithes and offerings 256, 374, 375, 382

    warn careless and unsuspecting of coming fate 15, 16

    young, having learned doctrines but not Christ 174, 175

    See also Workers.

Ministry, converted, needed 227

    teachers should adapt instruction for young men entering 27

Miracles, of Christ Jesus, feeds multitude 400, 413

    of Moses before Pharaoh counterfeited by magicians 696-698

Mission fields, means to support 369, 460

Missionaries, all church members to be 176

    can do good work if soul is purified 238

    example of Christ for 385

    foreign, learning foreign languages 392

    should gratefully accept help 392

    to be, men and women who walk and talk with God 598

    where God has placed them 184

    young men and women as 390-395

    See also Church; Workers.

Missionary, Christ the great model 385

    every minister to be a consecrated 381

    spirit 582

    all must be filled with 307, 308, 386

    decline in, among ministers and teachers 88

    is spirit of personal sacrifice 386, 387

    must not flag 129

    true, Dorcas actuated by 304

Nervous system—*continued*
undermined by use of tobacco
440
New birth, needed by many in
church and ministry 218-
220
results of 189, 218-220
transformation of nature 122
See also Conversion.
Newspaper stories as reading 516-
518
See also Reading.
Noah, days of, and ours 99, 100,
134, 218, 365
intemperance in day of 361
last days compared to time of 10
Noblemen, God's 578
Notoriety, error in working to gain
587
Nurses must stand scrutiny of Jehovah 448

OAKLAND, admonitions to
church in 532-541
Object lessons from nature, graft-
ing, union with Christ 47,
48, 591
seed sown produces harvest 120
vine and branches, Christ and
followers 47, 48, 229-231,
240, 591
Observation, no item of conduct
escapes God's eye 627
Obstacles, man to overcome, not
be molded by 312
Offerings, God will enable us to
make 282
heartless, indicate lack of connection with God 270
Israel's perfect, required 541
New Testament, Paul laid down
rule for, for all time
735
required in proportion to light
and privileges 150, 151
to be bound upon altar by willing obedience and pure
love 269

today, begrudged, not acceptable 285
trespass, bring to God if
wronged soul is dead 339
See also Benevolence; Giving;
Liberality; Tithes.
Oil of grace 220
Olympic games, lesson from 552
Omnipotence, prayer moves arm
of 453
One, spot or stain of sin 214
wrong trait of character 53
Opinions, difference of, leads to
deeper study 707
individual, not to be advanced
independently 534, 535
Opponents, how to meet 708
Opportunities, for service in helping those who have stum-
bled and fallen 420
success depends on use made of
God-given 321
Opposition, advances gospel
453
of apostates 463
open, less perilous than secret
enmity 273, 274
strengthens God's people 601
Oratory, modern, we need not
imitate 132
silver-tongued, not needed to
give this message 187
Order, God is God of 274
in church organization, Israel
an example of 274
in church services is taught to
people 500
Organization of Seventh-day
Adventists, not to hinder
any from work 461, 462
Ornaments, gold and silver, species of idolatry 499
Overcomers by making a strong
decided effort 340
Overcoming, Christ our pattern in
312
only hope of, is in uniting with
will of God 513-515

Parents—*continued*
responsibilities of, for souls of
children 36-45, 506
in preparing children for
camp meeting 164, 165
lesson regarding, from slay-
ing of first-born in Egypt
505
to develop strong character in
children 29, 39, 319, 324
to elevate standard of Christianity in children's minds
494
to guard and choose associations of children 544-546
to guide footsteps of children
in religious experience 40-
43
to mold mind and character
according to divine Model
29
to restrain children 319, 545,
546
to set right example before
children 128, 129, 319,
320, 498
to shield children from temptation 232, 233
to simplify and explain plan
of salvation to children
330
to stimulate weak and repress
wrong traits of children
319
to surround children with
right influences 505-507
to sustain the authority of
teachers 52, 89
to teach children, obedience
323-327
reverence for house of God
494
sacredness of religious
obligations 37, 38
that others' sins are no excuse
for them 37
to be honest, truthful, temperate, industrious, eco-

nomical 329
to respect experienced judgment and rightful authority
89
to respect hour of prayer and
religious things 424
unfaithfulness of, brings dishonor and bitterness to
324,325
consequences of, reach to
children's children 325
much backsliding is consequence of 38
proves ruin of children 39,
40, 305
results in loss of children's
respect 305, 319
revealed by children's defective characters 326, 423,
424
want of respect for, is marked
sin of this age 125
work of, is solemn and sacred
305
Partiality, parents not to show 319
Passion, unsanctified, results in
life of misery 366
Passions, Elijah subject to like 161
gratification of, enfeebles 135
kept fierce by Satan are bitter
fountain 488
only divine grace can quell 445
Pastors for churches, great need of
723
Patience, difficulty and trials develop 344, 345
divine, finally worn out 524
of God shown in parable of fig
tree 250
Patients benefited by blending
spiritual healing with
physical 443
Pattern, Christ our perfect 35, 37,
129, 235
faithfully follow Christ's
18
ministers to imitate divine 160-
162

Paul, bitterly opposes the cause of Christ 641

Christian experience of 223

example of, as man of faith 79

to churches 65

highly honored of God 223

influence of, as prisoner wider than if free 453, 454

inspired apostle 65, 684

set for defense of church 684

Peace, and safety cry 211

which no circumstance can change 487, 488

Penitence, genuine, and confession 342, 343

See also Repentance.

Pentecost, power of God's church at 239, 240

People of God, angels near, to aid in work 753, 754

angels preserve, if in path of duty 198

appeal to arouse 387, 464

God's care for 749, 753, 754

interests of, centered in world 277

not ready for last crisis 713-718

peculiarity of, lost to great extent 188

press together 236

professed, state of 79, 240

remarkable persistence in impenitence among 77

to be, educated regarding truth and duty 302

peculiar 591

taught self-sacrifice 373, 374

to stand in defense of truth and righteousness 136

See also Church.

Perceptions, moral, deadened 641

Perfection, not to be sought in men 333, 334

of character, a lifelong work 105, 500

Perils of last days 525, 601, 753

Periodicals, obtaining short subscriptions for 399

using premiums with 401, 402

Persecution, counsel regarding 135

to be repeated 449-451, 473, 712

Perseverance, need of, in any noble work 304, 391

to attain to high standard of efficiency 109, 110, 446

Persistence in finding Jesus 132

Peter, character of, after conversion 334, 335

before conversion 334

denies Jesus 427, 428

example of acting from policy 427, 428

miraculous escape of, from prison 748

Pharaoh, confession of 637

example of hardness of heart 119, 120

Pharisaism, no time for, to control humble efforts 462

Pharisees desired Jesus to silence children 462

Philosophers, conceited, so-called 79

Philosophy, false, knowledge needed to meet 390

moral, to be taught 522

Physician, Christ as, able to save to uttermost 194

of mind and body 449

resources of him who has close connection with 448

the Great, requires unquestioning submission 219

not everyone can make a successful 446, 447

young, has access to God of Daniel 448

Physicians and ministers, ignorance and indifference of health laws is sin in 441

influence of, constantly tells for or against moral reform 441

protest against every form
and degree of iniquity 441
teach patients that disease is
result of sin 444, 445
urge youth to overcome health-
destroying habits 440
Piety, education in, neglected 496
lacking natural bent toward 288
need more fervent 134
Pilot, need of, near harbor 105
Pioneer days, joy accompanied
534
of publishing work oppressed
by poverty 565
Pity, God's promises expression
of unutterable love and
635
Place for work, special, in service,
every Christian qualified
for 87
Plans, broader, for education of
workers 581
no larger than means to carry
out 567
Satan's, for weakening God's
people 592
to be broadened 11, 187, 203,
721, 722
Pleasure, and ease ruin many 70
fate of seekers of 435
Pledge, Bible on 284
God will enable us to pay 282
pay your 153, 281-285
sacredness of 149, 150
without faith 283
See also Vows.
Policy, acting from, in religious
things 427
incompatible with honesty 96
worldly 561-563
urges outward compliance
for sake of peace 712
Poor, provision for 150, 151
to sacrifice for the cause 733,
734
Poor rich men 259, 260
Popularity, a delusion 13
error of shaping our work to

gain 587
lowering standard to gain 31,32
Position, does not sanctify 536
keep clear of, which would ensnare 340, 341
most suited to talents 87
Possessions, all belong to God 736
God calls to sell 733
those having large, to work fast
734
time to decrease 152, 153
worldly, loving, more than
Jesus 340
See also Property.
Power, God's, to protect from
Satan's attacks 467-476
physical, responsibility for 179
Powers, of mind and body
proportionately taxed
522, 523
Praise, and flattery cannot but injure 75
never speak word of, to ministers 173
of men, loving, more than God
340
of world, soothes 430
thirsting for 435
peril of receiving 133
to be given during lifetime 490
to God, reason for 312, 315-319
Prayer, and effort 231
by parents for success in training children 324
constant 235, 596
ever in spirit of 235
for laborers 162
for preservation of liberty of
conscience 714
for sick by physicians 443
gives abiding confidence 443
God hears, of contrite heart 173
hurried, now and then 161
importunate, in great day of
atonement 472, 473
in, behalf of church 209, 210
hour of church's greatest
dangers 524

depends on spiritual health 265

unless forward, we will go backward 93

Progression, God's plan for His people 484

Promises of God, comfort in, in times of trial 578

conditional on obedience 630, 631

expression of unutterable love and pity 635

most positive, underlie all commands 445

set in framework of faith, place in memory's halls 630

Propensities, carnal, subdued by love of Christ 648

Property, all belongs to God 736

God gives man, to enable him to give 150

greed for, sign of the end 10

obtained by oppressing poor, God destroys 350

securing to the cause 154, 155

time to decrease 152, 153

using all for own purpose 151

when to sell 733, 734

See also Possessions.

Prophecy and history to be studied in our schools 525

Prosperity, God's purpose in 259-261

in agriculture 152

Lord sometimes tests His people with 261

work neglected in, must be finished in terrible crisis 463

Protestantism, making concessions to Rome 716

Romanism, spiritualism, union of 451, 525

Providence, movings of, we should watch 728

sinful repining over 309-315

Provocation, giving way to 347

Pruning knife of God 229

Publishing, association not to be all-controlling power 564

department, important branch of God's work 550

house, in Battle Creek, danger for youth in 408

danger of becoming narrow 417

pioneer, humble beginning of 565, 566

temptation for those in 407, 408

houses, duty of workers to attend meetings of 408

duty toward apprentices in 415, 416

economy in 413-416

employees, families of 423, 425

managers, competent, should be employed in 414

missionary work in 416

need of faithful foremen in 415, 416

relation of, to each other 417, 418

union of, with other institutions 535

workers in, to manifest zeal and energy 421-429

Punishment, speedy, coming 209

Pupils, unpromising, attitude of teachers toward 30

Purchase of blood of Christ, deal kindly with 614

Purification of church, hastening 80

Purity, of deportment to be maintained 592, 593

of, life, appeal to church members for 141-147

thought, urged 599

QUALIFICATIONS without divine co-operation avail nothing 583

RACE, human, Bible contains most comprehensive and authentic record of 25

practical, dwell more upon 539

talk of, avails little 227

worldly-minded made heavenly-minded by 345

See also Christian experience; Christianity.

Religion and scientific education 501-505

Religious, amendment movement is fulfillment of prophecy 719

liberty, effort of National Reformers against 711, 712, 715

mission of *American Sentinel* 718-720

Remedies, for sickness, natural, advantages of 443

proper use of water 195, 443

Remorse, cause of disease 444

Repentance, example of true, Peter 334, 335

exhortations to 77, 78, 218, 636

fruit of, required 226

thought that God will not accept, dishonors Him 633

See also Contrite; Humility.

Repining, sinfulness of 309-315

Reports, false, church not to be misled by 480

of statements by Ellen G. White 692-696

to be tested by her published work 696

Reproach, taking up, against brethren 58, 615

Reproof, for accuser of brethren 289

to church in all ages 689

through *Testimonies*, duty to give 676-678

first hated, then resisted 139

Holy Spirit insulted by disregard of 64, 210, 211, 235, 680

how to receive 682, 683

in public dare not resist Spirit of God 20

rejection of 678-680

some never fully submit to 673

unwise sympathy encourages rebellion 679

Republicanism the fundamental principle of United States 451

Requirements of God, not one twentieth of, fulfilled 11

Reserve, strict, to be observed by men and women 602

Respect for. parents, lack of, a sin 125

Respite for God's people may be granted 714

Responses, cheerful, from congregation during services 318

Responsibilities, every church member should help bear 303, 724, 725

of parents 498

See also Parents.

temptations in proportion to 428

Responsibility, individual, need of, in work 189, 190

measured by powers originally bestowed for improvement 459

men of, principles in selecting 549, 619

Restitution, duty to make 339, 343

for dishonesty 643

Retaliation, avoidance of, under provocation 347

spirit of, not to be possessed 342, 343

Revenge, spirit of, how can we cherish ? 170

Revenue of gospel, tithes and offerings 149

Reverence, children to be taught 494-497

for God's house almost extinct 495, 496

Review and Herald publishing house, councils at 418, 419

Selfishness—*continued*
cannot live with faith 48
hindrance to God's work 154
prevailing sin in church 204
rebuked by Christ's sacrifice 17
Senses, Satan's efforts to paralyze 493
Sensuality enfeebles youth 78, 91
Sentimentalism to be guarded against as leprosy 123
See also Courtship.
Separation, from world our only safety 431, 432
from worldlings 13
Sermon on the Mount, burning truths in 253
no parade of human eloquence 254
Sermonizing, less, more heart devotion 104
Serpents, rods changed to 696-698
Servants, Christ teaches through His 300
of God, opposition and falsehood will only strengthen 601
Service, acceptable, measured by love rather than greatness of 279
"ready for either," an illustration 307
Seventh-day Adventists, regarded as too insignificant to notice, but change coming 546
Severity, and faultfinding must be rebuked 609, 610
authority must be maintained by firm 45
in judging 355
Sexes, association of, strict reserve in 602
Shadows never lifted from an ill-mated home 363
Shaking time, precious souls revealed in 80, 81
Shepherd, touched with need of each sheep 346

Shepherds, asleep instead of warning others 234
neglected obligations of 346
to guard interest of church 241
Sick, physicians messengers of grace to 448, 449
physicians to lead, to better life 444, 445
sin sickness cause of suffering of many 444
Sickness, consulting spiritualistic physicians in 191-199
faith in God's ability to heal 196, 197
leads to prayer 315
See also Disease.
Sifting, mighty, soon to take place 80-84
Sign, for God's people to leave cities 464, 465
of limit of God's forbearance 451, 525
Simplicity, importance of, in presentation of message 159
of, Christ needed 566, 567
faith, church departing from 18, 19
Jesus to be acquired by soul winners 253, 254
to be taught to youth 89
Sin, and disease, relation between 444
better to die than to commit 53
difference between sinning and being controlled by 474
greatest, committed by those who say they cannot 139
instances of, presumption 436
thoughtlessness 593
nerve self for conflict with 309
not a light thing 540
pleasures of, are cords of Satan 53
professed Christians blinded to sinfulness of 141-147
regarded as righteousness by agents of Satan 143

Study, courses of, long, warning against 22
  short, for ministers 27
  in school of hereafter 301
  of books cannot give needed discipline 22, 23
Stumbling block to sinners 352
Stupor of death is upon many 387,388
  See also Slumber.
Submission and consecration only hope of salvation 586
Success, condition of, spotless character 579
  God's promises of, to His people 754
  road to, not smooth way 552
Suffering, caused by sin 444
  of Christ reward to sharers in 230
  result of familiarity with scenes of, to physicians 445
  See also Affliction; Tests; Trials.
Suggestions, impure, forsake society that breathes 146
Sunday, laws, enforce institution of papacy 137, 451, 464, 525, 712
  impending 452, 716
  legislators will yield to demand for 451
  sign of end 451, 464, 525
  worldly policy will urge outward compliance with 712
  observance, enforcement of, strikes against religious liberty 711
  instituted by papacy, decree enforcing 451, 464
  movements for enforcement of, in progress 753
  owes existence to mystery of iniquity 712
  Protestants working to enforce 449
  union of Protestants and papists for enforcement of 451, 712

Suspicion, evil of, among workers 379
  instilling, into minds of others 286
Switzerland, custom of teachers in 653
Sympathy, unwise, becomes snare 250
  causes sharing of sin 679
  leads to other mistakes 298
System, in work of home 181
  not to crowd out simplicity of gospel 461, 462

TABERNACLE, building of, example of liberality in 268
  order in service of 274
Talent, to be recognized 722
  true estimate to be placed on 551
  unfaithful servant with one, shows distrust in God 282, 283
Talents, buried in earth 276, 277
  each to invest, as God directs 564-566
  not given for self-gratification 457, 458
  physical, responsible for, as for means 179
  responsibility for use or abuse of 458-467
  Saviour guides into position best suited to 87
Talkers, flippant, of Bible truth 166
Tares, binding, in bundles 384
Targets of Satan, God-chosen men become 428, 429
Teacher, Christ as, manner of teaching of 588
Teachers, called to be missionaries 91
  compensation of, compared with ministers' 85
  co-operation between, and parents 89

Testimonies—*continued*
to bring out general principles, specify dangers and sins of individuals 660
to deal with minutae of life 667
to exalt word of God 665
to give clearer understanding of word of God 663
to separate rebellious from Israel 676
to simplify great truths of Bible 665
of reproof, despised because they reprove darling sins 49
how to receive 682
must live in church 676
read with prejudice, will not be understood 695, 696
rejection of 678-680
to be borne, whether men hear or forbear 19, 20, 74
why given 661, 662
origin of, obedient assured of divine 674
personal, contain instruction for others 660
dream regarding duty to write 657, 658
duty to deliver, faithfully 677
power of, lies in their simplicity 667
lost if fashioned to please anyone 667
precious rays of light from throne 67, 681
published that others may be warned, reproved, counseled 657-660
read again and again 681
rejected, because they reprove sins 49, 675
because they speak not smooth things 679
relation of, to Bible 663-665
Satan's settled purpose to cut off or weaken faith in 300, 672
should be in every Sabbath-keeping family 681
slighted 62-84, 664
straight, must be revived, and will cause separation 676
to be judged by fruits 671
unbelief in, because of backsliding 76, 217
because of erratic ideas accepted as new light 292
because of unwillingness to be corrected 74
shuts away light 674
will separate from church those at war with 676
writing and sending out of 657-660, 671
wrong use of 668, 669
by dissecting to suit your ideas 691
by taking out force of through criticism 691
Thanksgiving would make prayer powerful 317
Theology, popular, effects of 710
Theories, new, not to be promulgated independently 463
Theory, practical godliness more needed than 158, 159
Third, angel represents our work 383
angel's message, bread of life for last days 206
extent of 383, 455, 456
last message 206, 207
not understood by all our ministers 715
Power, corresponding to, given to every worker 591
secret of power of 453-455
Testimonies linked with, from first 654
to go with loud voice 252, 383
why represented by flying angel 206, 207

Thoroughness, in self-examination 332, 333
  in work to be taught by managers of publishing house 415
Thought, every, will meet us again 466
Thoughts, and feelings make up moral character 310
  brought into captivity and subjection to Christ 310
  evilspeaking begins with cherishing evil 176, 177
  honor God by good, toward others 488
  if wrong, feelings will be wrong 310
  impure, contaminate and destroy soul 177
    God solemnly denounces those who cherish 592
  not to dwell on suspicion, doubt, repining 310
  pure, through influence of religion of Christ 314
  should be elevated in harmony with truth 594
  to dwell on pure and holy things 595, 599
  unholy, must be instantly repelled 177
Thoughtfulness needs to be cherished 335
Thoughtlessness, one moment of, may turn life in wrong direction 398
  regarding undue familiarity, is sin 593
Three, angels, symbol representing God's people 455, 456
  angels' messages, last messages of warning 456
    mighty cleaver of truth, separating from churches and world 455
Time, of end, we are now living in 10
  of test and trial at hand 273

  of troubles God's people cannot sell in 152
    God's people secure from tempter's devices in 475
  prayer only defense of God's people in 473-476
  preparation of heart for 452-454
  redeeming, in making wrongs right 349-354
Timothy, Paul's exhortation to 593
Tithe, all left free to say how much is 149
Tithes and offerings 148-157, 267-272
  every member to consecrate 481
  ministers to teach obligation of 256, 374, 375
  paying of, withheld 643, 644
  to be presented more before people 275, 382
  See also Benevolence; Giving; Liberality; Offerings.
Tobacco, use of 440-443
Touch of faith 227, 228
Trades, proper attention to students learning 415
Traditions, present danger of holding to 707
Training, duty of parents in 36-45
  suitable, for all gospel workers 390-392
Traits reveal to whom we are allied 224, 225
Transformation is supreme process in conversion 219, 220
Transgressions, confess full demerit of 636
  See also Sin.
Translators, spiritual qualifications of 511
Treason, loyalty from others' 136
Treasure, earthly, affection upon 464

Wages—*continued*
See also Compensation.
Waiting, Christ's appearing to those who are 15
Waldensian training of youth in institutions of learning 584
Walking with God as did Enoch 596
"Wanting" written against name 116
Warfare, against pride, ambition, deceit, hatred, 175
  Christian life constant 183
  to make virtue desirable 597
Warmth to be gathered from coldness of others 136
Warning, against licentiousness 145-148
  first hated, then resisted 139
  last, to world 157
    message, years behind in giving 715
  of True Witness 233
  to church in last days 99, 101, 114-132, 235
Warnings, given to those having most light 661, 662
  make church better or worse 72
Watch, pray, work 235
Watchfulness, admonition to 100
  and prayer, are only safeguards of purity 141, 148
    victory through 148, 485, 486
  constant, only safety 141
  final result of neglecting 102
  lest Satan take fort 14
  over self, lest we become traitors 532
  over word and deed 200
Watchmen, duty of, in crisis 716
  solemn responsibility of 15-21
  uncontaminated by applause 263
Watchword, Christian's, watch, pray, work 235
Water is heaven-sent blessing when skillfully applied

195
Weaklings leave own homes to desolation 597
Weakness, greatest strength realized when we feel and acknowledge our 70
  no strength in brooding over 741
  Satan studies, previous to attack 97
Well-doing while in this life 488
White, Elder James, physical breakdown through overwork 67
White, Ellen G., difficulties and hardships of, circulation of false reports concerning her statements 692-696
  criticism for manner of giving reproof 677-679
  great cross to relate plain, cutting testimonies 656, 678
  indignation often kindled in heart of sinner reproved 678
  helped and encouraged by, promise of divine help for work 677
  receiving light while speaking 20, 678
  judgment of, educated regarding duties and perils of church 686
  responsibilities and labors of, as instrument in Lord's hands 691
    in earnest prayer for liberation of souls 625, 626
    in faithfully delivering God's messages 677
    in reproving wrongs of God's people 677-679, 691
Wholeheartedness requisite in fellowship with Christ 568-571
Wife, helped by husband's unselfish desire to promote her comfort and happiness 181

meetings for, should be sacred
occasions 607
order in 491, 492
reverence in 491-500
should be made interesting and
attractive 609
Wrath of God 210-212
believing in, but making no effort to escape 221
church first to feel stroke of 211
Wrongdoing, consciousness of,
degrading to mind and
character 396

YOUNG men, characteristics of,
adaptability 393
endurance 393
duty of, be burden bearers 585
gain solidity of character 321
qualify for work 87, 203
study Scriptures to become
strong 321, 322
exposed to temptations, open
your doors to 599
God calls, to share self-denial,
sacrifice, suffering 87
lack of, in soul winning, result
of selfishness 34, 35
means needed to train 156
needed, rooted in faith, who
could enter higher colleges
583, 584
Satan entangles, with unwise
attachments and marriage
114, 115
to serve, as pioneers in toil and
sacrifice 393
because free from cares 393
hundreds of, should have been
preparing 390, 391
in hard places 583-585
in missionary fields 393
in place of fallen standard-bearers 584, 585
training of, as missionaries 390-
393
for ministry 27-36, 390
for positions of trust 585

for usefulness in cause 392,
393
unsanctified teachers induce, to
cease ministerial training
60, 85
Youth, basis of thoroughness,
honesty, integrity, laid in
415
capabilities of, not to be under-
estimated 30, 31
characteristics of, bewitched
with mania for courtship,
marriage 60
easily influenced by associations 543
ignorant, inexperienced, love
of Bible not natural 329
condition of, contemplated by
Ellen G. White with sad-
ness 521
dangers of, at school, association with many 186
being allowed to follow natural bent 38
desire to be admired and flattered 112, 478
from skepticism 41, 186
hasty and unwise marriages
105-113, 121-123
See also Marriage.
have no sense of their danger
105, 106
in gaining education 186,
521
in improper association 41,
106, 111, 186, 505, 542
in indiscriminate association
of sexes 110, 111
in sentimentalism 60
indulgence and indolence,
41, 42, 45
infidelity 186, 187
influence of so-called good
society 78
lack of proper training is
greatest 38-41
lack of stability 114, 115
love of pleasure 38, 112

Youth—*continued*

moral polution 78

objects of Satan's special attacks 34, 41, 42, 105, 106

Permitting powers to be perverted 115, 116

regarding with levity their early vows of consecration 40

Satan blinds eyes, diverts from God 115

want of respect and reverence 125, 186

wrong habits 408

depravity of, is increasing 112

discipline of, parents to aid teachers in 112

to be of highest order 416

example for, Jesus 42

Joseph 321

exhorted to, become firm, unwavering, grounded in truth 115

feed on God's word 43, 401

go forth controlled by principle 87

follow Jesus, Ellen G. White's highest wish for 87

forming right habits in, is important 415, 416

have no true sense of danger 105, 106

influence of, if demoralizing, not to be in college 111

some, is fatal to spirituality and devotion 186

labors for, beware of flattering 478

encourage to gain education 556

guard from demoralizing influences 112

in kindness for the apparently uninteresting 30, 31

in publishing houses 408

look upon, as purchase of Christ's blood 34

place in most favorable circumstances 545

require tact, vigilance 60

shield from Satan's devices 34

with kindness, love, sympathy, patience 91, 92, 415

Mordecai's words to Esther apply to 321

most important period of life 543-545

neglected by young teachers in college 35

of Bethel mocked and derided Elisha 44

responsibilities of, for good they might do 115

to bear burdens left by older ones 128, 585

training of, in principles of present truth 525

to aim at perfection in labor 415

to include all faculties 115, 522, 523

Waldensian, example of 584

will meet faithful record kept 523, 524

younger members of Lord's family 91